# Wills, the Administration of Estates, Trusts & Solicitors' Accounts

# Wills, the Administration of Estates, Trusts & Solicitors' Accounts

*Fourth edition*

Byron Jones

Reader and Deputy Head of Professional Legal Studies, Cardiff University

Byron Jones has over 30 years' teaching experience on the LPC, GDL and LLB. He was the Legal Practice Course Leader at Cardiff University from 2004 to 2020 and Head of Professional Legal Studies from 2019 to 2024. He is a qualified solicitor (non-practising), having specialised in private client work. He teaches a range of related subjects, including wills, probate and administration, equity and trusts, and solicitors' accounts. He has extensive experience as an external examiner, has undertaken periodic reviews and other consultancy work for other universities, and has held various advisory roles, including current membership of the Law Society's Wills and Equity Committee.

OXFORD
UNIVERSITY PRESS

OXFORD
UNIVERSITY PRESS

Great Clarendon Street, Oxford, OX2 6DP,
United Kingdom

Oxford University Press is a department of the University of Oxford.
It furthers the University's objective of excellence in research, scholarship,
and education by publishing worldwide. Oxford is a registered trade mark of
Oxford University Press in the UK and in certain other countries



First edition 2021
Second edition 2022
Third edition 2023



Published in the United States of America by Oxford University Press
198 Madison Avenue, New York, NY 10016, United States of America

British Library Cataloguing in Publication Data
Data available

Library of Congress Control Number: 2024939142

ISBN 978-0-19-893305-2

*To Mum, Dad, Tracey, Tamsin, Grace, Ken and Andy.*

# Acknowledgements

Some content under Crown copyright regarding different court structures is reproduced by kind permission under the Open Government Licence (http://www.nationalarchives.gov.uk/doc/open-government-licence/).

Grateful acknowledgement is made to the Solicitors Regulation Authority for copyright material which appears in this book.

For the latest version of the SRA Standards and Regulations please visit their website (https://www.sra.org.uk/solicitors/standards-regulations/).

Every effort has been made to trace and contact copyright holders prior to going to press. If notified, the publisher will undertake to rectify any errors or omissions at the earliest opportunity.

I should like to acknowledge my thanks to those of my colleagues who assisted me with the writing and updating of the text. I am indebted in particular to Elinor Kerr-Smith for her assistance with the first edition and to Jane Chesterman for her help with this fourth edition.

Any responsibility for errors in the text are mine alone.

# Contents

# Table of Cases

# Table of Statutes

# Table of Statutory Instruments



## European Union

### Directives



### Regulations



## Table of Professional Conduct Rules

## International

### United Sates

# Exam Technique

## A.1 Introduction

The functioning legal knowledge (FLK) assessments for SQE 1 comprise two assessments of 180 questions each.

The FLK assessments will cover the following subject areas:

1 Business Law and Practice; Dispute Resolution; Contract; Tort; Legal System of England and Wales; Constitutional and Administrative Law; and EU Law and Legal Services.

2 Property Practice; Wills and the Administration of Estates; Solicitors Accounts; Land Law; Trusts; Criminal Law and Practice.

The objective of the assessments, which is linked to the Statement of Solicitor Competence, is to assess the depth and breadth of your knowledge of the law of England and Wales. The assessments are not just about nuggets of knowledge but about demonstrating how well you can apply that knowledge to demonstrate the threshold competence required of a newly qualified solicitor on day one of practice.

In practice, the reality is that you will often look up information which you need to know either to confirm your thinking, to refresh your memory or, indeed, to find out about an issue with which you are unfamiliar. However, the FLK assessments are closed book. This means that, without reference to books and notes, you are answering the questions based upon your knowledge derived from your prior learning, including that provided and supported through these manuals, and through the practise questions.

Each question in the assessment contributes to the overall validity of the assessment; that is, it allows you the opportunity to demonstrate your knowledge and understanding about the application of the law. Therefore, it should be possible to infer that a successful candidate has demonstrated their competence to meet the threshold and is thus capable of being a solicitor.

The purpose of this chapter is to talk you through the assessment questions: how they are structured, what to look for and what to avoid. Be encouraged; the questions in the assessments and the questions in the question bank are written by human beings so bear in mind that the same thinking process which has been used to generate the question can be used by you to determine the correct answer. Questions are not written in a way purposefully to catch you out, as the point of a question is to assess what you *do* know, not what you *do not* know. If you have prepared thoroughly, you should be in a position to respond positively to the assessment.

## A.2 Question structure

To begin, let us take a question from the SRA SQE 1 FLK sample questions published on 16 December 2019. These sample questions were published to give a guide as to what might be expected in the live assessment, and frequent reference will be made to them throughout this chapter.

The question is split into three parts, as illustrated in **Figure A.1**:

- the context;
- the stem; and
- the options.

In the course of a trial various arguments are put to the judge as to the exact meaning of a particular section of a relevant statute. When deciding the case, the judge first looks at the natural ordinary meaning of the words used. However, such an interpretation of those words results in an absurd meaning being given to the section.The judge, therefore, in coming to his decision, interprets the words in a different way which does not result in an absurd meaning. — **Context**

What method of statutory interpretation has the judge used? → **Stem**

A. The literal rule.
B. The mischief rule.
C. The extrinsic evidence rule.
D. The golden rule.
E. The intrinsic evidence rule.

— **Options**

**FIGURE A.1** Example of question structure (SRA sample question 15)

## A.2.1 **The context**

The context may be objective, for example, just a couple of generalised sentences before the stem, which puts the question to be answered and which aims to capture a particular piece of knowledge. SRA sample question number 6 demonstrates an objective context:

**EXAMPLE**

A decision is made by the Court of Appeal (Civil Division) in favour of the claimant. The defendant wishes to obtain permission to appeal.

Which of the following courts have the power to grant permission to appeal?

Or, as in question 15, the context may be subjective and contain more scene-setting for the question which follows, providing details about where, who and why something happened, as represented in **Figure A.2**.

You should read the context carefully because it will contain clues which have been laid by the question writer to help you answer the question.

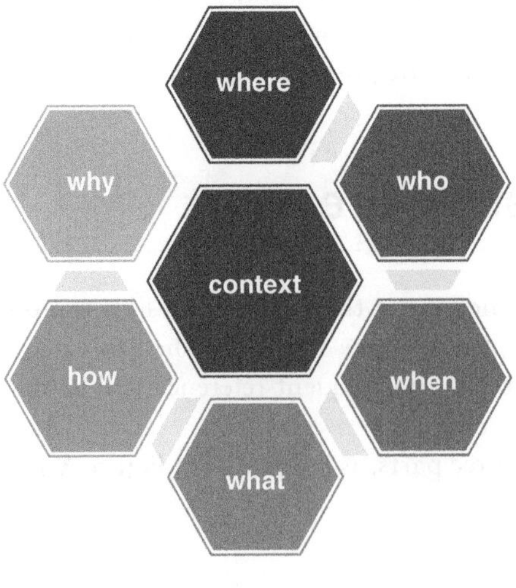


**FIGURE A.2** Subjective context

Here is the question 15 context again with highlighted relevant sections which give a good idea as to what is in the question writer's mind—the rules of statutory interpretation:

> **EXAMPLE**
>
> In the course of a trial various arguments are put to the judge as to the *exact meaning* of a particular section of a relevant statute. When deciding the case, the judge first looks at the *natural ordinary meaning of the words* used. However, such an interpretation of those words *results in an absurd meaning* being given to the section. The judge, therefore, in coming to his decision, *interprets the words* in a different way which *does not result in an absurd meaning*.
>
> What method of statutory interpretation has the judge used?

In this particular question, the stem itself also tells you that the question is about statutory interpretation but the stem might not always be quite so helpful. You may have to consider the facts carefully to establish which area of knowledge is being assessed; each assessment covers multiple subject areas, so you will not know what kind of question you are attempting until you read it. Having read the context carefully, you should be in the right mental zone as the context contains all of the relevant facts which are needed to give the correct answer to the stem which follows and which supports the answer.

## A.2.2 **The stem**

Look at the stem very carefully—after all, it is the link to the correct answer. Given its importance, the stem should be absolutely clear, should be connected to the context and include as much information as possible to be precise about what is being asked. Stems, properly written, should pass what is known as the *cover test*. The cover test means that the correct answer should, without seeing any of the options, pop into your head as soon as you read the stem. This is a very useful step to take as it prompts your memory to offer up the right answer without being conflicted by any distracting options. If you think of what you believe to be the correct answer and then, to your surprise, you do not see it in the options, double-check that you have read the stem correctly!

> **TIP**
>
> When you use the practise question bank, get into the habit of using the *cover test* as a technique as it is good for revision and will improve your recollection. A good habit to have! Having read the stem thoroughly, take a moment to pause and think what answer you expect to see amongst the options. When you read through the options, if that answer appears, you know you might be on the right track but pause again before you enthusiastically tick the box and move on to the next question! Check what you believe to be the answer very carefully to make sure that it matches what you had expected to see, then look through the other options to be doubly sure that you are correct in your selection. This is especially important in relation to single best answer questions which are discussed more fully later in the chapter; bear in mind that the 'best' answer might be very close to the second best answer giving you all the more reason to look carefully at all options. Only when this process is complete should you make your selection.

### A.2.2.1 Types of question

The SQE 1 FLK assessment contains what are described as single best answer questions. They are likely to be of two types. The stems for each are different although both lead to the selection of a single correct or a single best answer:

- a traditional multiple-choice question leading to a single correct answer; and
- a single best answer question leading to a single best answer.

## A.2.2.2 Traditional multiple-choice questions (MCQ)

For this type of question, there must be *only one unambiguously correct answer.* The answer is supported by the stem which will be worded in such a way that it can only lead to that one correct answer and is a heavy hint that you are looking for that one correct answer. As there is just one correct answer, these questions are an ideal way to practise using the cover test (see **A.2.2**).

Stem examples:

- Which of the following . . .
- What must X do . . .
- By when . . .
- What is the next step which should be taken . . .
- What is the correct advice to give . . .
- What is the correct procedure to . . .
- What is the accurate description of . . .

In question 15, the stem is worded: 'What method of statutory interpretation has the judge used?' The language is very precise: 'What method . . .'. It is an MCQ as there can only be one unambiguously correct answer.

## A.2.2.3 Single best answer questions (SBA)

A single best answer question may need a little more unravelling than a traditional MCQ. For an SBA, a range of responses might be possible or reasonable within the context of the question. However, only one will be the star option as it is the most preferable, reasonable and appropriate as the *single best answer* in the circumstances as provided by the context.

The context, here, is particularly important and is likely to require evaluation in order to determine what course of action is for the best. As there is no immediate stand-out correct answer, as for a traditional MCQ, the possible solutions require an evaluative judgement as to what is best to do in the situation. Each judgement-based option may be represented visually; see **Figure A.3** which shows how the options may be ranged from least suitable or worst option to the best option. Note that there is only *ONE* best option. You should bear in mind that the least suitable option, here B, may simply be wrong which is explanation in itself as to why it is the least suitable option!

In **Figure A.3**, A is identified as the best option on a given set of facts; B and E are identified as the least suitable options on the same set of facts with C and D somewhere in between. D is clearly challenging A for the star option spot but there is no provision to choose both options and so there will be a particular reason on the facts why option A trumps the other options.

As you can see, more thought is needed to work through and determine the best option in an SBA. The options are likely to be carefully nuanced and these types of questions demonstrate a higher degree of application in a professional context. For example, you can envisage a circumstance in which a solicitor needs to advise a client in the client's best interests. All options might present possible and plausible advice which might be given, although one option might definitely not be in the client's interests while another is recognisably the *best* advice.

Stem examples:

- Which of the following is the most appropriate ground upon which . . .
- Which of the following represents the best advice which might be given . . .

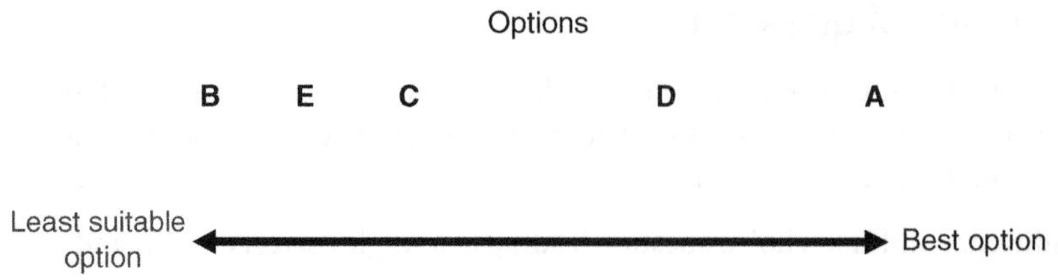


**FIGURE A.3** Range of responses

- What is the best course of action to recommend in these circumstances?
- How is the court most likely to determine the claimant's application?
- What approach is the most sensible to adopt on these facts?

**TIP**

As you work through the practise questions in the question bank, familiarise yourself with the stem types and see how the options differ so that you are best prepared. Remember that identifying the type of question you are being asked naturally links to the type of answer which is expected. If the stem looks to be an MCQ, then the expected answer should be an unambiguously correct response; if the stem looks to be an SBA, then the expected answer will be what is best in the circumstances. The feedback which is provided to the practise questions will help you to understand why a particular best option has been identified on the facts of the question.

## A.2.3 **The options**

After the stem come the five options lettered (A–E) from which you are to select your answer. Rest assured that the options will always include the right answer so there is some comfort in that! If the question has been carefully written, the answer should not stand out as being the correct answer, it should have been carefully embedded within the options which should all offer plausible alternatives to sway your choice. If you consider that the purpose of the question is to be able to infer competence, it is clear why it is unlikely that the right answer will stand out.

The remaining options are known as *distractors*, which is an apt description as they are there to distract you from the right answer. The distractors are likely to be plausibly based on common misconceptions or misunderstandings and be compatible with, and flow from, the stem. A distractor may look very similar to the right answer but will differ in a small but significant way, for example:

**EXAMPLE**

Which of the following is the correct explanation to provide about an unless order requiring filing and service of the defendant's list of documents by 4 pm on 21 May?

A. That unless by 4 pm on 21 May the defendant has filed and served its list of documents, the claim will be struck out.

B. That unless by 4 pm on 21 May the defendant has filed and served its list of documents, the defence will be struck out.

In this example there is a one-word difference between A and B. In the rush to answer and move on to the next question, the temptation may be to plump immediately for the first answer because it looks about right but, of course, it is wrong.

A distractor may also offer the wrong explanation for a definitive answer.

**EXAMPLE**

If the stem asks simply: 'Is the client entitled to take this course of action, and for what reason?', you know that the expected answer will be unambiguously correct because this is a traditional MCQ. The options might be presented as three 'Yes' options each followed by a different reason, one of which is correct, and two 'No' options each followed by a different reason.

A. Yes, because . . .

B. Yes, because . . .

C. Yes, because . . .

D. No, because . . .

E. No, because . . .

In some ways, these questions are quite helpfully structured because you might readily be able to eliminate the two 'no' options but you must still look carefully through the three remaining options to ensure that you home in on the correct reason for the 'yes' response.

> **TIP**
>
> If there are three positive options and two negative options, *do not immediately discount the negative options* and assume that one of the positive options is bound to be the right answer; the imbalance might be trying to lull you into a false sense of safety in numbers and prompt you to select a positive answer. Only eliminate options if you are sure that they are wrong.

The best distractors will also look similar to the answer in construction and length: they have symmetry. This is demonstrated in SRA sample question 15 where the options are given as:

A The literal rule.

B The mischief rule.

C The extrinsic evidence rule.

D The golden rule.

E The intrinsic evidence rule.

A distractor must work hard to distract you from the correct answer. In the same way that a stand-out correct answer does little to assess competence, a stand-out wrong option is also unhelpful to assessors because it can be eliminated from the running and so increases the chances of a candidate getting the question right without actually knowing the answer! In the FLK assessments, there are five options and you have a 1 in 5 chance of getting the answer correct even if you guess (more on this in **A.4.1**). If two of the options are implausible, the probability of selecting the correct answer increases to 1 in 3.

In SRA sample question 6 about appeals, these are the options:

A The Court of Appeal only.

B The Supreme Court only.

C The House of Lords only.

D The Court of Appeal and the Supreme Court.

E The Court of Appeal and the House of Lords.

There are two stand out options here, C and E, which can be eliminated as they are plainly wrong because they contain a reference to the House of Lords rather than the Supreme Court. The choice has now reduced to A, B and D.

Notice that A and B include the word 'only'. Be wary of such limiting phrasing and ask yourself whether this could possibly be correct in the context.

> **TIP**
>
> It is worth bearing in mind that options which include 'always' and 'never' are (almost) always wrong and never right. Do not discount them without some thought as such phrasing may be appropriate for the context, but bear in mind that such absolute phrasing often hints that the option is likely to be incorrect as it is inflexible and allows for no exceptions. This is often too rigid an approach in the field of law.

By this process of elimination, A and B include the word 'only' which is too absolute for the reality of those options. Therefore, only option D remains and that is the correct answer to the question.

The words 'must' and 'may' are frequently encountered in MCQs. Bearing in mind that the stem supports the answer and connects to the distractors, look carefully at whether either of those words appear in the options.

**EXAMPLE**

What is the likely costs order which the judge will make?

If any of the options contains the word 'must', for example:

A. The judge *must* make an order for the claimant to pay the defendant's costs in any event think carefully; costs are discretionary and, therefore, you would expect the correct answer to read:

A. The judge *may* make an order for the claimant to pay the defendant's costs in any event'.

**TIP**

Through use of the cover test technique, you will hopefully have in mind what you believe to be the answer and may mentally benchmark an option as soon as you see it. Do not bank that option too soon until you have reviewed the other options; use it as the measure against which the other options are considered as being correct/incorrect or better/worse. Then, eliminate options to narrow your choice further. Think logically, analyse the wording carefully and eliminate options based upon the *specific facts* you are given and not the general law, practice or procedure. The majority of questions will have a specific set of facts and the correct answer depends on those. If, after that analysis, you are still persuaded that your initial thought was correct, go ahead and bank the option!

## A.3 **Worked examples**

Now that you understand how a question is constructed, you can see that there are four simple steps to take to approach each question:

*Step 1.* Read the context carefully, taking note of key words to identify which topic area the question is about.

*Step 2.* Read the stem and identify whether this is an MCQ or SBA.

*Step 3.* From the stem, conduct the cover test.

*Step 4.* Read the options and identify the distractors.

Using these steps, have a look through these worked examples and try to think one step ahead.

**WORKED EXAMPLE: DISPUTE RESOLUTION**

A claimant, in proceedings in which they had raised a claim and a defence to counterclaim, does not attend court on the first day of trial.

What order should the defendant ask the court to make?

A. To adjourn the trial.

B. To give judgment on the counterclaim.

C. To make a wasted costs order.

D. To strike out the claim.

E. To strike out the claim and the defence to counterclaim.

*Step 1: Review the context.*

*A claimant*, in proceedings in which *they had raised a claim and a defence to counterclaim, does not attend court* on the first day of *trial.*

Your first thoughts might be that this is a very short fact-pattern and so unlikely to be a tricky question but it packs in a considerable amount of detail. The key words have been highlighted: we know that the claimant pursues a claim but is also defending a counterclaim, and does not attend court for the trial. Of those key words, perhaps the most significant is the presence of a counterclaim, which is a claim in its own right pursued by the defendant against the claimant and which can alter the dynamic between the parties. Having got a grip on the facts, read the stem.

*Step 2: Read the stem and identify whether this is an MCQ or SBA.*

What order should *the defendant* ask the court to make?

Is this an MCQ or an SBA? You might be thinking that this looks like an MCQ as it begins 'What order . . .' as if only one precise and correct answer is possible. However, look again; this is an SBA. The use of the word 'should' is a hint here. It is more or less asking: what is the best thing to do in these circumstances if you were the defendant. Note that the use of the word 'should' might also appear in an MCQ to indicate what should be done correctly in the circumstances—close reading of the fact-pattern and the stem will help you to decide what you are being asked. There is also a shift of context here: the fact-pattern sets up the scenario from the claimant's perspective but the question itself is asked from the defendant's perspective.

*Step 3: From the stem, conduct the cover test.*

Before looking at the options, try the cover test: what pops into your head as to what order the defendant should be seeking? Anything? Do not worry if not as we can now take a look at the options.

*Step 4: Read the options and identify the distractors.*

Read through all of the options once. This may provide an immediate prompt as to which of the options might possibly be the answer.

A. To adjourn the trial.
B. To give judgment on the counterclaim.
C. To make a wasted costs order.
D. To strike out the claim.
E. To strike out the claim and the defence to counterclaim.

Now go back and begin the process of elimination taking each option in turn and thinking from the defendant's perspective:

A cannot be right as, although a defendant can, of course, ask the court to adjourn the trial, there is no reason for a defendant to ask the court to adjourn the trial as the court may proceed with the trial in the absence of the claimant. Why would a defendant give up the opportunity to succeed against the claimant in their absence? B looks like a possibility, but this would not dispose of the claimant's claim, only the counterclaim; but something is beginning to emerge here as to what might be best for the defendant. C seems like a good idea to make the claimant pay but this is going down the wrong track because costs orders are consequential upon an event. Some event must occur first on which to hang the costs order. Also, there is something here that is not quite right as a wasted costs order is made against the legal representatives and there is nothing on the facts to suggest that the claimant's legal representatives are at fault. Let us look at D. This does not look right as it would leave the counterclaim live so let us look closely at E: asking for an order to strike out the claim and the defence to counterclaim looks to be a good answer on these facts as although the court may proceed with the trial in the absence of a party, if the claimant does not attend the trial, the court may strike out the claim and any defence to counterclaim. Got to the best answer, E, in the end!

## WORKED EXAMPLE: PROPERTY LAW

A solicitor is acting for the buyer of a house which has a registered title. The house was first registered in 2004 following a sale. The house was the subject of a further sale which was registered in 2012. The house is built on land which is near the church within a Church of England parish. There is no entry in the register as to chancel repair liability.

Which one of the following correctly describes whether the buyer's solicitor needs to carry out a chancel repair liability search?

A. No, because the title was registered under the Land Registration Act 2002.

B. Yes, because chancel repair liability takes effect as an overriding interest.

C. No, because there has been a registered transfer on sale subsequent to first registration of title.

D. No, because no entry has been made in the register in respect of any chancel repair liability.

E. Yes, because there has been no registered transfer on sale after 12 October 2013.

*Step 1: Review the fact pattern.*

A solicitor is acting for the buyer of a house which has a *registered* title. The house was first registered in *2004* following a sale. The house was the subject of a *further sale* which was registered in *2012*. The house is built on land which is near the church within a *Church of England* parish. There is no entry in the register as to *chancel repair liability*.

This fact-pattern sets the context for the question, which relates to a purchase of a house with registered title which is near a church. The key words and dates have been highlighted and these identify the issue—which is whether the house could be subject to chancel repair liability—and provide the important details which will be relevant to this issue. Those details include both dates and facts, so this should flag up to you that you will need to consider not just what events have taken place, but how the timing of those events could affect the outcome. With this in mind, you can now look at the stem.

*Step 2: Read the stem and identify whether this is an MCQ or SBA.*

Which one of the following correctly describes whether the buyer's solicitor needs to carry out a chancel repair liability search?

Is this an MCQ or an SBA? The key words here are 'correctly' and 'needs', which indicate that this is an MCQ rather than an SBA. Although the focus of the question is on whether a search is considered necessary, the determining factor is objective; that is, it is based on the underlying law rather than subjective judgement as to which of several courses of action might be 'best' in the circumstances.

*Step 3: From the stem, conduct the cover test.*

Before looking at the options, try the cover test: what pops into your head as to whether a search might be necessary? Anything? If so, apply this when considering your answer, but do not preempt your conclusion until you have read the options. Do not worry if nothing occurs to you at this stage, as we can now take a look at the options.

*Step 4: Read the options and identify the distractors.*

Read through all of the options once. This may provide an immediate prompt as to which of the options might possibly be the correct answer.

A. No, because the title was registered under the Land Registration Act 2002.

B. Yes, because chancel repair liability takes effect as an overriding interest.

C. No, because there has been a registered transfer on sale subsequent to first registration of title.

D. No, because no entry has been made in the register in respect of any chancel repair liability.

E. Yes, because there has been no registered transfer on sale after 12 October 2013.

Now go back and begin the process of elimination taking each option in turn and thinking from the solicitor's perspective:

A can be discounted because although the title was first registered in 2004, after the 2002 Act came into force, at that time chancel repair liability continued to be an overriding interest in the same way as it had previously.

B superficially looks as though it might be correct—chancel repair liability *was* originally within the list of overriding interests. But the key word here is 'was'—it ceased to be within the list after 12 October 2013. So, again, this option can be discounted.

C is a technical point where timing comes into play. Consider this option in conjunction with option B: when did chancel repair liability cease to be an overriding interest? In 2013—so if this transfer took place in 2009, the liability will have been binding on the transferee because it was an overriding interest at that time.

D looks, on the face of it, as though it could be a correct option: if chancel repair liability is no longer an overriding interest and there is no entry in the register as to any liability, will the buyer not take free of it? But again, remember the importance of timing here—the buyer has not yet completed their purchase, so is there still a risk? Bear in mind that just because chancel repair liability ceased to be an overriding interest in 2013, this did not mean the liability automatically ceased to exist.

E raises a technical point where again timing comes into play. Although there is currently no entry in the register and chancel repair liability no longer takes effect as an overriding interest after that date, the property remains subject to any existing liability until the next transfer on sale is registered. Consider whether there is a risk, at this stage of the transaction, that an application could still be made to register any such liability and the buyer would then be bound by it if they proceeded with their purchase.

Having evaluated the options, go back to the stem and check exactly what the question is asking. With this in mind, confirm the results of your evaluation and select the option you consider to be correct. In this instance, the correct option is E.

## WORKED EXAMPLE: BUSINESS LAW

A woman has been appointed to the board of directors of a private limited company (with unamended model articles). It is her first directorship and she wants to understand the legal requirements relating to decisions taken by the board of directors.

Which one of the following correctly describes the requirements of the company's articles and/or the Companies Act 2006 in respect of decisions taken by the board of directors of the company?

A. Only the directors can attend board meetings.

B. If the director cannot attend a board meeting, she can appoint a proxy.

C. The directors may take decisions by way of written resolution.

D. The directors can vote at board meetings on either a show of hands or by a poll vote.

E. Minutes of the board meetings must be filed with the Registrar of Companies.

*Step 1: Review the context.*

A woman has been appointed to the board of directors of *a private limited company* (with unamended model articles) and seeks your advice. It is her first directorship and she wants to understand the legal requirements relating to *decisions taken by the board of directors.*

When you look at the context, you will see that this is one of those generalised style questions which seeks to test your understanding of a particular topic. The key words have been highlighted for you: we are told that the woman is seeking advice about the requirements relating to decisions taken by the board of directors of a private limited company. It is important to recognise that the question focuses entirely on board decisions. This question is not asking about shareholder decisions so you should already be thinking about the difference in formalities and procedure of the two. It is also significant that we are told about this company's constitution: it has unamended model articles. Now that you have understood the context, you must read the stem.

*Step 2: Read the stem and identify whether this is an MCQ or SBA.*

Which one of the following correctly describes the requirements of the company's articles and/or the Companies Act 2006 in respect of decisions taken by the board of directors of the company?

Is this an MCQ or an SBA? The clue here is the use of the words 'Which one of the following' and 'correctly'. It is an MCQ as there can only be one correct answer. This stem does not ask you to advise the woman which is the best course of action when taking a decision as a director, but rather to confirm which one of the statements is a correct option.

*Step 3: From the stem, conduct the cover test.*

Before looking at the options, try the cover test: what pops into your head about the requirements for the decisions of the board of directors of private limited companies? What rules governing the taking of board decisions do you expect to see amongst the options? Now, move on to look at the options.

*Step 4: Read the options and identify the distractors.*

Carefully read through all of the options once. This may provide an immediate prompt as to which of the options might possibly be the answer.

A. Only the directors can attend board meetings.
B. If the director cannot attend a board meeting, she can appoint a proxy.
C. The directors may take decisions by way of written resolution.
D. The directors can vote at board meetings on either a show of hands or by a poll vote.
E. Minutes of the board meetings must be filed with the Registrar of Companies.

Now go back and begin the process of elimination, taking each option in turn.

A cannot be correct as others—for example, a company secretary, the company's lawyers or accountants—may also attend board meetings. Whilst they do not have a right to vote, they may attend. This option needs to be eliminated. This option also includes the word 'only'. Be alert to the use of this word as it is creating an exclusive category. It may be appropriate for a context but here it is clearly not appropriate as others may attend the meetings.

At first glance B might look like a correct answer; however, this is where a solid understanding of the differences between board decisions and shareholder decisions is important. If the director cannot attend a board meeting, she could, if the articles of association allow (and the model articles do not), appoint an alternate director to attend in her place. A proxy is the term used for someone who attends a shareholders' meeting on behalf of the shareholder, so this is not a correct option and this option needs to be ruled out. Furthermore, this option uses the word 'can'. Again, be alert to this. 'Can' means the same as to be able to do something but bear in mind that just because you can do something does not mean that you should or that it is the correct thing to do. Here, although the option is worded that the director 'can appoint a proxy' and, literally, she can do that, it would be the wrong thing to do in her position to meet requirements.

How about C? The model articles do allow the directors to take decisions either at a board meeting or in writing. This looks like it is a correct option. If you think that C is the correct answer, pause before you select the option and move on to the next question. Look through the final two options to be doubly sure that you are correct in your selection. The word 'may' is used in this option which is an expression of possibility and means that a choice may be exercised to do something or not to do something; there is no obligation to do a specific thing. Here, the directors have a choice as they may take decisions either at a board meeting *or* in writing and so C looks like a good contender for the correct answer as the option provides that the directors may take decisions by way of written resolution.

D is incorrect as directors can only vote for or against the resolution by a show of hands. A poll vote is an alternative way of voting at a general meeting of shareholders. Again, this is where a good understanding of the differences between board decisions and shareholder decisions is important. Here, again, we meet use of the word 'can'. In this context, just because the directors are physically able to vote by a show of hands does not mean that they should or that it is the correct thing to do to meet requirements.

Finally, E is incorrect as the minutes are a private record of the decisions taken by the board and there is no requirement under either the articles or the Companies Act 2006 for them to be filed with the Registrar of Companies. The use of the word 'must' creates an obligation, a necessity or requirement to do something. It may be appropriate to a given context but be alert to it being a categorical answer; there is no doubt or any choice but to do something.

Having carefully considered each of the options, go back to the stem and check exactly what the question is asking. Apply the results of your evaluation and select the option you considered to be correct. In this instance, the correct option is C.

## A.4 Time management

Each FLK assessment is likely to allow five hours and six minutes to answer 180 questions; just 1.7 minutes per question. So, it is clearly important to practise your time management. You can use the practise questions however you wish but to get the most from them you might:

- use the questions to support your learning as you work through the manuals. You might read a section or a chapter of the manual and then try your hand at answering some of the questions to reinforce your learning;
- come to the questions fresh and try your hand at a random selection of questions to keep you on your toes and to embed learning over a period of time and to highlight where you may need to look again at a topic to deepen your understanding. The feedback on each question and cross-referencing with the manual will be helpful here;
- practise the questions against the clock to replicate the assessment time constraint and to be sure that you can complete the assessment within the allocated time.

### A.4.1 Blind guessing against making an educated choice

This chapter would be incomplete without facing down the old chestnut that you can guess your way through a multiple-choice assessment. Statistically speaking, it has a basis in truth. Simply, there are five options and, by making a selection, you have a 1 in 5 chance of getting the answer correct. But blind guessing is a risky strategy to deploy throughout an assessment. Think of it this way: for every question answered by guessing, you have 4 chances in 5 of getting it wrong! Statistically, that would be 144 out of 180 questions wrongly answered on an FLK assessment. You may also have heard that selecting option C consistently is bound to improve your chances. This is not true. Options are often randomised so option C is no more likely to be correct than A, B, D or E.

It is far better to make an educated guess which may be necessary where you are struggling either against time, in the closing minutes of the assessment, or against a mental blank which is blocking progress. Making an educated guess involves narrowing down the options by the process of elimination leaving perhaps a choice between two or three options. You now have, respectively, a 1 in 2 or 1 in 3 chance of selecting the right answer, which has significantly improved the odds. But let us be realistic. Under time pressure, you may temporarily be at a loss even to make an educated guess. Your memory has not been prompted by reading the stem and nothing stands out when you read through the options. What should you do? Be positive and hold your nerve; recognise that this is a temporary block and there are other questions which need your attention which you will be able to answer—so get a move on to the next question. You may even find that, in working through the other questions, your memory suddenly gives up the answer which had eluded you before. Near the end of the assessment, go back to any missed questions and make an educated guess; there is no negative marking in the assessment, that is losing a mark for an incorrect answer, but, as a certainty, skipping a question loses you the chance to gain a mark.

## A.5 Summary

You will now appreciate that there is a method to the process of answering questions; just as there is a method to writing them. A methodical approach brings calm to the process; knowing that there is a structured approach to the creation of a question helps you to know that the question can also be deconstructed. An understanding of how that can be done, and the step-by-step process which has been outlined, will be a guide on your shoulder when you are either working your way through the question bank or working your way through the exam paper.

Of course, 'knowing your stuff' will provide the required bedrock of functioning legal knowledge, which is at the heart of the SQE assessments. The manuals, the question banks and your own preparation and practise will help put you into the best possible position to respond to the questions in the assessments.

**TIP**

This tip applies throughout the entire preparation process building up to sitting the FLK assessments. From studying the manual materials, going over a tricky area of law or procedure which you do not grasp at first, practising the questions until you know (and understand) why the answer is as given, to sitting the assessment: preparation and perseverance are key. *Remember, giving up assures a fail but the difference between failing and succeeding is trying one more time!*

Good luck!

# Ethics, Professional Conduct and Client Care

## FUNCTIONING LEGAL KNOWLEDGE

Candidates are required to demonstrate their ability to act honestly and with integrity, and in accordance with the SRA Standards and Regulations as follows:

- the purpose, scope and content of the SRA Principles
- the purpose, scope and content of the:
  - SRA Code of Conduct for Solicitors, Registered European Lawyers and Registered Foreign Lawyers
  - SRA Code of Conduct for Firms in relation to:
    - managers in authorised firms
    - compliance officers

## AUTHORITIES UNDERPINNING PRACTICE

The key authorities that underpin this area of practice are listed below. Note that for legislation you are linked to legislation.gov.uk.

Although much of the legislation on this government website is available in its amended form, the incorporation of new amendments into the text of legislation can be delayed. You should refer to legal databases to ensure you are referencing the most up-to-date legislation.

- SRA Code of Conduct 2019 for Solicitors, REL's and RFL's
  **https://www.sra.org.uk/solicitors/standards-regulations/code-conduct-solicitors/**
- Solicitors Regulation Authority Standards and Regulations
  **https://www.sra.org.uk/solicitors/standards-regulations**
- Criminal Finances Act 2017
  **http://www.legislation.gov.uk/ukpga/2017/22/contents**
- Data Protection Act 2018
  **http://www.legislation.gov.uk/ukpga/2018/12/contents/enacted**
- Legal Services Act 2007
  **http://www.legislation.gov.uk/ukpga/2007/29/contents**
- Money Laundering, Terrorist, Financing and Transfer of Funds (Information on the Payer) Regulations 2017 (SI 2017/692)
  **http://www.legislation.gov.uk/uksi/2017/692/contents/made**
- Proceeds of Crime Act 2002
  **https://www.legislation.gov.uk/ukpga/2002/29/contents**
- Terrorism Act 2000
  **https://www.legislation.gov.uk/ukpga/2000/11/contents**

# B.1 Introduction

This chapter introduces ethics, professional conduct and client care in relation to solicitors and law firms. A practical understanding of ethics and professional conduct are fundamental to being a good solicitor; indeed, it is paramount that solicitors act with integrity and honesty while recognising the need to be guided by certain moral principles. Client care is covered within this chapter because it is important for all businesses, even more so for law firms. As a solicitor, you have an obligation to take care of your clients, though these are not always thought of as ethical concerns. Clients are usually facing challenging life circumstances when they contact a solicitor and they need to have trust and confidence in them to be able to deal with their matter well, whether it is part of their ethical obligations or in addition to them.

# B.2 Introduction to ethics and professional conduct

Ethical principles have been recognised by the solicitors' profession for centuries. Many have argued the need to ensure a neutral partisanship: this holds that a solicitor must pursue a legal end for any client by any legal means. It is difficult, however, to balance the ethical conflicts between professional and personal morality. Ethics which arise by virtue of a solicitor's professional status are identified as professional or legal ethics. These ethics may at times be incompatible with what is morally required of non-professionals.

The Law Society was founded in 1825. At the Law Society's inception, the organisation was both the representative body and regulatory body for solicitors in England and Wales. It was only in 1960, however, that an actual text incorporating principles was published. It was called *A Guide to the Professional Conduct and Etiquette of Solicitors* and was written by the Law Society. The Solicitors' Practice Rules were then established in 1990 and were adhered to by solicitors until 1 July 2007, when the Code of Conduct 2007 was implemented.

The Solicitors Regulation Authority (SRA) is now the independent regulatory body overseeing the regulation of solicitors on behalf of the Law Society in England and Wales. It was created in January 2007, in anticipation of the Legal Services Act 2007 but also due to conflict within the profession and in an attempt to restore public trust in solicitors, which was an issue around that time. The SRA supports solicitors who are faced with moral dilemmas that arise in practice by setting out the principles and code of conduct which all solicitors and law firms in England and Wales must regulate and uphold. In the event of a conflict, the principles which safeguard the wider public interest take precedence over those relating to an individual client's interests. Solicitors should, where relevant, inform their client of the circumstances in which their duty to the court and other professional obligations will outweigh their duty to them. At the present time, the Code of Conduct 2019 is guided by trust, confidence and the protection of the public interest. It is as much about ethical values as moral principles.

## B.2.1 Changes to the Code of Conduct

Since the first Code of Conduct was implemented in 2007 there have been two updates, one in October 2011 and the second, most recently, in November 2019. These are discussed in more detail later.

## B.2.2 Code of Conduct 2007

The Code of Conduct 2007 was a lengthy and prescriptive code, supported by guidance. Along with the Code, there were also the Solicitors' Account Rules 1998, the SRA Recognised Bodies Regulations and the Client Financial Protection Requirements, which formed the regulatory authority to which solicitors had to adhere. Clearly, this was a lot of information placed in a number of different sources, and so it was time-consuming for solicitors to be able to understand and consult these when faced with an ethical dilemma.

## B.2.3 **Code of Conduct 2011 and SRA Handbook**

The Code of Conduct 2011 was contained in the SRA Handbook which came into force for all firms on 6 October 2011. The purpose of the Handbook was to provide an accompanying set of rules and regulations which supported the standards and requirements which all law firms, in-house legal departments and alternative business structures were expected to uphold. There were ten Principles. They were all-pervasive and underpinned all of the Handbook requirements. The Code of Conduct chapters showed how the Principles would apply in certain contexts and focused on the quality of the service a solicitor was delivering to a client, using outcomes and indicative behaviours to generate what is known as 'outcomes focused regulation'. The 2011 Code was shorter and less prescriptive. The SRA hoped that this would offer greater flexibility as solicitors would need to use greater professional judgement to ensure compliance with the SRA. It was more detailed in some areas than others, which created uncertainty and led to some criticism. However, it did reflect the overall aim of the SRA which was to focus on the quality of what a solicitor was delivering to a client rather than prescribing how the solicitor had reached that stage.

## B.2.4 **Code of Conduct 2019**

The SRA Standards and Regulations came into effect on 25 November 2019 and replaced the SRA Handbook. They can be found on the SRA website and, as they are published online only, they can be updated and amended regularly, so it is important to keep up to date with the website as there may have been changes since this manual was published. As well as making it easier to update, publishing the Standards and Regulations online was intended to make access to a solicitor or barrister easier for members of the public.

There was a change in this Code from a focus on indicative behaviour to one on ethical conduct, and there are now seven Principles rather than ten. There are also two types of Code of Conduct in the 2019 set of SRA Standards and Regulations.

Code of Conduct for Solicitors, Registered European Lawyers (RELs) and Registered Foreign Lawyers (RFLs) applies to those individuals who are authorised by the SRA to provide legal services.

Code of Conduct for Firms which applies to all bodies authorised by the SRA to provide legal services.

One of the reasons for creating a code for individual solicitors and another for firms is that the onus is now on a firm's management team to establish processes, structures and controls to ensure uniformity across the firm.

In light of the UK's withdrawal from the European Union (Brexit), the SRA's guidance on RFLs, initially published on 23 July 2019, was updated on 24 March 2021. See SRA Guidance: Registered Foreign Lawyers.

### B.2.4.1 The Principles

The Principles, alongside the Code of Conduct, are the basis of ethical behaviour which the SRA expects individual solicitors as well as law firms, managers and employees, to uphold. The Principles were established by the SRA Enforcement Strategy which underpins all the requirements set out in the Principles, Codes, and rules and regulations. It provides a detailed explanation of the approach to taking regulatory action in the public interest. If the Principles come into conflict, those which safeguard the wider public interest and public confidence in solicitors take precedence over an individual client's interest. It is important to explain this potential situation to a client.

**EXAMPLE**

To demonstrate how the Principles can come into conflict, suppose a solicitor is asked to allow a witness to give evidence in support of their client, in the knowledge that the evidence is untrue. The solicitor would have to refuse to do this as the wider public interest and public confidence take precedence over the client.

The Principles are mandatory, and so a breach of these Principles may constitute professional misconduct which could result in a warning, a financial penalty, a referral to the Solicitors Disciplinary Tribunal or some level of control or disqualification from acting in certain roles. When faced with an ethical dilemma in practice, the Principles are where a solicitor should look initially for guidance.

The seven current Principles are as follows.

1. To act in a way that upholds the constitutional principle of the rule of law, and the proper administration of justice.
2. To act in a way that upholds public trust and confidence in the solicitors' profession and in legal services provided by authorised persons.
3. To act with independence.
4. To act with honesty.
5. To act with integrity.
6. To act in a way that encourages equality, diversity and inclusion.
7. To act in the best interests of each client.

**EXAMPLE**

In a corporate firm, a solicitor may be approached by a firm of brokers to refer all clients to them. They may be offered a large financial incentive to do this. This, however, would compromise their independence and so would not comply with the Principles above, apart from where certain conditions are met (Code of Conduct paras 5.1–5.3)). In particular to act with independence and to act in the best interests of each client. The solicitor would usually need to decline to act and suggest that the brokers provide a list of corporate firms in the area or link to the Law Society Find a Solicitor webpage, to allow the client to decide who they wished to instruct. This would avoid any risk of compromising the solicitor's independence and would allow them to continue to act in the best interests of each client who instructed them.

### B.2.4.2 SRA Regulation

In line with the SRA Enforcement Strategy, the SRA seeks to:

- ensure a strong, competitive, and highly effective legal market
- ensure a focus on quality and client care
- promote a culture in which ethical values and behaviours are embedded

The SRA have a number of regulatory tools which are used in order to support compliance from law firms. The SRA Enforcement Strategy lists these as including:

- conducting thematic reviews of areas of risk
- publishing a risk outlook highlighting our priority risks
- providing advice and support through our Professional Ethics helpline and a range of toolkits and guidance
- SRA Innovate, a service which helps legal services providers to develop their business in new ways

In addition to the regulatory requirements set by the SRA Codes, Principles, rules and regulations, the SRA monitor and enforce the requirements relating to referral fees set out in s56 of the Legal Aid, Sentencing and Punishment of Offenders Act 2012. They also look at provisions relating to anti-money laundering which is mentioned at **B.3**.

## B.2.5 **Compliance officers**

There are two different types of compliance officers. Compliance officers for legal practice (COLPs) and compliance officers for finance and administration (COFAs). All practices authorised by the SRA must appoint a COLP and a COFA. They are both a fundamental part of a law firm's compliance and governance arrangements as well as the culture of compliance within the firm. They have a broad number of responsibilities and may be liable for regulatory action if they fail to meet them. The Law Society Practice Note on Compliance Officers sets out a full list of the compliance officer roles, and best practice as to how breaches should be recorded and monitored.

COLPs and COFAs have a duty to report a serious breach of compliance to the SRA. This may go against the wishes of the managers of the practice. They have a duty to keep records of all breaches in order to recognise when one may be a serious breach. Managers are, however, responsible for their firm's compliance with the Code of Conduct. This responsibility is joint and several, if they share management responsibility with other managers of the firm.

**EXAMPLE**

A potential new solicitor applies to a firm for a job and in his additional paperwork he gives details of a physical disability which will require various reasonable adjustments to be made by his employer. The day after he submits this paperwork, the firm withdraws the job offer, giving only a brief explanation as to the reasons behind this decision. The solicitor makes a formal complaint to the firm, alleging disability discrimination.

The firm's COLP has a duty to investigate the complaint and write a report with their conclusion. If the COLP is satisfied that there is no regulation issue, then they would not need to report this.

If the COLP is, however, concerned about being misled by any staff involved in the decision then this must be reported, as a regulatory concern has arisen regarding potentially being given misleading information relating to the job offer being withdrawn.

## B.2.6 **Complaints and the Legal Ombudsman**

If a client believes that their solicitor has not treated them fairly or professionally, they are entitled to complain. The main issues they may complain about are the way the case was handled or the costs for the services. If a client does complain then they will have been provided with details of how to complain by the law firm. The first step is usually to contact the solicitor to explain what the issue is and how it may be resolved. In most situations where a client complains, the matter will be resolved internally, and the complaint and file could be closed.

If the complaint has not been dealt with to the client's satisfaction or within eight weeks, then the client is entitled to complain to the Legal Ombudsman. The Legal Ombudsman deals with complaints across the entire legal profession, not just solicitors. There is a £400 fee potentially payable by the law firm which is being complained about. The aim of the Ombudsman is to use speed and informality to try and come to an agreement between the parties. If an agreement cannot be reached, then a decision is made by an officer of the Ombudsman. There are several remedies which may be available if the Ombudsman finds in favour of the complainant. There are also time limits (revised on 1 April 2023) which need to be adhered to by the client and the Ombudsman. Further details on remedies, limitations and the Legal Ombudsman can be found on the Law Society's website.

**EXAMPLE**

A client believes that his solicitor has not been honest with him about his chances for success and has not acted in his best interests. He feels that the solicitor encouraged him to take a matter to litigation and pay a large amount in legal fees; he subsequently lost the case and was told by the judge that he did not have a strong case in the first place. The client can lodge a complaint to the law firm but, if not satisfied with their response, then he could take it to the Legal Ombudsman.

If the client believes that a solicitor has breached the SRA Code of Conduct then they may contact the SRA direct in order to report it. Examples of breaches which a client may be concerned about include discrimination, fraud and dishonesty.

**EXAMPLE**

If a solicitor refused to continue acting for a client due to their religious belief, this would be a form of discrimination and thus a breach of the SRA Code of Conduct. The client could make a complaint to the law firm but, again, if not satisfied with their response then they could take it to the Legal Ombudsman and/or to the SRA.

## B.2.7 **Conflicts of interest**

A solicitor has a duty to act in the best interests of their client and to make sure that these interests do not conflict with each other. This is a key area within ethics and professional conduct as it is important for public protection and for acting in relation to the client's best interests. There will be occasions when you find that your firm already acts for a client whose interests conflict with a potential new client. When this happens, then it is almost impossible to be able to act for both in their best interests. The Code of Conduct 2019 (paras 6.1–6.2) prevents a solicitor acting where a conflict of interest exists, apart from in very limited circumstances.

As the SRA Guidance on Conflicts explains (SRA Case Studies: Conflict of Interest) there are two types of conflict of interest situations. The first is a conflict between two or more clients, known as a 'conflict of interest'. The second is a conflict between the client's interests and the solicitor's interests, known as an 'own interest conflict'.

A solicitor can never act in an 'own interest conflict'; however, in certain circumstances they can act in a 'conflict of interest' situation. The best interests of the clients continuously need to be considered. There is also another conflict to consider which relates to Principle 1, to uphold the law, as solicitors are also officers of the court. There could be occasions where there is a conflict between acting in the best interests of your client (Principle 7) and your duty as an officer of the court. This is more common when conducting litigation. In this situation, a person's duty to the court would outweigh their duty to the client. An example of this is calling a witness to give evidence when the solicitor knows they are lying.

Paragraph 6.2 of the Code of Conduct 2019 outlines the circumstances where a solicitor may be able to act in a 'conflict of interest' situation:

> You do not act in relation to a matter or particular aspect of it if you have a conflict of interest or a significant risk of such a conflict in relation to that matter or aspect of it, unless:
>
> - the clients have a substantially common interest in relation to the matter or the aspect of it, as appropriate; or
> - the clients are competing for the same objective,
> - and the conditions below are met, namely that:
> - all the clients have given informed consent, given or evidenced in writing, to you acting;
> - where appropriate, you put in place effective safeguards to protect your clients' confidential information; and
> - you are satisfied it is reasonable for you to act for all the clients.

In practice, it is important to carry out a conflict check as soon as possible. Ideally, this information should be obtained from the client before the interview:

- name, address and telephone number;
- area of law on which advice is needed (eg crime, property, contract);
- name and address of any potential opponent or other involved (if applicable).

If this information is not obtained in advance of the interview, a conflict check should be done when the client arrives at the office and then the interview may progress if there is no conflict of interest. On occasions a client may not understand who the other parties are in their case and so once you recognise who they are then a conflict check must be carried out as soon as practicable. Money laundering regulations (discussed in more detail at **B3.3**), also demand information being taken into account, which supports the notion of conflict checks.

The SRA provides a helpful case study—see SRA Case Studies: Conflicts of Interest: Solicitors Regulation Authority.

**EXAMPLE**

There are many ways in which a conflict can arise in practice and some areas of law have more likelihood of a conflict than others. In a family law situation, a person may come to a law firm for advice when they are thinking about leaving a relationship, despite the other person being unaware of it. The advice provided could simply be a one-off appointment. A conflict would arise if at a later date the other person in the relationship came to the law firm for advice. In criminal law, a conflict could be where the criminal department of a firm represents someone accused of assaulting their wife and the wife attends the family department for advice on separation. In both instances, a solicitor would have to decline the instructions and provide details of other solicitors in their area who could assist in that area of law and/or provide them with the Law Society Find a Solicitor webpage.

## B.2.8 **Confidentiality**

Confidentiality between a solicitor and client is one of the most important parts of their relationship. It is significant in the area of ethics and professional conduct as it is an area in which it is important that the solicitor receives all of the information from the client in order to provide the best advice, and that the client is confident that their solicitor will not release this to the public. The duty of confidentiality remains when the client retainer is terminated and even on the death of the client. Paragraphs 6.3–6.5 of the Code of Conduct 2019 state that a solicitor must keep the affairs of clients and former clients confidential apart from in limited situations. The main situations are if the client consents to the disclosure or if permitted by law.

Paragraph 6.2 the Code of Conduct 2019 outlines the situation when a solicitor may limit the information provided to a client:

> Where you are acting for a client on a matter, you make the client aware of all information material to the matter of which you have knowledge, except when:
>
> - the disclosure of the information is prohibited by legal restrictions imposed in the interests of national security or the prevention of crime;
> - your client gives informed consent, given or evidenced in writing, to the information not being disclosed to them;
> - you have reason to believe that serious physical or mental injury will be caused to your client or another if the information is disclosed; or
> - the information is contained in a privileged document that you have knowledge of only because it has been mistakenly disclosed.

Paragraph 6.5 of the Code of Conduct 2019 explains the limited circumstances when you can act for a client who has an adverse interest and where you hold confidential information:

> You do not act for a client in a matter where that client has an interest adverse to the interest of another current or former client of you or your business or employer, for whom you or your business or employer holds confidential information which is material to that matter, unless:
>
> - effective measures have been taken which result in there being no real risk of disclosure of the confidential information; or
> - the current or former client whose information you or your business or employer holds has given informed consent, given or evidenced in writing, to you acting, including to any measures taken to protect their information.

**EXAMPLE**

There are many ways in which an issue around confidentiality can arise in practice. In a criminal law firm, a person may come to a law firm for advice and you may overhear them on the telephone planning to sell drugs. In this case, in order to prevent a crime you would have to disclose this information to the police and would therefore be breaching confidentiality.

In a private client firm, a solicitor may have drafted a will for a lady who has now died. If her son contacts the solicitor after she has passed to ask if he has been left anything, then because of the duty of confidentiality the solicitor would be unable to tell him without the consent of the personal representatives of the will.

## B.2.9 **Undertakings**

An undertaking made by a solicitor is a commitment to do or not do something that someone places reliance upon. An undertaking is binding and does not necessarily have to be made by a solicitor or use the word 'undertake'. It is often made to clients or third parties in a matter. Once the undertaking has been relied upon, then it cannot be withdrawn without the agreement of both parties.

Many areas of practice, such as conveyancing and litigation, rely on the giving and receiving of undertakings to progress matters.

The solicitor giving the undertaking needs to be careful and is not obliged to give undertakings. If an undertaking is breached, then the solicitor could be sued personally for the money which was promised within the undertaking. The solicitor would have also breached the Code of Conduct and disciplinary proceedings would likely follow.

The SRA's Guidance on Undertakings, given by, or on behalf of, incorporated practice explains your obligations when undertakings are provided, by or on behalf of incorporated practices. This is because the Supreme Court decision in *Harcus Sinclair v Your Lawyers* [2021] UKSC 32 confirmed that the courts have no jurisdiction to enforce undertakings against incorporated practices. However, an incorporated practice could still face regulatory proceedings as there might have been a breach of our rules.

**EXAMPLE**

A solicitor is acting for a client in relation to debt matters and one large debt of £80,000 is owed by him to Jones Construction, who have written to ask for payment of the full amount within ten days. The client is in the process of selling a flat at auction, which has been valued at £100,000. The auction is in seven days and the solicitor provides an undertaking to Jones Construction to pay the £80,000 from the proceeds of sale from the flat.

The flat is only sold for £70,000 and Jones Construction has demanded the £80,000 from the solicitor. The solicitor must perform the undertaking and pay the full amount of £80,000. Failure to do so could be considered a breach of professional conduct.

In hindsight, what the solicitor should have done was to draft the undertaking but state that the payment would be limited to the amount received from the auction sale, or make it clear that they were not accepting responsibility for any personal liability.

## B.2.10 **Alternate Business Structures (ABSs)**

It is worth noting that all of these regulations also bind ABSs. ABSs were introduced by the Legal Services Act 2007 and the SRA began accepting applications from prospective ABSs in January 2012. This allowed non-lawyers to own or invest in a law firm, when previously only lawyers could seek to create and operate a law firm. At the time, this was seen to be a huge change in the way law firms could function. They are still overseen by the SRA and the SRA decides whether a firm or business can become an ABS.

There are two key distinct ABS roles, those which entail the appointment of a recognised lawyer and those which do not require a qualified lawyer. There was a great deal of scepticism by many in the legal profession when the ABS was introduced. It was feared that big businesses would reduce the quality of legal work provided and that 'Tesco Law'-type businesses would emerge.

# B.3 Money laundering

Money laundering is an illegal practice in which money generated from criminal activities is disguised and made to appear to have come from a legitimate source, in order to make it easier to spend the money and avoid suspicion. There are a wide variety of activities in which money may be attempted to be laundered. Examples of these are fraud, prostitution, robbery and the trafficking of drugs or people.

The purpose of anti-money laundering legislation is because solicitors' firms are often targeted in order to assist with money laundering. They can legitimise a transaction, have access to financial markets and often advise on property and business deals. It is therefore important for solicitors to understand the legislation, remain vigilant and to have the right training and processes in place in order to avoid the risk of facilitating this crime.

The Legal Sector Affinity Group (LSAG)'s Anti-Money Laundering Guidance for the legal profession, published in 2021, provides detailed guidance in this area.

Ensuring that solicitors do not facilitate money laundering is, of course, as much an ethical issue as a financial one. For more detail on money laundering regulations, see the financial services chapter in *Public Law, Legal Services & the Legal System.*

# B.4 Client care

Client care is a fundamental part of the role of a solicitor. A client is required to be given information in a way that they understand and allows them to make decisions about the services they need, how their case will be handled and the options which are available to them (para 8.6 of the 2019 Code). They are also required to be provided with information about costs both at the time of engagement and as the matter progresses (para 8.7 of the 2019 Code). Most complaints from clients are either regarding not being updated about how the matter is progressing or with issues about costs.

## B.4.1 General Data Protection Regulation

The UK General Data Protection Regulation (GDPR) sets out key principles, rights and obligations when processing personal data. It sits alongside the Data Protection Act 2018 and incorporates the EU GDPR, but, following Brexit, it allows the UK government the flexibility to review and amends its provisions. Personal data is essentially data that allows a living person to be directly or indirectly identified from information that is available. All solicitors hold personal data relating to both clients and employees. It is therefore crucial to be able to comply with the regulations. Knowing what personal data you have is the first step in compliance.

Further detailed guidance on the GDPR for solicitors can be found on the Law Society website.

## B.4.2 The first interview

Some practical considerations are necessary in relation to client care and when meeting the client for the first time, it is important to be fully prepared. Clients may have a range of emotions depending on the areas of law you are advising on. It is important that the client is reassured, offered an appointment promptly and also that the solicitor is fully prepared for the first interview.

Before the interview, the Law Society, in its client information requirements practice note, advises that when the client attends the interview the following information must be explained to them and confirmed in writing:

- name and status of the solicitor or other person conducting the interview;
- information on the costs for the interview;
- details of who to contact if they have a complaint including the right to complain to the Legal Ombudsman, the time frame and the contact details.

This information can be prepared in a pro forma document in advance. It is important to keep a copy on file.

In the first interview, you must remember to cover all of the professional conduct issues, money laundering regulations, the GDPR and legal issues as well as to obtain the basic details from the client.

## B.4.3 Client care letter

This letter is used by most law firms to set out the necessary client care information to a client. It is usually the first piece of correspondence you will send to your client and it is therefore an extremely important document. It must have certain regulatory information in it in order to comply with the Code of Conduct. It is usually also the retainer or contract between you and your client and is the beginning of the solicitor/client relationship. The Consumer Contracts (Information, Cancellation and Additional Charges) Regulations 2013 (SI 2013/3134) apply when you enter into a retainer with a consumer client who you have not met. This is often known as a distance contract.

## B.4.4 Fees and costs

In most circumstances, you will have a direct retainer with the client and the client will be responsible for paying your costs. In certain areas of law, this may be different such as criminal law, family law and personal injury. In those areas, a client may be eligible for Legal Aid or there may be a 'no win, no fee' arrangement. Legal aid is the provision of assistance to people who are unable to afford legal representation and/or access to the court system. Firms must have a legal aid contract in order to be able to offer this service to clients and legal aid is only available in certain areas of law (usually family law and criminal law) and for clients who, in most cases, have a low income. More information regarding legal aid and how it is assessed can be found on the Gov.uk website.

'No win, no fee', often called a conditional fee agreement, is a legal fee arrangement whereby the client agrees to pay only if they win their case and is generally used in personal injury law. A damages-based agreement is another legal fee arrangement under which the client agrees to pay the solicitor a set percentage of the compensation they receive if they win the case.

In the situation where a client is paying your costs, there are several options available regarding how to charge a client for work. The main two ways of charging a client are by hourly rates or a fixed fee arrangement. Whichever way you do charge, it is essential to communicate this to the client and to provide the client with a likely overall cost of the matter. If the likely overall cost changes then it is important to advise the client of this as soon as possible in order to avoid any issues which may give rise to a complaint or a potential breach of the Code of Conduct.

## B.4.5 Advertising

A solicitor cannot make an unsolicited approach to members of the public regarding the advertising of its legal services, but this does not apply to current or former clients. Any potential client referred to the firm by a current or former client will be seen as a member of the public (para 8.9 Code of Conduct for Solicitors, RELs and RFLs).

**KEY POINT SUMMARY**

- Ethics and professional conduct are fundamental to being a good solicitor.
- The Code of Conduct 2019 and the Principles provide the most up-to-date set of standards and requirements expected of solicitors, RELs and RFLs, and you should refer to them frequently.
- Breach of the Code of Conduct may constitute professional misconduct and could result in being fined, lead to criminal proceedings and/or being struck off from the roll of solicitors.
- It is crucial that solicitors have knowledge and understanding of the GDPR, money laundering and client care.

# PART A
# Introduction

# CHAPTER 1
# Introduction to Wills, the Administration of Estates, Trusts and Solicitors' Accounts

## 1.1 Introduction

This introductory chapter is a short one, designed to explain the structure of the manual and introduce the topics covered in it, as well as to discuss in outline some professional conduct and regulatory considerations relevant to these topics.

Unlike some of the other texts in this SQE series, this manual deals with a number of topics, not all of which are closely related to each other. You will see that the topics of **wills**, the administration of estates and **trusts** are all related to one another. However, Solicitors' Accounts is an entirely separate topic which is relevant to all areas of legal practice—including property, litigation, business and commercial—not just to wills, estates and trusts. In SQE Part 1, Solicitors' Accounts will be assessed in the contexts of (1) Wills and the Administration of Estates and (2) Property Law and Practice.

## 1.2 Wills, the administration of estates and trusts

### 1.2.1 An outline of what is covered in each topic

Mainly to have a title to this manual which is not overly long, the first few topics in this manual have been called 'wills', 'the administration of estates' and 'trusts'. However, these titles are not entirely accurate, and it is worth realising that there is considerable overlap between each of the three topics. Some explanation is needed, therefore, of what will be covered under each topic, and in this section there is also an explanation of how relevant taxation rules are covered in the manual.

#### 1.2.1.1 Wills

This is not an entirely accurate title for the topics which are covered under this heading. In fact, this topic covers the law and practice to succession to property on death, whether or not a person leaves a will. We will cover these rules of succession in **Chapters 2–5**:

- First, one of the ways that a person can provide for a transmission of their property on death is to make a document called a 'will'. In **Chapters 2** and **3** we will consider the requirements for making a valid will, as well as the typical contents of a will and ways in which a will may be changed. We will consider the interpretation of wills and ways in which **gifts** in wills might fail.
- However, many people do not make a will and, if they fail to do so or if they make a will which is not valid or not wholly valid, then the whole or part of their estate will be distributed according to a set of statutory rules, called the rules of **intestacy**. These rules are considered in **Chapter 4**.
- Also, many (quite important) forms of property will pass independently of a person's will, and independently of the rules of intestacy. There are other mechanisms and rules that provide who inherits such property on death. We will consider these forms of property and the rules which apply to them in **Chapter 5**.

#### 1.2.1.2 The administration of estates

When someone dies another person or persons (called **personal representatives**, or PRs) will have the responsibility for administering the estate. The PR(s) must collect in the assets of the deceased, pay the deceased's debts (and the expenses of the administration) and then distribute the estate in accordance with the terms of the deceased's will or, to the extent there is no will, in accordance with the rules of intestacy.

There are two types of PRs—**executors** and **administrators**. If the deceased made a will they will usually have appointed executors in the will. Failing that (if there is either no will or no valid appointment of executors), the HMCTS (HM Courts and Tribunals Service) will appoint one or more administrators.

The PRs will need to apply to the HMCTS for a '**grant of representation**'. This is a formal document which provides proof of the PR's authority to act in the estate.

The Administration of Estates will be covered in **Chapters 7–11**:

- In **Chapter 7** we will consider the preliminary steps needed in administering the estate, prior to making the application for the grant of representation. A very important aspect of this preliminary work is preparing and submitting the **inheritance tax account** to HMRC (HM Revenue and Customs).
- In **Chapter 8** we will look at the grant application to HMCTS itself. This is an area of practice that has seen rapid and major changes in recent years.
- In **Chapter 9** we will consider the work that is needed to administer the estate once the PRs have obtained the grant of representation from HMCTS. Now that the PRs have the grant, they will be able to collect in assets, pay debts and expenses and distribute what is left to the **beneficiaries** of the estate.
- In **Chapter 10** we will look at the taxation considerations when administering the estate after the grant has been obtained. This is in a separate chapter because it is quite a substantial topic in its own right.
- Lastly, in **Chapter 11** we will consider potential claims against the estate. After someone's death, there may be persons who are aggrieved that they have not been left anything in the deceased's will, or who do not stand to inherit anything on intestacy. Those persons may contest the deceased's will (by claiming it is invalid) or may apply to the court for a payment from the estate, usually based on their financial needs.

#### 1.2.1.3 Trusts

Again, the title to this topic is shorthand, in this case for the law of **Equity** and trusts. The Assessment Specification for Stage 1 of the SQE includes various aspects of the academic subject of Equity and trusts which would typically be covered by a student in their law degree or in a law conversion course, such as the Graduate Diploma in Law.

**Chapters 12** and **13** therefore are intended mainly as refreshers of topics which you are likely to have studied previously. These chapters contain brief summaries of the principles of Equity and trusts, although **Chapter 13** then goes into more detail on the powers and duties of **trustees** (something which is also relevant to PRs, who have many of the same powers and duties when administering an estate).

You might think that the refresher of the principles of Equity and trusts would normally appear before the other chapters in this manual. However, in practice, there is relatively little from the principles of Equity and trusts which is needed in order to understand the rules of succession to property on death, or to understand how to administer an estate. So, whilst Equity and trusts forms part of the Assessment Specification for the SQE, it is largely a separate topic to wills and the administration of estates, and it makes sense to deal with the more important practical legal topics before returning to a refresher of the academic topic. Also, the powers and duties of trustees (and PRs) only make sense once you know the general processes for administering an estate.

Another point to note is that neither the Assessment Specification for the SQE nor this manual cover the detailed rules on how to administer a trust. This is a separate topic to the administration of estates, and is itself very detailed (particularly when considering the taxation of trusts). So, this manual only covers certain aspects of trusts—just the principles from the academic subject and certain powers and duties of trustees (which, as said, are also relevant to PRs).

#### 1.2.1.4 How taxation is covered in this manual

The one chapter not mentioned so far is **Chapter 6**, which is on **inheritance tax** (IHT). A separate chapter is needed to cover the basic rules of this tax which is arguably the most important tax affecting succession to property on death and the administration of estates. You need to know about the basic rules to IHT before you begin to study the law and practice of administration of estates.

However, although the basic rules are covered in **Chapter 6**, IHT will crop up elsewhere in this manual. In **Chapter 7** you will look at how PRs provide HMRC with required information on the property of the deceased (and certain lifetime transfers). This is an extremely important preliminary step before obtaining the grant of representation, because HMCTS will not issue a grant of representation unless an IHT account has been submitted and any IHT due on the account has been paid.

Then, following the issuing of the grant of representation, there may be adjustments which need to be made to the amount of IHT payable, and the PRs will wish to obtain **clearance** from HMRC to confirm that all of the IHT has been paid. These steps are considered as part of **Chapter 10**.

**Chapter 10** also covers two other taxes that are particularly important when administering estates—**income tax** and **capital gains tax** (CGT). The PRs will have to finalise the income tax and CGT of the deceased for the period before death, and will have to account for any income tax and CGT due in respect of the administration period after death.

### 1.2.2 The background to wills, the administration of estates and trusts

Traditionally, solicitors have been the main source of professional advice and assistance in the making of wills, in the administration of the estates and in the administration of trusts. Although there are now other entrants into this field of work, the majority of work in this area is still conducted by solicitors.

In part, this is because of legal restrictions on undertaking certain types of legal work. Under the Legal Services Act 2007 only persons who are authorised or exempt may undertake any of the six specified 'reserved legal activities'. One of these activities is '**probate** activities', namely preparing any probate papers for the purposes of the law of England and Wales or in relation to any proceedings in England and Wales. Probate papers for this purpose means papers on which to found or oppose a grant of probate or a **grant of letters of administration**. In other words, although a person may apply for a grant of representation in person, if someone else is to make the application on their behalf, that other person must be authorised or exempt.

Historically, only solicitors were authorised to prepare these probate papers, although under the Legal Services Act 2007 it is possible for other persons to obtain authorisation. For example, certain types of qualified accountants have obtained authorisation in recent years to undertake probate activities. Nevertheless, solicitors remain the main source of professional assistance to PRs in obtaining grants of representation and in administering estates.

Similarly, solicitors are the main source of assistance to persons wishing to make their wills. Although a **testator** can draft their own will, most testators seek assistance with the drafting and preparation of their wills. Most wills are drafted by solicitors, acting on instruction from their clients. However, there are some unregulated companies which offer will-writing services. There is considerable concern that such companies are allowed to undertake this highly skilled and important work without being regulated by the Solicitors Regulation Authority (SRA) or by another regulator. Unregulated will-writing companies are not subject to the same stringent regulatory requirements as solicitors, are not bound by the codes of conduct and, unlike the clients of solicitors, their customers are not protected by professional indemnity insurance or the SRA Compensation Fund when things go wrong. Unfortunately, in 2013 the government rejected the Legal Services Board's (LSB) recommendation that will-writing services be made a reserved legal activity in England and Wales, as it is in Scotland. Thankfully, the majority of wills in England and Wales still continue to be drafted by solicitors.

Many solicitors will also undertake trusts work. This may be a testamentary trust, arising out of the estate of a deceased person, or an ***inter vivos*** trust created by the settlor during their lifetime. The solicitors may themselves be trustees or may be advising the trustees. Either way, solicitors need to know the basic principles of Equity and trusts, the powers and duties of trustees and the rights and remedies of beneficiaries.

## 1.3 Solicitors' Accounts

As already said, this is very much a separate topic to the other topics covered in this manual. The term 'Solicitors' Accounts' is not strictly accurate because what we are concerned with is a set of rules governing the accounts of any person or body that is regulated by the SRA. These rules are the SRA Accounts Rules 2019, and they are supplemented by guidance provided by the SRA. The main purpose of the rules is to protect the money of other persons when that money is being held and used by SRA regulated bodies, such as firms of solicitors.

Solicitors will receive and hold money which belongs to their clients, and solicitors must keep that money safe. To help achieve this, solicitors must keep the clients' money separate from the solicitors' firm's own money. This is achieved by keeping the money in separate bank or building society accounts. There is also the requirement for the firm to keep its own accounting records to record transactions using clients' money. We will see that there is independent oversight of the firm's accounting records, due to the requirement to obtain an accountant's report.

In **Chapter 14** we will look at the provisions of the SRA Accounts Rules 2019, followed in **Chapters 15** and **16** by a look at the accounting records kept by solicitors, and the entries that are made in those records in respect of a range of transactions. We will see that solicitors, like other businesses, will use the double entry bookkeeping system.

As said previously, the SRA Accounts Rules 2019 apply to all solicitors, regardless of their area of legal practice—not just to solicitors undertaking wills, estates and trusts work. In SQE 1, Solicitors' Accounts will be assessed in the context of Property Practice and Wills and Probate Practice.

## 1.4 Professional conduct and regulation in wills, the administration of estates and trusts

In this section, we will cover in summary the sorts of professional conduct and regulatory issues that are relevant to the practice of a solicitor working in the area of wills and the administration of estates. Because this manual does not cover the practice of administering trusts, the emphasis will be on rules which impact on the making of wills and the administration of an estate. Also, because the SRA Accounts Rules 2019 are themselves rules of professional conduct, it is not necessary to consider separately the relevance of professional conduct to Solicitors' Accounts in this chapter.

### 1.4.1 Professional conduct and ethical considerations

The rules of professional conduct are set out in the SRA Principles 2019, and in two codes of conduct: the SRA Code of Conduct for Solicitors, RELs and RFLs 2019, and the SRA Code of Conduct for Firms 2019. (NB: RELs stands for 'registered European lawyers' and RFLs stands for 'registered foreign lawyers'.)

The first code is aimed at individuals (solicitors, RELs and RFLs), and the second code is aimed at solicitors' firms and other bodies that are regulated by the SRA.

There is significant overlap between the two codes—for example, para 7.1 of the Code of Conduct for Firms expressly applies a number of paragraphs of the Code for Solicitors, RELs and RFLs to the conduct of firms and regulated bodies.

The SRA Principles comprise the 'fundamental tenets of ethical behaviour' that the SRA expects all those who the SRA regulates to uphold. Where two or more Principles come into conflict, those which safeguard the wider public interest should prevail.

The Principles and Codes are supported by the SRA's Enforcement Strategy, and the SRA also issues both guidance and warning notices in respect of conduct and regulatory issues.

In addition to the rules of professional conduct, solicitors and firms have to comply with a range of regulatory obligations. For example, solicitors must have a practising certificate (which is issued annually) in order to provide legal services to the public, solicitors' firms which are regulated by the SRA must also obtain professional indemnity insurance and solicitors' firms must contribute to a levy to maintain the SRA Compensation Fund.

There is regulatory oversight from more than one regulatory body. Solicitors are one of a range of legal professionals whose clients can complain to the Legal Ombudsman about the standard of service. Also, a solicitor may find themselves before the Solicitors' Disciplinary Tribunal, which may strike the solicitor off the Roll of Solicitors.

Firms must also comply with the general law which imposes obligations on businesses and organisations generally, such as the data protection requirements of the General Data Protection Regulation. Some general regulatory obligations are in later sections of this chapter, although it is important to realise that they apply to all solicitors and firms, regardless of their area of practice.

We will now look at some of the professional conduct issues particularly relevant to the practice of a wills and estates practitioner.

The professional conduct issues that arise whilst undertaking wills and administration work are noted in subsequent chapters as and when each particular issue arises. However, in summary, the sorts of issues that a solicitor might have to consider include the following (where the issue is discussed in more depth in a later chapter, the relevant section of that chapter is shown in brackets):

- Ensuring that a testator has the necessary mental **capacity** to instruct the solicitor to make a will, and confirming the testator's instructions if the instructions have been received from a third party (eg a relative who stands to inherit in the proposed will). A solicitor should also ensure that the client is not making the will as a result of force, fear or **undue influence**. These are all necessary to ensure that a solicitor meets Principle 7 (to act in the best interests of the client). The SRA has issued guidance on accepting instructions from vulnerable clients or third parties acting on their behalf. (See **2.4.1.4** and **2.4.2.2**.)
- Taking care when a client proposes to make a gift to the solicitor in the client's will. If the gift is a significant one, the solicitor should either refuse the gift or ensure that the client obtains independent legal advice before the solicitor drafts the will which includes such a gift. Paragraph 6.1 of each of the codes requires a solicitor not to act if there is an own interest conflict (ie a conflict between the interests of the client and the interests of the solicitor) or a significant risk of an own interest conflict. (See **2.4.2.4**.)
- Providing a testator with impartial advice on the choice of executor when the client is making a will. A solicitor should not promote their own firm as executor without advising the client on alternatives, such as appointing family members or friends as executors. Similarly, if a solicitor receives instructions for the preparation of a will from a trust corporation, the solicitor should advise on alternatives to the appointment of the trust corporation as executor. Principle 7 requires the solicitor and firm to act in the best interests of each client. In this context, this means not encouraging clients to appoint the solicitor or the firm as executor unless it is clearly in the best interests of the client to do so. (See **2.5.2**.)
- As with other areas of practice, solicitors are required to provide clear information regarding the likely costs of a matter. The administration of estates is one area of practice covered by the SRA Transparency Rules 2018, where the overall cost of administration services, and other information (eg the identity and level of the fee earners undertaking such work) has to be provided to potential clients, usually on the firm's website. (See **2.5.2.2** and **7.2.2**.)
- The SRA has issued guidance on the drafting and preparation of wills, and this also includes the storage of wills once they have been made. (See **2.12**.)
- As with all areas of practice, a solicitor needs to ensure they know who is their client, and must avoid conflicts of interest. With the making of a will, the client is the testator not the beneficiaries. In the administration of an estate, is the solicitor acting for the PR(s), or for a beneficiary, or perhaps for someone who is bringing a claim against the estate?

The above list concentrates on requirements of professional conduct arising from the Principles or the codes, and does not include other important considerations that solicitors should bear in mind in practice, such as drafting a will with sufficient speed following receipt of instructions (as those considerations are prompted by the case law on professional negligence rather than by the rules of professional conduct). Note that it is a requirement of all SQE assessments that candidates demonstrate their understanding and ability to act ethically as a solicitor and follow the SRA Standards and Regulations.

## 1.4.2 Financial services considerations

Solicitors will rarely be qualified to give advice on the merits of financial products or to make arrangements to buy and sell financial products. A solicitor who attempted to do so would probably be in breach of SRA Principle 7, because they would not be acting in the best interests of their client.

In addition to this, solicitors must comply with the requirements of the Financial Services and Markets Act 2000 (FSMA 2000), which regulates the financial services sector. The main thrust of FSMA 2000 is to protect persons who are investing in financial products and to ensure they obtain advice from a qualified person.

Solicitors undertaking wills and estates work will often not be engaged in regulated activities within the meaning of FSMA 2000, for the following reasons:

- a solicitor who is assisting a client with the drafting of the client's will is not providing financial services advice, because the client is not seeking to invest in financial products as part of the making of the will; and
- a PR who is administering the estate may do so by collecting in the deceased's assets, often converting those to cash by selling them and distributing the proceeds to the beneficiaries of the estate. The sale of assets from an estate is not usually regarded as a regulated activity due to relevant exclusions. It is only if the PRs decide to invest the sale proceeds that there will be FSMA 2000 considerations, and often the relatively short duration of the **administration period** will mean that the PRs will simply put the sales proceeds of the deceased's assets into a bank or building society account. Most activities with such accounts are not regulated activities. For these reasons, there will often be no FSMA 2000 difficulties for a solicitor who is acting as a PR or who is advising a PR.

In contrast, the trustee of a trust that might last for a period of years will want to consider how best to invest the trust fund. A trustee is much more likely to need to invest in specified investments, and so will have to consider the FSMA implications of those investments. However, the administration of trusts is outside the scope of this manual so the FSMA requirements relevant to the administration of trusts are not covered here.

#### 1.4.2.1 The Financial Services and Markets Act 2000

This is not a text on FSMA 2000, and specialist texts should be consulted for more detail. You will only need to know the very basics to answer FSMA-related questions in the context of wills and the administration of estates in the SQE.

#### 1.4.2.2 Financial services regulatory bodies

Since 2013 there have been three FSMA regulatory bodies. The most important of these for our purposes is the Financial Conduct Authority (FCA). If a solicitors' firm undertakes regulated activities then it must be regulated by the FCA.

In addition to the main regulatory bodies, professionals may be regulated by designated professional bodies (or DPBs). The Law Society is the DPB for solicitors but acts through its independent regulatory arm, the Solicitors Regulation Authority.

#### 1.4.2.3 Regulated activities and financial promotions

FSMA 2000 contains a prohibition on carrying out regulated activities (s19) and restrictions on making financial promotions (s21). The rest of this section deals only with regulated activities. We will not consider financial promotions any further as it is not normally relevant to solicitors undertaking wills and estates work.

#### 1.4.2.4 The general prohibition

Section 19 of FSMA 2000 prohibits a person from carrying on a regulated activity unless they are either:

- authorised (to do so by the FCA); or
- exempt (through conducting exempt regulated activities).

This is known as 'the general prohibition'.

A breach of the general prohibition is a criminal offence, and any agreement made in contravention of the general prohibition will be unenforceable.

### 1.4.2.5 Regulated activities

A business (eg a solicitors' firm) will conduct a regulated activity (for which FCA authorisation is required) if the activity is of a specified type, in respect of a specified investment and where no exclusion applies.

The different types of specified activities, specified investments and exclusions are set out the Financial Services and Markets Act 2000 (Regulated Activities) Order 2001 (RAO).

#### Specified activities

The specified types of activity include:

- dealing in investments as **agent**;
- arranging deals in investments;
- managing investments;
- safeguarding investments;
- advising on investments.

This is not a complete list.

#### Specified investments

Specified investments include:

- company stocks and shares;
- unit trusts;
- debentures;
- bonds;
- other financial products.

Again, this is not a complete list. However, significantly, interests in land are not included, and although bank and building society deposits are specified investments for some purposes, a solicitor will not be conducting a regulated activity in respect of such deposits.

#### Exclusions

The exclusions from regulated activities are also set out in the RAO. If an exclusion applies, there is no need to be authorised by the FCA in order to conduct the regulated activity.

We will only mention two exclusions here.

- Article 66—an important exclusion for our purposes is that applying to PRs (and trustees) in connection with the following activities: arranging, managing, safeguarding, advising and certain other activities. This will only benefit a solicitor who has been *appointed as* a PR or trustee: the exclusion does not apply to a solicitor who is *instructed by* a PR or trustee. Also, for the exclusion to apply, the activity must be conducted by the person themselves (ie by the solicitor who is the appointed PR/trustee), and not by another person within the same firm. The solicitor must not receive 'additional remuneration' for the activity; that is, on top of the fees the solicitor charges for their time in administering the estate. (Note that this explanation is a simplification and that there are other limitations on the exclusion not detailed here.)
- Article 67—the 'necessary' exclusion—activities carried out in the course of a profession or business. This applies to a number of activities, including advising, arranging and safeguarding. The activity must be seen as a necessary part of the other services provided in the course of the profession or business. This might benefit a solicitor who arranges the sale of assets from an estate in the course of administering the estate. It can apply to a solicitor who is not themselves a PR but who is acting for the PRs. Again, there must be no separate remuneration for carrying out the activity. This is not usually a problem as the solicitor will normally only charge for the time spent by them on the administration work.

### The exemption for professional firms

Most solicitors' firms will not be authorised by the FCA. If a non-authorised firm is conducting regulated activities, to avoid breaching s19 of FSMA 2000 the firm must be able to rely on either:

- one of the exclusions from the RAO; or
- be exempt.

We have considered the exclusions that are likely to be relevant to a solicitor conducting wills and estates work earlier in this section. In most cases, it should be possible to rely upon one of those exclusions. Alternatively, it might be possible to rely on the exemption for professional firms.

Under Part XX of FSMA 2000, there are exemptions for professional firms that carry out regulated activities incidentally in the course of their business—those activities are then described as 'exempt regulated activities'. For SRA regulated entities, such as solicitors' firms, this exemption is detailed in the SRA Financial Services (Scope) Rules. The SRA Financial Services (Conduct of Business) Rules also apply where the firm is carrying out an exempt regulated activity.

To fall within the professional firm's exemption, certain conditions must be met. These conditions are specified in s327 of FSMA 2000 and in the SRA Financial Services (Scope) Rules. In summary:

- the firm must account to the client for any pecuniary or other advantage received from a third party (eg it must not pocket any commission received as a result of conducting the regulated activity);
- the regulated activities must be incidental to the provision by the firm of its professional (ie legal) services, both in general terms when considering the work of the firm as a whole (ie for all of its clients) and in specific terms (ie when considering the work undertaken for the particular client);
- the regulated activities must be ones permitted by the SRA;
- there must be no specific prohibition on the particular activities (eg there are prohibitions in respect of certain insurance contracts, and so it is not possible to rely upon the exemption if the activity relates to an insurance contract); and
- the firm must not carry on other regulated activities.

Most solicitors' firms do not undertake what are called 'mainstream' regulated activities (ie as their core business), but only carry out regulated activities when it is incidental to their main work (ie the provision of legal services). So, if a firm undertaking administration work is not able to rely on one of the two exclusions mentioned earlier in this section, it will normally be able to rely on the professional firms' exemption. (Again, for the sake of brevity, the above explanation is a simplification of the rules, which are detailed and complex. In practice, care should be taken to ensure that any proposed regulated activity is covered by the exemption.)

## 1.4.3 **Money laundering**

Solicitors who draft wills for clients and who assist with the administration of estates are less likely to need to worry about criminals seeking to launder the proceeds of crime than solicitors undertaking other fields of work. For example, in property work or commercial work, clients may ask the solicitor to accept receipt of and hold large sums of money in the firm's client bank account. Similarly, there is less risk of money being used to finance terrorism or by someone who is seeking to evade paying tax.

A solicitor who is instructed to draft a client's will does not usually receive any sum of money from the client other than the payment of the solicitor's fees for drafting the will.

A solicitor who is acting for the PRs in the administration of an estate is not likely to receive any monies other than monies from the closure of the deceased's bank accounts or the sale proceeds of the deceased's existing assets. It is not the same as a situation where a living client wishes to put money (which may be the proceeds of crime) into the solicitor's bank accounts (in order to launder that money). Of course, the deceased may themselves have been a criminal and their assets may represent the proceeds of crime, but the risk is reduced compared with a request from a living client to bank large sums of money.

Situations where a solicitor may need to be particularly wary when undertaking administration work would be ones where someone involved in the estate is proposing to pay sums of money to the solicitor. For example, this might happen where the estate is requesting a loan from a PR or from a beneficiary to pay the inheritance tax due on submission of the inheritance tax account prior to applying for the grant of representation (see **7.6** for an explanation of why this might be necessary). Another situation may be where an asset is being sold to a beneficiary for more than the value of the beneficiary's interest in the estate: in such a situation, the beneficiary will have to pay to the estate the balance. However, as said, most of the money that flows into a solicitor's **client account** during the administration of an estate will be money on the closure of the deceased's own accounts and the sale proceeds of the deceased's assets.

Nevertheless, a solicitor undertaking wills and administration work must be alive to potential money laundering and comply with the relevant regulatory requirements.

The statutory regimes are not confined to money laundering that involves the proceeds of crime, but also seek to tackle both terrorist financing and tax evasion.

### 1.4.3.1 The statutory framework

The main authority is the Money Laundering, Terrorist Financing and Transfer of Funds (Information on the Payer) Regulations 2017 (as amended). As can be seen from the title, the regulations are concerned with the prospect of terrorist financing as well as that of money laundering (and also deal with tax evasion). The main statutes in this area are:

- the Proceeds of Crime Act 2002, which sets out various offences for non-compliance (see **1.4.3.6**);
- the Terrorism Act 2000 (relevant to terrorist financing); and
- the Criminal Finances Act 2017 (on the facilitation of tax evasion).

In addition to the primary and secondary legislation, there is guidance. The Legal Sector Affinity Group (a group of relevant organisations including the SRA) has issued Anti Money Laundering Guidance for the Legal Sector, most recently in 2023. The SRA has also issued guidance and warning notices in respect of money laundering, and has produced its own risk assessment document for the legal sector.

### 1.4.3.2 Risk assessment and management

As with other businesses, solicitors' firms must:

- undertake a risk assessment to identify and assess the risks of money laundering (it is worth noting that although risks with making wills and administering estates are usually low, the formation of trusts is regarded as one of the services most likely to be targeted by criminals or terrorists);
- have and maintain written policies, controls and procedures to mitigate and manage those risks effectively;
- appoint a member of senior management to be responsible for compliance;
- train their employees;
- screen employees to assess their competence and integrity; and
- keep specified records in respect of transactions.

### 1.4.3.3 Client identity checks (due diligence)

As with all areas of legal practice, a solicitor undertaking wills and estates work should undertake 'due diligence' to verify the identity of the client—whether this is the client who wishes to make a will or the PRs when instructions are received for the administration of an estate.

The verification of the client's identity should usually be completed before the establishment of the business relationship or the carrying out of the transaction. However, where (essentially) the risk of money laundering (or terrorist financing) is low, the identity of the client may be verified later, provided this is as soon as practicable after contact is first established.

Depending on the likely risk of money laundering, the due diligence may be 'simplified', 'standard' or 'enhanced'. Standard due diligence is most common, and in practice is done by asking the client to produce their passport or driving licence (in each case a form of official government document which has a photograph of the person as well as details such as the date of birth) and a document that verifies the person's address (eg a recent utility bill). There are different ways of verifying non-natural persons (eg limited companies) but this is rarely relevant to the making of a will or the administration of an estate. However, where a trust is involved, it may be necessary to verify the identity of the beneficial owners, which as defined includes the settlor, trustees (and certain other persons involved with the trust) as well as the beneficiaries of the trust.

Enhanced due diligence is required where there is a high risk of money laundering (or terrorist financing), perhaps where the client comes from one of the listed high-risk countries or has provided false identification documents. It may also be where the transactions are complex or unusually large, or the pattern of transactions is unusual, or where they have no apparent economic or legal purpose. This is not usually likely to be relevant to the making of wills or the administration of estates, but if enhanced due diligence is required, the solicitor will have to take additional steps which are not detailed here.

### 1.4.3.4 Ongoing monitoring

It is also necessary to continue to monitor the business relationship with the client on an ongoing basis. In particular, a solicitor should undertake checks on the source of funds to ensure that the client's transactions are consistent with the solicitor's knowledge of the client, the client's business and the client's risk profile. This check on the source of funds should occur before the solicitor gives the client the solicitor's bank account details.

### 1.4.3.5 Reporting suspicious activity

A solicitors' firm must also report suspicious activity to the National Crime Agency (NCA). Each firm is required to have its own nominated officer (also known as a money laundering reporting officer, or MLRO). Other persons within the firm, such as individual solicitors, may need to report suspicious activity to the MLRO. The MLRO will then consider the report made by the other member of the firm and consider whether or not a suspicious activity report should be made to the NCA.

When considering whether to make a suspicious activity report to the MLRO, a solicitor should consider the risk of money laundering having regard to the Legal Services Affinity Group guidance.

Chapter 5 of the 2023 Legal Sector Affinity Group guidance acknowledges that executorship and wills work may involve a lower risk of money laundering (section 5.6.3 of the guidance), but the risk factors in the guidance still need to be considered.

Under para 6.3 of the Code of Conduct for Solicitors, RELs and RFLs there is a duty to keep the affairs of current and former clients confidential. However, the duty in para 6.3 is qualified, as disclosure of the client's confidential information is allowed if it is either: (a) required or permitted by law; or (b) the client consents. In the context of money laundering and terrorist financing, disclosure of the client's information (by making a suspicious activity report to the NCA) is required or permitted by law and so is not a breach of the Code of Conduct.

### 1.4.3.6 Offences under the Proceeds of Crime Act 2002

There are various offences under the Proceeds of Crime Act 2002. The detail of these offences is outside the scope of this manual, but briefly the offences particularly relevant to a solicitor include the following:

- s328—entering into or becoming concerned in an arrangement which the person knows or suspects facilitates the acquisition, retention, use or control of criminal property by another person. This offence is particularly relevant to solicitors who could be seen to be assisting criminals in the laundering of money, such as by paying the proceeds of crime into the firm's client account. However, this is not the only way in which a solicitor may be seen to be involved in arrangements. An offence is not committed under s328 if the solicitor makes an 'authorised disclosure' (as defined in s338);

- s329—the acquisition, use or possession of criminal property. For a solicitor, this might include paying the proceeds of crime into the firm's general client account. Again, an offence is not committed under s329 if the solicitor makes an 'authorised disclosure' (as defined in s338). There is also a defence for a person who provides adequate consideration for the property (eg a solicitor who receives payment of their fees for the work undertaken for the client), but the defence does not apply if the person knows or suspects the services provided may help another to carry out criminal conduct;
- s330—a failure by a person to make an authorised disclosure (again, as defined in s338) where they know or suspect (or have reasonable grounds to know or suspect) that another person is engaged in money laundering. The information must have been obtained whilst working in the course of a 'business in the regulated sector' (this will include most solicitors' firms). An authorised disclosure is not required if the information is covered by legal professional privilege (the details of which are outside the scope of this manual);
- s333A—'tipping off'. It is an offence to disclose to a person that a suspicious activity report has been made (eg the solicitor tipping off the client). It is also an offence to disclose that there is an investigation into money laundering activities. In each case, the disclosure must be such that is likely to prejudice an investigation. Again, the information (on which the disclosure is based) must have come to the person in the course of a business in the regulated sector.

The penalties for the above offences include fines and, on indictment, maximum prison terms of between two and 14 years, depending on the offence.

Breach of the money laundering and terrorism financing legislation may also amount to a breach of professional conduct, for which a solicitor can be disciplined by the SRA.

## 1.4.4 Some other regulatory considerations

Perhaps unsurprisingly, there are other regulatory requirements which trustees (and PRs) will have to consider. These include responsibilities under the data protection legislation, and the requirement under a number of schemes to register a trust or provide information about the trust to relevant (usually tax) authorities.

### 1.4.4.1 Data protection (GDPR)

The current rules on data protection derive from the UK General Data Protection Regulation (UK GDPR) and the Data Protection Act 2018 (as amended). UK GDPR replaces the European Union's GDPR following Brexit. For the sake of simplicity, we will use the acronym GDPR to refer to UK GDPR in the following discussion.

The detailed rules on the GDPR are outside the scope of this manual and the discussion that follows is necessarily a simplification:

- The GDPR imposes requirements on the controllers and processors of the personal data of individuals. Such data must be processed in a way that protects the rights of those individuals (who are known as data subjects). Processing includes the recording and storage of data. When administering an estate or trust, PRs and trustees will record and store details of the beneficiaries of the estate or trust (eg their names and addresses) and will thus be processing personal data of the beneficiaries. However, the GDPR requirements only apply to the information of natural persons. This means, for example, that there are no GDPR requirements regarding the processing of the data of a charity that is a beneficiary of an estate or trust.
- It would seem that non-professional PRs and trustees (who do not receive payment for their services) fall within an exception to the GDPR requirements. This exception does not apply, though, to professional PRs and trustees (who are paid for their services).
- Solicitors who are instructed by the PRs and trustees in the administration of estates and trusts will also be processing the data of the beneficiaries.
- There must be a lawful ground for processing data. PRs, trustees and solicitors advising them will usually rely on the ground that the processing is necessary to comply with a legal obligation (ie the administration of the estate or trust).

- There is a prohibition on the processing of certain special category data (eg race, ethnic origin, religion or sexual orientation). However, there are exceptions to the prohibition, and it would seem that for PRs, trustees and solicitors advising them, the processing can be regarded as necessary for the 'establishment, exercise or defence of legal claims'.
- Data subjects have the right to be provided with certain information about how their data is being processed. The data subject should be provided with a privacy notice (containing specified information). PRs and trustees should normally provide beneficiaries with such privacy notices. The data subject may also make a data subject access request to be provided with a copy of all data held by the processor.
- When making their will, a testator will provide their solicitors with the personal data of individuals who are beneficiaries of the will, and often of persons who are excluded from benefit. The solicitor will thus be processing personal data. However, whilst there is a general requirement to provide data subjects with details of how their data is being processed, there are exceptions including one based upon confidentiality. Accordingly, a solicitor who has made a will for a client owes a duty of confidentiality to that client, and does not have to provide the data subjects with a privacy notice during the lifetime of the testator.
- The personal data of the data subject should be kept safe and protected from threats such as computer hacking.

#### 1.4.4.2 Trust registration and provision of information regimes

Trusts may need to register with or provide information to the appropriate authorities under one or more of a number of different regimes. The detail of these regimes is outside the scope of this manual, but briefly the regimes include:

- All UK resident **express trusts** and some non-UK resident trusts must register with HMRC's Trust Registration Service (TRS), unless the particular trust is a type that is excluded. Trusts have to register within 90 days of creation. The registration process is online and the trustee or advisor will need a 'Government Gateway' account. In addition, trustees must keep certain information on the trust and the beneficial owners, and provide that information on request to law enforcement authorities.
- Under the US Foreign Account Tax Compliance Act (FATCA), trusts outside the US, but with US taxpayers, must report information to the US tax authorities.
- Similarly, although applying to the taxpayers of EU and other countries, provision of information under the OECD's/EU's Common Reporting Standard (CRS) where a taxpayer's assets are held overseas.
- Disclosure of certain cross-border arrangements (under new UK regulations made in line with OECD mandatory disclosure rules, replacing regulations which implemented EU Directive 2018/822 (DAC6)).

### KEY POINT SUMMARY

- The topics of wills (or, more accurately, succession to property on death), the administration of estates, and trusts (or more accurately, Equity and trusts) are all related. A solicitor who drafts wills for clients is likely also to administer the estates of clients and to deal with the administration of trusts. However, Solicitors' Accounts is a separate topic: solicitors must comply with the SRA Accounts Rules no matter what area of law they practise in.
- Solicitors are the main source of professional advice and assistance for persons making wills and in the administration of estates. 'Probate activities' is one of the reserved legal activities under the Legal Services Act 2007, and solicitors are one of the types of professional persons authorised to prepare probate papers. Solicitors are also one of the main sources of advice and assistance in the drafting and administration of trusts.
- The SRA Accounts Rules 2019 are rules of conduct that all solicitors must comply with. The main objective of the Rules is to keep other people's money safe, because solicitors

will often hold money belonging to clients and others in the solicitor's client bank accounts. Solicitors must also maintain proper accounting records and obtain accountants' reports.

- Like everyone who is regulated by the SRA, solicitors working in the field of wills, estates and trusts must comply with the rules of professional conduct. The SRA has set out a number of Principles, which are supplemented by two Codes of Conduct (one for individual solicitors and registered overseas lawyers, and one for firms of solicitors). In particular, solicitors making wills for clients must provide impartial advice on the client's choice of executors and must take appropriate steps if the client intends leaving the solicitor a gift in the will. Where instructions for the will have come from a third party, the solicitor should check the instructions with the client (ie the testator) and should be satisfied that the testator has capacity and that the client wishes to make the will freely, without being pressured into doing so by others. Solicitors should provide clear information to the client about the costs of their services. The likely overall cost of administration services (and other related information) should appear on the firm's website.
- Solicitors need to comply with the requirements of the Financial Services and Markets Act 2000. There is a prohibition from undertaking regulated activities unless a solicitor is either authorised by the Financial Conduct Authority or is exempt. Most solicitors are not authorised by the FCA and, as a matter of professional conduct, are not properly qualified to provide investment advice to their clients. Solicitors may avoid undertaking regulated activities by using one of the exclusions under the Regulated Activities Order or by relying on the professional firms' exemption in Part XX of FSMA 2000 and the SRA's own Scope Rules. For solicitors undertaking estates or trusts work, the most likely exemptions are: (a) for solicitors who have been appointed as PRs or trustees (RAO art 66); or (b) for solicitors instructed by the PRs or trustees, the 'necessary' exclusion, where the regulated activity is incidental to the legal work undertaken for the client (RAO art 67). The professional firms' exemption also works on the basis that the regulated activity is incidental to the solicitor's legal work.
- Solicitors' firms have responsibilities to guard against money laundering. Criminals may seek to launder the proceeds of crime by passing money through a solicitor's bank accounts. Similarly, terrorists might seek to finance their activities through a solicitor's bank accounts or a client may be seeking to evade the payment of taxes. The Money Laundering, Terrorist Financing and Transfer of Funds (Information on the Payer) Regulations 2017 impose requirements on businesses (including solicitors) to put in place procedures to prevent money laundering, such as due diligence (verifying the identity of the client and other persons, eg beneficial owners of trusts), and to report suspicious activity. Individual solicitors should make suspicious activity reports to the firm's nominated officer, who will then consider whether to make a report to the National Crime Agency. There are a range of criminal offences for non-compliance. For example, the Proceeds of Crime Act 2002 includes offences of failing to report suspicious activity and of tipping off a client when a suspicious activity report has been made or an investigation is ongoing.
- Solicitors must comply with the obligations placed on the controllers and processors of personal data by the UK General Data Protection Regulation and the Data Protection Act 2018. Individual beneficiaries will be data subjects and PRs and trustees (and the solicitors advising them) will need to consider whether those beneficiaries should be provided with a privacy notice at the beginning of the estate or trust administration period. Data subjects can also make data subject requests. PRs and trustees (and the solicitors advising them) are likely to be seen as having a legitimate ground for processing the personal data. However, the personal data must be kept secure.
- Most express trusts will have to register with HMRC's Trust Registration Service. In addition, there are various overseas and multinational regimes which require trusts to provide information to the relevant authorities in specified circumstances.

# PART B
# Wills and Intestacy

# CHAPTER 2
# Making Wills

**FUNCTIONING LEGAL KNOWLEDGE**

This chapter covers the following functioning legal knowledge required to pass the SQE 1 assessments:

**Validity of wills and codicils:**

- **testamentary capacity**
- duress and **undue influence**
- formal requirements

**AUTHORITIES UNDERPINNING PRACTICE**

The key authorities that underpin this area of practice are listed below. Note that for legislation you are linked to legislation.gov.uk.

Although much of the legislation on this government website is available in its amended form, the incorporation of new amendments into the text of legislation can be delayed. You should refer to legal databases to ensure you are referencing the most up-to-date legislation.

- Wills Act 1837
  **http://www.legislation.gov.uk/ukpga/Will4and1Vict/7/26/contents**

## 2.1 Introduction

A will is a declaration or series of declarations by a person stating what should happen following that person's death, mainly with regard to that person's property. The person who makes the will is known as the '**testator**' or 'testatrix' if female. (For ease of reference, though, the term 'testator' is used in this manual except when referring to the facts of any reported case or if there is an example where the will has been made by a testatrix.)

In this chapter we will consider the purpose of a will and you will see a short example of a will with a selection of clauses that might be incorporated in a will. We will then consider the requirements for a valid will—**capacity**, **intention** and **formalities**—in some depth. After that we will look at the appointment of **executors** and **trustees** (although the duties associated with those roles are dealt with in later chapters—particularly **Chapters 7–9** and **13**). We will also consider the appointment of testamentary **guardians** briefly, the testator's wishes for their funeral and disposal of their body, and the storage of wills.

Then, in **Chapter 3** we will move on to look at how someone can change their will, at different types of **gift** and how clauses in wills are interpreted.

## 2.2 **Why make a will?**

There are a number of reasons for making a will.

1. The main reason is that the testator can decide who should benefit from their estate, and in what proportions. Without a will, the person's estate would be distributed in accordance with the rules of **intestacy** and this may produce results which the testator would be unhappy with. (A discussion of different types of gift is included in **Chapter 3**, and the rules of intestacy are covered in **Chapter 4**.) It is also important to realise that not all of the testator's assets will be distributed in accordance with the terms of the will. Certain property, such as the share of a **joint tenant in equity**, passes independently of the terms of the will (see **Chapter 5**). The testator has freedom to decide who should benefit from the estate and is not obliged to leave the estate to close relatives or persons who are financially dependent on the testator. However, close relatives and dependants are able to apply to court after a testator's death if they consider that the testator has not made **reasonable financial provision** for them (see **Chapter 11**).
2. A secondary consideration for making a will is that the testator can appoint **personal representatives** of their choice. Personal representatives have the job of administering the testator's estate, distributing the estate in accordance with the terms of the testator's will. These personal representatives, chosen by the testator, are called the 'executors'. (We will look at the appointment of executors in **2.5**.) If the testator does not choose executors, the identity of the personal representatives will be determined by the Non-Contentious Probate Rules 1987 (this is covered in **Chapter 8**).
3. The testator can appoint 'testamentary guardians' to look after any of their children who are under the age of 18 years at the date of the testator's death. (This is considered briefly in **2.10**.)
4. The testator can include tax-saving provisions in the will, particularly with regard to the potential **inheritance tax** charge on death. (Inheritance tax is covered in detail in **Chapter 6**.)
5. It is possible to extend the statutory powers of the executors (and the trustees of any continuing **trust**), and to remove certain inconvenient rules of law, thereby giving the executors and trustees greater freedom in administering the estate or trust. (For more detail on the powers of executors and trustees, see **Chapter 13**.)
6. The testator can include directions as to their funeral and regarding the disposal of their body. (This is considered briefly in **2.11**.)
7. There is also some comfort simply in putting your wishes down 'in black and white', namely in writing.

## 2.3 **The typical structure of a will**

Over time, a standard order has been developed for the clauses within a will. It is not necessary to follow this order when drafting wills, but it is advisable to do so as other legal professionals will expect to see the clauses in this order when they come to look at the wills you have drafted.

The traditional order is:

- the heading/opening words;
- a '**revocation**' clause;
- directions as to the funeral and disposal of the body (although this often comes later, towards the end of the will);
- the appointment of executors (and of trustees, if there is a trust created by the will);
- the appointment of testamentary guardians;
- '**non-residuary**' gifts, including:
  - gifts of sums of money (**pecuniary legacies**);
  - gifts of **chattels** and other personal property (**bequests**); and
  - gifts of land (**devises**);

- provisions relating to the rest (or '**residue**') of the estate (**residuary gifts**);
- extensions of the trustees' powers;
- declarations excluding or modifying certain inconvenient rules of law; and
- the **attestation** clause (followed by the signatures of the testator and the **witnesses**).

An example will follow in the next section.

## 2.3.1 Example will

Here are extracts from an example will. The extracts include examples of different types of clause that will be considered later in this chapter and in later chapters of this manual. However, it is not mandatory to include each of these types of clause in a will. For example, the extracts which follow include non-residuary gifts of money, of a watch and of a holiday cottage, but a testator is not obliged to include any non-residuary gifts in their will.

THIS IS THE LAST WILL AND TESTAMENT dated the 10th day of January 2024 of me HAYDN DAVIES of 19 Brynglas Close, Whitchurch, Cardiff.

1. I REVOKE all earlier wills and testamentary dispositions.
2. I APPOINT my brother GERAINT DAVIES of 4 Coryton View, Tongwynlais, Cardiff and my sister MARGARET PRICE of 59 Bishop's Lane, Llandaff, Cardiff as my executors and trustees.
3. If my wife MEGAN DAVIES fails to survive me I APPOINT my said sister MARGARET PRICE and her husband IOLO PRICE as testamentary guardians of any of my children who are under eighteen at the date of my death.
4. I GIVE the sum of ONE THOUSAND POUNDS (£1,000) to my good friend WYN JONES of 45 Park View South, Roath, Cardiff absolutely.
5. I GIVE my gold watch to my said brother GERAINT DAVIES absolutely.
6. I GIVE my holiday cottage at 12 Sea View, Tenby, Carmarthenshire to my said sister MARGARET PRICE absolutely.
7. MY EXECUTORS AND TRUSTEES shall hold the rest of my estate on trust:
   (a) to pay debts funeral and executorship expenses and legacies;
   (b) to pay my residuary estate to my said wife MEGAN DAVIES but if she dies before me;
   (c) to divide my residuary estate equally among those of my brother the said GERAINT DAVIES and my sister the said MARGARET PRICE as survive me but if either of them should die before me leaving a child or children of their own then that child or those children will take the share which their parent would have taken had he or she survived me and if more than one in equal shares.

[*NB—extensions of the executors' and trustees' statutory powers, and certain declarations by the testator would normally follow, although they are not included here. For a discussion of these clauses see* ***Chapter 13***.]

| | |
|---|---|
| SIGNED by the Testator<br>the said HAYDN DAVIES<br>in our joint presence and<br>attested by us in his<br>presence: | Haydn Davies |
| Peter Evans | Gwen Evans |
| PETER EVANS<br>17 BRYNGLAS CLOSE<br>WHITCHURCH<br>CARDIFF | GWEN EVANS<br>17 BRYNGLAS CLOSE<br>WHITCHURCH<br>CARDIFF |

The opening part of the will (the heading) indicates that the document is the last will of the testator and identifies the testator (Haydn Davies).

Clause 1 is a 'revocation' clause, which is used to cancel, or 'revoke', any earlier wills. See **Chapter 3** for a discussion of revocation.

Clause 2 is an appointment of executors and trustees. The testator has appointed family members (his brother and his sister) but testators have an open choice as to who to choose as executors and trustees. The executors and trustees will administer the testator's estate after the testator's death, and will carry out the testator's wishes. See **2.5** and **2.6** for more detail on the appointment of executors and trustees.

Clause 3 provides for an appointment of testamentary guardians, which is discussed in **2.10**.

Clauses 4, 5 and 6 include a series of 'non-residuary' gifts. They are, respectively, a **legacy** of money in clause 4, a 'bequest' of a chattel (a personal possession) in clause 5 and a 'devise' of land and buildings (the holiday cottage in Tenby) in clause 6. See **Chapter 3** for a discussion of these different types of non-residuary gifts.

Clause 7 creates a trust over the **residuary estate** of the testator. After payment of debts, expenses and legacies, the whole estate is left initially to the testator's wife, but if she dies before the testator, the estate is divided equally between his brother and sister. There is a further substitutional gift in clause 7(c) which provides for a gift of one half of the estate to the children of the testator's brother or sister, if the brother or sister die before the testator.

The clauses not shown are the clauses dealing with technical matters, rather than the main wishes of the testator. The missing clauses would extend the powers of the executors and trustees (to give them more powers than they would normally have under the general law), and would make a series of declarations, usually in order to simplify the administration of the estate. Such extensions of powers and declarations are discussed in **Chapter 13**.

The final clause shown is the signature clause, or 'attestation clause'. The signature of the testator and the two witnesses appear here. See **2.4.3** for a discussion of the requisite formalities for making a valid will.

## 2.4 The requirements of a valid will

There are three requirements for a will to be valid:

- First, the testator should have the relevant mental *capacity*, which is called 'testamentary capacity'.
- Secondly, the testator must have the *intention* to make the will (and the particular provisions of the will).
- Thirdly, the will must have been signed (or '**executed**') in accordance with the *formalities* set out in the relevant statutory provision.

We will consider each of these three requirements in turn in **2.4.1–2.4.3**.

### 2.4.1 Testamentary capacity

To make a valid will, a testator must have the requisite mental state, or 'capacity', at the date the will is made. This capacity is known as 'testamentary capacity'. With an ageing population and a more litigious society, there have been many recent examples of the validity of wills being challenged after the testator's death, on the basis that the testator lacked testamentary capacity. There are frequent reported cases: these usually add nothing of principle to this area of law, because they do not change the rules, and each case is decided by the judge on the basis of the facts. However, the number of reported cases shows that testamentary capacity is a very fertile ground for litigation.

#### 2.4.1.1 The testator's age

In addition to having testamentary capacity (discussed in **2.4.1.2**), the testator must be aged 18 or over at the date the will is made (s7 Wills Act 1837). This is with the exception of 'privileged wills' (s11 Wills Act 1837).

Privileged wills are wills which do not have to comply with the usual formalities for wills set out in section 9 of the Wills Act 1837 (see **2.4.3** for more detail on the usual formalities). The important point for this section on capacity is that a person under the age of 18 may make a privileged will. Privileged wills can only be made by persons in the armed forces whilst on active service or by sailors at sea. Testators of privileged wills do, though, have to meet the common law test for testamentary capacity, just like testators of standard wills.

### 2.4.1.2 The common law test for testamentary capacity

The traditional test for testamentary capacity was laid down in the 19th-century case of *Banks v Goodfellow* (1870) LR 5 QB 549.

To have testamentary capacity, a testator must understand three key things:

1 *the nature of the act and its effects* (in other words, the testator must understand that they are making a will, and that the effect of the will is to dispose of their property amongst their chosen **beneficiaries**);

2 *the extent of the property that they are disposing of by the will* (testators do not need to know exactly how much they own, ie down to the nearest pound or pence, but they should have a reasonable understanding of their own wealth); and

3 *the claims to which they ought to give effect* (ie the persons who would normally be expected to benefit from the will—such as spouses, children, other close family members). This does not mean that the testator has to leave something in the will to any of those persons—in English and Welsh law the testator has testamentary freedom and can decide on who should benefit in the will. However, it is necessary that the testator knows who normally would have a moral claim on their estate, even if the testator decides not to leave those persons anything in the will.

There is also a fourth aspect to the test, which is that the testator should not suffer from insane delusions which cause the testator to make provisions in the will which they would not have made if they had been of sound mind. In other words, for the delusions to affect the testator's testamentary capacity, the delusions must have had an effect on what is written in the will. So, in *Banks v Goodfellow* itself, it was held that the testator's insane delusions (that he was being followed by a man long since dead, and by spirits and demons), did not affect the validity of the will, because they did not influence the wishes expressed by the testator in the will.

It should be apparent from what has just been said about the facts in *Banks v Goodfellow* that a person may have significant issues with their mental health or mental capacity in general, and yet may still have sufficient understanding to make a will. Provided a person has the necessary elements of testamentary capacity listed above, they can make a valid will, and it does not matter that they lack the capacity to do other things, for example to manage their own property and finances.

### 2.4.1.3 At what point in time is testamentary capacity required?

Testamentary capacity is determined at a particular point in time. The testator needs to have the relevant understanding at the time the will is executed (ie signed and witnessed).

It is well recognised that a person's mental capacity is not constant and can fluctuate over time. For example, someone suffering from some form of dementia (eg Alzheimer's disease) will find their mental capacity gradually diminishing as their illness progresses. However, even though the general trend is a worsening of the condition, on a day-to-day basis a person's capacity can worsen or improve. People can have good days and bad days. A person who might not have capacity to make a will on one day, might have sufficient capacity to make it on the next day.

**EXAMPLE**

Letitia is suffering from Alzheimer's disease. As usual, the illness is progressive, but Letitia is in the early stages of the disease and so some days the effect on her memory and understanding is minimal. Letitia visits her solicitor on one of these good days, and gives the solicitor instructions for the will. The solicitor questions Letitia to see if she understands the effect of a will, if she has a good idea about the property she owns and about the persons who would normally be expected to benefit from her estate. She is able to demonstrate understanding of all these things. She returns to the office and the will is signed and witnessed, also on a good day. However, in between the two appointments, Letitia's condition deteriorated considerably, and for most of those days her memory was such that she would not have had testamentary capacity. Nevertheless, this does not affect the validity of the will because she had the necessary capacity at the date the will was executed (ie at the second appointment).

Although the basic rule is that the testator must have the necessary testamentary capacity at the date of executing the will, the rule in *Parker v Felgate* (1883) 8 PD 171 laid down an acceptable alternative. Under this rule, it is sufficient to show that:

1 the requisite capacity existed at the date of giving instructions for the preparation of the will;
2 the will was prepared in accordance with those instructions; and
3 at the time of execution the testator understood that they were signing a will for which instructions had previously been given (though it is not necessary for the testator at that time to be able either to remember what those instructions were or to understand the will if read over to them).

**EXAMPLE**

Abdul is suffering from senile dementia and lives in a residential care home. His solicitor visits him in early March and takes instructions from him for a simple will, making some small legacies and dividing his residuary estate amongst his children and grandchildren. At the time of giving instructions, Abdul is lucid and is able to demonstrate that he understands the effect of a will, roughly what he owns and who his nearest relatives are. He is not delusional.

However, when the solicitor returns to the residential care home a week later, there has been a marked deterioration in Abdul's condition. Abdul is much more confused, and unable to explain what property he owns or who his nearest family members are. Abdul does retain some understanding, though: he is still able to understand that by signing the will he is giving effect to his previous instructions. Based on the authority of *Parker v Felgate*, it should be possible for Abdul to make a valid will.

The common law rules detailed above predated the Mental Capacity Act 2005 which came into force in October 2007. The Mental Capacity Act 2005 provides for a single test of mental capacity, but the Code of Practice issued in relation to the Act indicates that the Act is to be read alongside existing common law tests of capacity. However, the statutory test differs in several respects from the common law test for testamentary capacity from *Banks v Goodfellow*, and for some years after the Act came into force there was doubt over whether the statutory test had replaced or altered the common law test. This question was eventually resolved in *Walker v Badmin* [2014] EWHC 71 (Ch) when it was held that the relevant test for testamentary capacity was the common law test from *Banks v Goodfellow*, and that this test had not been altered or displaced by the Mental Capacity Act. This has been confirmed in several cases, including *Baker v Hewston* [2023] EWHC 1145 (Ch), although it was suggested in that case to use the Act as a 'cross-check' against the common law test.

#### 2.4.1.4 Proof of capacity

At common law, the burden of proving that the testator had testamentary capacity is on the person who is seeking to prove the will, namely to have it accepted by the court as valid.

However, there are two rebuttable presumptions which will usually help a person who is seeking to prove the will. The first presumption is that capacity is assumed where the will appears to be rational, and the second presumption is that mental states are presumed to continue.

So, if the will appears to be rational and the testator had no history of mental capacity issues, the burden of proof will pass to the person who is seeking to prove that the testator lacked testamentary capacity. The person seeking to prove that the testator lacked testamentary capacity will have to adduce evidence to the court to prove this, on the balance of probabilities.

However, the second presumption can work against the person who is seeking to prove the will, because if the testator had a history of mental capacity issues prior to making the will, the presumption is that this mental state continued and that it would have affected the testator at the time the will was made. This means that the person seeking to prove the will must then adduce evidence to prove, on the balance of probabilities, that the testator had testamentary capacity at the date the will was made (or, under *Parker v Felgate*, when instructions were given for the preparation of the will). As said earlier, testamentary capacity is assessed at the date the will is made (or when instructions are given), so it is possible for someone to lack capacity on some days but have capacity on others. If the testator made the will (or gave instructions) on a day when they had capacity, that is sufficient for the will to be valid. However, the point is that the person seeking to establish testamentary capacity must prove this, with evidence, to overcome the presumption.

Under s1 of the Mental Capacity Act 2005, there is a statutory presumption of capacity, namely it is assumed that a person has capacity until the contrary is proved. This statutory presumption seemingly applies in all cases, and until *Walker v Badmin* in 2014 it was thought that this statutory presumption had changed the common law presumption in the previous paragraph. However, in *Walker v Badmin* it was confirmed that the common law test for testamentary capacity, and the common law presumptions referred to earlier, continue to apply and have not been replaced by the statutory presumption.

**CONDUCT POINT**

The SRA guidance note on Drafting and Preparation of Wills (amended 25 November 2019) indicates that a solicitor needs to make sure that clients have the necessary testamentary capacity and, where appropriate, that a doctor's opinion is obtained to evidence this.

If there is doubt about a testator's capacity, what evidence of capacity might be available? How might a solicitor seek to mitigate the potential for challenges after the client's death?

Helpfully, it has been stated (and confirmed recently by the Court of Appeal in *Hughes v Pritchard* [2022] EWCA Civ 386) that a will drafted by an experienced, independent lawyer should only be set aside on the clearest evidence of lack of mental capacity. The Court of Appeal also stressed the considerable importance of the evidence of such a lawyer, compared with that of a medical expert at trial who had never met the testator.

In *Kenward v Adams* [1975] 1 WLUK 39, Templeman J set out what he called 'the golden rule' that solicitors should follow when instructed by a testator where capacity may be in doubt. However, there are difficulties in following all the steps of the 'golden rule' in practice, and it is clear from other cases, including *Hughes*, that failure to follow the rule does not automatically invalidate a will.

According to Templeman J:

> In the case of an aged testator or a testator who has suffered a serious illness, there is one golden rule which should always be observed, however straightforward matters may appear, and however difficult or tactless it may be to suggest that precautions be taken: the making of a will by such a testator ought to be witnessed or approved by a medical practitioner who satisfies himself of the capacity and understanding of the testator, and records and preserves his examination and findings

Unfortunately, in practice, this is easier said than done, and doctors and other medical practitioners are often unwilling to witness a will. Hospital staff, and the staff of care homes, are often prohibited by their employer from doing so. The alternative is for a medical practitioner to make an assessment of mental capacity. However, many (but not all) doctors are reluctant to provide such assessments. Time has moved on since 1975—with increasing workloads, general practitioners (GPs) have less time to provide assessments of capacity. Also, doctors are concerned about being drawn into litigation after the testator's death. Lastly, many GPs lack the necessary expertise in mental capacity assessments.

It is possible to obtain a report from an expert in mental capacity but this is likely to prove expensive and the client may not be willing to pay. The solicitor will need to consider whether to proceed without a medical opinion (and face the prospect of being criticised by a judge if the matter goes to court). As said, though, it is clear from case law (including *Hughes*) that the golden rule is more of a guide to practitioners than an absolute requirement for validity of the will.

Ironically, after Templeman J (later Lord Templeman) died in 2014, there was a dispute (reported as *Goss-Custard v Templeman* [2020] EWHC 632 (Ch)) over his own will, made at a time when his memory was starting to deteriorate. Although the will was held to be valid, he failed to follow his own golden rule (which, remember, he said 'should always be observed') of ensuring there was a medically qualified witness!

There are other aspects of the 'golden rule' worth noting.

- First, if the testator has made a previous will, the legal and medical advisors should discuss this with the testator. Again, this is not an absolute requirement.
- Also, the instructions of the testator should be taken in the absence of anyone who may stand to benefit, or who may have influence over the testator. This aspect, though, is usually more relevant to the question of undue influence—see **2.4.2.2**—than to the question of capacity.
- Lastly, one precaution that should always be followed (and not just where the client is elderly or unwell) is for the solicitor to make and retain a full contemporaneous attendance note, which should be helpful in the event of any future challenge to the will. The note should record the questions asked by the solicitor in order to assess the client's capacity and the answers given by the client. The solicitor should check that the client understands the effect of a will, ask the client questions about the client's property and assets and ask the client questions about the nearest relatives, even if the client does not wish those relatives to benefit. In practice, an attendance note should always be taken and kept.

### 2.4.1.5 Statutory wills

Perhaps surprisingly, it is not always necessary for the testator to have testamentary capacity for a will to be valid. This is because the Court of Protection has the authority (under s16 Mental Capacity Act 2005) to make a '**statutory will**' on behalf of a person who lacks the necessary mental capacity to make a valid will for themselves. The details of statutory wills are outside the scope of this manual, and specialist texts should be consulted.

## 2.4.2 **Intention (knowledge and approval)**

The second requirement for a valid will is that the testator must have the **intention** to make the will. There are two aspects of this. First, the testator must have had a general intention to make a will and, secondly, the testator must have the specific intention to make the particular will, and the particular provisions contained in that will. Put another way, the testator must 'know and approve' the contents of the will for it to be valid. To the extent that such knowledge and approval are lacking, the will cannot be admitted to **probate**.

The necessary knowledge and approval must normally have existed at the date of the execution of the will. However, the rule in *Parker v Felgate* (see **2.4.1.3**) also applies in this context, so that it is sufficient if the testator had the necessary knowledge and approval at the time of giving instructions for the preparation of the will, even if this knowledge and approval was not apparent at the time the will was executed.

A court might find that the testator knew and approved part of their will, but lacked knowledge and approval of other parts of the will. In such circumstances, part of the will may be allowed for probate but part of the will would be invalid, and will be excluded. This happened in *Wintle v Nye* [1959] 1 WLR 284, where the House of Lords decided that a testatrix did not know and approve those gifts in her will which benefited the solicitor who had prepared the will for her. Nevertheless, the rest of the will was admitted to probate.

It is possible for words to be included or omitted from the will by mistake. A testator may lack knowledge and approval of an entire will (perhaps by executing the wrong will) or the testator may not know and approve of parts of a will (as in *Wintle v Nye*).

### 2.4.2.1 Proof

The burden of proving intention lies on the person seeking to obtain probate, namely on the person who is claiming that the will is valid. However, there is generally a rebuttable presumption that a testator with the necessary mental capacity also executed the will with the requisite knowledge and approval of its contents. Those who seek to challenge the will would have to prove that the testator made the will (or perhaps a particular provision in it) as a result of force, fear, fraud or undue influence or that the necessary knowledge and approval were lacking because of a mistake.

Having said this, there is no presumption of knowledge and approval in two situations:

1 where the testator is blind or illiterate, or someone has signed the will on the testator's behalf. As we will see (in **2.4.3** on formalities), a suitably drafted 'attestation clause' will assist in supplying the necessary evidence of knowledge and approval in such situations;

2 where there are suspicious circumstances—in particular where the will substantially benefits the person who prepared it (or a close relative of that person), such as in *Wintle v Nye*. In such cases, evidence will be required of the testator's knowledge and approval of the contents of the will: otherwise, the gift will fail.

There does not need to be evidence that the testator actually read the will—this can be inferred from the surrounding circumstances—and the court may consider that it is sufficient that the testator had the opportunity to read the will. This is what happened in *Fuller v Strum* [2001] EWCA Civ 1879, where the Court of Appeal overturned the decision of the trial judge, holding that it was improbable that the testator had not read what was a short and simple will, even though there was no evidence of the testator actually having read the will.

In contrast, in *Gill v Woodall* [2010] EWCA Civ 1430, the Court of Appeal held that the testatrix had lacked knowledge and approval, even though the will was prepared by solicitors and the testatrix attended the solicitors' office to sign and witness the will, and even though the sole beneficiary under the will (a charity, the RSPCA), played no part in the making of the will. In that case, there were other suspicious circumstances (including the testatrix's previously critical view of the RSPCA, the influence seemingly exerted by the testatrix's husband and the unexplained lack of provision for the testatrix's only daughter). Combined with the testatrix's severe anxiety disorder (agoraphobia), the result was that the testatrix was held not to have known and approved the terms of the will. The will was thus invalid and the daughter inherited the estate on the resulting intestacy.

As with questions of proof on capacity, the standard of proof when considering intention is the civil standard (the balance of probabilities), not the criminal standard (beyond reasonable doubt).

### 2.4.2.2 Force, fear, fraud and undue influence

If a will has been made as a result of force, fear, fraud or undue influence it will not be valid. However, it is always necessary to prove force, fear, fraud or undue influence. There are no presumptions that will assist the person trying to prove that a will is invalid for one of these reasons. Again, the standard of proof is the balance of probabilities, even though the behaviour alleged might also involve the commission of a criminal offence.

It is worth noting that this is a different approach compared with undue influence with lifetime gifts. With lifetime gifts, there is a presumption of undue influence where the donee is in a position of influence over the donor, for example a father and child or a solicitor and client. With gifts in wills, though, undue influence must always be proven.

A good example of possible undue influence is *Gill v Woodall* [2010] (see **2.4.2.1**). Although the Court of Appeal made its decision on the basis that the testatrix did not know and approve the contents of the will due to suspicious circumstances, an alternative reason for the decision could have been that the testatrix's husband had exerted undue influence over her in making her leave her estate to the RSPCA (and thereby excluding their only daughter). This was, in fact, the decision by the judge at first instance, but because the Court of Appeal decided the case on the basis of lack of knowledge and approval, it was not necessary for the Court of Appeal to decide whether or not there had been undue influence.

**CONDUCT POINT**

The SRA guidance note on Drafting and Preparation of Wills (amended 25 November 2019) indicates that you may need to manage situations where you are concerned about someone's undue influence on the client, and to monitor for frauds and scams (particularly if the solicitor provides online will-writing services). Under SRA Principle 7, the solicitor has a duty to act in the best interests of each client, and in the context of a will being prepared by the solicitor, the client is the testator of the will. The SRA has also issued separate guidance on Accepting Instructions from Vulnerable Clients or Third Parties Acting on their Behalf.

### 2.4.2.3 Rectification

**Rectification** involves the court in ordering the amendment of a will to correct an error in the testator's will. Applications for rectification are made to the court after the testator's death, when the error in the will is discovered.

Section 20 of the Administration of Justice Act 1982 provides that a court may order that a will be rectified if the court is satisfied that the will is so expressed that if fails to carry out the testator's intentions, due to:

- a clerical error; or
- a failure (by the person preparing the will) to understand the testator's instructions.

A clerical error includes typing errors—words included or omitted from the will by mistake. It does not cover a situation where the person drafting the will makes an error of law, by not appreciating the legal effect of the words chosen for inclusion in the will.

In *Marley v Rawlings* [2014] UKSC 2, the Supreme Court said that 'clerical error' should be given a wide meaning, and should include a mistake arising out of office work of a routine nature. In *Marley v Rawlings*, a husband's will was rectified in a situation where the husband had mistakenly signed his wife's will and the wife had mistakenly signed the husband's will.

An application for rectification must be made within six months of the date of the main **grant of representation** to the testator's estate, although the court may give permission for a later application. However, the personal representatives will be protected if they distribute after the initial six month period, and will not be personally liable to anyone who would become entitled as a result of an out-of-time rectification application. This does not preclude such persons being able to recover money and property from the beneficiaries who have already received distributions from the estate.

Rectification may not be necessary if the court can instead interpret the will in such a way as to ascertain and give effect to the testator's intention. In *Marley v Rawlings*, the more flexible approach taken by courts to the interpretation of contracts was applied to the interpretation of wills. Lord Neuberger said: 'the aim is to identify the intention of the party or parties to the document [this is the testator in the case of a will] by interpreting the words used in their documentary, factual and commercial context'.

Also, where part of a will is meaningless or ambiguous, there is statutory authority to enable the use of extrinsic evidence, including extrinsic evidence of a testator's intention, to assist in the interpretation of the will (s21 Administration of Justice Act 1982). (Extrinsic evidence is evidence outside, or extrinsic to, the words used in the will itself. For example, extrinsic evidence would include evidence of oral statements made by the testator around the time the will was made.)

For more detail on the interpretation of wills, see **Chapter 3**.

### 2.4.2.4 Gifts to solicitors

We have seen (in **2.4.2.1**) that there is a rebuttable presumption that a testator does not have knowledge and approval of a will, or parts of a will, where the will benefits the person who prepared the will. We have also seen the case of *Wintle v Nye*, where the House of Lords held that the testatrix lacked knowledge and approval of the gifts made to her solicitor in the will, and so those gifts were held to be invalid. In addition to this, there are also professional conduct considerations where a client is leaving a gift to their solicitor in the will.

**CONDUCT POINT**

A solicitor who drafts a client's will must abide by the SRA Principles and SRA Code of Conduct for Solicitors, RELs and RFLs 2019. Under the SRA Principles, solicitors and firms must act with honesty, integrity and in a way that upholds public trust and confidence in the solicitors' profession (Principles 4, 5 and 2 respectively) and in legal services provided by SRA authorised persons. Solicitors must also act in the best interests of each client (Principle 7).

A solicitor is not likely to be acting honestly, with integrity or in the best interests of their client if they are effectively helping themselves to the client's estate after the client's death, by persuading or allowing the client to leave gifts to them in the will.

The SRA has also issued guidance on the Drafting and Preparation of Wills (updated in November 2019 to reflect the 2019 Principles and Codes of Conduct). The guidance indicates that if a solicitor drafts a will where the client wishes to make a gift of significant value to the solicitor (or to a member of the solicitor's family or an employee of the solicitor's business or the employee's family), then the solicitor should satisfy themselves that the client has first taken independent legal advice with regard to making the gift. A gift may be of a significant value in relation to the size of the client's overall estate, but also where the gift is of significant value in itself. A solicitor will usually need to cease acting if the client does not agree to obtain independent legal advice.

The guidance reminds solicitors that para 6.1 of each of the codes (there is one code for solicitors and another for firms) requires the solicitor not to act if there is an own interest conflict or a significant risk of an own interest conflict (an 'own interest conflict' is a conflict of interest between the interests of the client and the interests of the solicitor).

What can present difficulties is the situation where a solicitor is asked by a family member (say, a parent) to make a will for that family member. This is a common, and understandable, request. A parent is likely to want to leave a substantial part of their estate to the child who is the solicitor. The safest course of action for the solicitor would be to ensure the parent instructed another solicitor to prepare the will. However, there is a recognition that there is not necessarily anything improper in the child preparing the will in these circumstances, as the parent is likely to want to benefit the child in any event. The guidance states:

> *There may be some exceptions where you can continue to draft the will even if the client has not received independent legal advice, for example if you draft wills for your parents and the surviving parent wishes to leave the residuary estate to you and your siblings in equal shares.*

Care should be taken, though, if there is the potential for disputes with, say, the other children of the testator (the solicitor's siblings) after the testator's death. This risk is likely to be greater if the solicitor is being given a greater proportion of the estate than the other children. The guidance on this issue concludes as follows:

> *However, whether it is appropriate to do so will depend upon the specific circumstances of each situation, and in each case you should consider whether your ability to advise, and be seen to advise, impartially is undermined by any financial interest or personal relationship which you have.*

The Law Society has also produced a practice note for solicitors—'Preparing a will when your client is leaving a gift for you, your family or colleagues'—which contains guidance on this issue.

## 2.4.3 **Formalities**

Section 9 of the Wills Act 1837 provides that:

> No will shall be valid unless—
>
> (a) it is in writing, and signed by the testator, or by some other person in his presence and by his direction; and
>
> (b) it appears that the testator intended by his signature to give effect to the will; and
>
> (c) the signature is made or acknowledged by the testator in the presence of two or more witnesses present at the same time; and

(d) each witness either—
 (i) attests and signs the will; or
 (ii) acknowledges his signature in the presence of the testator (but not necessarily in the presence of any other witness), but no form of attestation shall be necessary.

The section does not apply to 'privileged wills', which can be made informally—even orally—by members of the armed forces on active duty and by sailors at sea (see **2.4.1.1**). Nor does it apply to statutory wills under the Mental Capacity Act 2005, for which that Act lays down special rules (see **2.4.1.5**).

### 2.4.3.1 Attestation clauses

Most wills contain an attestation clause (it is to be hoped that all those prepared by professionals will do so), although it is not a requirement for validity. If the will contains an appropriate attestation clause, the task of proving the formal validity of the will should be straightforward, as it is presumed that the will has been executed in accordance with s9 of the Wills Act 1837, namely there is a presumption of 'due' execution.

There are a number of different forms of attestation clauses in common use, but all should show (as a minimum) compliance with the statutory requirements.

If you look back at the will of Haydn Davies in **2.3.1**, you will see that the will includes an attestation clause. The wording of that clause, when combined with the signatures of the testator and witnesses, indicates that the will has been executed in accordance with the requirements of s9 of the Wills Act 1837. Of course, it is not known for certain, from looking at the document, that both witnesses were actually present when the testator signed, but the attestation clause provides prima facie evidence that this was the case. In other words, the attestation clause provides a presumption of due execution, and it would then be up to a person challenging the validity of the will to prove (on the balance of probabilities) that the requisite formalities in s9 were not in fact complied with.

In contrast, if a will does not include an attestation clause (or only includes an inadequate one) compliance with the requirements of s9 will have to be proved. This will also be necessary if there is something on the face of the will, for example the testator's signature is not complete, to show that there were unusual circumstances at the time of execution. The process of how compliance with s9 is proved in the absence of an attestation clause is discussed in **Chapter 8**.

#### Blind or illiterate testators; signing on behalf of the testator

Where the testator was blind or illiterate, or someone else signed on behalf of the testator, we saw (in **2.4.2.1**) that there is no presumption of knowledge and approval, and that there will have to be proof of knowledge and approval if the will is to be admitted to probate. The simplest way of providing proof of knowledge and approval in these circumstances is to include a differently worded attestation clause in the will, stating that:

1 the will was read over to the testator in the presence of the witnesses;
2 the testator understood and approved the will;
3 the testator then signed the will, or it was signed by another in the testator's presence and at their direction; and
4 the witnesses attested the will as before.

If the will contains an appropriately adapted attestation clause, there will also be a presumption of due execution, despite the testator being blind or illiterate, or despite another person signing on behalf of the testator.

### 2.4.3.2 In writing

A will may be typed or handwritten (in ink or pencil—though the use of both will raise a rebuttable presumption that the parts written in pencil are 'deliberative only' and they will only be admitted to probate if there is evidence that the testator intended them to be final). There is no restriction as to the material upon which a will may be written (it could be written on an eggshell, for example!), or as to the language used: it may even be written in code, provided there is evidence available enabling it to be deciphered.

#### 2.4.3.3 Signature

The testator's usual signature is ideal, but any mark (eg a thumbprint or rubber stamp) made by the testator and intended to be a signature will suffice. One of the leading cases on this point is *In the Goods of Chalcraft* [1948] P 222, [1948] 1 All ER 700, where a dying testatrix managed to sign 'E. Chal' but was unable to complete her full signature. It was held that this was sufficient; the testatrix intended what she had written (as much as she could manage in the circumstances) to be her signature. In another case, *In the Estate of Cook* [1960] 1 WLR 353, [1960] 1 All ER 689, the will began with the name of the testatrix and ended with the words 'Your loving mother'. The court accepted that the testatrix intended this to be her signature.

However, as we have seen, testators do not need to sign their own wills; the Act allows signature by another—at the testator's direction and in the testator's presence. The person so signing (who may be one of the witnesses) may sign their own name or that of the testator.

In *Barrett v Bem* [2012] EWCA Civ 52, the Court of Appeal considered what it means for the will to be 'signed at the testator's direction'. After eight years of litigation, the Court of Appeal decided that a deathbed will, which had been signed by the dying man's sister (the sole beneficiary under the will) at his direction, was invalid. It was said that a court should not find that a will had been signed at the testator's direction 'unless there is positive and discernible communication (which may be verbal or non-verbal) by the testator that he wished the will to be signed on his behalf by the third party'. In the court's judgement, the evidence did not establish that the will had been properly executed. The court also confirmed as good practice in such cases that the attestation clause should show that the will had been signed by the third party at the testator's direction (see **2.4.3.1**).

#### 2.4.3.4 With intent to give effect to the will

It is usual (and logical) for the signature to appear at the end of the will, but this need not necessarily be the case. In *Wood v Smith* [1993] Ch 90, the testator wrote his signature at the beginning of the will, intending this to give effect to his will but written before he had made any provisions disposing of his estate. The Court of Appeal held that this could constitute a valid execution of the will provided the signing and the subsequently written dispositions all formed part of one transaction.

#### 2.4.3.5 Signature made/acknowledged in the presence of two or more witnesses present at the same time

Where the testator is (as is usually the case) signing the will, the signature must be completed in the presence of at least two witnesses, present at the same time. The witnesses do not need to be able to see the contents of the will or even to know that the testator is signing a will. They must, however, be able to see the testator writing the signature (for this reason a blind person cannot act as a witness), though it is not necessary for them to see the signature itself. Alternatively, the testator may sign the will and then acknowledge that signature (by words or conduct) in the presence of the (two or more) witnesses, who must be present at the same time and be able to see the signature. Again, ideally, this will be recited in the attestation clause. There are no special rules as to the capacity of the witnesses but they must be bodily and mentally present (eg not drunk or asleep). Although, by s15 of the Wills Act 1837, a beneficiary will normally lose a gift under a will where that beneficiary or their spouse has witnessed the will (see **3.5.5**), this does not affect the formal validity of the will.

#### 2.4.3.6 Witnesses attest and sign (or acknowledge their signatures) in the presence of the testator

Attestation is, in effect, the validation of the testator's signature. The witnesses need not sign (or acknowledge) in each other's presence, though in practice this is what usually happens. However, the presence of the testator (bodily and mentally) is required when the signature/acknowledgement is made.

In *Payne v Payne* [2018] EWCA Civ 985, the Court of Appeal held that it was not necessary for a witness to write their freehand signature on the will—it was sufficient that the witness had written their name in block capitals on the will.

### 2.4.3.7 Execution of the will

Undoubtedly, the best way of ensuring that the requirements of s9 of the Wills Act 1837 have been complied with is for the solicitor to take charge of the process themselves. The ideal is to have the testator attend the solicitor's office, where the solicitor can ensure that the will is executed in accordance with s9. The solicitor can ensure that there are two witnesses (typically two members of staff), that the testator signs in the presence of both witnesses present at the same time and that the witnesses sign in the presence of the testator. The solicitor can also double check with the client that the client wishes to include the terms in the will, and the solicitor can make an attendance note which is retained on file and which should be helpful if there are any future challenges.

If the client is not well enough to attend the solicitor's office, the solicitor can arrange to visit the client at the client's home, at a care home or in hospital. The solicitor can take sufficient members of staff with them to act as witnesses.

However, it is often not possible for the client to execute the will under the supervision of the solicitor. This has always happened in a proportion of cases but is far more prevalent today, due to the number of wills made online. Increasingly, solicitors do not meet their clients and the final will is sent out to the client for signature.

If the solicitor is sending the will to the testator for signature, it is clear that the solicitor needs to provide the testator with very clear instructions on how to execute the will. If the solicitor fails to do so and the client makes a mistake due to the solicitor's omission or incorrect instructions, the solicitor will be liable in negligence to the disappointed beneficiaries (the persons who would have benefited had the will been valid).

Also, the solicitor should ask to see the original will after it has been signed, or seek some proof that the will has been executed properly. In *Ross v Caunters* [1980] Ch 297, the solicitor made the mistake of failing to warn the testator that a spouse of a beneficiary should not witness the will (and it resulted in the failure of the gift to the beneficiary). This initial mistake was compounded by the failure to check the original will properly when it was returned to the solicitor for storage.

### 2.4.3.8 Incorporation by reference

As we have seen, for a will to be valid it must be executed in accordance with the requirements of s9 of the Wills Act 1837. This necessarily means that all of the terms of the will must appear in the will itself. It is not possible to make a will and then to add terms to the will subsequently in documents that have not themselves been executed in accordance with s9. However, a document that is already in existence at the time the will is executed may become part of the will under the doctrine of '**incorporation by reference**', even if that document has not been executed in accordance with s9.

For an unexecuted document to be incorporated by reference, three conditions must be met.

1 The document must be clearly identified in the will.

2 The document must already exist at the date of the will. The onus of proving this fact lies with the person seeking incorporation of the document.

3 The document must be referred to in the will as already in existence at the time of execution. If this is not the case (eg because the statement is equivocal or the reference is to a document to be prepared in the future), the document in question cannot be incorporated.

**EXAMPLE**

Clause 3 of a recently deceased testator's will (made in 2024) states 'I leave £10,000 to be held on the trusts set out in clause 5 of the Trust Deed dated 8 March 2020 and made between myself of the one part and Daniel Thomas and Ruth Brown of the other part'. The deceased's executor, Daniel Thomas, tells you that he has the trust deed mentioned in the will at home in his safe. It would seem that all the requirements for incorporation are satisfied; the gift under the will is prima facie valid and the trust deed would be admitted to probate with the will.

### 2.4.3.9 The effect of Covid-19: video witnessing of wills

In 2020, as everyone knows, the world was hit by the Covid-19 pandemic. This led to a series of lockdowns across the world, including in England and Wales. Most persons were told to stay at home and not to mix with persons from other households. Even when conducting essential transactions, social distancing rules had to be complied with.

This presented great difficulties for those who wanted to make a will and, given the greater prominence given to mortality, with the daily reported deaths from Covid-19, there was increased interest amongst the general public in making wills. This also presented great challenges for solicitors who were contacted by clients who wanted to make their wills, although solicitors undertaking will-making work were designated by the UK government as essential workers.

The problem was to do with the requirements of s9 of the Wills Act 1837, in that for the will to be valid, the testator and the witnesses had to be present at the same time. The interpretation of 'presence' was such that this meant physical presence, namely in the same physical location. However, the gathering together of the testator and the witnesses (and perhaps a solicitor who was assisting) had the potential to breach the social distancing requirements imposed during lockdown. It also had the potential to expose each of the participants to catching the virus from the other participants.

To counter this, solicitors' firms devised many ingenious ways of executing wills. The witnesses both need to see the testator sign (or witness the testator acknowledging their signature) and the testator needs to see each witness sign (or acknowledge their signature). To achieve this as safely as possible, wills were executed with the testator and witnesses being on different sides of a closed patio window, or watching each other through a car windscreen in a supermarket car park. Solicitors also ensured that the testator and each witness used their own pens, so that the only item that needed to pass from hand to hand was the will itself. Many other inventive solutions were found.

However, one solution that was apparently not allowed was to conduct the execution of the will using video conferencing technology, such as FaceTime, Skype, Teams or Zoom. This was because 'presence' meant that the testator and witnesses still had to be in each other's physical presence, even if this was through a pane of glass. This restriction was particularly important for residents of care homes because outside visitors to most care homes were banned during the lockdown, making it very difficult for a solicitor to take instructions from the resident or to supervise the signing of a will (although the care home staff could in those circumstances be used as witnesses).

As a result of the difficulties faced by persons wishing to make a will during lockdown, and the difficulties for those professionals who were advising them, the Ministry of Justice was lobbied over possible amendments or relaxations to the requirements of s9. After some delay, the Ministry of Justice announced in late July 2020 that it would introduce new secondary legislation, which it did in September 2020, with the Wills Act 1837 (Electronic Communications) (Amendment) (Coronavirus) Order 2020.

The amendment to s9 of the Wills Act 1837 made by the Order allowed wills to be conducted by video conference, provided the witnesses saw the testator sign and the testator could see each witness sign. The order amended s9 by temporarily adding a new subsection which provides that in relation to wills made on or after 31 January 2020 'presence' included 'presence by means of videoconference or other visual transmission'.

It was still necessary for each of them to sign the same document, so the document had to be moved from where the testator was (the testator must sign first) to where each witness was (if the witnesses were in separate locations, the will had to go on two journeys!). The will was not valid until the second witness signed.

Opinion in the solicitors' profession was divided as to the merits of this relaxation of the established rules. There were some concerns about the mechanics (what happened if the testator died before the will reached the second witness) and about the potential for fraud and abuse (with the possibility of persons off-camera exerting undue influence on the testator, literally or metaphorically pointing a gun to their head).

Although the order only came into effect in September 2020, the relaxation of the rules was backdated to cover any wills made since 31 January 2020 (the date of the first registered Covid-19 case in England and Wales).

There was a saving provision in that nothing in the Order affects a grant of probate already issued before the coming into force of the Order (on 28 September 2020), or anything which had been done pursuant to a grant of probate which was done prior to the Order coming into force.

However, there was no exception for cases where a **grant of letters of administration** had already been issued (or anything done pursuant to such a grant of letters of administration before the Order came into force). Potentially, existing grants of letters of administration (issued on the basis that video-witnessed wills were not valid) could have been revoked and replaced by grants of probate where wills had been witnessed using video technology. Also, acts undertaken by an **administrator** pursuant to what they thought was a valid grant of letters of administration (eg distributing the estate to persons entitled on an intestacy) may have had to be undone.

The relaxation of the rules was originally for a period of two years, to 31 January 2022. However, the Ministry of Justice subsequently extended this period for a further two years, to 31 January 2024. On 1 February 2024, in an answer to a question in Parliament, it was confirmed that there would not be an extension of the relaxation beyond 31 January 2024. The law has now returned to its original state and it is again only possible to make wills using the normal methods.

It is worth noting, though, the Law Commission's project on making wills. This is considering various updates of the law and should lead in time to the passing of a new Wills Act. The project stalled in 2018, due to the government instructing the Law Commission to focus on other work, but work on the wills project restarted in 2023.

## 2.5 The appointment of executors and trustees

In most wills, the testator will appoint one or more persons, or perhaps a **trust corporation**, to be their executor (and possibly also to be their trustee). In this section we will consider the choices of executor and trustee available to the testator, and some advantages and disadvantages of each type.

### 2.5.1 The need for executors and trustees

After the testator's death, the testator's estate will need to be 'administered'. This involves collecting in and securing the testator's assets, paying any debts of the testator and then distributing the testator's estate in accordance with the wishes expressed by the testator in the will. The person or persons who undertake this role are called the 'personal representative(s)'. If the testator does not choose personal representatives, then the Non-Contentious Probate Rules 1987 provide an order of entitlement as to who may be appointed as a personal representative (and such a person is called an 'administrator with the will'). It is much more common, though, for the testator to choose the personal representatives by naming or identifying them in the will, and the personal representatives so appointed by the testator in the will are called 'executors'. The testator need only appoint a sole executor, although the testator can appoint more than one executor.

Although it is possible for a testator to make a will that does not create a trust, most testators will also create trusts in their wills, and so will also need to appoint trustees to run the trust. It is common to appoint the same persons as both executors and trustees, although the roles are separate and distinct. As executors, the persons appointed will administer the estate, distributing part or all of the estate to the ongoing trust. As trustees, those same persons will receive the distribution from the estate, and will administer the trust (perhaps over many years) on behalf of the beneficiaries of the trust.

### 2.5.2 The choices of executors and trustees

There are various types of executors and trustees:

- non-professional (or 'lay') executors (family, friends, trusted acquaintances);
- professional executors (eg solicitors, accountants);
- a trust corporation (eg a subsidiary company of a high street bank); and
- the **Public Trustee**.

From the point of view of the solicitor who is advising the testator, it is important that the testator has a free and informed choice.

**CONDUCT POINT**

Under SRA Principles 3, 4 and 5, the solicitor must act with independence, honesty and integrity, and under SRA Principle 7 a solicitor must act in the best interests of each client. The solicitor who prepares the testator's will, therefore, should give full advice on the advantages and disadvantages of the different types of executor.

The SRA guidance note on Drafting and Preparing Wills (amended 25 November 2019) provides guidance to solicitors on this issue.

Although a client might decide to appoint the solicitor, the solicitor's firm or other people in the firm as executors in the will, the guidance makes it clear that the solicitor must not exploit a client's lack of knowledge by leading them to believe that appointing a solicitor as an executor is essential or that it is the default position for someone making a will. The guidance continues:

> Principle 7 . . . requires you to act in the best interests of each client. In this context this means not encouraging clients to appoint you or the business you work for as their executor unless it is clearly in their best interests to do so.
>
> In some cases it might be beneficial for a client to appoint a solicitor to act as an executor—for example, if their affairs are complex, or there are potential disputes in the family. However, in other cases there may be little or no advantage to the client—for example, if their estate is small or straightforward. A professional executor is likely to be more expensive than a lay person and the client should be advised about this.
>
> Before drafting a will which appoints you or your business (or someone else in the business) as the executor(s), you should be satisfied that the client has made their decision on a fully informed basis. This includes:
>
> - explaining the options available to the client regarding their choice of executor;
> - ensuring the client understands that an executor does not have to be a professional person or a business, that they could instead be a family member or a beneficiary under the will, and that lay executors can subsequently instruct a solicitor to act for them if this proves necessary (and can be indemnified out of the estate for the solicitors' fees);
> - recording advice that is given concerning the appointment of executors and the client's decision.

The Law Society has also produced a practice note for solicitors—'Appointment of a professional executor'—which contains further guidance on this issue.

### 2.5.2.1 Non-professional executors

'Non-professional' executors are executors who are typically members of the testator's family or trusted friends or acquaintances. There is no suggestion that these executors are 'unprofessional', in the sense of being careless or incompetent. It is simply that they are not undertaking the role as part of their job, and are not charging a fee for undertaking the work. In comparison, 'professional executors', such as solicitors, do undertake the work as part of their job and will charge a fee.

Non-professional (or 'lay') executors have the advantage of knowing the deceased and perhaps knowing the beneficiaries. The executor may even be a beneficiary of the will. If the executor is a beneficiary, then they will have a personal interest in ensuring that the estate is administered quickly.

One possible advantage of a non-professional executor is cost, because the executor will not charge for their work in administering the estate, although they will be entitled to the reimbursement of reasonable expenses.

On the other hand, the non-professional executor who is also a beneficiary may be tempted to 'cut corners' in the hope of an earlier distribution. This may lead to problems, for example if **creditors** of the deceased are not paid. There is also the potential for a conflict of interest if the executor/beneficiary disagrees with the other beneficiaries, perhaps over which assets should be sold.

In addition, the non-professional executor may not have the necessary knowledge, experience or aptitude to administer the estate efficiently. They may find difficulties with the paperwork, and may instruct a professional, such as a solicitor, to undertake the daily administration of the estate, thereby losing the advantage of lower cost, because the professional so instructed will charge a fee not dissimilar to the fee they would have charged had they been appointed as an executor in the will.

Another disadvantage of a non-professional executor is that they may die before the testator, or perhaps after the testator but before the administration of the estate is completed. If there is an ongoing trust created by the will, the non-professional trustee may die before the administration of the trust is completed (which may be some years after the death of the testator). Alternatively, the non-professional executor or trustee may lose the necessary mental capacity to do the job or have a change of heart and decide not to act.

### 2.5.2.2 Professional executors

A professional executor should have the advantage of being more experienced at administering estates and therefore be more efficient. A professional is also unlikely to 'cut corners' and should ensure that the estate is administered properly according to the law and the terms of the will.

A considerable advantage of a professional acting is that they will take out professional indemnity insurance, so if the professional executor makes a mistake and there is a consequent loss to the estate, the beneficiaries can recover the lost money from the professional's insurers. In addition, claims that might not be covered by the indemnity insurance (eg where the professional has taken money dishonestly) may be covered by claiming a payment from the SRA Compensation Fund, if the professional is in a firm or organisation that is regulated by the SRA.

The main disadvantage of a professional executor is that of cost. If a professional is appointed as executor then they will charge for administering the estate. Whilst these charges are not small, remember that many non-professional executors pass the legal aspects of the administration over to a professional in any event, so the difference in cost is usually not as great as it might be imagined.

If a named professional is appointed as executor and trustee then they may die or lose capacity in the same way that a lay executor and trustee might. For this reason, it has been traditional to appoint the partners in a particular firm as executors and trustees. This should avoid the problems associated with specifying particular individuals. Also, some firms have set up their own trust corporations, in which case the trust corporation will be appointed as executor (see **2.5.2.3**).

Another possibility is to appoint a combination of non-professional and professional executors. The benefits of this would be that the solicitor or other professional can undertake the legal work and other paperwork whereas the non-professional executor can do a lot of the 'legwork', such as reading the gas meter, although such jobs can be undertaken by a family member even where only professional executors are appointed. There can also be complications where a mix of non-professional executors and professional executors are appointed, and this combined appointment is probably becoming less common.

**CONDUCT POINT**

Under the SRA Transparency Rules 2018, solicitors' firms must publish information about their fees for undertaking estate administration work. This applies whether or not the solicitors are appointed as executors and trustees. The information must appear on the firm's website (or be made available on request, in the unusual case of a firm that does not maintain a website).

### 2.5.2.3 Trust corporations

The main trust corporations are subsidiaries of high street banks, such as Barclays, Lloyds, NatWest or HSBC, although increasingly solicitors firms are setting up their own trust corporations to manage the firms' probate work. Bank trust corporations offer a similar service to professionals and are only not 'professional' in the sense that they are companies and do not belong to a 'profession'. Clearly, a trust corporation set up by a solicitors' firm will be run by the solicitors who specialise in that area of work, and can be regarded as part of the legal profession.

Bank and similar trust corporations will bring expertise to the task but, like professionals, they will charge for doing this. Depending on the circumstances of the estate, they can be more expensive than solicitors and other professionals due to their charging structure. Bank trust corporations often charge a fixed percentage of the estate, plus a set amount per beneficiary or per transaction, whereas solicitors will normally charge according to the time spent (although solicitors may also charge a percentage where it is fair and reasonable to do so). It would be too simplistic to say that solicitors are always cheaper, though. Also, bank trust corporations increasingly instruct firms of solicitors to undertake the administration work on their behalf, and some solicitors' firms undertake a lot of administration work for their trust corporation clients.

One criticism which used to be levelled at bank trust corporations is that they were remote, because they concentrated their work in national or regional centres. As a result, they were perhaps not as accessible as local solicitors. However, with the development of email and other technologies, being at a distance from the client is not the problem that it once was. Clients often do not have the expectation that they will meet their legal advisor in person.

It is possible for there to be a joint appointment of a lay executor and a trust corporation, although in practice bank (and other) trust corporations are likely to discourage this.

A trust corporation has more continuity than individuals who are appointed as executors and trustees—the appointment will not fail as a result of the executor and trustee dying. Although a firm of professionals is likely to continue in business for some time to come, problems can still be experienced if the firm is a small one with only a few partners.

### 2.5.2.4 The Public Trustee

Another option is to appoint the Public Trustee as executor. The Public Trustee is an official appointment (and it is combined with the role of Official Solicitor). The Public Trustee administers trusts and estates where they have accepted the appointment to do so and act as:

- executor and administrator of the estates of the deceased;
- trustee of trusts in the interests of vulnerable individuals or disabled people;
- where there are differences between executors, trustees or beneficiaries.

However, the Public Trustee is really an executor and trustee 'of last resort', and should not be considered by testators if there are viable alternatives. In most cases, therefore, it is not worth mentioning to clients as an option. For more detail on the Public Trustee, see the government website.

### 2.5.2.5 Requirements to be an executor

There is no minimum age for an executor, but an executor who is under the age of 18 years of age at the date of the testator's death will not be able to apply for probate (someone else will have to apply for a grant of representation instead) and there would obviously be other difficulties in a child trying to administer the estate. See **Chapter 8** for more detail on the appropriate grant applications where an executor is under 18.

There is no rule preventing a person who lacks mental capacity from being appointed as an executor, although clearly they would not be competent to apply for a grant of probate.

There is no rule preventing someone who is bankrupt or a convicted criminal from being an executor, although clearly this might not be desirable.

The court has a discretion to pass over an executor who is considered unsuitable, and to appoint someone in their place (s116 Senior Courts Act 1981).

## 2.6 The role of an executor contrasted with the role of a trustee of a will trust

As mentioned previously, although a testator can make a will that does not include a trust, it is very common for testators to include trusts in their wills. If a trust has been included, the testator will need to appoint trustees of the trust, as well as appointing executors. Usually, the same persons are appointed as both executors and trustees.

As already explained, the roles are different. As executor, the appointee will administer and distribute the estate. As trustee, the person will run the ongoing trust created by the testator in the will. Sometimes, those will trusts will last for many years.

## 2.7 **Renunciation by executors and reservation of power to executors**

A person who is appointed as executor cannot be forced to act as executor following the death of the testator. An appointed executor can refuse to act and can step down from the position as executor. If an executor does not wish to act following the death of the testator, the executor can '**renounce**' the executorship. If the executor renounces the executorship (often this is referred to as 'renouncing probate') then the person ceases to be an executor, and will take no part in the administration of the testator's estate. At the same time, the person is also likely to refuse to act as a trustee of any ongoing trust.

It is only possible for an executor to renounce probate if they have not taken any steps in administering the estate. The old-fashioned way of describing this is to say that the executor must not have 'intermeddled' in the estate. If an executor has intermeddled in the estate, perhaps by contacting the deceased's bank or notifying the deceased's house insurers, then it is too late for the executor to renounce.

An alternative to renouncing probate is for 'power' 'to be reserved' to the executor. This is only possible where there is more than one executor. If there is more than one executor, and one of the executors does not wish to apply for a grant of probate, it is possible for the other executor(s) to apply for the grant, and **power is reserved** to the executor who does not apply. It is said that power is reserved to the non-proving executor—in a way, they act like a substitute in a football match—they stand to one side and let the proving executors administer the estate. Then, just like a substitute in a football match, they can be brought in to help with the administration at a later stage (although unlike a football match, they do not necessarily replace the original proving executor—instead they may just join the original proving executor).

Traditionally, precedent clauses for the appointment of a solicitors' firm have provided for an appointment of all of the partners in a traditional partnership, members of a limited liability partnership, or directors where the firm is incorporated. In large firms this could be tens (even hundreds) of persons—it would be unwieldy for all of them to prove the will (and, in fact, a grant of probate will be issued to a maximum of four persons). So, power is usually reserved to all but a couple of them, and it is those two persons who prove the will. If it becomes necessary at a later date, one of the non-proving executors (to whom power has been reserved) can apply for a grant.

So, an executor who renounces ceases to be an executor, but an executor to whom power is reserved continues to be an executor, even though they might not take an active role in administering the estate (either initially or, possibly, not at all).

There is more detail on renunciation and on reserving power to executors in **Chapter 8**, when we will look at the grant application process.

## 2.8 **Personal representative where there is no will: the administrator**

Where the deceased person has not made a will at all, or has made a will that is not valid for some reason (eg because the testator lacked the necessary testamentary capacity described in **2.4.1**), the person will die 'intestate', and a set of statutory rules (the intestacy rules) will determine what will happen to the whole estate of the deceased. The intestacy rules are discussed in **Chapter 4**.

Also, because there is no valid will, there will be no executor. The question then arises—'who will be the personal representative of the deceased?'; that is, 'who will have responsibility for administering the deceased's estate?'

The answer is that a person will be appointed by HMCTS (HM Courts and Tribunals Service) to be personal representative, and that person is called an 'administrator'. The administrator will distribute the deceased's estate according to the intestacy rules.

Rule 22 of the Non-Contentious Probate Rules 1987 determines who is entitled to apply to be appointed as administrator. The order of entitlement closely follows the entitlement of persons to benefit to the deceased's estate under the intestacy rules.

Normally, there is only the need for one administrator, but there are situations in which more than one administrator is required.

The detail on applications to be appointed as administrator is covered in **Chapter 8**.

## 2.9 Personal representative where there is a will but no executor: the administrator with the will

Alternatively, a testator may have made a valid will but for some reason there is no executor willing and able to apply for a grant of probate. There might be various reasons for the lack of an executor. First, although unlikely, there may be a will but no appointment of an executor in the will. Secondly, the testator might have attempted to appoint an executor in the will but the appointment has failed for some reason. This might be because there is a lack of **certainty** (the description of the executor is unclear). Thirdly, the testator might have appointed their spouse or civil partner as executor but the testator and the executor have since divorced, or the **civil partnership** between the testator and the executor has since been dissolved. In such circumstances, the appointment of the spouse or civil partner as executor will fail. Sections 18A and 18C of the Wills Act 1837 provide that the spouse or civil partner is treated as if they had predeceased the testator (more correctly, the spouse or civil partner is treated as if they had died on the date of the divorce or dissolution).

Another possibility is that there is a valid appointment of an executor but the executor has died before the testator, or the executor is under 18 years of age at the date of the testator's death, or the executor has lost the necessary mental capacity to undertake the role, or the executor simply does not wish to act and so renounces probate.

Whichever way it has occurred, the point is that there is a valid will but there is no executor to obtain probate and to administer the estate. In such circumstances, it will be necessary for someone to apply to HMCTS to be appointed as an administrator. In this situation, where the testator left a valid will, the administrator is called an 'administrator with the will'. The administrator who is appointed will administer the estate and distribute in accordance with the terms of the will.

Rule 20 of the Non-Contentious Probate Rules 1987 determines who is entitled to apply to be appointed as administrator with the will. The order of entitlement is linked, at least initially, with the entitlement of beneficiaries under the will (although it is ultimately possible for a creditor to apply).

As with an administrator of an intestate estate, normally there is only the need for one administrator with the will, but there are situations in which more than one administrator with the will is required.

The detail on applications to be appointed as administrator with the will is also covered in **Chapter 8**.

## 2.10 Testamentary guardians

If the testator has children who are under the age of 18, the testator will obviously be concerned about the arrangements for caring for those children in the event that the testator dies before the children reach 18. It is possible for the concerned parent to appoint one or more 'guardians' who will take over the parental role if this happens. Guardians can be appointed in different ways, but if the guardians are appointed by a will they are often called 'testamentary guardians'.

In some cases, the appointment of guardians will be the primary motivation for making a will, particularly where the client has very few assets.

A will is a convenient place in which to appoint guardians, but an appointment can be made other than in a will provided the appointment is in writing, is dated and is signed by the parent.

### 2.10.1 Parental responsibility

A parent can only appoint a testamentary guardian if that parent has 'parental responsibility' for the child in question. Not all parents have 'parental responsibility'.

Parental responsibility is defined in s3(1) of the Children Act 1989 as 'all the rights, duties, powers, responsibilities and authority which by law a parent of a child has in relation to the child and his property'.

Under the Children Act 1989, a mother always has parental responsibility for her children. However, a father only has parental responsibility if:

- he is married to the mother or married the mother subsequent to the birth of the child (the latter process is called 'legitimation'); or
- the mother has given the father parental responsibility by means of a parental responsibility agreement; or
- the father has acquired parental responsibility on the mother's death as a result of the mother appointing the father as testamentary guardian in her will; or
- he has been given it by court order.

There are similar rules applying to a second female parent. Under s42 of the Human Fertilisation and Embryology Act 2008, where two women are married or in a civil partnership at the time that one woman has the relevant fertility treatment, the other woman is treated as a parent of the child and will have parental responsibility. This is provided the other woman consented to the first woman's treatment.

It is also possible for a woman to become a second female parent by agreement with the woman receiving the relevant treatment, even if the two women are not married or in a civil partnership (s43 2008 Act). However, that second female parent would be in a similar position to an unmarried father, in that she would not have parental responsibility automatically but could acquire it by means of a parental responsibility agreement, being appointed as testamentary guardian by the other woman, or by court order.

There are also specific rules applying to surrogacy arrangements (where a woman agrees to carry a child on behalf of another), but the details, also to be found in the 2008 Act, are outside the scope of this manual.

### 2.10.2 Some considerations when appointing guardians

If there is only one parent who has parental responsibility for the child (eg a single mother) then that parent can appoint a guardian, and the appointment of that guardian will take effect on the parent's death. From that point on, the guardian will have parental responsibility for the child (and can, in turn, appoint a guardian).

However, if there are two parents with parental responsibility, the position is more complicated and there are various permutations. The main point, though, is that the appointment of guardians by one parent will be subject to the existing parental responsibility of the other surviving parent. So, it is the surviving parent not the appointed guardians who will have the rights and responsibilities of looking after the child after the death of the other parent.

Also, parents will often make wills appointing guardians at a time when the parents are divorcing (or dissolving a civil partnership). In such situations, the parents should consider appointing the same guardians in their wills as it is not ideal for the parents to appoint different guardians; this could lead to a dispute over which guardians should look after the children if both parents die.

Another consideration is the age of the guardians who are appointed. Ideally, guardians should be a similar age to the parents or younger. However, clients often choose the grandparents of the child as guardians. Whilst there are sound reasons for this, consideration needs to be given to the grandparents' ability to look after children if the grandparents are at an advanced age.

The testator should also check with the proposed guardians that they are willing to take on the role of guardian, and thought needs to be given to financial arrangements (usually, this is catered for by the gifts left to the child or children in the testator's will).

## 2.11 Wishes regarding the funeral and disposal of the body

The will is often a convenient (and logically appropriate) place to state directions as to the testator's funeral and as to the disposal of the testator's body. However, a will is not necessarily the best place to include such directions. The reason for this is that the relatives sometimes do not check whether anything is said in the will until the funeral arrangements have been made, or even until after the funeral has taken place!

Whilst it is not appropriate to refuse to include such directions in the will (or even to discourage a testator from doing so), it is prudent to advise the testator to consult the nearest relatives and/or friends so that they are aware of what the testator's wishes are and can act on these immediately after the testator's death.

Clients sometimes wish to leave their bodies (or parts of them) to medical science, and sometimes wish to restrict the uses to which their bodies can be put to purely therapeutic purposes (eg organ transplants). Some testators do not want their bodies to be used for research purposes or as practice or demonstration corpses for medical students. It is possible (although not necessary) to express these wishes in the will. However, once again, clients should make their views known in other ways, for example by speaking with their relatives—otherwise their wishes may not become known until it is too late.

In Wales, since December 2015, there has been implied consent to organ and tissue donation, with an opt-out available to those who do not wish to donate their organs and tissue. A similar deemed consent system was introduced in England in May 2020.

Lastly, any wishes or directions about the funeral or disposal of the body are not binding on the personal representatives, and the personal representatives do not have to carry out the testator's wishes. Usually, the personal representatives will endeavour to implement reasonable requests, but if the testator has specified something impractical, unwise or unreasonable, the personal representatives cannot be forced to comply with the testator's wishes.

## 2.12 Storage and review of the will

Although we will continue looking at wills in the next chapter (by focusing on the testator's instructions in regard to their property), it is worth mentioning the need to ensure the will is safely stored once it has been made.

For reasons that we will see in the next chapter, there can be problems if the testator keeps the original will at home and then the will is lost. If the testator does take away the original will, the solicitor should keep a copy. It may then be possible to prove the copy will in the absence of the original if it appears the original has simply been lost (as opposed to cancelled or revoked by the testator).

It is possible to store the original will with HMCTS for a fee (currently a one-off fee of £20), but this service is not used by most testators. A testator could put the original will in a bank safety-deposit box but there is a cost associated with this and relatively few persons have bank safety-deposit boxes. Another alternative is to store the original will with the firm of solicitors that prepared the will, and this is done quite frequently as firms will usually offer this service free of charge. Clearly, the firm of solicitors has responsibilities to ensure the original will is kept safe for the testator. There may be many years between the testator making the will and the death of the testator, and so the firm will have to keep the testator's will safe for a very long time indeed.

Testators should also be made aware of the need to review their wills as their circumstances change, or perhaps as a result of a change in the law (eg a change to the inheritance tax rules). However, it should be made clear to the testator that the firm does not have a 'watching brief'—namely, it is the testator's responsibility not the firm's to check the will periodically and seek further advice as appropriate. This is to avoid someone suing the firm of solicitors for failing to warn the testator that they needed to change their will as a result of a change in the law.

**CONDUCT POINT**

The SRA guidance note on Drafting and Preparing Wills (amended 25 November 2019) provides guidance to solicitors on storage of wills:

> Some clients may prefer you or your business to store the original copy of their will, particularly where it can be retrieved easily and quickly by their executors or if they wish to make an alteration. You should advise your client about storage options that are available. The most

important thing is to make sure your client understands the importance of their executor(s) knowing where to locate the original copy of the will following the client's death.

- make sure that all their executors know where to find the original version of the will;
- keep a copy of the will at their home with the relevant details;
- keep you informed of any changes to their address or contact details; and
- review their will regularly to make sure it still reflects their wishes and circumstances.

## KEY POINT SUMMARY

- A will is a document containing a series of declarations by someone as to what should happen following their death. For the most part, the will is concerned with the question of who inherits the assets that a person owns (their estate).
- The person who makes the will is called the testator (or testatrix if female).
- In a will the testator can choose who will administer the estate (the executor(s)), and who will administer any ongoing trust (the trustee(s)). Often the testator will choose the same person(s) as both executor(s) and trustee(s).
- For a will to be valid, three things are necessary:
  - the testator must have the required mental capacity ('testamentary capacity');
  - the testator must want to make the will and must want to include the provisions in the will—namely, the testator must 'know and approve' the terms of the will;
  - the formalities prescribed by s9 of the Wills Act 1837 must be complied with (these include all the terms of the will must be in writing, and the testator's signature must be witnessed by two witnesses present at the same time).
- The test for testamentary capacity is a common law one from the 19th-century case of *Banks v Goodfellow*. The testator needs to understand the effect of a will, the property that they have in their estate, the persons who they would normally be expected to leave their estate to and the testator must not have delusions which impact on their ability to make a valid will.
- Capacity is presumed unless there is evidence of mental issues that suggests incapacity. It is possible to overcome (or rebut) presumptions by adducing evidence and the standard of proof is the civil one (balance of probabilities).
- Similarly, a testator's intention (knowledge and approval) is usually presumed but not if there are suspicious circumstances (eg the will being drafted by the main beneficiary). Solicitors have professional conduct considerations if the testator is proposing to make a gift to the solicitor.
- It is possible to show that a will has been made as a result of force, fear, fraud or undue influence, but each of these must be proven.
- If a mistake is made in the drafting or preparation of a will, it is sometimes possible for the court to 'rectify' the will.
- The inclusion of an appropriate attestation clause will provide prima facie evidence that a will has been made in compliance with the formalities requirements in s9 of the Wills Act 1837. Special forms of attestation clause should be used where the testator is blind, illiterate or where someone else is signing on the testator's behalf.
- A will must be in writing and must be signed (or acknowledged) by the testator in the presence of two witnesses. Each witness must sign (or acknowledge) in the presence of the testator. Presence means physical presence. This caused difficulties during the Covid-19 lockdowns, with the result that a temporary relaxation of the rules (until 31 January 2024) was passed to allow wills to be made using video-conferencing technology.
- Testators may choose non-professional executors (typically friends or family) or may choose from a range of professional executors, including solicitors and trust corporations,

which will charge for their services. There are advantages and disadvantages of each type of executor and, as a matter of professional conduct, the solicitor should explain the choice to the testator so that the testator is able to make an informed choice.

- An executor administers and distributes the testator's estate in the period immediately following the testator's death. However, the testator may set up an ongoing trust in their will, in which case the testator should appoint trustees to run the trust on an ongoing basis. A trust may last many years after a testator's death, depending on the type of trust created.
- A person who is appointed as executor is not bound to carry out their duties. They may refuse to act and renounce probate (ie refuse to take any steps in administering the estate) or they may stand aside and let other executors undertake the administration, but without being removed as an executor (this standing aside is known as having 'power reserved').
- If the deceased left no valid will, then they will be intestate and their estate will be administered by someone appointed by HMCTS. Once appointed, that person is called an 'administrator'.
- There may, though, be a valid will dealing with all or part of the estate but the executor has died before the testator or is unwilling to act as executor (and so has renounced probate). In these circumstances, HMCTS will appoint someone to be the 'administrator with the will'.
- A will is a convenient place to appoint guardians of minor children, to take care of those children after the testator's death. However, the appointment of a guardian will be subject to the rights of the other parent if the other parent also has parental responsibility.
- The testator can specify wishes as to their funeral and the disposal of their body, but these wishes are not binding on the personal representatives. The testator should consider informing relatives and friends of their wishes before they die rather than relying on statements in the will.
- Care should be taken over the storage of a will, and it may be many years between the making of the will and the death of the testator. Testators should review their wills periodically to consider whether changes need to be made due to changed circumstances or changes in the law.

# CHAPTER 3
# Changing and Interpreting Wills

**FUNCTIONING LEGAL KNOWLEDGE**

This chapter covers the following functioning legal knowledge required to pass the SQE 1 assessments:

**Alterations and amendments to wills:**

- effect of alterations made to wills both before and after **execution**
- use of **codicils**

**Revocation of wills:**

- methods of revocation
- effect of marriage and divorce of a **testator**

**The interpretation of wills:**

- effect of different types of **gift**
- failure of gifts

**AUTHORITIES UNDERPINNING PRACTICE**

The key authorities that underpin this area of practice are listed below. Note that for legislation you are linked to legislation.gov.uk.

Although much of the legislation on this government website is available in its amended form, the incorporation of new amendments into the text of legislation can be delayed. You should refer to legal databases to ensure you are referencing the most up-to-date legislation.

- Wills Act 1837
  **http://www.legislation.gov.uk/ukpga/Will4and1Vict/7/26/contents**

## 3.1 Introduction

In this chapter we are continuing our look at wills, and we will consider the following topics:

- how alterations may be made to wills, and when attempted alterations will be invalid (**3.2**);
- how wills are cancelled or 'revoked'—this can happen as a result of a deliberate act by the testator, or automatically by the application of the law (**3.3**);
- the different types of gift that a testator may make in a will (**3.4**); and
- ways in which those gifts may fail, and what happens if they do fail (**3.5**).

## 3.2 Alteration of wills

A will is usually a typed document. A testator may wish to make handwritten amendments to the draft will before the will is signed (or, more accurately, 'executed'). Are those handwritten amendments valid?

Alternatively, a testator may look at their will after it has been executed, perhaps months or years later, and decide they want to make changes and so write amendments on the will. Are those amendments valid?

If it is not possible to change a will after it has been executed by adding handwritten amendments, how can a testator make changes to their will?

### 3.2.1 The effect of alterations made to wills both before and after execution

To comply with the Wills Act 1837, all of the terms of the will must be contained in the will (or possibly in another document **incorporated by reference**) at the time the will is executed.

This does mean that it is possible for a testator to make handwritten amendments to a draft will before the will is signed. Perhaps there is an error in the typed document that needs correcting or perhaps the testator has decided at the last minute to increase the amount of a monetary **legacy**, and so the testator changes the amount of the legacy by hand. This is perfectly acceptable, even though the amendment is handwritten, and the alteration will be valid and will be regarded as part of the will. The important point *legally* is that the alteration was made before the will was signed, and so the will, as executed, includes the alteration. The important point *practically* is that to provide evidence that the handwritten amendment was made before the will was executed, the testator and the two **witnesses** should write their initials next to each handwritten amendment, or in the margin next to each alteration. This is to provide evidence (or, at least, prima facie evidence) to HMCTS (HM Courts and Tribunals Service) that the amendment was made before the will was executed.

In contrast, an unattested alteration (ie one not signed or initialled by the testator and witnesses) is rebuttably presumed to have been made *after* execution. This is with the exception of where the 'alteration' is the filling in of a blank space, when the rebuttable presumption is that this was done *prior* to execution. The most common example of filling in a blank space is when the date of the will is handwritten into a blank space in the typed text when the will is executed. However, either presumption may be rebutted by adducing evidence to the contrary. The evidence may be 'intrinsic' (ie internal to the document, the will, itself) or 'extrinsic' (perhaps a statement from one of the witnesses).

So, if a handwritten amendment has not been initialled by the testator and the two witnesses when the **executors** are applying for the grant of **probate**, HMCTS will require evidence that the amendment was made before the will was signed. Such evidence would typically be extrinsic and traditionally has taken the form of a sworn written statement called an '**affidavit**'. The person making the affidavit swears to the truth of the contents on the Bible or another holy book, or formally attests to the truth of the contents if the person is not religious. Typically, the affidavit is provided by one of the witnesses to state that the amendment had in fact been made before the will was signed, even though the amendment had not been initialled. It is now possible to submit a '**statement of truth**' in place of an affidavit.

It follows that if the testator made the amendment after the will was executed, then the amendment may not be valid because it was not part of the will when the will was executed, and so does not comply with s9 of the Wills Act 1837. Not all amendments made after the will has been executed are invalid, though.

Section 21 of the Wills Act 1837 lays down the basic rule for alterations made after the will has been executed. Section 21 states that:

> no obliteration, interlineation, or other alteration made in any will after the execution thereof shall be valid or have any effect, except so far as the words or effect of the will before such alteration shall not be apparent, unless such alteration shall be executed in like manner as hereinbefore is required for the execution of a will . . .

Therefore, not every amendment made after the execution of the will is going to be invalid. Some amendments made after the execution of the will are going to be valid. The question is, which ones?

An alteration made after the will has been executed will be effective if:

1 the amendment itself is duly executed. In practice, to achieve this it is sufficient if the testator and two witnesses initial the alteration (or in the margin near to the alteration). It is relatively easy for the testator and the witnesses to initial a handwritten amendment if the testator wants to make a change to the wording only five minutes after the will has been executed, with the witnesses still present. It is much harder to do this some days, weeks, months or years later when the witnesses might not be available. In such circumstances, there are better ways to change a will than to make handwritten amendments; or

2 the amendment is an obliteration of the original wording and the original wording or effect of the will is, as a result of the 'alteration', not 'apparent'.

Wording is apparent if it can be deciphered by 'natural means' (such as holding it up to the light or using a magnifying glass) without resort to 'forbidden' methods (such as the use of chemicals or infrared photography) or by extrinsic evidence (such as a statement from a witness or drafts or copies of the will). If the amendment is an obliteration of the original wording and the original wording is not apparent using these natural means, the amendment will be effective and the will is read as if it does not contain the original wording. In effect, the testator will be deemed to have cancelled, or revoked, the wording that has been obliterated. The will is prima facie admitted to probate with a blank space where the obliteration has occurred.

In contrast, an alteration will be ineffective if:

- it is unattested and made by the testator after (or it cannot be established to have been made before) execution and does not amount to an obliteration;
- it is made by someone other than the testator and without their knowledge and approval; or
- it is made by the testator without an intention to revoke.

The consequences of an invalid alteration depend upon whether or not the original wording is 'apparent':

1 If the original wording is so apparent, it will be admitted to probate.

2 If it is not so apparent, the amendment will then amount to an obliteration and so will usually be effective to exclude the original wording. As said above, the will is then prima facie admitted to probate with a blank space where the obliteration has occurred. However, this might not be the case where there has been an attempted substitution in place of what has been obliterated.

In that situation, the doctrine of 'conditional revocation' may apply; this will allow the court to employ any of the forbidden methods mentioned earlier, including extrinsic evidence, in an attempt to ascertain and give effect to the original wording. (Significantly, this would enable the court to consider the wording of an unsigned draft of the will or a photocopy of the signed will before it had been amended.)

**EXAMPLE**

Kylie made a will in which she left a legacy of £1,000 to Bob. Two years later, Kylie decided to increase the amount of the legacy to £5,000. Kylie drew a line through the words and figures of the original amount, like so: 'I GIVE to my good friend Bob the sum of ~~ONE THOUSAND POUNDS (£1,000)~~', and hand-wrote the sum of £5,000 in words and figures just above the wording she had crossed out. The alteration was not executed as if it were a will and the alteration was not initialled by Kylie and two witnesses. Kylie has now died.

The alteration to the will is invalid and Bob will not receive a legacy of £5,000. However, the original wording and figure is still apparent (ie still readable) and so Bob will receive a legacy of the original amount (£1,000).

**EXAMPLE**

If, in the above example, Kylie had completely obscured the original wording rather than drawing a thin line through the wording, then the alteration might have amounted to an obliteration. This might mean that Bob would not be entitled to the original amount of the legacy because the original amount is not apparent from an examination of the will.

However, because Kylie wrote another amount above the obscured original wording, the court might consider this to be a conditional revocation of the legacy (ie that Kylie only obliterated the original wording so that the new wording should take effect). In this situation, although the alteration is not valid and Bob will not receive the new amount of £5,000, extrinsic evidence (such as looking at drafts or a copy of the will before the wording was obscured) could be used to confirm the original amount of the legacy. If there is such evidence, Bob could still receive the £1,000.

In practice, it is clearly sensible to have all alterations (even those made before execution of the will) initialled by the testator and the witnesses. Further, testators should be discouraged from attempting to make their own 'adjustments' to their wills. There are much better ways to amend wills than to make handwritten amendments, such as making a new will or adding a codicil to the will.

## 3.2.2 **Codicils**

Arguably, the best method of altering a will is to make an entirely new will, revoking the old one. See **3.3** for more detail on revocation.

However, if the testator is happy with most of the existing will it is possible to make amendments to the will by making a supplementary testamentary document called a 'codicil'. For example, a testator may wish to add a new legacy to their will due to the birth of a new grandchild or might wish to increase the amount of a legacy due to the effect of inflation since the date the will was made.

**EXAMPLE**

Fifteen years ago, Ayman made a will in which he left a monetary legacy of £5,000 to Zara. He is now reviewing his will and decides to increase the legacy to £10,000.

Ayman also decides to add a legacy of £3,000 to Umair.

Ayman can do both things without making a new will, by making a codicil to his existing will.

If, though, the testator wishes to make major changes or complex changes to the will, it is usually better for them to make an entirely new will, rather than to make the changes by codicil.

It is possible to make more than one codicil to a will. If, say, there are three codicils to a will, all three codicils can be proved alongside the will when the application is made for the grant of probate following the testator's death.

A codicil is a testamentary document like a will, and must be executed in accordance with the **formalities** in s9 of the Wills Act 1837 (so it must be in writing and must be signed by the testator in the presence of two witnesses etc). If the formalities of s9 of the Wills Act 1837 are not complied with, the codicil will not be valid.

A codicil also has the effect of 'republishing' the will at the date of the codicil. This means the effective date of the will becomes the date of the codicil not the date on which the will was executed initially. This might have an impact if there are, say, **beneficiaries** who are described in the will by their relationship to the testator, rather than being named.

**EXAMPLE**

David makes a will in which one of the gifts is to 'my brother's wife', without naming her. At the date of the will, David's brother, Michael, is married to Jane. Five years later, David makes a codicil to his will and the will is republished at the date of the codicil. However, between the date of the will and the date of the codicil, Michael divorced Jane and married Sophie. As a result of the codicil republishing the will, the reference in the will to 'my brother's wife' is taken to be Michael's wife at the date of the codicil. Sophie would therefore be entitled to the gift, not Jane. This might be exactly what David intended, but it is possible David intended to give a personal gift to Jane. If so, then this intention will have been frustrated by the republication of the will by the codicil.

# 3.3 **Revocation**

The process of cancelling part or all of a will is called 'revocation', and when it occurs it is said that the will, or part of it, is 'revoked'.

We have already considered the revocation of parts of a will when considering alteration of wills in **3.2**. An effective alteration to the will in effect revokes the part of the will that has been amended.

We will also see later (**3.4**) that parts of a will may be revoked automatically by operation of law where the testator divorces or on the dissolution of a **civil partnership**.

In this section, though, we will consider revocation of the will as a whole.

A will may be revoked deliberately by the testator by making a later will or a codicil (**3.3.1**). Alternatively, the testator may revoke a will by physically destroying it (**3.3.2**). In either case, for the revocation to be effective the testator must have the intention to revoke the will and must have the necessary mental **capacity** ('**testamentary capacity**') to do so.

The testator's intention may be to revoke the will with immediate effect or may be conditional on some condition being met (**3.3.3**).

We will also see that wills may be revoked automatically by operation of law when the testator marries or enters into a civil partnership (**3.3.4**).

## 3.3.1 **Revocation by a later will or by codicil**

If a testator wishes to revoke their will, the best method by far of doing so is to execute another testamentary document which does so. Section 20 of the Wills Act 1837 provides that a will is revoked (wholly or partially) by a later will or codicil.

Usually, a testator will want to make a new will containing provisions that are different from the existing will. In such circumstances, the testator makes a new will and includes a revocation clause in the new will which has the effect of revoking the old will.

A typical revocation clause might read as follows:

*I REVOKE all earlier wills and other testamentary dispositions.*

The term 'wills' is deemed to include any codicils and the term 'other testamentary dispositions' is intended to cover privileged wills (wills which can be made without the usual formalities by armed forces personnel on active service and by sailors (see **2.4.1.1**)).

Alternatively, although far less likely, a testator might wish to revoke a will without replacing it with a new will. Such a revocation could be achieved by executing a codicil revoking the existing will, using a revocation clause similar to the one shown above.

However, remember that codicils are usually used to supplement and amend an existing will. It is not common, therefore, to have a revocation clause in a codicil. A codicil would only have a revocation clause in the very rare situation where the testator wished to revoke an existing will without making a new one.

What happens if a testator makes a later will or a codicil but fails to include an appropriate revocation clause in the new will or in the codicil? Although the heading of a will usually states that the will is the last will and testament of the testator, this statement does not in itself invalidate any earlier will or other testamentary disposition, except to the extent that the new will is not consistent with or simply repeats the earlier will. Whilst this means that it is unlikely that the terms of an earlier will shall take effect, it does mean that the **personal representatives** may have to produce both wills when applying for a grant of probate. Practically, this is likely to be fiddly and time-consuming.

Also, as said, a later will or codicil impliedly revokes an earlier testamentary disposition but only to the extent that it is inconsistent with or merely repeats the terms of the earlier document. It is possible, therefore, that one or more of the provisions of the first will could still be valid.

**EXAMPLE**

Milly makes a will in which she leaves her whole estate to Jasmin. Subsequent to that, Milly makes a second will in which she leaves a number of legacies (gifts of specified sums of money) to her nephews and nieces. Milly's second will does not say what is to happen to the rest of her estate after the payment of the legacies. Also, Milly's second will does not include a revocation clause. On Milly's death, the legacies in Milly's second will are valid, but the rest of the estate would be distributed to Jasmin in accordance with the first will. Milly's personal representatives would have to prove both wills.

Clearly, it is best when making a new will to include a revocation clause and to include all of the dispositions and other provisions that the testator wants in the new will.

### 3.3.1.1 Foreign property and foreign wills

Care must be taken not to revoke any prior wills which the testator has made abroad in connection with foreign property. A new will made in England and Wales may inadvertently revoke an earlier foreign will, with adverse consequences.

Generally, the law of the testator's domicile applies to personal property whereas for real property (ie land) the law of the country in which the real property is situated applies.

For example, a testator may own a villa in Spain and may have already executed a Spanish will in respect of that property. If the standard revocation clause were included in a new English and Welsh will then this would revoke the earlier Spanish will. This could result in a range of problems for the testator's estate and beneficiaries, which in turn may lead to a negligence claim against the firm of solicitors which drafted the English and Welsh will.

So, if the testator owns foreign property, the standard revocation clause may need to be adapted to make it clear that the foreign will is not to be revoked or that the will is limited to real property in England and Wales, or to state that the will does not apply to real property in the foreign country.

### 3.3.1.2 Revocation by other documents

As already noted, s20 of the Wills Act 1837 provides the rule that a will is revoked (wholly or partially) by a later will or codicil. However, s20 also provides that a will (or part of one) may be revoked by any written document which declares an intention to revoke the will and which is executed in the manner in which a will is executed. For example, in *Re Spracklan's Estate* [1938] 2 All ER 345, the Court of Appeal held that a letter (signed by the testatrix and duly attested) to her bank manager, asking him to destroy the will which the bank was keeping for her, satisfied this requirement.

### 3.3.1.3 Mutual wills

In practice, it is common for married couples to make wills that mirror each other. For example, in his will a husband might leave his estate initially to his wife but provide that if she dies before him, his estate will be divided amongst their children. At the same time, the wife makes a will leaving her estate initially to her husband, providing that if he dies before her, her estate will be divided amongst their children. Such wills are sometimes called '**mirror wills**' because they are mirror images of each other. There is not usually an expectation that the will that each person makes is binding on them, and the couple do not usually have the intention that the survivor of the couple cannot change their will after the first death.

What the married couple in the above scenario are attempting to do is to provide first of all for the survivor after the first death, with their children inheriting everything after the second death. Both the husband and wife are, essentially, trusting the other to pass the combined estates to the children ultimately.

However, it may be that the husband and wife are less trusting and they may be worried that the survivor might fall in love with a new partner and might make a new will leaving everything to that new partner, effectively disinheriting the children.

If the married couple are more suspicious then they could seek to prevent each other from changing their wills in the future. In such circumstances, the married couple could choose to make what are called '**mutual wills**'.

Mutual wills might look superficially like mirror wills but are significantly different. If a couple make mutual wills, they are trying to bind each other to the terms of the mutual wills and to prevent each other from making new wills in the future.

Mutual wills are not confined to situations involving married couples—the above scenario is just for illustration purposes only—but apply wherever two people make wills and, at the same time, make an agreement not to revoke their wills without the other person's consent.

To be clear, even if two people make mutual wills, there is nothing preventing each of them revoking their wills unilaterally. Even if a will is a mutual will, it can be revoked by the testator in the normal way. However, the consequences of revoking the mutual will are that the testator will be in breach of contract (the contract with the other person making a will). A **constructive trust** will then arise to enable the contract to be enforced.

In *Charles v Fraser* [2010] EWHC 2154 (Ch), a case involving two sisters who had made mutual wills, the court confirmed the following points.

1 Mutual wills are wills made by two or more persons, usually in substantially the same terms and conferring reciprocal benefits, following an agreement between them to make such wills and not to revoke them without the consent of the other.
2 For the doctrine of mutual wills to apply, there has to be what amounts to a contract between the two testators that both wills shall be irrevocable and remain unaltered. The agreement may be incorporated in the will or proved by extraneous evidence, which may be oral or in writing.
3 The agreement is enforced in **equity** by the imposition of a constructive trust on the property which is the subject matter of the agreement. The beneficiaries under the will that was not to be revoked may apply to the court for an order that the estate is held on trust to give effect to the provisions of that will.

It should be noted that mutual wills can be problematic and are not popular with practitioners. Unless there are very good reasons to make mutual wills, they are best avoided. One of the problems with mutual wills is that they seek to restrict what the survivor can do after the first death, when there may be sound reasons for the survivor changing their will to take into account new and unforeseen circumstances. For example, to take the scenario of the married couple mentioned earlier, one of the children may become addicted to drugs or gambling and so it might be desirable to avoid that child inheriting money absolutely (ie without any restrictions on their ability to spend the money).

Another issue with mutual wills is the extent to which the survivor is able to deal with their estate during their lifetime. It is possible that the survivor could frustrate the agreement behind the mutual wills by giving away most of their estate during their lifetime, although there are judicial statements in case law that suggest this might be open to challenge by the court.

## 3.3.2 Destruction of the will

By s20 of the Wills Act 1837, a will is also revoked by 'burning tearing or otherwise destroying the same by the testator or by some person in his presence and by his direction with the intention of revoking the same'.

There are two essential elements for an effective revocation:

1 *An act of destruction.* An act of destruction is necessary; merely writing 'cancelled' or 'revoked' across the will is not enough; nor is putting a line through parts of the will, or even the signature of the testator (though it will be otherwise if there has been an effective obliteration). In *Re Adams (Dec'd)* [1990] Ch 601, the testator's signature had been heavily scored through with a ballpoint pen so as to render it illegible. The court held that a material part of the will had been destroyed with the intention to effect a revocation of the whole. Where part only of the will is destroyed, this may amount to a revocation of that part of the will only,

or of the whole will if of a sufficiently substantial or vital part (eg the testator's or witnesses' signatures: *Hobbs v Knight* (1838) 1 Curt 769). The court will admit extrinsic evidence of the testator's intention in determining the extent of any revocation and may infer this from the state of the will at the date of death. Destruction by someone other than the testator must, to be effective, be done in the testator's presence and at the testator's direction; if not, it is not possible for the testator subsequently to 'ratify' the act.

2 *An intention to revoke.* The testator must have the intention to revoke at the time of the will's destruction. The necessary mental capacity is the same as that required for the making of a will (see **Chapter 2**). Accidental revocation is, therefore, an impossibility; so is one based upon a mistaken belief that the will is invalid or has already been revoked. If a will is found mutilated at the date of death, this will be rebuttably presumed to have been done by the testator with the intention of revoking it (wholly or partially, depending upon the extent of the mutilation). There is a further rebuttable presumption that a will last known to have been in the testator's possession, but which cannot be found at the date of death, has been destroyed by the testator with the intention of revoking it. This is one good reason for a testator to leave their original will with the firm of solicitors which drafted it, only keeping a copy at home: otherwise, if the original will is kept by the testator but cannot be found after death, it is presumed that the will has been revoked. Although this presumption can be rebutted by evidence to the contrary, it is possible that there will be no such evidence and so the testator's intentions, as expressed in the will, would then be frustrated and the **intestacy** rules (see **Chapter 4**) would apply to the testator's estate.

## 3.3.3 **Conditional revocation**

When a testator revokes a will (whether by a testamentary instrument, such as a will or codicil, or by destruction), the testator may intend that the revocation should take effect immediately, regardless of any conditions being met. Alternatively, the testator's intention might be that the revocation is conditional on some condition being met, and that if the condition is not met then the original will is not revoked and will continue to be valid.

The condition might be, for example, the validity of a new will so that if the testator revokes one will and attempts to make a new will, but for some reason the new will is not valid (perhaps due to a failure to comply with the formalities in s9 Wills Act 1837), then the old will would not be treated as having been revoked. In such circumstances, it would have to be clear that the testator intended that the old will should still be effective in preference to the rules of intestacy applying to their estate. In other words, there would have to be evidence that the testator's intention to revoke the first will was conditional only.

**EXAMPLE**

Chan made two wills during his lifetime. In both the first and second wills he left half of his estate to Ling, but he changed the provisions relating to the other half of his estate in the second will. Unfortunately, Ling was one of the two attesting witnesses to the second will, and so she loses her entitlement to her legacy, due to s15 of the Wills Act 1837 (see **3.5.5**). The matter goes to court and the court makes a finding that Chan's intention to revoke that part of his first will that leaves half of the estate to Ling was conditional on Ling receiving half of Chan's estate under the second will. So, the first will is still valid to pass half of the estate to Ling, and the other half passes under the terms of the second will.

This result may seem surprising, but this is very similar to the outcome in *Re Finnemore (Dec'd)* [1991] 1 WLR 793.

Conditional revocation is also known as the 'doctrine of dependent relative revocation'. The doctrine applies also to alterations in a will, as well as to revocation of a whole will. So, if it is clear that an alteration is intended to be conditional on a particular condition being met, it is possible to revert to the original wording in the event of the condition not being met.

### 3.3.4 The effect of a subsequent marriage or a civil partnership

A will is revoked automatically by the subsequent marriage/civil partnership of the testator (ss18 and 18B Wills Act 1837). This is unless the will is made in contemplation of marriage/civil partnership (ss18(3) and 18B(3)) or a particular disposition in a will is made in contemplation of marriage/civil partnership (ss18(4) and 18B(4)).

Sometimes a testator is expecting to be married at the time of making a will but wishes the will to remain effective after the impending marriage/civil partnership. In such a case, it is possible to state in the will that the will is made 'in contemplation of' the intended marriage/civil partnership with the other person and that the will should not be revoked by that marriage/civil partnership taking place. The testator does not need to be formally 'engaged' at the time of making the will.

Under ss18(3) and 18B(3), the will has to be made in contemplation of marriage to/civil partnership with a particular person—in other words, the future spouse/civil partner must be identified in the will. It must also appear from the will that the testator is intending to marry/form a civil partnership with the other person, and the will should state that the will should not be revoked by the marriage/civil partnership.

It is quite common for solicitors in practice to make wills for clients in contemplation of marriage, and appropriate precedent clauses are easily available. Many couples marry in exotic locations around the globe but have fears about flying and so decide to make wills before they depart for their overseas wedding!

Under ss18(4) and 18B(4), it is possible to provide that certain dispositions in a will should not be revoked by marriage to/civil partnership with a particular person, but this is far less common because it would mean that the rest of the will would be revoked by the marriage/civil partnership, and it is unlikely that many persons would want to make a will in those terms.

Only intrinsic evidence is admissible to establish the testator's intention. In practice, an express declaration is included in the will to prevent revocation.

**EXAMPLE**

Brian made a will in January last year. His will contained the following clause:

> I DECLARE that I make this will in the expectation of my marriage to Steven Phillips and that I intend that this will shall not be revoked by that marriage.

Brian and Steven married in March last year. Unfortunately, Brian died in December last year.

Brian's will is not revoked by his marriage with Steven, as it complies with s18(3) of the Wills Act 1837.

Alternatively, a testator may intend that their will should only become effective if the marriage/civil partnership takes place. In this instance, the will can be expressed to be 'conditional' on the marriage/civil partnership taking place, and will not have effect until the couple are married/have registered the civil partnership. It is even possible to specify a period of time within which the marriage/civil partnership should take place.

Lastly, many same-sex couples who formed civil partnerships from 2005 onwards did so at a time when they were not able to marry. Since same-sex marriage became available in 2014, some civil partners have converted their civil partnership into a marriage. Section 18(5) provides that a will is not revoked by a marriage which results from the conversion of a civil partnership into a marriage.

## 3.4 The effect of different types of gift

In this section we will consider different types of gift—both in terms of the type of property being given to the beneficiary and in terms of where that property comes from. We will also look at the interpretation of gifts in wills, including considering some implied rules that apply where a clause is silent on a particular question (eg is the gift subject to, or free of, **inheritance tax**).

## 3.4.1 **Different types of gift: legacies, bequests and devises**

At the outset it is worth noting that the terminology in this area can be confusing. This is partly explained by the use at various times of Latin, 'Law-French' and English. As lawyers, you need to understand each of these technical terms but you need not, and should not, trouble clients with them! No matter what the technical term is for one of these gifts, they are all 'gifts'. It is also better to use the term '**specific gift**' with clients rather than the more accurate '**non-residuary gifts**', even though 'specific' has a particular technical meaning (on which see later).

## 3.4.2 **Pecuniary legacies**

These are gifts of money. Sometimes such gifts are referred to as 'monetary legacies' or just 'legacies'. The use of the prefixes '**pecuniary**' and 'monetary' are used to distinguish this type of gift from a gift of **chattels** or other personal property, which is also sometimes known as a 'legacy'.

Pecuniary legacies (in common with other non-residuary gifts) may be **general**, specific or **demonstrative**.

A general legacy is the most common, for example 'I give ONE THOUSAND POUNDS (£1,000) to ALICE'. The wording of the clause does not seek to identify which £1,000 is to go to Alice, or from where that £1,000 must be drawn—it is simply taken out of the estate as a whole.

A specific legacy in contrast would seek to determine exactly which £1,000 was meant to go to Alice, for example 'I give the ONE THOUSAND POUNDS (£1,000) in bank notes which I have deposited under the mattress in the spare bedroom to ALICE'. Clearly, this is an absurd method of providing for a legacy, given that most people do not keep the same bank notes for long periods of time and keep large sums of money not in bank notes but in bank or building society accounts. As a result, specific pecuniary legacies are rare and not to be recommended.

It is possible to identify the source of a legacy, though: such as 'I give ONE THOUSAND POUNDS (£1,000) to ALICE payable from my Barclays Bank plc account number 342521'. This is a demonstrative legacy. Although this sort of legacy makes more sense than a specific pecuniary legacy, it is still not advisable. The testator may well close the Barclays Bank account in question between the date of the will and the date of death. Although in such circumstances the gift would not fail (the legacy would be paid out of the estate generally), it is clearly introducing an unnecessary (and ineffective) complication to the terms of the will—much better just to frame the gift in general terms.

For an example of a pecuniary legacy, see clause 4 in the example will in **2.3.1**.

## 3.4.3 **Bequests**

**Bequests** are gifts of chattels (items of personal property or, to use an archaic term, 'personalty'). Confusingly, such gifts are also called legacies.

Bequests are much more likely to be specific in nature than are pecuniary legacies. The gift is usually intended to be of a specific item or items which the testator owns, for example 'I give my Sony widescreen television to JOHN'. It would be unusual for a testator to include a general gift, such as 'I give *a* Sony widescreen television to JOHN'. With the latter wording, the executors would have to use monies from the estate to purchase the item for the beneficiary.

For another example of a bequest, see clause 5 in the example will in **2.3.1**.

### 3.4.3.1 Incorporation by reference

The will is meant to include all of the wishes of the testator, subject to any changes made by codicil. Both wills and codicils have to be made in accordance with the formalities prescribed by s9 of the Wills Act 1837, which are imposed due to the particular importance attached to these testamentary documents. As a general rule, therefore, it is not possible to provide for testamentary dispositions in documents outside the will. However, in certain circumstances a document may be 'incorporated' into the will 'by reference', as we saw in **2.4.3.8**.

A good example of a document that might be incorporated is a list of chattels. Such a list has to have been made prior to the execution of the will, otherwise the testator would be held to be making a testamentary disposition without following the prescribed formalities. As we saw in **Chapter 2**, where it is sought to incorporate a document by reference, it is necessary to identify the document with certainty in the will, and to make clear in the will that the document in question is already in existence.

There are problems associated with this approach, though: the list of chattels cannot be altered (unless a new one is prepared and that new one is incorporated properly by a later codicil to the will); and the list has to be kept safe (ideally with the will), otherwise the list may be lost.

#### 3.4.3.2 Precatory trust

This can be seen as an alternative to incorporation by reference. The idea with a '**precatory trust**' (which is not in fact a trust at all) is to give property outright to a beneficiary but express the wish that the beneficiary should act in relation to that property according to directions given by the testator (usually by letter).

The hope is that the beneficiary will comply with these wishes, which might be to distribute a number of chattels among various family members, but this is no more than a hope: the beneficiary is not obliged (apart from morally) to follow the directions and is legally entitled to keep the subject matter of the gift for themselves. The disadvantages of adopting this approach are obvious.

#### 3.4.3.3 Division by beneficiaries

Another option when dealing with a number of chattels is for the testator to direct that those chattels are divided between the beneficiaries by agreement. The beneficiaries may well disagree, and so it is prudent to include a provision giving the final say to the executors (although this may not be appropriate where the executors are themselves beneficiaries).

### 3.4.4 **Other legacies (gifts of shares)**

As well as non-residuary gifts of chattels, it is possible to make gifts of intangibles such as 'choses in action', for example shares in a company. These gifts are also called legacies.

However, a company might issue bonus shares to its shareholders or the testator may be forced to exchange their shares in the company where the company is taken over by another. It is wise, therefore, to include provisions catering for such eventualities in the wording of any gift of shares.

### 3.4.5 **Devises**

A gift of land or of an interest in land is called a '**devise**'. Devises will almost always be specific, identifying a particular property, either by address or by some formula such as 'any house which I use as my principal residence at the date of my death'.

For an example of a devise, see clause 6 in the example will in **2.3.1**.

#### 3.4.5.1 Rights of occupation

It is also possible to create a **trust over land** in the will, under which the beneficiary is given a right to occupy the land for life or until the happening of a certain event, such as remarriage. The land will then either pass into **residue** or to named beneficiaries once the beneficiary in occupation ceases to occupy. This is sometimes done where a testator has married for a second time and gives their spouse a right to occupy the home for life, with the house ultimately passing to the testator's children from the testator's first marriage.

There must be clarity on which events result in the termination of the right to occupy (it is clear whether the beneficiary has died or remarried, but there can be uncertainty if the right to occupy ceases on the beneficiary entering into an informal relationship with another person). Also, consideration needs to be given to who insures and maintains the property whilst the beneficiary is living there—is it the beneficiary or is it the deceased's estate? Finally, the beneficiary is likely to need to use the items of household use (eg carpets, curtains and furniture).

### 3.4.5.2 Joint property: tenants in common

We will see in **Chapter 5** that there are two forms of joint ownership. With the first form, the owners are described as **joint tenants in equity**, and it is not possible for either joint tenant to leave their interest by will. With the second form, the owners are described as **tenants in common**, and it is possible for a tenant in common to leave their share of the property to a beneficiary by will. It is not essential for a tenant in common to make a non-residuary gift of the share in the property in order for it to pass by will. If no specific provision is made, the share in the property will pass as part of the testator's **residuary estate**.

### 3.4.5.3 Joint property: joint tenants in equity

In contrast, a joint tenant in equity cannot leave their interest in a property by will. If this is the testator's intention, it will be necessary to '**sever**' the joint tenancy. For more detail on **joint property**, see **5.2**.

## 3.4.6 Non-residuary gifts and residuary gifts

There are two ways in which the testator might theoretically provide for the distribution of their estate. The first is to identify every single item of property that they own and make specific provisions covering each and every item. The other method is to simply look at the underlying value of the estate as a whole and then divide the estate into portions or slices, just as if it were a cake.

In practice, a combination of these approaches is often used—the testator will identify certain items of property or sums of money and leave these to specified beneficiaries. These specified gifts are termed 'non-residuary gifts'. Then the testator will treat everything else (called 'the residuary estate' or 'the residue') as one big cake and leave it to one or more beneficiaries as they wish.

Often, the testator will leave this residuary estate to one person—usually their spouse. The will typically will also state what is to happen if that person dies before the testator. Generally, wills provide that if a spouse dies before the testator then the residuary estate is divided amongst the testator's children (and possibly grandchildren).

This does not have to be the case, though—under the law in England and Wales a testator has complete freedom to do as they wish with their estate, and can leave their estate to whoever they wish to benefit. The only limitation on this is that certain persons may apply to the court after the testator's death for **reasonable financial provision** from the estate, under the Inheritance (Provision for Family and Dependants) Act 1975 (see **Chapter 11**).

Where a testator provides for their children or grandchildren, or indeed any other group such as nephews and nieces, the clause will often be drafted as a class gift, identifying the class to benefit but not naming the individual members of that class. We will consider class gifts in **3.4.7**.

## 3.4.7 Class gifts

Class gifts are gifts to the members of a class. The class is identified in the will by a generic description, without naming the individual beneficiaries. For example, a testator might leave their whole estate (or their residuary estate) to be divided amongst their children. The children would not be named in the will: instead, the will would include wording similar to the following:

*I GIVE my residuary estate between those of my children who survive me.*

Under this clause, on the testator's death each of the testator's children to survive the testator would receive an equal share of the residuary estate.

Class gifts can be used for other groups—it is not just used for gifts to children. The class specified could instead be grandchildren, nephews and nieces, brothers and sisters or persons not related to the testators, such as the employees of a particular company or friends. Having said this, the most common class gift in wills is a class gift to children.

Where the gift is to the children, the will also usually provides for a substitute gift to grandchildren, to cover the situation where one or more of the children fails to survive. Usually, this is written so that if a given child dies before the testator, that child's share of the estate will pass to that child's children (usually, to those who survive the testator).

**EXAMPLE**

David makes a will, leaving his residuary estate to those of his children who survive him, with a provision that if a child of his dies before him then the share the child would have received will pass to the child's children, if there are any who survive David.

David is survived by one child, Louise. David had another child, James, who died before David. However, James had two children, Robert and Olivia. They will inherit the share that James would have received if he had survived David. So, David's daughter, Louise, will take one half of the residuary estate. The other half of the residuary estate (ie the half that would have gone to James) is divided between James's children (David's grandchildren), Robert and Olivia.

Louise also has a child, Harry, who has also survived his grandfather David. As Louise is still alive, though, she takes her gift under David's will, and her son, Harry, receives nothing.

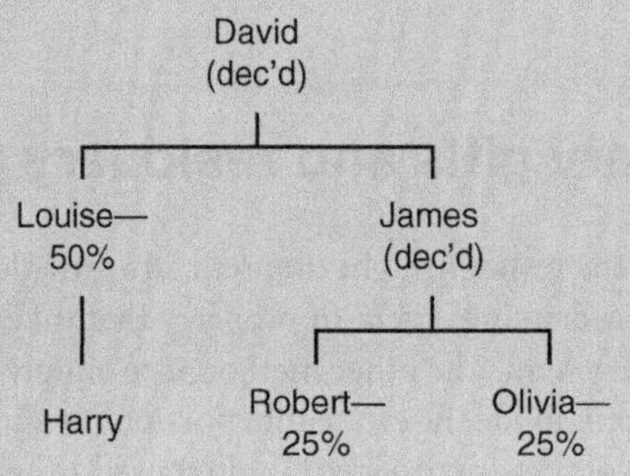


**EXAMPLE**

If we change the facts in the above example, what if Louise had also died before David?

In that situation, James' children (Robert and Olivia) would still share the half of the estate that would have been paid to James had he survived David. In other words, Robert and Olivia will each receive one-quarter of the estate.

However, Harry (Louise's child) will receive half of the estate (the share that would have gone to Louise).

So, the percentages of the estate going to each grandchild will be: Harry, 50 per cent, Robert, 25 per cent, Olivia, 25 per cent.

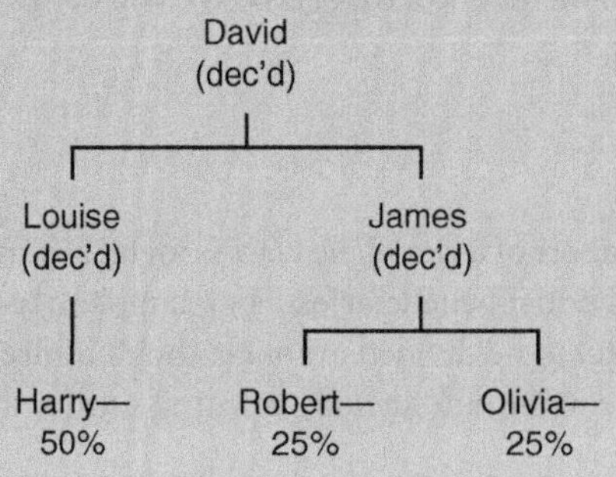


The type of division of the estate in the above example is known as a '***per stirpes***' distribution—it is a division according to branches of the family. The alternative type of division would be a '***per capita***' division—in other words, a per 'head' division. If a *per capita* provision was chosen by the testator, then the residuary estate in the second example above would have been divided equally between each of the surviving grandchildren, and each grandchild (Robert, Olivia, Harry) would get one-third of David's estate.

It is much more common to have provisions that divide the residuary estate according to branches of the family, namely a *per stirpes* provision.

### 3.4.7.1 Class gifts to children

For the purposes of class gifts (and indeed any other gifts in wills), a testator's children include any adopted children and also any children whose parents are not married to one another (historically, referred to as 'illegitimate' children). Any reference to 'children' or 'child' in a will is taken to include both categories of children.

It is, of course, possible to name the testator's children in the will. However, where a testator is still of an age to have more children, it is common practice not to name young children in a will but just to include a class gift to the testator's 'children'. If the testator is older, the children are themselves adults, and the testator is unlikely to have more children, it is more common to name the children in the will.

One reason for naming children in a will, rather than having a class gift that refers to them by description is if the testator wishes to exclude a particular child from benefiting. This might be because the child in question is dependent on alcohol or drugs, or has a gambling problem, or the child and the testator are estranged in some way. If a class gift to 'my children' is used, that child would be included in the class and that child would receive a share of the estate, but if the other children are named in the will, the other child (who is not named) will be excluded from benefit.

If a child (even an adult child) is not named by the testator and thereby excluded from benefit, that child may be able to bring a successful application for reasonable financial provision from the testator's estate under the Inheritance (Provision for Family and Dependants) Act 1975 (see **Chapter 11**).

### 3.4.7.2 How to recognise a class gift

As said earlier, a class gift is a gift of property to be divided among beneficiaries who fulfil a general description: for example, '£50,000 to the children of Zoe' or '£50,000 to the children of Zoe who attain the age of 18'. In such cases, the total value of the gift is clear: the problem is to know how to share it among those entitled. This will obviously depend upon how many people fit the description. In the examples given, it would not be possible to answer this question with certainty at least until the death of Zoe. In the meantime, no distribution would be possible.

A similar problem arises where the gift in the will takes the form of an individual gift to the members of a class, for example '£5,000 to each of the children of Zack'. Here, what the prospective beneficiaries are to take is identified but until the death of Zack it cannot be known how many children will qualify.

### 3.4.7.3 Class-closing rules

The courts have invented class-closing rules to overcome these problems and allow distribution at an earlier date. There are various rules (which apply to different types of gift), but each class-closing rule determines the point in time when the particular class chosen by the testator will close. In principle, this will generally happen when there is one person fitting the description who has a 'vested' interest (ie an absolute interest).

At whatever point the class closes, it does so to the exclusion of any potential beneficiary not then 'living'—a term which includes a child ***en ventre sa mère*** (ie already conceived but not yet born, provided the child is born alive). This closing of the class seems unfair to those persons thus excluded from benefit, but this disadvantage is considered to be outweighed by the advantage of ensuring an earlier distribution.

The class-closing rules may be excluded by a clear provision in the testator's will, such as 'to the children of Zoe living at my death' or 'to the children of Zack whenever born'.

As indicated, the rules (if not so excluded) differ according to the type of gift involved. Class gifts are most commonly used to provide for classes who are related to the testator, such as children, grandchildren, nephews and nieces. The class-closing rules will differ depending on whether the interests of the members of the class are **vested** (ie absolute) or conditional (ie dependent on meeting a specified condition).

For example, Michael leaves his residuary estate to be divided between 'such of my grandchildren as survive me'. Here, the interests of the members of the class (his grandchildren) are vested—all that the grandchildren have to do is to survive Michael (note that if there is a survivorship provision in the will—see **3.5.2.3**—this may mean the grandchildren have to survive Michael by a period of time specified in the will, such as 28 days). As far as the class-closing rules are concerned, the class would close when Michael died and would include those grandchildren alive at the date of his death (or at the end of the survivorship period if there is one). As said, this would include grandchildren *en ventre sa mère* (grandchildren conceived but not yet born at the time of Michael's death).

Alternatively, Michael may have concerns about his grandchildren spending their inheritances unwisely if they receive their money at the age of 18. This would occur with the vested interests given in the previous paragraph, as whilst the grandchildren could not control the money before reaching 18, once they do reach 18 they can demand the money from the executors and **trustees**, under the rule in *Saunders v Vautier* (1841) 49 ER 282. To avoid the grandchildren taking control of the money at a relatively young age, Michael might instead give the grandchildren a 'conditional' gift.

For example, Michael might provide in his will for a gift of the residuary estate 'to those of my grandchildren who survive me and attain the age of 21'. This means what it says—that for one of Michael's grandchildren to inherit, they must both survive him and reach the age of 21. A grandchild who had already reached 21 but who has died before Michael will not inherit because they have not survived Michael. Also, a grandchild who is alive but under the age of 21 at the date of Michael's death will have to wait until they reach the age of 21 before becoming entitled.

What are the class-closing rules with the second type of gift (ie the conditional gift)? In that situation, the class will still close at the date of Michael's death (or possibly at the end of a survivorship period specified in the will), but the members of the closed class (ie the grandchildren who have survived Michael, including those *en ventre sa mère*) will not inherit until they meet the relevant condition, namely reaching the age of 21.

However, if Michael had provided in his will a gift 'to those of my grandchildren who reach the age of 21' (ie not specifying that the grandchildren had to survive him), then this class could include grandchildren who were born (or, rather, conceived) after his death. This could include grandchildren born many years later. With a provision of this type, though, the class would have to close at some point, and the class will normally close at the point in time when the condition is first met by a beneficiary. In the case of Michael's gift to those of his grandchildren who reach the age of 21, the class will close when the first of his grandchildren reaches 21. The reason why the class closes at this point is that when that grandchild reaches 21, the executors and trustees will have to pay a proportionate share of the residuary estate to that grandchild. It has to be clear whether that grandchild is receiving one-quarter, one-sixth or one-tenth of the estate (or whatever proportion, depending on the number of beneficiaries in the class). For that reason, the class will close when the first grandchild reaches 21, and any grandchild born subsequently will fall outside the class.

**EXAMPLE**

To take the example provision just mentioned, Michael leaves his residuary estate to be divided between 'those of my grandchildren who attain the age of 21'.

When Michael dies, he has three living grandchildren—Katy (aged 17), Paul (aged 15) and John (aged 12). Two years after Michael's death, another grandchild, George, is born.

Unfortunately, Katy dies before reaching 21, and so she does not inherit any part of her grandfather's estate. Subsequently, Paul does reach the age of 21. At that point in time, there are three grandchildren—Paul, John and George. The class will close at this point and Paul will be paid one-third of the residuary estate. A year after this happens, another grandchild, Richard, is born but the class has already closed and Richard will not receive a share of the residuary estate.

There are other class-closing rules which apply to other types of class gift, but these are not considered here.

## 3.4.8 Some implied rules where the will is silent

### 3.4.8.1 Inheritance tax

Care should be taken to deal with the question of who should bear the **burden** of any inheritance tax attributable to each gift in the will. If a non-residuary gift is to an exempt beneficiary (eg a spouse or a charity), then this is not an issue. Similarly, if the type of property which is the subject of the gift is likely to qualify for 100 per cent IHT Agricultural or Business Property Relief (see **6.7.2** for more detail), then it is likely that this will not be a significant concern (however, a relief can be lost if the conditions for the relief no longer apply by the date of death).

If the gift is to a non-exempt beneficiary and is not covered wholly by a relief, it is necessary to determine who should bear the burden of the inheritance tax. The inheritance tax payable on the 'estate' is apportioned to each asset in the estate according to that asset's value. Although the personal representatives are '**liable**' to HM Revenue and Customs for the payment of the inheritance tax on the estate, the 'burden' of the inheritance tax may be shared between the beneficiaries of the estate according to the value of the property to which they are entitled.

The implied rule is that non-residuary gifts are free of inheritance (or other) tax, unless stated otherwise in the will. To make a non-residuary beneficiary pay the inheritance tax attributable to their gift, it is necessary to state in the will that the gift is 'subject to tax', or some similar wording. It is possible, for clarity's sake, to state that a non-residuary gift is 'free of tax' but this is not strictly necessary due to the implied rule.

#### 3.4.8.2 Costs of transport, insurance etc.

With bequests and devises there is another implied rule—that the beneficiary bears the cost of transport, insurance and similar costs unless stated otherwise in the will. So, if a beneficiary in Glasgow is left antique furniture by a testator in Cardiff, the normal rule is that the beneficiary has to pay the cost of transporting the furniture from Cardiff to Glasgow and the attendant costs of insurance. The testator can provide that the beneficiary takes the gift free of those costs, though.

To apply this rule to a devise, although it is the responsibility of the executors to complete an **assent** for the transfer of the land, it is the beneficiary's responsibility to register the transfer with the Land Registry and pay the registration fee.

#### 3.4.8.3 Secured debts and charges on property

Section 35 of the Administration of Estates Act 1925 provides that where property is subject to a secured debt or charge, any gift of that property will be subject to that debt or charge. This applies mainly to land, where there are mortgages, but can also apply to other types of property, particularly shares in a company.

Taking land as an example, where there is a gift of land, that land will pass to the beneficiary subject to any charges attaching to the land unless the testator has expressed a contrary intention. So, if there is a mortgage on the testator's house and the deceased leaves the house to their niece, the niece will have the benefit of the house but will have to take on board the obligations under the mortgage (this is assuming the mortgage has not been paid off through mortgage protection insurance or the proceeds of an endowment policy). The lender will also have to agree to the transfer of the mortgage to the niece. Lastly, the niece does not have to accept the gift—she can always disclaim the gift (see **3.5.6** for more detail on **disclaimers**).

If the testator wishes to pass on the land without the burden of the mortgage, it is necessary to state this in the will, in the clause providing for the gift in question. The mortgage would then typically be paid out of the residuary estate.

## 3.5 The failure of gifts

Gifts in wills may fail due to a variety of reasons, several of which are considered in this section. In this section we also consider the effect of a gift failing, which differs depending on the type of gift intended.

### 3.5.1 Uncertainty

You will no doubt remember the three certainties from your study of equity and trusts. If not, don't worry—a reminder of the rules is included in **Chapter 12**. The same certainties—intention, subject matter (ie property) and objects (ie the beneficiaries)—need to be certain when considering gifts in wills. The 'intention' will be either the intention to make a gift or the intention to make a trust in the will. We will next consider the other two certainties.

#### 3.5.1.1 Certainty of subject matter

It is important to describe the property which is the subject of the gift with **certainty**, otherwise the gift may fail. For example, if the will provided for 'A gift of one of my vintage Beatles long-playing vinyl records to JANE' the question would be asked 'Which one?' This question could not be answered with certainty and so the gift to Jane would fail.

It is possible to provide for some mechanism for determining which item should go to the beneficiary. The executors can be given the power to decide which Beatles LP to give to Jane—if such a stipulation were included in the clause, then the gift would not fail.

With pecuniary legacies it is important to be clear as to how much money the testator wishes to give to the beneficiary. The amount of such gifts is usually stated in words and figures.

With **residuary gifts** it is important to state clearly the proportion of the estate which is going to each beneficiary.

#### 3.5.1.2 Certainty of objects (beneficiaries)

It is an obvious, but nevertheless often overlooked, point that the beneficiaries (of all types of gift, including residuary gifts) must be described with sufficient accuracy. Best practice with adult beneficiaries is to state full name and address (current at the time the will is made—it does not matter that the beneficiary subsequently changes name, eg through marriage, or changes address).

As has been seen, sometimes beneficiaries can be referred to by description rather than being named. The most common examples of this are 'children' and 'grandchildren'. Where a testator is unlikely to have any more children, and where that testator's children are themselves adults, it is usual to name each child in the will. Where the testator is likely to have more children, or where the children are all minors, it is common practice not to name the children but rather to refer to them as a class.

### 3.5.2 **Lapse**

Another common reason for the failure of gifts is the beneficiary dying before the testator. This is a problem with non-residuary and residuary gifts alike, and the process is called **lapse**.

Generally, if the beneficiary of a non-residuary gift dies, the gift fails and the property which is the subject matter of the gift falls into residue. In other words, it will become part of the residuary estate and will be distributed in accordance with the testator's wishes regarding the residuary estate.

However, it is possible to provide for a substitutional gift in the will in the event of the death of the original beneficiary of a non-residuary gift. In most cases, though, the testator intends to benefit the named beneficiary and does not intend passing the same property on to another person if that named beneficiary predeceases.

If a residuary gift fails due to lapse, in the absence of express substitutional provisions the lapsed gift will usually give rise to a **partial intestacy**. As a result, the testator has lost control over that part of their estate, which may then pass to persons whom the testator did not wish to benefit. It is usual, therefore, to cater for this by including a series of substitutional gifts of residue.

#### 3.5.2.1 Section 33 of the Wills Act 1837

There is a statutory exception to the rule that the property of the lapsed gift falls into residue. This is where the gift in question is to the child or other lineal descendant of the testator (this would include a grandchild, great-grandchild etc). In the absence of contrary intention in the will, the gift will not lapse if the deceased beneficiary had children or other lineal descendants living at the date of the testator's death. Section 33 provides that the gift will pass *per stirpes* to the children or lineal descendants of the deceased beneficiary rather than falling into residue (with a non-residuary gift) or there being a partial intestacy (with a residuary gift).

Section 33 is subject to any contrary intention expressed in the will. With a non-residuary gift, the necessary contrary intention can be shown by including words such as 'but if s/he dies before me then [the property] shall form part of my residuary estate'. With a residuary gift, provisions are usually included to provide what will happen if a residuary beneficiary dies before the testator (this is common whether or not the beneficiary is one of the testator's **issue**). Such substitutional provisions will provide a contrary intention to s33, although often the terms of such substitutional provisions will have the same effect as if s33 had applied. Thus, if there is a residuary gift divided between the testator's children, it is common to have a 'gift-over' (ie substitutional provision) to the children of a child who predeceases the testator. This will result in the same *per stirpes* distribution as would have occurred had s33 not been overridden by the express provision in the will. (See **3.4.7** on class gifts for more detail on substitutional provisions in class gifts to children.)

### 3.5.2.2 *Commorientes*

As a gift normally lapses if the beneficiary predeceases the testator, it is useful to know who died first. In the vast majority of cases this will be quite clear. However, there may be limited circumstances where the order of death is not known, for example where the testator and beneficiary die in the same road accident. In these circumstances, s184 of the Law of Property Act 1925 (the ***commorientes*** rule) says that the elder of the two is deemed to die first. For example, in *Jump v Lister* [2016] EWHC 2160 (Ch), the bodies of a married couple were found in their house some considerable time after their likely deaths (the bodies were in a state of decomposition). As a result, the order of deaths was not known. Under the *commorientes* rule, the husband was deemed to survive the wife as he was the younger of the two.

### 3.5.2.3 Survivorship clauses

To deal with the situation where the beneficiary survives the testator, but dies very soon after, it is common to include a survivorship clause in the will. The beneficiary then has to survive the testator by a given period of time (commonly one month, or 28 days) in order to inherit.

Care should be taken with mirror wills that each contain survivorship clauses, if each will contains a series of non-residuary gifts. As mentioned earlier, in *Jump v Lister* [2016], the bodies of a married couple were found some time after their likely deaths and, under the *commorientes* rule, the husband was deemed to survive the wife as he was the younger of the two. However, the wife's will contained a standard survivorship clause whereby the husband was treated as if he had pre-deceased the wife for the purposes of her will, because he had not survived her by 28 days. The problem was that each will contained identical pecuniary legacies totalling £214,500 which were to be paid if the other spouse had pre-deceased. The effect of the combination of the *commorientes* rule and the survivorship clause was that the legacies mentioned in their wills would have to be paid twice—once from the husband's estate and once from the wife's estate. This was clearly not what the couple had intended. The likely outcome in such a situation, should it happen again, is a negligence claim against the solicitors' firm that drafted the clients' wills. In view of this problem, survivorship clauses should be modified to avoid double payment of pecuniary legacies in similar circumstances, where couples wish to make mirror wills.

## 3.5.3 **Ademption**

Another way in which gifts can fail is by **ademption**. This is really only significant for 'specific' gifts, namely bequests of specified items of personalty, and devises. Ademption is concerned with the subject matter of the gift (ie the property, whereas lapse is concerned with the object(s) of the gift, ie the beneficiaries).

Take the gift mentioned earlier: 'I give my Sony widescreen television to JOHN'. Aside from the fact that the description may not be adequate, and the gift may fail for lack of certainty, the gift might also fail as a result of ademption. If the testator replaces the Sony television with a Samsung television between the date of the will and the date of their death, the gift will fail. This is for the obvious reason that the testator no longer has the Sony television in their estate at the date of death. As the testator's stated intention was that John should get that particular Sony television, it cannot be said that John should now get the Samsung one, or even an equivalent amount of money instead, and so John will get nothing.

However, it is important to realise that a testator is not prevented from dealing with their estate by the making of a will. Some clients believe that once they have stated something in a will they are legally obliged to stick to their stated intentions, so that if a testator has made a gift of, for example a gold watch, the testator has to retain that gold watch until death and cannot give it away or sell it. It is worthwhile explaining to clients that they are still free to deal with their property as they wish during their lifetime, regardless of what is said in their will: this has been described as a will being 'ambulatory' until the testator dies.

Strictly, s24 of the Wills Act 1837 provides that the gift of a stated item or items by description is deemed to be a gift of such item or items that the testator owns at the date of death. Following this rule, you would think that a gift of 'my car' would mean a gift of the car (if any) which the testator owned at the date of their death. However, s24 is subject to a contrary intention, and it has been held that the use of the word 'my' in the case of a single item provides such a contrary intention, namely that it indicates that the testator is referring to the car which they own at the date of the will. Thus, a gift of 'my car' or 'my house' is subject to ademption if the testator changes car or moves house by the time they die. To avoid this, it is possible to state in the clause that the gift is of such car or house which the testator owns 'at the date of my death'.

This contrary intention is not usually implied where the reference is to a group of objects which is capable of increase or decrease: for example, 'my collection of china dolls' or 'my jewellery'. With such gifts, s24 will apply and the gift will be assumed to be of those dolls or jewellery that the testator owns at the date of death.

Also, it is possible to provide for a gift of chattels by reference to the description set out in s55(1)(x) of the Administration of Estates Act 1925. This is the same description of personal chattels that applies when considering the entitlement of a spouse or civil partner on intestacy (see **Chapter 4**). A gift by reference to this section will include most chattels, but not all.

The definition of personal possessions in s55(1)(x) changed relatively recently, due to the Inheritance and Trustees' Powers Act 2014. The Act changed the definition in s55(1)(x) to all tangible movable property other than: (a) money or securities for money; (b) property used solely or mainly for business purposes; and (c) property held solely as an investment. However, the Act will not affect any will which was executed before the Act came into force on 1 October 2014. For wills executed before that date, the old definition in s55(1)(x) will continue to apply, unless a contrary intention has been expressed (which is unlikely).

**EXAMPLE**

Clause 3 of Paul's will states, 'I give my 800 shares in PQR plc to my brother Robert'. It is likely that this will be construed as a specific gift of the 800 shares that Paul owned at the date of the will in PQR plc. If Paul sold 300 of those shares before he died, Robert would only take the remaining 500 shares.

Ademption can also occur where there has been a change in substance (ie in the very nature of the property) as opposed to a mere change in name or form. This distinction is not always easy to see.

**EXAMPLE**

Clause 4 of Paul's will provides, 'I give my 100 shares in BCD plc to my sister Susan'. Again, this is likely to be construed as a specific gift. Suppose before Paul died BCD plc subdivided its shares so that one original share was represented by five new shares. It is likely that this would be construed as a mere change in the form of the shares, and Susan would take the 500 (new) shares in BCD plc. If, however, BCD plc were taken over by another company (say, FGH plc), and FGH plc issued shares in FGH plc to replace those held in the original company, it is likely that this would be seen as a change in substance (ie shares in an entirely different company) and the gift of the BCD plc shares to Susan would fail.

### 3.5.4 The effect of divorce, or of dissolution of a civil partnership

Unlike marriage or the formation of a civil partnership, a will is not revoked by a divorce or a dissolution of a civil partnership. Instead, the divorce or dissolution will have the effect of revoking those provisions of the will that relate to the former spouse or civil partner.

Section 18A of the Wills Act 1837 provides (subject to contrary intention in the will) for this limited revocation on a decree absolute of divorce or nullity. Section 18C includes the equivalent provisions applying on the dissolution of a civil partnership.

Any provisions in the will as to the appointment of the former spouse or civil partner as executor or trustee take effect as if the former spouse or civil partner had died on the date upon which the marriage or civil partnership was annulled or dissolved and will thus be ineffective. Further, any property that is given by the will to the former spouse or civil partner passes as if that spouse or civil partner had died on that day, and will thus not pass to the former spouse or civil partner.

Under s6 of the Children Act 1989 (again, subject to expressed contrary intention), any appointment of the spouse or civil partner as guardian of the testator's children is similarly revoked on the annulment or dissolution of the marriage/civil partnership.

Note that these provisions do not apply on separation, nor do they affect any provisions of the will other than those indicated. So, if the will appointed other executors (in addition to the spouse/civil partner) the appointment of those other executors would still be valid. Also, any gifts in the will which are made to persons other than the spouse or civil partner will continue to be valid.

As indicated, the revocations provided by ss18A and 18C of the Wills Act 1837 and s6 of the Children Act 1989 are subject to a contrary intention being shown in a will, but it is rare for someone to express in a will that appointments of a spouse/civil partner and gifts to a spouse/civil partner should continue to apply following a divorce or dissolution.

It is worth noting that nothing in ss18A and 18C of the Wills Act affects the right of a former spouse or former civil partner to make an application for reasonable financial provision under the Inheritance (Provision for Family and Dependants) Act 1975 (on which, see **Chapter 11**).

Also, s18D of the Wills Act 1837 provides that appointments of and gifts to a civil partner are not revoked by the conversion of the civil partnership into a marriage (this may happen as same-sex civil partners take the opportunity to marry which has only been available to same-sex couples since 2014, whereas civil partnerships have been available since 2005).

## 3.5.5 Gifts to witnesses

A gift in a will fails if the beneficiary, or the beneficiary's spouse or civil partner, witnesses the will, though the validity of the will itself is not affected (s15 Wills Act 1837). However, the gift will not fail if, ignoring the attestation by the beneficiary or spouse or civil partner, the will is duly executed, namely because there are at least two other witnesses who are not beneficiaries or their spouses or civil partners. Further, a gift within the terms of s15 may be 'saved' if the will is subsequently confirmed by a codicil which is independently witnessed.

Where the beneficiary's spouse or civil partner has witnessed the will, s15 applies only if the beneficiary and the witness were married or civil partners at the date of the execution of the will; there will be no problem where they married or entered into a civil partnership after that date.

## 3.5.6 Disclaimer

No one can be forced to take a benefit under a will if they do not want it. Subject to certain limitations, a beneficiary is always able to refuse a gift under a will. This refusal is called a '**disclaimer**' and the beneficiary is said to 'disclaim' the gift.

A beneficiary cannot disclaim a gift until the death of the testator, as until the testator dies the beneficiary does not have an entitlement that they can disclaim (they merely have a hope or expectation of future benefit).

There are limitations on disclaiming a benefit under a will. First, it is not seemingly possible to disclaim part of a benefit under a will. It is, though, possible to accept one gift under a will and disclaim another gift under the same will if the two gifts are clearly separate. However, it would not be possible to disclaim entitlement to, say, half of the residuary estate if the beneficiary had been left the whole residuary estate in the will.

Secondly, it is only possible to disclaim a gift if the beneficiary has not already received a benefit from that gift. For example, if the gifted property produces an income (rent from rented property or dividends from company shares) the beneficiary cannot disclaim once they have already accepted some of that income.

Usually, where a beneficiary does not wish to receive a gift after the testator's death, it is because the beneficiary would prefer that the gift goes to a particular person that the beneficiary has in mind to benefit. In such situations, it is more common to make a post-death **variation**, rather than simply disclaiming the gift, because it is not possible for the beneficiary to control the destination of the gifted property by means of a disclaimer. In other words, a disclaimer is simply a rejection of the gift.

If a beneficiary disclaims a gift, then the gifted property will pass either into residue (if the gift disclaimed is a non-residuary gift), or according to substitutional provisions in the will, or under the rules of intestacy if there are no such provisions. If the beneficiary disclaiming is a child (or one of the issue) of the testator, then s33A of the Wills Act 1837 provides that the disclaiming beneficiary will be treated as if they had predeceased the testator, and under s33 the disclaimed gift will pass to the children (or, more accurately, issue) of the disclaiming beneficiary, subject to any contrary intention expressed in the will.

It is also possible to disclaim an entitlement under the intestacy rules. A beneficiary may be entitled under the will and under the intestacy rules if the gift in the will fails. A disclaimer of the gift in the will does not disclaim the entitlement under intestacy: the beneficiary must disclaim both.

For more detail on disclaimers and on post-death variations, see **10.5**.

## 3.5.7 **Forfeiture**

The **forfeiture** rule is a rule of public policy which precludes a person who has unlawfully killed another from acquiring a benefit in consequence of the killing. The rule applies also to someone who has unlawfully aided or assisted in the death or the unlawful killing of the person. The rule prevents a person who has murdered another from benefiting from the deceased's estate. The rule also applies to a person convicted of manslaughter or a person who has assisted the deceased person to commit suicide. In *Amos v Amos* [2020] EWHC 1063 (Ch), it was applied to a case of causing death by careless driving.

If a person has been precluded by the forfeiture rule from acquiring a benefit under a will, s33A of the Wills Act 1837 provides that the person is treated as having predeceased the testator. This is important because it means that standard substitutional provisions to be found in most wills can be applied, as gifts in wills are usually expressed so that they pass to other beneficiaries if the beneficiary dies. As the beneficiary is deemed to have predeceased the testator (due to s33A), the substitutional provisions in the will can thus take effect. This is subject to any contrary intention appearing in the will, but it is unlikely that many (if any) wills contain wording to state what would happen if a beneficiary were to unlawfully kill the testator!

If the beneficiary is one of the issue of the testator, s33 of the Wills Act 1837 provides that the issue of the beneficiary will inherit in their place. This is also subject to any contrary intention expressed in the will.

Under s2 of the Forfeiture Act 1982, the court has the power to modify or exclude the effect of the forfeiture rule. This is known as 'relief from forfeiture'. A person who has been convicted of murder is not able to apply for relief from forfeiture, but someone who has been convicted of manslaughter or has assisted another to commit suicide may apply to the court. Relief from forfeiture was granted in *Amos v Amos*, where the wife of an elderly couple was responsible for her husband's death when she was driving their car and he was a passenger.

The forfeiture rules are also particularly relevant to situations of terminally ill persons who travel abroad to countries where voluntary euthanasia is legal, such as in Switzerland. The terminally ill person is committing suicide under the laws of England and Wales, and may have been assisted by a relative who accompanied them to the clinic where the fatal procedure was carried out, and the relative may have assisted with making the booking and the travel arrangements. Has that relative assisted in the suicide and, if so, should relief from forfeiture be granted? These issues were considered in *Ninian v Findlay* [2019] EWHC 297 (Ch), when a wife helped her husband to end his life in the Dignitas clinic in Switzerland. She helped with the booking, made the travel arrangements and accompanied him to the clinic as he was not able to travel on his own. However, she did so reluctantly, after having tried to dissuade him from the course of action. She reported herself voluntarily to the police in the UK following her husband's death, and the decision was taken not to prosecute her as it was not in the public interest. The court in the reported case had to decide: (a) whether the forfeiture rule applied; and (b) whether relief from forfeiture should be given. On point (a), the court held that she had assisted her husband to commit suicide, but that on point (b) relief from forfeiture should be granted, so that she could inherit under her husband's will (she was the sole beneficiary). The court considered a number of factors derived from an earlier Court of Appeal decision in *Dunbar v Plant* [1998] Ch 412, although it was said that there was no constraint on what the court might regard as material when exercising its discretion under s2(1) of the 1982 Act.

Section 3 of the Forfeiture Act 1982 provides that the forfeiture rule does not preclude a person from making an application for reasonable financial provision under the Inheritance (Provision for Family and Dependants) Act 1975, although clearly the fact that the person had unlawfully killed the deceased is likely to be a factor that weighs heavily against them in any such application. Again, those persons convicted of murder do not benefit from this saving provision, and so cannot make an application under the 1975 Act.

## 3.5.8 The effect of failure of gifts

The effect of a failed gift differs depending on the reason for the failure and the type of gift that has failed.

If the reason for the failure of the gift is ademption (see **3.5.3**) then the testator no longer owns the item of property, and so there is no question of who else might receive the property. The beneficiary gets nothing and there is no transmission of the property to another beneficiary because the property is no longer part of the testator's estate.

With the other reasons for failure, the subject matter of the gift (ie the property which was to be given away) still exists, and is still part of the testator's estate. The gift has failed either because the property was not clearly described (so it fails for uncertainty) or because there is some problem with the beneficiary—perhaps the beneficiary has died before the testator (lapse), or the testator and the beneficiary have divorced/dissolved a civil partnership, the beneficiary has witnessed the will, the beneficiary has decided to disclaim the gift or the beneficiary has unlawfully killed the testator. As the subject matter of the gift is still part of the testator's estate, the question is: 'who should receive the property now the original gift has failed?'

The answer to this question differs depending on whether the gift was a non-residuary gift or was a gift of part or all of the residuary estate.

If the gift was a non-residuary one, then the usual rule is that the gift will fall into residue—that is, it will become part of the residuary estate and will pass to whoever is entitled to the residuary estate. This will not happen if the will provides otherwise, by indicating what is to happen to the subject matter of the non-residuary gift in the event of the gift to the original beneficiary failing. Also, if the original beneficiary was one of the testator's issue, then s33 of the Wills Act 1837 would direct the property to the issue of the beneficiary, in the absence of any contrary intention in the will.

With failure of residuary gifts, it is common practice to provide for certain eventualities (eg the death of a residuary beneficiary) by including one or more substitutional gifts. Often there is a series of such substitutional gifts. For example, the primary gift of the whole of the residuary estate may be to the testator's spouse, but if the spouse dies before the testator (or is treated as if they had died before the testator due to a divorce), there is often a substitutional gift to the testator's children. There is usually also a further substitutional gift to the children of any children who happen to die before the testator. Then, possibly, to prevent the possibility of an intestacy in a situation where the testator is not survived by spouse, children or grandchildren, the testator might leave the residuary estate to charity.

Obviously, the choice as to whether to have substitutional gifts of residue, and the choice of substitutional beneficiaries, is up to the wishes of the particular testator—the testator has freedom to choose what they want in the will. The point for present purposes, though, is that if the will contains substitutional provisions, those provisions will determine who will benefit in the event of one or more of the residuary beneficiaries dying before the testator.

The flip side of this is that if the testator fails to provide for substitutional gifts to cover the eventuality that a residuary beneficiary may die, then the will may fail to dispose of part or all of the residuary estate, and part or all of the residuary estate would be distributed in accordance with the intestacy rules.

### EXAMPLE

Della's will leaves '£2,000 to my niece Jane and the rest of my estate to my husband Neil but if he fails to survive me then to my son Mark'. Only Della's son Mark survives her; the gifts to Jane and Neil therefore lapse. Jane's gift will thus fall into residue, and Mark will take Della's entire estate.

### EXAMPLE

Ranjit's will divides his residuary estate between two of his children, Ajay and Puja. Ranjit has another child, Baljit, but Ranjit does not wish to leave anything to Baljit due to an argument between the two of them some years previously.

Ajay dies before Ranjit. Ranjit's will does not include substitutional gifts to say what is to happen in the event of one of the residuary gifts failing. Puja will take one half of the residuary estate under the will, but the gift to Ajay has lapsed and there will be a partial intestacy of the other half of the residuary estate. Under the intestacy rules, the second half of the residuary estate will be divided equally between Ranjit's closest relatives, Puja and Baljit. Clearly, this is not an outcome that Ranjit would have desired, and so it would have been better had Ranjit included substitutional gifts in his will.

### KEY POINT SUMMARY

- If a testator wishes to amend their will, they are best advised to make a new will. Failing that, the next best course of action is to make a codicil to supplement their existing will.
- Testators should avoid amending a will by hand, although handwritten amendments will be valid, provided they have been executed in accordance with the formalities for making a will (this is usually evidenced by the testator and two witnesses placing their initials beside the amendment).
- Alterations may amount to obliterations and so may result in the original wording being ignored when the will goes to probate. Alternatively, if the original wording is still apparent, the original wording may still be included.
- A testator may revoke a will if they intend to do so, and if they have testamentary capacity at the time of the revocation. The best way of revoking a will is to include an appropriate revocation clause in a new will. Revocation may be absolute or may be conditional (eg on the validity of a new will).
- A will may also be revoked by destruction provided there is an intention to revoke, but there are many problems associated with this method of revocation and so it is best avoided.
- A will is revoked by a subsequent marriage or civil partnership unless it is clear the will is made in contemplation of marriage to, or civil partnership with, a particular person.
- There are various ways of categorising gifts according to the type of property being given away and the funds from which the gift is derived. The most common type of gift is a specific gift of a sum of money, specified personal possessions, intangible property (eg shares in a company) or particular land and buildings. These are non-residuary gifts and are contrasted with the residuary gift, which is everything in the testator's estate which has not already been mentioned.
- Gifts may be left to named individuals or to a class of beneficiaries (eg 'my children'). If the gift is to a class of beneficiaries, there are rules to determine when the class of beneficiaries closes so that it is known which beneficiaries are included in the class.
- Gifts may be absolute (vested) or **contingent** upon the happening of a certain event, usually a beneficiary reaching a specified age.

- There are a series of implied rules which will apply if a will is silent on a particular question, for example is the gift subject to inheritance tax or free of inheritance tax?
- Gifts may fail for a number of reasons: the wording used in the will may be unclear or ambiguous (uncertainty); the property that is the subject of the gift may no longer be owned by the testator at the date of death (ademption); the beneficiary may die before the testator (lapse); the testator may divorce or a civil partnership may be dissolved; a beneficiary (or their spouse/civil partner) may witness the will; the beneficiary may reject the will (disclaimer); or the beneficiary may unlawfully kill the testator (forfeiture).
- If a non-residuary gift fails, it usually falls into the residuary estate. If the gift of part or all of the residuary estate fails, it depends if there are substitutional gifts specified in the will. If there are no substitutional gifts which apply, any part of the residuary estate not disposed of by the will is then distributed according to the rules of intestacy.

# CHAPTER 4
# Intestacy

**FUNCTIONING LEGAL KNOWLEDGE**

This chapter covers the following functioning legal knowledge required to pass the SQE 1 assessments:

**The intestacy rules:**

- s46 of the Administration of Estates Act 1925
- the **statutory trusts**

**AUTHORITIES UNDERPINNING PRACTICE**

The key authorities that underpin this area of practice are listed below. Note that for legislation you are linked to legislation.gov.uk.

Although much of the legislation on this government website is available in its amended form, the incorporation of new amendments into the text of legislation can be delayed. You should refer to legal databases to ensure you are referencing the most up-to-date legislation.

- Administration of Estates Act 1925 (particularly Part IV)
  **http://www.legislation.gov.uk/ukpga/Geo5/15-16/23/contents**
- Intestates' Estates Act 1952
  **http://www.legislation.gov.uk/ukpga/Geo6and1Eliz2/15-16/64/contents**

## 4.1 Introduction

The intestacy rules are a set of statutory rules which provide for the distribution of a person's estate in the absence of a valid **will**. According to research, less than half of adults in the UK have made a will. It is thus very important to have a good working knowledge of the intestacy rules, because they will apply to a significant proportion of estates.

If a person dies without a will, they are said to have died 'intestate', and sometimes the deceased person themselves is referred to as 'the intestate'.

Most of the rules on intestacy can be found in Part IV of the Administration of Estates Act 1925, which has been amended over time (eg significant changes were made in 2014 by the Inheritance and Trustees' Powers Act 2014).

There are particular rules which apply where the deceased is survived by a spouse or civil partner, and then other rules which apply to other specified categories of relative. We will look at the entitlement of the spouse or civil partner in **4.2**, and at the position of other relatives in **4.3–4.6**. First, though, some general points.

### 4.1.1 Total intestacy

If a person dies without leaving a will then they will die intestate, and the intestacy rules will govern how the whole estate is distributed. Similarly, if the person left a will but the will is not valid, or the will is valid but fails to deal with any part of the estate (perhaps because all of the **beneficiaries** named in it have died), then the person will die intestate and the intestacy rules will apply to the whole estate. If a person has a will but marries or forms a **civil partnership** subsequently, the marriage/civil partnership usually **revokes** the will and the person would then die intestate if they did not make a new will.

### 4.1.2 Partial intestacy

It is also possible to have a **partial intestacy**, where the person leaves a valid will but where the will does not dispose of all of the person's estate. This may be because the will contains no **residuary gift** or an incomplete residuary gift (that disposes of part of the **residue** but not all of it).

Alternatively, and more likely, there will be a **gift** of residue in the will but this residuary gift has failed entirely, or in part. This usually occurs where a residuary beneficiary has died before the **testator** and there is no effective express substitutional gift in the will (and no substitutional gift implied by law).

Where there is a partial intestacy, part of the estate is distributed in accordance with the will and the remaining estate (ie that part not covered by the will) is distributed in accordance with the intestacy rules.

**EXAMPLE**

Kiera has died leaving a valid will in which she gives £10,000 to charity and then divides the rest of her estate (her '**residuary estate**') equally between Jo and Olivia. However, Jo died before Kiera and the will does not say what is to happen in the event of one of the beneficiaries dying before Kiera. The will is valid in respect of the gift to charity of £10,000 and the gift of half of the residuary estate to Olivia. However, there will be a partial intestacy and the other half of the residuary estate, which had been left to Jo, will pass to Kiera's nearest relatives according to the intestacy rules.

### 4.1.3 What property is subject to the intestacy rules?

It is also important to remember that the intestacy rules will only apply to the estate that can be left by will. As we will see in **Chapter 5**, there are various types of property that pass independently of the will, and therefore also pass independently of the rules of intestacy. For example, the interest of a **joint tenant in equity** will pass to the surviving joint tenant(s) automatically by survivorship and will not be governed by the terms of a will *or* by the rules of intestacy.

### 4.1.4 Payment of the deceased's debts and expenses of the administration

Section 33(1) of the Administration of Estates Act 1925 (as amended) provides that the **personal representatives** hold the intestate's estate not disposed of by will on trust with a power to sell.

The personal representatives must pay the funeral, testamentary and administration expenses, debts and other liabilities of the deceased out of the intestate's ready money and from the net proceeds of any part of the estate which is sold.

The residuary estate (what is left after all the liabilities and expenses have been discharged) is then to be shared among those entitled according to the statutory rules.

## 4.2 The entitlement of a spouse or civil partner

A surviving spouse or civil partner has significant rights under the intestacy rules.

## 4.2.1 **Spouses and civil partners: general points**

### 4.2.1.1 Spouses

A spouse is a husband or wife, namely one of the parties to a valid marriage. The spouses may be of the opposite sex or of the same sex. Same-sex couples have been able to marry since 2014 due to the Marriage (Same Sex Couples) Act 2013.

### 4.2.1.2 Civil partners

A civil partner is a party to a civil partnership, which is a legal arrangement similar to a marriage. The Civil Partnership Act 2004 provides that a civil partner has the same rights to the intestate's estate as those enjoyed by a spouse.

Civil partnerships were introduced in 2005 to provide for same-sex couples, who were not at that time able to marry. Until recently, opposite-sex couples have not been able to form a civil partnership. However, following a legal challenge by an opposite-sex couple who wished to form a civil partnership, the Civil Partnerships, Marriages and Deaths (Registration) Act 2019 was enacted to allow opposite-sex couples to register a civil partnership as an alternative to marriage. The first opposite-sex civil partnerships were registered on 31 December 2019.

### 4.2.1.3 Former spouses and civil partners

A former spouse or civil partner (following a divorce in the case of a marriage or the dissolution of a civil partnership) has no entitlement under the intestacy rules. Only a current spouse or civil partner is entitled.

### 4.2.1.4 Judicial separation

Although it is comparatively rare, spouses and civil partners may wish to separate on a formal basis, but without bringing the marriage or civil partnership to an end, namely without a divorce or a dissolution. This is done by way of a **judicial separation** with a marriage and by a separation order with a civil partnership. Although the parties separate formally, the marriage or civil partnership continues. The details of judicial separation and separation orders are outside the scope of this manual, but in each case the entitlement under the intestacy rules is affected. So, a spouse will not have any entitlement on intestacy if the parties to the marriage have judicially separated, and a civil partner will not have an entitlement on intestacy if there has been a separation order in respect of the civil partnership.

### 4.2.1.5 Cohabitees and other partners

It is very important to realise that the intestacy rules only provide for spouses and civil partners. If the deceased left a partner who was not married to the deceased, and was not in a civil partnership with the deceased, that partner will have no entitlement whatsoever under the intestacy rules. This will be the case even if the partner had been cohabiting with the deceased, perhaps for a considerable number of years.

Given the large number of couples who live together without marrying (or forming a civil partnership), this is a very significant omission.

In very limited circumstances, if there are no surviving relatives the Crown may exercise a discretion to pay the estate (or part of it) to a cohabitee/unmarried partner (see **4.7**). Subject to that, a cohabitee or unmarried partner's only recourse would be to apply for **reasonable financial provision** from the estate under the Inheritance (Provision for Family and Dependants) Act 1975, as detailed in **Chapter 11**.

### 4.2.1.6 The survivorship provision applying to spouses and civil partners

To be entitled under the intestacy rules, the spouse or civil partner must survive the intestate by 28 days. If the spouse or civil partner fails to survive the intestate by 28 days then the spouse or civil partner is treated as if they had died before the intestate. Due to this 28-day rule, the ***commorientes*** rule (mentioned in **4.6.4** in connection with other relatives) does not apply to spouses or civil partners on intestacy.

#### 4.2.1.7 Has the deceased also been survived by 'issue'?

If the spouse or civil partner survives the intestate by 28 days (and assuming there has been no judicial separation or separation order), the exact entitlement of the spouse or civil partner will depend upon whether the deceased has also been survived by the deceased's '**issue**'.

The 'issue' is a category of relative that includes the deceased's children, grandchildren and other lineal (ie direct) descendants (eg great-great grandchildren, etc).

### 4.2.2 **The entitlement of a spouse or civil partner where the deceased is not survived by any issue**

This may occur either because the deceased never had any issue or because the deceased had issue but all of those issue have died before the deceased.

In either case, the distribution of the estate on intestacy is very simple: the spouse or civil partner will be entitled to the whole of the deceased's estate.

Even if there are other relatives, they will not be entitled to any part of the deceased's estate under the intestacy rules.

(Note that this is the position for persons dying on or after 1 October 2014. Different rules applied to persons dying before that date. It is now unlikely that you will encounter estates where the intestate died before 1 October 2014, though, so the rules which applied previously are outside the scope of this manual.)

### 4.2.3 **The entitlement of a spouse or civil partner where the deceased is also survived by issue**

In this situation, the intestacy rules may have the effect of dividing the estate between the spouse/civil partner and the issue. Much depends on the size of the estate, though. With small estates, the whole of the estate may still pass to the spouse/civil partner, as explained later.

Under the intestacy rules, currently the spouse/civil partner is entitled to the following:

- the deceased's personal possessions (or **chattels**) absolutely; and
- a '**fixed net sum**' (also known as a '**statutory legacy**') of (currently) £322,000, together with interest on that sum; and
- one half of the rest of the estate (the residuary estate) absolutely. (The deceased's issue are entitled to the other half of the residuary estate.)

(Again, note that this is the position for persons dying on or after 1 October 2014. Different rules applied to persons dying before that date. It is unlikely that you will encounter new estates where the intestate died before 1 October 2014, but you may encounter estates where there is an ongoing **trust** arising out of that estate, and so the relevant aspects of the old rules are covered in **4.2.5**.)

See **Figure 4.1** for a destination table where a spouse or civil partner survives by 28 days.

We will now look at the current entitlement of a spouse or civil partner in more detail.

#### 4.2.3.1 Personal possessions

The spouse/civil partner is entitled to the personal 'chattels' of the deceased. Chattels is an old fashioned word for possessions, and comes originally from the word 'cattle', from a time when livestock were among the most valuable personal possessions. Essentially, chattels are all the physical, 'movable' property of the deceased (as opposed to land and buildings, which are 'immovable' property). Chattels are also classed as a type of 'personal' property (whereas land and buildings are classed as 'real' property—hence the term 'real estate').

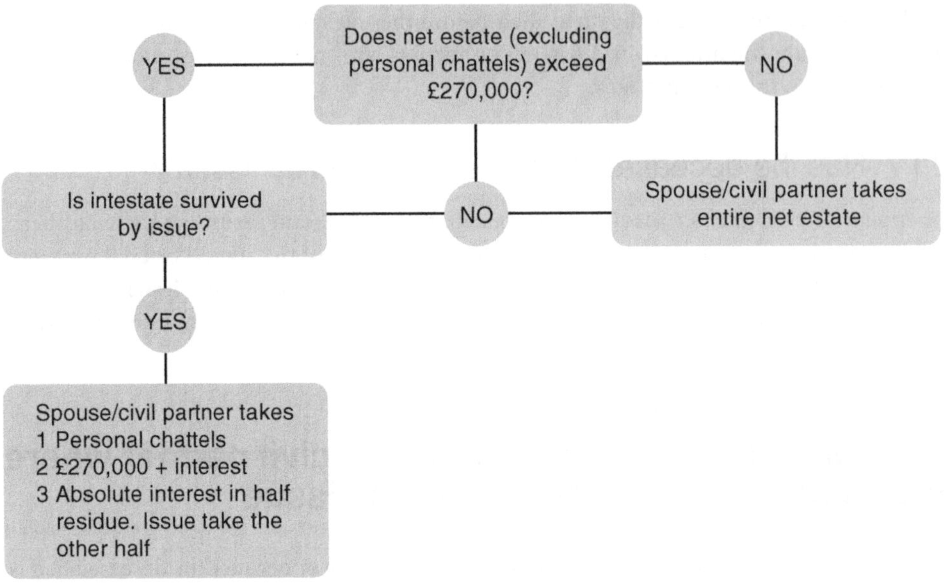


**FIGURE 4.1** Destination table where a spouse or civil partner survives by 28 days

Not all of the deceased's possessions are covered by the definition used by the intestacy rules. The spouse/civil partner is only entitled to the personal chattels as defined in s55(1)(x) of the Administration of Estates Act 1925. However, the definition is a very wide one, and so most of the deceased's possessions will therefore pass to the spouse/civil partner.

Section 55(1)(x) defines 'personal chattels' as:

> tangible movable property, other than any such property which—
>
> consists of money or securities for money, or
>
> was used at the death of the intestate solely or mainly for business purposes, or
>
> was held at the death of the intestate solely as an investment.

So, for example, if the deceased had their own business, any possessions used solely or mainly in that business would not be included in the possessions passing to the spouse/civil partner on intestacy.

**EXAMPLE**

Steven has died. His wife, Janet, has survived him by 28 days. Steven's personal chattels pass automatically to Janet. However, Steven was an electrician and the chattels used wholly or mainly for the business (eg the van he used and his tools) are not included in the chattels automatically passing to Janet under the intestacy rules.

**EXAMPLE**

Anthony has died. His wife, Helen, has survived him by 28 days. Anthony's personal chattels pass automatically to Helen. Anthony had invested in vintage wine bottles which were stored securely at the wine merchant's premises. Anthony did not keep the wine at his house or drink any of the wine. His sole intention was to sell the wine bottles at profit at some point in the future. The bottles would therefore have been held by him at his death solely as an investment and would not pass to Helen automatically.

(Note that the definition from s55(1)(x) set out earlier is from the current version of the subsection and applies to intestate estates of persons dying on or after 1 October 2014. Due to the time which has elapsed since then, you are unlikely to need to refer to the definition which applied to intestate estates before that date, although the previous definition is still relevant to testate estates where there are gifts of chattels in wills which specifically refer to s55(1)(x).)

### 4.2.3.2 The fixed net sum ('statutory legacy')

In addition to the personal possessions, the spouse/civil partner is entitled to a fixed net sum. This fixed net sum is often referred to as the 'statutory legacy'. You are more likely to hear practitioners use the term statutory legacy than to use 'fixed net sum'.

The current amount of the fixed net sum is £322,000. This applies to the estates of persons dying on or after 26 July 2023.

The fixed net sum was £270,000 for deaths from 6 February 2020 to 25 July 2023, and was £250,000 for deaths from 31 January 2009 to 6 February 2020.

You are unlikely to have to deal with the estate of a person dying before 31 January 2009, but you are likely to encounter estates of persons who died before 26 July 2023. If so, remember that the fixed net sum applicable will be either £270,000 or £250,000, rather than £322,000.

Under Sch 1A to the Administration of Estates Act 1925 (inserted by the Inheritance and Trustees Powers Act 2014), since October 2014 the Lord Chancellor has been required to review the amount of the fixed net sum at least every five years, or increase it in line with substantial increases in the Consumer Prices Index. To date, the Lord Chancellor has had to do this twice, in February 2020 and July 2023.

The fixed net sum is payable out of the residuary estate of the deceased, and is payable to the spouse/civil partner free of taxes (s46 Administration of Estates Act 1925 refers to 'death duties') and free of costs.

#### Interest on the fixed net sum

The spouse/civil partner is also entitled to interest on the fixed net sum. The interest payable is 'simple' interest, which is a straight percentage of the amount of the fixed net sum (as opposed to 'compound' interest, where interest is payable on unpaid interest as well as on the amount of the fixed net sum itself).

The interest rate is now specified by s46 of the Administration of Estates Act 1925 as the Bank of England rate that had effect at the end of the day on which the intestate died. At the time of writing (March 2024) the Bank of England base rate is 5.25 per cent, but the rate is reviewed monthly.

The interest is payable from the date of death to the date of payment.

**EXAMPLE**

Paula dies on 1 March 2024 leaving her husband, John, plus issue, when the fixed net sum was £322,000. This fixed net sum is paid to John on 28 February 2025. Exactly one year's worth of interest is payable. The Bank of England rate on 1 March 2024 is 5.25 per cent, so the amount of interest payable to John will be £322,000 x 5.25% = £16,905.

#### Estates worth less than the fixed net sum

Many estates will not be worth £322,000, especially after taking away the personal chattels from the total value of the estate. Where the estate is less than the fixed net sum of £322,000, the spouse/civil partner will not receive a full £322,000, but will of course receive the whole of the estate.

**EXAMPLE**

Javid dies, leaving his wife, Saira (who has survived him for 28 days), plus issue (his children). The estate, after taking away the personal chattels, is worth £275,000. Saira will receive the personal chattels. Saira will also receive the rest of the estate of £275,000 in part payment of the fixed net sum. Saira will not receive a full fixed net sum of £322,000, therefore. Also, the issue (the children) will get nothing because the estate does not exceed the fixed net sum.

#### 4.2.3.3 Half of the residuary estate

If the value of the estate does exceed the amount of the fixed net sum, then the spouse/civil partner will be entitled to half of the excess absolutely. The deceased's issue will be entitled to the other half of the excess. The excess is known as the residuary estate.

**EXAMPLE**

Sian and Wendy are civil partners, and Sian has issue (their children). Sian dies intestate. Her estate (after taking away the personal possessions, and accounting for her debts and costs of administration) is worth £370,000. As a civil partner, Wendy will be entitled to the fixed net sum of £322,000. Ignoring interest (for the benefit of simplicity in this example), the rest of the estate is worth £48,000. Wendy will be entitled to £24,000 of that absolutely, and Sian's issue (the children) will be entitled to the other £24,000.

### 4.2.4 **Appropriation of assets to the spouse or civil partner**

#### 4.2.4.1 Appropriation of the matrimonial home

The Intestates' Estates Act 1952 gives the spouse or civil partner the right to require the **appropriation** of the matrimonial home (or the deceased's interest in it) in satisfaction or part-satisfaction of the spouse's/civil partner's entitlement to the estate.

The details are set out in Sch 2 to the Intestates' Estates Act 1952. In effect, the Act enables the surviving spouse/civil partner to purchase the matrimonial home from the estate. The personal representative(s) would be exercising the power of appropriation from s41 of the Administration of Estates Act 1925.

However, the two spouses/civil partners will usually have been joint owners of the matrimonial home. It is rare for the matrimonial home to be in the sole name of one of them. If the couple owned the property jointly, as is likely, there are two possibilities:

- if the couple were beneficial **tenants in common**, then the deceased's interest in the matrimonial home will be part of the deceased's interest on intestacy, and the spouse/civil partner will be able to require the appropriation of the deceased's interest in the home in satisfaction/part-satisfaction of the spouse/civil partner's interest in the estate;
- it is much more likely, though, that the couple were beneficial joint tenants (ie joint tenants in equity). If so, it will not be possible for the deceased's interest in the matrimonial home to be appropriated, and in fact there will be no need to do so. This is because the deceased's interest as a joint tenant in equity does not form part of the deceased's estate for intestacy purposes. This would not be a problem for the spouse/civil partner, because the spouse/civil partner will be the other joint tenant in equity and the deceased's interest will pass automatically by survivorship to the spouse/civil partner anyway. So, if the couple were joint tenants in equity, there is no need to appropriate the deceased's interest in the home, because the spouse/civil partner will inherit the deceased's interest by other means.

If an appropriation is possible and is contemplated, there are several points to bear in mind:

- the spouse/civil partner has the right to require the personal representatives to appropriate the matrimonial home in partial or total satisfaction of the spouse/civil partner's fixed net sum *and/or* their absolute interest in the residuary estate;
- if the value of the deceased's interest in the estate is less than the value of the matrimonial home, the spouse/civil partner may make up the deficiency out of their own resources (ie pay the difference to the estate);
- the 'matrimonial home' is defined as that in which the surviving spouse/civil partner was resident at the date of death of the intestate (it does not matter whether the deceased was also resident);

- the relevant value for the matrimonial home is its value at the date of appropriation, not its value at the date of death (*Re Collins* [1975] 1 WLR 309);
- the spouse/civil partner must exercise the right within 12 months of the **grant of representation** (although the court has a discretion to extend the time limit), by giving written notice to the personal representatives. If the spouse/civil partner is one of the personal representatives, then written notice must be given to the other personal representative(s). In many estates, the spouse/civil partner will be the only personal representative, in which case there is no need for the spouse/civil partner to give written notice;
- the consent of the court is required before the election can be made in certain situations, for example where the matrimonial home was only part of a building owned by the deceased or was part of a farm or other business premises;
- usually, the spouse/civil partner will be the sole personal representative or one of the personal representatives, and so there is no danger of the matrimonial home being sold by the personal representatives without the spouse's/civil partner's consent. Where the spouse/civil partner is not a personal representative, the Schedule provides that the personal representatives cannot sell the matrimonial home without the consent of the spouse/civil partner during this 12-month period. This prohibition is subject to exceptions, such as obtaining the consent of the court to a sale.

### 4.2.4.2 Appropriation of other assets

The general power of appropriation under s41 of the Administration of Estates Act 1925 is also available to the personal representative, so that other assets in the estate may be appropriated to the spouse/civil partner in satisfaction or part-satisfaction of their entitlement in the estate. (See **9.7.2.1** for more detail on the general power of appropriation.) Remember that the spouse/civil partner will inherit the deceased's personal chattels anyway (**4.2.3.1**), so there is no need for an appropriation of those chattels.

### 4.2.4.3 Appropriation to the spouse or civil partner and the 'self-dealing' rule

Care should be taken where the spouse/civil partner is also a personal representative, because if certain assets are appropriated to the spouse/civil partner, the **self-dealing** rule will apply.

The self-dealing rule is covered in more detail in **Chapter 13**, but essentially provides that a **trustee** cannot be both seller and buyer in a transaction. The rule also applies to personal representatives and estates when personal representatives appropriate assets to themselves.

If there has been a transaction involving self-dealing then the transaction is voidable, and can be set aside (or voided) by the beneficiaries (or other beneficiaries) of the trust or estate.

In *Kane v Radley-Kane* [1999] Ch 274, the deceased died intestate in 1994, leaving a spouse (his widow) and issue (his children from an earlier marriage). The estate was valued at £93,000, which was less than the value of the widow's fixed net sum/statutory legacy (which in 1994 was £125,000). The estate included shares which were valued at the date of death at £50,000. The widow, who was also the personal representative, appropriated the shares to herself in part-satisfaction of her statutory legacy. However, she subsequently sold the shares for over £1 million. One of the sons (who would have been entitled to part of the estate as one of the issue if the shares had been valued at £1 million instead of £50,000) sought to set the appropriation of shares aside, on the basis that the appropriation amounted to self-dealing. The son was successful in that the court held that the transfer of shares to the widow was self-dealing and should be set aside, with the effect that the £1 million sale proceeds of the shares were to be treated as part of the assets in the estate.

Schedule 2, para 5(1) of the Intestates' Estates Act 1952 provides that the self-dealing rule does not apply to the appropriation of the matrimonial home in a situation where the spouse/civil partner is one of two or more personal representatives. In such a case, the appropriation of the matrimonial home (or the deceased's interest in it) is not voidable at the instance of another beneficiary. Unfortunately, it would seem that this protection is not available if the spouse or civil partner is the sole personal representative. The protection from Sch 2 is also not available for appropriation of other assets.

If the protection from the Schedule is not available, the spouse or civil partner should seek the consent of the other potential beneficiaries (ie the issue). If this is not possible (perhaps because one or more of the issue are under 18 and so cannot give consent), an application can be made to obtain the consent of the court.

Lastly, there is apparently not a problem of self-dealing with appropriations of certain types of asset, such as government bonds or shares quoted on the Stock Exchange, because they are regarded as equivalent to cash. The value of those assets will be known due to those assets having an open market price. The problem in *Kane v Radley-Kane* arose because the shares were in a private company and the true value of those shares was not appreciated at the time of the appropriation.

## 4.2.5 The entitlement of the spouse or civil partner where the deceased died before 1 October 2014: life interest trusts

Although you are not likely to have to deal with the administration of the estate of a person who has died intestate before 1 October 2014, you may encounter an ongoing trust arising out of such an estate. This is because of one particular aspect of the entitlement of a spouse or civil partner under the old rules—a **life interest**.

For deaths before 1 October 2014, where the deceased was survived by the spouse/civil partner and issue, the spouse/civil partner was entitled to the following:

1 the deceased's personal possessions (or chattels) absolutely (but according to a previous version of s55(1)(x) Administration of Estates Act 1925, with a different definition to the current version);

2 a fixed net sum of £250,000 (for deaths on or after 1 February 2009—different lower amounts applied previously), plus interest; and

3 a life interest in one half of the rest of the estate (the residuary estate).

Under these old rules, the deceased's issue were entitled to:

- the other half of the residuary estate; *and*
- a **remainder interest** in the half of the residuary estate in which the spouse/civil partner had a life interest.

The life interest would have given the spouse or civil partner the right to the income for life on half of the residuary estate. This would have required the personal representatives to invest this half of the residuary estate, and the income generated by those investments would have been paid to the spouse/civil partner.

However, the capital sum invested would remain untouched as the spouse/civil partner would not be entitled to the underlying capital sum but only to the income on that capital sum. The spouse's/civil partner's interest would come to an end on their subsequent death, which is why it is called a 'life interest'. The capital sum of this half of the estate would then pass to the issue, as 'remainder' beneficiaries.

There may be intestate estates where the personal possessions and statutory legacy have been paid to the spouse/civil partner some years ago, and where one half of the residuary estate has passed outright to the issue some years ago, but where the other half of the residuary estate is still being held on trust for the spouse/civil partner for life. Any such trust will continue until the spouse/civil partner dies. As a result, you may still encounter life interest trusts in intestate estates which are subject to these old rules.

### 4.2.5.1 The right of the spouse/civil partner to redeem the life interest

In practice, many of these ongoing life interest trusts will have been avoided by the spouse or civil partner electing to have their life interest redeemed or 'capitalised'. This means that a capital value is placed on the spouse's/civil partner's right to receive income for life, and the spouse/civil partner then takes the capitalised value of the life interest outright. The capitalised value of the life interest is paid to the spouse or civil partner out of that half of the residuary estate, and whatever is left from that half of the residuary estate is paid to the issue. This is difficult to understand without an example, so here is one to help you.

**EXAMPLE**

Brian died in 2008, leaving his wife, Fiona, plus issue (his children). The estate, after taking away the personal chattels, was worth £225,000. Fiona received the personal chattels. Fiona also received the fixed net sum, which at that time was £125,000. Ignoring interest (for the benefit of simplicity in this example), the rest of the estate was worth £100,000. Fiona was entitled to a life interest in half of the residuary (ie £50,000). Brian's issue (the children) were entitled to the remainder interest in that £50,000 when Fiona dies, and were entitled immediately (subject to the statutory trusts) to the other £50,000. However, rather than receiving the income on the £50,000 for life, Fiona decides to redeem her life interest. The capitalised value of her life interest is calculated as being £20,000. Fiona takes this £20,000 from the estate absolutely, and the remaining £30,000 from that half of the residuary estate is added to the other half of the residuary estate (£50,000) passing to the issue. As a result of Fiona's decision to capitalise her life interest, the issue will not have a remainder interest in £50,000 on Fiona's subsequent death, but will get an immediate payment of the £30,000. In total, therefore, the issue will have received £80,000—the £50,000 half of the residuary estate they were entitled to initially under the intestacy rules, and the £30,000 left over from the other half of the residuary estate after Fiona redeemed her life interest.

The spouse or civil partner had to make an election to redeem the life interest within 12 months of the date of the grant of representation, so there will not be any estates now where the spouse or civil partner can still exercise this right.

#### 4.2.5.2 Breaking the life interest trust

Under general trust law, if all of the beneficiaries (the spouse/civil partner and the issue) are adults and of sound mind, then they can always agree between themselves to 'break' the trust, and bring the life interest to an end during the lifetime of the spouse/civil partner. This can be done at any time, even if it is several years after the deceased passed away and even if the income of that half of the residuary estate has been paid to the spouse/civil partner in the intervening years. The beneficiaries would agree on how much of the underlying capital of that half of the residuary estate would be paid to the spouse/civil partner, and how much would be paid to the issue, and the life interest would be brought to an end.

## 4.3 The issue of the deceased

### 4.3.1 The meaning of 'issue'

The 'issue' is a category of relative that includes the deceased's children, grandchildren and other lineal (ie direct) descendants (eg great-great grandchildren).

As well as biological children and descendants, this includes adopted children and descendants (see **4.6.1**). It also includes children and descendants whose parents were not married or in a civil partnership at the time of birth (see **4.6.2**). In addition, see **4.6.3** for the effect of the Human Fertilisation and Embryology Act 2008.

However, stepchildren have no entitlement to the estate of their step-parent under the intestacy rules. As is the case with unmarried cohabitees, if there are no surviving relatives and the estate is **bona vacantia**, the Crown may exercise a discretion to pay the estate (or part of it) to a stepchild (see **4.7**). Subject to that, a stepchild's only recourse would be to apply for reasonable financial provision from the estate, under the Inheritance (Provision for Family and Dependants) Act 1975, as detailed in **Chapter 11**.

### 4.3.2 The entitlement of issue where there is a spouse or civil partner

As has already been seen, where the deceased was survived by a spouse/civil partner and issue, the issue will take one half of the residuary estate. We have seen, though, that many estates will not exceed the amount of the spouse's/civil partner's fixed net sum of £322,000, and if that is case then there will be no residuary estate and the issue will get nothing. Where there is a spouse/civil partner, therefore, the issue will only be entitled to part of the estate if the estate exceeds the fixed net sum.

See the Javid example in **4.2.3.2** for an illustration of a situation when the spouse/civil partner inherits everything and the issue receive nothing, and the Sian example in **4.2.3.3** for an illustration of a situation where the issue are entitled to half of the residuary estate.

As also mentioned earlier (in **4.2.5**), in older estates (of persons dying intestate before 1 October 2014), the issue might have a remainder interest in the other half of the residuary estate. Thus, when the life interest of the spouse or civil partner comes to an end, that other half of the residuary estate will be payable to the issue.

**EXAMPLE**

Diana died in 2011, leaving her husband, William, plus issue (her children). The estate, after taking away the personal chattels, was worth £450,000. William received the personal chattels. William also received the fixed net sum (which was then £250,000). Ignoring interest (for the benefit of simplicity in this example), the rest of the estate was worth £200,000. William was entitled to a life interest in half of the residuary (ie £100,000). Diana's issue (the children) were entitled immediately (subject to the statutory trusts) to the other £100,000. William receives the income on the first £100,000 until his subsequent death, in 2024. When William dies the remaining capital from this half of the residuary estate (due to how the capital has been invested, this may be more or less than £100,000) now passes to Diana's issue, because they have the remainder interest in this half of the residuary estate. In other words, the issue will have received part of their entitlement from Diana's estate in 2011 when Diana died, and then the rest in 2024 when William dies.

### 4.3.3 The entitlement of issue where there is no spouse or civil partner

Where there is no spouse/civil partner, the issue is the highest category of relatives under the intestacy rules, and so the issue will be entitled to the whole of the estate on intestacy.

As with the other categories of relatives mentioned later, the entitlement of the issue is subject to 'the statutory trusts' (see **4.5**).

## 4.4 The entitlement of other relatives

### 4.4.1 The order of entitlement

If there is no surviving spouse/civil partner or issue, the order of entitlement to share in the estate is as follows:

1 parents (equally if both alive); but if none then
2 brothers and sisters of the **whole blood** (ie who share the same parents as the deceased) on 'the statutory trusts'; but if none then
3 brothers and sisters of the **half blood** (ie who share only one parent with the deceased) on 'the statutory trusts'; but if none then
4 grandparents (equally if more than one); but if none then

5 uncles and aunts of the whole blood (ie brothers and sisters of the whole blood of one of the intestate's parents) on 'the statutory trusts'; but if none then
6 uncles and aunts of the half blood (ie brothers and sisters of the half blood of one of the intestate's parents) on 'the statutory trusts'.

Apart from parents or grandparents, members of each class take on 'the statutory trusts' (see **4.5**).

Note that only 'blood' relatives of the intestate are entitled, not those related only by marriage (or by civil partnership). So, for example, the son-in-law or daughter-in-law of the intestate will not be entitled under the intestacy rules. Similarly, there is no entitlement for a father-in-law, mother-in-law, brother-in-law, sister-in-law or uncle or aunt by marriage.

As mentioned earlier, the list of specified relatives does not include cohabitees, unmarried partners, stepchildren and other persons who may have been financially dependent on the deceased. Such persons may be able to apply for reasonable financial provision from the estate under the Inheritance (Provision for Family and Dependants) Act 1975 (see **Chapter 11**).

Persons may be entitled by reason of adoption, even though they are not related by blood (see **4.6.1**). Also, see **4.6.2** when the parents are not married or in a civil partnership at the time of birth and **4.6.3** on the Human Fertilisation and Embryology Act 2008.

## 4.4.2 **Relatives in a higher category take to the exclusion of relatives in a lower category**

If there are relatives in a higher category of relative, they will take the entire exclusion of relatives in lower categories. So, if the deceased left issue, the issue will be entitled to the whole estate and the other relatives mentioned earlier will receive nothing. If there are no issue but the parents (or a parent) survive, then the parents (or parent) will take the whole estate, to the exclusion of the other categories of relative, and so on.

The effect of this is seen most starkly when comparing the entitlement of relatives of the 'whole blood' compared to relatives of the 'half blood'. These now outdated terms (bear in mind the rules date from 1925) signify the following:

- 'whole blood'—a relative who shares the same two parents as the deceased (in the case of a brother or sister) or who shares the same parent as the deceased's parent (in the case of an uncle or aunt); and
- 'half blood'—a relative who shares only one parent with the deceased (in the case of a brother or sister) or who shares only one parent with the deceased's parent (in the case of an uncle or aunt).

**EXAMPLE**

Carlton dies intestate, leaving a sister, Janine, and a brother, Kenwyn. Both are adults. However, Janine and Carlton shared the same mother and father and so are of the whole blood, whereas Kenwyn had a different father and so is of the half blood. Janine is therefore in a higher category of relative (brothers and sisters of the whole blood) and will take to the exclusion of Kenwyn who is in a lower category of relative (brothers and sisters of the half blood). The whole estate will pass to Janine, and Kenwyn will get nothing.

This is the case even if relatives in the higher category are taking by substitution under 'the statutory trusts' (see **4.5**), as seen in the following example.

**EXAMPLE**

Louisa dies intestate, leaving a nephew, Timothy, and a brother, Peter. Both are adults. Louisa and Timothy's mother (Louisa's sister, Jane, who has predeceased) shared the same mother and father and so were of the whole blood. This also means that Timothy, Louisa's nephew, is of the whole blood. In contrast, Peter had a different father to Louisa and so is of the half blood.

The nephew, Timothy, is therefore in a higher category of relative (brothers and sisters of the whole blood, *and their issue*) and will take to the exclusion of the brother, Peter, who is in a lower category of relative (brothers and sisters of the half blood, and their issue). The whole estate will pass to the nephew, Timothy, and the brother, Peter, will get nothing.

See **Figure 4.2** for a destination table where there is no spouse or civil partner or where a spouse or civil partner fails to survive by 28 days,

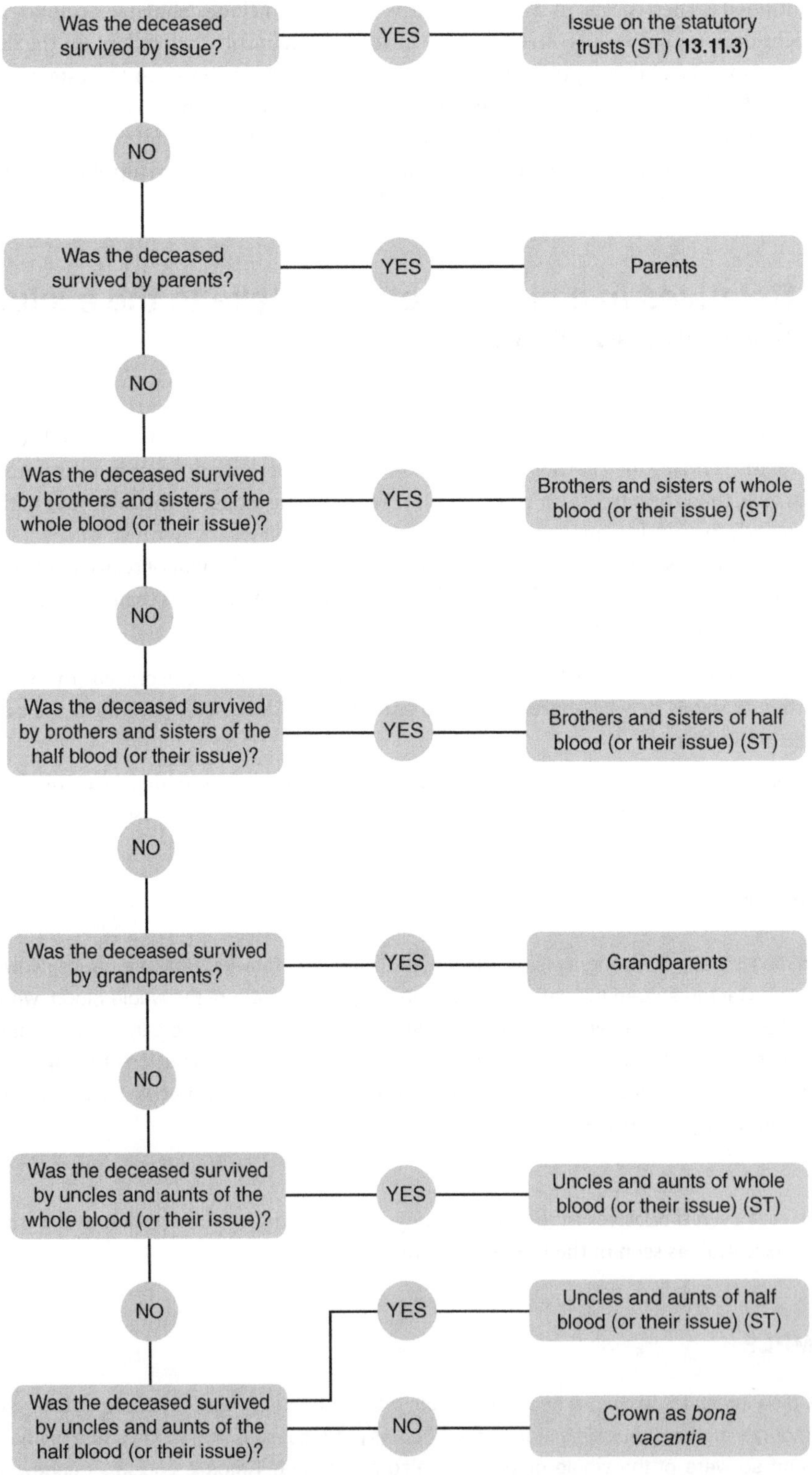


**FIGURE 4.2** Destination table where there is no spouse or civil partner, or where the spouse or civil partner does not survive by 28 days

## 4.5 The statutory trusts

In the case of most classes of relatives—issue (children, grandchildren, etc), brothers and sisters, uncles and aunts—their entitlement is held 'on the statutory trusts'. Section 47 of the Administration of Estates Act 1925 defines this expression as meaning:

- equally for all members of the class of relatives concerned living, or ***en ventre sa mère*** (ie conceived but not yet born—see **4.6.5**), at the date of the intestate's death, who attain the age of 18 or marry or enter into a civil partnership under that age. (The minimum age to marry/form a civil partnership is now 18, but prior to 27 February 2023 it was possible to marry/form a civil partnership at 16, with parental or judicial consent.);
- the issue of any class members who predecease (ie die before the intestate dies) take ***per stirpes*** their parent's share, provided they (ie the issue) attain 18 (or marry or enter into a civil partnership earlier). (*Per stirpes* is explained in **4.5.1**.)

### 4.5.1 *Per stirpes* distributions under the statutory trusts

*Per stirpes* is Latin, and means 'according to the branches'. A *per stirpes* distribution is thus a distribution according to the branches of a family. It can be contrasted with a ***per capita*** distribution, which is an equal distribution to every member of a class. Although we have considered this in the context of residuary gifts in wills in **Chapter 3**, it is helpful to consider it again here in the context of an intestacy.

**EXAMPLE**

Jonathan dies intestate. He did not leave a spouse or civil partner and his two children, Mandy and Giles, died before him. His nearest relatives are his three grandchildren—Georgia, Michael and Liam. Georgia is the daughter of Mandy, and Michael and Liam are the sons of Giles.

The statutory trusts provide for a *per stirpes* distribution of the estate. Each branch of the family will receive an equal amount. This means that Georgia will inherit 50 per cent of the estate (the 50 per cent share which her mother, Mandy, would have inherited had she survived Jonathan), and Michael and Liam will each inherit 25 per cent of the estate (they share between them the 50 per cent share that their father Giles would have inherited). (A *per capita* distribution in contrast would have given one-third shares to each of Georgia, Michael and Liam.)

This *per stirpes* distribution is shown below.

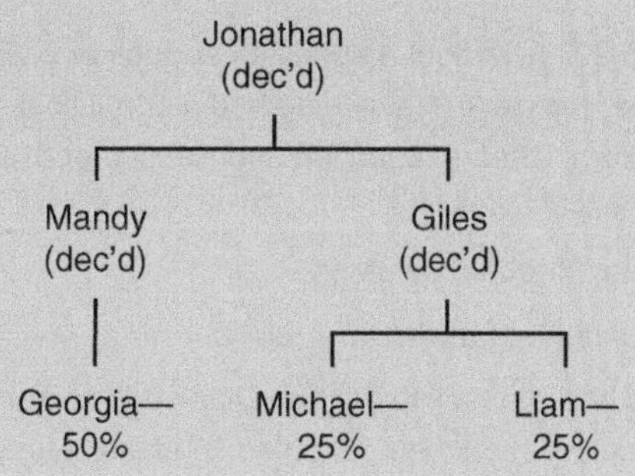


One aspect of the statutory trusts, and of *per stirpes* distributions in general, is that the children of the member of the class of beneficiaries will not inherit anything if their parent is still alive and can inherit themselves.

**EXAMPLE**

Using the Jonathan example again, if we change the facts so that Jonathan's daughter Mandy survives him, then she will take 50 per cent of the estate instead of her daughter, Georgia. Georgia would inherit nothing, because her parent, Mandy, had survived.

Each branch of the family still receives an equal amount, but with Mandy inheriting 50 per cent instead of Georgia. Michael and Liam will each still inherit 25 per cent of the estate (they share between them the 50 per cent share that their father Giles would have inherited). This is shown below.

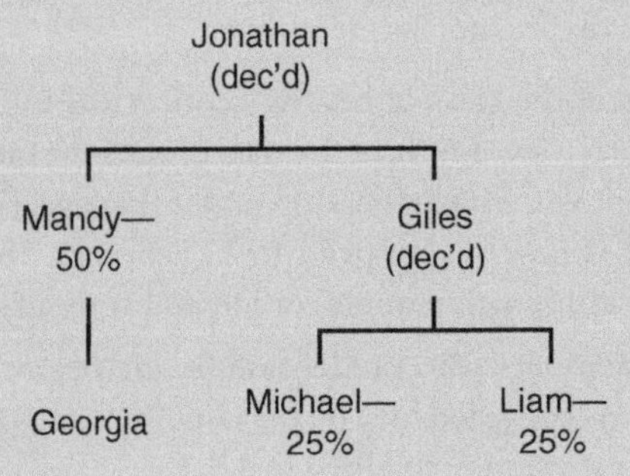


However, the rule that children will not inherit if their parent is still alive is modified in circumstances where the parent has disclaimed their entitlement (ie decided to refuse the entitlement) or where the parent has **forfeited** their entitlement (due to unlawfully killing the intestate). The Estates of Deceased Persons (Forfeiture Rule and Law of Succession) Act 2011 made changes, with effect from 1 February 2012. If a beneficiary of an estate disclaims their entitlement, or forfeits their entitlement due to unlawfully killing the intestate, then the beneficiary is treated as if they had predeceased the intestate. This enables the issue of the beneficiary to inherit under the statutory trusts.

## 4.5.2 The death of a potential beneficiary before the death of the intestate

The statutory trusts discussed in the previous section will apply where a potential beneficiary dies before the intestate. So, if the potential beneficiary leaves issue of their own, there will be a substitution to their issue.

Here is another example, which is used also in the sections which follow.

**EXAMPLE**

Naina dies intestate in March 2024, without a surviving spouse or civil partner, leaving two adult daughters, Meera and Laksha. However, Naina also had a son, Dipak, but he died before Naina. Dipak left two children of his own, Chetan (aged 14) and Ranjit (aged 10).

Naina's estate will be divided as follows:

- one-third to her daughter Meera absolutely;
- one-third to her other daughter Laksha absolutely;
- one-third (which would have passed to her son Dipak had he survived) to Dipak's two sons, Chetan and Ranjit, conditional on them reaching 18 years of age. If both Chetan and Ranjit reach 18, then they will each inherit one-sixth of Naina's estate. (NB: neither Chetan nor Ranjit can marry or form a civil partnership before they reach 18, as the minimum age for marriage/civil partnership was increased from 16 to 18 on 27 February 2023.)

## 4.5.3 The death of a beneficiary with a contingent interest after the death of the intestate

What happens, though, if a beneficiary survives the deceased but dies after the deceased and before becoming fully entitled? This could happen where the beneficiary is under the age of 18 (and is unmarried and not in a civil partnership) at the date of the deceased's death. That beneficiary's interest will be **contingent** on reaching 18 (or earlier marriage/civil partnership before 27 February 2023).

**EXAMPLE**

To return to Naina's estate from the previous example, she has been survived by her grandchildren, Chetan and Ranjit. Both of them are under 18 and they have one-sixth shares which are contingent on reaching 18. What would happen to Chetan's one-sixth share if he were to die before reaching 18?

The law is more complicated than where the potential beneficiary died before the deceased. There are several possibilities, which we will consider in **4.5.3.1** and **4.5.3.2**.

### 4.5.3.1 Where the potential beneficiary has no issue of their own

Where the potential beneficiary has no issue of their own, and the potential beneficiary dies before reaching 18 (or earlier marriage/civil partnership before 27 February 2023), the estate will be dealt with as if the potential beneficiary never existed, and the estate will be distributed accordingly among the remaining members of the class.

**EXAMPLE**

If Chetan dies before reaching 18, and if Chetan does not have issue of his own, then for the purposes of distributing Naina's estate he will be treated as if he never existed, and his one-sixth share will pass to Ranjit. This means Ranjit would receive one-third of the estate.

### 4.5.3.2 Where the potential beneficiary leaves issue of their own

The potential beneficiary may die before reaching 18 (or earlier marriage/civil partnership before 27 February 2023), but might leave issue of their own. For obvious reasons, this will not happen that frequently. However, the question then arises—will the issue of the potential beneficiary take the potential beneficiary's interest in the estate by substitution under the statutory trusts?

Where the intestate died before 1 February 2012, the position is the same as if the potential beneficiary had no issue, namely the estate will be dealt with as if the potential beneficiary never existed, and the estate will be distributed accordingly among the remaining members of the class. The issue of the potential beneficiary will receive nothing.

Where the intestate died on or after 1 February 2012, the position depends on whether the issue of the potential beneficiary were living (or *en ventre sa mère*, ie had been conceived) at the date of death of the intestate. (Note that it is the date of death of the *intestate* that is relevant, not the date of death of the potential beneficiary.)

The two situations are considered in more detail in the following two sections.

#### Issue (of a potential beneficiary) living at the death of the intestate

If the issue of the potential beneficiary were born (or *en ventre sa mère*) at the date of death of the intestate, then there will be a substitution to the issue of the beneficiary if the beneficiary dies before reaching 18 (or earlier marriage/civil partnership before 27 February 2023). This is as a result of changes made to the Administration of Estates Act 1925 by the Estates of Deceased Persons (Forfeiture Rule and Law of Succession) Act 2011. The potential beneficiary will be treated as if they had predeceased the intestate.

However, the issue (of the potential beneficiary) have to be living (or *en ventre sa mère*) at the date of death of the intestate for this substitution to occur.

**EXAMPLE**

Harry died intestate in 2022, survived by one brother, Philip. Harry had another brother, Anthony, who died before Harry. Anthony had a daughter, Jenny. Jenny is aged 16 at the date of Harry's death, she is not married (or in a civil partnership) and she has a young child, Jac, who is aged 1 at the time of Harry's death.

Anthony has an absolute interest in one half of Harry's estate, and Jenny has a contingent interest in one half of Harry's estate.

Jenny dies before reaching 18, and does not marry or form a civil partnership before 27 February 2023.

Under s47 of the Administration of Estates Act 1925 (as amended), Jenny is treated as having predeceased Harry (even though she did, in fact, survive him). As Jac was living at the date of Harry's death, Jenny's one half share will thus pass to Jac on the statutory trusts. (Note that Jac's interest will be conditional on reaching 18.)

We are obviously looking at a comparatively rare situation here, because the potential beneficiary must be both under 18 and must have a child or children of their own at the date of death of the intestate. The potential beneficiary must therefore be of an age themselves to have their own children, so this would exclude any potential beneficiaries who are very young and who have not reached puberty.

### Issue (of a potential beneficiary) not living at the death of the intestate

If the issue of the potential beneficiary were born (or conceived) after the death of the intestate, then there will be no substitution to the issue of the beneficiary if the beneficiary dies before reaching 18 (or earlier marriage/civil partnership before 27 February 2023).

This is the same as if the potential beneficiary had no issue, namely the estate will be dealt with as if the potential beneficiary never existed, and the estate will be distributed accordingly among the remaining members of the class. The issue of the potential beneficiary will receive nothing.

**EXAMPLE**

To return again to Naina's estate in the earlier example. You will recall that her two grandsons, Chetan and Ranjit, each had one-sixth contingent interests in her estate. Chetan was 14 at the time of Naina's death. When he is 17, Chetan has a son, Adil. Chetan dies before reaching 18.

For the purposes of distributing Naina's estate, Chetan will be treated as if he never existed, and his one-sixth share will pass to Ranjit. This means Ranjit would receive one-third of the estate. There will be no substitution to Chetan's son Adil, who will receive nothing.

## 4.6 Other rules applying to relatives generally

### 4.6.1 Adoption

For the purposes of entitlement under the intestacy rules, an adopted child is treated as a child of its adoptive parent(s) and not as the child of its natural parents.

For example, this means that the issue of the deceased will include any adopted children, grandchildren or other direct descendants who are adopted.

**EXAMPLE**

Oscar dies intestate, without a spouse or civil partner, but with issue. He had two children—Morgan and Penny. Morgan has survived Oscar, but Penny died before Oscar. Penny had two children—Thomas (who is her natural child) and Lily (who is adopted). Both Thomas and Lily are under the age of 16.

Morgan will take half of the estate absolutely and the other half of the estate (the share which Penny would have taken had she survived Oscar) will be held on the statutory trusts for Thomas and Lily, who will each have a one-quarter share contingent on them reaching 18 or marrying/forming a civil partnership under that age. It does not matter that Lily is adopted—she has the same rights as Thomas.

This does not just apply to the issue of the deceased. It could also apply to determine who is within one of the other classes of relative. For example, brothers and sisters 'of the whole blood' would include brothers and sisters who had been adopted by the parents of the intestate.

**EXAMPLE**

Sophie dies intestate, without a spouse or civil partner or issue. Her nearest relatives are her two adult sisters, Phoebe and Hermione. Phoebe is Sophie's natural (blood) sister, but Hermione was adopted by Sophie's parents. Nevertheless, Sophie's estate will be split equally between Phoebe and Hermione.

Generally, a person who is adopted loses any entitlement on the intestacy of their natural parents or of any member of their birth family. There are some saving provisions, though, to protect the interests of persons who had existing entitlements in estates at the time of the adoption.

Section 69 of the Adoption and Children Act 2002 preserves a number of interests, including 'any interest vested in possession' that the person has prior to the adoption. However, this does not include a contingent interest that a child would have under intestacy, where the child's interest would be contingent on reaching 18 (or earlier marriage/civil partnership before 27 February 2023).

To address this, s69 of the Adoption and Children Act 2002 was amended by the Inheritance and Trustees' Powers Act 2014, in respect of adoptions on or after 1 October 2014. Section 69 now also preserves 'any contingent interest (other than a contingent interest in remainder) which the adopted person has immediately before the adoption in the estate of a deceased parent'. This is so whether the parent was testate or intestate. For present purposes, the important thing is that it preserves the contingent interest of an adopted child under an intestacy, but only of the child's parent. It does not preserve any contingent interest the child might have under the intestacy of any other member of the birth family.

### 4.6.2 **Persons whose parents were not married or in a civil partnership at the date of birth**

Section 18 of the Family Law Reform Act 1987 provides that the distribution of assets on intestacy is to be determined without regard to whether the parents of a particular person were (or were not) married or in a civil partnership at the time of the person's birth. As with adoption, this applies not only to the intestate's issue but to all other relatives who may be entitled under the intestacy rules.

However, there is a presumption (in s18(2)) that a child (whose parents were not married or in a civil partnership at the date of birth) is not survived by the father, or any person related to that child only through its father, unless the contrary is shown. This presumption of death does not apply if a person is recorded as the child's father in an official register or record of births.

## 4.6.3 The Human Fertilisation and Embryology Act 2008

Section 42 of the Act (as amended) provides that where two women are married or in a civil partnership, and one of the women receives fertility treatment and bears a child, the other woman (the other party to the marriage or civil partnership) is also to be treated as a parent of the child (unless she did not consent to the other woman having the fertility treatment).

Also, s43 of the Act provides that two women who are not married or in a civil partnership may agree that the women who is not bearing the child is also to be a parent of the child, provided certain conditions are met.

Section 48 of the Act provides that the second female parent (recognised under ss42 and 43) is to be treated as the child's parent for all purposes. This would include the intestacy rules, and affects the application of the rules beyond a mere parent–child relationship. For example, if the second female parent had children of her own (from another relationship, not involving the natural mother of the child), then the children of the other relationship would be treated as brothers and sisters of the half blood of the child.

The presumption in s18(2) of the Family Law Reform Act 1987 (see **4.6.2**) that applies to fathers of children whose parents were not married/in a civil partnership also applies to a second female parent who is treated as a parent under s43 of the 2008 Act (it does not apply to a female spouse or civil partner who is treated as a parent under s42). There is thus a presumption that the child is not survived by the second female parent, or any person related to that child only through its second female parent, unless the contrary is shown. As with an unmarried father, this presumption of death does not apply if the second female parent is recorded as the child's parent in an official register or record of births.

## 4.6.4 *Commorientes*: when the order of death is not clear

The *commorientes* rule (where the order of death is uncertain) applies to testate estates and to cases where there is a total or partial intestacy.

Section 184 of the Law of Property Act 1925 states that where two persons have died in circumstances where it is uncertain which of them survived the other, the younger shall be deemed to have survived the elder for all purposes affecting title to property. So far as intestate succession between spouses/civil partners is concerned, the spouse/civil partner must survive the deceased by 28 days, so the *commorientes* rule is not relevant.

In the case of intestate succession between other relatives, though, the *commorientes* rule will apply in the usual way, as there is no requirement that other relatives survive the deceased by 28 days in order to become entitled.

## 4.6.5 *En ventre sa mère*: children conceived but not yet born

*En ventre sa mère* is a French phrase that can roughly be translated as 'in the mother's womb'. It is used to describe a child who has been conceived but not yet born. Section 55(2) of the Administration of Estates Act 1925 provides that references to a child or issue living at the death of any person include a child or issue *en ventre sa mère* at the death. Persons who have been conceived but not yet born will therefore fall within a class of specified relatives under the intestacy rules.

**EXAMPLE**

Francesco died intestate, leaving a spouse, Claudia, and issue. Francesco and Claudia already had two children, Marco and Dina, but Claudia was pregnant at the time Francesco died, and another child, Lucca, is born after Francesco's death. However, Lucca will be one of the issue entitled on Francesco's intestacy, because Lucca had been conceived before Francesco's death (put another way, Lucca was *en ventre sa mère* at the time of Francesco's death).

## 4.7 *Bona vacantia*: where there are no surviving relatives

This Latin phrase (pronounced 'boh-nah vah-kan-tee-ah' or 'boh-nah vah-kan-shee-ah') is used to describe the situation where the intestate is not survived by any of the relatives listed previously. Given the comprehensive list of specified relatives, this situation is comparatively rare.

*Bona vacantia* (which roughly means 'vacant goods' but is best translated as 'ownerless goods') describes a situation where there is no owner of property. The intestacy rules provide for a default mechanism to prevent the deceased's property being ownerless: the default mechanism is for the property to pass to the Crown.

If the intestate is not survived by a spouse/civil partner or issue, or any of the other relatives qualifying to share in the estate in any of the categories described at **4.4**, then the Crown (ie the King) takes the residuary estate as *bona vacantia*. However, if the intestate died resident within the Duchy of Lancaster or in Cornwall, the Duchy of Lancaster (the King is the current Duke of Lancaster) or Duke of Cornwall (the title is usually held by the Prince of Wales,) respectively take as *bona vacantia* instead of the Crown. (For ease of reference, the term 'the Crown' is used here but should be taken to include the Duchy of Lancaster or the Duke of Cornwall, where relevant.)

This does not necessarily mean that the Crown will keep the deceased's property. Section 46 of the Administration of Estates Act 1925 gives the Crown a discretion to make provision for the intestate's dependants (who need not be related to the deceased) and for 'any other person for whom the intestate might reasonably have been expected to make provision'. So, this discretion might be exercised in favour of a cohabitee of the deceased or a stepchild of the deceased, neither of whom would be entitled under the intestacy rules.

There is more information on how to claim against an estate which is *bona vacantia* on the Government Legal Department webpages.

### KEY POINT SUMMARY

- The intestacy rules determine the distribution of any part of a person's estate that is not determined by the terms of a valid will.
- A person may be wholly intestate (where there is no valid will, or the will fails to deal with any part of the estate) or partially intestate (where there is a valid will which deals with part, but not all, of the estate).
- Certain property passes independently of the terms of a will or the rules of intestacy (eg **joint property** passing by survivorship).
- Spouses and civil partners have significant rights under the intestacy rules, but the extent of their entitlement depends on whether the deceased was also survived by the deceased's issue (children and other direct descendants).
- Where there is no issue, the spouse or civil partner takes the whole estate.
- Where there is a spouse/civil partner and there is issue, the spouse/civil partner will be entitled to the personal possessions, a fixed net sum (currently £322,000), interest on the fixed net sum, and half of the rest of the estate, with the other half of the rest of the estate passing to the issue.
- Where there is no spouse/civil partner, the closest surviving specified relatives share the estate. Relatives in a higher category inherit to the exclusion of relatives in a lower category. The deceased's issue is the highest category of specified relatives.
- The 'statutory trusts' apply to most of the categories of relatives, and provide for substitute gifts to the issue of relatives who do not survive the deceased. Relatives who are under 18 have contingent interests until reaching 18 (or marrying/forming a civil partnership under that age prior to 27 February 2023).
- If there are no surviving specified relatives, the deceased's estate passes *bona vacantia* to the Crown (although the Crown has a discretion to provide for dependants etc of the deceased).

# CHAPTER 5
# Property Passing Outside the Estate

**FUNCTIONING LEGAL KNOWLEDGE**

This chapter covers the following functioning legal knowledge required to pass the SQE 1 assessments:

**Property passing outside the estate:**

- **joint property**
- life policies
- pension scheme benefits
- **trust** property

**AUTHORITIES UNDERPINNING PRACTICE**

Although this is a very important area, there are no key rules or legislation which underpin this area of practice.

## 5.1 Introduction

This is the shortest chapter in the book, yet it is one of the most important. You should not skim over this chapter thinking that the lack of detail means that it is not important. Many students make this error and do not pay sufficient attention to this topic. You need to know the rules covered in this chapter extremely well.

This is because it is vital in practice to understand that certain, very common, types of property do not pass on death according to the terms of a person's **will** or according to the rules of **intestacy**, but pass instead according to other legal mechanisms.

These types of property pass independently of the terms of any will, *even if the terms of the will state what is to happen to that property*: in other words, the terms of the will are of no effect in determining the distribution of the property.

These types of property also pass independently of the rules of intestacy.

For many persons these assets are the most valuable assets that they will leave on their death, far exceeding the value of the assets which are subject to a will/the rules of intestacy.

You have to know these types of property well, because if you do not, you run the risk of not achieving a client's objectives for how their assets should be distributed on their death. Also, you (and/or your firm) could face a professional negligence claim by disappointed **beneficiaries** if you fail to take account of these important rules.

For example, if a solicitor drafts a will for a client but does not arrange for the **severance** of a **joint tenancy in equity** (see **5.2** for more detail), the deceased's interest in the joint property will pass automatically by survivorship to the surviving joint tenant, and will not pass according to the terms of the will. If the **testator**'s wishes were to leave their interest in the joint property by will, then the solicitor will have been negligent. The solicitor's firm will then be liable to compensate the disappointed beneficiary (who was supposed to receive the testator's share of the property under the terms of the will).

You therefore need to understand when property and assets pass independently of a will/the rules of intestacy. You need to be able to advise the client on the implications of this. You also need to know how to make changes (where this is possible) so that the asset or property in question does then form part of the estate that passes by will/intestacy.

However, although the rules covered in this chapter are very important, you do not need to know the primary sources for the rules, so there are relatively few references to authority in this chapter.

As the property listed in **5.2–5.7** does not form part of the deceased's 'succession estate', it is not payable to the deceased's **personal representatives**, but will usually pass directly to the persons who are entitled to benefit under the alternative succession arrangements described here.

Also, some (but not all) of these types of property are not taxable to **inheritance tax** on a person's death. Inheritance tax is covered in detail in **Chapter 6**. However, the question of whether these types of asset are subject to inheritance tax, or are free from inheritance tax, is also covered later in **5.9**.

## 5.2 Joint property passing by survivorship

### 5.2.1 The two forms of joint ownership

There are two forms of joint ownership of property in **equity**. Persons owning property jointly can either own the interest in property as:

- **tenants in common**; or
- joint tenants in equity.

This can be the case with any type of property (including money in bank accounts, **chattels** and shares in limited companies), but the rules most commonly apply in relation to land or interests in land.

The most common situation involving a jointly owned asset is where a couple (whether or not they are married or in a **civil partnership**) own their home together. If the property is registered in their joint names, then they will always hold the *legal title* jointly. However, there are two ways in which they can share the underlying *equitable, or beneficial, interest* in the property.

### 5.2.2 Tenants in common

If the joint owners are tenants in common, then they will each have their own defined shares in the equity in the property and, significantly, each of the joint owners will be able to leave their own share in the property to the beneficiaries of their will. So, when the joint owner (who is a tenant in common) dies, their share in the joint property will pass according to the terms of that person's will.

If a tenant in common dies without leaving a will, then the rules of intestacy will determine what happens to the person's share in the property.

The share of a tenant in common does not have to be an equal share, but could be a defined percentage (eg one tenant in common owns 60 per cent and the other owns 40 per cent).

### 5.2.3 Joint tenants in equity

The form of equitable ownership that we are concerned with in this chapter, though, is the other type, which is where the joint owners are 'joint tenants *in equity*'. This is to distinguish the equitable ownership from the legal ownership. This is necessary because all joint owners will be joint owners at law (eg on the legal title of the land), regardless of the form of their underlying equitable ownership.

Persons who are joint tenants in equity are also referred to as 'equitable joint tenants' or 'beneficial joint tenants'.

### 5.2.3.1 The doctrine of survivorship

When a person who is a joint tenant in equity dies, their interest in the joint property passes automatically to the surviving joint tenant(s) in equity. So, if a husband and wife are joint tenants in equity of the matrimonial home, and the husband dies, the wife will inherit the husband's share automatically, simply by virtue of being the surviving joint tenant.

The same would be true if there were two friends who were not in a relationship—in other words, the joint tenants in equity do not have to be a couple.

Usually there will be only one surviving joint tenant, as we are usually dealing with a property owned by a couple, but it is possible for more than two people to own property jointly.

Importantly, when a joint tenant in equity dies, the surviving joint tenant will inherit regardless of the terms of the deceased's will, if there is one. This is the case even if the testator has included provisions in the will which indicate what should happen to the property. Any **gift** of the property in the will is of no effect, because the property passes independently of the will.

Similarly, if the deceased died intestate, the deceased's interest as joint tenant in equity will pass independently of the intestate estate, and so will not be governed by the rules of intestacy.

### 5.2.3.2 *Commorientes*: where the order of deaths is not known

Where two joint tenants have died in circumstances where the order of death is uncertain, the ***commorientes*** rule (from s184 Law of Property Act 1925) will apply. The *commorientes* rule provides that the younger person is deemed to have survived the older.

For example, this rule was applied in a case where the bodies of two persons were found in their house some weeks after their likely deaths, where their bodies were in a state of decomposition, but where the exact order of deaths was not known.

The question of which joint tenant has survived the other is important, because the joint tenant who is deemed to have survived will inherit the interest of the other joint tenant by survivorship.

### 5.2.3.3 Severance of joint tenancies

There is a problem for someone who is a joint tenant in equity if they wish to leave their interest in the property to someone other than the other joint tenant(s). The only way to achieve this is to convert the form of equitable ownership from a joint tenancy in equity to a tenancy in common. This process of conversion is known as 'severing' the joint tenancy, or 'severance'.

#### Notices of severance

By far the best method of severing a joint tenancy (and the one that you should follow in practice) is for the one joint tenant to give the other joint tenant a simple document, called a 'notice of severance', indicating the intention to sever. (The notice does not have to be handed over physically—it can be served by post or email.)

You will encounter situations in practice where you will have to sever a joint tenancy at the same time as you are making a will for a client. Severance of a joint tenancy is also often dealt with by the lawyers in the matrimonial or family department of the firm. Where different fee earners are dealing with the client's matters, care should be taken to ensure that the notice of severance is not overlooked.

#### Other methods of severance

Although a notice of severance is the best way of severing a joint tenancy in equity, severance can occur in a number of other ways—by mutual agreement or by action taken by one or both joint tenants that is inconsistent with a continued joint tenancy in equity. The detail on this is outside the scope of this manual, but there is case law on when a joint tenancy is severed by these other methods.

In particular, there is an issue over whether wills made by the joint tenants, in which the joint tenants make provisions disposing of their interests in the joint property, has the effect of severing the joint tenancy. Normally, the making of wills does not sever a joint tenancy in equity, but there are cases in which this has happened (eg *Dunbabin v Dunbabin* [2022] EWHC 241 (Ch)).

Care needs to be taken to check whether a joint tenancy in equity might have been severed in one of these ways. This is particularly important when you are administering the estate of the deceased joint owner, because if the joint tenancy in equity had been severed, the deceased's share of the property (as tenant in common) would form part of the estate, and the personal representatives would have a duty to secure that share and include it in the distribution of the estate under the terms of the will or the rules of intestacy.

Note also that the making of one special type of will—'**mutual wills**'—does have the effect of severing a joint tenancy in equity if the testators include provisions in the wills dealing with their respective shares in the joint property. The making of mutual wills involves a contract between the two testators to abide by the terms of the mutual wills, and so in effect the severance of the joint tenancy becomes part of the contractual arrangement between the two testators. However, it should be noted that most wills are not mutual wills. Married (and unmarried) couples often make wills that appear to be similar, and those wills are often referred to as '**mirror wills**', but it is rare for couples to make 'mutual wills', in the technical sense of that term. (See **Chapter 2** for more detail on mutual wills.)

## 5.2.4 **Examples of joint ownership**

Here are two examples to show the difference between property owned jointly as joint tenants in equity and property which is owned jointly as tenants in common.

**EXAMPLE**

Avril and Peter, who are not married, live together with Avril's daughter, Susan (aged 18), who is Avril's only child. Avril has a joint bank account (beneficial joint tenancy) with Peter and they jointly own their home as tenants in common. Avril dies intestate, survived by Peter and Susan. Avril's share of the money in the bank account will pass by survivorship to Peter. Avril's share in the home, however, will form part of her succession estate, which passes under the intestacy rules to Susan.

As said, in most cases a couple will own their property as joint tenants in equity and so in most cases the interest of the deceased will pass to the other independently of the deceased's will or of the rules of intestacy. For many persons, their joint interest in their own home is likely to be their most valuable asset, perhaps leaving very little else to be distributed under the terms of their will or by the rules of intestacy.

**EXAMPLE**

Shona and Rhian are in a relationship but they are not married or in a civil partnership. They are joint tenants in equity of their house, which is worth £300,000. Shona dies. The mortgage on the property is paid off on her death, due to a mortgage protection policy. Shona's interest in the property, worth around £150,000, will pass automatically to Rhian, as the surviving joint tenant. Shona did not leave a will and her whole estate will pass under the rules of intestacy to her nearest relatives, who are her parents, Margaret and Dennis. Shona's estate is modest in comparison to the value of her interest in the house. The only other assets Shona has are her personal possessions (worth approximately £10,000) and savings of £15,000.

## 5.2.5 **Transferring legal title to a surviving joint tenant**

It is not necessary to produce a grant of **probate** or a grant of administration in order to secure title to joint property passing by survivorship. Instead, following the death of the deceased joint tenant, the surviving joint tenant may claim the property by providing an official copy of a **death certificate**. If the joint property is land, then the surviving joint tenant will also need to be registered as the sole owner of the property at HM Land Registry.

## 5.3 Life assurance policies

Life assurance policies are a common form of asset. Under these policies, a person pays sums of money, called 'premiums', to the life assurance company in return for a sum of money which the life assurance company pays out on the death of a person. (The premiums may be by way of a single lump sum or regular payments over a period of time, or a mixture of the two.)

Usually, the payment by the life assurance company ('the sum assured') is made on the death of the person who has taken out the life assurance policy, and the person is then also called 'the life assured'.

It is possible to take out life assurance on another person's life, in which case the other person would be the life assured. We will assume for the rest of this section, though, that the person taking out the policy has insured their own life and that they are also the life assured. The sum assured is often referred to as 'the policy proceeds', or 'the death benefits'.

There are various life assurance products on the market and it is possible for the sum assured to go to different beneficiaries.

### 5.3.1 Life policies payable to the estate

The simplest situation is where the sum assured is payable to the deceased's estate, in which case the life assurance company will pay it to the deceased's personal representatives, and the personal representatives will distribute the sum assured in accordance with the terms of the will, if there is one, or the rules of intestacy if there is no will.

Note that the deceased's will does not have to mention the sum assured specifically, as the sum assured will usually simply form part of the deceased's **residuary estate** and will pass to the residuary beneficiaries as part of their entitlement.

### 5.3.2 Life policies written in trust

Our concern in this chapter, though, is with the other type of life assurance policy—one which is written in trust for named beneficiaries. If a life assurance policy is written in trust, then the sum assured belongs to those named beneficiaries on the deceased's death. In other words, the sum assured does not belong to the deceased's estate and so will not be governed by the deceased's will or the rules of intestacy.

**EXAMPLE**

Brian has a will in which he leaves everything to his second wife, Barbara. Brian also takes out a life assurance policy on his own life, and the policy is written in trust for the benefit of his two children from his first marriage, Ffion and Jamie. The sum assured of £100,000 under the life assurance will be paid to Ffion and Jamie on Brian's death, even though he has left everything to Barbara in his will.

If a life policy is written in trust, this could be written expressly for named beneficiaries or alternatively the policy could be written under s11 of the Married Women's Property Act 1882. Under that Act, a policy may be written in trust in favour of the life assured's spouse, civil partner and/or children.

Where a life policy has been written in trust, the sum assured is payable directly to the named beneficiaries on proof of death, by sending a death certificate and completed claim form to the life assurance company.

### 5.3.3 Converting a life policy into a trust policy

It is also possible for a policyholder to 'convert' an existing life policy (that is payable to the estate) into a trust policy by assigning the benefits of the life policy, either under s11 of the Married Women's Property Act 1882 or expressly in favour of named beneficiaries. This conversion has to be during the life of the life assured.

One of the main reasons for taking out a life policy which is written in trust, or converting an existing non-trust policy into a trust policy, is the favourable inheritance tax treatment of life policies written in trust (on which, see **5.9**).

# 5.4 **Pension schemes**

Many people will be entitled to a State retirement pension, based upon the National Insurance contributions they have made during their working lifetime. In addition, many people will have a private pension. This may be an occupational pension scheme, arranged via their employment, or a pension scheme taken out privately with a commercial provider. Many people have an occupational pension scheme by virtue of being civil servants, NHS staff, teachers or otherwise working in the public sector.

## 5.4.1 **Pension scheme benefits**

In return for making contributions to the pension scheme during their working lives, pension schemes generally offer the following benefits:

- a regular income on retirement (the pension);
- a lump sum payment on the death of the pension scheme member if the member dies before reaching pension age.

### 5.4.1.1 Pensions

The main reason a person takes out a private pension is in order to provide a regular income during that person's retirement, with a regular (usually monthly) payment which is used by the person to cover living costs now that the person is no longer in employment and so no longer has any wages or salary. Generally, the regular pension payments are made from the date the person retires to the date of the person's death.

Often, a person can decide to take a reduced monthly pension in exchange for receiving a lump sum on or shortly after retirement.

### 5.4.1.2 Lump sum payments before retirement age

However, a person might die before reaching retirement age, in which case they will never receive any pension from the scheme. The person would have made substantial contributions to the scheme during their working life (with an occupational scheme, a percentage of a person's salary is deducted to pay for these contributions, and a person's employer will usually contribute to the scheme each month too). To reflect the fact that the person had contributed to the pension scheme, and as a kind of compensation for never having drawn their pension, a lump sum is often paid on that person's premature death.

Note that this is not compensation to reflect the exact amount that someone has lost, but is compensation in a looser sense, so that the person, their estate or someone close to them, will receive some money on their death.

With occupational pension schemes, this lump sum payment is often called a 'death-in-service' payment, because the pension scheme member will often have died whilst still working for the employer.

## 5.4.2 **Lump sum payments due to the deceased's estate**

With some pension schemes, the lump sum payment (on the death of a pension scheme member) may be due as of right. In other words, the deceased member, or their estate, may have an entitlement to that payment. If that is the case, then the lump sum is added to the estate that is subject to the will/the rules of intestacy.

### 5.4.3 Discretionary lump sum payments

However, many pension schemes, particularly occupational pension schemes, do not give the deceased member, or their estate, a *right* or entitlement to the death-in-service payment. Instead, the **trustees** of the pension scheme are given a *discretion* to make a payment on the member's death. The pension scheme is, in effect, a large **discretionary trust** and the members (as beneficiaries) have only a mere hope that they and their estate will be benefited by the trust.

This sounds like a considerable disadvantage for the pension scheme member and their estate, but one reason for structuring pension schemes in this way is the preferable inheritance tax treatment. As we will see in **5.9**, a discretionary death-in-service payment is inheritance tax-free, simply because it is discretionary and not paid as of right.

The other impact of a death-in-service payment being discretionary is that it does not necessarily form part of the deceased member's estate, and so is not governed by the terms of the will or the rules of intestacy. The pension scheme trustees might make the discretionary death-in-service payment to the personal representatives of the deceased member's estate, in which case the payment will be subject to the terms of the will or the rules of intestacy. More commonly, however, the pension scheme trustees will make the payment direct to one or more relatives or dependants of the deceased member.

### 5.4.4 Pension schemes and nominations

Usually, the member of the pension scheme will have completed a nomination form specifying the person(s) to benefit from a death-in-service payment if one is made. Typically, the member will specify their spouse (or civil partner or unmarried partner) and/or the member's children. Each pension scheme will have its own nomination forms and the form will be submitted to the pension scheme administrators, acting on behalf of the trustees. If the member has nominated one or more persons to receive the death-in-service payment, the pension scheme trustees will usually make the payment to the person(s) nominated by the member.

If the death-in-service payment is made to the nominated person(s) (as opposed to the deceased member's estate), then the money belongs to the nominated person(s) and is not governed by the terms of the deceased member's will or the rules of intestacy.

### 5.4.5 The significance of pension scheme payments

Next to the value of a person's interest in jointly held property, a death-in-service payment is often the largest asset that a person can expect to pass on when they die. This is because it is common for a death-in-service benefit to be a multiple of the person's salary.

**EXAMPLE**

Helen is a member of her employer's pension scheme. Under the terms of the scheme, there is provision for a discretionary death-in-service payment of three times salary. Helen dies before reaching retirement age. Her current salary is £50,000. She has nominated her husband, George, to receive any payment from the scheme. The pension scheme trustees exercise their discretion and make a payment of £150,000 to George. This does not form part of Helen's estate, and is not governed by the terms of her will. Once the payment has been made, the money belongs to George absolutely.

### 5.4.6 Claiming pension scheme payments after death

Where there is a discretionary payment there is no need to produce a grant of probate or grant of administration (unless the payment is being made to the personal representatives). Usually, the nominated beneficiary simply provides the trustees of the scheme with proof of death (an official copy of the death certificate) to enable payment to be made.

### 5.4.7 Personal pension schemes

There are special rules, under the Taxation of Pensions Act 2014, that apply to 'personal pension schemes' (ones purchased from a commercial provider, as opposed to an occupational pension scheme which is linked to the person's employment). Under a personal pension scheme, the member builds a pension fund and they have various options on using that fund on and after retirement. It is possible to pass that pension fund on to beneficiaries using a nomination. However, this can be done with unused pension funds even after retirement, although the tax position differs after the age of 75. The detail of the rules is outside the scope of this manual. The rules apply to pension fund benefits paid on or after 6 April 2015: different rules (which are also outside the scope of this manual) applied before that date.

## 5.5 Interests in trust property

The deceased might have been the beneficiary or trustee of a trust before their death. There are various possible situations where it will be necessary to consider the transmission of the trust property on the deceased's death. These are considered in the following sections.

### 5.5.1 Life interest trusts

The deceased might have had a limited interest in a trust during their lifetime, either:

- entitling the deceased to the income of the trust as and when it arose; or
- to otherwise enjoy the trust property (eg having the right to live in a house owned by the trust).

Such an interest is called a '**life interest**', and this usually comes to an end on the death of the beneficiary. The beneficiary is called the 'life tenant'.

When the life tenant of a life interest dies, the trust property will pass in accordance with the terms of the original trust deed or instrument. It will not form part of the life tenant's own death estate and so does not pass in accordance with the terms of the life tenant's will, or according to the rules of intestacy if the life tenant has died intestate.

### 5.5.2 Powers of appointment

Some trust instruments give a **power of appointment** to the life tenant, which gives them the power to determine what is to happen when the life interest ends. Sometimes, the life tenant may exercise the power in their will, namely by including the appointment of the next beneficiary(ies) of the trust property as a clause in the will.

However, the trust property does not form part of the life tenant's estate, and this is so even if the life tenant exercises the appointment in their will.

### 5.5.3 Reversionary or remainder interests

A different type of interest that a person might have in a trust is a **reversionary** or **remainder interest**. Typically, this is an interest that will only vest on the death of another person, usually on the death of another person who is the life tenant of the trust. If a person with a reversionary or remainder interest dies before the life tenant dies, then the reversionary or remainder interest will **lapse** and will not form part of the deceased's estate that is subject to their will or the rules of intestacy.

### 5.5.4 Where the deceased is a trustee of a trust

Another possibility that may arise is that the deceased is a trustee of a trust. Although the deceased, as trustee, will have had legal title to the trust property, the beneficial interest in the trust property belongs to someone else (the beneficiary(ies) of the trust), and so the trust property will not form part of the deceased's estate.

### 5.5.5 Beneficial interests claimed by third parties

A further possibility is that the deceased appears to be the sole legal and beneficiary owner of property, but another person may claim part or all of the beneficial entitlement to the trust property.

For example, a farmer might be the sole owner of a farm but one of the farm workers might bring a claim for some or all of the value of the farm on the basis of the equitable claim of **proprietary estoppel**. Alternatively, someone might claim a beneficial interest in the deceased's property on the basis of a **resulting** or a **constructive trust**. See **12.5–12.8** for more detail on these claims.

To the extent that a claim is successful, the beneficial entitlement of the other person will not belong to the deceased and so will not be part of the deceased's estate.

## 5.6 Nominated property

This section explains what is meant by '**nominated property**'. Nominated property is not to be confused with the pension scheme nominations mentioned previously in **5.4**. Pension scheme benefits following a nomination by a pension scheme member are not 'nominated property', in the technical sense of that phrase.

'Nominated property' refers to certain investments where, over time, it has been possible for the owner of the investment to make a binding nomination in favour of someone else. The investment holder (the company that holds the investment) will then pay the investment to the nominated person on the death of the investment owner.

This offers an alternative to including a gift of such property in a will. The rules on nominated property date from a time when there were concerns that ordinary people might be reluctant to make wills or might simply not get round to doing so.

However, nominated property is now quite rare and is largely historical. There are few types of property where it is still possible to make a nomination of this type. Many of those who have made nominations in the past have since died, and so nominated property is encountered infrequently in practice. Nevertheless, they need to be mentioned, for completeness' sake.

### 5.6.1 Nominations

In the case of certain investments, a person who is aged 16 or over may pass the property concerned on death under a statutory nomination made in writing and **attested** by one **witness**. Such a nomination is **revoked** by subsequent marriage, a later nomination or if the nominee predeceases the nominator; however, it is unaffected by any subsequent will.

### 5.6.2 What property can be nominated?

It is now only possible to make such a nomination of monies deposited in 'friendly societies' and 'industrial and provident societies', and even then only up to a limit in each case of £5,000. It used to be possible to nominate funds in 'trustee savings banks' (this facility was withdrawn on 1 May 1979) and National Savings Certificates and the National Savings Bank (this facility was withdrawn on 1 May 1981). However, nominations made before these dates remain effective (unless revoked) but, as said earlier, many of the persons who will have made those nominations will have since died.

If property capable of nomination in this way is not so nominated, it forms part of the property passing on death under the terms of the deceased's will or the intestacy rules.

### 5.6.3 Claiming nominated property after death

If a valid nomination has been made, then the nominated beneficiary does not have to produce a grant of probate or grant of administration to claim the money: all that is required is proof of death (an official copy of the death certificate).

# 5.7 Donationes mortis causa

This Latin phrase is used to describe gifts ('*donationes*') made shortly before death which are both in contemplation of death ('*mortis*') and conditional on death.

***Donationes mortis causa*** are comparatively rare, and they are not a recommended method of passing on property to a beneficiary. It is much better if property is left to a beneficiary as part of a clearly written will.

The rules on *donationes mortis causa* derive from Roman Law (hence the Latin). *Donationes* is the plural ('gifts') and *donatio* is the singular ('gift').

We will not consider the rules on *donationes mortis causa* in any depth here, but for the purposes of this chapter, it is sufficient to say that any property that is the subject matter of a valid *donatio mortis causa* will not be part of the estate that is governed by a will or the rules of intestacy. Instead, any property passing under a valid *donatio mortis causa* passes directly to the donee of the gift on death.

Many (but not all) types of property can pass by means of a *donatio mortis causa*: even land can pass by means of this type of gift (as in *Sen v Headley* [1991] Ch 425 (CA Civ)).

**EXAMPLE**

Rohan is gravely ill with a terminal disease. Believing that he is due to die soon, he hands his son, Fergus, the keys to Rohan's vintage MG motorcar, telling Fergus that the car is Fergus's when Rohan dies. Rohan dies two days later. The elements of a valid *donatio mortis causa* appear to have been met. Rohan made the gift in contemplation of his death, which appeared reasonably imminent; the gift presumably was conditional on death in that it would not have been a completed gift had Rohan recovered; and Rohan gave 'dominion' of the car to Fergus by giving him the keys. On this basis, the vintage MG motorcar would pass to Fergus direct, and the car would not form part of Rohan's estate for will or intestacy purposes.

As said earlier, it is much more preferable to include all of a person's wishes in a properly drafted will, rather than use less reliable methods such as *donationes mortis causa*.

# 5.8 Gifts with the reservation of benefit

This is an inheritance tax concept—it basically means that the deceased has given away property in their lifetime but has retained some benefit in the gifted property. Although the inheritance tax rules (which are covered in detail in **Chapter 6**) may mean that the property is still taxed on the deceased's death, for succession purposes the asset will no longer form part of the deceased's estate. The asset will already belong to the person(s) who received the gift (the donee(s)) and so the asset will not be governed by the terms of the deceased's will or the rules of intestacy.

# 5.9 Inheritance tax on property passing outside the estate

Although the detailed inheritance tax rules are covered in **Chapter 6**, it is important to realise the difference between the estate for succession purposes (ie the estate that is subject to the will or to the rules of intestacy) and the estate for inheritance tax purposes (ie the estate that is taxable). We will see that the estate for inheritance tax purposes includes some types of property that pass independently of the will or of the rules of intestacy.

## 5.9.1 Property not forming part of the succession estate but forming part of the deceased's estate for inheritance tax purposes

Although the following property is not payable to the deceased's personal representatives, it nevertheless must be included in calculating the value of property passing on death for inheritance tax purposes; that is, it forms part of the deceased's taxable estate.

1 Property held by the deceased as beneficial joint tenant. The value of the deceased's share only is counted, not the whole value of the property. In the first example in **5.2**, the value of Avril's share of money in the bank account (not the total amount in the account) would be included in her estate for tax purposes. The value of her interest in the house (part of her succession estate) would, of course, also form part of her taxable estate on death.
2 Nominated property.
3 *Donationes mortis causa.*
4 Some life interests in trust property (the rules on whether or not a particular life interest is subject to inheritance tax are complex, and are covered in brief in **Chapter 6**).
5 Gifts with a reservation of benefit.

## 5.9.2 Property not forming part of the deceased's estate for succession or inheritance tax purposes

These are:

- Life assurance policies written in trust. Sums assured under such policies are not subject to inheritance tax because the sum assured belongs to the nominated beneficiary(ies) of the policy. Put another way, the deceased was not beneficially entitled to the sum assured immediately before death. Sums assured under policies payable to the deceased's estate would, however, form part of the taxable estate.
- Pension scheme benefits payable at the discretion of the pension trustees. This is not taxable for the same reason, namely the deceased was not beneficially entitled to the payment immediately before death. The deceased (or their estate) only has a hope that a lump sum will be paid to them: there is no entitlement to a payment. However, if the terms of the pension scheme provide for a payment to the deceased's estate as of right, the lump sum will be included in the estate for inheritance tax.

Also, and subject to meeting certain conditions, reversionary or remainder interests are excluded property for inheritance tax purposes and so are not subject to inheritance tax as part of the person's estate on death.

**TABLE 5.1** Summary of commonly encountered property

| Asset | Does the asset form part of the estate? | Is the asset taxable to inheritance tax? |
|---|---|---|
| Deceased's interests as beneficial joint tenant | No | Yes (but exempt if passing to spouse/civil partner) |
| Deceased's interests as tenant in common | Yes | Yes (but exempt if passing to spouse/civil partner) |
| Life policy not written in trust | Yes | Yes |
| Life policy written in trust | No | No |
| Pension benefits passing to estate | Yes | Yes |
| Discretionary pension benefits | No | No |

## KEY POINT SUMMARY

- There are some important types of property that pass independently of the terms of a will or the rules of intestacy. These can often be the most valuable assets passing following someone's death.
- With jointly owned property, the share of tenant in common is part of a person's estate which is governed by a will or the rules of intestacy. However, the interest of a joint tenant in equity, which is more common when couples own property together, will pass automatically by survivorship to the surviving joint tenant(s).
- Life assurance policies may be written into trust, in which case the policy proceeds will not form part of a person's estate: instead, the policy proceeds will be paid direct to the beneficiaries of the trust.
- Lump sum benefits under some pension schemes will be paid by the pension scheme trustees in the exercise of their discretion, and so will not form part of the deceased's estate. Usually, the payment is made direct to persons nominated by the pension scheme member during their lifetime.
- The proceeds of life assurance policies written in trust and discretionary payments from pension schemes will also be free of inheritance tax (because the deceased had no beneficial entitlement to those assets immediately before death).

## KEY POINT SUMMARY

# PART C
# Inheritance Tax

# CHAPTER 6
# Inheritance Tax

**FUNCTIONING LEGAL KNOWLEDGE**

This chapter covers the following functioning legal knowledge required to pass the SQE 1 assessments:

**Inheritance tax:**

- lifetime transfers that are immediately chargeable and those that are potentially exempt
- transfers on death
- exemptions and reliefs
- the scope of anti-avoidance provisions

**AUTHORITIES UNDERPINNING PRACTICE**

The key authorities that underpin this area of practice are listed below. Note that for legislation you are linked to legislation.gov.uk.

Although much of the legislation on this government website is available in its amended form, the incorporation of new amendments into the text of legislation can be delayed. You should refer to legal databases to ensure you are referencing the most up-to-date legislation.

- Inheritance Tax Act 1984
  **http://www.legislation.gov.uk/ukpga/1984/51/contents**

## 6.1 Introduction to inheritance tax (IHT)

This chapter deals with the charge to **inheritance tax**.

This text is aimed at preparing you for a multiple-choice test (one of the functioning knowledge tests in Stage 1 of the SQE). As a result, this manual, unlike texts which were written for the Legal Practice Course, does not include lengthy example calculations of IHT. Instead, this chapter focuses on the main IHT principles and rules, and some simple example calculations appear later in the chapter (in **6.10**) to illustrate how those rules work in combination with each other.

Nevertheless, IHT is a detailed topic and this is a long chapter as a result. Also, this chapter provides the foundation for your study of IHT across the whole of this series of SQE manuals, and this is another reason for the greater length of this chapter. You will need to know the basics of IHT in this chapter in order to understand the discussion of IHT in the *Business Law & Practice* manual, for example.

Whilst it is difficult to divide this topic into two smaller chapters, you may wish to study this chapter in stages rather than trying to cover all of it in one go.

### 6.1.1 What is IHT?

IHT is commonly thought of as a tax paid only on death. Certainly, **liability** to the tax is often triggered by death but it is also triggered when a person makes certain transfers of money or property during their lifetime, such as lifetime transfers to certain types of **trust**.

In this chapter we will look at the following occasions on which IHT is charged:

- on a chargeable transfer made during a person's lifetime (a **lifetime chargeable transfer**);
- on other lifetime transfers that are not chargeable when they are made but which become chargeable because the transferor dies within seven years of the date of the transfer; and
- on a person's 'estate' on their death.

We will look at what is a **transfer of value**, and consider each of the above transfers in turn. We will also consider how these chargeable transfers are valued, what exemptions and reliefs apply, what the rates of tax are and how the tax payable on one chargeable transfer may be affected by earlier chargeable transfers, due to the principle of cumulation.

### 6.1.2 Sources of inheritance tax law

The sources of IHT law are:

1. Statute: the principal charging Act is the Inheritance Tax Act 1984 (IHTA 1984). As with other taxes, annual Finance Acts have made changes to the Act, although most of these result in amendments to the IHTA 1984 itself.
2. Case law: as with other taxes, the courts and tribunals are meant to interpret the tax legislation only. There is no common law, as such, namely there is no tax law that has been developed by the courts that is independent of the legislation.
3. HMRC statements: as with other taxes, HMRC produce a range of official statements which set out HMRC's view on the application of the law or indicate HMRC's policy and practice.

### 6.1.3 Administration and collection of IHT

IHT is administered by HMRC. The main HMRC office which deals with IHT is in Nottingham. It used to be called the Capital Taxes Office, and you might hear practitioners still using that name.

IHT is collected by direct assessment; that is, details of a chargeable transfer are reported to HMRC and payment of the amount of IHT calculated is sent to HMRC. There are different reporting regimes for lifetime chargeable transfers when they are made, compared with the tax liabilities arising on death. The tax liabilities on death may be in respect of both: (a) the death estate; and (b) lifetime transfers which have become chargeable retrospectively as a result of death. We will consider the process of reporting details following a death in more detail in **Chapter 7**.

## 6.2 Outline steps in calculating IHT

The first step is to identify that there is a chargeable transfer of value. The question of what is a chargeable transfer is considered in **6.3**, and also in **6.4** (lifetime transfers) and **6.5** (transfers on death).

Having identified that there has been a chargeable transfer, to calculate the IHT payable on that chargeable transfer there are five basic steps to follow:

1. Calculate the value transferred. (See **6.6** on valuation.)
2. Identify any available 'exemptions' and deduct them from the value transferred. (See **6.7.1** on exemptions from IHT.)
3. Identify any available 'reliefs' and deduct them from the value transferred. (See **6.7.2** on reliefs from IHT.)
4. Calculate the transferor's 'cumulative total' as at the date of the transfer and the amount of the '**nil rate band**' remaining. (See **6.9**.)
5. Calculate the IHT payable by applying the appropriate rate or rates of tax to the value of the transfer for IHT purposes. (The rate, or rates, will depend on whether the tax is being paid on the date of the transfer or on the death of the transferor.) (See **6.8** on the rates of tax.)

The five basic steps remain the same regardless of the occasion on which the tax is being charged (the three occasions are as listed in **6.1.1**). Depending on which occasion is the relevant one, there may be additional steps to go through. These are set out later when examples of calculating the tax are worked through for each of the three occasions on which IHT is charged. (See **6.10** for example calculations.)

# 6.3 Transfers of value

Section 1 of the IHTA 1984 states that 'Inheritance tax shall be charged on the value transferred by a chargeable transfer.' This raises two questions: 'what is a chargeable transfer?' and 'how is the value transferred calculated?' The answers to these questions differ depending on whether the transfer of value is made during the transferor's lifetime or whether the transfer of value is on the transferor's death.

## 6.3.1 Lifetime transfers

For lifetime transfers, s2 of the IHTA 1984 provides that 'A chargeable transfer is a transfer of value which is made by an individual but is not . . . an exempt transfer.' Section 3 then defines a transfer of value as:

> a disposition made by a person (the transferor) as a result of which the value of the transferor's estate immediately after the disposition is less than it would be but for the disposition; and the amount by which it is less is the value transferred by the transfer.

In other words, a transfer of value occurs when the transferor's estate (ie everything that they own) is worth less as a result of the transfer, and the value transferred is the amount by which their estate is reduced. This is easiest to understand in the context of a **gift** by the transferor to the transferee, when the transferor's estate will be reduced (the gifted property no longer belongs to them) and the value of the transfer will be the value of the gifted property (as this is usually the same as the amount by which the estate is reduced).

**EXAMPLE**

Helen gives a valuable painting, worth £200,000, to her daughter, Jessica.

Helen's estate has been reduced by the lifetime transfer. There has thus been a transfer of value, and the value of the transfer is £200,000.

So, if a transferor makes a gift, it will be a transfer of value. What, though, if the transferor sells an asset, but at a deliberate undervalue?

**EXAMPLE**

Changing the facts of the previous example, what if Helen sold the valuable painting, worth £200,000, to her daughter, Jessica, for a nominal sum of £1?

There would be a transfer of value here too. Helen's estate has been reduced by the lifetime transfer. There has thus been a transfer of value, although the value of the transfer is £199,999 (£200,000 minus £1).

As has been seen, a transfer must reduce the value of the transferor's estate. It follows that a sale of an asset for its true value will not result in a transfer of value, and so will not be subject to an IHT charge.

**EXAMPLE**

Simon sells shares which are listed on the London Stock Exchange. These are valued at £50,000 and Simon receives £50,000 from the sale. Simon's estate has not fallen as a result of the transaction, and so there is no transfer of value. (Note that the incidental costs of sale are ignored.)

So, there needs to be a gift, or a gift element, for a lifetime transfer to be a transfer of value for IHT purposes. Also, the transferor must intend to confer a gratuitous benefit on the transferee. Clearly, Helen in the first two examples above is intending to confer a gratuitous benefit on her daughter, Jessica. However, where there has been a sale on the open market, there is not likely to be an intention to confer a gratuitous benefit. In such situations, there will be no transfer of value even if the transferor's estate is reduced. See **6.3.4.1** for more detail on situations where the transferor has made a 'bad bargain' and, although their estate has been reduced, there is no transfer of value because there is no intention to confer a gratuitous benefit.

## 6.3.2 The transfer on death

When a person makes a transfer during their lifetime, they take active steps in transferring the property to the transferee—in other words, there is an actual transfer. On death, however, the transferor is dead and there is no actual transfer. The law of succession provides that the deceased's estate (that is covered by their **will** or the rules of **intestacy**) passes to their **personal representatives** and then ultimately to the **beneficiaries** of the estate. As we have seen in **Chapter 5**, other types of property pass independently of the will or intestacy rules, according to other rules of succession, such as the interest of a **joint tenant in equity** passing automatically to the surviving joint tenant(s). There is thus no actual transfer of assets on death from the deceased to the beneficiaries of those assets. Where then is the transfer for value for IHT?

The Act answers this question by providing for an assumed, or 'deemed', transfer of value on the death of the transferor. Section 4 of the IHTA 1984 states:

> On the death of any person tax shall be charged as if, immediately before his death, he had made a transfer of value and the value transferred by it had been equal to the value of his estate immediately before his death.

We will see in **6.5** what is included and excluded from the death estate for IHT purposes.

## 6.3.3 Excluded assets

The Act specifically excludes some assets from the charge to tax. This applies to lifetime transfers and to the estate on death.

The categories of excluded property are set out in ss6, 47, and 48 of the IHTA 1984. Section 6 includes property situated outside the UK where the person beneficially entitled to it is domiciled outside the UK. Sections 47 and 48 deal with **reversionary interests** in settled property. The term 'reversionary interest' is used to describe the situation where X leaves some property in a **settlement** so that Y enjoys the income from that settlement during their lifetime but, on Y's death, the property goes to Z absolutely. Prior to Y's death, Z's interest in the settled fund is referred to as a 'reversionary interest'. This interest is excluded property so far as Z is concerned. In some cases, the reversionary interest will not be excluded property. One example would be if it was purchased for money or money's worth.

## 6.3.4 Dispositions which are not transfers of value

The Act also details dispositions which are not transfers of value. These apply to lifetime transfers only (because they are not relevant to the estate on death).

#### 6.3.4.1 No intention to confer a gratuitous benefit

A disposition is not a transfer of value if the transferor had no intention to confer a gratuitous benefit (s10 IHTA 1984). This principle is relevant where there has been a sale at an undervalue. If the transferor can prove that they made a bad bargain (eg through not recognising how much the asset was really worth) and had no intention of conferring a gratuitous benefit on the transferee, then the loss resulting to the transferor's estate arising from the bad bargain will not have any IHT implications.

**EXAMPLE**

Baljit owns a property which she rents out to tenants. Baljit decides to sell the property. She advertises the property on the open market and sells it to Nigel for £250,000. Baljit and Nigel are not connected to each other—the sale is an arm's length transaction. After the sale, it becomes clear that Baljit has sold the property for much less than it was worth, as its true value is more like £300,000. However, although Baljit's estate has been reduced as a result of the transaction (she has £250,000 cash instead of an asset worth £300,000), she will not have made a chargeable transfer of value because she did not intend to confer a gratuitous benefit on Nigel.

#### 6.3.4.2 Dispositions for family maintenance

Under s11 of the IHTA 1984, payments by a transferor to spouses, civil partners, children and dependent relations which result in a loss to the transferor's estate are not chargeable in the following circumstances:

- if the payment is by one spouse or civil partner for the maintenance of the other (this provision includes any disposition for maintenance made on the occasion of a divorce); or
- if the payment is for the maintenance, education or training of a child of the marriage or **civil partnership** (or of any other child not in the care of its parents); or
- if the payment represents reasonable provision for the care and maintenance of a dependent relative.

**EXAMPLE**

Jack's son, Timothy, is a pupil at a private school (which charges fees). Jack pays £15,000 per year on school fees for Timothy. Although this is a significant amount of money, the payment is for the education of Jack's child and so is not chargeable to IHT, due to s11 of the IHTA 1984.

## 6.4 Lifetime transfers

Much inheritance tax planning involves taking advantage of the inheritance tax rules by making large lifetime gifts and then surviving those gifts by seven years. In general, if a person survives a lifetime transfer by seven years then the value of that transfer will fall out of consideration for IHT and will either not be taxed at all or (if some tax has already been paid in respect of a lifetime transfer) there will be no additional IHT to pay. In contrast, if a person holds on to all of their assets until they die then, above a certain figure, there is a straight rate of tax of 40 per cent.

In this section we will consider the two types of lifetime transfer that can be made—a **potentially exempt transfer** (PET) and a lifetime chargeable transfer (LCT). A person does not have a choice as to whether a particular lifetime transfer is a PET or an LCT—a lifetime transfer either qualifies as a PET or, if it does not qualify as a PET, it is an LCT. Instead, the nature of the transfer (which is dependent on the identity of the transferee) will determine whether it is a PET or an LCT. (Obviously, the person can structure the transfer in such a way that it qualifies either as a PET or an LCT, and so to this extent the person has a choice.)

The third type of lifetime transfer we consider in this section is actually an overlay on top of the other two types of transfer. A transfer that is a PET or an LCT may also be a **gift which is subject to a reservation.** The rules on gifts subject to a reservation are anti-avoidance rules. Other anti-avoidance rules are considered in **6.12**, but it is convenient, and logical, to consider gifts subject to a reservation at the same time as looking at lifetime transfers.

## 6.4.1 Potentially exempt transfers

Some transfers of value made during a person's lifetime are classified by the Act as potentially exempt transfers (s3A IHTA 1984). If the transferor survives by seven years or more, the PET becomes an exempt transfer. Conversely, if the transferor dies within seven years of making the PET, it becomes chargeable. A PET is called a PET because the transfer is 'potentially exempt' until either the transferor survives by seven years or dies within seven years.

Essentially, a PET is a lifetime transfer of value made to one of the following:

- another individual; or
- the **trustees** of a trust for the benefit of the disabled.

An outright gift by an individual to another individual is the PET you are most likely to come across.

An outright gift to an individual can include a transfer to a bare trust for the individual. A bare trust is where the trustee is holding the property on trust absolutely for the beneficiary. Such a beneficiary could easily bring the trust to an end by exercising their right to require the trustees to terminate the trust, under the rule in *Saunders v Vautier* (1841) 49 ER 282, if the beneficiary is an adult and of sound mind. Bare trusts for adults are rare, but bare trusts for children are more common. A bare trust will arise when absolute gifts are made to children (as children cannot look after the gifted property themselves).

With the exception of gifts to disabled trusts or bare trusts, gifts made during a person's lifetime into trust will be lifetime chargeable transfers. LCTs are considered in the next section.

IHT is charged on a PET when the transferor does not survive for a period of seven years from the date of the PET. If the transferor dies within that period, the transfer becomes a chargeable transfer and IHT is payable at the full rates at the date of death.

Due to the fact that PETs become exempt once the transferor survives them by seven years, they are a very powerful tool to avoid paying IHT. It does not matter how large the PET is—provided the transferor survives by seven years, the transfer will become exempt. For this reason, lifetime giving is an extremely important tool for wealthy persons wishing to reduce or avoid paying IHT. This is an entirely legitimate way of avoiding IHT.

**EXAMPLE**

Ida makes a gift of £10 million to her son, Jose. Ida survives the gift by seven years (she dies seven years and one day after the gift is made).

The gift to Jose is a PET when it is made. As Ida has survived the PET by seven years, it has now become exempt. There will be no IHT payable on the £10 million as a result of Ida's death. Ida has managed, therefore, to pass £10 million to her son without any IHT being payable on that money.

## 6.4.2 Lifetime chargeable transfers

Most gifts made during a person's lifetime into trust will be LCTs. Examples of LCTs include:

- a lifetime transfer to a **discretionary trust**; and
- a lifetime transfer giving a beneficiary an interest in possession (eg right to income for life).

Such trusts are subject to a different charging regime during the lifetime of the trust. These trusts are called 'relevant property' trusts. In addition to any IHT charge when the trust is set up (by LCT), the trust may be subject to other IHT charges throughout its existence. There are periodic charges every ten years and 'exit charges' whenever there is a distribution of property from the trust. The details of the relevant property regime are outside the scope of this manual as they are not assessed in the SQE.

Also, lifetime transfers to companies (eg private limited companies) will be LCTs.

When an LCT is made, there will be IHT payable (depending on the value of the LCT and the value of any earlier chargeable transfers in the seven years before the LCT). Above a certain value, the rate on IHT on an LCT is 20 per cent.

Whilst this might seem relatively straightforward, the amount of tax paid will depend on whether the transferor or the transferee pay the tax. Also, if the transferor dies within seven years of making the LCT, there will be a recalculation of IHT. We will now consider these points.

### 6.4.2.1 Grossing up

As mentioned earlier, the value transferred is the amount by which the transferor's estate is reduced by the disposition. The transferor is primarily liable for any IHT due on an LCT, but the transferee can pay. Usually it is the transferee who pays the IHT out of the property which has been received. As most LCTs are transfers to trusts, the transferees are usually the trustees of the trust set up by the transferor.

Where the transferee pays the IHT, the loss to the transferor's estate is limited to the value of the gift itself. However, if the transferor pays the IHT due on an LCT then the loss to the transferor's estate will be the total of the gift *plus* the IHT which is due on the transfer.

The value of the gift must then be '**grossed up**' to find the value transferred. If the transferor is paying the IHT, then the property gifted is generally described as the 'net chargeable transfer' and the loss to the transferor's estate is described as the 'gross chargeable transfer', being the net chargeable transfer *plus* the attributable tax.

The steps to follow when grossing up a transfer are:

1 Calculate the net chargeable transfer (NCT).

2 Calculate the amount of the NCT that is taxable at 20 per cent (this will be the amount of the NCT that exceeds the 'nil rate band'—see **6.8** on rates of tax for more detail).

3 Calculate the IHT payable. The formula to use is:

   *IHT* = ¼ × *amount of NCT which is taxable at 20%*

4 Calculate the gross chargeable transfer (GCT). This is done by adding the net chargeable transfer to the IHT payable: *NCT* + *IHT* = *GCT*. This is the loss to the transferor's estate.

This is very difficult to understand without an example.

**EXAMPLE**

Hussain creates a discretionary trust during his lifetime and transfers property to the trust. This is an LCT. The net chargeable transfer is £100,000. The whole of the £100,000 is taxable at 20 per cent (due to Hussain having made earlier chargeable transfers).

If the trustees of the trust pay the IHT, the IHT will be £100,000 × 20% = £20,000.

However, if Hussain pays the IHT, the tax will have to be grossed up. One-quarter of £100,000 is £25,000.

So, if Hussain pays the IHT, the IHT charge will be £25,000 (£5,000 more than if the trustees had paid IHT).

The gross chargeable transfer will be £125,000 (£100,000 + £25,000).

Should the transferor make other gifts or die within the next seven years, the *gross* chargeable transfer (not the net chargeable transfer) must be brought forward as part of the 'cumulative total' (see **6.9** on the process of cumulation).

### 6.4.2.2 The charge to tax where the transferor dies within seven years of the LCT

If the transferor survives by seven years from the date of the LCT, there will be no recalculation of tax and there is no further IHT to pay.

However, if the transferor dies within seven years of making the LCT, then the tax on the LCT is recalculated, using the main death rate of IHT of 40 per cent. This may result in more IHT being payable on the LCT. Also, as a result of the deceased's death, other lifetime transfers which were originally PETs may now have become chargeable. If any of these were in the seven years prior to the LCT, this will also affect the amount of additional IHT payable on the LCT (because the 'cumulative total' of the LCT will have changed).

So, in addition to the initial tax charge on an LCT when it is made, there may be a second, retrospective tax charge when the transferor dies.

**EXAMPLE**

Ruth creates a trust during her lifetime and transfers £400,000 (after exemptions and reliefs) to the trust. At the time she made the LCT, she had made no previous chargeable transfers, although she had given £325,000 to her daughter, Bella, a year earlier. That gift to Bella would have been a PET so no IHT is due (yet) on the PET.

IHT is due on the LCT of £400,000 to the trust, though. The first £325,000 of the LCT is within the 'nil rate band' and is 'taxed' at 0 per cent. The remaining £75,000 is taxed at 20 per cent, and so the IHT is £15,000. This is because the transferees, namely the trustees of the trust, paid the IHT. The IHT charge would have been more if Ruth (the transferor) had paid the IHT.

Ruth dies within seven years of making the LCT (and within seven years of making the PET to Bella).

The IHT on the LCT must be recalculated. First, the cumulative total of the LCT has changed, because as a result of Ruth's death there is now another chargeable transfer in the seven years before the date of the LCT (the gift to Bella, which was a PET but is now chargeable).

This has the effect of using up the nil rate band of £325,000. Although no IHT will be payable on the gift to Bella, there is no nil rate band left to set against the LCT. The whole of the LCT of £400,000 is taxable, and at the death rate of 40 per cent. The tax charge will be £160,000.

Assuming the trustees pay the IHT, they will have a credit for the £15,000 already paid and will now have to pay £145,000 (£160,000 – £15,000) to HMRC.

Sometimes, however, there will no additional tax payable when the transferor dies within seven years of making the LCT. This is because of **taper relief** (see **6.8.2.4**), which may mean that the recalculated charge to IHT is less than (or no more than) the amount of IHT paid on the LCT in the first place.

However, it is not possible to reclaim any of the IHT paid on the LCT initially—this money is lost and cannot be recovered from HMRC.

**EXAMPLE**

The above example was deliberately vague on dates but to change the facts let us assume that Ruth died six years and one month after the LCT, and seven years and one month after the gift to Bella.

The initial tax charge on the LCT (£15,000) would be exactly the same as earlier.

However, the recalculation of tax would differ markedly. First, the gift to Bella was a PET and Ruth survived the PET by seven years. It has now become exempt, and so does not affect the recalculation of tax on the LCT.

Applying the death rates to the LCT of £400,000, the first £325,000 will be at 0 per cent, and the remaining £75,000 would be at 40 per cent, leading to IHT of £30,000. But IHT taper relief also applies (see **6.8.2.4**) and only 20 per cent of this £30,000 (ie £6,000) would be payable. This is less than the £15,000 tax paid initially on the LCT, so no further IHT is now payable on the LCT as a result of Ruth's death. However, the trustees of the trust cannot reclaim the difference between the £15,000 paid and the new calculation of £6,000 (ie they cannot recover the £9,000 difference from HMRC).

It is possible that the value of the property transferred by the LCT may go down between the date of the gift and the date of the transferor's death. If this is the case, then usually the lower (date of death) value is used to calculate the additional tax payable (s131 IHTA 1984). The lower value is only used to calculate the additional charge to IHT as a result of the donor's death. The original value at the date of the LCT is used in all other calculations, for example the calculation of the donor's 'cumulative total'.

## 6.4.3 Gifts subject to a reservation

A gift of property is subject to a reservation if, after gifting the property, some benefit is still enjoyed or retained by the transferor.

It would be tempting under the IHT legislation for the transferor to give away property to another individual but to continue to retain an interest in it. That way, the property would not form part of the transferor's estate liable to IHT on death. Also, provided the transferor survived seven years from the date of the gift, the property would escape IHT altogether. Even if the transferor died within seven years of making the gift, then no more IHT would be payable on the death than would have been paid had the gift not been made.

A good example of a gift where a benefit is retained would be a parent who makes a gift of a holiday home to a child but continues to use the holiday home frequently throughout the year without paying any rent to the child.

There are rules to prevent taxpayers trying to avoid IHT in this way (s102 Finance Act 1986). These rules provide that if the property is still subject to a reservation at the transferor's death, then the value of the property at the date of death will be aggregated with the value of the transferor's estate. In other words, the value of the property will be taxed alongside the transferor's estate on death. For IHT purposes, it is as if the transferor had not given the property away at all, and the attempt to avoid IHT being paid on the property will have failed.

### 6.4.3.1 The possibility of double taxation

Even if a gift is treated as a gift subject to a reservation, the original gift of the asset will also be a lifetime transfer (an LCT or a PET, depending on the recipient of the gift). If the original gift was made in the seven years preceding the transferor's death, IHT or additional IHT may be payable on the original gift as a result of the death. This IHT on the original lifetime transfer is in addition to the IHT payable on the gifted property at the date of death when it is aggregated with the death estate. There is thus a possibility of double taxation—the same property is being taxed as a chargeable transfer during the deceased's lifetime and being taxed again on the deceased's death because it is gifted property subject to a reservation.

If, in the earlier example of the gift of a holiday home, the parent was still enjoying visits to the property at the time of death, which was six years after the original gift, the original PET would become chargeable as a result of the death. In addition, the value of the property would also be aggregated with the value of the parent's estate at the date of death. There would therefore be a double charge to IHT.

As the making of a gift with a reservation can result in a double charge to IHT, there are provisions in the legislation giving some relief for this.

### 6.4.3.2 Where the reserved benefit is released before death

If the reservation in the gifted property ceases before death, then the transferor will be treated as making a PET on the date the reservation ceases. In the earlier example, if the parent ceased using the holiday property five years after having made the original gift, there would be a PET at the date the parent stopped using it. The value of the PET would be the value of the property at that date. If the parent died one year after ceasing to use the property, both PETs would become chargeable as they would have been made in the seven years preceding the parent's death, so there could still be an element of double taxation but there are provisions in the legislation giving some relief.

### 6.4.3.3 Legitimate methods of avoiding a gift with a reservation

Due to the very serious consequences noted above, care should be taken to avoid giving advice to a client which could result in a gift with a reservation being made.

However, there are legitimate ways to avoid there being a reservation of benefit in a gifted asset, such as the transferor paying market rent when continuing to live in a house that has been given away. The detail of this and of other aspects of inheritance tax planning are outside the scope of the SQE and of this manual.

### 6.4.4 Incidental expenses of transfer and capital gains tax

There may be expenses incurred in connection with the gift or a sale at an undervalue (eg legal costs). There may also be a liability to **capital gains tax** (CGT) as well as to IHT. The rules for deduction of expenses or CGT from the value transferred are as follows:

- if the expenses or CGT are paid by the transferor, they do not reduce the value transferred;
- if they are paid by the transferee, they reduce the value transferred.

## 6.5 Transfers on death

Let us now consider the transfer of value on death in more detail. You will recall that the transfer on death is a deemed transfer of the deceased's 'estate', and that this deemed transfer is assumed to be of the estate 'immediately before death'.

What, though, is meant by the 'estate'?

Section 5 of the IHTA 1984 provides that, subject to some exceptions, 'a person's estate is the aggregate of all the property to which he is beneficially entitled'. What then does this mean? What is the deceased 'beneficially entitled' to 'immediately before' death?

### 6.5.1 What is included in the estate for IHT

It is very important to realise that the person's 'estate' for IHT is wider than the 'estate' for succession purposes.

#### 6.5.1.1 Assets passing independently of the will or rules of intestacy

The estate for succession purposes means everything that the deceased can leave by will, and which will be distributed in accordance with the rules of intestacy in default of a will.

As we have seen in the earlier chapters, for succession purposes the estate does not contain such property as the interest of a joint tenant in equity (which passes automatically by survivorship to the other joint tenant(s)) or the subject of a valid **donatio mortis causa** (which passes direct to the intended beneficiary of the gift). However, such property *is* owned beneficially by the deceased immediately before their death, and so *is included* in the estate that is subject to IHT.

A mistake made commonly by students is to assume that such property, for example the interest of a joint tenant in equity, is not subject to IHT on a person's death, when in fact it is subject to IHT. However, often no IHT will be payable on the interest of a deceased joint tenant, because the surviving joint tenant is often the spouse or civil partner, but the reason no IHT is payable in those cases is because of the IHT exemption for transfers between spouses and civil partners (discussed in **6.7.1.1**). If the surviving joint tenant was, say, an unmarried cohabitant, then there would be no spouse/civil partner exemption and the interest of the deceased joint tenant would be subject to IHT.

#### 6.5.1.2 Settled property

The deceased's estate also includes the value of certain interests which the deceased had in settled property (ie an interest in a trust). We have already seen, in **6.3.3**, that '**remainder**' interests are excluded property. What we are concerned with here, therefore, is 'interests in possession' that the deceased had in settled property. An example of a deceased having an interest in possession is where the deceased was the sole life tenant of a will trust. An 'interest in possession' is defined as 'the present right to the present enjoyment' of the trust property. A life tenant of a **life interest** trust has the right to the annual 'income' generated by the trust assets but is not entitled to the underlying 'capital' (the underlying assets themselves, ie the assets that generate the income).

Although a beneficiary of an interest in possession does not own the underlying capital, historically there was a rule which said that for IHT purposes (but not for other purposes) the beneficiary would be treated 'as if' they owned the underlying capital. The effect of this was that if a person with an interest in possession died, the value of the underlying trust assets would be aggregated with the value of their death estate, for the purposes of calculating IHT.

**EXAMPLE**

Michael died in 2005. In his will he left a life interest in his estate to his son, Kyle, with remainder interests to Kyle's children, Betty and Holly, after Kyle's death.

Kyle therefore has an interest in possession in the trust that Michael created, and will be entitled to the income that is produced by the trust assets during his (ie Kyle's) lifetime.

Kyle dies in May 2024, at which point the capital value of the trust fund is £4 million. Kyle will be treated for IHT purposes as if he had owned the underlying capital, so the £4 million value of the trust fund will be aggregated with the value of Kyle's own estate on Kyle's death.

However, there were major changes to the IHT rules in 2006. The detail of most of these changes are outside the scope of this manual as they relate to the IHT treatment of trusts, which is not part of SQE. The changes date from 22 March 2006 (the reason for this odd date is that this was the date of the annual government budget in 2006). The effect of the changes for present purposes is that, for most new interests in possession, the beneficiary is not treated as if they own the underlying capital for IHT purposes. This means that the deeming rule (that a beneficiary of an interest in possession is treated as if they own the underlying capital) now only applies to certain interests in possession.

This deeming rule only now applies to the following categories of interests in possession:

- interests in possession already in existence before 22 March 2006 (eg Kyle's life interest in the above example);
- transitional serial interests—where, on or before 5 April 2008, an interest in possession arises on the ending of another interest in possession that was in existence before 22 March 2006;
- an immediate post-death interest in possession trust (eg an interest in possession trust created in the will of the deceased which begins immediately after the **testator**'s death);
- the interest in possession of a disabled person in a disabled person's trust.

It follows that with any other interest in possession (eg an interest in possession created in a lifetime trust on or after 22 March 2006), the value of the underlying trust assets will not be liable to IHT on the death of the beneficiary. (This is because another IHT regime, the relevant property regime, applies and the relevant property regime provides for different methods of charging IHT.)

**EXAMPLE**

In the previous example, Kyle's interest in possession was created before 22 March 2006 and so is one of the categories of interest in possession where the 'old' IHT rules apply.

However, even if Michael had died on or after 22 March 2006, the IHT treatment would be the same and the £4 million value of the trust fund would be aggregated with Kyle's estate on Kyle's death. This is because the interest in possession would qualify as an immediate post-death interest in possession.

If, though, Michael had made a trust during his lifetime (and did this on or after 22 March 2006) the 'old' IHT rules would not apply on Kyle's death so the £4 million trust fund would not be aggregated with Kyle's own estate. Instead, the trust would qualify as a 'relevant property trust' and would be taxed according to the relevant property regime.

### 6.5.1.3 Gifted property subject to a reservation

Also aggregated with the deceased's estate will be the value of any property subject to a reservation of a benefit (see **6.4.3**). The value of that gifted property at the date of death (not at the date of the gift) is taken into account.

**EXAMPLE**

Sergey dies in June 2024. Ten years earlier he transferred the title to his house (which was then worth £600,000) to his daughter, Jayne, although Sergey continued to live in the house. At the date of Sergey's death, the house was worth £750,000.

The gift of the house to Jayne was a gift subject to a reservation and Sergey has continued to reserve a benefit in the property until his death.

The value of the house at the date of his death (£750,000) will be aggregated with the value of his own estate and will be subject to IHT.

## 6.5.2 **What is excluded from the estate for IHT**

However, some types of property are both outside the estate for succession purposes and outside the estate for IHT purposes.

So, any payment from an occupational pension scheme on the death, that is made solely at the discretion of the pension scheme trustees, is not part of the estate for succession purposes and is also not part of the estate for IHT purposes.

The reason why it is not included as part of the estate for IHT purposes is, quite simply, that the deceased was not 'beneficially entitled' to the pension scheme payment immediately before death. This is because the pension scheme payment is discretionary—the deceased had no entitlement to the payment. In other words, the deceased, and the deceased's personal representatives, cannot demand the payment as of right. The payment is wholly at the discretion of the pension scheme trustees, and the trustees might decide not to make the payment.

The other example of property that is not part of the IHT estate is the death benefit paid by a life assurance company on a life assurance policy that is written in trust. As the policy proceeds are payable to specified beneficiaries, those beneficiaries are beneficially entitled to the policy proceeds, not the deceased.

The effect of this is beneficial for the persons inheriting on the death of the deceased, because quite sizeable assets (occupational pension scheme benefits and the proceeds of life policies written into trust) will escape IHT altogether.

**EXAMPLE**

Aaron died recently. He lived with his long-term partner, Cathy, and their young children, Joshua and Sophie. Aaron and Cathy were not married. Aaron and Cathy owned their house jointly, as joint tenants in equity. Aaron's share of the house was worth £250,000.

Aaron was also a member of his employer's occupational pension scheme. Under the scheme's rules, the trustees have a discretion to make a payment of three times salary on the death of a pension scheme member. Aaron's salary was £50,000 and so the possible payment from the scheme is £150,000. The trustees indicate they will exercise their discretion and make a payment of £150,000 to Cathy.

Aaron had also insured his life for £100,000. The life policy is written in trust for his two children, Joshua and Sophie.

Aaron's £250,000 share of the **joint property** will be included in his estate for IHT purposes. However, both the pension scheme payment of £150,000 and the life policy proceeds of £100,000 will not form part of the IHT estate, because Aaron was not beneficially entitled to either payment.

We have also seen, in **6.3.3**, that certain types of 'excluded property' are not subject to IHT, even though the deceased was beneficially entitled to that property.

### 6.5.3 Liabilities and expenses

So far we have only considered the value of assets, but it is possible to deduct liabilities and expenses from the 'gross' value of the estate to work out a 'net' value of the estate. It is the net value that is taxed.

Liabilities will include any debts that the deceased owed at the date of their death. This could be relatively minor amounts, such as small credit card bills or 'utilities' bills (gas, electricity, water, telephone, broadband and other media). There could also be sizeable liabilities (such as any mortgages on property, although often there will be some form of life assurance that will pay off a person's mortgage debt).

There are rules which prevent the deduction of certain liabilities (eg debts artificially created) but the details are outside the scope of this manual.

Expenses will include reasonable funeral expenses and mourners' expenses (ie the cost of a reception for mourners after the funeral) and a gravestone or tombstone. However, general administration expenses (eg the cost of employing a solicitor to undertake the legal work necessary to administer the estate) cannot be deducted for IHT purposes.

## 6.6 Valuation

Inheritance tax is a tax on value. The more valuable a chargeable transfer, the more IHT is payable. We will see that there is an initial tax rate of 0 per cent (see **6.8**), but above that IHT is charged at a flat rate of, usually, 40 per cent. So, it is very important to HMRC that correct values are established for assets which have been transferred. For every extra £1 of value, there will be an extra 40 pence of IHT going into government coffers!

It is very easy to establish the value of some assets. For example, the value of a person's savings in a bank or building society account when they die can be determined very easily by finding out the balance on that account at the date of death (and adding the amount of any accrued interest on the account up to the date of death). This information is easily obtained from the bank or building society and there is not likely to be any dispute over the value.

Similarly, the death benefit payable on a life assurance policy will be certain—the life assurance company will be able to confirm the relevant figure.

So, the value of many assets will be clear.

### 6.6.1 Market value

The relevant value for many other assets will be 'market value' at the date of the transfer (s160 IHTA 1984). What is market value? Essentially, it is what it is thought the asset would be sold for if it was sold on the open market at the date of the transfer.

The market value of quoted shares that are listed on the London Stock Exchange can be found very easily, as the value is determined by reference to share prices that are public and are readily available. (The valuation rule for quoted shares is that the value is found by taking the lowest listed value for the day of death or nearest day on which stock prices are published, plus one-quarter of the difference between the lowest price and the highest price).

However, there are other assets where there will be no public record that provides an objective value for the asset. This will apply to land and buildings owned by the transferor, to the transferor's personal possessions and to any unquoted shares (shares not listed on a recognised stock exchange or other market).

In the case of these assets, a valuation will have to be obtained from someone who is qualified or experienced to provide a professional opinion as to value. So, land and buildings might be valued by a surveyor or an estate agent. Personal possessions might be valued by an auctioneer. Unquoted shares might be valued by an accountant.

Remember that the transfer of value on death is of everything the deceased was beneficially entitled to *immediately before* death. So, in this case, assets are to be valued at their market value *immediately before* death. This date-of-death value is often referred to as the '**probate** valuation'.

## 6.6.2 Joint property

When an individual has only a share in an asset, it is more difficult to sell the share than it would be to sell the whole. To take account of this difficulty, the value of the individual's share in the asset is reduced by between 10 and 15 per cent. For example, Joan and Ruth own a house as **tenants in common** in equal shares. The house has a market value of £640,000. The value of Joan's share in the property for IHT purposes is in the region of £288,000 (one half of the property is worth £320,000; 10 per cent of this is £32,000 and so the discount leaves a value of £288,000).

This can be an advantage to the transferor if the transferor's share in a property is gifted to another or the transferor dies; the loss to the transferor's estate is smaller because of the discount.

When the joint owner is the transferor's spouse or civil partner, the related property rules apply and no discount is given (see **6.6.3**).

## 6.6.3 Related property

Some assets are worth more when valued together as a set than they would be if they were owned by more than one person. Six dining chairs could be worth £3,600 as a set, giving an individual value of £600. However, if they are not kept as a set the value of each chair would be only £200, giving a total value of only £1,200. A transferor could use this to their advantage. For example, Mr Evans owns a pair of antique side tables. The market value of the pair is £50,000 but if they were separated they would each be worth only £15,000. Mr Evans wants to give the side tables to his daughter. If he made a gift to her of the pair then he would have made a PET of £50,000 (ignoring any exemptions or reliefs). However, if Mr Evans were to give away one of the side tables to his wife, the loss to his estate would be £35,000 (£50,000 less £15,000, being the value of the side table he retained). As the gift was to his wife, it would be exempt for IHT purposes (see **6.7.1.1**). Mr Evans could then gift the remaining side table to his daughter; this would be a PET of £15,000 as the side table is no longer one of a pair and so has a lower value. His wife could gift the side table she received to their daughter, also making a PET of £15,000. The potential liability to IHT is therefore smaller than it would have been had Mr Evans made the gift to his daughter of both of the side tables.

Section 161 of the IHTA 1984 prevents transferors from avoiding IHT in this way. Property in one spouse's estate is related to property in the other spouse's estate. Where any property in one spouse's estate would be worth more if valued together with related property in the other spouse's estate, the property is valued as a proportion of the related property valued together.

This means that, on the facts of Mr Evans above, when he makes the gift of one side table to his daughter, the side table is valued with the side table in his wife's estate, as the related property rules apply, and so the loss to his estate is ½ × £50,000 = £25,000, rather than £15,000.

Shareholdings are a good example of assets affected by the related property rules. The related property rules apply mainly to property in the estates of spouses or civil partners, but the rules do cover other situations where the transferor makes gifts to other exempt transferees, for example charities, and stands to benefit from a similar tax advantage.

Section 176 of the IHTA 1984 gives some relief to the related property rules. If property in the deceased's estate is valued as related property and is sold within three years of the date of death, then, provided the sale meets the conditions set out in the section, s 176 of IHTA 1984 allows the property to be revalued without it being treated as related property. This means that the lower value can be substituted for IHT purposes.

## 6.6.4 Value immediately before death

As said earlier, s4 of the IHTA 1984 states that 'the value transferred is the value of the deceased's estate immediately *before* death'. However, some assets are valued immediately *after* death in order that any changes in the value of the asset by reason of the death can be taken into account. Section 171 of the IHTA 1984 provides that changes in the value of the estate which have occurred by reason of the death are to be taken into account as if they had occurred before the death.

One example of how this provision works is a life policy. Where the deceased has taken out a life policy and the proceeds to be paid out on death form part of the estate, it is the policy proceeds which are taxable, even though the proceeds are not due immediately before death; they are only due as a result of the death and the insurance company does not in fact pay out until after death. However, as a result of s171, the policy proceeds are taken into account as if they had been payable before death and so therefore are deemed to be something that the deceased was beneficially entitled to immediately before death.

Another example is the loss of 'goodwill' in a business. Where the deceased was a proprietor of a business, it will frequently be the case that the business will suffer as a result of the deceased's death through loss of goodwill (because customers associate the business with the proprietor and may be less inclined to do business with a new owner). Consequently, the value of the business will fall. The legislation permits this factor to be taken into account when valuing the business at the date of death.

### 6.6.5 Sale of land within four years of death

The usual market value rules apply to land held in a deceased's estate. However, if an interest in land is sold within four years of the date of death for less than the probate value, the lower value can, in certain circumstances, be substituted for the probate value (ss190–198 IHTA 1984).

### 6.6.6 Sale of qualifying shares within 12 months of death

Again, the usual market value rules apply to shares held in a deceased's estate. If the shares are shares in a company which is quoted on a recognised stock exchange or holdings in an authorised unit trust (qualifying shares) and are sold within 12 months of the date of death for less than the probate value, the lower value can, in certain circumstances, be substituted for the probate value (ss178–189 IHTA 1984). When calculating the overall loss to the estate by virtue of the qualifying shares being sold for less than the probate value, it is the aggregate, or net, loss to the estate taking into account the proceeds of sale of all qualifying shares sold during the 12 months.

## 6.7 Exemptions and reliefs

We have already seen that some types of property are not subject to IHT because they are excluded property (**6.3.3**) and that some transfers are not considered transfers of value for the purposes of IHT (**6.3.4**). Also, we will see when looking at the rates of tax in **6.8** that the first rate of tax applied is 0 per cent, and the application of that 0 per cent rate (on the various nil rate bands) acts like an exemption, even though it isn't officially an exemption, but is a rate of tax.

In this section we will consider other reasons why the IHT charge may be extinguished or reduced, by considering exemptions and reliefs from IHT.

Taking exemptions first, part or all of a transfer of value may be exempt from IHT due to one or more of the available exemptions from IHT. These are applied at Step 2 of the calculation, and are considered in **6.7.1**.

In addition, there are a number of reliefs, which operate in different ways. Some reliefs (eg business property relief) operate by reducing the value of particular items of property owned by the transferor. Other reliefs, though, operate like exemptions and mean that all of a transfer is not charged to IHT. Reliefs are normally applied at Step 3 of the calculation, and are considered in **6.7.2**.

### 6.7.1 Exemptions

A transfer of value made by an individual will not be a chargeable transfer if it is an exempt transfer. There are a number of exemptions available; some cause the whole transfer to be exempt, while others cause part of the transfer to be exempt with the remainder of the transfer being a chargeable transfer or a PET.

The transfer of value may qualify for exemption by virtue of the fact that it is a disposition to an exempt transferee (these are applicable on lifetime dispositions *and* on death) or because it comes within one of a number of limited *lifetime* transfers which qualify for exemption.

The full range of exemptions can be found in Part II of the IHTA 1984, although the main exemptions are mentioned in this section.

### 6.7.1.1 Exemptions which apply to lifetime transfers and to the estate on death

The exemptions which are available for both lifetime transfers and the estate on death depend upon the nature of the transferee. Put another way, these exemptions are given based on the special nature of the recipient of the gift or transfer.

The effect of these exemptions is that everything that is given to the particular transferee is exempt from inheritance tax, regardless of how much is transferred. So, for example, a testator may give their whole estate to charity and it will be exempt from IHT, whether the estate is worth £300,000, £3 million or £3 billion.

The main exemptions are:

1 Transfers between spouses or civil partners (s18 IHTA 1984). Transfers between spouses or civil partners are exempt provided that the gift takes effect immediately. It is common for a spouse or civil partner to state in their will that the estate will pass to the other spouse or civil partner only if the other spouse or civil partner survives for a specified period. As long as the specified period does not exceed 12 months, the spouse or civil partner exemption will still apply. However, there are other reasons, to do with the taxation treatment of trusts, why it is not advisable to have a survivorship period of more than six months. For practical reasons, so that the estate can be administered within a reasonably short period of time, it is preferable to have a shorter survivorship period of, say, 28 days or 30 days. (Even then, care needs to be taken with spouses/civil partners and survivorship periods in wills, as if the spouses/civil partners both die within a short period of time, there may be double payment of any legacies included in the couple's wills (see **Chapter 3**, and the discussion of *Jump v Lister* [2016] EWHC 2160 (Ch) at **3.5.2.3**).) If both the transferor and the spouse or civil partner are domiciled in the UK, there is no limit on the amount of the exemption. However, the exemption is limited if the transferor was domiciled in the UK but the spouse or civil partner was not domiciled in the UK. Currently, the exemption is limited to the nil rate band that applies at the date of the transfer, so for the 2024/25 tax year the exemption is £325,000. It is possible for the non-UK domiciled spouse or civil partner to make an election to be treated as UK domiciled, although this brings with it other tax consequences which should be considered (but which are outside the scope of this manual).
2 Gifts to charities (s23 IHTA 1984).
3 Gifts to political parties (s24 IHTA 1984).
4 Gifts for national purposes (to any of the bodies listed in Sch 3 IHTA 1984, eg the British Museum or the National Museum of Wales) (s25 IHTA 1984)).

There are also exemptions for gifts to other non-profit-making bodies, such as community amateur sports clubs and housing associations.

Lastly, there are conditional exemptions available for property regarded by the Treasury as of national, scientific, historic or artistic interest (Part II, Chap II, IHTA 1984). The taxpayer must give an undertaking to take steps to preserve the property and to secure reasonable access to the public. Tax becomes payable if an undertaking is broken, for example if there is a disposal of the property.

### 6.7.1.2 Exemptions which apply to lifetime transfers only

In addition to the exemptions mentioned above (which apply both to lifetime transfers and to the estate on death), there are other exemptions which apply to lifetime transfers only. One of the most common mistakes made by students is to apply one or more of these exemptions (usually the annual exemption) to the death estate.

#### The annual exemption

The first £3,000 of transfers made by a transferor in any one tax year are exempt (s19 IHTA 1984). Where the transfers of value exceed £3,000, the first £3,000 is taken to be exempt. If the total transfers fall short of £3,000, the unused part of the exemption may be carried forward to the following tax year. However, in the following tax year the £3,000 exemption for that year must be used before the amount brought forward. There is no further carry forward if the amount brought forward cannot be used in the following tax year. The exemption is applied chronologically if there is more than one transfer of value in a tax year. If there are several gifts on one day, the exemption is apportioned among them in proportion to the values transferred.

### Small gifts exemption

A transferor is allowed to make any number of gifts per annum, each of up to £250, provided they are to different people, without affecting the cumulative total (s20 IHTA 1984). The gifts must be outright (ie absolute rather than on trust). The gift itself must be no more than £250—the exemption cannot be used to cover the first £250 of a larger gift, namely if the gift is greater than £250, it is not an exempt transfer under the small gifts exemption.

### Gifts in consideration of marriage or civil partnership

Gifts 'in consideration of' marriage or civil partnership are exempt up to certain limits (s22 IHTA 1984). Basically, we are concerned here with gifts made to the bride and/or groom (or to one or both civil partner). The limits are dependent on the relationship of the donor to the parties to the marriage or civil partnership. If the value of the gift exceeds the limit, the excess is chargeable. The limits are:

- £5,000 if the gift is by a parent of one of the parties to the marriage or civil partnership;
- £2,500 if the gift is by a remoter ancestor of one of the parties to the marriage or civil partnership (eg a grandparent or great-grandparent) or by one of the parties to the marriage or civil partnership; or
- £1,000 if the gift is by any other person (eg a guest).

### Normal expenditure out of income

Transfers of value are exempt if they can be proved to be part of the normal expenditure of the transferor, made out of income and of such a size that, after allowing for all such transfers, the transferor is left with sufficient income to maintain the standard of living which the transferor is used to (s21 IHTA 1984).

One example of expenditure which falls into this exemption is where the transferor takes out a life assurance policy which insures the transferor's own life for the benefit of, say, the transferor's children. When the policy matures (on the death of the transferor), the proceeds of the life policy do not pass through the transferor's estate (and thus do not attract IHT), but instead they go directly to the children. Because the policy is ultimately for the benefit of the children, the transferor is deemed to make a gift to the children every time a premium on the policy is paid. However, the transferor will frequently be able to establish that such a gift does not represent a transfer of value because it can be exempted under the 'normal expenditure out of income' provisions. The transferor is paying the premiums out of income and is left with sufficient income to maintain the transferor's usual standard of living. As the premiums are paid regularly, the payments are part of the transferor's normal expenditure.

A taxpayer, or their estate, must claim the normal expenditure out of income exemption—it is not applied automatically—and it must be shown that the expenditure is out of income and it is something which the taxpayer could afford without affecting their standard of living.

## 6.7.2 **Reliefs**

In this section we will concentrate on two of the IHT reliefs—business property relief (BPR) and agricultural property relief (APR). These reliefs are available both on lifetime transfers and on deemed transfers of value on death.

There are other, less common, reliefs that are referred to briefly in **6.7.2.3**. Those reliefs are not available on some or all lifetime transfers.

Generally, any exemption is deducted before any available relief. However, if the disposition is a lifetime disposition and BPR or APR is available at 50 per cent, the relief is given before deducting the annual and other exemptions. This ensures that the exemptions are maximised.

#### 6.7.2.1 Business property relief

Business property relief (Part V, Chap I, IHTA 1984) operates to reduce the value transferred by a transfer of relevant business property by either 100 per cent (ie no charge to IHT) or 50 per cent.

The following categories of property qualify as 'relevant business property' for BPR:

1 a business or interest in a business, for example the business of a sole proprietor or a partner's interest in a business;

2 shares in an unquoted company;

3 shares in a quoted company, which give the transferor control of the company; or

4 land, buildings, machinery or plant used for the purposes of a business carried on either:
   - by a company (unquoted or quoted) of which the transferor has control; or
   - by a partnership of which the transferor was a partner (NB: in contrast to a company, control of the partnership is not required).

'Quoted shares' are defined as shares which are listed on a recognised stock exchange (eg the London Stock Exchange). A requirement of listing on the London Stock Exchange is that a company should be a public limited company (or plc), although not all plcs are listed on the London Stock Exchange (or on another recognised stock exchange). However, this requirement to be a plc in order to list means that shares in private limited companies (ie companies whose names end in 'Limited' rather than 'plc') will be treated as 'unquoted shares' for the purposes of BPR. Also, shares which are listed on AIM (the Alternative Investment Market), which is the London Stock Exchange's secondary market in shares of smaller companies, are treated as 'unquoted'.

The business (whether a company or not) must essentially be a trading business as opposed to a business that simply deals in or holds investments (eg stocks, shares, land and buildings). This is an important point often overlooked by students.

The reduction in the value transferred is 100 per cent for business property coming within categories (1) and (2) and 50 per cent for business property coming within categories (3) and (4). (NB: it is unlikely that many shareholdings will qualify within category (3) as it is not likely that many individuals will have voting control of a public limited company whose shares are listed on the London Stock Exchange.)

Under the related property rules (see **6.6.3**), holdings of spouses or civil partners are treated as one holding and if their total holding gives control then each of them will be deemed to have control for the purposes of the relief.

To qualify for the relief, the transferor must have owned the 'relevant business property' for two years prior to the transfer.

If the relevant business property is a replacement for other relevant business property, then the relief will be available if the combined period of ownership is two years or more (although the relief is restricted to the value of the original property until the replacement property has been held for two years).

The period of ownership of a spouse or civil partner can be taken into account where the transferor had inherited the business property on the death of the spouse or civil partner.

Also, where a lifetime transfer is made (either a lifetime chargeable transfer or a PET where the transferor does not survive by seven years) and IHT (or additional IHT) becomes payable because the transferor dies within seven years, then the relief is not available unless the property originally transferred (or replacement property which qualifies as relevant business property) is owned by the transferee at the date of the transferor's death (or transferee's death, if earlier).

**EXAMPLE**

At the time of his death Mr Khan was the owner of a building used by an unquoted trading company in which he had a controlling shareholding. The value of the land at the date of his death is £350,000. The shareholding in the company has a value of £450,000.

On his death there is a deemed transfer of value. The shares are relevant property for the purposes of BPR and so BPR is available. Their value transferred is reduced by 100 per cent. The value transferred is nil.

As Mr Khan has a controlling interest in the company, the building is also relevant property for the purposes of BPR and so BPR is available. The value transferred is reduced by 50 per cent. The value transferred is 50 per cent × the value of the buildings at the date of death: 50% × £350,000 = £175,000.

**EXAMPLE**

Mr Tang holds 40 per cent of the shares in an unquoted trading company. Mr Tang gives his holding to his son.

This gift is a PET. Should Mr Tang die within seven years of making the gift then the PET will become a chargeable transfer. The shares are relevant property for the purposes of BPR and so BPR is available. Their value transferred is reduced by 100 per cent. However, Mr Tang's son will have to still own the shares (or replacement business property) at the date of Mr Tang's death, otherwise the relief will be lost. So, if the son has sold the shares at the time of his father's death, BPR will be lost if the son has kept the sale proceeds as cash, but BPR would still be available if the son had invested the sale proceeds in property that qualifies as relevant business property (eg unquoted shares in another company). (Note also that other conditions need to be met to retain BPR in this situation, but the details of this are outside the scope of this manual.)

### 6.7.2.2 Agricultural property relief

Agricultural property relief (APR) (Part V, Chap II, IHTA 1984) is extremely important in rural areas, and an understanding of APR is very important for any solicitor involved in advising the farming community.

APR operates in a similar way to BPR. It reduces the value transferred by a transfer of agricultural property by either 100 per cent (ie no charge to IHT) or 50 per cent.

Agricultural property is defined in the IHTA 1984 and, basically, is agricultural land or pasture and farm buildings occupied for the purposes of agriculture. The latter include 'such cottages, farm buildings and farmhouses, together with the land occupied with them, as are of a character appropriate to the property'. In practice, there is often much dispute between the estate and HMRC over whether a farmhouse or farm building is occupied for the purposes of agriculture or appropriate to the agricultural property: for example, is it of a size and character that is needed for the purposes of a working farm or is it in effect just a house which happens to be sited in the middle of agricultural land?

The agricultural value of the property is taken as the value at which the property would be valued if it was subject to a perpetual covenant prohibiting its use otherwise than as agricultural property. This is to prevent estates from claiming APR for the development value of the farmland (the value of the land if it were sold, say, to housing developers), which could be considerably more than the agricultural value of the same land.

To qualify as agricultural property, the property must have been:

- occupied by the transferor for agriculture throughout the two years immediately before the transfer (there is no condition on the time of ownership: the transferor may have rented the property initially and only purchased the property shortly before selling it—the transferor will still qualify for APR provided the total period of occupation was at least two years); or
- owned by the transferor for seven years before the transfer and occupied by someone for agriculture throughout that seven-year period.

The period of ownership of a spouse or civil partner can be taken into account where the transferor had inherited the agricultural property on the death of the spouse or civil partner.

Relief at 100 per cent is, broadly, available for transfers if:

- the transferor was either the owner or tenant in possession, or the transferor had the right to obtain vacant possession from the tenant within 12 months (by extra-statutory concession, this has been extended to 24 months); or
- the property is let on a tenancy beginning on or after 1 September 1995.

Relief at 50 per cent is available on any other qualifying agricultural property.

As with BPR, where a lifetime transfer is made (either a lifetime chargeable transfer or a PET where the transferor does not survive by seven years) and IHT (or additional IHT) becomes payable because the transferor dies within seven years, then APR is not available unless the property originally transferred (or replacement property which qualifies as relevant agricultural property) is still owned by the transferee at the date of the transferor's death (or transferee's death, if earlier) and the property qualifies for the relief at the date of the transferor's death.

**EXAMPLE**

Joe owns his farm, which he works, and has done so for many years. The agricultural value of his farm is £800,000. If Joe were to gift the farm, or on his death, agricultural property relief at 100 per cent is available. The agricultural value of the farm in Joe's estate is reduced to nil.

### 6.7.2.3 Other reliefs

There are two reliefs which apply only on death and which operate in different ways to BPR and APR. The details of these reliefs are outside the scope of this manual, but in summary:

- It is possible to obtain woodlands relief on land on which trees or underwood are growing but which is not agricultural property (Part V, Chap III, IHTA 1984). Woodlands relief only defers payment of IHT following a death until such time as there is a disposal of part or all of the trees or underwood (whether with or without the land on which they were growing).
- If persons die within five years of a transfer to them (whether on someone's else's death or a lifetime transfer), it is possible to claim a relief that is known as 'quick succession relief' (s141 IHTA 1984). This reduces the tax payable on death according to a scale—the shorter the period of time between the transfer and the death of the transferee, the greater the relief (the relief is 100 per cent if the death is within one year of the transfer).

In addition, there is a series of reliefs which seek to give relief to estates by providing that no IHT will be charged on those estates. Although called reliefs, and although being listed in Part V rather than Part II of the IHTA 1984, these reliefs operate more like exemptions, in that the whole of the estate is free of IHT.

The reliefs apply to the estate on death, to PETs made within seven years of death that would otherwise become chargeable and to the possible second charge to IHT on LCTs made within seven years of death (where normally there would be a recalculation of IHT at the death rates). If there has been an LCT within seven years of death, there is no additional tax charge on the transferor dying, but there is no refund of any tax paid on the LCT when it was made.

The reliefs apply where someone in the relevant category has lost their life or where their life has been shortened due to injuries sustained or disease contracted whilst undertaking their duties. The reliefs apply to the estates of the following persons:

1 a member of the armed forces on active service (s154 IHTA 1984);

2 an emergency responder (eg ambulance crew or fire service personnel) responding to emergency circumstances (s153A);

3 a person targeted and killed or injured due to their status as a police constable or member of the armed forces (155A).

Relief (1) is a longstanding relief, but reliefs (2) and (3) were introduced relatively recently, in 2015 (and with effect for deaths on or after 19 March 2014). Relief (3) was introduced to cover circumstances such as the death of Fusilier Lee Rigby who was murdered in 2013 whilst off duty outside his army barracks, and who had been targeted because he was a soldier. Relief (2) could include a fire officer dying when attending a fire or perhaps a nurse dying as a result of contracting the disease Ebola whilst responding to an epidemic in Africa.

There are other reliefs, not all of which are mentioned here, but one worth mentioning is the relief that removes from tax any 'qualifying payment' to someone who was a victim of persecution during the Second World War, such as a Holocaust survivor (s153ZA). Again, this is relatively new, having been introduced in 2016 in respect of deaths on or after 1 January 2015. Qualifying payments are listed in Sch 5A and include payments from a range of specified funds set up in Germany and elsewhere to compensate victims of the Holocaust.

# 6.8 Rates of IHT

We are going to bypass Step 4 (cumulation) and consider Step 5 (the rates of tax) first. This is because an understanding of the rates of tax (and the existence of the various 'nil rate bands') is essential to understanding cumulation. We will consider the rates of tax in this section, and then look at cumulation in **6.9**.

The rates of IHT are comparatively simple. There is an initial rate of 0 per cent (meaning no tax is payable) on the first portion of the transfer (or on the cumulative total if there have been earlier transfers in the previous seven years). The portion that is covered by the 0 per cent rate is called the 'nil rate band'.

We will see that every person has their own standard nil rate band, but also that the standard nil rate bands of spouses or civil partners can be transferred to the other spouse or civil partner. We will also see that there is another, additional nil rate band, called a '**residence nil rate band**' which applies in particular circumstances and which is also transferable between spouses and civil partners.

To the extent that a chargeable transfer of value exceeds the available nil rate band(s), the excess will be taxed at one of the following three rates:

1 40 per cent on the death estate, and on lifetime transfers made within seven years of the date of death (this will include both PETs which have become retrospectively taxable as a result of the transferor dying, and LCTs made within seven years of death where there is a recalculation of tax due to the transferor's death);

2 20 per cent on LCTs, payable at the time the LCT is made (as said earlier, there may be a recalculation of IHT on the LCT using the rate of 40 per cent if the transferor dies within seven years);

3 36 per cent on the death estate (instead of 40 per cent), provided at least 10 per cent of the net estate has been left to charity.

However, point (1) is a simplification because where tax is payable on PETs which have become chargeable, or more tax is payable on LCTs as a result of death, IHT taper relief may be available to reduce the rate of IHT payable (see **6.8.2.4**).

## 6.8.1 The nil rate bands

As said previously, there is a standard nil rate band and a residence nil rate band, and each of these is transferable between spouses and civil partners. We will look at each in turn.

### 6.8.1.1 The standard nil rate band

The first rate of tax applied to the transfer (or the cumulative total if there have been earlier transfers affecting the position on the current transfer) is 0 per cent. This 0 per cent is applied, currently, to the first £325,000.

Prior to 2010, the standard nil rate band was usually increased each year, normally by a relatively small amount, but there were significant increases in some years (eg in April 1996 the nil rate band increased from £154,000 to £200,000).

However, as part of the austerity measures taken following the economic downturn in the late 2000s (initially by the Conservative/Liberal Democrat coalition government in 2010, and then by the Conservative governments which followed), the nil rate band has been kept at £325,000 since April 2010. The tax year 2020/21 was meant to be the last tax year in which the nil rate band was £325,000. From 6 April 2021 onwards, the nil rate band should have been increased in line with inflation, as measured by increases in the Consumer Prices Index (CPI), rounding up to the nearest £1,000. At least this is what *should* have happened, but due to the current economy the government has decided to keep the nil rate band at £325,000 until and including the 2027/28 tax year.

For the sake of simplicity, a nil rate band of £325,000 is used in all examples in this manual, but bear in mind that the nil rate band before April 2010 was lower, and that it should be higher in future (from 6 April 2028 onwards).

### 6.8.1.2 The transferable nil rate band

For deaths on or after 9 October 2007, a claim can be made to transfer that part of the nil rate band unused on the earlier death of a spouse or civil partner (s8A IHTA 1984, as amended). The relevant death is the death of the second spouse or civil partner—it does not matter if the first spouse or civil partner died before 9 October 2007.

The effect of this is that where the first to die used none of their nil rate band on the first death, the surviving spouse/civil partner has double the nil rate band available on the second death. So, for deaths in the 2024/25 tax year, when the nil rate band is £325,000, the effect of having a standard nil rate band and a transferable nil rate band is that the first £650,000 (£325,000 + £325,000) of the cumulative total will be subject to 0 per cent (and so free of tax).

If part of the nil rate band had been used on the first death, a proportion of the nil rate band at the date of the second death is available on the second death. So, if the first spouse/civil partner to die had used 40 per cent of their nil rate band, the estate of the second spouse/partner could have a transferable nil rate band of 60 per cent of the current nil rate band, in addition to 100 per cent of their own nil rate band.

**EXAMPLE**

Lorna dies on 1 July 2024. Lorna was married to Francis who died in August 2007.

When Francis died, he left everything he owned to Lorna, with the exception of a car, worth £30,000, which Francis left to their son, Jeremy.

As there was a transfer between spouses, the exemption in s18 of the IHTA 1984 would have applied to make most of Francis' estate (everything but the car) exempt from IHT. The gift of the car to the son, Jeremy, would not have been exempt from IHT but it would have been covered by part of Francis's nil rate band so no IHT would have been payable.

As a result of giving the car to his son, Francis used £30,000 (or 10 per cent) of his nil rate band (which, when he died in the 2007/2008 tax year, was £300,000, not £325,000). Put another way, 90 per cent of Francis' nil rate band was unused.

On Lorna's death, her personal representatives will be able to use Lorna's own nil rate band of £325,000 and they will be able to claim a transferable nil rate band of 90 per cent of the *current* nil rate band (not 90 per cent of what the nil rate band had been at Francis's death). The current nil rate band is £325,000, and 90 per cent of this is £292,500. Ignoring any possible residence nil rate band, the nil rate bands that will apply to Lorna's estate amount to £325,000 + £292,500 = £617,500.

It does not matter that Francis died before 9 October 2007—the rules apply because Lorna has died on or after 9 October 2007.

It is possible that there may be two, or more, unused nil rate bands available for a transfer where the deceased had been married or in a civil partnership more than once in their lifetime (their previous spouses/civil partners having died, rather than there having been a divorce of dissolution). In such circumstances, the maximum that can be transferred is 100 per cent of the nil rate band at the date of death of the surviving spouse or civil partner. So, if Lorna in the above example had remarried after Francis's death but then her new husband had died before her without using his nil rate band, the maximum transferable nil rate band would be £325,000, namely 100 per cent of the current nil rate band.

The other very important point to realise with the transferable nil rate band is that it can only be transferred on the death of the second spouse or civil partner. In other words, it cannot be used to reduce the IHT payable on an LCT when the LCT is made.

However, like the standard nil rate band, the transferable nil rate band is set against the *cumulative total* of the transfers made by the deceased, not just against the deceased's death estate. This means that the standard and transferable nil rate bands will be set against lifetime transfers (such as PETs which have become chargeable retrospectively due to the transferor dying within seven years and any LCTs made in the seven years prior to death) before being set against the death estate.

As a result, the transferable nil rate band could well reduce or eliminate any IHT charge on any PETs that are now chargeable, and reduce or eliminate any *additional* charge to tax on any LCTs.

### 6.8.1.3 The residence nil rate band

For deaths on or after 6 April 2017, an individual is entitled to an additional nil rate band, termed the residence nil rate band (RNRB) (ss8D–8M IHTA 1984). This is available if:

- the individual owned a 'qualifying residential interest' (essentially a home or a share of one), and it is included in their death estate; and
- the individual's qualifying residential interest is 'closely inherited' on their death ('closely inherited' means inherited by direct descendants such as children or grandchildren, or by the spouse or civil partner of a direct descendant).

An estate may also be entitled to the RNRB when an individual no longer has a qualifying residential interest at the date of their death, because they have downsized to a less valuable home or sold or given away their home on or after 8 July 2015, provided:

- the individual's interest would have qualified as a 'qualifying residential interest' at the date of death, had it been retained rather than sold or given away; and
- the individual leaves replacement property or assets of an equivalent value which are 'closely inherited' on their death (again, this means inherited by direct descendants such as children or grandchildren, or by the spouse or civil partner of a direct descendant).

The amount of the RNRB was increased over a number of tax years. For deaths in the tax year 2017/18, the RNRB was £100,000. For deaths in the tax year 2018/19, it increased to £125,000 and for deaths in the tax year 2019/20 to £150,000. For deaths in the 2020/21 tax year, the maximum £175,000 RNRB was available.

From April 2021 onwards, as with the standard nil rate band, the RNRB should have been increased yearly in line with inflation (based again on the CPI), rounded up to the nearest £1,000, but the government decided to fix the RNRB at £175,000 until and including the 2027/28 tax year.

As is the case with the transfer of any unused standard nil rate band (see **6.8.1.2**), any unused RNRB when someone dies can be transferred to the deceased's spouse or civil partner's estate. This can also be done even if the first of the couple died before 6 April 2017, and even though the RNRB was not available at that time.

For estates valued at more than £2 million, the RNRB (and any transferred RNRB) will be gradually withdrawn or tapered away. The RNRB is reduced by £1 for every £2 over £2 million. This taper has also been fixed until and including tax year 2027/28.

## 6.8.2 **The rates of tax above the nil rate band**

Now let us turn our attention to the rates of tax that apply when the nil rate bands have been exhausted or, put another way, to the excess value of the chargeable transfer above the amount of the applicable nil rate band(s).

### 6.8.2.1 The main rate of tax

The main rate of IHT is 40 per cent.

This rate applies to the death estate (unless the relief detailed in **6.8.2.3** applies—ie where 10 per cent of the net estate is left to charity). In addition, the main rate applies to any gifted property which is subject to a reservation (as the value of that property is aggregated with the value of the death estate).

The main rate of 40 per cent also applies to lifetime transfers made within seven years of death. This includes two types of lifetime transfer:

- a PET which has become a chargeable transfer as a result of the transferor dying within seven years of making the PET; and
- an LCT. Although tax (at 20 per cent) may have been paid on the LCT when it was made, there is now a recalculation of IHT (using the main rate of 40 per cent) due to the transferor dying within seven years of making the LCT.

### 6.8.2.2 The rate applicable to lifetime chargeable transfers

The rate applicable to LCTs when they are made is 20 per cent. As said, there may be a recalculation of tax subsequently, using the main rate of 40 per cent, if the transferor dies within seven years of making the LCT.

### 6.8.2.3 The reduced rate where 10 per cent of the net estate is left to charity

Schedule 1A to the IHTA 1984 provides for a reduction of the rate of IHT from 40 per cent to 36 per cent where at least 10 per cent of the net estate goes to charity. The rules for working out whether the relief applies are complex. For the purposes of calculating the percentage of the estate that passes to charity, the estate is divided into three components. The components reflect the different ways in which assets can be owned and are:

1 the survivorship component (ie joint assets passing by survivorship);
2 the settled property component (ie assets in trust);
3 the general component (ie assets owned outright; including a share in joint property held as tenants in common).

Each component can be looked at separately with the reduced rate being applied to the assets falling into the component, provided at least 10 per cent of the total value of the component passes to charity. It is also possible to merge components to maximise the benefit of the 36 per cent rate.

### 6.8.2.4 Taper relief

As a general principle, tax will usually be saved by making a transfer during a person's lifetime rather than on death. If the transferor survives seven years after making the gift, then no tax will be payable on the gift if it was a PET, and tax at only 20 per cent will have been paid if it was an LCT.

Even if death occurs within seven years, the full charge to IHT may be mitigated by taper relief (s7(4) IHTA 1984). Taper relief will reduce the tax payable to a given percentage if the transferor survives the date of the lifetime transfer by at least three years.

| Transferor survives the lifetime transfer by | Percentage of IHT chargeable |
|---|---|
| More than 3 years but not more than 4 years | 80% |
| More than 4 years but not more than 5 years | 60% |
| More than 5 years but not more than 6 years | 40% |
| More than 6 years but not more than 7 years | 20% |

**EXAMPLE**

Javid died recently. Four and a half years before he died, Javid made a large gift to his son. This would have been a PET when made but it has become chargeable retrospectively as Javid has failed to survive the gift by seven years. The IHT payable on the gift would be £100,000 if the main rate of 40 per cent was applied without taking into account any taper relief (NB: *the £100,000 is the amount of the tax not the value of the transfer, which would have been much higher*). However, as Javid made the transfer more than four years but not more than five years before he died, taper relief will apply so that now only 60 per cent of the IHT is payable. The IHT would have been £100,000 so the IHT payable as a result of taper relief is 60 per cent of that, namely £60,000. Put another way, there has been a reduction in IHT of £40,000 as a result of applying the taper relief.

However, it is important to understand that taper relief reduces the IHT attributable to the chargeable transfer, not the value of the chargeable transfer itself. Therefore, taper relief is only applicable if IHT is payable on the chargeable transfer. Also, taper relief does not reduce the IHT payable on the death estate.

IHT will only be payable on the chargeable transfer if the value of the transfer, taking into account the transferor's cumulative total at the date the transfer was made, exceeds the transferor's nil rate band. If the chargeable transfer (taking into account the cumulative total at the date of the gift) does not exceed the nil rate band available at the date of chargeable transfer, no IHT is payable and so taper relief is inapplicable.

**EXAMPLE**

Dennis died recently. Six years and three months before he died, he made a gift of £300,000 to his daughter. The gift would have been a PET when made but it has become chargeable retrospectively as Dennis has failed to survive the gift by seven years. However, Dennis had not used any part of his nil rate band on any earlier chargeable transfers so there was a full nil rate band at the date of making the PET. As the nil rate band (of £325,000) exceeds the value of the gift (£300,000), there is no IHT to pay in respect of the gift. Taper relief is therefore irrelevant.

## 6.9 Cumulation

We are now at Step 4 of the IHT calculation. As said earlier, it made sense to skip over this step and consider the rates of IHT at Step 5 first. This is because a knowledge of the rates of tax (in particular, the various nil rate bands) is vital to an understanding of the significance of cumulation.

It is very important to understand that IHT operates on a cumulative basis. The cumulation period is, effectively, every seven years.

The rate (or rates) of tax applicable to a chargeable transfer depends on the 'cumulative total' of all chargeable transfers made by the transferor in the seven years preceding the transfer currently being charged. (*It is worth re-reading the previous sentence again, several times if necessary, because this is crucial to an understanding of IHT.*)

As a consequence of the cumulation principle, the most recent chargeable transfer is taxed as the top slice of the aggregate of the cumulative total and the chargeable transfer.

Put another way, the cumulative total eats into the nil rate band, and may in fact use up the whole nil rate band, leaving no part of the nil rate band for the most recent transfer. So, for example, if the most recent transfer is of the death estate, and there are lifetime transfers within the seven years prior to death (whether LCTs, or PETs which have become chargeable due to death), the lifetime transfers may use up all of the available nil rate bands, meaning that the whole of the death estate is taxed at 40 per cent.

Cumulation can, though, also affect the IHT payable on lifetime transfers if there have been earlier chargeable transfers within the seven years prior to the date of the lifetime transfer.

In general terms, to calculate the rate (or rates) of tax at which a chargeable transfer is to be taxed, the cumulative total is deducted from the nil rate band. If, after deducting the cumulative total from the nil rate band, there is some nil rate band remaining, then the amount of the transfer equal to the remaining nil rate band is taxed at 0 per cent and the remainder of the transfer is taxed at the rate applicable to the occasion of the charge (20 per cent if an LCT, 40 per cent in most other cases).

It is important to emphasise that the cumulative total is relevant only in determining the rate (or rates) of tax. Once this has been determined, the rate(s) is then applied only to the value transferred by the current chargeable transfer. It is not applied to the cumulative total.

To calculate the transferor's cumulative total at the date of the current transfer, therefore, it is necessary to look back over the seven years preceding the date of the transfer and identify the chargeable transfers, if any, which the transferor made during that period.

This concept of cumulation is one of the most difficult aspects of IHT for students to understand. It can only be understood by considering example calculations, and a number of these follow in **6.10** so you should work through them carefully.

# 6.10 Example calculations of IHT

In this section we have some simple examples of how inheritance tax is calculated, followed by a longer, more detailed example showing the inheritance tax calculation on a death estate.

**EXAMPLE**

Desmond, a bachelor with no children, dies on 1 September 2024 leaving an estate worth £425,000 to his brothers and sisters. No exemptions or reliefs apply. He made no chargeable transfers in the seven years before his death.

The transfer of value here is the estate on death.

**Step 1: calculate the value transferred**
We are given the value of the estate—£425,000. Presumably, this includes everything that he was beneficially entitled to immediately before death.

**Steps 2 and 3: identify exemptions and reliefs**
We are told that none apply.

**Step 4: calculate the cumulative total**
There is no cumulative total as there were no chargeable transfers in the seven years prior to death.

**Step 5: calculate the IHT payable by applying the appropriate rate(s) of tax**
Desmond was a bachelor (ie he never married or entered into a civil partnership), so there is no possibility of a transferable nil rate band. He is leaving his estate to his brothers and sisters. They are not specified relatives for the purposes of the residence nil rate band, so his estate will not have a residence nil rate band. He will just have his own standard nil rate band of £325,000. The whole of that nil rate band is available to set against the death estate, due to there being no cumulative total (ie no chargeable transfers in the seven years before death).

This means the calculation will be a simple one.

**Desmond—IHT on death estate of £425,000**

£325,000 @ 0% = Nil

£100,000 @ 40% = £40,000

So, IHT of £40,000 will be payable by Desmond's personal representatives.

**EXAMPLE**

Nadia, a spinster, gave a gift of £425,000 cash (after exemptions and reliefs) to her brother on 1 September 2022. Nadia dies on 1 September 2024 (her estate passes to her sister). She made no other chargeable transfers in the seven years prior to the gift.

Nadia's estate has fallen in value as a result of the gift, so there has been a transfer of value. It was a PET when it was made in 2022 but has become chargeable as a result of Nadia dying within seven years.

**Step 1, 2 and 3: calculate the value transferred and identify exemptions and reliefs**
We are told that having applied exemptions and reliefs (eg perhaps Nadia has used her annual exemption for this tax year to reduce the transfer by £3,000), the chargeable amount remaining is £425,000.

**Step 4: calculate the cumulative total**
There is no cumulative total as there were no chargeable transfers in the seven years prior to the making of the gift.

**Step 5: calculate the IHT payable by applying the appropriate rate(s) of tax**
Nadia was a spinster (ie she never married or entered into a civil partnership), so there is no possibility of a transferable nil rate band. No residence nil rate band applies as the gift was a lifetime one

and was of cash—also, the residence nil rate band would not apply to the death estate as Nadia's death estate passes to her sister.

Looking at the tax on the lifetime gift, the whole of the £325,000 nil rate band is available to set against the PET which has become chargeable, due to there being no cumulative total (ie no chargeable transfers in the seven years before the date of the gift).

This means the calculation will again be a simple one.

**Nadia—effect of death on lifetime transfer (PET) of £425,000**

£325,000 @ 0% = Nil

£100,000 @ 40% = £40,000

So, IHT of £40,000 will be payable on the lifetime transfer.

As we will see in **6.11**, this liability for IHT might be met by the transferee (Nadia's sister) or by Nadia's personal representatives.

Note that Nadia died only two years after making the gift. This means there is no IHT taper relief. If, however, she had lived for longer (but still died within seven years of making the gift), then IHT taper relief would have applied. The relief is greater the longer she lives. For example, if she had survived the gift by more than four years but less than five years, the IHT payable would only be 60 per cent of the £40,000, namely £24,000.

Note that the calculation in this example is solely of the IHT due on Nadia's lifetime transfer, but the lifetime transfer will also affect the amount of IHT due on Nadia's death estate. See the next example for how a lifetime transfer affects the tax on the death estate.

## EXAMPLE

Reuben, a bachelor, made a gift of £100,000 (after exemptions and reliefs) to his nephew, on 1 September 2019. Reuben dies on 1 September 2024, leaving an estate worth £425,000 (after exemptions and reliefs) to his brothers and sisters. He made no other chargeable transfers in the seven years prior to the gift or prior to his death.

There are two transfers of value here.

1. The gift to Reuben's nephew. This is a lifetime transfer. It was a PET when it was made in 2019 but has become chargeable as a result of Reuben dying within seven years. Reuben's estate has fallen in value as a result of the gift, so there is a transfer of value.
2. Reuben's death estate: here there is the usual deemed transfer of value on death.

First, we need to consider the IHT charge on the lifetime transfer and then separately consider the IHT charge on the death estate.

(1) THE TAX CHARGE ON THE LIFETIME TRANSFER

**Steps 1, 2 and 3: calculate the value transferred and identify exemptions and reliefs**
We are told that having applied exemptions and reliefs, the chargeable amount of the lifetime transfer remaining is £100,000.

**Step 4: calculate the cumulative total**
There is no cumulative total as there were no chargeable transfers in the seven years prior to the making of the gift.

**Step 5: calculate the IHT payable by applying the appropriate rate(s) of tax**
Applying the tax rates to that, the £100,000 comes within the nil rate band, so a tax rate of 0 per cent applies, and there is no tax on the £100,000.

**No IHT on the lifetime transfer itself**

£100,000 @ 0% = Nil

Although Reuben survived the gift by five years, IHT taper relief is not applicable as IHT taper relief only works by reducing a tax charge on the lifetime transfer. If there is no IHT charge, as here, then there is nothing for IHT taper relief to reduce.

(2) THE TAX CHARGE ON THE DEATH ESTATE
We then need to calculate IHT separately on the later chargeable transfer, namely on the estate on death.

**Steps 1, 2 and 3: calculate the value transferred and identify exemptions and reliefs**
We are given the value of the estate—£425,000. Presumably, this includes everything that he was beneficially entitled to immediately before death. We are told that exemptions and reliefs have already been taken into account already in reaching the figure of £425,000.

**Step 4: calculate the cumulative total**
There is a cumulative total as there was a chargeable transfer in the seven years prior to death (the gift to his nephew in 2019—this is a PET which has become chargeable).

**Step 5: calculate the IHT payable by applying the appropriate rate(s) of tax**
Reuben is a bachelor so there is no transferable nil rate band, and he has left his estate to brothers and sisters so there is no residence nil rate band.

As for Reuben's own standard nil rate band of £325,000, this will be eroded by the cumulative total (the lifetime gift), which has used up £100,000 of the nil rate band, so only a portion of the nil rate band (the remaining £225,000) it is left to set against the death estate. So, although there was no IHT payable on the lifetime gift, the very existence of the lifetime transfer will increase the IHT charge on the death estate.

**Reuben—effect of lifetime transfer of £100,000 on estate of £425,000**

The IHT on estate will be:

£225,000 @ 0% = Nil

£200,000 @ 40% = £80,000

If Reuben had survived seven years from the gift, then the tax charge on the estate would only be £40,000, namely the same as in the Desmond example earlier.

Note that IHT taper relief will not reduce the tax payable on the death estate. IHT taper relief will only reduce tax which is payable on a lifetime transfer.

Also, you will notice that the entire **burden** of the IHT which has to be paid (£80,000) will fall on the beneficiaries of the death estate (his brothers and sisters), whereas the recipient of the lifetime gift (his nephew) will pay no IHT.

## EXAMPLE

Li, a widower, gave £325,000 (after exemptions and reliefs) to his son on 1 September 2022 and £100,000 (after exemptions and reliefs) to his daughter on 1 September 2023. He dies on 1 September 2024 leaving an estate worth £1,350,000 (after exemptions and reliefs) to his grandchildren. The estate included his house (which is worth £500,000). He made no other chargeable transfers in the seven years prior to either gift or prior to his death. However, his late wife used her full nil rate band when she died in 2019 (by leaving £325,000 to their children), although she left everything else she owned (including her interest in the couple's home) to Li.

This scenario shows the effect of cumulation on lifetime transfers. In Li's situation, he has died within seven years of making two lifetime transfers. Although both lifetime transfers would have been PETs when made, when he died both of them became chargeable transfers.

There are therefore three chargeable transfers here—the two lifetime transfers and the death estate. We need to calculate the tax on each transfer in turn, starting with the earliest.

(1) THE TAX CHARGE ON THE FIRST LIFETIME TRANSFER (THE GIFT OF £325,000 TO THE SON IN SEPTEMBER 2022)

**Step 1, 2 and 3: calculate the value transferred and identify exemptions and reliefs**
We are told that having applied exemptions and reliefs the chargeable amount of the lifetime transfer remaining is £325,000.

**Step 4: calculate the cumulative total**
There is no cumulative total as there were no chargeable transfers in the seven years prior to the making of the gift.

**Step 5: calculate the IHT payable by applying the appropriate rate(s) of tax**
Li does not have a transferable nil rate band because, although he is a widower, his wife used up her full nil rate band on her death. We are considering here the IHT on a lifetime transfer, so the residence nil rate band is not relevant to this calculation (although it will be relevant to the calculation of IHT on the death estate).

Applying Li's own standard nil rate band of £325,000, the value of the lifetime transfer is (just) covered by this, so tax rate of 0 per cent applies, and there is no tax on the £325,000.

**No IHT on the first lifetime transfer (to the son in September 2022)**

£325,000 @ 0% = Nil

(2) THE TAX CHARGE ON THE SECOND LIFETIME TRANSFER (THE GIFT OF £100,000 TO THE DAUGHTER IN SEPTEMBER 2023)

**Step 1, 2 and 3: calculate the value transferred and identify exemptions and reliefs**
We are told that having applied exemptions and reliefs the chargeable amount of the lifetime transfer remaining is £100,000.

**Step 4: calculate the cumulative total**
There is a cumulative total for the gift to the daughter in 2023 as there was a chargeable transfer in the seven years prior to date of the 2023 transfer (ie the gift to his son in 2022).

**Step 5: calculate the IHT payable by applying the appropriate rate(s) of tax**
As said above, Li does not have a transferable nil rate band because although he is a widower, his wife used up her full nil rate band on her death. We are considering here the IHT on a lifetime transfer, so again the residence nil rate band is not relevant to this calculation (although it will be relevant to the calculation of IHT on the death estate below).

Applying Li's own standard nil rate band of £325,000, we will see that none of this is left to set against the second lifetime transfer in 2023 because Li already has a cumulative total of £325,000, due to the earlier chargeable transfer in 2022. Put another way, the 2022 gift to the son has used up Li's nil rate band in its entirety, and so there is no nil rate band left for the second gift to his daughter in 2023. This means that the whole of the 2023 gift will be taxed at the relevant rate of IHT, which is 40 per cent for lifetime transfers made within seven years of death.

**IHT on the second lifetime transfer (to the daughter in September 2023)**

£100,000 @ 40% = £40,000

As we will see in **6.11**, this liability for IHT might be met by the transferee (Li's daughter) or by Li's personal representatives.

However, the burden of the IHT falls entirely on the recipient of the second gift, namely the daughter. She will end up keeping only £60,000 out of £100,000 after she pays the IHT, whereas the son gets to keep the whole £325,000, without paying any IHT.

(3) THE TAX CHARGE ON THE DEATH ESTATE
We then need to calculate IHT separately on the third chargeable transfer, namely on the estate on death.

**Steps 1, 2 and 3: calculate the value transferred and identify exemptions and reliefs**
We are given the value of the estate—£1,350,000. Presumably, this include everything that he was beneficially entitled to immediately before death. We are told that exemptions and reliefs have already been taken into account in reaching the figure of £1,350,000.

**Step 4: calculate the cumulative total**
There is a cumulative total as there are two chargeable transfers in the seven years prior to death (the gift of £325,000 to Li's son in 2022 and the gift of £100,000 to Li's daughter in 2023, both of which were PETs which have become chargeable). Li's cumulative total is therefore £425,000.

**Step 5: calculate the IHT payable by applying the appropriate rate(s) of tax**
Li was married, but there is no transferable nil rate band because Li's wife used her nil rate band on her death. Li's own standard nil rate band has been used up by the cumulative total (in fact, as we have seen, it was used up by the first of the two lifetime transfers, the gift to the son in 2022).

There is, however, a residence nil rate band (because Li's house has been left to his direct descendants) and there is a transferable residence nil rate band because Li's wife didn't use her residence nil rate band on her death. Li's combined residence nil rate bands amount to £350,000 (2 × £175,000). Note, though, that the residence nil rate band is deducted from the value of the residence (whereas the standard nil rate band is deducted from the estate as a whole), so the residence has to be worth at least £350,000 for the full residence nil rate bands to be applied. Here, the residence is worth £500,000 so the full residence nil rate bands of £350,000 can be used.

**Li—IHT on death estate of £1,350,000**

£350,000 @ 0% = Nil

£1,000,000 @ 40% = £400,000

## EXAMPLE

Orla transfers £425,000 (after exemptions and reliefs) to a discretionary trust on 1 September 2024. She made no other chargeable transfers in the seven years prior to this transfer.

The transfer to the discretionary trust will not qualify as a PET. It will therefore be an LCT and IHT is payable immediately on the transfer. Orla's estate has fallen in value as a result of the transfer, so there has been a transfer of value.

**Step 1, 2 and 3: calculate the value transferred and identify exemptions and reliefs**
We are told that having applied exemptions and reliefs the chargeable amount remaining is £425,000.

**Step 4: calculate the cumulative total**
There is no cumulative total as there were no chargeable transfers in the seven years prior to the making of the LCT.

**Step 5: calculate the IHT payable by applying the appropriate rate(s) of tax**
Orla is making a lifetime transfer. She has not died so the transferable nil rate band does not apply, even if she is a widow. Put another way, the transferable nil rate band does not apply to lifetime transfers unless the transferor has died. Also, because she has not died, the residence nil rate band is not relevant. She will, however, have all of her main nil rate band of £325,000 because there is no cumulative total (ie chargeable transfers in the seven years before the date of this transfer).

The rate of IHT on LCTs above the nil rate band is 20 per cent, not 40 per cent.

**Orla—lifetime chargeable transfer (LCT) of £425,000**

£325,000 @ 0% = Nil

£100,000 @ 20% = £20,000

The IHT payable will be £20,000 if the transferees of the LCT (ie the trustees of the discretionary trust) pay the IHT out of the £425,000 that they have received.

However, if Orla pays the IHT, she will have to pay more than £20,000 as the IHT will have to be 'grossed up'.

Also, if Orla dies within seven years of making the LCT, the IHT will be recalculated, using death rates, but the trustees would get a credit for the £20,000 already paid. No IHT would be refunded, though if, as a result of IHT taper relief, the amount of recalculated IHT is less than £20,000.

Now let us look at a more detailed example of the calculation of IHT on a death estate.

## EXAMPLE

Martin Jones dies on 1 October 2024. He leaves the following assets (all in his sole name):

| | |
|---|---|
| House | £750,000 |
| Personal possessions (including house contents and car) | £50,000 |
| Bank and building society accounts | £85,000 |
| Portfolio of quoted shares | £240,000 |
| Unquoted shares in a trading company | £300,000 |

He also had taken out a life assurance policy for £75,000 which was written in trust and payable on his death to his grandchildren.

Three years before his death, he gave £100,000 to his adult daughter who was already married.

The cost of his funeral and the reception for the mourners was £5,000.

In his will, Martin Jones left gifts totalling £20,000 to charity and then divided the rest of his estate between his children and grandchildren.

He had been a director and shareholder of a family run company for over 25 years (the value of his shareholding in unquoted shares is listed above).

When his wife died five years ago she left everything to him.

### IHT calculations

There are two chargeable transfers to consider here. As well as the transfer on death, there is the PET (the gifts three years ago to his daughter) which has become chargeable as a result of his death.

(1) THE TAX CHARGE ON THE LIFETIME TRANSFER (THE £100,000 GIFT TO HIS DAUGHTER)

**Step 1: calculate the value transferred**
We are told that the gift was for £100,000. Without more information we can assume that the amount by which his estate has been reduced was £100,000.

**Steps 2 and 3: identify exemptions and reliefs**
Let us assume that Martin Jones had not used his annual exemptions for the tax year in which the transfer was made or for the previous tax year. Working on this assumption (we might have to prove it to HMRC), we can deduct £6,000 from the £100,000, leaving a net chargeable transfer of £94,000. We will assume no other exemptions apply (we are told in particular that the gift was not on the occasion of a marriage or civil partnership, so that particular exemption definitely does not apply). There is nothing to suggest reliefs will apply either.

**Step 4: calculate the cumulative total**
There is no cumulative total as there were no chargeable transfers in the seven years prior to the making of the gift.

**Step 5: calculate the IHT payable by applying the appropriate rate(s) of tax**
Applying the tax rates to that, the £94,000 comes within the nil rate band, so tax rate of 0 per cent applies, and there is no tax on the £94,000.

**No IHT on the lifetime transfer itself**

£94,000 @ 0% = Nil

Taper relief is not applicable as there is no IHT on the lifetime transfer in the first place.

(2) THE TAX CHARGE ON THE DEATH ESTATE
We then need to calculate IHT separately on the later chargeable transfer, namely on the estate on death.

**Step 1: calculate the value transferred**
We are given values for various assets and liabilities, so we need to work out the value of the estate.

Most of the assets listed above are subject to IHT. However, the life policy of £75,000 is not subject to IHT because it is written in trust for the grandchildren, and so Martin Jones was not beneficially entitled to the policy proceeds.

Taking into account the other assets and liabilities, the value of the estate will be:

| | |
|---|---|
| House | £750,000 |
| Personal possessions (including house contents and car) | £50,000 |
| Bank and building society accounts | £85,000 |
| Portfolio of quoted shares | £240,000 |
| Unquoted shares in a trading company | £300,000 |
| Gross estate | £1,425,000 |
| Less: funeral and mourners' expenses | (£5,000) |
| Net estate | £1,420,000 |

**Step 2: identify exemptions**
There is one exemption available—Martin Jones has left £20,000 to charity and so this is deducted from the £1,420,000 to leave a net estate after exemptions of £1,400,000.

**Step 3: identify reliefs**
Business property relief will be available in respect of his shareholding in unquoted shares. The company is a trading company and he has owned the shares for at least two years before death. The value of the shares for IHT purposes will be reduced by 100 per cent. This means we deduct £300,000 from the £1,400,000 to leave a net estate after exemptions and reliefs of £1,100,000.

**Step 4: calculate the cumulative total**
There is a cumulative total as there was a chargeable transfer in the seven years prior to death (the gift to his daughter). The cumulative total is £94,000. Effectively, this means the first £94,000 of his nil rate band is used up.

**Step 5: calculate the IHT payable by applying the appropriate rate(s) of tax**
Martin Jones's wife left everything to him when she died. Her whole estate would have been covered by the IHT exemption for transfers between spouses. As a result, her nil rate band and her residence nil rate band will transfer to him.

Martin Jones's estate will thus have the benefit of two residence nil rate bands (his and his late wife's), so £350,000 can be deducted from the value of the house (and hence from the value of the estate). This will reduce his estate from £1,100,000 to £750,000. The residence nil rate bands are available because his house is passing (as part of his estate) to his direct descendants (children and grandchildren).

His estate will then have his nil rate band of £325,000 and his wife's nil rate band of £325,000, so a total of £650,000. However, the nil rate band is a rate of tax and the rate of tax is applied to the cumulative total. As Martin Jones has a cumulative total of £94,000, only £556,000 of the nil rate band (£650,000 – £94,000) is available to set against his estate.

**Martin Jones—IHT on the death estate**

The IHT on estate (of £750,000) will be:

£556,000 @ 0% = Nil

£194,000 @ 40% = £77,600

This will be the IHT payable by Martin Jones's personal representatives.

## 6.11 Liability, burden and payment of IHT

The question of *liability* concerns who can be required to send to HMRC any IHT that is due. In contrast, the question of *burden* concerns who should ultimately bear the cost of the tax. The question of burden is a matter of no concern to HMRC but is of considerable interest to, for example, the beneficiaries of a deceased's estate.

Typically, IHT payable following a death is collected from the personal representatives (PRs) of a deceased, as the PRs cannot obtain a **grant of representation** until they have paid the IHT due on the death estate. PRs are also liable for IHT in respect of property passing outside the estate (eg joint property passing by survivorship) and certain lifetime transfers (if the person(s) with primary liability fail to pay the IHT within a certain period of time). Whilst the PRs have the right of recovery from beneficiaries of property passing outside the estate, the PRs have no statutory right to recover IHT in respect of lifetime transfers.

In this section we will also consider the due dates for payment of IHT.

Overdue IHT (ie IHT unpaid as at the due date for payment) attracts interest (s233 IHTA 1984). This is with the exception of IHT due on certain assets, where the **instalment option** is such as to defer interest payments (see **6.11.5**).

## 6.11.1 IHT on lifetime chargeable transfers when they are made

IHT due on the value transferred by an LCT normally falls due six months after the end of the month in which the LCT takes place. However, if the LCT occurs between 6 April and 30 September (inclusive) in the tax year, then the IHT is due on 30 April in the following year (s226 IHTA 1984).

The primary liability for IHT in respect of an LCT lies with the transferor (s199). The majority of LCTs will involve the transferor transferring property to trustees. The trustees are also liable for the tax, if the transferor does not pay the IHT by the due date. If the trustees are unable to pay the tax, then HMRC have power to seek payment from persons who have an interest in the settlement.

However, if the transferor pays the IHT the transfer must be grossed up (see **6.4.2.1**) and the amount of IHT will be more than if the trustees had paid the IHT. For this reason, it is usual for the trustees to pay the IHT out of the property they have received, rather than the transferor paying.

The burden of IHT on an LCT will fall on whoever pays the tax (transferor or trustees), although if the trustees pay the IHT, in reality the burden is falling on the beneficiaries of that trust because the IHT paid will come out of the trust fund.

## 6.11.2 Additional tax due on LCTs made within seven years of death

Where a person dies within seven years of making an LCT, additional tax may become payable. If so, this tax is due six months after the end of the month in which death occurred.

The primary liability for this additional tax lies with the transferee (ie the trustees). However, if the tax remains unpaid after the due date, HMRC can seek payment from persons who have an interest in the settlement. As a final recourse, if the tax remains unpaid 12 months after the end of the month of death, HMRC can seek payment from the personal representatives of the transferor's estate. This means that personal representatives must be careful not to distribute the estate until they are satisfied that all such IHT liabilities have been paid. PRs are only liable to the extent of the assets that they have received (or would have received).

Although the burden should fall on the persons who have benefited from the LCT, the personal representatives have no statutory right to recover IHT from those persons.

## 6.11.3 PETs which have become chargeable

IHT falls due six months after the end of the month in which the transferor's death occurs.

The transferee is primarily liable (and bears the burden of the tax). If the tax remains unpaid 12 months after the date of death, then the PRs of the deceased's estate are liable, leaving them to try to recover the tax from those who have primary liability. Again, the PRs must be careful not to distribute the estate until they are satisfied that all such IHT liabilities have been paid. PRs are only liable to the extent of the assets that they have received (or would have received).

Although the burden should fall on the persons who have benefited from the PET, the PRs have no statutory right to recover IHT from those persons.

## 6.11.4 The transfer on death

IHT on death is due six months after the end of the month in which death occurs.

The liability and burden depend on the property bearing the IHT.

### 6.11.4.1 The deceased's free estate

The PRs are liable for the IHT on the deceased's free estate (ie the estate that the deceased could leave by will or intestacy) (s200 IHTA 1984).

If the will is silent as to burden, tax on the free estate in the UK is normally borne by the **residuary estate**. However, if the testator has specifically provided that particular gifts in the will are to bear their own tax, that direction will normally prevail.

### 6.11.4.2 Property passing other than under the deceased's will or intestacy

The PRs are also liable for IHT on property passed outside the will, for example the deceased's share of a house owned as beneficial joint tenants (s200 IHTA 1984). PRs are only liable to the extent of the assets that they have received (or would have received).

Unless the deceased has left a will that provides otherwise, the burden of IHT should be borne by the beneficiary of the asset, for example the surviving joint tenant. If the personal representatives have paid the IHT to HMRC, therefore, the PRs have a statutory right to reimbursement from the beneficiary of the asset (s211(3)).

### 6.11.4.3 Gifted property subject to a reservation

If the deceased had retained an interest in property given away during their lifetime, then, as we have seen, the value of that property at the date of death is aggregated with the value of the deceased's estate.

The donee of the property is primarily liable for the IHT attributable to the gifted property which is subject to the reservation, but if the donee does not pay the IHT within 12 months after the end of the month of death, the deceased's PRs will also be liable. The PRs therefore must be satisfied that the IHT on the gifted property has been paid by the donee before the PRs distribute the estate. Again, the PRs are only liable to the extent of the assets that they have received (or would have received).

However, the burden should fall on the persons who have benefited from the gift subject to a reservation, and the PRs have a statutory right to recover the IHT from those persons (s211(3)).

### 6.11.4.4 Settled property in which the deceased had an interest

If IHT is due, as a result of the death, on assets in a trust fund in which the deceased had an interest, then the trustees of the settlement are liable for the IHT due.

The burden falls on the trust property. The PRs will not be liable for this IHT.

## 6.11.5 The instalment option

In certain cases, IHT may be paid by ten equal annual instalments, the first instalment due on the normal due date for payment (ss227–228 IHTA 1984).

Only certain assets qualify for the instalment option. The list of assets is long and complicated, and it is unlikely you would be able to remember the finer details for the SQE. In brief, the instalment option is available in respect of land and buildings, a business or an interest in a business (eg a share in a partnership) and certain specified shareholdings. The latter include shares (unquoted or quoted) which gave the transferor control immediately before the transfer and certain non-controlling shareholdings (unquoted shares only).

The categories of non-controlling shareholdings listed in the Act include ones where HMRC are satisfied that the tax attributable to the shares cannot be paid in one sum without undue hardship, but there are other categories. See s228 of the IHTA 1984 for the full list.

The instalment option is available in respect of:

- transfers on death;
- LCTs, but only where the transferee pays the IHT; and
- PETs which have become chargeable, or the additional IHT payable on an LCT, due to the transferor dying within seven years, provided the transferee pays the IHT and still owns the property at the date of the transferor's death.

**EXAMPLE**

Colin dies on 20 November 2024. Part of his estate comprises 20,000 shares in an unquoted company which gave Colin control of the company. The shareholding is valued at £75,000 at the date of Colin's death. The IHT payable in respect of shares is, say, £27,400.

If the instalment option is not opted for, IHT falls due on 31 May 2025 (six months after the end of the month of death).

However, if the instalment option is opted for, £2,740 (1/10 × £27,400) is payable on each 31 May from 31 May 2025 until 31 May 2034.

Where land is concerned (other than land on which agricultural property relief is available), interest accrues on the balance of IHT outstanding from the date when the first instalment becomes due for payment. However, in respect of the other categories of property qualifying for the instalment option, the general rule is that no interest is payable provided that each instalment is paid by the due date.

Note that if any type of property (on which the instalment option has been claimed) is sold, then the whole amount of IHT remaining on the property becomes payable immediately. This stands to reason, as the instalment option was only available in the first place because the asset in question is one that might have been difficult to sell.

## 6.12 **Anti-avoidance rules**

We have already considered one of the main anti-avoidance provisions in **6.4.3**, when we looked at the rules on gifts subject to a reservation. As said earlier, the effect of those anti-avoidance rules is to tax the value of the gifted property at the date of death, the value being aggregated with the value of the death estate to work out the tax charge. The effect, for IHT, is just as if the gifted property had never been given away and was still owned by the transferor.

There are other anti-avoidance rules, though. Some of these are specifically related to IHT, whereas others also apply to other taxes. We will not consider these rules in detail and they are just listed here so you have a basic awareness of them:

1. The pre-owned assets regime: under s84 of and Sch 15 to the Finance Act 2004, a taxpayer may be charged to **income tax** on the annual benefit assumed to be derived from a capital asset, where the taxpayer had previously owned that asset and is still enjoying a benefit. This regime is intended to counter arrangements whereby taxpayers have retained a benefit in an asset but have somehow managed to avoid the IHT gift with reservation rules discussed at **6.4.3**. If the taxpayer is caught by the pre-owned assets rules, they can elect to leave the pre-owned assets regime (to avoid an ongoing income tax charge) but the taxpayer would then be covered by the IHT rules on gifts subject to a reservation.
2. Associated operations: s268 of the IHTA 1984 includes anti-avoidance provisions relating specifically to IHT. The detail of what are considered 'associated operations' is outside the scope of this manual.
3. Control by the courts: there is a difference between tax evasion (eg hiding capital or income from HMRC), which has always been illegal (and criminal), and tax avoidance, which is the structuring of your affairs in such a way as to take advantage of loopholes in the tax legislation, which is legal. The traditional view taken by the courts was that tax avoidance was

entirely legitimate. However, this view has been challenged over a long period of time, and we now have regimes like DOTAS and the GAAR (see points (4) and (5)) that seek to prevent and counteract tax avoidance. In addition, there is a line of cases (starting with the House of Lords decisions in *WT Ramsay Ltd v IRC* [1982] AC 300 and *Furniss v Dawson* [1984] AC 474) where the courts have struck down tax avoidance arrangements in situations where tax avoidance schemes had steps inserted which had no commercial purpose other than to avoid tax. The rules from these cases apply also to other taxes, not just to IHT.

4 Disclosure of tax avoidance schemes (DOTAS): the DOTAS regime (originally introduced by Part 7 of the Finance Act 2004) places requirements on promoters and users of tax avoidance schemes to disclose the schemes to HMRC. This gives HMRC 'early warning' of tax avoidance schemes and enables HMRC to take action much more quickly to challenge those schemes through the courts and to make changes to the legislation to prevent future usage of such schemes. DOTAS applies to a number of taxes, not just IHT.

5 GAAR (the General Anti Avoidance Rule): this was introduced by Finance Act 2013. The stated purpose of GAAR is to counteract 'tax advantages arising from tax arrangements that are abusive'. So, the arrangements have to lead to a tax advantage and be abusive. The obtaining of a tax advantage has to be the main purpose of the arrangements. If tax arrangements are caught by GAAR, then HMRC may take action to counteract the tax advantages. GAAR applies to a number of taxes, not just IHT.

6 Sanctions for 'enablers': the Finance (No 2) Act 2017 introduced sanctions (including financial penalties) that can be imposed against 'enablers' of tax avoidance schemes that are defeated by HMRC. 'Enablers' includes tax advisors and could include solicitors involved in acting for their clients. These rules apply to other taxes, not just IHT.

## KEY POINT SUMMARY

- Inheritance tax is a tax payable on death and also in respect of certain lifetime transfers.
- IHT is payable on chargeable transfers of value. Not all transfers of value are chargeable—for example, maintenance payments by a person to their spouse or civil partner or child are usually not chargeable transfers of value and so will not be subject to IHT.
- During a person's lifetime, a transfer of value is the amount by which a person's estate is reduced as a result of the transfer. On death, there is a deemed transfer of value which is of everything the deceased was beneficially entitled to before death.
- There are various exemptions and reliefs which apply to exempt a transfer from IHT or reduce the value of the transfer for IHT purposes. Some exemptions apply on death and to lifetime transfers (these include exemptions for transfers between spouses and civil partners and gifts to charities). Other exemptions apply only to lifetime transfers (eg the annual exemption and gifts in consideration of marriage). The main reliefs operate to reduce the value of business or agricultural property.
- Most lifetime gifts to individuals will qualify as potentially exempt transfers. If the transferor survives the PET by seven years, the transfer becomes exempt and will not be subject to IHT. However, if the transferor fails to survive the PET by seven years it becomes chargeable retrospectively
- Lifetime gifts to most trusts and to companies will be lifetime chargeable transfers, and will be chargeable when they are made. If the transferor dies within seven years of making the LCT, the tax will be recalculated, and there may be more IHT to pay.
- If the transferor retains a benefit in the property which is given away during their lifetime, this may be considered a gift subject to the reservation, and the property may be taxed alongside the transferor's estate on their death as if they had not given it away. This is one example of the anti-avoidance measures: there are others.
- The rates of IHT are 40 per cent on transfers on death (or on transfers taxable retrospectively as a result of death) and 20 per cent on LCTs when they are taxed during the transferor's lifetime. If a proportion of a person's estate is left to charity, the death rate on the estate is reduced from 40 per cent to 36 per cent.

- A rate of 0 per cent is applied first, though, before applying any of the other rates. The portion that this 0 per cent is applied to is called the 'nil rate band'. Each person has their own standard nil rate band, currently of £325,000. The survivor of two spouses or civil partners may use a transferable nil rate band where the first spouse to die has not used their nil rate band on the first death. There is also a 'residence nil rate band', provided certain conditions apply, and this residence nil rate band is also transferable between spouses and civil partners.
- IHT is cumulative. Any chargeable transfer of value within the seven years prior to the most recent transfer of value will have an effect on the tax rates applied to the most recent transfer of value. For example, any lifetime transfers within seven years prior to death will have an effect on the tax rates applied to the estate on death.
- There are rules regarding liability for IHT (who can be required to pay the IHT to HMRC), although this is different from the question of who bears the burden of IHT (ie out of the transferees and beneficiaries of the deceased, who has to bear the cost of the tax ultimately).

# PART D
# Probate and Administration Practice

# CHAPTER 7
# Preliminary Steps in Administering the Estate

**FUNCTIONING LEGAL KNOWLEDGE**

This chapter covers the following functioning legal knowledge required to pass the SQE 1 assessments:

**Probate and administration practice**
**Grants of representation:**

- valuation of assets and liabilities
- **excepted estates**
- methods of funding the initial payment of **inheritance tax**

**AUTHORITIES UNDERPINNING PRACTICE**

The key authorities that underpin this area of practice are listed below. Note that for legislation you are linked to legislation.gov.uk.

Although much of the legislation on this government website is available in its amended form, the incorporation of new amendments into the text of legislation can be delayed. You should refer to legal databases to ensure you are referencing the most up-to-date legislation.

- Inheritance Tax Act 1984
  **http://www.legislation.gov.uk/ukpga/1984/51/contents**
- Inheritance Tax (Delivery of Accounts) (Excepted Estates) Regulations 2004
  **http://www.legislation.gov.uk/uksi/2004/2543/contents/made**

## 7.1 Introduction

In **Chapters 7–11** and **13** we will consider the process of administering an estate after someone has died. In this chapter we will consider the initial steps in administering the estate, and some important work that has to be undertaken in preparation for the grant application. In particular, it is often necessary to complete an inheritance tax (IHT) account, and send that account to HM Revenue and Customs (HMRC) together with payment of the IHT due. The grant application should not be made until this has been done.

Then, in **Chapter 8** we will look at the grant application itself. The grant is needed as it is proof of the **executors'** authority to act and confers the authority to act on **administrators**. In **Chapter 9** we will look at the process of administering and distributing the estate once the grant has been obtained. However, some aspects of administration will be covered in detail in other chapters. The finalising of the IHT position of the estate and dealing with **income tax** and **capital gains tax** are covered in **Chapter 10**. Many of the powers and duties of the **personal representatives** (PRs) are dealt with in **Chapter 13** because those powers and duties also apply to **trustees**.

Finally, the PRs may face claims against the estate, particularly applications for **reasonable financial provision** under the Inheritance (Provision for Family and Dependants) Act 1975. These claims are dealt with in **Chapter 11**.

## 7.2 Preliminary steps following a death

In this section we will consider in outline the preliminary steps that are commonly taken in the administration of a person's estate immediately following death, and leading up to the application for the **grant of representation**. A more detailed consideration of some of those steps (eg completing the **inheritance tax account** and paying the IHT) is then covered in the following sections.

### 7.2.1 Registering the death

Following a death, the death is registered, usually by a close family member. The solicitor will not usually be involved with this process but it is useful for you to know the basic process in outline.

The death should usually be registered within five days of the death, specifying whether there is to be a burial or cremation. The death is registered at a local register office, part of the General Register Office of England and Wales.

There are register offices in many locations.

The register office will issue the person registering the death with a **death certificate**. The person registering the death may request a number of copies of the death certificate. There is a small charge for each additional copy. It is useful to have a number of copies of the death certificate as it means it is then possible to notify more than one organisation at a time, for example the deceased's bank, building society etc.

The person registering the death may use the Tell Us Once service if the service is available in that area. Tell Us Once enables the person registering the death to inform various government departments, such as HMRC and the Department of Work and Pensions (which deals with payment of State Retirement Pension) without the need to notify each government department separately. If the service is available in the area, the register office will either complete the Tell Us Once service with the person registering the death or give them a unique reference number to use online or by phone. The person then contacts Tell Us Once, giving certain details about the deceased, such as National Insurance number, driving licence number, vehicle registration number and passport number. Then, the Tell Us Once service informs each relevant government department.

If the death was sudden or unexpected, or if the cause was violent or unexplained, the death may be reported by someone (eg by a doctor, a hospital or the police) to the **coroner**. The coroner is a specialist type of judge. The coroner's office will consider whether or not to hold an **inquest** (an inquiry by the coroner at a public court hearing into the circumstances and cause of death). The coroner may also order a **post-mortem** examination of the body. The coroner may decide there is no need for either a post-mortem or an inquest, in which case a relative can proceed to register the death. There may be a post-mortem but no inquest, in which case the coroner will issue the relative with a form to provide to the register office to register the death. If there is an inquest, it is not possible to register the death until after the inquest. As the inquest is not likely to be held for some weeks or months, the coroner will usually issue a form to enable burial or cremation so that the funeral can take place.

Importantly for the administration of the estate, if the coroner has decided there needs to be an inquest, the coroner will issue a certificate of the fact of death, often called an 'interim death certificate', which the PRs can use to report the death to the holders of the deceased's assets. This enables the PRs to proceed to establish the value of the estate and apply for the grant of representation.

### 7.2.2 Taking initial instructions (and obtaining information)

Usually, the solicitor is first aware of the death when they are contacted by a relative or friend of the deceased. This is normally after a relative has registered the death with the register office.

The firm may be holding the original of the deceased's **will**, in which case the solicitor will release the will to the appointed executors or the solicitor will take instructions from the executors to assist in the administration of the estate.

Alternatively, the will might not be stored with the firm, but the executors instead approach the firm, seeking advice and assistance, and bringing the will with them.

Where there is no will, usually a relative will make an appointment with the solicitor to obtain advice and assistance.

The solicitor will need to obtain details of the assets and liabilities of the deceased and to enquire as to the **beneficiaries** named or referred to in the will, or the nearest family members if there isn't a will (or if there is a **partial intestacy**).

Often, the solicitor will ask the relative or other person who has contacted the firm to complete a questionnaire before any meeting or discussion. The questionnaire will ask for information regarding the deceased's assets and liabilities, and the members of the deceased's family. Frequently, the person will have some questions about the questionnaire and will require some assistance from the solicitor to complete it.

The solicitor will usually then have a meeting or discussion with the person about the information provided in the questionnaire and will give advice on the likely distribution of the estate and on any other relevant issues (eg whether there is a potential claim against the estate).

The person contacting the solicitor is likely to be grieving following the loss of someone who might have been very close to them. The solicitor must bear this in mind and should deal sensitively with the new client, expressing sympathy for their loss and leading them through the process of administering the estate as supportively as possible.

However, as with any new client, the solicitor will need to verify the client's identity and will need to send the client a client care letter and terms and conditions of business, including an indication of the firm's charges for the administration work. There is also a requirement that solicitors provide costs information online for any prospective client.

**CONDUCT POINT**

Paragraph 8.7 of the SRA Code of Conduct for Solicitors, RELs and RFLs 2019 provides that a solicitor must ensure that a client has the best possible information about how their matter will be priced and about the likely overall cost of the matter and any costs incurred. This applies both at the time of engagement and as the matter progresses. Paragraph 8.6 provides that the information must be given to clients in a way which the client can understand, and enables them to make informed decisions about the services they need, how the matter will be handled and the options available to them.

Paragraph 7.1 of the Code of Conduct for Firms applies these rules to firms of solicitors.

Also, under the SRA's Transparency Rules 2018 solicitors firms (and any other body authorised by the SRA) must provide certain information about the firm, including costs information, on the firm's website. This is so that prospective clients have accurate and relevant information to enable the prospective client to make an informed choice on whether or not to instruct the firm. The Transparency Rules also apply to solicitors who are providing services outside an SRA-authorised body (ie so called 'freelance' solicitors—see **Chapter 1**).

The information should be clear and accessible and in a prominent place on the firm's website. If, unusually, a firm does not have a website, then the firm must provide the information on request. The Transparency Rules relate to certain areas of work only, but one of those areas is uncontentious probate and administration work.

Under the Transparency Rules, the costs information must include the total cost or, if this is not practicable, the average cost or range of costs. There should be information about the basis for charging, including any hourly rates or fixed fees and the experience and qualifications of anyone carrying out the work and their supervisors. There should be information about likely **disbursements**, such as probate application fees.

The SRA has published guidance on transparency and service, including area-specific tips and templates. The Law Society has also published practice notes for solicitors on information for firms' websites and on price transparency.

## 7.2.3 The funeral and the deceased's wishes (for the funeral and for disposal of the body)

If there is a will, this should be checked to see whether the deceased had expressed a wish as to their funeral and/or as to the disposal of the body. The will should be checked before the funeral as it will be too late if the deceased's wishes are only discovered after the funeral has taken place!

Some **testators** wish to be buried, others wish to be cremated. Sometimes, the testator will even specify particular music to be played. Generally, though, testators should be encouraged to communicate their funeral wishes to their relatives clearly during their lifetime, rather than rely upon a statement in the will. This is because the relatives might not think of checking the will before making the funeral arrangements or holding the funeral. (It might also not be possible to follow all of the deceased's wishes, due to restrictions on what is permitted at a funeral.) Alternatively, the deceased might have specified the arrangements via a pre-paid funeral plan.

The testator may also have expressed a wish in the will to leave their body (or parts of it) to be used for medical purposes. In Wales since 2015 and in England since 2020, there has been an opt-out system for organ donation—namely, consent to use of the person's organs is presumed unless the person indicates that they do not wish to donate their organs. In practice, the deceased's family is often still asked for permission before removing organs, despite this presumed consent.

## 7.2.4 **Identifying and informing the beneficiaries**

As said previously, it is necessary for the solicitor to enquire as to the beneficiaries in a will or the nearest family members if there is no will or if there is a partial intestacy. From the information provided (and the will if there is one), the solicitor will advise the PRs and the beneficiaries on who appears to be entitled to the deceased's estate.

Most of you will have seen television programmes (usually murder mysteries) where the family gather around a large oak table at the solicitor's office for the reading of the will. This rarely (if ever) happens in practice. Usually, the beneficiaries are informed of their entitlement by email or letter.

## 7.2.5 **Securing assets and practical steps**

### 7.2.5.1 The deceased's property, personal possessions and pets

After a person dies there may be an immediate need to secure their home, to protect the house itself and to protect the contents of the home. It will be necessary to check whether the house and contents are insured and to contact the insurance company to let them know that the house is empty. This obviously applies if the person was living on their own when they died. If the person's partner was living there, the house will usually be held jointly so then it will be the responsibility of the surviving partner to sort these matters out.

The deceased may have obligations to a landlord, though—either under a short-term lease where the deceased was living in rented accommodation or to a freeholder under a long lease where ground rent is payable. If the deceased had an apartment in a larger building, there may be service charges due to the freeholder or management company for the building. If the deceased was in rented accommodation, then consideration needs to be given to ending the rental agreement and removal of the deceased's possessions.

One problem that can arise following someone's death (again if they were living on their own) is that relatives, friends and neighbours might have access to the deceased's property. Although this could be beneficial as those persons could undertake regular checks on the property and undertake tasks which it would be impractical for the solicitor to do (eg checking the mail and reading the gas and electricity meters), there is the danger that they could help themselves to items. Usually this is not a problem but it might be if the deceased had, say, valuable antiques. As a result, locks may need to be changed. The other consideration, however, is ensuring that the property is secure from burglary, so ensuring there are adequate locks etc in the first place may prove necessary. Again, solicitors will seek the assistance of relatives and friends of the deceased to ensure such jobs are done.

Similarly, if the deceased had a car or other vehicle, this will have to be kept secure, although usually this is left in place in a garage, on a drive or outside the property.

Also, arrangements may need to be made to care for any pet of the deceased (ie the deceased's cat, dog or python, rather than a PET, or **potentially exempt transfer**!). The solicitor will not normally be involved in such arrangements. Usually, arrangements for a pet are made by the deceased's relatives or friends.

### 7.2.5.2 Notifying asset holders of the death

It is necessary to inform the companies holding the deceased's assets of the death. Many banks now have online portals for this purpose. Otherwise, the solicitor will write to each asset holder, sending an official or certified copy of the death certificate and will request information about the value of the deceased's assets. The solicitor will also request a withdrawal form for signature by the PRs in due course. The asset holder will also return the official or certified copy of the death certificate.

Asset holders include a variety of organisations but mainly banks, building societies, National Savings & Investments, life assurance companies and unit trust managers.

It is also necessary to obtain a value for the asset from the asset holder because the PRs will have to establish the value of the estate for probate, to decide which inheritance tax account is required and what the value of the estate is for inheritance tax purposes, in order to calculate any IHT which is due. With bank and building society accounts, it is necessary to find out the balance on the account at the date of death and, for IHT purposes, the amount of any interest which is unpaid at, but which has accrued to, the date of death.

### 7.2.5.3 Obtaining valuations of assets

With some assets it is not possible to simply write to a company and obtain a value for the asset.

#### Shares

Whilst a bank can say what the balance was at the date of death on each of the deceased's bank accounts, a company registrar will either not need to tell the PRs the value of the deceased's shareholding in a company or will not be able to.

If the company's shares are listed on a stock exchange, there is an established method for valuing the shares. This is by reference to the published prices of the shares on the date of death—information which is publicly available. The value of the shares will usually be the 'quarter-up value'. The published prices will give a lowest price for the shares on the day, and the highest price for the shares on the day (if the deceased died on a non-trading day, then the prices for the nearest trading day are taken). The probate value (also taken for IHT purposes) will be the lowest price plus one-quarter of the difference between the lowest price and the highest price. This is more easily understood by looking at a simple example.

**EXAMPLE**

Abayomi dies on 1 October 2024. He held shares in a public limited company listed on the London Stock Exchange. On 1 October 2024, the lowest price per share was £15 and the highest price was £17 per share. The difference between the lowest and highest price is £2. One-quarter of that is £0.50. The probate (and IHT) value of each share will be one-quarter up from the lowest price, so £15 + £0.50 = £15.50.

As it is possible to value such shares using publicly available information, it is not necessary to write to the company registrars to notify them of the death. In fact, such shares are normally traded via the London Stock Exchange's electronic CREST system, and so the shares will be held by a nominee company for the deceased. It is still possible to write to notify the company registrars of the death, but this is not always done for the above reason. The main reason for writing would be so that the company registrars, or the nominee company, were aware of the death and that the solicitors were acting for the PRs.

The position, however, is very different for shares in companies which are not listed on a recognised exchange. Smaller private limited companies will not have their shares listed on any market and so it will not be possible to apply the 'quarter-up' rule. Instead, it will be necessary to obtain a valuation of the shares by some other means.

The basic valuation rule for probate and IHT purposes is the market value at the date of death. What is the market value depends on what a buyer is willing to pay for the asset if it is sold on the open market. The difficulty with shareholdings in small companies is that there is not often a ready market for the shares. The shares are not available to the public to buy them—someone has to know about the company and want to buy the shares. Usually, the only option is to sell the shares to other persons who are already involved with the company as directors and/or shareholders. Even if there is a ready buyer, an appropriate value for the shareholding needs to be established. It is necessary, therefore, to obtain a valuation from an expert—a professional with an understanding of the company, such as an accountant. Practically, this means that the PRs (or their solicitor) will need to instruct an expert to provide a valuation for probate and IHT purposes, so it will be necessary to identify a suitable expert and contact them to request a valuation. There is likely to be a cost associated with this as the expert is likely to charge for their valuation services.

### Land and buildings

Similarly, there is usually no objective basis for valuing land and buildings. It is not possible to obtain a definite figure from an asset holder and it is not possible to look up the prices of the land in a publicly available list of prices. As a result, land and buildings will have to be valued by an appropriate expert. Again, the value needed will be the market value at the date of death, but this is also dependent upon what a buyer is willing to pay for the land and buildings. The same applies where the deceased had an interest in land and buildings (eg the share of a **tenant in common** in jointly owned property).

The sorts of experts who would be consulted include chartered surveyors and estate agents. If the estate is one where IHT is payable, the valuation of a surveyor may be preferable. If the estate is smaller, or is covered by exemptions, then an estate agent's valuation may be sufficient, but it may be worth getting three estate agents' valuations and taking an average of the three. A surveyor will charge for a valuation, whereas estate agents will usually provide valuations free of charge, in the hope of securing business when the estate comes to sell the property.

## 7.2.5.4 Notifying creditors of the death and funeral expenses

The solicitors acting for the PRs will also need to contact any known **creditors** of the deceased to inform the creditors that the deceased has died, to indicate that they have been instructed by the PRs and to ask for confirmation of the amount owed to the creditor. It is not necessary to send a death certificate to a creditor. It is obviously necessary to check the amount which the creditor says is owed.

The creditors should be advised that there will be a delay in payment of the debt until after the grant has been obtained and that payment is also dependent on there being sufficient funds in the estate to pay all of the deceased's debts and relevant expenses.

For the position on unknown creditors and on protecting the PRs, see **9.8.1**.

In many estates, the debts will be comparatively minor—unpaid credit card balances, utility bills (gas, electricity, broadband)—but in some estates there will be more significant debts, such as PCP agreements on motor vehicles and mortgages on land.

Mortgages, though, may be covered by life assurance. It is common for borrowers to take out life assurance to cover an unpaid mortgage balance on the death of the borrower or, where there are joint borrowers, on the death of one of them. If the mortgage is a repayment mortgage (where each month the borrower pays off part of the capital balance as well as paying interest), then there may be a mortgage protection policy which will pay off the unpaid capital. With an interest-only mortgage, where the capital sum is not paid off during the term of the mortgage, the borrowers might have taken out an endowment policy which should pay off the capital in the event of a borrower's death. However, some borrowers, whether due to lack of common sense or an inability to afford endowment insurance, will have interest-only mortgages with no insurance cover, meaning the whole of the capital sum borrowed will be due on their death.

As noted earlier, the deceased might have been living in rented accommodation, where rent is due, and will continue to be due, under the lease. Even if the deceased owned a long lease of a property, there may be ground rent due to the freeholder or service charges.

If the deceased was in business, in their sole name or in partnership, there will be personal liabilities. Some protection is afforded by limited liability if the business was run through a company, but the company's bank might have secured second charges over the deceased's personal property, usually the home.

One liability in particular that must be discharged is the cost of the funeral. The funeral expenses are not strictly a debt of the deceased but are an expense of the estate. Funerals are expensive. The Money Advice Service website reported that in 2020 the average cost of a funeral using a funeral director was £3,837, although the costs vary significantly from one funeral to another, depending on what is included and in which area the funeral is taking place. For example, in London the cost of simple burial was reported as being £7,259!

Often the relatives of the deceased will be concerned about how the funeral expenses will be paid, and will not have the financial resources themselves to do so. The solicitor can assure the relatives that the funeral expenses are commonly paid from the deceased's estate. The solicitors should contact the funeral directors to explain there may be a delay in payment whilst the grant is obtained, although it is often possible to secure the release of funds from the deceased's bank accounts before the grant is obtained, in order to pay the funeral directors. Alternatively, the relatives might already have paid the funeral bill and will thus obtain a reimbursement from the estate (provided the funeral expenses were reasonable!). Another possibility is that the cost of the funeral will have been covered by a pre-payment plan.

#### 7.2.5.5 Checking for assets which pass independently of the estate

As well as establishing the value of the assets which pass on death via the PRs under the will or **intestacy**, it is necessary to check whether there are any other assets which pass independently of the estate (eg interest in **joint property** which passes by survivorship or property which is the subject of a valid ***donatio mortis causa***) and the value of that property. This is not just to establish the distribution of that property (eg if there is a valid *donatio mortis causa*, the asset that has been given away by the deceased will not be part of the estate), but is also because the property may be taxable to inheritance tax, and the PRs will be **liable** for IHT on certain property which passes independently of the estate.

#### 7.2.5.6 Checking whether there were any lifetime transfers

Similarly, it is necessary to check whether the deceased made any lifetime transfers. Were those lifetime transfers ones which were covered by an IHT exemption or relief?

Alternatively, if the transfers qualified as potentially exempt transfers, did the deceased survive them by seven years or were the transfers in the seven years before death? Did the deceased make any **lifetime chargeable transfers**? Did the deceased make lifetime transfers that were subject to a reservation of benefit (in which case the value of that property at the date of death will be aggregated with the value of the deceased's estate)? Depending on the answers to these questions, the lifetime transfers may affect the IHT payable on the death estate and the PRs could be liable for any IHT or additional IHT on those transfers.

### 7.2.6 Submitting an inheritance tax account and paying IHT

Depending on the size and complexity of the estate, including whether there have been any substantial lifetime transfers, the PRs may need to complete and submit an IHT account.

#### 7.2.6.1 IHT 400

The main inheritance tax account is IHT400.

An IHT400 is required for any estate which does *not* qualify as an 'excepted estate' (see **7.4**).

IHT400 will be needed for any estate where IHT is payable but may also be needed in other estates where no IHT is due. For example, if PRs wish to claim the **residence nil rate band**, they will have to submit an IHT400.

If an IHT400 is needed, the PRs (or more likely, their professional advisors) must submit IHT400 (together with a number of supporting schedules) to HMRC before it is possible to make the grant application to HMCTS. The PRs will also need to arrange for the payment to HMRC of any IHT which is due.

The IHT400 must usually be delivered within 12 months of the end of the month in which the deceased died, and there are penalties for late delivery.

In practice, the PRs are likely to want to deliver the IHT400 sooner than this, as until the IHT400 has been delivered (and any IHT paid), the PRs will not be able to apply for the grant of representation. Also, the due date for inheritance tax is six months from the end of the month of death, and after that date interest will be payable on overdue IHT, so the PRs will want to submit the IHT400 before the due date for paying IHT.

#### 7.2.6.2 Excepted estates

There is now no longer a need to submit an inheritance tax account for excepted estates (see **7.4**). There is no need to submit an IHT400 (or, indeed, any IHT account) for excepted estates where the death was on or after 1 January 2022.

For deaths prior to 1 January 2022, though, there was another IHT account: IHT205. You are unlikely to have questions on older estates in SQE, but you might occasionally see one in practice.

IHT205 was the most common short account used, although Form IHT207 was used for foreign-domiciled estates. Where the PRs of an older excepted estate claim a transferable **nil rate band**, they also have to submit Form IHT217.

For excepted estates where the deceased died before 1 January 2022, there is no requirement to submit the IHT205 to HMRC prior to making the grant application. Instead, the PRs should send the IHT205 direct to HMCTS when they make the grant application.

#### 7.2.6.3 Penalties for failure to establish and report accurate values

It is very important that the PRs establish accurate values for assets and liabilities in the IHT400 or when valuing an excepted estate. It is possible to provide estimated values for some assets and liabilities but if it is not possible to obtain accurate values before submitting the account, HMRC may impose penalties on PRs (and third parties, such as relatives, who provide the PRs with information in the first place) if estimated values prove to be wrong and there is an understatement of the liability to IHT. Similarly, PRs should ensure they have made sufficient enquiries regarding any lifetime transfers that the deceased made. Failure to report these could also lead to penalties for PRs and third parties. The penalties in each case are sizeable—a percentage of the amount of the tax not paid due to the underreporting, for example at least 30 per cent of the underpaid tax where the underreporting has been careless, and at least 70 per cent of the unpaid tax where the act was deliberate.

### 7.2.7 Submitting the application for a grant of representation

Once HMRC have confirmed that they have checked the IHT400 and that any IHT due has been paid, the PRs can proceed to apply for the grant of representation. HMRC will confirm by letter that the IHT400 has been checked and that the IHT has been paid. HMRC will provide the PRs with a unique code that the PRs will have to quote to HMCTS in the probate application. The HMRC letter will also confirm the gross and net values of the estate for probate purposes, which must also be included in the probate application.

Alternatively, if the estate is an excepted one (and the deceased died on or after 1 January 2022), there is no need to submit an IHT account: the PRs can proceed to make the grant application to HMCTS without first sending an IHT account to HMRC.

(For excepted estates where the death was before 1 January 2022, the PRs will need to send IHT205 (and possibly IHT217) to HMCTS with the rest of the grant application. However, the PRs will not need to send IHT205 (and IHT217) to HMRC before making the grant application.)

The grant application process is covered in detail in **Chapter 8**.

## 7.3 Inheritance tax accounts

The purpose of an inheritance tax account is to inform HMRC about the composition and value of the deceased's IHT estate (and any relevant lifetime transfers) and, if there is IHT due, to calculate the amount of tax to be paid.

As indicated previously, there are two types of IHT account—the main account is the IHT400, which is a detailed form supplemented by a series of additional forms (or schedules). The IHT400 is needed when there is IHT to be paid, and also in situations where there is no IHT to be paid but the estate does not qualify as an 'excepted estate'. The rules on when an estate is excepted are discussed in **7.4**.

As stated, it is no longer necessary to complete and submit an IHT account if the estate is excepted. No account is required where the death was on or after 1 January 2022. The shorter form of IHT account (IHT205) must be submitted for excepted estates of persons who died before that date, but IHT205 is much shorter and simpler than IHT400 and, for the most part, there are no supporting schedules. A different form, IHT207, is required for excepted estates where the deceased was domiciled outside the UK (see **7.4.4** for details).

The inheritance tax accounts and other forms can be found on the gov.uk website, under 'Inheritance tax'.

There are also guides on how to complete each account and schedule, available on this website, but those guides are very detailed. You do not need to know the detail covered in those guides, but obviously in practice you should consult them if you are completing an IHT account for an estate.

## 7.3.1 The IHT400 account and supporting schedules

The IHT400 account is, essentially, a summary of the assets and liabilities of the estate. The detail is often found in the supporting schedules. We will consider the supporting schedules first, and then the IHT400 form itself.

### 7.3.1.1 The supporting schedules

It is unlikely you will need to know the number or name of most of the supporting schedules for the SQE assessment, but the schedules listed here are examples to give you a sense of how many schedules have to be completed for a typical estate, and what these schedules cover.

The schedules can, perhaps, be broken down into different categories based on their main function.

First, there are a number of schedules that provide information about the values of assets and liabilities in the estate, such as the following:

- IHT405: houses, land, buildings and interests in land;
- IHT406: bank and building society accounts;
- IHT407: household and personal goods;
- IHT410: life assurance and annuities;
- IHT411: listed stocks and shares;
- IHT412: unlisted stocks and shares and control holdings;
- IHT417: foreign assets;
- IHT419: debts owed by the deceased.

Then, there are schedules which detail assets which pass independently of the will or intestacy, whether subject to IHT or not, and lifetime transfers:

- IHT404: jointly owned assets (which will include interests as a **joint tenant in equity** which pass by survivorship);
- IHT409: pensions (often there will be a discretionary payment from the deceased's pension on death, which will not be subject to IHT, but HMRC still want to know about it—similarly, on IHT410 (life assurance and annuities), the PRs will have to report details of any life assurance payment under a life policy written in trust, even though this is not subject to IHT);
- IHT418: assets held in **trust** (this would include where the deceased has a **life interest** in a trust at the time of death);
- IHT403: **gifts** and other transfers of value (this is the form to report lifetime transfers).

There are also schedules which are used to claim some form of relief or other benefit for the estate, such as:

- IHT435: residence nil rate band;
- IHT402: transfer of unused nil rate band (on the death of a surviving spouse or civil partner);

- IHT413: business relief, business and partnership interests and assets (NB: business property relief is claimed on relevant shareholdings on IHT412 mentioned earlier);
- IHT414: farms, farmhouses and farmland (used to claim agricultural property relief).

Not all of the supporting schedules have been listed—there are others.

As can be seen, it will often be necessary to complete and submit a large number of these schedules, as many of them will be relevant to the deceased's estate.

Why not go to gov.uk now and browse through the schedules to get a sense of the amount of information that is required by HMRC. You need not spend long on this, but you will find it helpful to see what the forms look like. All the forms are available from the following link: https://www.gov.uk/government/collections/inheritance-tax-forms.

## 7.3.1.2 The IHT400 account

Similarly, you should look at the IHT400 account itself. It is also available from the above link. You will find it helpful to keep referring back to the IHT400 as you read through this section. As mentioned, there are also detailed guides on how to complete the IHT accounts but you do not need to refer to those whilst reading this section, or for the SQE. Also, you are unlikely to need to know the structure of the IHT400 form for the SQE assessment, but for practical purposes you will find a knowledge of the basic layout useful.

The IHT400 is, currently, 16 pages long. As said, it is largely a summary document, the detail being provided in the supporting schedules just mentioned. The IHT400 form is divided into the following parts:

1. On pages 1 and 2, the PRs must provide personal details about the deceased (eg name, address, gender, domicile, marital status).
2. Page 3 is for details of the persons dealing with the estate (ie details of the solicitors' firm), and indicating whether or not the deceased left a will. There are various questions about the will on pages 3 and 4, including space to list any items which were referred to in the will but which are not included in the estate (ie items which have been given away by the deceased during their lifetime).
3. Pages 5 and 6 are important and useful as they list the supporting schedules which may be needed. The pages act as a useful prompt to the solicitor to check whether or not a particular schedule is needed. If a supporting schedule is needed, the relevant 'Yes' box is ticked, otherwise the relevant 'No' box must be ticked, to confirm that the particular schedule is not required.
4. Pages 7 and 8 are for a summary of the deceased's UK assets—this includes any interest which the deceased had in any joint property passing by survivorship, and the assets in the deceased's sole name.
5. On pages 9 and 10 there are boxes to report deductions from the UK estate, due to the deceased's debts and liabilities, and funeral expenses.
6. On pages 10 and 11 there are boxes to indicate if the PRs are claiming IHT exemptions and reliefs (eg charity exemption or agricultural property relief).
7. Page 11 continues with a section for 'Other assets taken into account to calculate the tax'—this includes foreign property, assets held in trust and **gifted property subject to a reservation**.
8. Page 12 includes boxes for a simple inheritance calculation, although this can only be used in certain circumstances. If the calculation is more complicated, another form (IHT400 Calculation or IHT430) must be used. For example, the simple calculation on page 12 cannot be used if any part of the IHT is being paid by instalments. Also, if the estate wishes to pay IHT at the reduced rate of 36 per cent (due to leaving 10 per cent of the net estate to charity), Form IHT430 Reduced Rate of Inheritance Tax will have to be used.
9. Page 13 has a question to determine if the PRs wish to use the Direct Payment Scheme. Pages 13 and 14 then set out the declaration by the PRs or their agent, together with boxes for their details and signatures.
10. Lastly, pages 15 and 16 contain a checklist to remind the PRs of the actions they should take and the additional information they should include when sending the IHT forms to HMRC. There is also space for any additional information.

You will also have noticed that the IHT400 requires the PRs to report the values of assets and liabilities either in Column A or in Column B in various sections of the form. This is because of the **instalment option** (which is explained in **7.5.3**). Assets which do not attract the instalment option are reported in Column A, and assets which do attract the instalment option are reported in Column B.

### 7.3.2 The IHT205 (and IHT207) accounts

These IHT accounts are used where the estate is excepted, but only for deaths before 1 January 2022. For deaths on or after 1 January 2022, there is no need to submit an IHT account in an excepted estate.

IHT 205 is used where the excepted estate is either a low-value estate or an exempt estate (see **7.4** for an explanation). If the excepted estate is a foreign domiciled estate, Form IHT207 is used instead of Form IHT205. However, we will not consider IHT207 any further in this section.

There is only one supporting schedule that might accompany Form IHT205, which is Form IHT217 Claim to transfer unused nil rate band for excepted estates.

If you look online, you will see several versions of IHT205, as the form changed over time, but the earlier versions are shown as they are still relevant to estates where the deceased died some years ago—obviously, none of the IHT205 forms are likely to be needed frequently now.

IHT205 is much simpler than IHT400. IHT205 is only eight pages long and includes the following sections:

- details of the person who has died;
- a series of questions about the estate, designed to check that the estate is indeed an excepted estate or whether an IHT400 is needed instead;
- assets and liabilities that are part of the IHT estate, but for which no grant of representation is required (eg joint property passing by survivorship);
- assets and liabilities for which a grant of representation is required (ie the estate passing by will or intestacy);
- a section for claiming spouse and/or charity exemption (NB: an IHT400 will be required if business property relief or agricultural property relief is to be claimed);
- a declaration section, with space for the PRs to sign.

## 7.4 Excepted estates

An IHT400 will be required where there is IHT to pay on the death of the deceased, but a full IHT400 may also be required even when there is no IHT to be paid. An IHT400 is only not required where the estate is an excepted estate.

Where an estate is excepted, it is not necessary to deliver an IHT400 and supporting schedules to HMRC prior to making the grant application to HMCTS. Instead, for deaths on or after 1 January 2022, the PRs will simply confirm certain values in the probate application itself. For deaths before 1 January 2022, Form IHT205 or Form IHT207 is still needed, but is sent to HMCTS with the rest of the grant application.

However, even if the estate is excepted, HMRC may subsequently demand an IHT400 from the PRs. HMRC have 60 days from the date of the grant of representation in which to do this.

Also, if the PRs subsequently realise that the estate should not have been an excepted estate, the PRs have six months from the discovery of this to submit an IHT400.

For an estate to be excepted, certain requirements have to be met. These are set out in the Inheritance Tax (Delivery of Accounts) (Excepted Estates) Regulations 2004 (as amended). These regulations were amended most recently in 2021, introducing new rules for deaths on or after 1 January 2022. The regulations are very detailed and the summary in this section is a simplification of the rules, which is more appropriate to what you can remember for the SQE exam. In practice, when dealing with a person's estate you should check the exact requirements of the regulations to determine whether or not the estate is an excepted one.

There are, in fact, three categories of excepted estate:

1 low-value estates;
2 exempt estates; and
3 foreign domiciled estates.

Some requirements are common to low-value estates and exempt estates, but do not apply to foreign domiciled estates.

## 7.4.1 Low-value estates

Low-value estates are ones where the gross value of the estate (ie the total value of the assets before any expenses and liabilities are deducted, and before any exemptions are applied) does not exceed the relevant excepted estates threshold.

There is an excepted estates threshold for low-value estates and for exempt estates. This excepted estates threshold currently is the same as the standard nil rate band for IHT, namely £325,000.

However, if the deceased was the survivor of a married couple or registered civil partners, and the deceased's spouse/civil partner had not used their nil rate band on the first death, the excepted estates threshold can be doubled to £650,000. (For deaths on or after 1 January 2022, if the deceased's spouse/civil partner had used part of their nil rate band on the first death, then the excepted estates threshold can be increased by the proportion of the nil rate band that has not been used. For deaths before 1 January 2022, it is only possible to increase the threshold if the deceased spouse/civil partner had not used any part of their nil rate band on the first death.) Other conditions must also be met to claim the higher threshold in an excepted estate, and in practice you should check those conditions carefully.

**EXAMPLE**

Javid dies on 1 September 2024, leaving an estate worth £275,000 before taking into account the funeral expenses or debts. No exemptions apply. Javid was a bachelor (ie he never married). His estate will be a low-value estate, as the gross estate (£275,000) does not exceed the excepted estates threshold, which in his case will be £325,000. The estate will be an excepted estate, and IHT400 will not be needed. Instead, Javid's PRs will confirm several values as part of the grant application.

**EXAMPLE**

Nerissa dies on 1 October 2024, leaving an estate worth £500,000 before taking into account the funeral expenses or debts. No exemptions apply. Nerissa was a widow, her husband Pablo having died two years before her. Pablo left most of his estate to Nerissa when he died but did use 10 per cent of his nil rate band on gifts to other beneficiaries.

The excepted estates threshold applicable to Nerissa's estate will be £617,500. This is made up by Nerissa's 'own' £325,000, plus 90 per cent of a second £325,000 (ie £292,500) due to Pablo only having used 10 per cent of his nil rate band. Nerissa's estate will therefore be a low-value estate, even though the gross estate (£500,000) exceeds the usual excepted estates threshold of £325,000.

The estate will be an excepted estate, and IHT400 will not be needed. Nerissa's PRs will confirm several values as part of the grant application.

## 7.4.2 Exempt estates

An exempt estate is one where the *net* estate after deduction of expenses and liabilities, and after the application of spouse exemption and/or charity exemption, does not exceed the excepted estates threshold.

Again, the threshold is £325,000, unless the deceased's spouse/civil partner did not use their full nil rate band on an earlier death, in which case the threshold is increased to up to £650,000.

In addition to this stipulation concerning the net estate, the *gross* estate must not exceed £3 (£1 million for deaths before 1 January 2022) million for the estate to qualify as an exempt estate.

**EXAMPLE**

Mina dies on 1 November 2024, leaving an estate worth £900,000 before taking into account the funeral expenses or debts, or exemptions. Mina was married to Carl. Apart from her jewellery of £5,000 that she left to her daughter, Alice, Mina left her whole estate to Carl. Both Alice and Carl have survived Mina.

There are funeral expenses and debts totalling £10,000, which will be deducted from the £900,000. Of the remaining £890,000, nearly all of it (£885,000) is left to Carl, and this amount will be covered by spouse exemption. This leaves a net estate of £5,000 which is the value of the jewellery passing to Mina's daughter, Alice.

The estate qualifies as an exempt estate. The gross estate (£900,000) does not exceed £3 million. The net estate (after deduction of expenses, debts and the application of spouse exemption) is £5,000. This net estate does not exceed the excepted estates threshold of £325,000.

The estate will be an excepted estate, and IHT400 will not be needed. Mina's PRs will instead confirm several values as part of the grant application.

**EXAMPLE**

Wei died on 1 December 2021, leaving an estate worth £1,500,000 before taking into account the funeral expenses or debts, or exemptions. Wei was single (never having married or formed a **civil partnership**). In her will, Wei has left her whole estate to charity.

However, Wei's estate does not qualify as an exempt estate. Although the net value of the estate will be £0, or nil, because of the charity exemption, the gross value of the estate exceeds £1 million (which was the limit applying to deaths before 1 January 2022).

The estate will not be an excepted estate, and IHT400 will be required.

### 7.4.3 Other requirements common to low-value estates and exempt estates

The following conditions must also be met for an estate to qualify as a low-value estate or an exempt estate:

- the deceased's IHT estate must consist only of property passing:
  - by will or intestacy;
  - by statutory nomination (these are now rare—see **5.6**);
  - under a single **settlement** where the deceased had an interest in possession (ie no more than one settlement); or
  - by survivorship (ie where there is a joint tenancy in equity);
- no more than £250,000 (£150,000 for deaths before 1 January 2022) of the deceased's estate immediately before death was settled property (an exempt estate may have up to £1 million in settled property provided no more than £250,000 passes to non-exempt beneficiaries);
- no more than £100,000 of the deceased's estate immediately before death was situated outside the UK; and
- the deceased did not make chargeable transfers during their lifetime other than 'specified transfers' totalling no more than £250,000 (£150,000 for deaths before 1 January 2022).

These requirements do not apply to foreign domiciled estates.

### 7.4.4 Foreign domiciled estates

An estate may also be excepted if the deceased was not domiciled in the UK and owned a relatively small amount of UK assets.

Essentially, with a death on or after 1 January 2022, for the estate to be excepted:

- the deceased must never have been domiciled or treated as domiciled in the UK;
- the gross value of the deceased's estate in the UK must not exceed £150,000;
- the UK estate must consist only of cash or quoted shares or securities;
- those assets must pass by the deceased's will, on intestacy, or be joint property passing by survivorship;
- the deceased must not have had an indirect interests in UK residential property; and
- the deceased must not have made chargeable transfers during the seven years prior to death (other than those covered by the £3,000 per annum IHT annual exemption)

If the estate meets these conditions, then the PRs do not have to submit an IHT400, but will report certain values as part of the grant application. For deaths before 1 January 2022, the last two bullet points above do not apply, and there is a different form for foreign domiciled excepted estates: Form IHT207 is required instead of Form IHT205.

## 7.5 Submission of the IHT400 and payment of IHT

Once the PRs (or their advisors) have completed Form IHT400 and its supporting schedules, the IHT400 and schedules will be sent to HMRC. PRs (or their advisors) will also make arrangements for payment of the IHT due on the account. The IHT payable may be reduced by claiming an instalment option in respect of certain property.

### 7.5.1 Procedure for submission of the IHT400

Surprisingly, at the time of writing there is no HMRC online process for completion of IHT accounts, compared with, say, **Self Assessment** tax returns for income tax and capital gains tax. (During the Covid lockdowns, HMRC did accept delivery of the IHT400 electronically via Dropbox, but only when it was not possible or practical to send the forms to HMRC by post.)

Therefore, a set of paper forms must be sent to HMRC, at the following address: Inheritance Tax, HM Revenue and Customs, BX9 1HT.

Also, due to Covid lockdowns, HMRC accepted IHT400 accounts without the signature of the PRs, who should sign a declaration at the end of the form, because it was difficult to obtain the PRs' 'wet' signatures due to social distancing measures and the switch to remote working. HMRC thus accepted IHT400 forms from professionals which contained the typed names of the PRs, provided there was a clear and unambiguous statement from the professional to confirm that all the PRs had seen the account and had agreed to be bound by the declaration. This temporary change of procedure has now been made permanent.

At the same time as submitting the IHT400 and schedules to HMRC, the PRs (or their advisors) will need to make arrangements for payment of the IHT which is due on delivery of the IHT400.

This may involve the PRs (or their advisors) sending a payment to HMRC, or perhaps utilising one of the direct payment schemes, whereby one or more of the deceased's asset holders (such as a bank or building society) is asked to transfer funds direct to HMRC out of the deceased's account or holding. For more detail on direct payment schemes, see **7.6.1**.

Alternatively, IHT may be paid by electronic transfer, cheque, or using online banking or a mobile banking app. However, it is not possible to make payment by online banking or mobile app from the deceased's own bank accounts, where the direct payment scheme should be used. HMRC have advised that cheques should be sent separately from the IHT400 to avoid delays in payment.

Whichever method of paying the IHT is used, the PRs will first need to obtain an IHT reference number from HMRC at least three weeks before making the payment. The PRs can apply for the reference number online (at www.gov.uk) or by post, using Form IHT422 (Application for an Inheritance Tax reference).

Following submission of the IHT400, and once HMRC have checked that the figures in the IHT400 are correct and the right amount of IHT has been paid, HMRC will write to the PRs to confirm payment of the IHT. In their letter, HMRC will provide the PRs with a unique code for the probate application to HMCTS, together with the gross and net probate values that will be needed for the grant application. (This is a new process that replaces the previous need to submit a Form IHT421 to HMRC with the IHT400. Previously, HMRC would have receipted Form IHT421 to show the IHT had been paid and return it to the PRs. The PRs then sent IHT421 to HMCTS with the grant application. More recently, HMRC liaised directly with HMCTS to confirm that the IHT had been paid. Both of these processes have now been replaced by the HMRC letter to the PRs mentioned earlier.)

## 7.5.2 Time for payment of IHT

The due date for payment of any IHT due on the estate is six months from the end of the month of death. So, if the deceased died on, say, 12 April 2024, the due date would be six months from the end of April 2024, so 31 October 2024.

Interest on unpaid IHT will run from this date (so from and including 1 November 2024 in the above example). The interest rate is much higher than the rates that might be payable on savings accounts. At the time of writing, the rate is 7.75 per cent.

However, if the IHT400 is delivered to HMRC before the due date, the IHT will be payable when the account is delivered, even though this is earlier than the due date. Interest only runs from the due date, though.

Also, as we will see in the next section, it is possible to claim the instalment option in respect of certain types of property. If the instalment option is claimed, then the due date for the first instalment is the same as the standard due date, namely six months from the end of the month of death. Significantly, if the IHT400 account is delivered before the due date, it is not necessary to pay the first instalment on the earlier delivery of the IHT400, although it is common practice to do so.

The due date for payment of IHT on a potentially exempt transfer which has become chargeable as a result of death, and on additional IHT due on a lifetime chargeable transfer as a result of death, is also six months from the end of the month of death. The PRs are not primarily liable for this IHT (the primary liability rests with the transferee), but the PRs will be liable to pay from the estate any IHT due on these lifetime transfers if it is not paid within 12 months from the end of the month of death. The PRs should take steps therefore to check that the transferee pays this IHT. Often, though, there will be no IHT due on the lifetime transfers themselves, and the main effect of the lifetime transfers will be to reduce the amount of the nil rate band available for the death estate, thereby increasing the IHT due on the death estate.

## 7.5.3 The instalment option

If the PRs claim the instalment option where it is available, they will be able to reduce the amount of money that is needed to pay IHT on delivery of the IHT400.

It is possible to claim the instalment option in respect of certain types of property. We have already seen previously that the IHT400 form distinguishes between property which attracts the instalment option and property which does not attract the instalment option, and there are different columns in the sections of the IHT400 form for each type of property.

If the instalment option is claimed on the instalment option property, then the IHT that is attributable to that property may be paid by ten equal annual instalments. Commonly, the first instalment is paid on the submission of the IHT400 to HMRC, but if the IHT400 is delivered before the due date for IHT, then it is not even necessary to pay the first instalment on delivery of the IHT account.

Although the IHT attributable to the non-instalment option property is payable in full on submission of the IHT400, claiming the instalment option where it is available will reduce the amount of money that needs to be found to pay IHT. This is important because the PRs will not be able to realise the deceased's assets until the grant is issued, yet the IHT has to be paid on submission of the IHT400 before the grant is issued.

**EXAMPLE**

James dies on 1 January 2025, leaving a substantial estate. The IHT due on the estate is £100,000. However, of this £100,000, three-quarters of the tax (£75,000) is attributable to instalment option property (James's house). The remaining quarter of the tax (£25,000) is attributable to the rest of James's assets (bank accounts, quoted shares, personal possessions), which do not attract the instalment option.

James's PRs submit the IHT400 to HMRC on 1 March 2025, and claim the instalment option in respect of the house.

The due date for payment of the IHT will be 31 July 2025, which is six months from the end of the month in which James died. However, the IHT of £25,000 on the non-instalment option property must be paid on the delivery of the IHT400 on 1 March 2025, even though this is earlier than the due date of 31 July 2025.

The first instalment of the IHT on the instalment option property (£7,500) does not have to be paid, though, until 31 July 2025, so does not have to be paid on the earlier delivery of the IHT400 on 1 March 2025. For convenience's sake, the PRs decide to make the payment of the first instalment on delivery of the account.

As a result, on submission of the IHT400 the PRs will only need to find £32,500 (£25,000 in respect of the non-instalment option property, and the first one-tenth instalment of £7,500 on the instalment option property).

Prior to the grant being issued, it is likely to be easier for the PRs to find £32,500 than to find the whole £100,000. (As said, the first instalment of £7,500 was paid on delivery of the IHT400 out of convenience, but if funds were more limited, it would be possible to deliver the IHT400 and only pay the £25,000 due on the non-instalment option property.)

Only certain assets qualify for the instalment option. There is a detailed list in the Inheritance Tax Act 1984 (IHTA 1984) but, in summary, the main categories of instalment option property are:

- land and buildings;
- a business or an interest in a business (eg a share in a partnership);
- certain specified shareholdings, including:
  - shares (unquoted or quoted) which gave the transferor control immediately before the transfer; and
  - certain non-controlling shareholdings (unquoted shares only), provided certain conditions apply.

The instalment option is allowed for these types of property because it is recognised that the PRs may have difficulty selling these assets quickly. It may take years to sell the deceased's house or to sell a shareholding in an unquoted company.

(Having said that, many shareholdings in unquoted companies will be covered by IHT business property relief at a rate of 100 per cent, so that those shareholdings have a nil value for IHT purposes, meaning no IHT will be due on those shares anyway. The question of paying by instalments then becomes irrelevant, because there is no tax to pay on those shares.)

We will see in **Chapter 10**, that interest may be payable on the unpaid instalments, and that it is not possible to continue to pay by instalments where the property is sold by the PRs because the PRs then have the sale proceeds which can be used to pay the remaining instalments. The importance of the IHT instalment option for present purposes, however, is that claiming it will reduce the amount of money that the PRs need to find in advance of obtaining the grant of representation.

The instalment option may also be available in respect of IHT due on lifetime transfers as a result of death (PETs which have become chargeable and additional tax on lifetime chargeable transfers) provided certain conditions are met.

## 7.6 Methods of funding the initial payment of inheritance tax

The PRs face a practical problem when paying the inheritance due on the submission of the IHT400. The IHT400 has to be submitted before the PRs can apply for the grant of representation and this means the IHT due on the IHT400 also has to be paid before the grant is issued.

However, until the grant is issued the PRs will not be able to realise many of the deceased's assets, either because the asset holders (such as banks, building societies, insurance companies, unit trust managers) will require sight of the grant before releasing funds or because a grant will be needed to sell assets (eg shares or land) to third parties.

If the PRs are not able to realise the deceased's assets in order to pay the IHT, what other sources of finance are there? There are various options which may or may not be available to the PRs, depending on the particular circumstances of the estate.

### 7.6.1 Direct payment schemes

There is more than one direct payment scheme that might be of use. Under these schemes the PRs ask the asset holder to transfer to HMRC sufficient monies from the deceased's accounts or holdings to meet the IHT liability.

The most commonly used scheme is for direct payment of IHT from the bank account or building society account of the deceased to HMRC. The scheme also applies to National Savings & Investments (NS&I) products. The scheme is voluntary and so banks and building societies do not have to operate the scheme: most will do so, though. To take advantage of the scheme, there will also need to be sufficient funds to pay the IHT in one or more of the deceased's accounts with the bank, building society or NS&I.

For the PRs, and for their solicitors, the scheme has the benefit that payment of IHT can be arranged without the PR or solicitor having to arrange for the funds to pass through their own accounts, or to make the payment themselves. However, the scheme does have the disadvantage that the PRs (or their solicitors) are reliant on other parties—the bank, building society, NS&I and HMRC—working effectively together, and the process can be slow.

The PRs will first need to obtain an IHT reference number from HMRC online or using Form IHT422, as mentioned earlier. Then the PRs will send a completed Form IHT423 (quoting the IHT reference number) to the bank, building society or NS&I. The IHT423 will identify the account from which funds are to be taken, and state the amount that is to be transferred to HMRC. The PRs will send Form IHT423 to the bank, building society or NS&I at the same time as sending the IHT400 and supporting schedules (including IHT421) to HMRC. (However, the PRs should have also made contact with the bank, building society or NS&I some time before sending Form IHT423, to check that the bank or building society is part of the scheme and to satisfy the asset holder's requirements regarding proof of the PRs' status.) PRs may also need to sign a separate authority, depending on the requirements of particular asset holders.

The bank or building society will transfer the amount requested on IHT423 to HMRC in payment of the IHT. Once HMRC are satisfied that the IHT has been paid, HMRC send a letter to the PRs with the unique code for the probate application and the gross and net probate values.

There is a similar direct payment scheme for payment of the IHT out of British government stock held by the deceased, although the process is different: the PRs must write to Computershare Investor Services, which run the British government stock scheme, to request payment from the deceased's holding. The procedure is detailed at: https://www.gov.uk/paying-inheritance-tax/british-government-stock.

### 7.6.2 Informal arrangements

For many years, banks and building societies were willing to provide the solicitor with a cheque made payable to HMRC for the amount of the IHT, drawn on an account of the deceased. This was usually only possible where the bank or building society had a good working relationship with, and trusted, the solicitors' firm. It may be possible to obtain funds from the bank or building society informally, by electronic transfer (direct to HMRC) out of the deceased's accounts. Similarly, if there are life assurance monies payable to the estate, the life assurance company may be willing to make a payment direct to HMRC.

Also, although historically banks and building societies have required sight of the grant of representation before releasing large sums from the deceased's accounts, many banks have changed their practice in recent years and will now release substantial amounts from the deceased's accounts purely on production of a death certificate. This would enable the PRs to obtain money from the deceased's bank and it may be that the amount the deceased's bank is willing to release will cover the amount needed to pay the IHT due on submission of the IHT400, with the PRs using this money to pay HMRC. Building societies may be less willing to release large sums without production of a grant.

## 7.6.3 Small payments

If the amount of the IHT to be paid is small, it might be possible to obtain small payments under the Administration of Estates (Small Payments) Act 1965 and/or the Building Societies Act 1986, as detailed in **8.2.2.1**. However, in most cases this will either not be possible (because the deceased does not have assets of the requisite type or the balance on each account exceeds £5,000), or the IHT due is more than £5,000 (and so any funds released in this way would be insufficient to pay the IHT).

## 7.6.4 Loans from beneficiaries

It might be possible to borrow money from one or more of the beneficiaries of the estate. Beneficiaries may be willing to do this in order to ensure the grant is obtained as quickly as possible, and a beneficiary may be willing to lend money to the PRs interest-free.

Of course, the beneficiaries will need to have the financial resources to be able to lend this money to the PRs, as well as being willing to provide such a loan. Many beneficiaries will not have the financial resources to be able to lend money in this way.

However, it is possible that some beneficiaries may have received property on the death of the deceased which has passed independently of the deceased's estate. So, a beneficiary might have received a discretionary payment from the deceased's pension scheme, or the death benefit of a life assurance policy that was written in trust. These payments would, potentially, provide the beneficiary with funds which could be used to lend money to the estate for the payment of IHT, always provided the beneficiary was willing. Similarly, if the deceased had a joint bank account, the monies in that account would pass automatically to the surviving joint account holder, who could then lend money to the PRs. (Having said that, sometimes banks will freeze joint accounts following a death.)

The 'loan' could take the form of the beneficiary paying the IHT out of their own bank account, using online or mobile banking, and then claiming the money back from the estate.

## 7.6.5 Bridging loan from a bank

If none of the previous options is available, another option is to obtain a loan from a bank. This form of short-term loan is often called a 'bridging' loan. The loan is short-term because the PRs take it out solely to pay the IHT and will then seek to pay the loan off as soon as possible after the grant, once the PRs are able to realise the deceased's assets.

However, there are problems with this option. First, banks may be reluctant to provide such a facility and, if they do, will charge an arrangement fee and interest on the loan. The bank will require undertakings from the PRs, and any solicitors acting for the PRs, that the loan will be paid off out of the first proceeds of the estate. There may be other conditions imposed.

Given these problems, and the likely availability of the Direct Payment Scheme mentioned previously, this option should be seen as one of last resort.

## 7.6.6 Direct transfer of heritage property to HMRC

In a small number of estates, it might be possible to transfer special kinds of property to HMRC, instead of some or all of the IHT which is due (s230 IHTA 1984). Only certain types of property will be accepted in lieu of IHT. Essentially, the property (whether land or movable property such as works of art) will only be accepted if it is pre-eminent for its national, scientific, historic or artistic interest.

### 7.6.7 Obtaining a grant on credit

In theory, it is possible to obtain a grant without first paying the IHT which is due on the IHT400. In exceptional cases, HMRC will permit PRs to obtain a grant without paying the IHT first. From 1 April 2024, it is no longer necessary to have sought commercial loans to pay IHT prior to requesting a grant on credit. In most estates, though, it will be possible to use one of the other options to raise money to pay the IHT.

**KEY POINT SUMMARY**

- Following a death, usually a relative of the deceased registers the death and obtains the death certificate. The relative will then contact solicitors, who will take initial instructions from the relative or personal representative, and obtain relevant information from them about the deceased's assets and liabilities and details of the beneficiaries.
- The funeral will often have taken place before the solicitor is instructed but the will should be checked to see if the deceased expressed any wishes in it as to the funeral or disposal of the body. A will is not the best place for such wishes, which the deceased should ideally have communicated to their family during their lifetime.
- The solicitor will need to notify the holders of the deceased's assets of the death and will need to ascertain the value of the deceased's assets for probate and IHT purposes. The asset holder will be able to confirm the value of certain assets (eg the balances on bank and building society accounts).
- Other assets (eg land and shares) will have to be valued. Quoted shares have a standard method of valuation based on publicly available information, but unquoted shares and land will have to be valued by an expert.
- Creditors will also be notified of the death and the value of liabilities ascertained. Contact should be made with the funeral directors if the funeral expenses have still to be paid.
- PRs will need to know about assets which pass independently of the will or rules of intestacy, and about relevant lifetime transfers, as both might affect the amount of IHT for which the PRs are liable.
- IHT400 is the main inheritance tax account and is used in any estate which is not 'excepted'. IHT400 is supplemented by a large number of supporting schedules.
- No IHT account is required where the estate is an excepted estate and the death was on or after 1 January 2022.
- Where the estate is an excepted estate and the deceased died before 1 January 2022, a shorter, simpler account (IHT205 or IHT207) is used.
- There are three types of excepted estate: low-value estates (where the gross value is below the relevant threshold); exempt estates (where the net value of the estate, taking into account spouse and charity exemption, is below the threshold); and foreign domiciled estates.
- If the estate is not excepted, PRs (or their advisors) will submit IHT400 and the supporting schedules to HMRC, and will make arrangements for the payment of any IHT which is due on delivery of the account. HMRC will confirm payment of the IHT by letter, providing a unique code and the gross and net estate figures to be used in the grant application.
- The IHT on the estate is due six months from the end of the month of death. Interest on unpaid tax will be payable after this due date. However, if the IHT400 is submitted before the due date, the IHT must be paid on the due date subject to any IHT where the instalment option has been claimed.

- The IHT instalment option applies to certain types of property that may be difficult to sell, such as land and buildings. If the instalment option is claimed, IHT is payable in ten annual instalments. The first instalment is due on the standard due date for IHT. Claiming the instalment option may significantly reduce the IHT which has to be paid on the delivery of the IHT400.
- There is a practical problem in paying IHT when submitting the IHT400. The IHT400 must be submitted, and IHT paid, before the PRs can apply for the grant. However, until the grant is issued the PRs may not be able to realise many of the deceased's assets. Prior to the grant there may therefore be a shortage of funds with which to pay the IHT.
- Despite this, there are various methods of funding the IHT. There are direct payment schemes, whereby monies can be transferred directly by the asset holder (in particular, a bank or building society) to HMRC. Alternatively, funds may be accessed using informal arrangements with banks and building societies. If these options are not available, it might be possible to obtain a loan from a beneficiary or from a bank: these loans will then be repaid once the grant has been issued and the PRs are able to realise the deceased's assets.

# CHAPTER 8
# Obtaining the Grant of Representation

**FUNCTIONING LEGAL KNOWLEDGE**

This chapter covers the following functioning legal knowledge required to pass the SQE 1 assessments:

**Probate and administration practice**

**Grants of representation:**

- need for grant
- the relevant provisions of the Non-Contentious Probate Rules
- application procedure

**AUTHORITIES UNDERPINNING PRACTICE**

The key authorities that underpin this area of practice are listed below. Note that for legislation you are linked to legislation.gov.uk.

Although much of the legislation on this government website is available in its amended form, the incorporation of new amendments into the text of legislation can be delayed. You should refer to legal databases to ensure you are referencing the most up-to-date legislation.

- Senior Courts Act 1981
  **http://www.legislation.gov.uk/ukpga/1981/54/contents**
- Non-Contentious Probate Rules 1987
  **http://www.legislation.gov.uk/uksi/1987/2024/contents/made**

## 8.1 Introduction

In **Chapter 7** we looked at the initial work that is needed when taking instructions for the administration of an estate, prior to obtaining the grant of representation. That initial work included the completion of the **inheritance tax account** (IHT400 or IHT205), the submission of an IHT400 to HMRC and the payment of IHT. In this chapter we will consider the process of applying to HM Courts and Tribunals Service (HMCTS) for the grant of representation. Then, in **Chapter 9**, we will consider the work involved in administering and distributing the estate once the grant of representation has been obtained.

The rules on applications for grants of representation are contained mainly in a statutory instrument—the Non-Contentious Probate Rules 1987 (NCPR 1987). Although these rules date originally from 1987 there have been significant changes to the rules, especially in recent years. For example, in September 2020 significant changes were made by the Non-Contentious Probate (Amendment) Rules 2020 with effect from 2 November 2020. These amendments were significant in three respects. First, the rules require all grant applications which are made by probate professionals (eg solicitors) to be made online, unless the application is one of a number of listed types of application which can also be made via a paper application (see **8.4**). Secondly, the rules enable the use of **witness** statements, supported by a **statement of truth**, instead of **affidavits** (see **8.6** on additional evidence).

Thirdly, the amendment rules introduce a new overriding objective for non-contentious probate business. This idea of an overriding objective is one that has been used for many years in the rules applying to contentious civil litigation (the Civil Procedure Rules). The amendment rules insert a new r3A into the NCPR 1987, which states that the overriding objective of the Rules is 'to enable non-contentious and common form probate business to be dealt with justly and expeditiously by the court and the registry'.

## 8.2 Grants of representation and personal representatives

There are two types of **personal representative** and three main types of grant of representation.

In most estates, it will be necessary to obtain a grant of representation from HMCTS as the deceased will have assets which cannot be realised without production of a valid grant of representation. It will not be possible to cash in most investments without a grant; also, it will not be possible to sell the deceased's house or sell any stocks and shares without a grant. In some estates, though, it may be possible to administer the estate without obtaining a grant at all.

The grant will either confirm the authority of the personal representatives (if they are the **executors** of the deceased) or confer authority on the person(s) who have applied to be **administrator**(s) of the deceased.

There are rules and conventions which determine the number of personal representatives (PRs) in different estates and who can act as personal representatives. We will look at a number of these rules and conventions in this section.

### 8.2.1 The main types of grant of representation and personal representatives

There are two types of PRs:

- executors; and
- administrators.

Executors are appointed by the **testator** in the **will** (or **codicil**), and so are chosen by the testator. Administrators are appointed by HMCTS following a death, and a person's right to apply to be appointed as an administrator depends upon the provisions of the NCPR 1987.

However, administrators may be either:

- 'administrators with the will', if the deceased left a will but there are no executors willing and able to prove the will; or
- administrators without the will (called, simply, 'administrators') where the deceased did not leave a will and died wholly intestate.

We will consider the main types of grant that will be issued to each type of personal representative in more detail in **8.3**.

### 8.2.2 When a grant is not required

A grant of representation is not needed in all estates. For example, if the estate is very small, with very few assets, it may be possible to administer the estate without HMCTS issuing a grant. There are statutory rules that enable small sums to be realised without production of a grant, and there has been a change to banking practice in recent years which means it may be easier to obtain funds solely on production of a **death certificate**.

Also, as we saw in **Chapter 5**, there may be assets which pass on death independently of the will or the rules of **intestacy**, and it follows that it is not necessary to obtain a grant to realise those assets. Also, some assets which are part of the estate may be realised (ie sold) without a grant.

#### 8.2.2.1 Small sums due to the estate

Under the Administration of Estates (Small Payments) Act 1965, it may be possible for the PRs to obtain payment of sums due to the estate on production of a copy of the death certificate. However, where orders have been made under this Act, there is an upper limit (currently £5,000) in respect of each account—and if this is exceeded a grant will be necessary to establish title to the whole sum in the account, not just the excess. The Act allows such payment to be made to the person appearing to be entitled to the grant or to be beneficially entitled to the asset concerned. The Act merely permits payment without a grant—it is not obligatory.

Monies which are covered by orders under this Act include:

- money held in the National Savings Bank, National Savings Certificates or Premium Savings Bonds (NB: small balances in accounts with the high street banks are not covered by orders under the Act);
- monies payable on the death of a member of a trade union or in an industrial or provident society or a friendly society;
- civil servants' salaries, wages or superannuation benefits; and
- service, police and firemen's pensions.

Similar provisions apply under the Building Societies Act 1986 to funds invested in a building society.

Although requirements vary from one asset holder to another, typically the asset holder will require some form of declaration from the person who is claiming the funds or additional proof (such as a certified copy of a will or a marriage certificate to show a spouse's entitlement on intestacy).

#### 8.2.2.2 Current banking practice

The practice of many banks relating to the release of funds from a deceased person's account has changed in recent years. At one time, banks were reluctant to release any monies from the deceased's bank accounts without production of a grant of representation. One example of an exception to that was where the solicitors acting in the estate requested a cheque from the bank, payable to HMRC, to pay the **inheritance tax** due on the delivery of the IHT400. Another example was when there was a request for a cheque to pay the funeral directors. However, recently banks appear to be taking a different approach to the release of monies following a death. It is apparent that some banks will release significant sums of money (often tens of thousands of pounds) from the deceased's accounts simply on production of a death certificate, without the need to produce a grant. There is obviously a risk of fraud or abuse here, and banks may face claims subsequently for allowing such payments if they make a payment to someone who is not entitled to the money. However, banks appear to be taking a commercial decision that the risk of fraud is low and that the bank can meet the relatively few claims that are likely to arise.

Even if a bank is willing to release substantial sums from the deceased's accounts without production of a grant, in most cases a grant should or must be obtained. It is usually preferable for an executor to obtain a grant, and an administrator derives their authority from the grant.

#### 8.2.2.3 Assets which pass independently of the estate

It may be that most of the deceased's assets will pass independently of the deceased's will or of the rules of intestacy. These assets are discussed in more detail in **Chapter 5**, but include:

- the deceased's interest as a **joint tenant in equity** in jointly owned property—the deceased's interest will pass by survivorship to the surviving joint tenant(s);
- any payment made by the **trustees** of a pension scheme, where the payment is being made at the discretion of the trustees—such payments are often made to individuals named, or nominated, by the deceased;
- a life assurance policy that is written in **trust** (either for named **beneficiaries** or under s11 of the Married Women's Property Act 1882 for the spouse/civil partner or children of the deceased);

- statutory nominations in certain investments, such as deposits in friendly societies (these statutory nominations are now relatively rare); and
- property which is the subject of a valid ***donatio mortis causa*** (a **gift** in contemplation of death).

A grant of representation is not needed to realise any of the above assets, and the assets will not devolve on the PRs but will pass outside the estate.

So, although there may be substantial assets passing on the deceased's death, there may be no need for a grant to deal with those assets, as can be seen in the following example.

**EXAMPLE**

Harriette has died, leaving a will. She was married to Geoffrey who has survived her. She is also survived by two adult children, Nina and Pauline.

Harriette and Geoffrey owned their house (and its contents) as joint tenants in equity. Harriette's share of the house (and contents) is valued at £250,000. Her interest will pass by survivorship to Geoffrey as the surviving joint tenant. Also, the couple had joint bank accounts. Harriette's share of the balance on these at her date of death was £50,000. Again, her interest in the accounts will pass automatically to Geoffrey by survivorship.

Harriette was a member of her employer's occupational pension scheme. There is no entitlement to a payment from the scheme, but the pension scheme trustees have indicated they will make a discretionary payment of £150,000 from the scheme to Geoffrey (in accordance with a nomination form completed by Harriette). This payment will be made by the trustees of the pension scheme direct to Geoffrey.

Harriette had also insured her own life, and there is a payment of £80,000 due from the life assurance company. However, the life policy was written in trust for her two children. The death benefit therefore belongs to the children, not to Harriette's estate, and the life assurance company will make the payment direct to the children.

There is no need to obtain a grant of representation to deal with any of the above assets, because they all pass independently of Harriette's estate.

Harriette's only other assets are her personal possessions, and there is no need for a grant of representation to deal with these, either, even though they form part of her estate. In her will, Harriette appointed Geoffrey as her executor. She divided her jewellery among Nina and Pauline, and Geoffrey will take the rest of her personal possessions as he is the residuary beneficiary. As executor, Geoffrey can deal with the personal possessions without the need of a grant.

#### 8.2.2.4 Assets of the estate which may be realised without a grant

In very limited situations, such as in the above example, an executor may be able to realise or transfer certain assets without needing a grant. Personal possessions may be sold or transferred to the beneficiaries of a will without the need of a grant (although if assets are to be sold, the buyer might insist on seeing a grant). If the deceased had any cash in their possession (as opposed to in a bank or other account), the executor could distribute this cash without a grant.

This is not the case for estates where there is no executor because administrators derive their authority from the grant, so will not have the authority to deal with the deceased's assets without a grant, although the prospective administrator may take steps to safeguard the deceased's assets.

## 8.2.3 The effect of a grant of representation

The effect of the grant of representation differs depending on whether the personal representatives are executors or administrators.

### 8.2.3.1 Executors

The executors of the will have been chosen and appointed by the testator of the will, and so executors receive their authority to act from the testator and from the will. This means that executors have the authority to act as PRs on behalf of the deceased (and the estate) from the date of death.

Although it will usually be necessary to apply for a grant of representation (a grant of probate), the grant merely *confirms* that the executors have this authority. (This is why it is called a grant of probate—'probate' comes from the Latin for proof, and so the grant simply provides proof, or evidence, that the executors have the authority to act.)

The executor can in theory collect in and distribute the estate without need of a grant of probate but in practice a grant will be necessary because asset holders will usually demand sight of the grant of probate as proof of the executor's authority. Similarly, purchasers of assets from the estate (particularly land and shares) will require sight of the grant of probate. An executor may also start legal proceedings on behalf of the estate before the grant is issued.

#### 8.2.3.2 Administrators

In contrast, a person who wishes to be appointed as an administrator (of whatever type) has no authority to act until the **grant of letters of administration** (with or without the will) is issued by HMCTS. So, with an administrator the grant *confers* authority on the administrator who will not be the deceased's personal representative until the grant has been issued.

Until the grant of letters of administration is issued, the deceased's estate vests in the **Public Trustee** (s9 Administration of Estates Act 1925).

This has some practical consequences, in that appointed executors can do things prior to the issuing of a grant that prospective administrators cannot do. As solicitors acting for a person who is applying to be an administrator, you are not, before the grant, strictly acting for the deceased's PR—you are merely acting for someone who hopes to be appointed as the deceased's PR. However, in practice, this is not usually a problem.

This is because the authority of the administrator will relate back to the period before the appointment to validate acts undertaken by the administrator which were for the benefit of the estate. However, there are some acts that a prospective administrator may not do before the grant, such as distribute the deceased's property or bring court proceedings on behalf of the estate.

### 8.2.4 The number of personal representatives

A grant will not be issued to more than four persons in respect of the same property (s114 Senior Courts Act 1981). This rule applies to executors and to administrators, but as HMCTS usually appoint only one administrator (or sometimes two), the limitation of four persons is more relevant to executors. Different considerations apply to executors and administrators so they are considered in turn.

#### 8.2.4.1 Executors

It is unwieldy and impractical for there to be a large number of executors in an estate. For example, every time there is a document which needs to be signed by the executors, the more executors there are, the more signatures that will be needed. It is largely for this reason that a grant of representation will be issued to a maximum of four persons.

A testator can appoint any number of executors in the will, although there are obviously practical considerations with naming a large number of individuals, so this is rarely done.

There will, though, be significant numbers of existing wills (of persons who have not yet died) which appoint the partners in a particular solicitors' firm as executors. The firm in question may have many partners, and in theory all of them (usually, all of the partners at the date of death) will be appointed as executors. Where the partners in a firm of solicitors are appointed as executors, it is common for the appointment clause to indicate a wish that only two of the partners should prove the will, with **power being reserved** (see **8.2.8**) to the other partners.

#### 8.2.4.2 Administrators

Although more than one administrator can be appointed in any estate, the practice is to appoint one administrator only, except in certain specified situations. There is no need for more than one administrator in most estates.

The exception is where the estate contains a minority interest and/or a **life interest**, when usually a minimum of two administrators must be appointed (s114 Senior Courts Act 1981). That is unless the court considers it expedient to appoint a sole administrator. However, a trust corporation can be always be appointed as sole administrator even where there is a minority and/or life interest.

A minority interest is where any beneficiary of the estate is under the age of 18 years. This could be where such a beneficiary has been given a gift or share of the **residuary estate** in a will, or where the beneficiary has an interest in the estate under the intestacy rules.

**EXAMPLE**

James has died leaving a will. He appointed his brother, Kevin, as his executor and left his residuary estate to his three children, Arthur, Lorna and Ruth. Arthur and Lorna are aged 20 and 18 respectively, but Ruth is aged 15. There is therefore a minority interest (Ruth's interest in one-third of the residuary estate).

If Kevin survives James, and if Kevin is able and willing to take out a grant of probate, Kevin can act as sole executor of James's will, even though there is a minority interest. There is no need for a second personal representative to be appointed.

However, if Kevin dies before James, or if Kevin is unable or unwilling to take out a grant of probate, there will need to be two administrators appointed under a **grant of letters of administration with the will annexed**, because of the minority interest. It is likely that Arthur and Lorna, as adult residuary beneficiaries, will be appointed as administrators.

**EXAMPLE**

Tabitha has died intestate. She is survived by her husband, Aaron, and by their two children, Isobel and Oliver, who are aged 19 and 16 respectively.

Tabitha's estate exceeds the **statutory legacy** payable to Aaron. The excess will be divided equally between Aaron (who will get one half of the excess) and the children (who will share the other half of the excess). As Oliver is under 18 there is a minority interest.

It will be necessary to appoint two administrators. Most likely, this will be Aaron, as surviving spouse, and Isobel, the adult child.

A life interest would occur where there is a will, which gives one or more beneficiaries the right to income for life: this is not particularly common, not least because usually in the will the testator will have appointed at least one executor who is able and willing to act, so there is no need to appoint administrators.

Two administrators used to be necessary in some intestate estates but this is no longer the case. Under old rules which applied where the deceased died before 1 October 2014, the spouse had a life interest in part of the estate if the estate exceeded the amount of the spouse's statutory legacy. There is no such life interest under the current intestacy rules.

## 8.2.5 Minors

A minor is a person under the age of majority, namely a person under the age of 18. A grant of representation will not be issued to a minor. Different considerations apply depending on whether the minor has been appointed as an executor or is a person entitled to apply for a grant of letters of administration.

### 8.2.5.1 Executors

Although it is not advisable to do so, a testator may appoint a minor as executor in their will. If the person appointed is still a minor at the time that the grant application is made, the grant will not be issued to the person who is still a minor. Put another way, an executor who is under 18 at the time of the grant application cannot obtain a grant of probate themselves.

Where the minor was the sole executor appointed by the deceased, a grant of letters of administration will be issued to another person 'for the use and benefit' of the minor until the minor reaches 18 (r32 NCPR 1987). Rule 32 sets out a list of persons who may take out such a grant: this includes the parents or guardians of the minor. However, if the minor is an executor but not a beneficiary of the will, the person(s) entitled to share in the residuary estate of the testator may be appointed as administrator.

A grant for the use and benefit of the minor will be limited in time (usually until the person reaches 18), and the grant for use and benefit will automatically cease to have effect at that point in time (see also **8.7.3**). If the administration of the estate has not been completed by the time the person reaches 18, the person who is now an adult on reaching 18 will apply for a '**cessate grant**' in order to complete the administration of the estate (see **8.8.3**).

Alternatively, where the minor is a co-executor with one or more adult executors who are able and willing to take out a grant of probate, r33 of the NCPR 1987 provides that a grant of probate may be issued to the other executor(s), with 'power reserved' to the executor who is a minor (see **8.2.8**). If the administration of the estate has not been completed by the time the person becomes an adult (ie reaches 18), the minor can then apply for a grant of probate themselves. In this situation, this second grant of probate is called a 'grant of **double probate**', and the person will administer the estate alongside the executors who obtained the original grant of probate (see **8.8.4**).

Although normally the estate of the testator will vest in the executor(s) as PRs of the testator on the testator's death (so that the executor(s) have authority to act from the date of death), s118 of the Senior Courts Act 1981 says that the testator's property does not vest in a minor executor until such time as a grant of probate is issued to them (which, as said, will not happen until they have reached the age of 18).

#### 8.2.5.2 Administrators

A grant of letters of administration (whether simple administration on an intestacy or administration with the will annexed) will not be issued to a person under the age of 18.

Where the person with the best entitlement to a grant of letters of administration is a minor, a grant of letters of administration may be issued, again for the use and benefit of the minor until the minor reaches 18. If the administration of the estate has not been completed by the time the minor reaches 18, then the grant for the use and benefit of the minor will usually expire at that point in time, and the person (who is now an adult) will then apply for a cessate grant of letters of administration themselves.

Usually, however, more than one person will be entitled to apply for a grant of letters of administration. Where a minor is only one of the persons who is entitled to apply for a grant of letters of administration but there are adults able and willing to take out a grant, the grant will be issued to an adult (or adults) in preference to issuing a grant to the parent or guardian of the minor (r27(5) NCPR 1987).

### 8.2.6 **Mental incapacity**

Similar issues apply with adults who lack the necessary mental **capacity** (within the meaning of the Mental Capacity Act 2005) to apply for a grant.

If the person is an executor but there are other executors able and willing to take out a grant of probate, power can be reserved to the person who lacks capacity.

However, if there are no other executors able and willing to take out a grant, a grant of letters of administration for the use and benefit of the person who lacks capacity may be issued (r35 NCPR 1987). Under r35, a grant may be issued to someone who has been given authority over the person's finances (as a deputy appointed by the Court of Protection or an attorney appointed by the person under a lasting power of attorney or an enduring power of attorney). If there is no one who has been so appointed as deputy or attorney, then the grant may be issued to a person entitled to the residuary estate.

Similarly, if the person lacking capacity is entitled to apply for letters of administration (whether simple administration on an intestacy or administration with the will), it is possible to issue a grant to a deputy or attorney for the use and benefit of the incapacitated person. However, if there are other persons who have an equal entitlement to the grant as the person who lacks capacity, the grant will normally be issued to one or more of those persons.

**EXAMPLE**

Declan has died intestate leaving three adult children—Barbara, Janice and Laurence. Under the intestacy rules, each of the children is entitled to a one third-share of Declan's estate, and each of them has an equal entitlement to apply for a grant of letters of administration.

Barbara has learning difficulties and lacks the necessary mental capacity to be an administrator. Ranjit is her deputy, having been appointed by the Court of Protection.

Under r35 of the NCPR 1987, it is likely that the grant of letters of administration will be issued to either Janice or Laurence, rather than issuing a grant to Ranjit for the use and benefit of Barbara.

## 8.2.7 Renunciation by executors

A person who is appointed as executor by the testator can refuse to act following the testator's death. The executor cannot be forced to apply for a grant of probate or to administer the estate. A person is free to decide not to act if they do not wish to do so. If an executor does not wish to act, they may '**renounce**' probate. They will cease to be an executor and personal representative.

However, this 'renunciation' by the executor is only possible if the executor has not undertaken any steps in administering the estate. The old-fashioned phrase used is that the executor must not have 'intermeddled in the estate'. So, for example, an executor who had sent copies of the death certificate to the deceased's bank and other asset holders, or who had instructed an estate agent to value the deceased's house for probate purposes, would most likely be regarded as having 'intermeddled' and so the executor would not then be able to renounce probate. It can sometimes be unclear whether the steps undertaken by an executor amount to intermeddling, and so it is not always clear whether an executor still has the right to renounce probate.

A renunciation must be in writing, signed by the executor and witnessed by an independent witness. It is necessary to produce the renunciation to HMCTS to show that the executor named or referred to in the will has renounced. There is a standard form (PA15: renunciation (will)) which is available from the gov.uk website.

The executor should give the completed and signed form to the person(s) applying for the grant who then submits the form to HMCTS with the grant application papers.

If the executor renounces successfully they will take no further part in the application for the grant of probate or the administration of the estate as a PR (and they must declare on the PA15 form that they will not attempt to do so).

The executor may also be entitled to a grant of administration with the will if they have also been appointed as a trustee of the residuary estate. If that is the case, the person will also have to renounce their entitlement to a grant of letters of administration as a trustee, but the renunciation form mentioned above provides for a renunciation as both executor and trustee.

There is a separate form (PA16) for a spouse or civil partner to renounce their right to be administrator in an intestacy where the deceased was survived by a spouse and issue.

## 8.2.8 Power reserved to executors

What happens if the testator has appointed more than four executors? The grant will only be issued to four of the executors, so what is the position of the other executors who are not named on the grant itself? Similarly, what if one or more of the executors named in the will has decided that they do not wish to take an active role in the administration of the estate, at least initially?

We have already seen that an executor who has not intermeddled in the estate may renounce probate, and then they will cease to be an executor.

However, there is an alternative to renunciation, which is for 'power to be reserved' to an executor who does not, initially, prove the will. When power is reserved, the executor to whom power is reserved stands on the side lines. They do not take part in the administration of the estate as a proving executor, but they can be brought in at a later date to act as executor if needed.

So, if there are, say, six named executors in a will, the grant of probate will be issued to only four of those executors and power may be reserved to the other two executors. As already mentioned in **Chapter 2**, the executors to whom power has been reserved, namely the non-proving executors, effectively act like substitutes in a football match. If there is a need at some point in the future, one of those non-proving executors can be issued with a second grant of probate (called a grant of 'double probate') and from that point on they will act alongside the other proving executors.

Unlike in a football match, though, where substitutions are standard practice, an executor to whom power has been reserved will only usually become a proving executor in circumstances where there is a problem with one or more of the original proving executors. For example, there may have been one proving executor and one non-proving executor but the proving executor may have since died. In such a situation, a grant could be issued to the non-proving executor who will take over the administration of the estate. Alternatively, one of, say, two proving executors might have died but the other proving executor might still be able to administer the estate. However, it might be thought best to have two executors working together, so the non-proving executor is issued with a grant of double probate so that they can work alongside the surviving proving executor.

**EXAMPLE**

Gurvinder had died. In his will, he appointed Anul, Reshmi and Darshit as his executors. Anul and Reshmi apply for a grant of probate but power is reserved to Darshit.

Anul dies subsequently, before the administration of the estate is completed. Darshit can apply for a grant of double probate and will then complete the administration alongside the surviving original proving executor, Reshmi.

### 8.2.9 Overlooking applicants and removing personal representatives

Under s116 of the Senior Courts Act 1981, the High Court may pass over a person who has a prior claim to a grant, if the court considers it is necessary or expedient to appoint some other person as administrator. This might happen, for example, where there are serious concerns about the honesty and integrity of the person with the prior claim to the grant. Alternatively, the person might not be suitable to be a PR for another reason, as in the case of the infamous Dr Crippen, who had murdered his wife and so was deemed unsuitable to be the administrator of her estate (*Re Crippen* [1911] P 108).

The High Court also has the power, under s50 of the Administration of Justice Act 1985, to remove an existing personal representative and appoint a substitute.

## 8.3 The main forms of grant and the relevant provisions of the Non-Contentious Probate Rules 1987

There are three main forms of grant:

1 a **grant of probate**—issued to the proving executors of the deceased's will;

2 a **grant of letters of administration**—appointing one or more administrators to the estate of a person who has died intestate; and

3 a **grant of letters of administration with the will annexed**—appointing one or more administrators to the estate of a person who has left a will, but where there are no executors able and willing to obtain a grant.

There are other, more specialised forms of grant, or variations on the above, which we will consider in **8.7** and **8.8**.

Note that where a person has died **partially intestate**, they will have left a valid will which will govern the distribution of part of the deceased's estate even if another part of the deceased's estate is governed by the intestacy rules. As there is a valid will, there may be proving executors who will apply for a grant of probate: those executors would then carry out the testator's wishes over the testate part of the estate, and those executors will distribute the rest in accordance with the intestacy rules. Nevertheless, the grant will still be a grant of probate.

Similarly, if the deceased died partially intestate but left a valid will, but there are no executors able and willing to apply for a grant, a grant of letters of administration with the will annexed will be issued to one or more administrators. The administrator(s) will then apply the terms of the will to the testate part of the estate and will apply the intestacy rules to the intestate part of the estate.

It is even possible, although unlikely, for a person to have made a valid will appointing executors who are able and willing to act but the will fails to govern the distribution of any part of the deceased's estate. In such a situation, the executors would still obtain a grant of probate but would apply the intestacy rules to the whole of the estate.

The rules on applying for grants of representation come mainly from a statutory instrument—the NCPR 1987. Although these rules date from 1987, they have been amended over time, for example by replacing **oaths** with statements of truth in November 2018. Originally, there had been proposals to replace the NCPR 1987 with a new set of rules and a set of draft rules were published in 2013. However, these draft rules have not been implemented—instead, to date, revisions have been made to the NCPR 1987 themselves.

### 8.3.1 Grant of probate

Where the deceased left a valid will, the executors of the will normally have priority to a grant of representation, according to the order of priority in r20 of the NCPR 1987.

### 8.3.2 Grant of letters of administration with the will annexed (r20 NCPR 1987)

The deceased may have left a valid will but there may be no executors who are able and willing to apply for a grant of probate. This may be for a number of reasons, including:

- the testator may have failed to appoint an executor validly in the will;
- the executor(s) may have died before the testator;
- the executor(s) may have died after the testator but before making the grant application;
- the executor(s) may not wish to act and have renounced probate;
- the executor is the spouse or civil partner of the deceased, and the appointment of the spouse (or civil partner) has failed under s18A of the Wills Act 1837 due to divorce (or a dissolution of the **civil partnership**).

In any of the above circumstances, it will be necessary to appoint one or more administrators with the will (also known as 'administrators with the will annexed'). The administrators with the will, once appointed by HMCTS, will carry out the wishes of the testator as expressed in the will.

It is possible also that the testator might have died partially intestate, in which case the administrator with the will carries out the testator's wishes for the testate part of the estate and applies the intestacy rules to the intestate part of the estate.

Rule 20 of the NCPR 1987 sets out the order of priority to a grant. As we have seen, executors have priority above other persons, and the executors will apply for a grant of probate. However, if the executor is not able and willing to apply for a grant, r20 of the NCPR 1987 then sets out the order of priority to a grant of letters of administration with the will. The basic order will be listed first, using the rather old fashioned language of r20, and then each category is explained in **8.3.2.1–8.3.2.5**.

The order of priority is as follows:

1 any residuary legatee or devisee holding in trust for any other person;

2 any other residuary legatee or devisee or, where the **residue** is not wholly disposed of by will, a person who is entitled to share in the undisposed of estate;

3 the PR of a residuary legatee or devisee or of a person entitled to share in the undisposed of estate;

4 any other legatee or devisee, or a **creditor** of the deceased;

5 the PR of any other legatee or devisee or of a creditor of the deceased.

This is an order of priority so persons falling within a higher category have priority to the grant over persons in a lower category. For example, a person who is a residuary legatee or devisee (para (2) above) would have priority over the personal representative of a residuary legatee or devisee (para (3) above).

However, persons falling within a particular category will have an equal entitlement to apply for the grant, for example in para (4) above a creditor of the deceased has an equal entitlement to apply for the grant as a (non-residuary) legatee or devisee.

When applying for a grant, an applicant must show that there is no one in a higher category who is able and willing to apply for a grant. This process is known as 'clearing-off'. The applicant must also state the basis of their entitlement to the grant.

Note that the above list is a simplification of the categories in r20. The following sections explain each category in more detail.

#### 8.3.2.1 Any residuary legatee or devisee holding in trust for any other person

This wording is quite confusing because the terms 'legatee' and 'devisee' are usually used to describe someone who is a beneficiary (a legatee is a beneficiary of personal property, a devisee is a beneficiary of real property or land). This first category is, however, referring to someone who is a trustee and who is holding part or all of the residuary estate on trust for another person.

In wills, as we have seen, it is common to appoint trustees of the whole residuary estate. Normally, the testator will appoint the same person(s) as executor(s) and trustee(s), so if that person is not able or willing to apply for a grant as executor, they will not be able or willing to apply for a grant as trustee. (As said, if an executor who is also appointed trustee renounces probate they must also renounce their right to apply for a grant as trustee, but this is provided for by the PA15 renunciation form mentioned earlier.)

However, sometimes the testator will appoint different people as executor(s) and trustee(s), and so if the executor is not able or willing to apply for a grant of probate, the trustee of the residuary estate will be able to apply for a grant of letters of administration with the will instead.

#### 8.3.2.2 Any other residuary legatee or devisee, or a person entitled to share in the undisposed of estate

This category includes the true beneficiaries of the residuary estate (as opposed to legatees and devisees who are holding on trust for someone else).

It also includes residuary beneficiaries who have life interests as well as beneficiaries who have absolute interests.

Normally, a beneficiary with a vested interest will be preferred to a beneficiary with a **contingent** interest.

Where the estate is not wholly disposed of by will, namely there is a partial intestacy, this category also includes the persons who are entitled under the rules of intestacy to the intestate part of the estate. This is the meaning of 'a person entitled to share in the undisposed of estate'. Such persons have the same entitlement to the grant as a residuary beneficiary of the will. However, if most of the estate is disposed of by the will, the probate registrar may overlook a person who is entitled to a share of the intestate part of the estate.

#### 8.3.2.3 The personal representative of a residuary legatee or devisee or of a person entitled to share in the undisposed of estate

If none of the persons in the previous categories is able or willing to apply for a grant, the PR of a residuary beneficiary may apply for a grant. However, this does not include the PR of a residuary legatee or devisee who was holding on trust for another person, or the PR of a residuary beneficiary who only had a life interest.

The PR of a person entitled on a partial intestacy is also able to apply under this category.

This category is only relevant if a beneficiary (under the will or partial intestacy) dies after the deceased, as otherwise the beneficiary's interest will **lapse**.

#### 8.3.2.4 Any other legatee or devisee, or a creditor of the deceased

This category is also a hybrid category, including both beneficiaries of the will and creditors of the deceased who have equal entitlement to apply for the grant.

The beneficiaries in this category are non-residuary beneficiaries, for example beneficiaries who have been left a **specific gift** in the will of personal property or of land, or a specified sum of money. This category includes legatees and devisees who have life interests and legatees and devisees who are holding on trust for another person. Beneficiaries with vested interests are normally preferred to beneficiaries with contingent interests.

#### 8.3.2.5 The personal representative of any other legatee or devisee, or of a creditor of the deceased

This category includes the PR of any person from the previous category, namely non-residuary beneficiaries and creditors. However, this does not include the PR of a beneficiary who had a life interest or who themselves was holding the property on trust for another person.

For the PR of a beneficiary, this category is only relevant if the beneficiary dies after the deceased, as otherwise the beneficiary's interest will lapse.

### 8.3.3 Grant of letters of administration (r22 NCPR 1987)

A grant of letters of administration is the appropriate grant where the deceased did not leave a valid will. It is sometimes called 'simple' administration to distinguish it from the letters of administration with the will annexed.

Where the deceased did not leave a valid will, as we saw in **Chapter 4**, their estate will be distributed according to the rules of intestacy, and the order of entitlement to benefit in the estate under s46 of the Administration of Estates Act 1925. The order of priority to the grant of letters of administration is set out in r22 of the NCPR 1987 and closely follows the order of entitlement to the intestate's estate. As a rule of thumb, someone who is entitled to the estate or to a share of the estate will also be entitled to apply for the grant of representation.

The order of entitlement to apply for the grant in r22 is as follows:

1. the surviving spouse or civil partner;
2. the children of the deceased (and the issue of any child who died before the deceased);
3. the father and mother of the deceased;
4. brothers and sisters of the **whole blood** (and the issue of any brother or sister of the whole blood who died before the deceased);
5. brothers and sisters of the **half blood** (and the issue of any brother or sister of the half blood who died before the deceased);
6. the grandparents of the deceased;
7. uncles and aunts of the whole blood (and the issue of any uncle or aunt of the whole blood who died before the deceased); and
8. uncles and aunts of the half blood (and the issue of any uncle or aunt of the half blood who died before the deceased).

In the unlikely event that there are no such relatives and the estate passes to the Crown ***bona vacantia***, the Treasury Solicitor may apply for a grant.

If there is more than one person in a particular category, any one person within that category may apply for the grant of letters of administration, without notice to the others. For example, if the nearest relatives are the children of the deceased, and there are three of them, then any one of them may apply for the grant.

When applying for a grant of letters of administration, it is necessary to 'clear off' categories of persons who might have priority to the grant. This does not mean that those persons exist—rather, the clearing-off process is to tell the Probate Registry that there is no one within those higher categories. For example, a brother or sister of the whole blood would have to state in the grant application that the deceased was not survived by a spouse, civil partner, '**issue**' (this word includes the deceased's children, grandchildren etc) or parent.

Rule 22 also contains some complicated rules regarding persons in a lower category being able to apply in certain circumstances, and rules as to applications by PRs of beneficiaries who have died after the intestate.

# 8.4 Grant application procedure

It is possible for private individuals to apply personally for a grant of representation. Personal applicants apply directly to the Probate Registry and apply by means of a standard application form. This has been the case for many years.

The alternative method is to apply via a professional who is permitted to lodge grant applications on behalf of others. Such work is regarded as a form of 'reserved legal activity' under the Legal Services Act 2007. Only those who are authorised to undertake reserved legal activities may do so. For many years, only solicitors could undertake grant applications on behalf of another, but in recent years other professionals (including accountants) have also been given the right to conduct this activity. However, the majority of grant applications by professionals are still undertaken by solicitors.

Historically, grant applications (whether by personal applicants or professionals) have been paper applications, sent by post to a district probate registry. In recent years, though, HMCTS have closed district probate registries and developed online application processes for both personal applicants and professionals. These online application processes are comparatively new and are still under development: at the time of writing, it is not possible to apply online in all estates. HMCTS have begun by allowing online applications in more straightforward cases (eg a grant of probate application where there is one or more named executor proving), whereas more complicated or unusual applications still have to be made via a paper application.

Although HMCTS prefer applications to be made online where an online application is allowed, the online application is currently an alternative to the paper application for personal applicants, who can choose whether to apply online or on paper. Where online applications by professionals are allowed, they are also mandated, meaning that the professional applicant must apply online and cannot choose to apply on paper. It has to be said that there are significant advantages to the online application process: there are benefits of convenience and administration to both the applicant and HMCTS.

In August 2020, the Ministry of Justice (MoJ) issued a consultation on proposals to require all applications by professionals to be made online. Following this consultation, the MoJ indicated that it would proceed with these proposals, and these were enacted in September 2020 as part of the Non-Contentious Probate (Amendment) Rules 2020, the amendments taking effect on 2 November 2020.

The 2020 Amendment Rules amend the NCPR 1987 to provide that all grant applications made by professionals must be made online, except for: (a) applications where the professional is invited by the registry to apply by post; and (b) those types of application which are listed in a new Third Schedule to the NCPR 1987.

The reason for the exemptions is that the online system is not yet able to cope with certain applications. Although in general the system is set up to deal with some types of application, it may be that in other individual cases the system will not enable the particular application to be made. In such a situation, HMCTS will invite the professional to make a postal application instead. This would be on a case-by-case basis.

Also, the MoJ knows that the online system is not set up currently to manage some generic types of application, and this is the reason for having the exemption for those types of application listed in the Third Schedule.

The Third Schedule does, in fact, contain some fairly major exceptions, including grants of letters of administration (with or without the will), although the guidance on gov.uk indicates that some online applications for grants of administration are possible, provided certain conditions are met. Also, grant of probate applications by trust corporations are listed in the Third Schedule. Increasingly, more law firms are acting for external trust corporations or setting up their own trust corporations, so this will represent a significant number of grant applications that do not have to be made online (although since August 2021 it has been possible for trust corporations to apply online).

It is likely that the list of exemptions in the Third Schedule will shrink over time as the online system is developed further, and is able to cope with more types of grant application.

In view of the fact that paper applications are still possible for some types of application, the following sections cover both online and paper processes.

## 8.4.1 The application: what must be submitted to HMCTS

The grant application will involve providing HMCTS with the following:

- *The application itself*—this is either a standard paper application form or the application is made via an online portal on the gov.uk website. Both paper and online application processes require the provision of factual information about the deceased and the applicants, and about the will if there is one. Each process includes a statement of truth by the applicant(s) confirming the truth of the information provided in the application.
- If the application is for a grant of probate or a grant of letters of administration with the will annexed, the applicant(s) must deliver *the original will* (and the originals of any codicils) to HMCTS. Wills and codicils are, currently, paper documents and so have to be sent to HMCTS by post even if the application itself is made online. (NB: it used to be necessary to 'mark' the original will but this requirement was removed in 2018, and it also used to be necessary to send A4 copies of the will and codicils, but this is no longer necessary.) However, it is extremely important to retain a copy of the will when the original is sent to HMCTS.
- There is no longer a need to provide HMCTS with IHT421 confirming that IHT has been paid following the submission of IHT400 to HMRC. Instead, HMRC will have provided the PRs by letter with a *unique code* to quote in the probate application, together with the gross and net probate values.
- If the estate is an **excepted** one, for deaths on or after 1 January 2022 there is no need to send Form IHT205 (IHT207 for a foreign domiciled estate), to HMCTS, although this is still needed for deaths before 1 January 2022. Instead, for deaths on or after 1 January 2022, the applicant must declare that the estate is an excepted one and confirm the following:
  - the gross value of the estate for IHT purposes;
  - the net value of the estate for IHT purposes (after deduction of debts and expenses);
  - the net qualifying value of the estate (the net value of the estate minus any spouse exemption or charity exemption); and
  - if applicants are claiming part or all of a transferable nil rate band (where the deceased had a late spouse or civil partner and the net qualifying value of the deceased's estate is between £325,000 and £650,000).
- *Any additional evidence* that is likely to be required by the probate registrar. This is likely to take the form of an affidavit (or more likely a statement of truth)—see **8.6**.
- Payment of *the probate fees*—traditionally, payments were made by cheque, but payment is now usually made online. Professionals must have an online account with HMCTS.

As can be seen, grant applications have become something of a hybrid between online processes and postal applications—until the rules for a valid will under the Wills Act 1837 are changed to allow electronic wills this will remain the case. We will now look at paper applications and online applications separately.

## 8.4.2 Paper applications

Until fairly recently, there was no option to make online applications, and so all applications for grants of representation were made on paper by sending a paper application and supporting documents through the post.

Personal applications (ie applications by the executor(s) or prospective administrator(s) themselves, without the assistance of a professional) were made using a standard application form.

Until March 2020, there was no standard application form for applications made by professionals.

Prior to November 2018, the grant application through a professional was made via an 'oath'. This was a document drafted by the professional. It was not in a standard application form with boxes but was a text document which included some standard wording but also different wording according to the particular circumstances of the application. These oaths might have looked quite different, depending on the type of paper, font and point size used by each solicitors' firm. However, there was a common core to the wording of the oaths and, before the widespread use of word processors, practitioners used to use standard oath forms produced by law stationery companies. These standard oath forms were printed forms which had the core wording included, and gaps into which the solicitors' firm would type the information particular to the estate, such as names, addresses and date of death. With the greater use of word processors, firms largely abandoned the use of these law stationers' forms and produced wholly word-processed oaths.

Oaths had to be 'sworn' or 'affirmed' by the person(s) making the oath (the PR(s)). Swearing involved swearing to the truth of the statement on a holy book, such as the Bible. Affirming was the secular (ie non-religious) equivalent.

(NB: although personal applicants would apply initially using a standard application form, HMCTS would then produce an oath for the applicant to swear, so an oath was made for all grant applications.)

In November 2018, changes were made to the NCPR 1987, replacing oaths with 'statements of truth'. However, this did not change the essential requirement for the solicitor to draft a document. All that changed was how that document was executed (there was now no need to swear or affirm the statement), with minor changes to the wording included at the very beginning and end of the document. The bulk of the wording of statements of truth remained the same as the wording of oaths, save that the applicant merely signed a statement of truth at the end of the statement, whereas an oath had to be formally sworn (or affirmed) by the applicant at the end of the oath.

In March 2020, statements of truth were themselves replaced by standard application forms for professional applicants. In fact, the application forms contain a statement of truth at the end of the form, but the salient difference is that the professional no longer needs to draft a bespoke statement of truth from scratch.

From 18 May 2020, paper applications from professionals have had to be on one of the new forms. As mentioned in **8.4**, the MoJ has now introduced amendments to the NCPR 1987 to require all applications by professionals (subject to some exceptions) to be made online.

The HMCTS forms for paper applications by professionals are very similar to the forms used for personal applicants, just with some variations.

Currently, the paper application forms for professional applicants are:

- PA1P: this is used for an application where the deceased left a will. It is used for an application by executors for a grant of probate and by an application by a prospective administrator for a grant of letters of administration with the will annexed. The form is available from the gov.uk website.
- PA1A: this is used for an application where the deceased did not leave a will (essentially where there is a total intestacy). To be more precise, it is where the deceased did not leave a will dealing with assets in England and Wales—it is possible that the deceased may have a will dealing with foreign property only, and if that was the case this form would still be used (rather than the PA1P). The form is available from the gov.uk website.

Confusingly, both forms PA1P and PA1A are called 'Probate Application', although each form is clear at the start that it is either for a situation where the deceased left a will or did not leave a will.

Note also that the paper application forms for personal applicants have the same titles as, and look very similar to, the forms for professionals, although there are some differences. However, it is obvious from the gov.uk website which forms are applicable to professionals as the links to the forms for professionals include the wording 'Probate practitioners'.

The application forms are available in English and in Welsh.

Given that the intention is to require all applications by professionals to be made online in time, the details of the current paper application forms are not considered further. You are also unlikely to have SQE 1 questions on the specifics of the forms.

### 8.4.3 Online applications

Online applications are relatively recent. HMCTS, in consultation with relevant stakeholders such as the Law Society, have been developing processes to enable applicants to apply for grants online. The pilot scheme enabled personal applicants to apply in comparatively simple situations (eg where there is a will which appoints one or more named executors), and has gradually been expanded to allow applications in other situations.

A smaller pilot was undertaken for professionals, with the involvement of selected probate professionals including some solicitors' firms. Online applications are now available to all probate professionals but, again, only in certain situations. For example, at the time of writing, it is not possible for a professional to apply online for many grants of administration. The intention is, though, to expand the situations in which online applications may be made, and over time more and more applications will be possible online. As mentioned, the MoJ introduced amendments to the NCPR 1987 so that all applications by professionals (subject to exceptions) must be made online.

A personal applicant can pay the probate fees online when they make the application online, but a professional applicant can only use the online application process if they already have a PBA (Payment By Account) account with HMCTS.

It is possible to apply online in English or in Welsh.

As mentioned earlier, whilst it is possible to apply for the grant online, it is still necessary to send paper documents to HMCTS. Although the application may be via the relevant online portal, it is still necessary to send the following documents to HMCTS in the post:

- the original will (and any codicils) (remembering to keep copies for the PRs);
- if the deceased died before 1 January 2022 and the estate is an excepted one, the IHT205 (and IHT217), or IHT207. However, personal applicants can submit the IHT205 information online; and
- any additional evidence (either an affidavit or, currently, a statement of truth).

## 8.4.4 **Grant application fees**

The level of 'probate fees' (this term is used to cover the fees for all grant applications) has been a controversial issue in recent years.

### 8.4.4.1 Current probate fees

Probate fees are relatively modest. Since 26 January 2022, there has been one flat fee initially £273, but now £300 that applies irrespective of whether the application is being made by a personal applicant or professional. No fee applies if the net estate, after payment of funeral expenses and debts, does not exceed £5,000. The fee used to differ depending on whether the applicant was a personal applicant (£215) or a professional (£155).

In addition to the fee of £300, applicants will usually order a number of extra copies of the grant (copies with the seal of the Probate Registry) alongside the original grant itself. Each extra copy costs £1.50.

### 8.4.4.2 Previous proposals to increase probate fees

In 2016, the government announced that it intended to replace these relatively low rates of fees with a sliding scale of fees, with much higher maximum fees.

Although estates that have a probate value up to £50,000 would pay no probate fees, the fees levied on other estates would have been significantly greater, with estates worth more than £2 million paying probate fees of £20,000!

Whilst from its title, the Legal Aid, Sentencing and Punishment of Offenders Act 2012 (LASPO) might seem to have nothing to do with probate matters, LASPO gives HMCTS the right to levy fees at a level that exceeds the cost to HMCTS of providing a service. This is so that the fees can be used to help pay for the courts and tribunals in general.

However, whilst it makes some sense for litigants to pay a bit more to cover the costs of the courts and tribunals they use, the case for imposing much higher fees on the estates of deceased persons was less clear. The proposed increases were opposed by a range of stakeholders, including the Law Society, not least on the basis that it was argued that the government was attempting to levy an additional tax on death 'by the back door'.

In the event, these proposals were not implemented, but only due to a general election being called in 2017.

Subsequent to this, in 2018, HMCTS put forward new proposals, on similar lines, but with lower fees than originally proposed. Nevertheless, these amended proposals would still have seen a significant hike in probate fees, with a maximum fee of £6,000 on an estate worth more than £2 million. The same objections were raised—that this was a tax not a fee for a service. The new fees were due to come into force in April 2019 but due to the upheavals caused by debates and votes in Parliament over Brexit during 2018 and 2019, the amended proposals were not implemented.

Happily, HMCTS then consulted in 2021 on proposals for a more modest increase in probate fees, and introduced a new flat fee of £273 increased in May 2024 to £300. One of the unhappy consequences of the proposed fee increase in April 2019 was a scramble by probate practitioners to submit grant applications before the introduction date, because the fees were based on the date of the grant application not the date of death. This resulted in a surge of grant applications at the same time as a raft of district probate registry closures, HMCTS staff job cuts and glitches in the new HMCTS probate IT system. The combination of these factors has led to very lengthy delays in the issuing of grants by HMCTS from 2019 onwards. Whilst the situation has improved to a degree, probate applications are still taking considerably longer than they did before the 'modernisation' programme began. These delays continue to cause considerable difficulties in many estates and for the solicitors instructed by the PRs of those estates.

## 8.5 Grants of representation and official copies

If the application is successful, HMCTS will issue the grant of representation.

### 8.5.1 The grant of representation

The form of the grant of representation itself has changed recently, in March 2019.

Prior to this, grants were signed by the registry staff and embossed with the seal of the Probate Registry (or rather the district probate registry) that issued the grant. Grants of simple administration were single sheets, double-sided. Grants of probate and grants of letters of administration were booklets with a photocopy of the deceased's will (and any codicil) bound between two covers.

Since March 2019, HMCTS have been issuing a new form of grant certificate which is a single sheet in all cases. This has a digital seal (instead of the old, embossed seal), a standard digital signature (instead of a wet signature on the old-style grant), a validation telephone number for stakeholders to call and validate the grant, and a high security hologram at the bottom of the page for extra security.

If the applicant requests it, HMCTS will produce bilingual grants (in English and Welsh).

### 8.5.2 Wills and codicils become public documents

The original will (and any codicil) is retained by HMCTS and is not returned to the applicant. For that reason, it is imperative that the PRs retain a copy of the will when sending the original to HMCTS. The will (and any codicil) becomes a document of public record: it is available to the public and copies can be obtained by enquirers.

### 8.5.3 Official copies of the grant

It is usual also to request a number of extra 'official' copies of the grant, which can then be sent to asset holders.

Official copies historically have always been just a single sheet—a photocopy of the grant embossed with the seal of the Probate Registry. In the case of a grant of probate or letters of administration with the will, the official copy reproduced the information on the front and back covers of the original grant booklet, but not the photocopy will (and codicils, if any) which appeared inside the old-style original grant.

The features of the new-style grant mentioned previously in **8.5.1** also appear on the official copies, which now look the same as the grant itself.

## 8.6 Additional evidence

There are a number of situations when HMCTS will require additional evidence regarding the grant application. This is evidence in connection with a will, so is only relevant to applications for grants of probate and grants of letters of administration with the will. Under the NCPR 1987, the evidence was originally provided by means of a sworn statement, called an 'affidavit'. Under the Draft Probate Rules published in 2013 it was proposed that affidavits be replaced by witness statements, but these were never enacted. However, in April 2020, as part of the temporary measures designed to implement social distancing during the Covid pandemic, it was announced that statements of truth would be accepted in place of sworn affidavits in a number of situations where the NCPR 1987 require affidavits. This then led to a permanent change of procedure, with effect from 2 November 2020, due to changes made by the Non-Contentious Probate (Amendment) Rules 2020. The effect of these rules is that additional evidence can be provided by means of a 'witness statement' which is supported by a statement of truth, instead of by a sworn affidavit. One major advantage of a statement over an affidavit is that a statement can be included as part of the online application process, whereas an affidavit cannot.

Examples of additional evidence which might be required include:

1 A statement of due execution (r12 NCPR 1987)—if there is a concern that the **formalities** of s9 of the Wills Act 1837 have not been complied with, perhaps due to the will not containing an appropriate **attestation** clause. As we have seen in **2.4.3.1**, an appropriate attestation clause raises a rebuttable presumption that the will has been executed in accordance with the requisite formalities. In the absence of such an attestation clause, someone who was involved with the execution of the will—one of the attesting witnesses ideally, but possibly someone else who was present if the attesting witnesses are dead, lack capacity or cannot be found—should provide a statement. In the absence of evidence from someone present at the time the will was executed, HMCTS can accept a statement from any person whom they see fit.

2 Execution of the will by a blind or illiterate testator (r13 NCPR 1987)—this would be a statement that the testator knew and approved the terms of the will, in spite of their inability to read it. However, as we saw in **2.4.3.1**, it is common practice to include an adapted attestation clause in the will of a blind or illiterate testator that raises the presumption that they did know and approve the contents of the will, and so this form of additional evidence should not then be required.

3 Obliterations and alterations (r14 NCPR 1987)—where there are 'obliterations, interlineations and alterations which are not authenticated in the manner prescribed by . . . the Wills Act 1837'. This would be relevant where, say, the testator had crossed out some wording from the will or had amended some wording in the will by hand. The crossing out and/or handwritten amendments might have been made by the testator before the will was executed, but (as we saw in **3.2.1**) if the testator and the witnesses have not initialled the crossing out or amendment then the presumption is that the testator has made the amendments after the will has been executed and the change has thus not been made in accordance with the requirements of the Wills Act. HMCTS would then require a statement to explain when and how the alterations were made to the will to determine whether they form part of the final will or whether they should be disregarded.

4 Attempted **revocation** (r15 NCPR 1987)—this would be required where there is any appearance of attempted revocation of a will by burning, tearing or otherwise destroying. (We considered revocation by this method in **3.3.2**.) HMCTS will require a statement to help determine whether or not the testator had in fact revoked the will by their actions or whether the will is still valid despite the apparent attempt at revocation.

5 Where the will has marks on it that require some explanation—for example, staple marks that suggest that the pages of the will have been separated at some point in the past. However, the probate applications form PA1P and online process have questions that enable the probate practitioner to explain why the staple had been removed (usually this has been done in order to scan the will before re-stapling it).

Affidavits in categories (3), (4) and (5) have traditionally been called 'affidavits of plight and condition', so presumably statements will be known as 'statements of plight and condition' too.

The probate practitioner should try to anticipate what additional evidence will be required by HMCTS and obtain a relevant statement before submitting the application for a grant. The additional evidence is usually submitted with the rest of the grant application if a paper application is being made. Currently, it is not possible to make the application online if additional affidavit evidence is provided, but as statements can now be provided instead of affidavits, the additional facts can be added to the statement of truth that is made when submitting the application via the online portal.

# 8.7 Limited grants

Most grants cover the whole of a deceased's estate and are unlimited in time. However, it is also possible to obtain limited grants, which may be: (a) limited to certain property; (b) for a specific purpose; or (c) limited in time.

## 8.7.1 Grants limited as to particular property

It is possible that more than one grant may be issued in respect of a single person's estate. For example, an author might appoint literary executors who will administer the author's literary estate whereas the author's general estate might be administered by the author's general executors.

It is also necessary to have a separate grant solely in respect of **settled land** (land under a **strict settlement**, according to the Settled Land Act 1925). Settled land, within the meaning of the 1925 Act, is rare and so we will not consider the detail here. You should consult a specialist text if the deceased had an interest in settled land.

## 8.7.2 Grants for a specific purpose

It is possible to apply for a grant to collect and preserve certain assets of the deceased (known as a grant *ad colligenda bona*) in advance of an application for a full grant. For example, it might be necessary to have a grant to continue to run the deceased's business, pending the issuing of a full grant.

It is also possible to obtain grants in order to pursue litigation or to obtain a temporary grant until the completion of a probate action (eg an action disputing the validity of a will).

## 8.7.3 Grants limited in time

We have already seen one example of these—a grant of letters of administration for the use and benefit of a minor until they reach 18. On the person reaching 18, the grant ceases automatically, and the person who was a minor but is now an adult, will have to apply for a new grant if this is needed to complete the administration of the estate.

Similarly, a grant for the use and benefit of a person who lacks capacity (within the meaning of the Mental Capacity Act 2005) will be limited to until such time that the person acquires or regains capacity, although sadly in most cases the person's mental capacity does not improve sufficiently for them to have the capacity to apply for a grant themselves.

# 8.8 Grants to complete the administration of an incompletely administered estate and the chain of representation

Sometimes a PR will die before the administration of an estate has been completed. If the deceased PR was not the only PR and there is (at least) one surviving PR, then the surviving PR(s) may complete the administration of the estate on their own. So, for example, if there were two executors and one dies, the surviving executor may complete the administration of the estate.

However, it is usual to only appoint one administrator, so if an administrator dies before completing the administration, usually it will be necessary to appoint a replacement administrator.

Also, where there is a minority interest or a life interest in the estate, it is usually necessary to have at least two administrators, so if one of the two administrators dies it may be necessary to appoint a replacement so that there continue to be two administrators (s114 Senior Courts Act 1981).

## 8.8.1 Grants *de bonis non administratis*

This Latin name for this type of grant means grants of ('*de*') goods ('*bonis*') that have not been ('*non*') administered ('*administratis*'). Despite the literal meaning of 'goods', such a grant applies to land as well as to personal property. It is common to drop the '*administratis*' and refer to these grants as grants ***de bonis non***. As the grants appoint administrators, they are grants of letters of administration (as opposed to grants of probate).

A grant *de bonis non* will be needed where the sole personal representative (executor or administrator) has died before completing the administration of the estate. However, in the case of a deceased executor, this is only if the **chain of representation** does not apply (see **8.8.2**).

The grant *de bonis non* will be either a grant of simple administration (if there is an intestacy) or a grant of letters of administration with the will (if there is a will).

The grant *de bonis non* will be issued to the person(s) entitled to apply for the particular type of grant of letters of administration (under rr20 and 22 NCPR 1987). This will either be person(s) who were in the same category of priority as the original PR, or person(s) in the next relevant category of priority, as seen in the following examples.

**EXAMPLE**

Manish died intestate. His nearest relatives were his sons Anil, Kapoor and Amjad.

Anil was appointed as Manish's administrator but Anil has since died without completing the administration of Manish's estate.

Anil, Kapoor and Amjad were all in the same category of persons with priority to the grant under rule 22 of the NCPR 1987 (ie Manish's issue). Either Kapoor or Amjad may apply for a grant of letters of administration *de bonis non* in order to complete the administration of Manish's estate.

**EXAMPLE**

Brandon has died leaving a will. He appointed his sister, Felicity, as his sole executor but although Felicity obtained a grant of probate, she has died before completing the administration of his estate.

The residuary beneficiaries are Felicity's adult children, Nadia and Peter. Under rule 20 of the NCPR 1987, as there is no executor, either Nadia or Peter may apply for a grant of letters of administration with the will *de bonis non* in order to complete the administration of Brandon's estate.

The grant of administration *de bonis non* will be limited to that part of the estate that remains to be administered (ie the new administrator will not have duties and liabilities in respect of the estate which has already been administered by the original PR).

## 8.8.2 Executors and the chain of representation

A grant *de bonis non* is often not necessary where the deceased PR was an executor. This may be due to the number of executors appointed or due to what is called the '**chain of representation**'.

If there had been more than one proving executor, the surviving proving executor(s) will be able to complete the administration. This is the case even if there is only one surviving proving executor. There will be no need to issue a grant to another executor as long as there is one proving executor left.

Alternatively, there may be non-proving executors; that is, executors who have had power reserved to them. Those executors can apply for a grant of 'double probate' instead of a grant *de bonis non*.

Where there was only one executor appointed in the will, or where all but one of the executors have renounced probate, the death of the single proving executor may mean that there is no one left to administer the estate. There are then two possibilities:

- the first possibility is that the executor who has died has not left a will or has failed to appoint executors of their own or, having appointed executors of their own, none of those executors are able or willing to act as executor. In any of those situations, it will be necessary for someone to be appointed as administrator *de bonis non* in order that they may complete the administration of the estate;
- the second possibility, though, is that the deceased executor themselves makes a will, appoints one or more executors of their own and those executors obtain a grant of probate to the will of the deceased executor. If that happens, then the executors of the deceased executor will be able to complete the administration of the original testator's estate due to the chain of representation (s7 Administration of Estates Act 1925).

The chain of representation only applies from proving executor to proving executor. The executor of a deceased administrator cannot administer the first estate, and similarly the administrator of a deceased executor cannot administer the first estate: it must be the *proving* executor of the deceased *proving* executor.

**EXAMPLE**

Martin makes a will in which he appoints Oliver as his sole executor. Oliver obtains a grant of probate and begins to administer Martin's estate. However, Oliver dies before completing the administration of Martin's estate.

Oliver also made a will in which he appointed Stephanie as his sole executrix. Stephanie obtains a grant of probate of Oliver's estate.

The chain of representation applies. As Oliver's proving executor, Stephanie can also complete the administration of Martin's estate without having to apply for a special grant of representation.

**EXAMPLE**

Karol makes a will in which he appoints Jiri as his sole executor. Jiri obtains a grant of probate and begins to administer Karol's estate. However, Jiri dies before completing the administration of Karol's estate.

Jiri died intestate. Lara obtains a grant of letters of administration to Jiri's estate.

The chain of representation is broken—although Lara is Jiri's personal representative, she cannot administer Karol's estate. Someone will have to apply for a grant of letters of administration *de bonis non* in order to complete the administration of Karol's estate.

### 8.8.3 Cessate grants

A cessate grant is seen in one of two situations, both relevant where there has been an earlier grant of administration for the use and benefit of the person who is entitled to the grant. For example, where the person entitled to a grant is a minor and someone else has to take out a limited grant for the use and benefit of the minor until the minor reaches 18 years of age, a cessate grant may be needed.

As we have seen, when the minor reaches 18, the grant for the use and benefit of the minor will cease automatically. The minor is now an adult and must apply for a fresh grant, and this fresh grant is a type of cessate grant.

**EXAMPLE**

Hussain dies intestate. His niece, Zainab, is entitled to his whole estate but she is 15 years old and cannot apply for a grant herself. Zainab's father, Azam, obtains a grant of letters of administration for the use and benefit of Zainab.

If Zainab reaches 18 before the administration of the estate is completed, the grant to Azam will cease and Zainab must apply for a cessate grant.

The other type of cessate grant is where the administrator (who is acting under a grant for the use and benefit for another person) dies (eg if Azam were to die before Zainab reaches 18 and before he has completed the administration of the estate).

### 8.8.4 Grants of double probate

A grant of double probate is relevant where there has already been a grant of probate issued to one or more proving executors, and then subsequently another executor wishes to join the proving executors in administering the estate.

This could happen because power has been reserved to an executor and, subsequent to the issue of the original grant of probate, the executor to whom power has been reserved wishes to take an active involvement in the administration of the estate. The executor to whom power had been reserved will apply for what is called a grant of double probate.

Where an executor is a minor, we have seen that the executor cannot apply for probate, but it is possible there is also one or more adult executors who are able and willing to prove the will. Subsequently, the non-proving executor who was a minor may reach 18, and at that point may apply for a grant of double probate.

The newly proving executor under the grant of double probate will then work alongside the executors who had obtained the original grant of probate.

## 8.9 Caveats, citations and standing searches

There are a number of other applications which are relevant to probate practice, often in connection with contentious probate and disputes over the estate. Although these applications tend to be related to 'contentious' work (ie litigation), they are still governed by the NCPR 1987.

### 8.9.1 Caveats

A person will 'enter' a **caveat** if they wish to stop a grant being issued in an estate.

Why would someone wish to prevent a grant being issued in an estate? Often, this will be because there is a dispute over the validity of a testator's last will. A person may allege that the deceased's will is not valid, perhaps because the requisite formalities have not been complied with or because it is contended that the testator lacked the necessary mental capacity to make a will (**testamentary capacity**), and/or that the testator did not know and approve the terms of the will because the will was obtained by fraud, force, fear or **undue influence**.

Alternatively, there may be no dispute of the validity of the will but a person may have concerns about the suitability of the executor or prospective administrator to be a PR, perhaps due to a history of financial impropriety.

A caveat is only appropriate if the person entering the caveat has an interest in the estate (eg a beneficiary) or has an adverse interest (eg someone who will benefit under the intestacy rules if the deceased's will is held to be invalid).

If a caveat is entered then the grant applicant will not be able to obtain a grant until the caveat is withdrawn or removed. However, it is still possible to obtain an emergency grant for a particular purpose, such as an *ad colligenda* grant (see **8.7.2**), even if a caveat has been entered.

The procedure for caveats is provided by r44 of the NCPR 1987. A person may enter a caveat by applying online (there is a link on the gov.uk website) or by completing Form PA8A (Application to stop a grant of representation) and submitting it by post. There is a fee of £3. The person entering the caveat must provide some basic details online, or on Form PA8A, such as the deceased's name, address and date of death.

Once the caveat is entered, it is valid for a period of six months and can be renewed, each time for a further six months. A caveat is renewed by post—it is not currently possible to do this online—and there is a further fee of £3.

It is obviously unsatisfactory that a person could prevent a grant being issued indefinitely, and so there is a process whereby a caveat may be cleared away so that a grant may be issued. To clear away a caveat, the grant applicant may issue a '**warning**'. The relevant form (based on Form 4 Sch 1 NCPR 1987) can be obtained from the Leeds District Probate Registry. Once issued, the warning must be served on the person who entered the caveat.

If the person entering the caveat does not respond to the warning within 14 days (ie they do nothing), then the person warning may file an affidavit (or a statement of truth). The caveat will be 'warned off' and a grant may then be issued.

However, the person entering the caveat may respond to the warning in one of three ways:

1 They may withdraw the caveat. A grant may then be issued.
2 They may enter an '**appearance**' (the relevant form (based on Form 5, Sch 1 NCPR 1987) is also available from the Leeds District Probate Registry)—this would be the appropriate course of action if the caveator has an interest contrary to the person wishing to apply for the grant (eg if the caveator is contesting that the deceased's will is invalid). If an appearance is entered, it will prevent a grant being issued and will continue in force until a probate action is commenced. (A probate action involves formal litigation proceedings and will itself prevent a grant being issued until the litigation is completed.)
3 They may issue a summons for directions by a district judge or probate registrar—this would be the appropriate action if the caveator has no interest contrary to the estate so would not be contesting a will, but instead the caveator had concerns about the suitability of the person applying for the grant.

## 8.9.2 Citations

Alternatively, a person may have an interest in ensuring that a grant is in fact issued, so that the estate can be administered and distributed.

Executors or potential administrators may be slow in applying for a grant because they are lazy or incompetent. Or, perhaps they may not want to take on the burdens of administering the estate yet are doing nothing to step aside and let others do this job.

The **citation** is a process whereby the reluctant PR can be forced to apply for a grant. The person citing is called the 'citor'.

There are different types of citation:

- A citation to accept or refuse a grant (r47 NCPR 1987)—this is where the person with a better entitlement to the grant than the citor is failing to apply for a grant. The citation is to force the person to apply for the grant, failing which the citor can apply for a grant themselves. For example, a residuary beneficiary of a will may use this to force the executor to apply for a grant, failing which the residuary beneficiary can apply for a grant.
- A citation to take a grant of probate (r47 NCPR 1987)—this is where an executor has intermeddled in the estate but is failing to apply for a grant of probate.
- A citation to propound a will (r48 NCPR 1987)—this is where the citor has an interest which is contrary to the executors and to the persons entitled under the will.

In all cases, it is necessary to enter a caveat (see **8.9.1**) first, before a citation will be issued. The citation must also be 'settled' (ie the wording checked and agreed) by the probate registrar before it is issued. The procedure is set out in r46 of the NCPR 1987.

However, there may be little benefit in forcing an unwilling executor or prospective administrator to take out a grant. It might be better to see if the court will appoint someone else in their stead, which the court has the power to do, as under s116 of the Senior Courts Act 1981 it can pass over a person with a prior claim to the grant.

### 8.9.3 Standing searches

A **standing search** is useful for anyone who wishes to know whether a grant has been or will be issued. The person searching will find out if a grant has already been issued or if one is issued within six months from the date of the search. After six months the standing search expires, but it can be renewed for a further period of six months.

A standing search is made using Form PA1S, which is sent by post to the Leeds District Probate Registry. The fee is £3.

**KEY POINT SUMMARY**

- There are two types of personal representative: executors who are appointed by a testator in a will, and administrators who are appointed by the Probate Registry. The administrator may be with or without a will depending on whether the deceased left a will.
- It is necessary to obtain a grant of representation so that the PRs can administer the estate, in particular realising the deceased's assets. In some smaller estates, a grant may not be necessary if the deceased's only assets are relatively small balances in bank and other accounts, which can either be realised using the Administration of Estates (Small Payments) Act 1965 or taking advantage of the practice and policy of the asset holder to release monies on production of a death certificate. Other assets fall outside the estate and do not devolve on the personal representatives (eg the interest of a joint tenant in equity). Some assets within the estate (eg personal possessions) can be sold without a grant.
- Executors derive their authority from the deceased's will and will have that authority from the date of death. The grant of probate will confirm this authority (providing official proof of their right to act). In contrast, a grant of letters of administration (of whatever type) will confer authority on the administrator and the applicant has no authority before the grant is issued.
- A grant will be issued to a maximum of four individuals. If there are more than four executors, power may be reserved to the non-proving executors or the executors may renounce probate if they have not intermeddled in the estate. A grant of letters of administration will normally appoint only one administrator, although there are situations in which two administrators are required (eg where the estate contains a minority interest, ie one or more beneficiaries are under the age of 18).
- A grant will not be issued to a minor but it is possible for the grant to be issued to other persons who have an equal entitlement to the grant. If the minor is one of a number of executors, the grant can be issued to the other executors with power being reserved to the minor. If there is no one else entitled to a grant other than the minor, a grant of administration for the use and benefit of the minor may be issued. This will last until the minor reaches 18, and the minor would then apply for a second grant (a 'cessate' grant) on reaching 18 if the administration of the estate has not been completed.
- Similar considerations apply to adults who lack mental capacity. A grant for the use and benefit of the person may be issued.
- An executor cannot be compelled to apply for probate. An executor can renounce probate provided they have not intermeddled in the estate.
- Alternatively, an executor might not apply for the grant of probate initially, relying on other executors to obtain the grant: power is reserved to the non-proving executor who can subsequently apply for a grant of 'double probate' to be added as a proving executor.
- The rules on grant applications come from the Non-Contentious Probate Rules 1987 which have been amended significantly in recent years.

- There are three main forms of grant: (1) a grant of probate, for the executor(s) proving the deceased's will; (2) a grant of letters of administration, appointing the administrator(s) to an intestate estate; and (3) a grant of letters of administration with the will annexed, appointing the administrator(s) in a situation where the deceased has left a valid will but where the executor(s) are not able or willing to apply for a grant of probate.
- The order of entitlement to be appointed as administrator with the will annexed is set out in r20 of the NCPR 1987. This is based in large part on the entitlements of the beneficiaries to the estate, with residuary beneficiaries having priority.
- The order of entitlement to be appointed as administrator is set out in r22 of the NCPR 1987. The order of entitlement closely follows the order of beneficial entitlement to the estate on intestacy under s46 of the Administration of Estates 1925.
- Grant applications can be made by executors and prospective administrators themselves, as personal applicants. Alternatively, grant applications can be made via professionals, such as solicitors, who are authorised to undertake the reserved activity of making grant applications on behalf of clients.
- Most grant applications may be made online, but some may also be made on paper, using a standard form. There are slightly different forms for personal applicants and professionals. There is one form for when the deceased left a will (PA1P) and another for when the deceased did not leave a will (PA1A). The paper application is submitted to the Probate Registry together with the original will (if there is one) and a cheque for payment of the probate fees.
- In recent years, it has become possible and more common for personal applicants and professionals to apply online. HMCTS have been introducing this facility in stages, moving from simpler situations (eg a will appointing named individuals as executors) to encompass more complicated situations. Professionals need to sign up to an online payment account in order to make online applications. HMCTS encourage applicants to apply online where possible, and recent amendments to the rules require most applications by professionals to be made online. However, if there is a will, the original will (and any codicil) still has to be sent to HMCTS by post even if the rest of the application is made online.
- Both paper and online applications can be made in English or Welsh, and HMCTS will issue bilingual grants if requested.
- There is now one flat fee of £300 for all grant applications, regardless of whether the applicant is a personal one or a professional.
- Applicants will usually order a number of official copies of the grant from HMCTS. The official copies are sent to asset holders when collecting in the deceased's assets.
- In some estates, it will be necessary to submit additional evidence with the grant application. This evidence takes the form of either a sworn statement, called an affidavit, or, more likely, a statement of truth. The affidavit or statement is typically obtained by someone who was involved in the execution of a will, and may be needed to explain that a will was executed in accordance with the requisite formalities despite the lack of appropriate wording or the poor physical state of the will.
- There are other less common forms of grant. These may be grants which are limited, for example to part of the deceased's estate only (as opposed to a general grant over their whole estate, which is more common). Also, there are special grants to cater for particular circumstances, such as a grant of double probate (where an executor to whom power has been reserved wishes to join, or replace, the original proving executor(s)).
- Where an executor dies, it is possible for the other appointed executors to complete the administration of the estate. If the sole or sole surviving executor dies before completing the administration of the deceased's estate, it may be necessary to appoint an administrator with the will to complete the administration. However, if the deceased executor has themselves appointed an executor who proves their will, the executor of their will can complete the administration of the first estate due to the chain of representation.

- A person who wishes to claim against the estate (eg by claiming that the deceased's will is invalid) will wish to prevent a grant being issued. To do this, the person can enter a 'caveat'. The persons wishing to apply for a grant can clear the caveat by issuing a warning to the caveator.
- If the person entitled to apply for a grant is failing to do so, it is possible to issue a citation to force the person to make the grant application. Alternatively, the person entitled to the grant may be passed over by the court.
- It is possible to find out if a grant has already been issued or if a grant is issued in the following six months, by lodging a standing search. Standing searches can be renewed for further periods of six months.

# CHAPTER 9
# Administering the Estate After the Grant Has Been Obtained

**FUNCTIONING LEGAL KNOWLEDGE**

This chapter covers the following functioning legal knowledge required to pass the SQE 1 assessments:

**Probate and administration practice**
**Administration of estates:**

- duties of **personal representatives**
- liabilities of personal representatives and their protection
- the sale of assets to raise funds to pay funeral expenses, tax, debts and legacies
- distribution of the estate

**AUTHORITIES UNDERPINNING PRACTICE**

The key authorities that underpin this area of practice are listed below. Note that for legislation you are linked to legislation.gov.uk.

Although much of the legislation on this government website is available in its amended form, the incorporation of new amendments into the text of legislation can be delayed. You should refer to legal databases to ensure you are referencing the most up-to-date legislation.

- Administration of Estates Act 1925
  **http://www.legislation.gov.uk/ukpga/Geo5/15-16/23/contents**
- Trustee Act 1925
  **http://www.legislation.gov.uk/ukpga/Geo5/15-16/19/contents**
- Trustee Act 2000
  **http://www.legislation.gov.uk/ukpga/2000/29/contents**

## 9.1 Introduction

In **Chapter 7** we looked at the work that needs to be done immediately following a death, and in preparation for making the grant application. Then, in **Chapter 8**, we looked at the grant application itself. In this chapter we will consider the work that has to be undertaken by the **personal representatives** (PRs) (and their legal advisors) following the issuing of the **grant of representation**. We will consider the core duties of the PRs, and how those duties are carried out. The chapter will provide a framework for the work undertaken during the **administration period**. However, some aspects of this work will be looked at in more detail in other chapters—for example, the settling of the tax liabilities of the deceased and of the estate is considered in depth in **Chapter 10**. Also, a number of the powers and duties of the PRs will be covered in **Chapter 13** when discussing the powers and duties of PRs and **trustees**.

# 9.2 The main duties of the personal representatives

Under s25 of the Administration of Estates Act 1925, PRs are under a duty to 'collect and get in the real and personal estate of the deceased and administer it according to law'.

In effect, PRs have three main or core duties:

1 to collect in, secure and realise (ie convert into cash) the assets of the deceased;

2 to pay the deceased's debts, and expenses, such as funeral expenses and the expenses of administering the estate; and

3 to distribute the estate in accordance with the terms of the deceased's **will** or the rules of **intestacy** (NB: sometimes there will be a **partial intestacy**, where the estate will be distributed according to a combination of a will and the intestacy rules).

In many estates, the work required to discharge these duties is relatively straightforward, but this is not always the case. We will consider each of the duties in turn. It is also worth mentioning that under s1 of the Trustee Act 2000, the PRs have a duty to exercise care and skill in the performance of many of their functions (for more detail on s1 of the Trustee Act 2000, see **Chapter 13**).

## 9.2.1 To collect in and realise the deceased's assets

Once the grant has been obtained, the PRs will want to collect in the deceased's assets.

Remember that certain property does not pass by will or intestacy and so will not form part of the estate under the control of the PRs. The PRs will not be able to collect in these assets and will have no duties in respect of them. These types of property are discussed in detail in **Chapter 5**, and they include:

- the deceased's interest as a **joint tenant in equity** in jointly owned property (the deceased's interest will pass automatically by survivorship to the other joint tenant(s));
- any payment made at the discretion of pension scheme trustees (the trustees will have the discretion over who should receive any such payment, although the deceased will often have expressed a wish by nominating one or more persons);
- the death benefit under a life assurance policy which is written in **trust** (the monies will belong to the **beneficiary** of the policy, not to the deceased's estate);
- property which is the subject of a valid ***donatio mortis causa***;
- any interest the deceased had as a life tenant under a **life interest** trust (the trust instrument will govern who benefits on the death of the deceased); and
- certain '**nominated property**' (in certain forms of savings accounts—comparatively rare).

Regarding the assets which do form part of the deceased's estate, we will look at the process of collecting in these assets in **9.3**.

## 9.2.2 To pay the deceased's debts (and the expenses of the administration)

The PRs will be liable for all of the debts of the deceased. PRs will also have to pay the funeral expenses and any administrative expenses out of the assets in the estate. PRs must pay the debts and expenses with due diligence (ie they should not delay payment unduly). However, PRs will have very different considerations depending on whether the estate is solvent (the assets exceed the debts and expenses) or **insolvent** (the debts and expenses exceed the assets). We will look at both situations in **9.4**. Also, PRs will be liable for all of the debts of the deceased even if the PRs are unaware of those debts. We will see in **9.8** how PRs can obtain protection against unknown creditors.

### 9.2.3 To distribute according to the will or the rules of intestacy

Having collected in the assets and paid the debts and expenses, the PRs should be in a position to distribute the estate. This may involve paying monetary legacies to beneficiaries, which we will consider in **9.7.1**. It may involve the PRs transferring particular assets to beneficiaries, which we will look at in **9.7.2**. Lastly, payments (both interim and final) will be made to residuary beneficiaries (considered in **9.7.3**) and the PRs will produce a set of **estate accounts** summarising the finances of the estate (**9.7.4**).

## 9.3 Collecting in and realising assets

We will now look at the process of collecting in the assets, considering some of the more common types of assets found in estates.

### 9.3.1 Converting assets into cash

Often the deceased's assets will be converted into cash. So, the deceased's bank and building society accounts will be closed, and the sums held in those accounts will be transferred to the PRs.

Other assets (eg unit trust investments) can be easily converted into cash, with the asset holder transferring the money to the PRs. If there is a death benefit payable to the estate under a life assurance policy, the life assurance company will pay the death benefit to the PRs.

Alternatively, assets may have to be sold by the PRs. If the deceased had stocks and shares, valuable personal possessions (eg antiques) or land and buildings, these will have to be sold if they are to be converted into cash. Under s39 of the Administration of Estates 1925, PRs have the power to sell the assets of the deceased (and the power to mortgage or charge those assets, although this will rarely be required).

The PRs may not, though, wish to convert all of the deceased's assets into cash. Certain assets may have been left specifically to particular beneficiaries in the deceased's will, and in that situation it would be inappropriate to sell those assets (unless the beneficiary consents). Even if assets have not been left specifically to a beneficiary in the deceased's will, the PRs may wish to consult with the beneficiaries to see if one of them would wish to have certain property transferred to them in lieu (ie instead) of part of that beneficiary's entitlement in the estate. Another possibility is that the PRs decide not to sell assets immediately, even though they intend to sell the asset at some future point in time during the administration period.

### 9.3.2 Securing assets

It may be, therefore, that certain of the deceased's assets will not be realised (ie converted into cash), but instead the PRs will wish to secure those assets (ie make sure they are held securely) pending any transfer or future sale.

Securing intangible assets is relatively straightforward: because there is a virtual record of those assets and the assets are already being held by someone else (eg a nominee company which is holding shares quoted on the Stock Exchange). It may, however, be necessary to ensure that proofs of title and other documentation relating to the assets, for example share certificates, are kept securely.

It is harder to secure tangible (ie physical) property. We have already seen (in **Chapter 7**) that following a death it may be necessary to check that the deceased's house is secure, and that appropriate buildings and contents insurance (such as specialist, and expensive, 'unoccupied property' insurance) is maintained. Is the house secure from burglars, and from the elements (ie wind- and watertight)? Is the property visited regularly? (This may be a condition of specialist insurance.) As said previously, locks might have to be changed to protect valuable possessions from light-fingered relatives! Heating systems might have to be left on or water systems drained to avoid frost damage.

Regarding the legal title to land, there is no need for PRs to apply to HM Land Registry to be registered as the proprietors of registered land unless the will includes a trust over the property. The PRs may sell or transfer (by **assent**) the land without having been registered as the proprietors. However, the PRs may apply to be registered as the proprietors (using Land Registry form AP1: application to change the register) if they wish to do so.

## 9.3.3 **Digital assets**

One relatively recent development is the growth of 'digital assets'—for example, a person's profile on Facebook, Twitter or WhatsApp, or the information stored on their Apple account. These 'digital assets' present new challenges for PRs who are often not able to access those digital assets due to the standard terms and policies of digital providers, such as Facebook or Apple, not to release information to relatives, except where express permission had been given previously by the deceased, which is not usually the case. The 'digital assets' just mentioned may have no more than personal or sentimental value to the family of the deceased (eg photographs) but the deceased may also have had digital assets that have a real, commercial value (eg cryptocurrency, like Bitcoin). It may be difficult to know that the deceased has such assets in the first place, let alone being able to secure those assets after the person's death! It is fair to say that the law needs modernisation in this respect, although some will precedents now include the appointment of digital executors.

## 9.3.4 **How to collect in and realise assets**

The methods of how to collect in and realise assets vary from one type of asset to another.

### 9.3.4.1 Bank and building society accounts and investments easily converted into cash

With many assets (eg a bank or building society account, a life assurance policy, holdings in a unit trust) the process of collecting in the asset is quite simple. The PR (or the advisor acting for them) will write to the asset holder (bank, building society, life assurance company, unit trust managers) and request a payment from the asset holder for the value of the asset. This payment will be for the closing balance on a bank or building society account or the amount of the death benefit payable under a life assurance policy. With a holding in a unit trust, the deceased's holding will be sold by the unit trust managers at their current value and the sale proceeds will be paid to the PRs (or their advisor).

The asset holder in question will usually require sight of the grant of representation (or an official copy). It is standard practice to order a number of official copies of the grant from HMCTS so that these can be sent to the asset holders.

As well as the grant (or an official copy), it is standard practice to send a signed withdrawal form to the asset holder. These forms are not standard documents but are produced by the asset holder in question so they differ from one asset holder to another. The form will need to be signed by the PRs. Despite the greater use of technology in many walks of life, at the time of writing this can still be a paper process, although not always. Some asset holders have online processes and it is likely that the use of online processes will become more widespread over time.

### 9.3.4.2 Stocks and shares

Other assets of the deceased are not so easily converted into cash. If the deceased owned stocks and shares, then these will need to be sold to a buyer in order to convert them into cash. The process of selling shares differs depending on whether the shares are in a company listed on a stock exchange or not. Shares in those public limited companies that are listed on the London Stock Exchange can be sold very easily by the PRs, via the Stock Exchange's electronic CREST system. The deceased's shares will actually be held by another company that will have been acting as nominee for the deceased (and so that company will also act as nominee for the PRs). All that is needed is to instruct the nominee company to sell the shares. It is not necessary for the PRs to have the shares transferred into the PRs names first before selling the shares—the shares can be sold even if they are still registered in the name of the deceased.

Shares on the London Stock Exchange's Alternative Investment Market (AIM) may also be sold relatively easily, due to their being listed on the market, but may be harder to sell than shares quoted on the main Stock Exchange due to the fact that AIM companies are less well-established companies (meaning the investment in AIM shares would be riskier for a buyer).

Shares in companies that are not listed on any market or exchange may be much harder to sell. If the company is a private limited company, it is not possible to offer those shares to the public and so the pool of potential buyers is much more limited. However, there may be persons already involved with, or who have knowledge of, the company in question and those persons may be interested in purchasing the shares. So, although it might be possible to sell shares in a private limited company easily, it is also possible that the PRs may struggle to find a buyer. As with quoted shares, there is no need to formally transfer the shares into the name(s) of the PRs, as the PRs can sell the shares even if the shares are still officially registered in the name of the deceased.

### 9.3.4.3 Personal possessions

Personal possessions present particular challenges to PRs. Often, although the possessions are given a value for probate and IHT purposes, and although IHT may have been paid on the value of those possessions, in reality it is not practical, or financially worthwhile, to sell many of those possessions. Traditionally, possessions were sold at auction via firms of auctioneers. This may still be appropriate in some cases. However, this is only really viable if the possessions are worth selling, and many possessions are not. Antiques may have a ready market, but not everyday household items such as furniture, or personal items such as clothes. Often, PRs end up relying on the family of the deceased to deal with the personal possessions or the PRs might engage (and pay) a house clearance firm to remove furniture and other household items prior to the completion of a sale of the deceased's home.

With the availability of second-hand sales sites on the internet, such as eBay or Gumtree, it is in theory possible to sell much of what the deceased owned but this is not something that a solicitor would do as the hourly rate of paying the solicitor to sell the items would outweigh the sale proceeds, probably by some considerable margin.

### 9.3.4.4 Land and buildings

Usually, the main asset that is sold by the PRs is the deceased's own home. Land and buildings normally have to be sold on the open market (unless there is a ready buyer who is willing to buy at a fair price). We have already seen that prior to submitting the IHT accounts and applying for the grant, it is necessary to obtain valuations of the deceased's house (and any other land and buildings). Often this valuation is obtained from an estate agent who is then instructed to market the property to prospective buyers. Assuming this is done, then the PRs will have to wait for buyers to view the property and make a satisfactory offer—this can take months, and sometimes years. The PRs then have to wait for the conveyancing process to complete, which usually takes several months, even if the sale does not fall through at some point due to the buyer withdrawing or due to problems further down the chain of related property transactions. The sale of the deceased's home is, therefore, one of the factors most likely to result in a delay to the distribution of the estate, particularly in a slow or stagnant housing market.

## 9.4 Paying debts and expenses

As mentioned earlier, the PRs are liable for all of the debts and expenses of the estate. We will now consider the difference between debts and expenses and then the different considerations when paying the debts and expenses of a solvent estate compared with an insolvent estate.

### 9.4.1 Funeral and administration expenses

Reasonable funeral and administration expenses take priority over the debts of the deceased.

Funeral expenses by convention are paid first. What is reasonable depends upon the circumstances, such as whether or not the estate is solvent, what the deceased's religious beliefs were and whether the deceased expressed any wishes as to the funeral arrangements. In general, funerals do not come cheap and usually cost several thousands of pounds. In addition, mourners' expenses (paying for refreshments after the funeral) and the cost of a headstone have priority, like funeral expenses. The headstone will not be installed for some months (until after the ground has settled), so it is wise to pay in advance or retain sufficient funds, getting a quote at the outset. This is also useful so that the headstone cost can be included as a deduction in IHT400.

After payment of the funeral and related expenses, the costs of administering the estate are paid next. Again, these expenses must be reasonable, and what is reasonable depends upon the circumstances of the estate. Administrative expenses will include the costs of obtaining the grant of representation, the costs of solicitors and other professionals engaged during the administration and the **inheritance tax** which is payable on the estate which passes by will or intestacy.

## 9.4.2 Paying the debts of the deceased

Regarding the known debts of the deceased, it is usually possible to discharge these relatively quickly once the grant has been obtained and some of the deceased's assets have been cashed-in. It is usually not necessary to wait until the end of the administration to pay the deceased's debts, and indeed it would be wrong to do so because PRs are under a duty to pay the debts with 'due diligence', which means as soon as it is practicable (and prudent) to do so.

Sometimes the PRs may have difficult decisions as to which assets to sell in order to discharge the debts and expenses, but usually there are sufficient funds in the estate from the deceased's liquid assets or those easily converted into cash (eg bank and building society accounts and life assurance payments).

Markedly different issues arise depending on whether the estate is solvent (ie the value of the assets exceed the value of the debts and expenses) or insolvent (the debts and expenses exceed the value of the assets). We will look at each in turn.

## 9.4.3 Solvent estates

An estate is solvent if there is sufficient money to pay all of the debts and expenses, even if it is not possible to pay any legacies.

Although the assets will exceed the debts and expenses in a solvent estate, it is necessary to ascertain which part of the estate should bear the cost of paying the debts and expenses. In the vast majority of cases, this is not an issue.

It is necessary, though, to distinguish between unsecured debts and secured debts. Secured debts are those which are secured on a particular item of property, such as a mortgage on a house.

### 9.4.3.1 Unsecured debts

On an intestacy, s33 of the Administration of Estates Act 1925 provides that the debts and expenses should be paid before the **residuary estate** is divided among the nearest relatives.

In a testate estate, a properly drafted will should indicate clearly which part of the estate will bear the cost of any debts and expenses—usually the will states that the debts and expenses will be paid from the residuary estate before the residuary estate is divided amongst the residuary beneficiaries. This keeps things simple. (If there is a partial intestacy, usually the will contains a similar direction as to payment of debts and expenses before the residuary estate is divided.)

In the very unlikely event that a will does not contain a clear direction on payment of debts and expenses, the statutory rules in s34(3) of and Sch 1, Part II to the Administration of Estates Act 1925 apply. The detail of these rules is not considered here as in practice they will very rarely apply. If you find yourself in practice in the highly unusual situation of having a will (perhaps a home-made one) which does not include a clear direction on payment of debts and expenses, you should consult a more detailed practitioner text.

### 9.4.3.2 Secured debts

If there is a secured debt (eg a mortgage secured on the deceased's house) then different rules apply. Section 35 of the Administration of Estates Act 1925 provides that debts which are secured on property should pass with that property to the beneficiary, rather than being paid out of the residuary estate. This is only really significant where a **testator** has made a **specific gift** of that property in their will. The effect of s35 is that the beneficiary will inherit the property subject to the secured debt, namely the beneficiary will receive the asset but will also acquire a liability (ie the secured debt). So, if the property is a house and there is a mortgage on that house, the beneficiary will have to take on the liabilities under the mortgage when the house is transferred to them by the PRs. Normally, the mortgage cannot be transferred to the beneficiary so the beneficiary will have to pay the mortgage off, and may need a new mortgage to be able to do this.

However, s35 is subject to any contrary intention expressed in the will, and so the testator may specify that a particular secured debt should be paid out of, say, the residuary estate so that the beneficiary of a specific gift of the property takes the property free of the burden of the debt. A general statement that debts and expenses should be paid out of the residuary estate is not sufficient to provide a contrary intention to s35: what is needed is a statement clearly stating that the particular property should pass free of debts, or a clear statement that the debt should be paid out of **residue** or some other specified fund.

Also, s35 has very little relevance where the property is part of the residuary estate, because in that situation the property is likely to be sold in order to divide the residuary estate amongst the residuary beneficiaries. It matters little, therefore, whether the secured debt is paid out of the sale proceeds of the property or out of the residuary estate generally, because the effect is the same. (This is unless the property is to be **appropriated** to a particular beneficiary—in that case, the question of who bears the burden of the secured debt will be important.)

Another point to make in connection with secured debts is that often they do not survive the deceased. Many (if not most) people who have mortgages will also have taken out some form of life assurance to cover the outstanding mortgage in the event of their death. So, on the death of the person, the mortgage will be paid off by the life assurance and so there will be no debt that is still secured against the property.

## 9.4.4 Insolvent estates

An estate is insolvent if there is insufficient money to pay the debts and expenses in full.

Clearly, in an insolvent estate there will be no money left over for the beneficiaries of the estate—the beneficiaries will receive nothing.

However, the creditors of the deceased will not necessarily be paid in full either, as there may be a considerable shortfall between the assets of the estate and the debts of the deceased, once the reasonable expenses of the estate have been paid. In insolvent estates, it is usual for many creditors to only receive a proportion of the money they are owed.

Again, we must distinguish between secured debts and unsecured debts. Secured creditors are in a much better position than unsecured creditors.

A secured creditor has the advantage of being able to rely on their security. The debt will be secured on a specific item (or items) of property and the secured creditor can require a sale of that property and can expect payment of the debt in full, from the sale proceeds. If the sale proceeds are less than the amount of the debt, then the secured creditor will receive the whole of the sale proceeds and will be able to claim against the rest of the estate as an unsecured creditor for the balance of the unpaid debt.

In contrast, an unsecured creditor must notify the PRs of their claim and then wait to see how much of the debt will be paid by the estate. As said, this will only be a proportion of the debt, as the nature of an insolvent estate is that there is insufficient to pay everyone in full. This is exacerbated by the effect of secured creditors relying on their security—often the deceased's most valuable assets will be charged or mortgaged, and if the secured creditor is paid in full, that means less for the unsecured creditors.

In practice, you must take great care when administering an insolvent estate, to protect the PRs (and the solicitors as the advisors to the PRs). Care must be taken to ensure that claims from secured creditors are satisfied or part-satisfied, usually through the secured creditor relying on its security (ie the property that is subject to the secured debt). Sufficient monies must also be available for the reasonable funeral and administrative expenses. Then, an accurate calculation must be made of how much money (if any) is left for unsecured creditors, so that it is clear how much each creditor can be paid. Payment to all the unsecured creditors is generally made at the same time, at the very end of the administration, once each creditor has confirmed that they will agree to the proposed distribution by the PRs. Receipts and discharges should be obtained from each creditor, releasing the PRs from their duties.

There is a statutory order of priority for payment of the unsecured creditors (ie they do not all rank equally). The order of priority is determined by a statutory instrument—the Administration of Insolvent Estates of Deceased Persons Order 1986—and by the Insolvency Act 1986.

The order of priority is as follows:

1 reasonable funeral, testamentary and administration expenses (NB: expenses which are reasonable to incur in a solvent estate may not be regarded as reasonable in an insolvent estate);
2 ordinary preferential debts (eg the unpaid wages and salaries of the deceased's employees for a four-month period, and up to a certain maximum figure, currently £800 per employee);
3 secondary preferential debts (eg liabilities owed to HMRC in respect of Value Added Tax (VAT));
4 ordinary debts—this will be the majority of the unsecured creditors (including HMRC for most other unpaid taxes, and employees for wages and salaries which exceed the maximum figure for preferential debts);
5 interest on preferential and ordinary debts;
6 deferred debts (these include loans from the deceased's spouse or civil partner).

In general, creditors falling within a category will rank *pari passu*, namely proportionately, according to the size of their respective debts.

Usually, an insolvent estate will be administered out of court by the PRs. It is possible, although less common, for the estate to be administered in accordance with the court's directions following the making of an 'administration order'. The estate may also be administered by a trustee in bankruptcy under the formal bankruptcy regime, following the making of an 'insolvency administration order'. It is usually most economical and straightforward for the PRs to administer the estate out of court, but an insolvency administration order would have the benefit that a trustee in bankruptcy can take action that a PR could not, for example applying to set aside transactions at an undervalue under s339 of the Insolvency Act 1986. A trustee in bankruptcy may also apply to court to recover the deceased's interest as a joint tenant which has passed by survivorship, whereas a PR only has control over the deceased's estate which passes by will or intestacy. Difficulties can arise where an estate is administered initially by the PRs but then an insolvency administration order is made subsequently.

As can be seen, the rules on insolvent estates are extremely complex; you should take great care if you have an estate that is, or may be, insolvent, and you should consult practitioner texts for the detailed rules on this topic. Many professional PRs will not wish to take probate if there is a danger that the estate will be insolvent: care should be taken to avoid intermeddling in an estate so that the **executors** can **renounce** probate. Ultimately, a creditor may obtain a **grant of letters of administration** (with or without the will) if the executors and other persons entitled to apply for a grant do not wish to do so.

## 9.5 Investment by the personal representatives during the administration

There may be some delay (of months or even years) before the PRs can distribute the estate. Having converted many of the deceased's assets into cash, and having paid the deceased's debts, the PRs may well be holding substantial sums of money. The PRs may therefore have to invest the estate's money during the administration period. The investment may be quite simple—such as in an interest-bearing deposit savings account with a bank or building society—but the PRs may need to consider more sophisticated (and possibly riskier) investments, such as company stocks and shares.

PRs will have powers of investment, either from statute or from the deceased's will. Also, PRs have duties in respect of investment from statute and from the common law. For example, the statutory duty of care and skill from s1 of the Trustee Act 2000 applies to PRs when they are exercising their powers of investment (unless s1 has been excluded by the will). PRs' powers and duties of investment are considered in detail in **Chapter 13**.

It is worth mentioning that solicitors who are acting as professional executors or who are acting for the PRs must also have regard to the requirements of the Financial Services and Markets Act 2000. In addition, because the solicitor will be holding other people's money, the solicitor must comply with the SRA Accounts Rules 2019.

## 9.6 Taxation during the administration of the estate

Personal representatives will have to clear any remaining tax liabilities and claim any tax refunds or rebates before they can distribute the estate. These may include the following:

- The PRs may have to finalise the inheritance tax (IHT) position (if the estate is one where IHT is due).
- In virtually all estates, it will be necessary to finalise the deceased's pre-death **income tax** position, as well as to account for any income tax due on the income of the post-death administration period.
- In some estates, the deceased may have made chargeable **disposals** pre-death and/or the PRs will have made chargeable disposals post-death during the administration period: in either case, the PRs will have to finalise the **capital gains tax** (CGT) position.
- Other taxes may be relevant, such as where the deceased owned a business and was registered for VAT, the PRs will have to deal with the VAT which is due to, or from, HMRC.

As taxation during the administration of the estate is a substantial topic in its own right, it is covered in detail in **Chapter 10**.

## 9.7 Distribution of the estate

Once the PRs have collected in the deceased's assets and have paid all of the deceased's debts and expenses, the PRs will need to distribute the estate.

Under s44 of the Administration of Estates Act 1925, PRs are not bound to distribute the estate before the first anniversary of the deceased's death. This is known in practice as 'the executor's year', although it applies to **administrators** as well as executors.

The PRs will need to pay any **pecuniary** (ie monetary) legacies left by the deceased in the will (and the **statutory legacy** on an intestacy) (**9.7.1**). PRs will need to transfer specific items of property to beneficiaries who have been left assets specifically in the deceased's will (or the personal possessions to the spouse/civil partner on intestacy) (**9.7.2**). The sort of property left specifically by will include **chattels**, land and buildings, or choses in action (eg company shares). Alternatively, the PRs may transfer property to a beneficiary by way of an appropriation, in part or full satisfaction of the beneficiary's financial entitlement to part or all of the estate (**9.7.2.1**). In either case, the PRs will assent to the transfer of property if the property is not otherwise needed for the administration of the estate (**9.7.2.2**). Finally, whatever is left will be paid to the residuary beneficiaries who might receive their entitlement in stages, receiving one or more interim distributions before the final distribution on the conclusion of the administration (**9.7.3**).

When making the final distribution of the residuary estate, the PRs will produce a set of estate accounts for the residuary beneficiaries to approve (**9.7.4**). These show the property and money of the estate, and the outgoings of the estate (the deceased's debts and the expenses of the estate), and summarise how the estate has been distributed.

### 9.7.1 Payment of legacies

In this section we are concerned with the payment of pecuniary (ie monetary) legacies, such as a legacy of '£1,000 to my niece Alice'. For the most part, we are concerned with legacies that the deceased has included in their will, but where the deceased died intestate there is also the statutory legacy payable to the spouse/civil partner in certain situations (see **4.2.3.2**).

#### 9.7.1.1 When must legacies be paid?

As said, due to s44 of the Administration of Estates Act 1925, the PRs are not bound to pay legacies within the first 12 months after the death of the deceased. This is a practical measure because there are often sound reasons why it will not be possible, or prudent, for the PRs to make payment to a beneficiary earlier than that.

For example, the PRs might have to wait to see if there are applications made for **reasonable financial provision** under the Inheritance (Provision for Family and Dependants) Act 1975. Applicants have a time limit of six months from the date of the grant of representation, which might not be issued for several months after the date of death (particularly when there are lengthy delays by HMCTS in issuing grants, such as have occurred since 2019). It could easily be a year from the date of death before this time limit had expired, and it is only after that time limit has expired that PRs may feel safe to distribute any monies from the estate. (Note that this is just one example—there are many other reasons why payment of legacies might be delayed.)

Also, practically, the PRs do not have to pay the legacy as soon as the executor's year has ended—there may still be good reasons for delaying payment. Provided the PRs have good reasons for delay, the beneficiaries cannot force the PRs to make the payment. However, as we will see in the next section, interest on the legacy may be payable to the beneficiary if payment is delayed.

Lastly, if the legacy is contingent on a future event (say, the beneficiary reaching a specified age, such as 21) then the legacy will not be payable until that future event, even though this may be more than 12 months from the date of death.

#### 9.7.1.2 Interest on pecuniary legacies

In certain circumstances, the beneficiary of a pecuniary legacy will be entitled to interest on the amount of the legacy.

As a result of s44 of the Administration of Estates Act 1925, the beneficiary will not usually be entitled to any interest on an unpaid legacy until 'the executor's year' has expired. Interest will start to become due on the legacy from the first anniversary of death in most cases, therefore.

However, some legacies will carry the right to interest from the date of death, even though the PRs are not bound to make the payment until 12 months has expired, or perhaps later.

In particular, the statutory legacy for the spouse/civil partner on intestacy carries interest from the date of death onwards.

Legacies in wills carry the right to interest from the date of death in the following four cases:

1 where the legacy is to a creditor of the testator in satisfaction of a debt owed by the testator to the creditor (this will be quite rare);

2 where the legacy is charged on land owned by the testator (this will be very rare);

3 where the legacy is to the testator's minor child (or where the testator is *in loco parentis* to that child). This is unless there is a separate fund provided for the maintenance of the child; and

4 where the legacy is to any minor child (whether the child of the testator or not) and the legacy is being provided for the maintenance of the child.

Note this is a simplification of the rules, and the categories are subject to exceptions—for example, interest will not run from the date of death in (1) and (2) above if the testator specifies a later date for payment.

It is also possible for the testator to provide in the will that interest should be payable on a particular legacy from the date of death, even if this would not normally be the case.

The interest rate on legacies in wills is usually the same rate as paid on funds in court, which was 5 per cent at the time of writing. However, the testator may specify another rate of interest in the will if desired.

The interest rate on the statutory legacy on an intestacy is specified by s46 of the Administration of Estates Act 1925 as the Bank of England rate that had effect at the end of the day on which the intestate died. At the time of writing, the Bank of England base rate was 5.25 per cent.

#### 9.7.1.3 The incidence of legacies in wills

If a will has been drafted by a professional, such as a solicitor, it will usually include a provision that indicates that any legacy will be paid out of the residuary estate before the residuary estate is paid to the residuary beneficiaries. Such a provision will override the common law and statutory rules regarding which part of the deceased's estate should be used to pay a legacy.

In the very unlikely event that the will does not include a clear provision on payment of legacies, it will be necessary to work out which part of the deceased's estate will be used to pay the legacy. The likelihood is that the legacy will still be paid out of the residuary estate, but common law rules may provide that personal property (eg cash, shares, chattels) should be used first to pay the legacy, before any real property (land) is sold to raise funds to pay the legacy.

If there is a partial intestacy, with some of the testator's estate being undisposed of by will, then s33 of the Administration of Estates Act 1925 will apply. Section 33(2) basically provides that the legacy should be paid from the undisposed of portion of the estate (ie the part that is intestate) before using the portion of the estate which is governed by the terms of the will (ie the testate part of the estate).

The law in this area is far from clear, though, and so if you have the very unusual situation where a will does not indicate clearly which property should be used to pay a legacy, then you should consult more specialised texts.

#### 9.7.1.4 Obtaining a valid receipt

When the PRs pay money or transfer property to any beneficiary, the PRs will want to obtain a **valid receipt** from the beneficiary and a discharge of the PRs' duties in respect of that beneficiary. This applies whatever the form of the **gift**, whether it is money or some form of property, and whether the beneficiary is a non-residuary legatee or a residuary beneficiary.

With the payment of a vested pecuniary legacy, the process of obtaining a valid receipt and discharge is usually straightforward. The PRs will send the payment (by cheque or electronic transfer) to the beneficiary and will ask the beneficiary to reply acknowledging receipt and confirming that the PRs are discharged from their duties in respect of the legacy.

This is perfectly possible with a beneficiary who is an adult and who has **capacity**, but there are problems where the beneficiary of a vested legacy is a minor or where the beneficiary is an adult but lacks capacity.

A minor beneficiary (ie someone under the age of 18) cannot give a valid receipt for a capital payment and so cannot discharge the PRs from their responsibilities. A minor who is married, or in a **civil partnership**, can give a valid receipt for income, but this will not assist in this context as the payment of the legacy will be a capital payment.

However, if professionally drafted, hopefully the testator's will contains a clause, known as an 'infant receipt clause', which typically allows the PRs to accept a receipt from a beneficiary who has reached 16, or alternatively from the parent or guardian of the child. Effectively, the PRs are given permission to do this by the testator through the inclusion of the clause in the will. This only applies to **vested gifts**.

If there is no infant receipt clause, there is some suggestion that a parent with parental responsibility can give a valid receipt under the authority of s3 of the Children Act 1989, but many professionals may be wary of relying on this as it is far from certain that the Children Act 1989 gives parents the automatic right to provide a valid receipt.

Another, arguably safer, option would be to use the power under s42 of the Administration of Estates Act 1925 and to appoint two or more trustees of the legacy by means of a simple trust deed. The trustees will typically be the parents or guardians of the beneficiary, and the PRs can pay the legacy to the newly appointed trustees who will give the PRs a valid receipt. The PRs will be discharged from their duties when the appointment is made. This power also only applies if the beneficiary has a vested gift. The PRs can instead use s42 to appoint a **trust corporation** as sole trustee for the beneficiary's legacy, but this is likely to happen infrequently as trust corporations are likely to be reluctant to act as trustee in these circumstances. (In theory, the power in s42 would also apply to a beneficiary's share of the residuary estate but, where minor beneficiaries are also residuary beneficiaries, the testator will usually have appointed the PRs as trustees in respect of the beneficiary's entitlement in the will.)

There are other alternative courses of action. The PRs could simply hold the legacy for the beneficiary until the beneficiary reaches 18 (although they would have to invest it to produce an income to cover the interest due on the legacy). Often, the sums involved will make this impracticable and the PRs (especially if they are professionals) will not want to delay the completion of the administration and will want to be discharged from their duties as soon as practicable. Another option would be to appropriate an asset to the beneficiary in satisfaction of their legacy, but this will rarely be a suitable option (see **9.7.2.1** on appropriation). Finally, the PRs could pay the beneficiary's legacy into court under s63 of the Trustee Act 1925, but this will rarely be a suitable option when other options (eg using s42 Administration of Estates Act 1925) are available.

Obtaining a valid receipt for a legacy can also arise where the beneficiary is an adult but lacks the necessary mental capacity to give a valid receipt (perhaps because the beneficiary has senile dementia or a learning disability). Under the Mental Capacity Act 2005, capacity is assessed on a decision-by-decision basis, so the question is whether the beneficiary has sufficient capacity to understand and provide a valid receipt (even though they might lack capacity to do other things). Where an adult has capacity issues, there may be another person who has authority to give a valid receipt on behalf of the beneficiary, for example an attorney appointed under a lasting power of attorney or a deputy appointed by the Court of Protection. If there is no existing attorney or deputy, it will be necessary for an attorney to be appointed or, if the beneficiary lacks the capacity to appoint an attorney, an application will have to be made by someone to be appointed by the Court of Protection as a deputy.

### 9.7.1.5 Bankrupt beneficiaries

If a beneficiary becomes bankrupt after the deceased's death, then the PRs should make payment of the legacy to the trustee in bankruptcy of the beneficiary, and not to the beneficiary themselves. If the PRs pay the legacy to the bankrupt beneficiary direct, then the PRs will be personally liable to the trustee in bankruptcy for the amount of the legacy. Similarly, if the beneficiary was already bankrupt at the time of the deceased's death, it is most likely that the PRs should pay the legacy to the trustee in bankruptcy and not to the beneficiary. (In such a situation, the trustee has to give a notice to the beneficiary to claim the legacy, but this notice is likely to have been given in most cases.)

However, if the beneficiary had been bankrupt at some time in the past but had already been discharged from bankruptcy by the time of the deceased's death, the PRs can pay the legacy to the beneficiary in the usual way and the trustee in bankruptcy will not have any claims on the money.

If the PRs know that the beneficiary is bankrupt, or was bankrupt at the date of death, then the PRs can contact the trustee in bankruptcy and arrange payment of the legacy to the trustee in bankruptcy who will be able to give the PRs a valid receipt for the legacy. (NB: if the beneficiary had been bankrupt at the time of the deceased's death, the PRs will have to check that the appropriate notice mentioned earlier was given.)

Even if there is nothing to suggest that a beneficiary is (or was) bankrupt, the PRs should also undertake bankruptcy searches against the name of each beneficiary shortly before distributing any legacy to the beneficiary. This is the same search as is commonly undertaken in conveyancing transactions—a Land Charges Department search on Form K16 (Application for an official search (bankruptcy only)). The search can also be made electronically via HM Land Registry. Each search is inexpensive so the costs of undertaking these searches are definitely justified given the potentially significant personal liability of the PRs if they distribute to a beneficiary who is, or was, bankrupt.

The result of the bankruptcy search will show if the beneficiary is bankrupt or has been made bankrupt within the past five years. It is necessary to know if the beneficiary has been bankrupt in the past, as even if a beneficiary has been discharged from bankruptcy, it is possible the legacy is still properly payable to the trustee in bankruptcy. The search should be against the full name of the beneficiary and against variations of the beneficiary's name (eg omitting one or more of the beneficiary's middle names, if they have any).

It is also possible to check the Insolvency Service's register of bankruptcies but this will only reveal current bankruptcies and ones discharged recently.

Foreign bankruptcy searches may need to be undertaken against foreign beneficiaries, although these searches are likely to be much more expensive to undertake and the accuracy of the search depends on the country where the beneficiary is living.

Similarly, care should be taken if a beneficiary is the subject of an Individual Voluntary Arrangement (IVA), a form of insolvency procedure sometimes used instead of bankruptcy. Depending on the particular situation, it may still be possible to obtain a valid receipt from a beneficiary who is subject to an IVA.

Beneficiaries subject to a Debt Relief Order (a relatively new, but now common, form of insolvency procedure) can provide a valid receipt (although they will have to tell the Insolvency Service if they receive a legacy).

#### 9.7.1.6 Abatement of legacies

Although an estate might be solvent so that all of the debts and expenses can be paid in full, there may be insufficient left over to pay all of the legacies in full. In such a situation, there are rules on how the legacies should **abate**, namely which legacies are paid and in which proportion. Usually, if there are a number of non-residuary legacies, there is no priority within those legacies, and the legacies will abate proportionately.

However, where the will also contains specific gifts of property, the pecuniary legacies will abate before the specific gift.

This situation will be comparatively rare as most estates are not only solvent but also have more than enough assets to pay all of the **non-residuary gifts** in full, with plenty left over to be divided amongst the residuary beneficiaries.

**EXAMPLE**

Magda's estate is not insolvent, but after payment of the debts and expenses there is only £6,000 left in the estate. In her will, Magda left non-residuary legacies of £20,000 to Frances and £10,000 to Graham. The residuary estate is divided between Magda's young nephews and nieces.

The legacies to Frances and Graham will abate proportionately, so Frances will receive £4,000 and Graham will receive £2,000.

There is no money available for the residuary estate, so Magda's nephews and nieces will get nothing.

**EXAMPLE**

Let us say that Magda's will also includes a specific gift of her jewellery to Denise but the value of Magda's estate is as above, so there is only a surplus of £6,000 as before, but this is a mixture of jewellery and cash.

The jewellery is valued at £1,500. Denise will receive this jewellery in full. This leaves only £4,500 cash in the estate. The legacies to Frances and Graham will again abate proportionately—Frances will receive £3,000 and Graham will receive £1,500.

### 9.7.2 Transferring assets to beneficiaries

For the most part, the PRs will convert the deceased's assets into cash and then distribute cash to the beneficiaries of the estate. However, a beneficiary may be entitled to a specific item of property in the will, in which case the PRs will transfer that property to that beneficiary. Alternatively, a beneficiary may wish to take a specific item of property in lieu of part or all of the beneficiary's financial entitlement from the estate.

When property is transferred to a beneficiary, the PRs will need to obtain a valid receipt for the property. The PRs will also need to check whether the beneficiary is not, or has not been, bankrupt before transferring the property, in the same way as when paying a legacy (see **9.7.1.4**).

#### 9.7.2.1 Appropriation

If the PRs transfer property to a beneficiary in lieu of part or all of the beneficiary's financial entitlement, the PRs will be exercising their power of appropriation. There is a statutory power of appropriation under s41 of the Administration of Estates Act 1925, although executors may also be given an express power of appropriation by will.

The power under s41 can only be exercised if it does not prejudice any other beneficiary. For example, it would not be possible to appropriate an asset that had been left specifically to another beneficiary.

Also, under s41 the PRs must obtain the consent of the beneficiary (or the consent of the beneficiary's parent or guardian) to the appropriation. It is common for wills to vary this so that the PRs can appropriate an asset to a beneficiary without obtaining formal consent. However, in reality, it stands to reason that the PRs should not force unwelcome property on an unwilling beneficiary and that the PRs should obtain the agreement of the beneficiary (or their parent or guardian) to the appropriation.

Any kind of property may be the subject of an appropriation but usually it will be personal property, such as jewellery or items of sentimental value to the beneficiary, or the appropriation could be of a house (eg where the matrimonial home is appropriated to the surviving spouse or civil partner on an intestacy), or the property could be intangible property such as stocks and shares.

Care needs to be taken if there is an intended appropriation of property to a beneficiary who is also a personal representative, as the '**self-dealing**' rule will apply (see **13.4**) and the transaction may be voidable at the instance of the other beneficiaries of the estate. We have already seen this in connection with the surviving spouse/civil partner on intestacy (see **4.2.4.3**, and the discussion of *Kane v Radley-Kane* [1998] 3 WLR 617). If an appropriation to a PR is contemplated, the PR should obtain the consent of the other beneficiaries or the consent of the court. Obviously, there would be legal costs associated with obtaining the consent of the court, so obtaining the consent of the other beneficiaries would be preferable, but this might not be possible if, say, one of the other beneficiaries was a minor. In *Kane v Radley-Kane*, it was said that an appropriation to a PR should still be possible if the appropriation was of assets that are regarded as the equivalent of cash (eg quoted shares which can be sold very easily, and at a published market price). Despite this, it would still be prudent to obtain the consent of the other beneficiaries, if this is possible.

Importantly, under s41 assets are appropriated at their value at the date of the appropriation not at their value at the date of death. This has practical implications. First, it may be necessary to obtain a valuation of the assets—quoted stocks and shares will have a published market price so there is an objective method of valuing them on any given date, but items of personal property, or land and buildings, will need to be valued professionally. For land and buildings, it will be necessary to obtain the valuation of an estate agent or surveyor, just as had been necessary when trying to establish the probate value at the date of death. Similarly, unquoted shares will have to be valued again by an appropriate professional (probably an accountant).

Secondly, market conditions may result in pressure from the beneficiary to appropriate the asset sooner, or later. For example, if the asset is a house and house prices are rising rapidly, then the beneficiary will want the PRs to appropriate the house sooner rather than later, as the more valuable the house, the greater the loss by the beneficiary from their financial entitlement.

**EXAMPLE**

Basil makes a will in which he leaves his estate to his two children, Jennifer and Scott. After payment of debts and expenses, Basil's estate is worth £2 million, so Jennifer and Scott are each entitled to £1 million. Jennifer would like to have Basil's house in part satisfaction of her interest in the estate. The house was valued at the date of death at £700,000. Since Basil's death, the house market is buoyant and house prices are increasing rapidly. Jennifer will want the PRs to appropriate the house to her as soon as possible because the more valuable the house is when it is appropriated, the less money Jennifer will receive from her half share of the estate in addition to the house (in effect, more of the estate will go to her brother, Scott).

Under s41, the asset must be appropriated in part or full satisfaction of the beneficiary's legacy or interest, and seemingly an appropriation is not possible if the asset is worth more than the beneficiary's legacy or interest. However, in such circumstances the PRs could still sell the asset to the beneficiary.

### 9.7.2.2 Assents

The mechanism by which PRs transfer property to beneficiaries is known as an **assent**. An assent is simply an indication by the PRs that they do not need the item of property for the general administration of the estate (in particular, for the payment of the deceased's debts and the expenses of the administration).

An assent is used whether the PRs are transferring property to a beneficiary who has been left that property specifically in the will or where PRs are transferring property which is being appropriated to the beneficiary in part or full satisfaction of the beneficiary's financial entitlement under the estate.

We will see that the term 'assent' has another meaning, in connection with assents of land where there is a specific document called an assent. However, generally, there is no particular form of assent—the assent in most cases is just an indication by the PRs that they do not need the item of property for the other purposes of the administration of the estate.

In theory, an assent will transfer the equitable interest in the property to the beneficiary, and the PRs will hold the legal title on trust for the beneficiary until the legal title is transferred. In practice, however, the assent will be accompanied by a transfer of the legal title by the PRs to the beneficiary.

The **formalities** for transferring the legal title in assets depend upon the type of property in question.

Legal title to chattels, or personal possessions, may be transferred by physical delivery of the items to the beneficiary. Typically, the beneficiary will be required to acknowledge receipt of the item and to discharge the PRs from any further liability to the beneficiary in respect of the beneficiary's entitlement. (Solicitors are unlikely to effect the delivery themselves, but may ask lay executors to hand the items to the beneficiary or engage **agents** to effect delivery.)

Stocks and shares may be transferred using the appropriate transfer process, for example for shares in unquoted companies this would involve a stock transfer form signed by the PRs, together with handing over the form and the share certificate to the beneficiary (who then approaches the company to arrange registration in the company's register of members), or sending those documents direct to the company so that the registration of the beneficiary as the new owner can be effected. (The PRs may also need to provide the company with the grant, or an official copy, as proof of their title to the shares.)

An assent, once made, relates back to the date of death if it is made in favour of a beneficiary of a specific legacy (but not in the case of an appropriation). So, if a beneficiary is given a specific gift of shares in the will, the beneficiary will be entitled to the income from those shares from the date of death.

Seemingly, only executors and administrators with the will have a common law power to assent in respect of personal property (ie property other than land). In reality, an administrator on an intestacy can also transfer personal property to beneficiaries, providing the requisite formalities for transferring the legal title are followed.

### 9.7.2.3 Assents of land

The position is different for real property (land and buildings). Section 36 of the Administration of Estates Act 1925 gives all PRs (including administrators on an intestacy) the power to assent.

Also, for land and buildings, there is a formal document called an 'assent'. Whilst a deed is normally required to pass the legal title to land (s52(1) Law of Property Act 1925), s36 of the Administration of Estates Act 1925 gives PRs the power to transfer legal title by means of an assent, even if the assent is not made in the form of a deed. Under s36(4), the assent must be in writing, signed by the PRs and must name the person in whose favour it is given. Therefore, there is no need for the assent to be by deed, although there is nothing preventing the assent being made by deed and there may be good reasons for the assent to be made by deed, such as where the PRs require indemnity covenants from the beneficiary.

In practice, most land is registered land and the assent will take the form of a standard Land Registry transfer form (usually, Form AS1: assent of whole of registered title(s) by personal representative(s)). For the legal title to pass, there will also need to be an application to HM Land Registry to register the beneficiary as the new proprietor of the registered title.

If the land is not registered, Form AS1 can still be used or an assent can be drafted using precedents. It will also be necessary to lodge an application for first registration of the title (using Form FR1: application for first registration, and accompanying documents), because an assent of unregistered land triggers compulsory first registration of the title.

Strictly, the costs of transferring title (eg the cost of registration at HM Land Registry) should be borne by the beneficiary unless otherwise provided in the deceased's will. So, although it will be for the PRs to produce the assent, it will be for the beneficiary to deal with the registration (and pay the registration fee). However, wills often provide that such costs will be borne by the residuary estate, and it is common practice for the solicitors for the PRs to arrange for registration at HM Land Registry and for the estate to pay the costs of registration, to ensure that the land has been transferred.

Section 36(5)–(7) contains provisions which are aimed at the protection of the beneficiary in whose favour an assent has been made, and of purchasers of the legal title to the land. In particular, s36(5) provides some protection for a beneficiary if a memorandum (ie note) of the assent is endorsed (ie written on) the original grant of representation. The beneficiary is entitled to require the PRs to endorse the grant with such a memorandum, and is entitled to production of the grant to check this has been done. Section 36(6) and (7) contains provisions protecting purchasers. However, with registered land, the register is conclusive evidence of title, and so subs(5)–(7) are not relevant to registered land, and are also of limited relevance to unregistered land given that an assent triggers first registration of title.

Under s36(2), an assent (whether to a specific legatee or where there has been an appropriation) relates back to the date of death so that the beneficiary will be entitled to any rent or profits on the land between the date of death and the date of the assent. However, this can be displaced by a contrary intention.

Under s36(10), as a condition of the assent, the PRs may require the beneficiary to provide security for the payment or discharge of any debts to which the property is subject (eg a mortgage). The PRs cannot refuse to make an assent if 'reasonable arrangements' are made for the payment of the debts. This is only really relevant to the situation where a beneficiary has been left a specific property on which there is a mortgage or similar charge. In the case of an appropriation, the PRs have no obligation to appropriate the property to a beneficiary, and so could insist on discharge of any debt as a condition of making the appropriation.

## 9.7.3 **Interim and final distributions**

There is a range of reasons why it might take some months, or even years, to complete the administration of the estate. However, as well as being in a position to pay any pecuniary legacies, and to transfer property to specific legatees, it may be that the PRs will be able to make payments to residuary beneficiaries before the administration is completed.

The PRs have to be sure that any monies paid will not be needed by them for the purposes of the administration (including the deceased's debts), but provided the PRs are satisfied they will not need all of the monies in the estate, they can make interim distributions to the residuary beneficiaries. Sometimes, these interim distributions can amount to a sizeable proportion, perhaps most, of the estate. For example, nearly all of the work in the estate might have been completed and all that is left is to finalise the income tax liabilities of the estate (which may be comparatively small). In such circumstances, the PRs could distribute almost all of the estate by way of interim distributions, leaving a small final distribution for when the income tax liabilities have been sorted out.

Whether a distribution to the residuary beneficiaries is an interim one, or a final one, the PRs will need, as they did with any pecuniary legacies, to obtain a valid receipt from the beneficiaries and a discharge of the PRs' liabilities to those beneficiaries. The PRs will thus want to obtain a formal written receipt and discharge from each beneficiary.

As we have seen, this is only possible with adult beneficiaries with capacity. If, say, a beneficiary is under 18 then a receipt will have to be obtained from a parent or guardian, perhaps in accordance with an infant receipt clause, or perhaps by appointing trustees of the child's entitlement, under s42 of the Administration of Estates Act 1925. There are similar issues if the residuary beneficiary is an adult but lacks mental capacity. Also, care must be taken to check that the residuary beneficiaries are not, or have not been, bankrupt. See earlier at **9.7.1** on payment of legacies for a full discussion of these points.

As with any distribution, care should also be taken to confirm each beneficiary's identity and to ensure that any bank transfer is paid to the correct account (eg by telephoning the beneficiary on the day of transfer to confirm their bank details).

Alternatively, there may be a continuing trust created by the deceased's will. The PRs may also have been appointed as the trustees of that trust. If so, there will need to be a formal transfer of assets from the estate to the trust: the money then ceases to be held by the PRs as PRs—instead their duties as PRs will be discharged and they will hold the money from that point on as trustees.

### 9.7.4 Estate accounts

When the residuary estate is distributed, the PRs will need to produce a set of estate accounts showing the assets and liabilities of the estate, the income and expenses, and the payments to the beneficiaries.

The estate accounts have limited relevance to beneficiaries who have a fixed entitlement, such as a beneficiary of a pecuniary legacy of £1,000, because that is all that the beneficiary is entitled to. Provided they receive their £1,000, they are content. In contrast, the residuary beneficiaries will be most interested in how much money is in the estate and how much money has been spent by the estate. Every £1 spent on the administration of the estate will be £1 less for the residuary beneficiaries at the end of the day.

In practice, as solicitors for the PRs you will be producing a set of estate accounts for the PRs to approve. However, because the residuary beneficiaries have a direct financial interest in the administration of the estate, the estate accounts will also be sent to the residuary beneficiaries. Best practice, and the case of *Kenig v Thomson Snell and Passmore LLP* [2024] EWCA Civ 15, suggest that residuary beneficiaries should be asked to confirm in writing their agreement to the solicitors' costs, otherwise residuary beneficiaries could challenge a firm's costs subsequently.

There is no prescribed form of estate accounts, which vary in their complexity from one estate to another, but they should be easy to understand. Commonly, a set of the estate accounts will contain the following:

- a basic narrative, summarising important information, such as the date of death, the date on which the grant was issued, an outline of the terms of any will and important events during the administration;
- a capital account that shows the assets of the estate and the debts and expenses of the estate (or at least, those expenses properly attributable to capital);
- an income account showing the income earned by the estate (NB: some expenses may be shown in this account instead of in the capital account because they are properly attributable to income rather than to capital); and
- a distribution account showing the distributions (of specific property and money) to the beneficiaries of the estate. This will record the payment of legacies and the transfer of specific gifts to non-residuary beneficiaries, and will show any interim distributions to residuary beneficiaries. The distribution account (and the estate accounts) will end with an indication of the proposed final distributions to the residuary beneficiaries.

The PRs should send the estate accounts to the residuary beneficiaries just prior to the final distribution, and will ask the residuary beneficiaries to sign the estate accounts, indicating their approval to the accounts. Once this is done, and the PRs have received their discharge from the beneficiaries, the PRs will make the final distribution to the residuary beneficiaries (and obtain a valid receipt for that distribution). At that point, the PRs will have completed their duties and the administration period will be at an end.

## 9.8 The liabilities of personal representatives and their protection

In this section we will consider some specific situations where the PRs may face particular difficulties in respect of their liabilities, and methods of protecting the PRs against those liabilities.

PRs will be liable in respect of any breach of their duties. A breach of duty by a PR is called a *devastavit*. The breach of duty may be fraudulent (through misappropriating the property and assets of the estate), 'maladministration' (eg mistakenly paying the wrong beneficiaries) or negligent (not carrying out their duties properly).

In addition to the specific situations discussed here, PRs may obtain protection from liability for breach of duty in the ways described in more detail in **Chapter 13**, including:

- protection from a trustee exemption clause which is contained in the will;
- obtaining the agreement of the beneficiaries (provided the beneficiaries are capable of giving such consent); and
- the court grants relief for a breach of duty, under s61 of the Trustee Act 1925.

PRs may also be protected by the relevant limitation periods under the Limitation Act 1980 (the details of these are outside the scope of this manual).

## 9.8.1 Unknown creditors and beneficiaries

PRs are liable for all the debts of the deceased. After collecting in the deceased's assets, the PRs will pay the debts of which they have knowledge. However, the PRs will also be liable for debts of which they had no knowledge. So, if the PRs distribute the deceased's estate to the beneficiaries and subsequently discover another creditor of the deceased, the PRs will be in breach of duty and will be personally liable to pay that creditor. Because the estate has already been distributed, the PRs can no longer pay the creditor out of the monies of the estate and so the PRs will have to pay the creditor out of the PRs' own personal resources. Clearly, this is a very unsatisfactory situation for PRs, and quite rightly the law provides a mechanism to protect PRs from liability to pay those creditors who are unknown to the PRs at the time of distributing the estate.

PRs can obtain protection against the claims of unknown creditors by making what are known as '**statutory advertisements**', under the authority of s27 of the Trustee Act 1925.

Essentially, the PRs place one or more advertisements notifying potential creditors that the deceased has died and giving creditors a period of time within which they should notify the PRs of the debts. Once this period of time has expired, the PRs may distribute the estate without being personally liable to any creditors of which the PRs have no knowledge at the time of distributing the estate.

The minimum period of time that must be given is two months from the date of the advertisement (although the minimum period is stated in the advertisement is usually two months and one day).

However, the PRs will still be liable to a creditor who notifies the PRs of their debt after the expiry of the statutory advertisement period if the creditor does so before the PRs distribute the estate.

**EXAMPLE**

Martin is the sole executor of George's will. Martin makes the necessary statutory advertisements on 1 November, giving creditors until 2 January to notify Martin of their claims against George's estate. Martin is planning to distribute George's estate on 1 February. No creditors notify Martin of their claims by 2 January. However, on 31 January, Steven contacts Martin and notifies him of a debt that George owed to Steven. Although Steven did not contact Martin in the period specified in the statutory advertisements, Martin now has notice of Steven's claim and cannot ignore it. Martin will have to make payment to Steven and adjust the amounts that Martin had planned to distribute to the beneficiaries of the will. If Martin goes ahead with the original distribution, and does not pay Steven out of the estate, Steven will be able to claim the debt personally from Martin.

Martin pays Steven and then distributes the estate on 15 February. On 1 March, Jonathan notifies Martin of a debt that he was owed by George. Martin is not personally liable to Jonathan, though, as Jonathan failed to notify Martin within the period specified in the statutory advertisements and Martin had no knowledge of Jonathan's claim at the time Martin distributed the estate.

In most cases, the statutory advertisements will be straightforward and will be relatively inexpensive. The cost is an administration expense, borne out of the estate, and not paid for by the PR personally, even though the purpose is to protect the PR from personal liability.

The main statutory advertisement is to place a notice in the *Gazette*. The *Gazette* was originally a newspaper but for many years it has been simply a publication for placing a range of legal notices (statutory advertisements in estates being just one example). The notices are now, essentially, online.

The next most frequent statutory advertisement is to place a notice in a newspaper that circulates in the district in which the deceased owned land. Note that the location of the newspaper is based on where the land is owned not where the deceased lived or died. Again, such notices tend now to be placed online, accessible on the online versions of the newspapers rather than the print version.

These are the most common form of statutory advertisement, but other advertisements may be necessary depending on the circumstances of the estate. Section 27 refers to 'such other like notices, including notices elsewhere than in England and Wales, as would, in any special case, have been directed by a court of competent jurisdiction in an action for administration'. It may be necessary, therefore, to consider what notices should be undertaken in other jurisdictions if the deceased owned assets outside England and Wales. If the PRs are in any doubt as to what other advertisements would be appropriate, they can apply to the court for directions.

Section 27 of the Trustee Act 1925 does not free the PRs from the obligation to undertake the sort of searches that an intending purchaser of land would make. One of these is a bankruptcy search against the name of the deceased. It is also advisable to undertake other searches that a normal purchaser of land would undertake. If the land is to be sold, though, arguably there is no need for the PRs to undertake a separate set of searches, as the purchaser of the land will be undertaking those searches and these will reveal if there are problems, which would then be raised by the purchaser's solicitors.

Importantly, although the statutory advertisements will protect the PRs from personal liability, the creditor can still claim against the beneficiaries of the estate who have received their inheritance.

Whilst so far we have only considered claims by unknown creditors, the same considerations apply to beneficiaries of which the PRs have no knowledge at the time the estate is distributed (eg in their will, the deceased leaves their estate to be divided equally between their children and, after distributing the estate, another child from another relationship is discovered). The PR would be personally liable to that newly discovered beneficiary.

The s27 statutory advertisements will protect the PRs against the claims of unknown beneficiaries as well as the claims of unknown creditors. As with creditors, although a newly discovered beneficiary would have no personal claim against the PRs, the newly discovered beneficiary could bring a claim against the other beneficiaries of the estate.

Due to the need to give a minimum period of two months in which creditors and beneficiaries should notify the PRs of any claims, the PRs should undertake the statutory advertisements shortly after the grant is obtained. As executors derive their authority from the will, executors could make the statutory advertisements before the grant of probate is obtained, but given that there are other factors that will delay the administration of the estate (eg waiting at least six months from the date of the grant due to potential applications under the Inheritance (Provision for Family and Dependants) Act 1975), these advertisements can usually be made after the grant is issued.

## 9.8.2 Missing creditors and beneficiaries

A different problem, however, is posed by a person who is known to be a creditor or beneficiary of the estate but whose whereabouts are not known. Perhaps, the deceased left part of their estate to their uncle who was last seen 20 years ago on an expedition to the Amazon rainforest. Or, more likely, the deceased's child had run away from home when a teenager ten years ago and has not been seen since. In each case, the PRs have knowledge of that beneficiary's claim to part of the estate, so the PRs will obtain no protection from the s27 advertisements. If the PRs distribute the whole estate to the other beneficiaries of the estate and then the missing beneficiary reappears, the PRs would be personally liable to that beneficiary for the amount of that beneficiary's inheritance.

Clearly, this is also an unsatisfactory position for the PRs to be in, but there are mechanisms that can be employed to provide protection for the PRs.

The safest course of action for the PRs would be to apply to court to obtain what is known as a *Benjamin* order (named after the case of *Re Benjamin* [1902] 1 Ch 723). This will enable the PRs to distribute the estate on a particular assumption: in this case, that the missing beneficiary died before the deceased (meaning the beneficiary would not be entitled under the intestacy rules and any gift to the beneficiary in a will would have **lapsed**). To obtain such an order, the PRs must first have undertaken appropriate enquiries, including s27 advertisements and notices in newspapers circulating in the locality where the beneficiary was last heard of. If the beneficiary then reappears after the PRs have distributed the estate, the court order will protect the PRs from personal liability to the beneficiary.

An alternative to seeking a *Benjamin* order would be to see if the PRs can obtain appropriate insurance which will cover the amount of the beneficiary's claim if the beneficiary reappears after the PRs have distributed the estate. This may be a more appropriate course of action in some circumstances, especially where the beneficiary's entitlement is small, and also depending on the cost of the insurance premium compared with the costs of the court application. It is likely that the PRs would still have to undertake appropriate enquiries before taking out the insurance, in order to meet the terms and conditions of the insurance policy. The insurance does not prevent the PRs from being personally liable but will provide a sum of money to enable the PRs to meet the claim of the beneficiary. Care needs to be taken to ensure that the sum assured is sufficient to cover the amount of the claim (eg that it will cover interest on the missing beneficiary's entitlement as well as the entitlement itself).

A third option would be for the PRs to simply hold on to the missing beneficiary's entitlement under the estate, investing it in the meantime, but this is not likely to be a popular option with the other beneficiaries and, of course, the missing beneficiary may never reappear. It is not likely to be a popular option with the PRs either, especially if they are professionals, as the PRs will not wish to be holding on to part of the estate for longer than is necessary. It is possible to pay the missing beneficiary's entitlement into court, rather than for the PRs to hold the money informally, but again this is not likely to be popular with the other beneficiaries, and a *Benjamin* order or insurance would almost certainly be a better option.

It is also possible that the PRs could distribute the estate to the other beneficiaries and seek an indemnity from them, but the indemnity may prove worthless if, say, the other beneficiaries spend their entitlements. PRs should not, therefore, rely on such indemnities.

Although in this section we have so far looked at missing beneficiaries, the same considerations and options apply to missing creditors.

As with unknown creditors and beneficiaries, missing creditors and beneficiaries will always be able to claim against the beneficiaries who have received distributions of the estate. In other words, the protections mentioned in this section are protections for the PRs from personal liability as PRs.

### 9.8.3 Other sources of liability and forms of protection

PRs will need to take into account a range of potential claims against the estate. Again, PRs will be personally liable if they distribute the estate without regard to those claims.

1. We have already looked at the position of creditors, who will be owed a debt by the deceased. Another possibility is that some form of litigation may be brought against the estate, perhaps in connection with the disputed ownership of an asset. The deceased might have owned a property according to the land register, but another person may be claiming an equitable interest in part of the property. Clearly, in such a situation, the PR would be wise to delay distributing the estate until the dispute is settled or the litigation is concluded. Similarly, the PRs may be aware of a claim that the deceased's will is invalid, in which case PRs should delay distribution. Where a will may be challenged, it might be possible to obtain a court order protecting the PRs from personal liability if a claimant does not issue proceedings within a certain period of time (*Sherman v Fitzhugh Gates (A Firm)* [2003] EWCA Civ 886).
2. As we will see in more detail in **Chapter 11**, under the Inheritance (Provision for Family and Dependants) Act 1975, certain categories of person may bring an application for reasonable financial provision from the estate of the deceased. Such applications should be brought within a time limit of six months from the date of the grant of representation. The court may also allow applications out of time, namely after the six-month period has expired, but importantly the PRs will be protected from personal liability from late applications if the PRs distribute the estate after the six-month time limit has expired. It follows that PRs should be wary of distributing the estate earlier than six months after the date of the grant of representation, because the PRs may be personally liable if they distribute before this time limit has expired. (In practice, PRs would be well advised to delay distribution slightly beyond six months, to allow time for applications to be processed by the court.) However, the PRs'

liability under the Act is limited to the assets which were in the estate (or which would have been in the estate but for the PRs' neglect).

3 The position is similar where there is a claim for **rectification** of a will under s20 of the Administration of Justice Act 1982—if the PRs wait for six months from the grant of representation before distributing then they will be protected from personal liability.

4 Section 27 of the Trustee Act 1925 will not protect the PRs against future or contingent liabilities that the PRs are aware of. PRs can more easily manage a future liability (ie a liability that they know will have to paid at a given point in the future) than a contingent liability (ie a liability that may or may not have to be paid, depending on circumstances, such as where the deceased was the guarantor on a loan, and the liability will only arise if the borrower of the loan defaults). The PRs could protect themselves against a future liability by setting aside a separate fund to pay that liability when it becomes due. However, a contingent liability may never become due, and although the PRs could set aside a fund to cover the possibility of it becoming due, this is not likely to be popular with the beneficiaries of the estate. It also might not be possible to accurately estimate the amount of the contingent liability and so it would be difficult to know how much to set aside. As with the situation of a missing creditor or beneficiary, the PRs could distribute the whole estate and seek an indemnity from the beneficiaries in case the contingent liability becomes due, but this is not recommended for the same reasons as mentioned above. Alternatively, it might be possible to obtain insurance cover or to apply to the court for directions.

5 Care should also be taken to protect PRs against claims by HMRC in respect of additional inheritance tax (IHT) liabilities, caused by the discovery of lifetime transfers, after the PRs have distributed the estate. PRs have secondary liability for the IHT due on certain lifetime transfers where the recipients of those transfers do not pay the IHT within 12 months of the date of death. Also, the lifetime transfers may increase the IHT payable on the death estate. If the PRs have already distributed the estate at the point at which the lifetime transfers are discovered, the PRs will be personally liable and may not be able to recover any money from the recipients of the lifetime transfers and/or the beneficiaries of the estate. HMRC have indicated that they will not usually enforce this personal liability of the PRs if the PRs have undertaken appropriate enquiries—'the fullest enquiries that are reasonably practicable in the circumstances to discover lifetime transfers'.

6 PRs are not liable to a beneficiary who is entitled as a result of an adoption which the PR was not aware of at the time of distributing the estate (s72 Adoption and Children Act 2002). However, the beneficiary may claim against the other beneficiaries who have received the estate.

7 The PRs may also have representative and personal liabilities for rent and breaches of covenant where the deceased was a leaseholder or tenant. Section 26 of the Trustee Act 1925 may provide protection for PRs once they have assigned the lease, but again this does not protect the beneficiaries of the estate against claims.

## KEY POINT SUMMARY

- The main duties of the personal representatives are to collect in the estate of the deceased, to pay the debts of the deceased and the expenses of the estate, and to distribute the estate in accordance with the deceased's will and/or the rules of intestacy.
- The PRs have a duty to collect in, secure and realise the assets of the deceased. Some important forms of property on death are not included in the estate which passes to the PRs (eg the interest of a joint tenant in equity).
- Some assets are easily converted into cash (eg bank and building society accounts, certain investments). Other assets (including shares and land) will need to be sold to realise cash. It may not be necessary to sell all of the assets as some assets may be transferred to beneficiaries. It will be impractical to sell some assets (eg most personal possessions). Assets which are not sold will need to be kept secure.
- The PRs must pay the deceased's debts with due diligence and must also pay the funeral and administration expenses. The debts and expenses are usually payable out of the

residuary estate before it is divided between the residuary beneficiaries. Great care must be taken if the estate is or appears to be insolvent, when the statutory order of priority must be followed. PRs may administer an insolvent estate informally, although there are alternative formal procedures.

- PRs will need to consider whether and how to invest the estate's funds, particularly if there is likely to be a lengthy delay in distributing the estate.
- It will be necessary to finalise the PRs' tax liabilities—in particular, income tax and inheritance tax but also other taxes, such as capital gains tax.
- PRs are not bound to pay legacies within the first 12 months after death, but can do so if they wish. Interest on legacies is generally not payable until the first anniversary of death, but some legacies carry interest from the date of death. Legacies are usually paid out of the residuary estate before it is divided between the residuary beneficiaries.
- PRs will want to obtain a valid receipt from any distribution that they make—whether a non-residuary legacy, the transfer of an item of property or a distribution of the residuary estate. Adult beneficiaries with capacity can give a valid receipt but there are issues obtaining a valid receipt if the beneficiary is a minor or is an adult who lacks capacity. Care is needed to ensure that payments are not made to bankrupt beneficiaries.
- Beneficiaries might be entitled to specific items of personal and real property under the terms of a will. Alternatively, the PRs may appropriate property to a beneficiary in part or total satisfaction of the beneficiary's financial entitlement in the estate. Specific property is transferred to the beneficiary by means of an assent, which is an indication by the PRs that they no longer require the property for the general purposes of the administration. In addition to the assent, the PRs must comply with the requisite formalities for transferring legal title to that type of property.
- The PRs may make interim distributions to the residuary beneficiaries if there is likely to be a delay before the administration can be completed, and provided the PRs do not need the funds for the remaining administration of the estate.
- The PRs will provide the residuary beneficiaries with a set of estate accounts, showing the assets, debts, expenses and income of the estate, and how the estate has been distributed. The residuary beneficiaries will be asked to sign the accounts to discharge the PRs from their responsibilities and to agree the solicitors' costs.
- PRs are personally liable for any breach of duty, even if this is not fraudulent and even if the PRs have acted in good faith. PRs can obtain protection from the law in respect of their personal liability towards particular claimants. PRs can protect themselves from liability to unknown creditors and beneficiaries by making statutory advertisements (in compliance with s27 Trustee Act 1925). PRs can obtain protection against the claims of missing creditors and beneficiaries by obtaining a court order or by taking out appropriate insurance cover. If distribution is delayed until six months after the date of the grant of representation has passed, PRs can obtain protection against applications under the Inheritance (Provision for Family and Dependants) Act 1975 and rectification claims. Certain other liabilities and methods of protection are detailed at **9.8**.

# CHAPTER 10
# Taxation During the Administration of the Estate; Post-Death Changes

**FUNCTIONING LEGAL KNOWLEDGE**

This chapter covers the following functioning legal knowledge required to pass the SQE 1 assessments:

**Inheritance tax:**

- transfers on death

**Income and capital gains tax in respect of the period of the administration of an estate:**

- **personal representatives'** liability to **income tax** and **capital gains tax**
- **beneficiaries'** liability to capital gains tax on inherited assets

**AUTHORITIES UNDERPINNING PRACTICE**

The key authorities that underpin this area of practice are listed below. Note that for legislation you are linked to legislation.gov.uk.

Although much of the legislation on this government website is available in its amended form, the incorporation of new amendments into the text of legislation can be delayed. You should refer to legal databases to ensure you are referencing the most up-to-date legislation.

- Inheritance Tax Act 1984
  **http://www.legislation.gov.uk/ukpga/1984/51/contents**
- Income Tax (Trading and Other Income) Act 2005
  **http://www.legislation.gov.uk/ukpga/2005/5/contents**
- Taxation of Chargeable Gains Act 1992
  **http://www.legislation.gov.uk/ukpga/1992/12/contents**

## 10.1 Introduction

In this chapter we will consider the taxation of the estate after the **grant of representation** has been obtained. We will look at the responsibilities of the personal representatives (PRs) for clearing tax liabilities, and the position of the beneficiaries of the estate as they may also be liable for tax on certain income and **gains**. We will also look at post-death events which affect the distribution of the estate and which, as a result, may also affect the taxation of the estate and the beneficiaries.

We will consider the following four main areas:

1 adjusting and clearing the inheritance tax liabilities of the estate (**10.2**);

2 the income tax liabilities of the PRs and beneficiaries (**10.3**);

3 the capital gains tax liabilities of the PRs and beneficiaries (**10.4**); and

4 post-death events that affect the distribution of the estate and which may affect the inheritance tax and capital gains tax liabilities of the PRs and beneficiaries (**10.5**).

## 10.2 Finalising the inheritance tax (IHT) position

We have already considered IHT in some detail. In **Chapter 6** we looked at the basic charge to IHT, both on lifetime transfers and on the estate on death. Then, in **Chapter 7** we looked at the process of reporting details of the deceased's estate to HMRC and at methods of paying the IHT due on the submission of the **inheritance tax account** (the IHT400).

However, the payment of IHT on submission of the IHT400 is not the end of the story, because:

- there may be reasons for adjusting the valuation of the assets in the estate and reporting adjustments to HMRC. This may result in more IHT to pay, or even an IHT refund;
- at some point, the PRs will wish to obtain '**clearance**' from HMRC in respect of their IHT liability, so that the administration of the estate can be completed;
- the PRs may have claimed the IHT **instalment option**, and either those instalments will need to be paid over a number of years or the remaining IHT will have to be paid in one sum if the instalment option assets are sold.

### 10.2.1 Corrective accounts

As we saw in **Chapter 7**, in estates which are not **excepted** it is necessary to submit an inheritance tax account (IHT400) to HMRC prior to making the application for the grant of representation. If there is IHT due on the submission of the IHT400, the PRs also need to make arrangements for the payment of that IHT.

In theory, the amount of IHT paid on delivery of the IHT400 should always be the correct amount of IHT, based on accurate valuations of everything in the deceased's estate. However, there are often reasons why the amount of IHT paid on the delivery of the IHT400 will not be the correct amount of IHT, either because the IHT400 will not include the values of every asset (or liability) in the estate or because the original values reported in the IHT400 are inaccurate.

If there is a need to adjust the values reported in the IHT400 after it has been submitted, then the PRs should report the adjustments on a '**corrective account**' (Form C4).

The reasons for reporting an adjustment include the following.

- The PRs discover another asset, the value of which was not included in the IHT400. For example, after submitting the IHT 400, when clearing the deceased's house, the PRs discover a valuable painting hidden in the attic.
- A **creditor** might notify the PRs of a debt owed by the deceased (one that the PRs were not aware of at the time of submitting IHT400). This will reduce the estate for IHT purposes.
- Additional lifetime transfers within the seven-year period prior to death may be discovered after the IHT400 has been submitted.
- There is reason to suggest that an estimated value for an asset reported in IHT400 is not an accurate value for that asset. As has been explained in earlier chapters, the IHT valuation will be the market value of an asset at the date of death. The market value is whatever value the asset can be sold for on the open market. With certain assets, such as land and buildings and unquoted shares, there is usually no objective means of establishing the value and a professional valuation will have to be obtained. The opinion of a surveyor or estate agent will typically be obtained to value land and buildings. The opinion of an accountant will often be obtained to value unquoted shares. However, these values are just the best guess of the professional valuer, although the guess is likely to be an informed one based on the valuer's professional knowledge and experience. Where such estimated values are reported in the IHT400, HMRC will investigate and seek help from their own professionals to see if the value reported in IHT400 is acceptable. HMRC will instruct District Valuer Services (DVS) for the area in which the land and buildings are located, and HMRC will instruct their own Shares and Assets Valuation (SAV) team to look more carefully at the reported values of shareholdings. It may be that DVS or HMRC SAV will disagree with the opinion of the estate's own professional valuers. What might then happen is that there will be a process of consultation and negotiation between HMRC and the estate to seek to establish an agreed value for the assets. The agreed value is likely to be more than the value reported in IHT400 and this might result in more IHT being due (this would usually be the case if the value of land and buildings

is adjusted, but if the value of unquoted shares is adjusted, often there will be 100 per cent business property relief (see **6.7.2.1**) on the shares, and so no further IHT will be due).

- The other possibility is that there is a sale of an asset on the open market shortly after death for a figure which is greater than the value in the IHT400. The sale of the asset at the higher figure may call into doubt the accuracy of the value reported in the IHT400. Remember that the IHT value is the market value at the date of death, and the market value is what an asset will fetch on the open market. If an asset is sold for a higher figure shortly after death, then it suggests that the sale price is a better guide to the IHT value than the valuer's professional opinion reported in the IHT400.
- The PRs might settle the income tax or other tax liabilities of the deceased for the period leading up to the date of death. This may result in tax (eg income tax) which has to be paid to HMRC (and which will reduce the value of the deceased's estate for IHT purposes) or alternatively there may be a refund of tax to the estate (which will increase the value of the estate for IHT purposes).
- There may be a sale of assets within a certain period of time after death, where the PRs can claim IHT loss relief, although this is reported on Forms IHT35 or IHT38, not Form C4 (see **10.2.2**).

**EXAMPLE**

Rupert has died, leaving an estate which includes a large manor house in the countryside. His **executors** obtain a professional valuation of the house at £2 million. The executors submit an IHT400 form (and schedules) reporting the house at that value, and the executors arrange for the payment of the IHT due on submission of the IHT400. HMRC confirm that the IHT has been paid and the grant application is made to HMCTS.

However, HMRC also instruct District Valuer Services to give an opinion on the value of Rupert's manor house. DVS forms the view that the house is worth £2.5 million.

There are then negotiations between HMRC and the executors, and eventually a figure of £2.3 million is agreed between HMRC and the executors. The executors then submit Form C4, reporting the increased value, and the executors pay the IHT due on the additional £300,000 (ie the difference between £2 million and £2.3 million).

## 10.2.2 IHT loss relief

IHT loss relief only applies to shares of certain assets but, in general, if the asset is sold within a specified period after death for less than the value reported in the IHT400, the lower sale value can be substituted and this may result in a repayment of IHT.

There are two types of assets which attract IHT loss relief:

1. *Qualifying investments sold within 12 months of death* (ss178–189 IHTA 1984). Qualifying investments include quoted shares (ie shares listed on a recognised stock exchange, such as the London Stock Exchange) and units in an authorised unit trust. (This is not a comprehensive list and specialist texts should be consulted in practice.) In some cases, transfers of shares to beneficiaries will be treated as if they are sales for the purposes of the relief. The aggregate sale value of all qualifying investments sold within 12 months is counted for the purposes of the relief, rather than individual sales of investments being considered in isolation. For example, the PRs of an estate sell two shareholdings, one for £10,000 less than the IHT400 value and one for £6,000 more than the IHT400 value. The aggregate loss is £4,000 and the PRs will be able to claim IHT loss relief based on this figure, not on the £10,000 loss on the one shareholding. The claim for loss relief on sales of qualifying investments is made on Form IHT35 (not on Form C4).
2. *Land sold within four years of death* (ss190–198 IHTA 1984). This would include interests in land (and any buildings on the land). There are restrictions preventing relief where the sale has been to a person beneficially entitled to the land or the close relative of such a person. Also, a claim for loss relief on sales of land is not possible if the amount of the loss is below certain limits. If the sale is within three years of death, other sales of land within the same period may be taken into account to work out if there has been an aggregate loss or an aggregate increase in value, and if there is an aggregate increase in value a claim for IHT loss relief

might result in more IHT becoming due. Care needs to be taken before making a claim for loss relief on the sale of land as it is not possible to withdraw a disadvantageous claim once it has been made. Claims for loss relief on land are made using Form IHT38 (not Form C4).

There are rules to restrict both types of loss relief where the same type of asset is purchased within a certain period of time of the qualifying sale.

Lastly, where loss relief is claimed, the lower sale value of the asset is substituted for the higher value at the date of death for capital gains tax (CGT) purposes.

## 10.2.3 **Paying IHT by instalments**

We considered the instalment option in **6.11.5** and again in **7.5.3**. You will recall that it is possible to pay the IHT attributable to certain types of property (land, unquoted shares) by ten annual instalments, rather than having to pay the full amount of tax on the delivery of the IHT400.

If the instalment option has been claimed, then it will be up to ten years before all of the remaining instalments (and any interest) is paid. This means the PRs will not be able to distribute all of the estate until they have paid all of the IHT. The PRs will need to retain assets until such time that they have been able to clear the remaining IHT liability.

Obviously, this is a far from ideal situation, especially with any IHT on land and buildings, as interest will be accruing on the amount of IHT outstanding (this is not a problem with IHT attributable to unquoted shares when interest is only payable on overdue instalments).

However, if the instalment option property is sold, and thus converted into cash, all remaining IHT on that property must be paid immediately—it is then no longer possible to pay the IHT related to that property by instalments.

## 10.2.4 **Liability for IHT on lifetime transfers**

As already mentioned in **6.11**, the PRs' liability for IHT extends beyond the assets which pass to them as part of the deceased's estate which is governed by the deceased's will or rules of **intestacy**. The PRs are liable to account to HMRC for the IHT due in respect of other property that the deceased had (eg the interest of a **joint tenant in equity** which passes by survivorship), and in respect of IHT due on certain lifetime transfers.

Although the PRs do not have primary liability for IHT due in respect of those lifetime transfers, the PRs may be liable for that IHT if the person with primary liability (usually the transferee of the lifetime transfer) does not pay the IHT due within 12 months of the end of the month of the deceased's death.

This means that the PRs may have to account to HMRC for IHT in respect of one or more of the following:

- the IHT due in respect of a **potentially exempt transfer** (PET) that has become chargeable due to the deceased dying within seven years of the transfer;
- the additional IHT due in respect of a **lifetime chargeable transfer** (LCT) as a result of the deceased dying within seven years of the LCT;
- the IHT due in respect of gifted property which is subject to a reservation.

However, the PRs will only be liable for the IHT on the above transfers to the extent of the property that the PRs have received, or that they ought to have received but for their neglect.

Even so, the PRs will need to be satisfied that the IHT on the above forms of transfer have been paid to HMRC by someone (typically the transferee(s)) before the PRs distribute the estate. Otherwise, the PRs will have to retain sufficient property to meet those IHT liabilities in case the persons primarily liable fail to pay the tax due.

## 10.2.5 **IHT clearance**

'Clearance' is the term often used to describe the process by which the PRs obtain confirmation from HMRC that there is no further IHT to pay. This is important to the PRs, as they will want to distribute the estate to the beneficiaries whilst being satisfied that there are no outstanding liabilities for IHT to HMRC.

Once the PRs are satisfied that they have paid all of the IHT, including any IHT due as a result of submitting a corrective account, the PRs should apply for a certificate of discharge (also called a 'clearance certificate') from HMRC. This is done by submitting Form IHT30.

PRs should only apply for a clearance certificate when they believe that they have reported all the assets, liabilities and **variations** in the estate, and they believe that the IHT position will not require further amendment. The inheritance tax legislation says that clearance should only be sought after two years from the date of death, but HMRC have advised that it is possible to apply sooner than this, although not usually earlier than one year from death. The IHT30 should not be submitted at the same time as the corrective account C4, but only after HMRC have accepted any amendments to the estate.

HMRC will issue a certificate (form SL120) confirming that HMRC discharge the applicants who signed IHT30.

The clearance certificate will mean the PRs will not have to pay any more IHT on the transfers reported to HMRC, but the certificate will not cover any additional IHT due, for example to the discovery of additional assets after the date of the certificate, in situations where there has been fraud or where the PRs have failed to disclose material facts.

A limited form of clearance certificate can be obtained where the PRs are continuing to pay IHT by instalments. This will provide a discharge in respect of all of the IHT, except for the outstanding instalments.

It is not necessary to obtain a clearance certificate where the estate is an excepted estate, as there is normally an automatic discharge 35 days after the issue of the grant, unless HMRC call for an account or it transpires that the estate was not in fact an excepted estate.

Also, HMRC may issue a 'closing letter' or non-statutory assurance when they consider that all IHT has been paid. HMRC have indicated that PRs should treat the closing letter as having the same effect as a clearance certificate, although it would probably still be advisable to submit IHT30 and obtain a formal certificate.

## 10.3 Income tax

In this section we will consider the PRs' duties in respect of income tax liabilities of the deceased and of the estate. We will also look at the position of the beneficiaries who will often have to include their share of the estate's income in their own personal tax returns. However, we will not consider the detail of any income tax liabilities which arise from any continuing **trust** that has been set up by a **testator** in a **will**. That is a specialist subject and is outside the scope of this manual.

Also, this section only considers the income tax rules that apply particularly to estates in the process of being administered. The basic charge to income tax is not covered in this manual, but is covered in the companion manual in this series, *Business Law & Practice.*

### 10.3.1 Finalising the deceased's income tax liabilities

The PRs are liable for the debts and other liabilities of the deceased. This will include any tax liabilities that the deceased owed to HMRC in respect of the period before death. This will include the income tax that the deceased was liable to pay to HMRC. One of the jobs of the PRs, therefore, is to ascertain whether there are any outstanding tax liabilities of the deceased, or indeed whether there is a refund of tax due to the estate.

This is the case in respect of many different taxes. For example, if the deceased was a sole trader and was registered for **value added tax** (VAT), the PRs might have to pay HMRC any outstanding VAT, or alternatively claim a refund of VAT.

Only a relatively small proportion of estates will involve the finalising of the deceased's VAT position, because most persons are not registered for VAT (at least personally—often, if they have a business this will be run through a company, and then it is the company that will be registered for VAT). However, nearly all estates will involve the finalising of the income tax position, as most persons have income of some sort—even if it is just their pension. So, in the majority of estates the PRs will have to ascertain the income tax position, paying any income tax that is still due or claiming any refund of income tax to which the estate is entitled.

#### 10.3.1.1 Distinguishing between income of the deceased and income of the administration period

PRs will have to distinguish between income that is taxable as part of the deceased's income of the pre-death period and income that is taxable as part of the income of the **administration period**.

Certain sources of income (eg bank and building society interest) are taxed to income tax based on when the income has been received (even though they may be apportioned between the pre-death and post-death periods for other purposes, such as IHT).

Employment or pension income will cease on death (although there may be additional salary or pension due from the employer/pension scheme, given that salary and pension are usually payable in arrears and the deceased will have died part way through the salary or pension month). This type of income will be part of the deceased's income and will not be part of the income of the administration period.

Other sources of income, such as rental income from property which is received after death, may be partly income of the pre-death period and partly income of the administration period. Dividends which are due before death are income of the deceased, even if received after death.

We will not consider the rules in detail, but in summary it is necessary to work out whether income belongs to the period before death or the period after death.

#### 10.3.1.2 Reasons why there might have been an overpayment of income tax for the period before death

It is very common for there to have been an overpayment of income tax for the period before death. This will result either in a rebate of income tax (a deduction from the amount of tax otherwise payable by the PRs) or even a refund (ie a repayment) to the estate.

The reason for this is linked, very often, with the Pay As You Earn (PAYE) system. PAYE is used to deduct income tax (and National Insurance contributions, or NIC) from the monthly salary of an employee, or the monthly pension of a pensioner (who is a member of a private pension scheme—PAYE does not apply to the State retirement pension). However, every taxpayer has an annual allowance to income tax—that is, an amount of income that they are allowed to have tax-free. The annual allowance for the 2024/25 tax year (and for each tax year up to and including 2027/28) is £12,570. Under PAYE, each month in which an employee/pensioner is paid their salary/pension, one-twelfth of the person's annual allowance is taken into account in working out the amount of income tax to deduct from the monthly payment. For a taxpayer who survives the whole tax year (which runs from 6 April in one calendar year to 5 April in the next calendar year, eg 6 April 2024 to 5 April 2025), this ensures that the employee/pensioner receives the benefit of the whole of their annual income tax allowance.

Of course, that is the position if the taxpayer survives the whole (or nearly the whole) tax year (much depends on the day when the salary or pension is paid each month), as the employee/pensioner will have received 12 payments of salary/pension in the year. It will be obvious, though, that most people do not die conveniently at the end of a tax year—on the law of averages most people die part-way through a tax year.

If a person does die part-way through the tax year, then they will not have had the benefit of a full income tax annual allowance in the tax year in which they died. However, they are *entitled* to a full income tax annual allowance in the tax year of their death. Put another way, this means that they will have paid too much income tax on their salary/pension in the period leading up to the date of death, because not all of their income tax annual allowance will have been deducted from their salary/pension.

**EXAMPLE**

Joanne dies on 10 October 2024. She was an employee and her salary was paid monthly on the last day of each calendar month. She will have received six monthly salary payments since 6 April 2024 (at the end of April, May, June, July, August and September). Her salary would have been paid using PAYE, and she would have had the benefit of 6/12ths (or one half) of her annual allowance of £12,570. So, she has had the benefit of £6,285 of her annual allowance in her six monthly payments, but has effectively been taxed on the other £6,285. Her PRs will be able to claim a refund of income tax by reference to the unused portion of her annual allowance (note that this will be claiming back tax paid on that £6,285, not claiming back the £6,285 itself).

(This is, of course, a simplification, because Joanne's estate will be entitled to part of her salary for October (from 1 to 10 October), and this will take into account part of her annual allowance when paid by her employer.)

#### 10.3.1.3 Reasons why there might be have been an underpayment of income tax for the period before death

Alternatively, because most sources of income are now received *gross* of income tax (ie no tax is deducted from the income before it is received), income tax may have to be paid on any income which the deceased had received in the period leading up to their death.

The types of income which are paid gross of income tax include income from a trade or profession, rental income, dividend income on shareholdings and bank and building society interest.

Having said this, the deceased will usually have a 'personal savings allowance' which makes the first portion of savings income (eg interest on bank and building society accounts) tax-free. The amount of the personal savings allowance varies—in simple terms, it is £1,000 for 'basic rate taxpayers' and £500 for 'higher rate taxpayers', but is not available for 'additional rate taxpayers' (currently, the additional rate of income tax is paid if a person's income exceeds £125,140).

Also, the deceased will have a 'dividend allowance': in the tax year 2024/25, the first £500 of dividend income is tax-free (the dividend allowance was initially £5,000 when first introduced in 2016 but has been reduced incrementally over time).

The personal savings allowance and dividend allowance might mean that although the deceased had some savings income and dividend income, that income did not exceed the relevant allowance, and so the PRs will not have to pay income tax on the deceased's income from those sources.

**EXAMPLE**

Layla dies during the 2024/25 tax year. In the period leading up to the date of death, she received savings interest of £400 on her bank and building society accounts, and dividends of £350 from her portfolio of shares. She was also employed, and her income overall is £70,000, meaning she was paying some income tax at the higher (but not additional) rates of income tax.

However, there will be no income tax on her savings income because of her personal savings allowance of £500. This is the allowance for 'higher rate taxpayers'—if her top rate of income tax had been the basic rate of tax, she would have had a personal savings allowance of £1,000 (not that this would have been needed), and if her top rate of tax had been the additional rate then she would not have had a personal savings allowance at all, making the £400 savings income taxable.

Also, Layla had a dividend allowance of £500, so her dividend income of £350 will not be taxed either. It does not matter how large her overall income was for this allowance.

Due to the delay in finalising a person's income tax liabilities through the **Self Assessment** system, PRs might find that they also have to deal with the tax liabilities of an earlier tax year, not just the first part of the tax year in which the deceased died. Under Self Assessment, a taxpayer must submit their tax return (reporting details of their income) by 31 January following the end of the tax year. Therefore, someone dying during the 2024/25 tax year (like Joanne in the above example) might not have submitted their Self Assessment tax return for the previous tax year (2023/24), because the due date for submission of the 2023/24 tax return is 31 January 2025. Joanne's PRs would thus have to submit a Self Assessment tax return for the 2023/24 tax year (and pay any income tax due) as well as sorting out Joanne's income tax liabilities for the 2024/25 tax year.

Another aspect of Self Assessment that may be relevant is the system of payment by instalments. A person who has a regular source of taxable income (but not employment or pension income, as this is taxed at source) will often have to pay regular instalments of income tax (on 31 January and 31 July each year), based upon the amount of income earned in previous tax years, but also taking into account exact tax calculations in each year's Self Assessment tax return on 31 January. If the deceased had been paying tax by instalments, and because the instalments are partly based on a previous year's income, it is possible that tax will have been overpaid, in which case the PRs will seek a refund to, or a rebate for, the estate.

#### 10.3.1.4 Individual savings accounts (ISAs)

Many individuals will have invested in **Individual Savings Accounts** during their lifetime. They will have done this due to the favourable income tax (and CGT) rules that apply to ISAs. Any income earned on an ISA is free of income tax.

Despite their name, ISAs can take two main forms. One is a savings account (a bank or building society account) that pays interest just like any other savings account. However, the other type of ISA is a Stocks and Shares ISA, which is not a savings account at all but is instead an investment in stocks and shares, often through the medium of an investment called a 'unit trust'. These investments are called unit trusts because the investor purchases units in the trust and the managers of the unit trust invest the money received from the investors in a range of stocks and shares. Both types of ISA attract the income tax (and CGT) benefits.

So, if the deceased had ISAs, the PRs would not have to account for income tax on income earned by the ISAs in the period before death.

#### 10.3.1.5 The effect of income tax overpayments and underpayments on the IHT position of the estate

The income tax position of the deceased will also affect the IHT position of the estate. If the estate is one where IHT has been paid, the finalising of the deceased's income tax position may affect the amount of IHT which must be paid. An additional liability to income tax (ie one that the deceased was liable to pay on income up to the date of death) will reduce the value of the estate for IHT purposes, and so it might be possible to claim a refund of IHT from HMRC. Conversely, a refund of income tax will result in an additional asset for the estate (the income tax refund) and this will itself be taxed to IHT, so more IHT will have to be paid.

It can take some time to finalise the income tax position of the deceased, and this is usually done some time after the grant of administration has been obtained, and therefore after the submission of the IHT400 to HMRC. We have seen in **10.2.1** that the settling of the deceased's income tax position is something that may result in an adjustment to the IHT liability, and the submission of an IHT corrective account (Form C4).

#### 10.3.1.6 Informing HMRC of the death

After someone has died, it is necessary to inform HMRC of the death. This can be done in one of two ways.

- As we saw in **Chapter 7**, following the registration of a person's death at a register office, it is possible to take advantage of the **Tell Us Once** service (in areas where it is available). As said, the idea behind this service is that the death is notified once, and then the information is passed automatically to several government agencies, such as HMRC and the Department for Work and Pensions (the latter deals with State welfare benefits, including the State retirement pension). This avoids having to notify each of these government agencies separately. The Tell Us Once notification can be online or by telephone. It is necessary to provide certain details about the deceased, including the deceased's National Insurance number, and details of the PRs. The Tell Us Once service will then notify HMRC in respect of the personal taxes of the deceased (but not in respect of business taxes, such as VAT). If the Tell Us Once service has been used, then HMRC will initiate contact with the PRs.
- Alternatively, if the Tell Us Once service has not been used, the PRs will need to initiate contact with HMRC, providing HMRC with details including the National Insurance number and, if there is one, the deceased's UTR (Unique Taxpayer Reference) number, which can be found on letters and payslips from HMRC.

#### 10.3.1.7 Authorisation to act as an agent

Where solicitors' firms are acting as **agents** for the PRs, it will be necessary to obtain authorisation to act as agent on behalf of the estate. When HMRC write to the person who has registered the death or to the PRs, they will send a form (P1000 or P1001) to enable the PRs to give authorisation to an agent. This can also be done by completing and submitting Form 64-8 to HMRC.

#### 10.3.1.8 Reporting details of the deceased's income

The steps that need to be taken to finalise the deceased's pre-death income tax position then depend on whether or not the Self Assessment system has to be used. The Self Assessment system may need to be used because the deceased was already submitting Self Assessment tax returns during their lifetime. If not, and assuming the deceased's income tax affairs are relatively straightforward, a simpler process of reporting can be followed. We will consider the simpler process first, before looking at Self Assessment.

##### Reporting details where Self Assessment returns are not needed

Many taxpayers will pay the majority, if not all, of their income tax via the PAYE scheme mentioned earlier. There may be other income, such as bank and building society interest or dividends from shares, but as we saw there are allowances that mean that such income is not taxable. As the taxpayer themselves had no need to submit Self Assessment tax returns during their lifetime, there is little to be gained by HMRC requiring the PRs to submit Self Assessment tax returns for the period before death.

If there is no need to submit Self Assessment tax returns, then the PRs will simply report details of the income in the period to the date of death to HMRC.

HMRC will then send the PRs a letter confirming the income tax position to the date of death and indicating whether there is an overpayment or underpayment. The PRs should check HMRC's calculation carefully, and then arrange to make payment of any underpayment. If there is an overpayment, this will either result in a refund or, alternatively, a rebate from the income tax that the PRs will have to pay on income of the administration period.

##### Reporting details where Self Assessment returns are required

Where the deceased was already submitting Self Assessment tax returns (or it becomes clear to the PRs that the deceased ought to have been doing so), the PRs will complete and file a Self Assessment tax return for the period before death (and possibly for previous tax years).

Self Assessment tax returns may be submitted in paper form or online. However, if an agent (eg a firm of solicitors working on behalf of the PRs) wishes to submit returns online, the agent must be registered for the Self Assessment for Agents online service, and must have purchased commercially available software to be able to submit the tax returns.

A firm (as an agent of the PRs) will usually submit Form 64-8 first, to show the firm has authority to act. (Form 64-8 is needed even if the returns are submitted online.)

HMRC will then send the paper Self Assessment tax return to the solicitors and HMRC will confirm the date the return needs to be submitted. Returns must be completed and submitted to HMRC within one month of the grant of representation.

### 10.3.2 The personal representatives' liability to tax on the income of the estate

As well as sorting out the deceased's liability for income tax on income earned up to the date of death, the PRs will also have to account for income tax on income that is earned by the estate after death. During the administration period, the estate will usually include assets which produced income, whether these are the original assets owned by the deceased or new assets created when the PRs have invested the money received on sale or closure of the deceased's assets. As we have seen, usually the deceased's assets are converted into cash, and that cash is then invested, even if only temporarily, in investments such as bank and building society accounts, until the estate can be distributed by the PRs.

### 10.3.2.1 Rates of income tax paid by personal representatives

PRs do not pay income tax at the higher rate of tax or additional rate of tax. They are instead liable for the basic rates of tax on the estate's income.

PRs are liable for basic rate of 20 per cent on most sources of income (including bank and building society account interest). The only source of income where there is a different rate is dividend income, where PRs pay the dividend ordinary rate of 8.75 per cent. These are the same rates of income tax that would be paid by a 'basic rate taxpayer'.

In the case of most estates, the only income post-death will be bank and building society interest (and similar savings income, such as interest on unit trust investments) and dividends from shares. Any employment or pension income would have ceased on death, and any business income is likely to relate to the pre-death period. Sometimes, the deceased will have rental income which will continue whilst the deceased's property is still let out to tenants.

Prior to April 2016, bank and building society interest was taxed at source (ie the tax was deducted by the bank and building society before the interest was paid), and dividends were assumed to have been paid subject to a notional 'tax credit'. The PRs' liability to income tax on the bank and building society had therefore already been paid, through the tax deducted at source, and the tax credit on the dividends covered the PRs' liability to income tax on the dividends. The result was that many estates did not have to account to HMRC for any income tax and this simplified the administration of those estates.

However, since April 2016 both bank and building society interest and dividends are paid gross of tax, with the result that PRs have to account to HMRC for the income tax on the income. This is an extra administrative burden compared to the pre-April 2016 position.

### 10.3.2.2 The trusts and estates allowance

HMRC recognise that many estates will receive small amounts of income and that the administrative burden of reporting that income and paying the income tax is not proportionate, given the small amount of tax due.

As a result, HMRC introduced a Trusts and Estates Allowance in 2016, whereby PRs did not need to report income or pay tax where:

- the only source of income was savings interest; and
- the tax liability did not exceed £100. As the rate of income tax paid by PRs on savings income is 20 per cent, this meant that up to £500 of income could be earned. However, the allowance applied to the whole of the administration period—ie it was not an annual allowance that applied for each tax year of the administration. With record low interest rates on savings income until 2022, this arrangement was adequate to cover the income of many estates but has proved less useful now that savings interest rates have risen again.

In 2023, HMRC announced that they would be replacing the above arrangements from the beginning of the 2024/25 tax year. From 6 April 2024, there is a new £500 allowance which applies to all sources of income, not just savings income. This means that PRs with other sources of income (eg dividends) may take advantage of the allowance. Also, PRs now have a £500 allowance per tax year of the administration period—so if the administration period runs across three different tax years, the PRs will have a £500 allowance for each of those tax years. However, if the income of the tax year exceeds £500, then tax will be payable on the full amount of the income (ie the first £500 of income will not be tax free).

**EXAMPLE**

Nyssa's PRs have income of £600 in the 2024/25 tax year. The PRs will not have a tax-free allowance of £500 for the 2024/25 tax year, because their income for the tax year exceeds £500. The PRs will have to pay income tax on the whole £600, including on the first £500.

If the allowance applies, there is no need to report the income to HMRC. Also, when working out if the allowance is available, ISA income which continues to be exempt (see **10.3.2.3**) is not counted as part of the estate's income. For example, if the estate has £400 of non-ISA income and £800 of exempt ISA income, the allowance would be available, as the exempt ISA income is ignored.

### 10.3.2.3 Individual savings accounts after death

Whilst it used to be the case that the favourable income tax (and CGT) treatment of ISAs ended on the death of the investor, since April 2015 it has been possible for the ISAs to be transferred to the spouse or civil partner of the deceased without losing those tax benefits (ie the spouse or civil partner continue to enjoy ISA status on those investments).

Also since 6 April 2018, the tax-free ISA status of all ISAs continues for a period after death, meaning that the income earned on the ISA during the administration period may not be subject to income tax. This is very important considering the popularity of ISA investments with investors, and ISAs are likely to feature in a significant proportion of estates. The ISA status will continue after death until the end of the administration period, or when the PRs close the ISA (ie if the PRs convert the ISA to cash) or for a period of three years from the date of death, whichever is sooner. The income earned on the ISA in the interim will not be taxed to income tax, therefore.

### 10.3.2.4 Informal procedure for reporting income of the administration period

If you do not need to submit Trusts and Estates tax returns (see **10.3.2.5**), the PRs can use the 'informal arrangements' for reporting and paying income tax. Essentially, the PRs write once only to HMRC, at the end of the administration period, with details of the income of the estate during the whole administration period. In other words, the PRs do not report details of income separately for each tax year of the administration period. Instead, PRs wait until the end of the administration period and report the income of (possibly) more than one tax year in one single communication.

HMRC will then provide a payment slip and reference number which the PRs will use to pay the income tax which is due. HMRC have advised practitioners that they should wait for a payment slip from HMRC before making payment of the tax due.

### 10.3.2.5 Formal procedure for reporting income of the administration period

If the estate is a large one, or has a lot of income, the PRs might instead have to submit SA900 Trusts and Estates Self Assessment tax returns to HMRC, with a separate tax return for each tax year of the administration period.

This formal procedure of submitting tax returns each year must be used if the estate is regarded as a 'complex estate'. This will be if one or more of the following conditions apply:

- the estate was worth more than £2.5 million at the date of death;
- the total income tax (and CGT) due for the whole of the administration period exceeds £10,000; and/or
- the proceeds of assets sold by the PRs in any one tax year exceeds £500,000 (for deaths before 6 April 2016, the relevant figure was £250,000).

If the estate does *not* exceed £2.5 million, the total income tax (and CGT) of the administration period does *not* exceed £10,000 *and* asset sales within any one tax year do *not* exceed £500,000, the informal procedures noted in **10.3.2.4** can be used.

How and when do the PRs know whether the above limits will be exceeded? It should be obvious from the outset if the estate is worth more than £2.5 million, as it is necessary to value the estate for the purposes of submitting the IHT400 and for **probate**. Even if the total value of the estate is less than £2.5 million, there may be a house which is worth more than £500,000, so the sale of that asset alone would exceed that limit (alternatively, if a number of assets are to be sold in a given tax year, this could exceed £500,000). However, it is less easy to determine at an early stage whether or not the total income tax (and CGT) for the whole administration will exceed £10,000.

If the formal procedure has to be used, the estate must be registered with HMRC by 5 October after the tax year of the first tax return. The formal procedures involve submitting Form SA900 (the Trusts and Estates tax return) for each tax year of the administration period. The filing dates for the SA900 are the same as for the standard Self Assessment tax return (SA100) submitted by individuals: paper returns must be submitted by 31 October following the end of the tax year, with online returns submitted by 31 January following the end of the tax year. If a solicitors' firm is to submit online returns, it must be registered with HMRC as an agent and the firm will have to purchase commercially available software to be able to submit the returns (it is not possible to use HMRC's free online service).

## 10.3.3 The beneficiaries' liability to tax on the income of the estate

Although the PRs will be liable for income tax on the income from the estate during the administration period, beneficiaries of the estate may also be liable for income tax on some or all of the same income. A double charge to tax is avoided, though, as the beneficiaries will be given a credit for the amount of income tax already paid by the PRs.

The income tax position of the beneficiaries depends upon the nature of their entitlement—are they entitled to specific assets of the estate, specific sums of money or do they have an entitlement to all or part of the **residuary estate**? Also, are beneficiaries entitled absolutely or is their interest a limited one? We will look at different types of beneficiary and their liability to income tax, but arguably the most important are beneficiaries who have an absolute interest in all or part of the residuary estate.

Except for where the estate pays interest to a legatee (on which see **10.3.3.4**), the beneficiaries will only be liable for income tax on income that has been taxed in the hands of the PRs. As income earned on ISAs is not taxable in the hands of the PRs, the beneficiaries are not subject to income tax on that income. Similarly, if the estate income is tax-free in the hands of the PRs due to the application of the trusts and estates allowance (because the annual income does not exceed £500—see **10.3.2.2**), the beneficiary will also not be taxed on that income.

### 10.3.3.1 Beneficiaries with absolute entitlement to all or part of the residuary estate

A beneficiary with an absolute interest in the residuary estate is one who is entitled to a share of both the capital and the income of the estate. For example, if there are three residuary beneficiaries with equal shares, each beneficiary will be entitled to receive one-third of the (capital of the) estate and will also be entitled to one-third of the income earned by the estate. There are detailed rules on what is regarded as capital and what is regarded as income.

In simple terms, however, when the PRs distribute the income to the beneficiaries (typically when making interim or final distributions of the estate), the beneficiaries will have to include their share of the estate's income in their own tax returns. (As mentioned earlier, if the income in question was not taxable due to the trusts and estates allowance, the beneficiaries will not have to pay tax on that income and so will not have to include that income in their tax returns.)

Where PRs have paid tax on estate income, the PRs will provide the beneficiary with information, on a 'tax deduction certificate' (Form R185: estate income) showing how much income tax has been paid by the PRs on the beneficiary's share of the estate's income. The beneficiary can then claim a credit for the tax paid by the PRs. If the beneficiary is liable to tax at the basic rate of 20 per cent and dividend ordinary rate of 8.75 per cent, there will be no further income tax for the beneficiary to pay, but equally no refund. However, if the beneficiary is liable to tax at the higher rate of 40 per cent and dividend higher rate of 33.75 per cent (or the additional rate of 45 per cent and dividend additional rate of 39.35 per cent), then the beneficiary will be liable to pay HMRC the difference between what the PRs paid and the amount the beneficiary owes. Conversely, if the beneficiary's income is so low as to mean that the beneficiary has not otherwise used their annual personal allowance to income tax (currently £12,570), or has not used their personal savings allowance or dividend allowance, the beneficiary will be able to claim a refund of some or all of the tax paid by the PRs.

The beneficiary will count the income in the tax year in which the income is distributed (ie paid) to the beneficiary, rather than in the tax year when the income was first received by the PRs.

**EXAMPLE**

Clinton has died leaving his estate to be divided between his two adult children, Lisa and Jamal.

During the administration period, the estate receives savings income (bank and building society interest) of £1,000, and dividends from shareholdings of £2,000. Both sources of income are received gross of income tax. The income of each tax year exceeds £500 so the trusts and estates allowance is not available. The PRs follow the informal arrangements for payment of income tax, submitting details of the income to HMRC at the end of the administration period. The PRs pay tax at 20 per cent on the savings income, namely £200 (£1,000 × 20%), and tax at 8.75 per cent on the dividend income, namely £175 (£2,000 × 8.75%).

When the estate (including the income) is distributed to the two beneficiaries, Lisa and Jamal, the PRs will provide each of them with a Form R185 (estate income) showing how much has been deducted from the income paid to each beneficiary.

Lisa's share of the income will be £500 savings income (on which £100 tax has been paid by the PRs) and £1,000 dividend income (on which £87.50 tax has been paid by the PRs).

Similarly, Jamal's share of the income will be £500 savings income (on which £100 tax has been paid by the PRs) and £1,000 dividend income (on which £87.50 tax has been paid by the PRs).

Lisa has significant sources of income in her own right. She pays tax on most of her income at 40 per cent. She has used her personal savings allowance of £500 already on her own savings income and has used her dividend allowance of £2,000 already on her own dividend income.

Lisa will have to pay more income tax therefore on the income she has received from the estate. Her liability for income tax on her share of the estate's savings income will be £500 × 40% = £200. She will be able to claim a credit for the £100 tax paid by the PRs on her share of the savings income, but will have to pay a further £100 to HMRC. Then, on her share of the estate's dividend income, she will be liable for £1,000 × 33.75% = £337.50. She will be able to claim a credit for the £87.50 tax paid by the PRs but will have to pay a further £250 to HMRC.

In contrast, Jamal has less personal income. He pays tax at the basic rate of 20 per cent on most of his income and tax at 8.75 per cent on dividend income. These are the same rates of tax paid by the PRs on Jamal's share of the estate's income. Significantly, Jamal has not used his personal savings allowance of £1,000 and has not used his dividend allowance of £1,000. This means he will be able to reclaim the income tax paid by the PRs on his share of the estate's income. He will be able to recover the £100 paid by the PRs on his share of the estate's savings income and the £87.50 paid by the PRs on his share of the estate's dividend income.

### 10.3.3.2 Beneficiaries with limited interests

Beneficiaries with limited interests might be entitled to the income of the estate (or to the income of any continuing trust that has been created by the testator's will). It is possible that a beneficiary will have been given a right to income only (if they have been given a 'life interest'). Such beneficiaries have what is called an 'interest in possession'. Although they will not be entitled to any part of the capital of the estate, because they are entitled to the income, any payments to them will be treated as distributions of the estate's (or trust's) income and the position is then similar to the position of beneficiaries with an absolute interest.

Other beneficiaries might not have an interest in possession, so they have no entitlement or right to the income of the estate, for example a beneficiary of a **discretionary trust**. That beneficiary only has a mere hope that the **trustees** will exercise their discretion in favour of the beneficiary. However, if the trustees do exercise their discretion in favour of the beneficiary and make an appointment of money from the trust in favour of the beneficiary, and if that payment is income, the beneficiary will include the payment in their taxable income for the year in which the payment is made.

Where a payment of income to a beneficiary is made from a continuing trust, rather than from the estate, the trustees will provide the beneficiary with a tax deduction certificate, but in this case it will be Form R185 (trust income).

### 10.3.3.3 Beneficiaries entitled to a specific income-producing asset

If a beneficiary is entitled to an asset due to a **specific gift** in the will (eg a house) and that asset produces income (eg rental income), the beneficiary will be entitled to the income produced by the asset from the date of death onwards. It follows that the beneficiary will be liable for the income tax on the income derived from that asset. If the PRs have received any of this income, they will be liable for income tax on that income but the beneficiary will receive a credit for the income tax paid by the PRs.

#### 10.3.3.4 Beneficiaries entitled to a specified sum of money

Sometimes interest is payable to the beneficiaries of monetary legacies. This is quite a different situation to the ones considered previously, as in this instance the beneficiary's income is derived from the estate rather than being part of the income earned by the estate. The estate is therefore the source of the income. In other words, it is income as far as the beneficiary is concerned, but is an expense as far as the estate is concerned. The income will be paid by the PRs to the beneficiaries gross of income tax, and the beneficiaries will have to include it in their overall income for the tax year when it is paid to them, although in most cases the amount of income is likely to be very small as it is at the rate of interest payable by the Court Funds Office on monies paid into court (currently 5 per cent).

**EXAMPLE**

In her will, Sally left a **legacy** to Gerald of £10,000. It takes two years to distribute the legacy to Gerald, and under the law interest is payable on the legacy from the first anniversary of Sally's death, so interest is payable for the second year of the administration period.

Sally's PRs pay interest at the Court Funds Office rate of 5 per cent, namely £500. So, when they make the payment of the legacy to Gerald, they will pay him £10,000 plus £500. The £500 is paid by the PRs gross of income tax (ie they will not deduct any part of the £500 before paying it to Gerald).

Gerald will have to include this income of £500 in his tax return, although as it is treated as savings income it may well be that it will not be taxed due to Gerald having not used his personal savings allowance (of £1,000 if he is a basic rate taxpayer or £500 if he is a higher rate taxpayer).

Clearly, in most cases legacies will be paid on or before the first anniversary of death (although interest on some legacies runs from the date of death itself). Given the personal savings allowance of most beneficiaries, many payments of interest on legacies will not be taxed to income tax.

## 10.4 Capital gains tax

As we did with income tax, we will now consider the PRs' duties in respect of the CGT liabilities of the deceased and of the estate. We will also briefly consider the CGT position of the beneficiaries.

Again, this section only considers the CGT rules that apply particularly to estates in the process of being administered. The basic charge to CGT is not covered in this manual, but is covered in the companion manual in this series, *Business Law & Practice*.

The principal charging Act for CGT is the Taxation of Chargeable Gains Act 1992 (TCGA 1992).

We will look first at the pre-death position, then the effect of death for CGT purposes, and then the CGT position post-death, both for the PRs and for the beneficiaries.

### 10.4.1 Finalising the deceased's CGT liabilities

We have already seen that the PRs will need to finalise the income tax liabilities of the deceased. This is also true of the deceased's CGT liabilities for the period prior to death. However, whilst the deceased is likely to have had one or more sources of income, the deceased is far less likely to have made chargeable gains which are taxable to CGT.

Most people will have income of some sort, and most people will have an annual allowance to income tax (which might only be partly used). It is necessary in most (if not all) estates for the PRs to sort out the income tax liabilities of the deceased. It is far less common, though, for a person to have made chargeable gains which are taxable to CGT.

Many everyday transactions, like selling your home or car or giving money to a relative, are not subject to CGT. In most cases, the principal private residence relief (under s222 TCGA 1992) means that the sale of your house does not give rise to a chargeable gain. A car is usually a wasting asset that depreciates in value rather than increases in value (and so is covered by the exemption in s45 TCGA 1992). The car might also be a **chattel** (personal possession), and therefore be subject to an exemption from CGT if sold for £6,000 or less (s262 TCGA 1992). If you give cash (in sterling, ie £s) to someone, sterling is not a chargeable asset for CGT purposes (s21 TCGA 1992).

Also, even if the deceased made a chargeable **disposal** (say, the sale of some quoted shares), every taxpayer has a CGT annual exemption (the annual exempt amount). In 2022/23 this was £12,300, but was reduced to £6,000 for 2023/24 and to £3,000 for 2024/25. Unless the deceased has made aggregate chargeable gains in the tax year which exceed that figure, no CGT will be due.

All of the above means that in most estates the PRs will not have to concern themselves with reporting chargeable gains or settling CGT liabilities of the deceased.

If the PRs need to report chargeable gains of the deceased, for the most part this will be done in the same way that the PRs report the income of the deceased (see **10.3.2**). Either the PRs will simply provide details of the gains under the simplified procedure specified earlier or the PRs will report the deceased's chargeable gains in the deceased's Self Assessment tax return, as Self Assessment tax returns are used for reporting capital gains as well as income.

However, disposals of UK residential property (other than a person's own home, if it is covered by the personal private residence exemption) must be reported to HMRC within 60 days of the completion of the sale. Any CGT due must also be paid within the same 60 days. HMRC have developed an online process for the reporting of such disposals, although a paper return can be made in certain circumstances. If the deceased disposed of UK residential property (other than their principal private residence) shortly before death, the PRs might need to report details of the sale very soon after death in order to report the disposal and pay the tax within the 60-day period, or as soon as possible thereafter if the 60-day period has already expired.

## 10.4.2 No disposal on death

CGT is charged on gains which have been made as a result of a 'disposal'. However, death is not treated as a disposal for CGT purposes. As death is not a 'disposal', there can be no CGT charge on death.

Although there is no disposal on death, the PRs are deemed to acquire the deceased's assets at their value at the date of death. The relevant value will be the market value at the date of death, which is the same value used for IHT purposes.

If the value of an asset has been 'ascertained' for IHT purposes then that same value will be used for CGT purposes. The value will usually have been ascertained for IHT purposes if the value was reported to HMRC in the IHT400, because HMRC will have had reason to consider the valuation of the asset. However, the value will not have been ascertained if the estate had been considerably below the level at which IHT was payable, or where an exemption or relief meant that there would have been no IHT chargeable on the asset. In those cases, HMRC would not have considered the values of an asset carefully, and so the value will not have been 'ascertained'.

One of the consequences of the PRs acquiring the deceased's assets at their value at the date of death is that any gains accrued by the deceased during their lifetime will be free of CGT. There is effectively an uplift, so that on subsequent disposals of the asset, the acquisition cost used will be the value of the asset at the date of death not the original acquisition cost of the deceased when the deceased first acquired the asset. This is obviously beneficial because it means that any increase in value in an asset during the deceased's lifetime will never be taxed to CGT.

**EXAMPLE**

Reshma owned a residential property which she let out to tenants. Reshma bought the property in 2005 for £150,000. She died in 2021 when the property was worth £250,000. Her PRs did not sell the property but transferred it to the residuary beneficiary, Nadia. Nadia sells the property in 2024 for £275,000.

There was no disposal in 2021 when Reshma died, although her PRs acquired the property at its then market value of £250,000. As we will see later, there is also no chargeable CGT disposal when her PRs transferred the property to the beneficiary, Nadia.

However, there will be a chargeable disposal when Nadia sells the property in 2024. Nadia's base cost, or acquisition value, will be the market value of the property at the date of Reshma's death, namely £250,000. The gain that Nadia has made (ignoring any incidental costs) will be £25,000 (£275,000 – £250,000).

The increase in value in the property during Reshma's lifetime (£100,000) will not, and will never, be chargeable to CGT.

## 10.4.3 The personal representatives' liability to CGT on gains made during the administration of the estate

There is no disposal when the PRs transfer assets to a beneficiary. This is the case whether the beneficiary is entitled to the asset under a specific gift in a will or if the PRs **appropriate** the asset to the beneficiary in satisfaction of part or all of the beneficiary's entitlement under the will or intestacy.

The same is true where the deceased's will creates a trust. There is no disposal when the PRs transfer assets to the trustees of the trust.

Therefore, the PRs will only make chargeable disposals if they sell chargeable assets of the estate (eg shares or land and buildings) during the administration period. They may do this when converting the deceased's assets into cash as a precursor to distributing the estate to the beneficiaries, or the PRs may be forced to sell assets in order to raise cash to pay expenses of the administration.

PRs have an annual exemption from CGT which is the same as an individual's annual exemption (£3,000 in 2024/25), but PRs will only have an annual exemption from CGT for the tax year in which the deceased died, and in the following two tax years. The PRs will not have an annual exemption for any subsequent tax year of the administration period if the administration period lasts that long.

PRs pay CGT at 20 per cent on the disposal of most assets. For disposals of UK residential property, though, the rate is 24 per cent for disposals on or after 6 April 2024, and 28 per cent for disposals before that date.

The main residence exemption applicable to individuals under s222 of the TCGA 1992 is available to PRs but only if the conditions of s225A apply. Broadly, the property must have been occupied before and after death by beneficiaries who are entitled to at least 75 per cent of the proceeds of sale of the property.

If the deceased had investments in an ISA, the tax-free ISA status will last until the end of the administration period (or, if earlier, three years from the deceased's death). Any disposals by the PRs of those investments within that timescale will be exempt from CGT.

PRs can deduct allowable expenditure in the usual way (eg the incidental costs of disposal). They can also deduct a proportion of the cost of valuing the assets of the estate.

PRs may make losses rather than gains when they dispose of assets. Losses can be set against other gains that the PRs make during the administration period, but any unrelieved losses at the end of the administration period cannot be passed on to the beneficiaries.

As PRs are liable to CGT on sales of assets, and because PRs pay higher rates of CGT, they should consider whether it would be preferable to transfer assets to beneficiaries rather than selling those assets. The beneficiaries may pay lower rates of CGT than the PRs, and so it would make sense for the beneficiaries to sell assets rather than the PRs. If the beneficiary is a charity, charities are exempt from paying CGT so it would be preferable for PRs to transfer the asset to the charity and for the charity to sell it, than for the PRs to sell the asset first and incur a CGT liability. Even if an asset has fallen in value, it might be preferable to transfer the asset to a beneficiary so that the beneficiary can take advantage of the loss, rather than for the PRs to sell the asset at a loss but not be able to pass that loss on to the beneficiary.

The PRs will report most of their chargeable disposals in the same way that they report the income of the administration period. Either the details will be reported to HMRC at the end of the administration period using informal arrangements or the PRs will include details of the disposals in the SA900 Self Assessment Trusts and Estates tax return for each tax year of the administration period. See **10.3.2.5** for the rules on whether the PRs can follow HMRC's informal arrangements or whether they are required to submit Self Assessment tax returns.

However, if the PRs dispose of UK residential property (this can include the deceased's private residence, as the principal private residence relief might not apply to the property now that the owner is dead), the PRs will have to report the disposal and pay any CGT due within 60 days of the disposal. A UK property paper return can be submitted in certain circumstances but in most cases the UK property return is submitted online. PRs will have to register with HMRC to use the online service if the PRs do not have an existing Government Gateway account.

### 10.4.4 **The beneficiaries' liability to CGT on inherited assets**

We saw earlier that there is no disposal when the PRs transfer an asset to a beneficiary, and so there is no CGT for the PRs to pay. What, though, is the effect on the beneficiary?

The beneficiary will be deemed to acquire the asset, but not at the value at the time of the transfer. Instead, for CGT purposes the beneficiary will acquire the asset at its value at the date of death. Effectively, this means that on a future disposal of the asset by the beneficiary, the beneficiary's gain will be the increase in value between the date of death and the date of disposal.

Hopefully, you will be able to see the admirable simplicity of CGT in connection with death estates: the deceased's assets pass to the PRs at the market value at the date of death; all pre-death gains on those assets are effectively wiped out and will never be subject to CGT; the PRs can pass those assets to the beneficiaries without the PRs having to pay CGT; and the beneficiaries have the value at the date of death as their starting point.

As mentioned in the previous section on the PRs' liability for CGT on sales during the administration, there may be good reasons for the PRs to transfer assets to beneficiaries, so that the beneficiaries sell the assets rather than the PRs. The beneficiaries may pay a lower rate of CGT or, if a charity, pay no CGT at all. It might also be beneficial to transfer assets that have fallen in value since the date of death so that the beneficiary can utilise a loss against other gains made by the beneficiary rather than the loss be realised by the PRs, as the PRs cannot pass the loss on to the beneficiary.

In many estates, there will be a continuing trust created by the testator in their will. At some point, the PRs will transfer assets from the estate to the trustees of the trust. The PRs and the trustees may even be the same persons, but their roles are distinct. As with transfers to beneficiaries, there is no disposal when the PRs transfer an asset to trustees.

## 10.5 **Post-death events and taxation**

A number of post-death events may affect the IHT, CGT and income tax positions of the estate and its beneficiaries.

These events include:

- orders made by the court under the Inheritance (Provision for Family and Dependants) Act 1975 (see **Chapter 11**);
- where the deceased created a discretionary trust in their will, the exercise of the trustees' discretion within two years of death, in accordance with s144 of the IHTA 1984;
- **disclaimers** by beneficiaries within two years of death; and
- variations to the distribution of the estate within two years of death.

Where the court makes an order under the 1975 Act, or where the trustees of a discretionary trust exercise their discretion to benefit certain beneficiaries within two years of death, the resulting distribution of the estate will be read back to the date of death for the purposes of IHT. This may mean that more or less IHT is payable, depending on the nature of the beneficiary. For example, the deceased may have left nothing to their spouse or civil partner in their will. If the spouse or civil partner brings a successful application for **reasonable financial provision** under the 1975

Act, any property which the court orders should pass to the spouse or civil partner will be covered by an IHT exemption, when previously it would not have been subject to an exemption. This could lead to a reduction in IHT, and the estate may be due a repayment of IHT from HMRC.

**EXAMPLE**

Hugo has died leaving nothing in his will to his husband, Jack. (Hugo made the will shortly before his death and after he married Jack, so it was not a pre-existing will that had been **revoked** by the marriage.)

Jack applies to the court for reasonable financial provision under the Inheritance (Provision for Family and Dependants) Act 1975 and is successful. The court awards Jack £500,000 from Hugo's estate (which was worth £750,000).

Hugo's estate was originally subject to IHT, as it exceeded his **nil rate band** of £325,000. As a result of Jack's successful application, the IHT exemption from s18 of the IHTA 1984 (transfers between spouses and civil partners) applies to the £500,000 awarded to Jack by the court. The remaining estate of £250,000 falls within Hugo's nil rate band, and so Hugo's executors can reclaim from HMRC any IHT that has been paid.

A similar result would have been achieved had Hugo set up a discretionary trust in his will and, within two years of his death, the trustees had decided to pay £500,000 from the trust to Jack. The resulting distribution by the trustees would be read back to the date of death, and there would be a similar repayment of IHT because the IHT exemption would apply to the £500,000 that the trustees had appointed to Jack.

For CGT purposes, the only difference is that a different beneficiary is acquiring the asset, but the acquisition cost for the beneficiary will always be the market value of the asset at the date of death. Neither the court order nor the exercise of the trustees' discretion is a disposal for CGT purposes.

These post-death events do not necessarily take effect from the date of death for the purposes of income tax.

## 10.5.1 Disclaimers

As mentioned in earlier chapters, a disclaimer is a rejection by the beneficiary of their entitlement under the will or intestacy. Disclaimers are 'all or nothing'. It is not possible to disclaim part of a benefit: the beneficiary must disclaim the whole **gift**. However, if the beneficiary has been given more than one separate gift, the beneficiary can disclaim one but accept the other(s). Also, a beneficiary cannot disclaim an entitlement once they have started to enjoy the benefit of their entitlement (eg by receiving income from an asset).

The taxation rules on disclaimers are a bit different to the post-death events mentioned previously. For IHT purposes, the effect of the disclaimer will be read back to the date of death under s142 of the IHTA 1984 but only if the disclaimer is made within two years of death, is made in writing and is not made for a consideration (money or money's worth). Again, this could affect the IHT payable. Taking the above example, let's say that Hugo left two-thirds of his estate (or £500,000) to his sister, Pamela. However, Pamela thinks that Hugo was being irrational in not providing for Jack and so Pamela disclaims her entitlement in writing within two years of Hugo's death. Hugo's will does not state what should happen if Pamela does not inherit and so that part of Hugo's estate (ie £500,000) passes to Jack under the intestacy rules. Again, the IHT exemption on transfers between spouses and civil partners would mean that IHT is repayable by HMRC to the estate.

If a disclaimer does not comply with the requirements in s142 (eg it is not in writing or is not made within two years of death), then the disclaiming beneficiary is treated as having made a lifetime transfer for IHT purposes.

For CGT purposes, the disclaiming beneficiary will be treated as making a disposal, unless the requirements of s62(6) of the Taxation of Chargeable Gains Act 1992 are met. These conditions are the same as the conditions for IHT in s142 of the IHTA 1984, so if the disclaimer is in writing, within two years of death and not for consideration, there will be no disposal by the disclaiming beneficiary.

For income tax purposes, disclaimers should be effective from the date of death. As stated previously, a beneficiary cannot disclaim once they have received a benefit (eg income).

## 10.5.2 Post-death variations

Disclaimers are a very blunt instrument and are not to be recommended in most cases. The disclaiming beneficiary cannot disclaim part of an entitlement, and the disclaiming beneficiary cannot control the destination of the property after the disclaimer. Also, the beneficiary cannot disclaim if they have already accepted a benefit from the property.

So, taking Hugo's estate again, if Pamela had been entitled to the whole estate of £750,000 she could not have disclaimed part of it (£500,000) and kept the rest (£250,000). Also, even if Pamela had only been entitled to £500,000, if she disclaims the £500,000 will then be distributed according to the terms of Hugo's will or the rules of intestacy if the will is silent on the matter. So, if Hugo's will provides for a substitutional gift to another beneficiary, Martin, in the event of Pamela not inheriting, then the terms of the will prevail and Martin will receive the £500,000. In other words, there is no guarantee that Jack will get the £500,000 as a result of Pamela disclaiming.

As a result of these problems, the recommended action usually is to make a 'variation' of the estate rather than for the beneficiary to make a disclaimer. With a variation it is possible for a beneficiary to accept part of an entitlement but provide that the other part should go to another beneficiary. The variation can specify who that other beneficiary will be rather than leaving the question to the existing terms of the deceased's will or the rules of intestacy.

Many students are shocked to discover that it is possible for the beneficiaries of a will to completely change the distribution of a person's estate after their death. This is perhaps less alarming with an estate which is intestate, as any variation of such an estate would be a means of avoiding the unwanted application of the statutory intestacy rules. However, it is also possible to effectively ignore what is in a testator's will. If the beneficiaries of the will agree, they do not have to follow the wishes of the testator at all and can radically alter the distribution of the estate.

Although there is an argument that this is an unwarranted attack on the principle of testamentary freedom, the important point is that the variation must be agreed by all the beneficiaries (or at least by all of the beneficiaries who stand to receive less as a result of the variation). Also, those beneficiaries have to be adults and of sound mind. Looked at this way, a variation is just a more sophisticated form of disclaimer.

In practice, a variation is made in writing by means of a formal 'deed of variation'.

Section 142 of the IHTA 1984, which we looked at earlier in relation to disclaimers, is also relevant to variations. Again, certain conditions must be met for the variation to be read back to the date of death for IHT purposes.

If the conditions are not met, then the variation is treated as a lifetime transfer by the beneficiary whose entitlement is reduced as a result of the variation. This is likely to be regarded as a PET for IHT purposes, as usually the variation is in favour of another individual, so it is just as if the original beneficiary is making a gift to the new beneficiary.

As with disclaimers, for the variation to be read back to the date of death the variation must be within two years of death, be in writing and not be for consideration. However, there is an additional requirement, and this is that the document which makes the variation must contain a statement by the person making the variation (and, in some cases, the PRs of the deceased) that the variation is to be read back to the date of death.

What this means is that the beneficiary making the variation has a choice—they can seek to read the variation back to the date of death or treat the variation as a lifetime transfer (which will most likely be a PET). There may, in fact, be benefits in treating the variation as a PET, but a detailed discussion of the choice is outside the scope of this manual.

If there is more IHT payable as a result of a variation being read back to the date of death, the PRs have to join in the statement that the variation is to be read back to the date of death. However, the PRs can only refuse to join in the statement if there are insufficient assets still held by them to pay the additional IHT.

Also, where the variation results in more IHT, there is a duty to send a copy of the written variation to HMRC and to notify HMRC of the extra IHT due.

HMRC have also expressed the view that s142 of the IHTA 1984 does not apply to a variation that redirects property that has already been subject to an earlier variation. So, although a second variation would be effective to transfer the property to the new beneficiary, the second variation would be treated as a lifetime transfer for IHT purposes. It is not be possible to have the second variation treated as if it was read back to the date of death.

The position for CGT (s62(6) TCGA 1992) is similar to the IHT position in several respects, but there are important differences. The same basic conditions (writing, within two years, not for consideration) apply, and the beneficiary making the variation has a choice whether to treat the variation as being read back to death or to treat the variation as a CGT disposal. Of course, if the beneficiary chooses the latter, there may be CGT to pay but there might be benefits of adopting this course of action. You just need to know there is a choice, and see other texts for more detail.

Unlike IHT, however, there will be no additional CGT liability for the PRs if the variation is read back to the date of death. Accordingly, there is no requirement for the PRs to be joined in the relevant statement regarding the CGT effect of the variation.

It is possible to elect to read the variation back to the date of death for IHT but not for CGT purposes, and vice versa. In other words, different elections can be made for the two taxes in respect of the same variation.

For income tax purposes, variations are only effective from the date of the variation and are not read back to the date of death. A beneficiary who makes a variation may be liable for income tax on the period between the date of death and the date of the variation, therefore.

## KEY POINT SUMMARY

- The PRs must report all assets and liabilities of the deceased in the IHT400, which is submitted to HMRC before the grant of representation is obtained. There are various reasons why the figures provided in the IHT400 may need to be adjusted subsequently. For example, additional assets might be found or the value of an asset might be agreed with HMRC following a period of negotiation. The PRs will report the changes in a corrective account and this may result in the payment of more IHT.
- PRs need to seek IHT clearance from HMRC once they consider that all the IHT has been (or will be) paid. PRs also need to ensure that they retain sufficient assets in the estate to pay any IHT instalments and also to cover the potential liability of IHT on lifetime transfers where the transferee does not pay HMRC.
- PRs will have to clear any income tax liabilities of the deceased for the period before death, as well as account for income tax on income of the administration period.
- If the deceased was already submitting tax returns via Self Assessment during their lifetime, the PRs will continue to do this for the period before death. Otherwise, there is a simpler process by which PRs provide details to HMRC. With many smaller estates, there is likely to have been an overpayment of income tax by the deceased due to the PAYE system.
- In relation to the income of the administration period, PRs have a small annual trusts and estates income tax allowance of £500. If the allowance applies, PRs do not need to report details of their income to HMRC. If income exceeds £500, the allowance does not apply and tax is paid on the full amount of income. PRs pay income tax at basic rates. Income is received gross, so PRs have to account to HMRC for any income tax due. PRs will do this either once at the end of the administration period by using HMRC's informal arrangements or by submitting Trusts and Estates Self Assessment tax returns for each tax year of the administration period.
- The income tax position of a beneficiary depends upon the beneficiary's exact entitlement. The beneficiaries of the residuary estate will each be liable for income tax on a proportion of the income earned by the residuary estate if the PRs have been taxed on that income. The PRs will provide beneficiaries with information on the amount of income tax that has been paid by the PRs and the beneficiaries will be able to claim a credit for this when working out their own income tax liabilities.

- For CGT purposes, the PRs acquire the deceased's assets at their market value at the date of death, but there is no CGT disposal on death. There is also no disposal when the PRs transfer those assets to the beneficiaries, and beneficiaries will use the market value at the date of death as their acquisition cost on any subsequent disposal. The PRs will only make chargeable disposals if they sell assets during the administration of the estate.
- Certain post-death events (eg post-death variations by the beneficiaries) may result in a change to the IHT position of the estate. These events can also affect the CGT position of the beneficiaries. With the exception of an order of the court under the Inheritance (Provision for Family and Dependants) Act 1975, post-death events have to take place within two years of death. Disclaimers and variations have to be in writing and variations must comply with certain requirements to be effective from the date of death for IHT and CGT purposes.

# CHAPTER 11
# Inheritance Act and Other Claims Against the Estate

**FUNCTIONING LEGAL KNOWLEDGE**

This chapter covers the following functioning legal knowledge required to pass the SQE 1 assessments:

**Claims against estates under the Inheritance (Provision for Family and Dependants) Act 1975:**

- time limit
- applicants
- ground

**AUTHORITIES UNDERPINNING PRACTICE**

The key authorities that underpin this area of practice are listed below. Note that for legislation you are linked to legislation.gov.uk.

Although much of the legislation on this government website is available in its amended form, the incorporation of new amendments into the text of legislation can be delayed. You should refer to legal databases to ensure you are referencing the most up-to-date legislation.

- Inheritance (Provision for Family and Dependants) Act 1975
  **http://www.legislation.gov.uk/ukpga/1975/63/contents**

## 11.1 Introduction

This chapter looks in detail at claims that may be made against the estate after a person's death. The main focus of this chapter is the Inheritance (Provision for Family and Dependants) Act 1975. This is a very important piece of legislation, because the Act gives certain categories of relatives and dependants the right to bring an application to the court for an order that the estate should provide some form of financial assistance to the applicant. Any order that the court makes will override what is said in the deceased's **will** (or the **intestacy** rules if the deceased died intestate). Applications under the Act are covered in detail in **11.2–11.10**.

However, there are other types of claim that may be brought against an estate, and whilst these are not covered in detail, they are mentioned in brief in **11.11** just so that you are aware of them.

As with other chapters in this manual, references to statutory provisions and to selected cases are included in the text. However, you do not need to remember the numbers of the statutory provisions or the names of the cases when preparing to sit the SQE 1 functional knowledge test.

## 11.2 The Inheritance (Provision for Family and Dependants) Act 1975

As said, the main focus of this chapter is the Inheritance (Provision for Family and Dependants) Act 1975. For ease of reference, we will refer to it as 'the Act' for the rest of this chapter. In practice, applications under the Act are often called '**family provision claims**' as a useful shorthand, or the Act is referred to as 'the Inheritance Act' or 'the 1975 Act'.

The Act allows certain categories of person (specified in **11.4**) to bring an application to the court against the deceased's estate, claiming what is called '**reasonable financial provision**'. We will see in **11.5** that the meaning of 'reasonable financial provision' differs depending on the particular category of applicant, but for most categories of applicant 'reasonable financial provision' is linked to the applicant's financial situation and needs.

Why might someone apply to the court? In simple terms, they would do so if they felt that the deceased's will (or the rules of intestacy if the deceased died intestate) did not provide adequately for them. For example, a child of the deceased (even an adult child) may have been disinherited by the parent, with the parent leaving them nothing in the parent's will. In English and Welsh law, there are no fixed rules of inheritance for family members which take precedence over a valid will, and **testators** have the freedom to leave their estate to whoever they so wish. Perhaps the parent in the example just given had left their entire estate to charity and left nothing to their child. This is perfectly possible, and legal, because the parent has testamentary freedom. However, in those circumstances the child could bring an application under the Act for 'reasonable financial provision' from the estate.

To give another example, a person might die intestate leaving an unmarried partner who may have been living with the deceased for many years prior to the deceased's death. As we saw in **Chapter 4**, that unmarried partner would have no entitlement whatsoever under the intestacy rules. The partner could, though, make an application to the court under the Act for 'reasonable financial provision'.

The Act only applies if the deceased was 'domiciled' in England and Wales at the date of their death. The detail on how domicile is established is outside the scope of this manual, but the Act would not apply, for example, to a deceased whose was domiciled in France or even in Scotland or Northern Ireland.

Another point to note at the outset is that the applicant's rights under the Act are personal and do not survive the applicant if the applicant dies. It is not possible, therefore, for the **personal representatives** (PRs) of an applicant to bring an application after the applicant's death or to continue with an application if the applicant dies after making an application.

**EXAMPLE**

Simon died last year, intestate. His unmarried partner and cohabitant Julie (who has no entitlement under the intestacy rules) brought an application under the Act for reasonable financial provision from his estate. However, Julie has now died. Julie's PRs cannot continue the application against Simon's estate because the application is personal to Julie. Her application effectively 'dies' with her.

We will now look at important aspects of the rules from the Act in more detail.

## 11.3 Time limit for applications

The time limit for applications under the Act is six months from the date of the **grant of representation** (s4). It is important to realise that the time period runs from the date on which the grant of **probate** or administration is issued by HMCTS, *not* from the date of death (students often make this mistake).

Not all grants count for the purposes of the time limit—in simple terms, the six months will usually run from the date of a *general* grant of representation (dealing with the estate as a whole), but will not run from an earlier *limited* grant that is taken out for a particular purpose (eg a grant which is limited to **settled land**). Section 23 lists the types of limited grant that are ignored for the purposes of the six-month time limit.

Although the time limit is stated as six months from the date of the grant of representation, s4 makes it clear that it is possible to make an application to the court before the grant is issued. If it was not possible to apply until a grant has been issued, the PRs could frustrate a potential application under the Act by deliberately delaying their grant application. There are practical difficulties with making an application before the grant is issued, mainly in terms of identifying the respondent to the application, but the details are outside the scope of this manual. It is sufficient that you know that an application can be made before a grant is issued. Further, it has been decided recently that a court can make an order before a grant is issued (*Antonio v Williams* [2022] EWHC 2383 (Ch)).

In practice, when administering estates it is common to wait until the six-month period has expired before distributing the estate. This is in order to protect the PRs, who would be personally liable if they distributed the estate before the six-month period expired. Under s20, PRs are protected from personal liability if they distribute the estate after the expiry of the six-month time period.

However, the PRs may pay the debts of the deceased, and pay the expenses of the administration, even before the expiry of the six-month period. This is because any order in favour of an applicant will be made against the deceased's net estate, namely the value of the estate after debts and expenses have been deducted.

Also, the court may give permission to allow applications to be made outside (ie later than) the time limit. There have been reported cases where the court has allowed an applicant to bring an application some considerable time after the expiry of the standard six months. In *Re Bhusate* [2019] EWHC 470 (Ch), a widow was allowed to bring an application even though it was nearly 26 years after the expiry of the six-month time. However, the facts of the case were unusual in that the widow had limited English language skills and limited understanding of financial matters, and the main asset of the estate (the house) had not been sold (in fact, the widow was still living in it).

The Act does not provide guidance to the court on how it should exercise its discretion to give permission to apply out of time. Instead, the court will consider a set of guidelines that have been developed in the case law. In *Cowan v Foreman* [2019] EWCA Civ 1336, the Court of Appeal said that the purpose of the time limit was not designed to protect the court from stale claims, but to avoid unnecessary delay in the administration of estates and complications from distributions being made from estates before proceedings were brought. It was said that the question of whether to grant an extension is substantive, rather than procedural, and that it is essential that the applicant seeking the extension show a real prospect of success rather than a fanciful one. It was also said that an extension may be granted even if there is no good reason for the delay. This approach was followed by the Court of Appeal in another 2019 decision, *Begum v Ahmed* [2019] EWCA Civ 1794.

Importantly, though, s20 of the Act still protects PRs against personal liability if they distribute the estate after the expiry of the six-month time limit, even if the court subsequently grants permission to an applicant to apply out of time.

## 11.4 Categories of applicant

It is very important to realise that only certain persons can bring an application under the Act. There is no general right for persons to bring an application simply because they are unhappy about being left out of a will or of not being entitled on intestacy. If a person is to bring an application under the Act, they have to come within one of the categories of applicant specified in s1 of the Act.

For example, a brother of the deceased (who was not financially dependent on the deceased) would not fall within one of the categories of applicant, set out later, and so would not be able to bring an application under the Act.

**EXAMPLE**

Jonathan has died. In his will, he left his whole estate (worth £1 million) to charity. His nearest surviving relative is his brother, David. David is financially secure and was not reliant on Jonathan financially. David does not fall within any of the categories under the Act and so will not be able to bring an application for reasonable financial provision.

The categories of applicant are:

1 the spouse or civil partner of the deceased;

2 a former spouse or civil partner of the deceased;

3 a cohabitant of the deceased;

4 a child of the deceased;
5 a person treated as a child of the family by the deceased;
6 a person being maintained by the deceased.

See **11.7** for more detail on each category of applicant and on applications made by them under the Act.

# 11.5 Ground for application

There is only one ground for an application under the Act. The ground (stated in s1) is that the disposition of the deceased's estate (under the terms of the deceased's will or the rules of intestacy, or a combination of the two) does not make 'reasonable financial provision' for the applicant.

## 11.5.1 Reasonable financial provision

What amounts to 'reasonable financial provision' depends on the category of applicant. There is a different standard of provision for most current spouses/civil partners (and some former spouses/civil partners) compared with the other categories of applicant.

Whichever standard of provision applies, it has been established that reasonable financial provision is to be determined on an objective basis by the court—in fact, this is implicit from the use of the word 'reasonable' in 'reasonable financial provision', as 'reasonable' implies an objective test. In other words, it is not what the deceased thought was reasonable, or what the applicant considers is reasonable, it is what the court assesses is reasonable, on an objective basis.

Also, the reasonableness to be considered by the court is the amount of the financial provision not the conduct of the testator. The testator might have acted reasonably but there may not be reasonable financial provision for the applicant. Conversely, the testator might have acted unreasonably yet there is reasonable financial provision for the applicant. Put another way, the focus is on what provision for the applicant is seen to be reasonable, taking all the circumstances of the case into consideration.

Also, the court will assess what is reasonable as at the date of the court hearing not as at the date of death.

**EXAMPLE**

Faisal has died. In his will, he left everything to his wife, Husna, and nothing to his daughter, Samira. Samira is a child of the deceased and can apply under the Act. She is an adult who is financially independent of Faisal, although she is of limited means. It could be said that Faisal has acted reasonably in making no financial provision for Samira in the will, as when he dies it is thought his estate is quite modest. However, shortly after his death it is discovered that Faisal had won £10 million on a lottery. In view of the greatly increased size of the estate, a court might decide that it might now be reasonable for Samira to receive some financial provision from the estate.

### 11.5.1.1 Spouses and civil partners

Reasonable financial provision for most current (and some former) spouses and civil partners is defined as whatever is 'reasonable in all the circumstances' for the spouse or civil partner to receive, 'whether or not that provision is required for [their] maintenance' (s1(2)(a) and (aa)). The application is not limited by the maintenance needs of the spouse or civil partner, therefore. When this rule is combined with the special guideline of what the spouse might have expected to receive on a divorce (or a civil partner might have expected to receive on a dissolution of the **civil partnership**), the reasonable financial provision awarded by the court could be a very sizeable proportion of the deceased's estate. See **11.7.1** for more detail.

Although this higher standard of reasonable financial provision applies mainly to current spouses and civil partners, it does not apply to all current spouses and civil partners, and it may also apply to some former spouses and civil partners.

- The higher standard of reasonable financial provision will not normally apply to judicially separated spouses or to civil partners following a separation order (s1(2)(a) and (aa)). This is even though, technically, they are still current spouses and civil partners because there has been no divorce or dissolution. However, where the deceased dies within 12 months of the date of a separation order, and there has been no financial provision order made in the family proceedings, the court considering the application under the Act has a discretion to apply the higher standard of reasonable financial provision (ss14 and 14A).
- Similarly, even after a divorce or a dissolution of a civil partnership, the court considering the application under the Act has a discretion to apply the higher standard of provision to former spouses and civil partners. This is again only if the deceased died within 12 months of the divorce/dissolution and no financial provision order has been made in the family proceedings (ss14 and 14A again).

That said, most former spouses and civil partners are treated like the other categories of applicant and the maintenance standard of reasonable financial provision will apply to them (on which, see **11.5.1.2**).

### 11.5.1.2 Other categories of applicant

The standard of reasonable financial provision for all other categories of applicant is linked to the applicant's maintenance needs. The wording is superficially similar to the standard of maintenance for spouses/civil partners, but if you read carefully you will appreciate the difference.

In the case of all other categories of applicant, reasonable financial provision is defined as such financial provision as it would be 'reasonable in all the circumstances ... for the applicant to receive for [their] maintenance' (s1(2)(b)).

Maintenance is not defined in the Act and there are no guidelines given to the court (other than the special guidelines, considered in **11.7**, relevant to particular categories of applicant). The meaning of 'maintenance' has been considered in case law, including by the Supreme Court in *Ilott v Blue Cross* [2017] UKSC 17, but there is no single definition of maintenance. The word implies provision to meet the everyday expenses of living rather than everything which it would be desirable for the applicant to have. However, maintenance is not limited to a subsistence level. Instead, what is regarded as an appropriate level of maintenance is flexible and will be assessed by the court on the facts of each case. *Miles v Shearer* [2021] EWHC 1000 (Ch) is a recent example of applicants (adult children) failing to show they had any maintenance needs.

## 11.6 The common and special guidelines

The court has a very wide discretion and can consider all the circumstances of the case in making its decision. However, the court must take into account certain guidelines that are set out in s3 of the Act. The court must consider the guidelines both when determining whether the applicant has established that no reasonable financial provision has been made for them by the deceased, and in determining what order, if any, the court should make under s2.

Some of the guidelines are relevant to all applicants—these are often referred to as the common guidelines. Other guidelines relate only to a particular category of applicant and these are known as special guidelines.

Section 1(5) provides that the court shall take into account the facts known at the date of the hearing when considering the common and special guidelines.

### 11.6.1 The common guidelines

The common guidelines apply to all categories of applicant, and are set out in s3(1). The court is directed to consider the following factors.

### 11.6.1.1 The financial resources and financial needs of the applicant and other persons

The court has to consider the relative financial resources and needs of a number of persons who might be affected by the making of an order by the court. Section 3(1)(a)–(c) provides that the court must consider the financial needs and resources of:

- the applicant; and
- any other applicant; and
- the **beneficiaries** of the estate of the deceased (ie the persons entitled to the estate of the deceased under the deceased's will or intestacy, or persons inheriting under some other means, eg a surviving joint tenant).

The court must consider the financial resources and financial needs of each of them at the date of the hearing and what those resources and needs are likely to be in the foreseeable future.

The court therefore has to balance the needs and resources of the applicant against, in particular, the needs and resources of the beneficiaries of the estate. This means a needy applicant will have greater prospects of success if the beneficiaries of the estate are well off.

### 11.6.1.2 Any moral obligation of the deceased to any applicant or beneficiary

The court might find that the deceased had a moral obligation to make reasonable financial provision for an applicant. For example, in *Re Callaghan* [1985] Fam 1, an application was made by an adult 'child of the family' against his stepfather's estate. The stepfather died intestate and his estate passed to his three sisters whom he had not seen for ten years. The court held that the deceased's greatest obligation was owed to the applicant who had kept in close touch with him and looked after him in his last illness. The court also took into account that many of the assets of the estate came from the applicant's mother who had died some years previously, and ordered a lump sum payment of £15,000 to the applicant to enable him to buy his council house outright.

The question of moral obligation often arises in relation to applications by adult able-bodied children. Clearly, a parent has a moral obligation to provide for their infant children (ie those under 18 years of age), but is there a moral obligation to provide for an adult child who can be expected to provide for themselves? This question is discussed in **11.7.4** when considering applications by children of the deceased.

### 11.6.1.3 The size and nature of the net estate of the deceased

The larger the estate, the easier it will be for the court to order reasonable provision for an applicant. Conversely, as costs will usually be awarded out of the estate, the court will discourage claims where the estate is small (*Re Coventry* [1980] Ch 461).

The source of the deceased's estate may be relevant, as in *Re Callaghan* [1985] Fam 1, where, as mentioned earlier, the deceased was the applicant's stepfather and the stepfather's estate derived from assets which had belonged to the applicant's mother.

### 11.6.1.4 Any physical or mental disability of any applicant or beneficiary

If an applicant has a disability which affects their ability to provide financially for themselves, then it potentially puts them in a stronger position to obtain reasonable financial provision from the estate. Conversely, the interests of a beneficiary with a disability may weaken the applicant's case, because the needs of the beneficiary are greater than they would otherwise be.

### 11.6.1.5 Any other relevant matter

The full wording of the guideline is: 'any other matter, including the conduct of the applicant, or any other person, which in the circumstances of the case the court may consider relevant'.

Effectively, this common guideline allows the court to take into account anything and everything that it considers is relevant (and begs the question why the Act specifies any other guidelines if the court can take anything into account). This common guideline gives the court unfettered discretion to consider all the circumstances of the case and to use these as reasons for making or not making an order for reasonable financial provision, and for how much financial provision to award an applicant if an award is being made. It gives the court the freedom to decide cases on the basis of what the court perceives are the merits of the application.

The court is directed, though, to consider in particular the conduct of the applicant or any other person. The term 'any other person' includes the deceased, so the conduct of the deceased can be taken into account by the court.

If an applicant is seen to have acted badly in some way, then this will count against them. For example, in *Wellesley v Wellesley* [2019] EWHC 11 (Ch) the court held that a **legacy** of £20,000 left by the deceased in his will to his adult daughter was reasonable financial provision, and the court refused to make an order in favour of the daughter for more provision from the estate. The court's decision was influenced by a 30-year estrangement between the 56-year-old daughter and her father, the deceased. The estate was large (which would normally count in favour of the applicant). Also, the daughter had been diagnosed with ADHD (and so had a disability). She was also unemployed and reliant on State welfare benefits (and so had limited financial resources). Nevertheless, the court refused to make any further provision for the applicant, basing the decision largely upon the conduct of the applicant. The court took into account the finding that the 30-year estrangement was due to the daughter's 'lifestyle of drink, drugs and bohemia' and her 'disruptive influence and behaviour'.

This conduct guideline can be applied the other way and work in favour of the applicant, if the applicant's conduct has been good and they are seen as being meritorious, such as in *Re Callaghan* [1985] Fam 1. The court might also consider the deceased's conduct, which might be open to criticism because they have acted harshly or unfairly towards the applicant, and this might count in the applicant's favour.

### 11.6.2 The special guidelines

The court is also directed to consider a number of special guidelines that apply to the different categories of applicant. The special guidelines are set out in s3(2)–(4).

Some special guidelines effectively apply to more than one category of applicant. For example, the education and training needs of the applicant are relevant to an application by a child of the deceased and to an application by a 'child of the family'.

The special guidelines relevant to each category of applicant are set out in **11.7** when applications by each category of applicant are discussed in more detail.

## 11.7 Applications by different categories of applicant

In this section we will consider in more detail the meaning of each category of applicant, the special guidelines applicable to each category of applicant and some case law on claims by each category of applicant.

### 11.7.1 Spouse or civil partner

The special guidelines applicable to a spouse/civil partner (s3(2)) are:

- the age of the applicant and the duration of the marriage or civil partnership;
- the contribution made by the applicant to the welfare of the family, including any contribution made by looking after the home or caring for the family; and
- the provision which the applicant might reasonably have expected to receive if the marriage had been terminated by divorce (or if the civil partnership had been terminated by a dissolution order) rather than by death.

The third special guideline does not apply to a spouse who was judicially separated from the deceased (in circumstances where that separation was continuing at the date of death). Similarly, the third special guideline does not apply to a civil partner where at the date of death a separation order was in force and the separation was continuing at the date of death.

Remember that a spouse or civil partner (other than one who has been judicially separated) is arguably in a stronger position when making an application than most other categories of applicant. This is due to the standard of reasonable financial provision appropriate to a spouse/civil partner mentioned in **11.5**, namely 'such financial provision as it would be reasonable in all the circumstances of the case for the [spouse/civil partner] to receive, whether or not that provision is required for his or her maintenance'. (In contrast, remember also that the applicable standard of reasonable financial provision for judicially separated spouses or civil partners is the ordinary standard, namely 'linked' to maintenance.)

The court is not limited, therefore, by the amount which the spouse/civil partner requires to meet their everyday needs and can, but doesn't have to, decide that a more substantial amount would be reasonable.

In deciding what is reasonable for a spouse/civil partner to receive, the court has to consider the common and special guidelines. The third special guideline, namely what the spouse/civil partner would have obtained if the marriage/civil partnership had been terminated by divorce/dissolution, is particularly significant due to the importance that has been attached to it in the reported cases.

What would an applicant have received if the marriage had ended on divorce/dissolution rather than on the death of the one party? This will vary in each case, but the House of Lords held in *White v White* [2001] 1 AC 596 that the yardstick for achieving a fair outcome between the parties to a divorce is an equal division of those assets, and equality should only be departed from if there are good reasons for doing so. (This case predated the introduction of civil partnerships but similar rules would apply to a dissolution.)

An example of the court departing from the principle in *White v White* is the case of *Cunliffe v Fielden* [2005] EWCA Civ 1508, which dealt specifically with a widow's claim under the Act. In this case, the Court of Appeal decided that equality, as in *White v White*, was indeed only a yardstick when deciding how to divide up an estate. The notion of equality could be departed from if there was good reason. In *Cunliffe v Fielden*, the marriage had been relatively short and the widow had contributed little to the deceased's wealth. Since the obligation under the Act was for the deceased to make reasonable financial provision for his widow, she received less than half the estate. So, depending on the value of the estate (which was relatively large in that case), what is reasonable financial provision may not necessarily be based on equality. Indeed, with smaller estates the reasonableness of the situation may result in the spouse/civil partner taking most if not all of the estate, when this would not have happened on a divorce/dissolution of the civil partnership. This is because on a divorce/dissolution you have to consider the financial needs of both spouses/ civil partners, whereas following the death of one spouse/civil partner, it is only the surviving spouse's/civil partner's financial needs that are relevant.

Note also that judicially separated spouses and civil partners might not be able to apply at all under the Act. This would be the case if the separation order (or a court order made whilst the separation is continuing) restricted the right of each party to the marriage/civil partnership to bring applications under the Act (under s15 or 15ZA).

## 11.7.2 **Former spouse or civil partner**

The special guidelines applying to a former spouse or civil partner (s3(2)) are:

- the age of the applicant and the duration of the marriage/civil partnership; and
- the contribution made by the applicant to the welfare of the family including any contribution made by looking after the home or caring for the family.

Both of these guidelines also apply to applications by current spouses and civil partners (see **11.7.1**). What is different for former spouses and civil partners is that the third guideline (what the spouse or civil partner would have received on divorce or dissolution) does not apply, at least in most cases. However, if the court exercises its discretion under s14 or 14A, the third guideline would also apply to an application by a former spouse or civil partner. As noted in **11.5.1.1**, under ss14 and 14A the court may apply the higher standard of reasonable financial provision to applications by former spouses and civil partners within 12 months of the divorce/dissolution, essentially where there had been no financial provision order already made in the matrimonial proceedings. If the court exercises its discretion under s14 or 14A, then the third guideline becomes relevant to the application by the former spouse or civil partner.

The next point to note is that a former spouse can only apply provided that they have not since remarried or formed a civil partnership and, similarly, a former civil partner can only apply provided they have not since formed another civil partnership or married. If an order is made under the Act for maintenance from the estate of the deceased to the former spouse/civil partner, then the maintenance will cease if the former spouse/civil partner subsequently marries or forms a civil partnership.

As with judicially separated spouses/civil partners, there are often restrictions imposed on applications by former spouses and civil partners. This is because the financial settlement on a divorce (or dissolution of the civil partnership) will often expressly exclude the possibility of a former spouse/civil partner making an application under the Act. This is allowed by ss15 and 15ZA of the Act. In practice, you need to check the terms of any order made in the divorce or dissolution proceedings to see if the former spouse is prohibited from applying under the Act.

Even if there is no such prohibition in a court order, a number of reported cases (including the Court of Appeal decision in *Re Fullard* [1981] 2 All ER 796), have shown that the chances of a successful application are likely to be greatly reduced where the divorce/dissolution settlement was intended to be a 'clean break' and occurred many years before the deceased's death. In such circumstances, the former spouse or civil partner faces similar hurdles as an adult child (on which, see **11.7.3**) and probably has to show more than mere financial hardship to succeed.

In practice, most applications by former spouses and civil partners are not likely to succeed. However, if a former spouse or civil partner is still receiving maintenance payments from the deceased at the date of the deceased's death, then (always subject to the consideration of the common and special guidelines) it is possible that the application will be successful.

## 11.7.3 Person cohabiting with the deceased

The applicant must have been living 'as the husband or wife' (or 'as the civil partner of the deceased') in the same household as the deceased throughout the period of two years prior to the date of death of the deceased (s1(1)(ba), (1A) and (1B)).

The phrases 'as husband and wife' and 'as civil partner of the deceased' require some explanation. Spouses (husbands and wives) and civil partners are, of course, able to apply in their own right as spouses or civil partners, and so do not need to apply as a cohabitant. What is meant in s1(1A) and (1B) is that the applicant was living with the deceased in the same household *as if* they had been married or had been civil partners. In other words, the relationship was such that was similar to, or akin to, marriage or civil partnership, even though the applicant and the deceased were not in fact married or civil partners.

The special guidelines applicable to cohabitants (s3(2A)) are:

- the age of the applicant and the length of the period during which the applicant lived as the husband or wife or civil partner of the deceased and in the same household as the deceased; and
- the contribution made by the applicant to the welfare of the family of the deceased, including any contribution made by looking after the home or caring for the family.

In one reported case on an application by a cohabitee (*Re Watson* [1999] 1 FLR 878), the trial judge held that it was not necessary for a couple to have shared the same bedroom or to have enjoyed sexual relations for them to be living together as husband and wife.

The special guidelines are similar to the first two special guidelines applying to surviving spouses/civil partners. However, there are significant differences between applications by spouses/civil partners and applications by cohabitants. With the former, the court is directed specifically to consider what the spouse/civil partner might have received on divorce/dissolution of the civil partnership, but there is no equivalent guideline for cohabitants. Also, the surviving spouse/civil partner may be awarded such financial provision as is reasonable in all the circumstances: this could amount to one half of the deceased's estate if the principle of equality (as referred to in *White v White*—see **11.7.1** on applications by spouses and civil partners) is applied. In contrast, a cohabitant may only be awarded 'such financial provision as it would be reasonable in all the circumstances of the case for the applicant to receive for his or her maintenance'. Although maintenance does not mean only what is needed for mere subsistence (and no more), it will be more difficult for a court to justify a high award to a cohabitant than to a spouse/civil partner. For an example of a substantial award to a cohabitant which went beyond a mere subsistence level (a mortgage-free flat plus a lump sum of £200,000), see *Negus v Bahouse* [2008] 1 FLR 381.

Under s1(1A) and (1B), the cohabitant must have been living with the deceased in the same household for the period of two years ending 'immediately' before the date of death. This wording suggests that if there is a gap in time, even a very short gap, between the ending of the period of cohabitation and the date of death, then the cohabitant would not be able to apply. For example, the deceased and the cohabitant have been living together for 30 years but, as a result of an argument, the cohabitant moves out of the house a week shortly before the deceased's death. On the face of the wording of s1(1A) and (1B), the period of cohabitation did not end immediately before the date of death, and so you would think that the cohabitant would not be able to apply. However, the courts have taken a more sensible approach to this question and short gaps between the ending of the period of cohabitation and the date of death are ignored by the court. For example, in *Gully v Dix* [2004] EWCA Civ 139 the Court of Appeal held that a three-month gap prior to the date of death did not prevent an application: regard was to be had to the settled state of affairs existing during the relationship and not to the immediate situation at the moment of death. In *Kaur v Dhaliwal* [2014] EWHC 1991 Ch, where the applicant and the deceased had been living together for only one year and 49 weeks immediately before death, an earlier eight-month gap was ignored for the purpose of meeting the two-year requirement.

It is also clear from the case law that the couple do not need to actually live together in the same house all the time—it is sufficient if they are regarded as part of the same 'household', which can be done even if they have their own homes and sometimes stay overnight in their own homes rather than together (*Swetenham v Walkley* [2014] WTLR 845).

## 11.7.4 Child of the deceased

Both natural children (including children ***en ventre sa mère***, ie conceived but not yet born at the deceased's date of death) and adopted children can apply under this head. However, adopted children lose the right to apply for reasonable financial provision from the estates of their natural parents.

Despite what might be seen as the implication of the word 'child', 'children' of all ages can apply, namely the 'child' need not be a minor.

However, applications by adult able-bodied children are less likely to succeed than those by disabled adult children or minor children.

In *Re Coventry* [1980] Ch 461, an application was brought by the adult son of the deceased. The Court of Appeal affirmed the decision of the judge to dismiss the application on the basis that the son (who was self-employed) was capable of earning his own living. In the absence of some moral obligation or special circumstance indicating that the deceased should have provided reasonable financial provision for the son, it was not unreasonable for the deceased to fail to make provision for him. This approach was followed in *Re Dennis* [1981] 2 All ER 140, where Browne-Wilkinson J said that the court is inclined to ask of the applicant:

> Why should anybody else make provision for you if you are capable of maintaining yourself?

In order for an adult able-bodied child to succeed, therefore, it has often been seen as necessary for the applicant to show some moral obligation or special circumstance to show why the deceased should have made provision, beyond mere financial hardship.

However, in *Re Hancock (sub nom Snapes v Aram)* [1998] 2 FLR 346, Butler-Sloss LJ pointed out that:

> the 1975 Act [does] not require . . . that an adult child [has] in all cases to show a moral obligation or other special circumstance.

Although this is correct, it is probably fair to say that whilst the need for a moral obligation or special circumstance is not an absolute requirement for an adult able-bodied child to succeed in an application under the Act, the chances of a successful outcome for the applicant are reduced without such an obligation or circumstance. This was acknowledged by Butler-Sloss LJ in *Re Hancock*, when she also said:

> if the facts disclose that the adult child is in employment, with an earning capacity for the foreseeable future, it is unlikely he will succeed in his application without some special circumstance such as a moral obligation.

There has only been one case on the Act to reach the Supreme Court (at the time of writing), and that is *Ilott v Blue Cross* [2017] UKSC 17 (also known at earlier stages of the litigation as *Ilott v Mitson*), which involved an application by an adult child. The applicant was the only child of the deceased but had been estranged from the deceased for many years (although there had been several failed attempts at reconciliation). The applicant, and her immediate family, were in poor financial circumstances but they were able to live within their means with the assistance of a number of State welfare benefits. The applicant had insufficient money, though, to pay for new household appliances or for the family to go on holiday. Due to the estrangement, the deceased left most of her estate to a number of charities (one of which was the Blue Cross). Although the applicant was successful in claiming reasonable financial provision, this was assessed as only £50,000 out of an estate of £486,000. The Supreme Court overruled the Court of Appeal's more generous award (£143,000 for the applicant to purchase her house from the Housing Association and a further £20,000) and reinstated the award of £50,000 that had been made by the district judge. The estrangement was taken into account as a factor limiting the amount of the award.

One point that has been made in the cases is that there is no requirement for the court to take into account the potential to save public funds by replacing State benefits with a payment from the estate.

Lastly, there is only one special guideline applying to children of the deceased, which is the manner in which the applicant was being or might expect to be educated or trained. This might be particularly important in the situation where an adult child is still in full-time education.

## 11.7.5 Child of the family

This is someone who is not the natural or adopted child of the deceased, but instead is someone who the deceased treated as a child of 'the family'. Previously, the family relationship had to be in the context of a marriage or civil partnership but this changed in 2014 to add 'any family in which the deceased at any time stood in the role of a parent' (s1(1)(d)).

This category essentially covers 'stepchildren' and gives them the right to apply for reasonable financial provision from the estate of a step-parent, whether or not the step-parent was married to (or in a civil partnership with) the child's parent. However, this category also allows applications by persons who have been looked after by someone other than their parents, for example in a situation where there is someone (say, a grandparent) who is effectively fulfilling the role of parent in the absence of the natural parents.

The wording of the Act also allows for a situation where there has only been one person fulfilling the role of parent—in other words, it is not necessary for there to be two persons fulfilling the role of parents in the 'family'.

The special guidelines applicable to a child of the family (s3(3)) are:

- the manner in which the applicant was being or might expect to be educated or trained (this is the same special guideline which applies to children of the deceased); and
- the extent to which and the basis upon which the deceased assumed responsibility for the applicant's maintenance and the length of time that the deceased had discharged that responsibility;
- whether the deceased assumed and discharged that responsibility whilst knowing the applicant was not their own child; and
- the liability of any other person to maintain the applicant.

Although you would think that the position of a child of the family would be substantially the same as that of a child of the deceased, the principle from *Re Coventry* that an adult able-bodied applicant has to show a moral obligation or special circumstance was not applied in two reported decisions concerning claims by children of the family (*Re Callaghan* [1985] Fam 1 and *Re Leach*

[1986] Ch 226). In each case, the (successful) applicant had been an adult at the time of the relevant marriage: at the time of the hearings the respective ages of the applicants were 47 and 57. In practice, however, it is probably best to regard an application by an able-bodied adult 'child of the family' as being similar to an application by an able-bodied adult 'child'.

## 11.7.6 Person being maintained by the deceased

This category is for persons who are dependants of the deceased but who do not fall within one of the other categories of applicant. Having said this, it is common practice for unmarried cohabitants to apply both as a cohabitant (under s1(1)(ba)) and as a 'person . . . being maintained' (ie under s1(1)(e)).

A person who falls outside one of the other categories of applicant may apply if they were being maintained by the deceased immediately before their death. For example, a niece who was caring for an elderly aunt but who was reliant on the aunt for accommodation would not qualify under any of the other categories of applicant. Nevertheless, the niece could apply as a person being maintained by the deceased.

For a person to claim under this category, they need to have been maintained by the deceased in some way, whether by direct financial assistance or by the provision of other assistance, such as rent-free accommodation.

The special guidelines are:

- the extent to which, and basis upon which, the deceased assumed responsibility for the maintenance of the applicant; and
- the length of time for which the deceased had discharged that responsibility.

Examples of successful applications include:

- *Re B (Deceased) (sub nom Bouette v Rose)* [2000] 1 All ER 665, a claim by the mother (and principal carer) of the deceased (who had been brain damaged at birth; the child had received substantial damages and was in effect supporting the mother financially); and
- *Re Lankesheer (sub nom Rees v Newberry)* [1998] 1 FLR 1041, a claim by a tenant of the deceased who had been allowed to occupy premises owned by the deceased at a very low rent.

Taking a literal interpretation of s1(1)(e) of the Act, which says states that an applicant under this category is a person who is being maintained 'immediately before the death of the deceased', the applicant would have to show that the deceased was maintaining them right up to the date of death. On this reasoning, if there was a short gap between the cessation of the maintenance and the date of death, the applicant would not be able to apply, on the basis that they were not being maintained immediately before death. However, as with applicants who are cohabitants, it is established that a short gap prior to the date of death is not fatal to an application, and the courts will look at the settled nature of the relationship between the deceased and the applicant.

Under s1(3) of the Act, an applicant in this category must also show that the deceased was providing this assistance otherwise than 'for full valuable consideration pursuant to an arrangement of a commercial nature'. So, for example, a full-time carer employed by the deceased would be paid a salary for the care provided. This would amount to 'an arrangement of a commercial nature', and the salary paid to the carer would not be regarded as maintenance by the deceased so, in the absence of any other form of maintenance provided, you would not expect that the carer would be able to apply to court for reasonable financial provision.

Prior to 1 October 2014, non-commercial arrangements were also caught by this requirement that the applicant should not have given 'full valuable consideration' to the deceased. This had the unfortunate consequence that an applicant who had been loving towards, and had perhaps cared for, the deceased was in theory placed in a worse position when applying under the Act than an applicant who had been parasitically living off the deceased without having done anything for the deceased in return. The courts did try to address this problem. In *Bishop v Plumley* [1991] 1 All ER 236, it was said that the care provided by one person to another is often part of the 'mutuality of the relationship' and should not, in many cases, be counted as 'full valuable consideration' by the applicant. Nevertheless, the concern remained until s1(3) was amended in 2014. As said, only commercial arrangements are now caught by the 'full valuable consideration' rule.

## 11.8 Orders that the court can make

Section 2 sets out the orders that the court may make, which include orders for:

- periodical payments to the applicant;
- the payment of a lump sum to the applicant;
- the transfer of property from the estate to the applicant;
- the **settlement** of property for the benefit of the applicant (ie the creation of a **trust** in favour of the applicant);
- the purchase of property using funds from the estate, with the property transferred to the applicant or settled on trust for them;
- the **variation** of existing trusts under the deceased's will or intestacy.

The most common monetary orders are for lump sum cash payments. Orders for periodical payments are less common. The reason for this is that the court usually considers that a 'clean break' between the estate and the applicant is desirable.

Under s5, interim periodical payment orders are possible pending the determination of the final order.

Where property has been transferred to the applicant, this is usually a house because the question is one of 'where will the applicant live'. For example, a cohabitant who lives in a house owned by the deceased would have no entitlement on the deceased's intestacy or if the deceased had not provided for them in the will. An appropriate order in such circumstances might be to transfer the deceased's house to the cohabitant.

Alternatively, the court might order that the house is held on trust, giving the applicant a right to occupy (ie reside, or live in) the house for the duration of the applicant's life or at least until the applicant no longer wishes to live there or no longer needs the right to occupy.

Under s6, a court may vary or discharge an existing order for periodical payments. It is not possible to vary or discharge other types of order (eg orders for the payment of a lump sum or transfer of property absolutely to the applicant).

Section 19(1) provides that for all purposes, including **inheritance tax**, the variation to the estate resulting from the court's order is deemed to be effective as from the deceased's death. In effect, the order is 'read back', as if the deceased had made the provision ordered by the court. If, for example, the court orders that provision be made for a surviving spouse, the estate's liability for inheritance tax will be reduced. This is because the property passing to the surviving spouse will be exempt from inheritance tax. If an award is made, the court can direct whether any inheritance tax is to be borne by the applicant or the estate.

## 11.9 Property that may be subject to an order

The deceased's 'net estate' from which any order for financial provision is made is widely defined in s25. It comprises the following:

- all property of the deceased owned at the date of death and which could have been disposed of by will, less:
  - funeral testamentary and administration expenses;
  - debts and liabilities; and
  - inheritance tax;
- the deceased's **severable** share of a joint tenancy (which normally passes by survivorship) provided the court orders (under s9) that it should be treated as part of the 'net estate'. When considering how to value the deceased's severable share in a property, the court will, as a general rule, have regard to its value at the date the claim is heard but the court retains the discretion to choose a different date if appropriate;
- any property which the court has ordered under the anti-avoidance provisions to be available (under s10 or 11); and

- any property in respect of which the deceased made a statutory nomination or a ***donatio mortis causa***, or which the deceased could have appointed in their lifetime under a general **power of appointment** which has not been exercised.

# 11.10 Making and defending family provision applications

## 11.10.1 Advising a client who is making a will

It is possible to take steps during a client's lifetime to anticipate and mitigate the possibility of a family provision claim after their death. For example, steps can be taken when a solicitor is preparing a will for a client. It is important to take full details of the client's close family and to enquire about any person or persons who may be financially dependent on the client in some way. If this information is compared with the details of the client's intended provisions in the will, it may be possible to identify someone who would have a potential claim for reasonable financial provision under the Act on the death of the client.

If there appears to be such a person with a potential claim, then the client should consider leaving something to that person in the will. The **gift** could be a substantial one designed to meet the perceived needs of the potential applicant; alternatively, the client could leave that person a small gift in the hope that this will deter that person from making an application under the Act.

If the client is certain that they wish to exclude the potential applicant from benefiting under the will, or restrict the person's benefits in some way, then the client should be advised to put their reasons for doing this in writing. A letter (a 'letter of wishes') setting out these reasons should be prepared and kept with the original will. If, after the testator's death, the person applies for financial provision under the Act, the letter of wishes can be produced to the court. Although such a letter will not prevent or stop a claim, it will be admitted to the court as evidence of the testator's intentions and wishes.

It is worth noting that the testator's reasons for disinheriting the potential applicant are not normally set out in the will itself, because when the will is admitted to probate the will becomes a public document.

## 11.10.2 Advising an applicant after the death of the deceased

As explained earlier, in **11.3**, an application under the Act must be made within six months of the grant of representation, although it is possible to apply for leave to issue out of time.

### 11.10.2.1 Citations

As also explained in **11.3**, it used to be the case that an application could not be made before a grant is issued, but this is now possible. However, there are practical difficulties in bringing an application before a grant is issued and so it may be necessary to force a reluctant PR to take out a grant. The appropriate action in such a case would be to apply to HMCTS for the issuing of a **citation**. (For more detail on citations, see **8.9.2**.)

Forcing a reluctant PR to take out a grant may not be the best course of action, though, and there is an alternative which is to apply for an order under s116 of the Senior Courts Act 1981 to pass over the PR and to appoint an alternative **administrator** in their place.

### 11.10.2.2 Standing searches

In most cases, however, the PRs will proceed to obtain a grant fairly quickly. Given the relatively short time limit for applications under the Act, it is important to know whether a grant has been issued and, if so, the date on which it was issued. To do this (short of receiving a copy from the solicitors acting for the PRs), it is possible to lodge a '**standing search**' with the Probate Service (see **8.9.3**).

The searcher will be provided with a copy of any grant issued in the name of the deceased within six months after the date of the search. The search is renewable for further periods of six months at a time.

#### 11.10.2.3 Challenging a will: caveats

In some circumstances, the client may be able to apply under the Act for reasonable financial provision but may also contest the validity of the deceased's will (or **revocation** of the deceased's will) on the basis that the **formalities** were not complied with or that the deceased lacked the necessary **intention** or **capacity**. In such a case it is advisable, as a preliminary, to try and prevent a grant being issued in the estate.

The first step here would be to apply to enter a '**caveat**' with HMCTS (see **8.9.1**). This has the effect of preventing anyone from obtaining a grant without taking further action to '**warn off**' the person who has lodged the caveat.

### 11.10.3 Advising the personal representatives

Once a grant has been obtained, it is usually best to wait and see whether the applicant makes an application within the six-month time limit. During this time, the PRs will be able to collect in the assets of the estate and pay debts, but they would be unwise to distribute anything to the beneficiaries until the six months has expired. This is because the PRs will be liable personally to the extent of any property of the estate which they distribute within this first six months.

It is often possible to negotiate with the applicant (usually in consultation with the beneficiaries) over a possible settlement. The costs of defending an application can be expensive—if the applicant has a reasonable case, the court usually orders that the applicant's costs be met out of the estate.

Also, it is important to realise that the interests of the PRs do not necessarily coincide with the interests of the beneficiaries, and that in some cases it will be appropriate for the PRs to obtain separate legal representation. The dispute is then effectively conducted between the solicitors for the applicant and the solicitors for the beneficiaries, with the solicitors for the PRs standing on the sidelines.

### 11.10.4 Issuing and defending proceedings

This is a specialist area of practice and the procedure and practice of bringing and defending applications under the Act are outside the scope of this manual.

## 11.11 Other possible claims against the estate

Applications under the Act are not the only form of litigation or potential litigation that the PRs may face. There are a range of actions which may be taken against the estate, or against the PRs personally, and some of these are mentioned briefly in this section just so that you are aware of them. The detail on these claims is outside the scope of this manual, though, and you should consult specialist texts in practice.

### 11.11.1 Claims contesting the validity of wills

If the deceased left a will, it is possible that someone might contest the validity of the will. This could be by claiming one or more of the following:

- that the testator did not have the necessary testamentary capacity to make a will; or
- that the testator did not know and/or approve the terms of the will (perhaps due to fraud or being forced, or being afraid of someone, or due to **undue influence**); or
- that the necessary formalities for a valid will under s9 of the Wills Act 1837 have not been complied with.

The person claiming the will is not valid will seek to prevent a grant of probate being issued. Usually, that person will stand to inherit all or a greater share of the deceased's estate if the will fails, either under the rules of intestacy or under an earlier will.

### 11.11.2 Claiming a beneficial interest under a trust

The PRs (whether there is a will or not) may face a claim from someone who is claiming a prior beneficial interest in property that is in the name of the deceased. Typically, this would be a house, where the title is in the sole name of the deceased but a beneficial, equitable interest is claimed by another person. Essentially, the claimant would be claiming that the deceased held the asset on trust for the claimant (or perhaps on trust for the deceased and the claimant), and that now the deceased had died, the deceased's PRs should pay the claimant's beneficial interest to the claimant or perhaps even transfer the whole asset to the claimant.

### 11.11.3 Creditors

PRs may also face claims by **creditors** of the deceased. The liability of PRs for the debts of the deceased is discussed in **Chapter 9**.

### 11.11.4 Claims against the personal representatives and trustees over the conduct of the administration of the estate or of any consequent trust

Lastly, the beneficiaries of the estate may take action against the PRs because the beneficiaries wish to remove the PRs or because the beneficiaries consider the PRs have failed in their duties in some way, leading to a financial loss to the estate.

**KEY POINT SUMMARY**

- Certain categories of relatives and persons who are financially dependent on the deceased are able to apply to the court if the deceased's will (or the rules of intestacy) does not make 'reasonable financial provision' for the applicant.
- There is a time limit for applications, which is six months from the date of the grant of representation but the court has the power to allow applications that are out of time.
- The applicant applies for 'reasonable financial provision' which is linked to the applicant's maintenance needs, except in the case of surviving spouses and civil partners who can apply for what is 'reasonable in all the circumstances'.
- Unmarried partners can apply if they are either 'cohabitants' (having lived with the deceased for at least two years) or 'persons being maintained by the deceased' (again for a period of at least two years).
- Adult children can apply, but one factor taken into account by the court is that adult children (if they do not have a disability) should normally be expected to provide for themselves and should not be reliant on the estate of their parent.
- The court can take a wide range of factors into account in making its decision, but is directed by the Act to consider certain common guidelines (applying to all categories of applicant) and special guidelines (applying to particular categories of applicant). The common guidelines include the financial resources and needs of the applicant and of beneficiaries of the estate, the size and nature of the estate and whether the deceased had a moral obligation to the applicant. However, the court can take into account any matter that it considers relevant in exercising its discretion.

- The court also has a wide discretion on the orders it can make, including (but not limited to) the payment of a lump sum to the applicant, regular maintenance payments and the right to occupy a property for life. Lump sum payments are preferred as this ensures a clean break between the applicant and the estate.
- The personal representatives of an estate may face other claims against the estate, such as claims contesting the validity of the deceased's will, a claim by a person to a beneficial interest in one or more assets of the estate, claims by creditors and claims by beneficiaries that the PRs are not doing their job properly.

# PART E
# Trusts

# CHAPTER 12
# Core Principles of Equity and Trusts

## FUNCTIONING LEGAL KNOWLEDGE

This chapter covers the following functioning legal knowledge required to pass the SQE 1 assessments:

**Creation and requirements of express trusts:**

- the three certainties of **intention**, subject matter and objects:
  - fixed interest trusts
  - **discretionary trusts**
- **formalities** to create express ***inter vivos*** trusts
- **constitution** of express *inter vivos* trusts and exceptions to the rule that **Equity** will not assist a **volunteer**

**Beneficial entitlement:**

- fixed, discretionary, vested, contingent interests
- the rule in *Saunders v Vautier*

**The distinction between charitable trusts and non-charitable purpose trusts**

**Resulting trusts:**

- how they arise and when they are (or are not) presumed

**Trusts of the family home:**

- establishment of a common intention **constructive trust**:
  - legal title in the name of both parties/sole party
  - express declaration or agreement as to equitable ownership
  - direct and indirect contributions
- requirements to establish **proprietary estoppel**

## AUTHORITIES UNDERPINNING PRACTICE

Most of the law on Equity and trusts is derived from case law. There are relatively few statutory provisions, compared with other topics; however, the following legislation is relevant to charitable trusts. Note that for legislation you are linked to legislation.gov.uk.

Although much of the legislation on this government website is available in its amended form, the incorporation of new amendments into the text of legislation can be delayed. You should refer to legal databases to ensure you are referencing the most up-to-date legislation.

- Charities Act 2011
  **http://www.legislation.gov.uk/ukpga/2011/25/contents**

## 12.1 Introduction

In this chapter we will consider some of the core principles of the law of Equity and **trusts**. We will look at different types of trust (express and implied, trusts for people and for purposes and informal trusts relating to property). Other core principles, though, will be covered in **Chapter 13**, when we look at the powers and duties of **personal representatives**, **trustees** and other fiduciaries, and the rights and remedies of **beneficiaries**.

It should be stressed that this manual is not a textbook on Equity and trusts. Although there is a comprehensive list of Equity and trusts topics in the assessment specification for SQE 1, it is likely that most questions in the SQE 1 functioning knowledge test will concentrate on the practical aspects of **wills**, estates and trusts which are covered in the other chapters of this manual. Therefore, this section of the manual will only set out the core principles in basic terms. It is very much a summary of some of the main points and a reminder of your previous study of Equity and trusts. For a detailed treatment of the subject, you should consult one of the established textbooks on Equity and trusts.

## 12.2 The creation and requirements of express trusts

An express trust is a trust set up by a person on purpose, as opposed to an **implied trust** that arises by operation of law out of particular circumstances.

The person who creates the express trust is called the 'settlor' in a lifetime, or *inter vivos*, trust and the '**testator**' (or 'testatrix' if female) in a testamentary trust, namely one created by will.

With an express trust, the settlor/testator indicates expressly (usually in writing) that they intend to create a trust and what the terms of that trust will be.

A will trust must be in writing (to comply with the general formality that a will and all its terms has to be in writing).

However, an *inter vivos* trust does not have to be in writing—the expression of the person's intention to create a trust, and of the terms of the trust, can be oral (in other words, *inter vivos* trusts can be created via the spoken word).

We will see in **12.2.1** that a number of things need to be clear, or 'certain', for an express private trust to be valid.

Also, some trusts have to meet statutory formalities requirements in order to be valid. We have already considered the formalities requirements for making wills in **2.4.3**. We will consider the formalities for *inter vivos* trusts in **12.2.2**.

Depending on who is appointed as trustee of the trust, it may also be necessary for the settlor of an *inter vivos* trust to transfer the legal title of the intended trust property to the trustee. Once this is done, the trust is said to be 'constituted' (or 'fully constituted'). We will consider the rules on constitution of trusts (and the related issue of '**perfection**' of **gifts**) in **12.2.3** and **12.2.4**.

With testamentary trusts, there will be an automatic transfer of the legal title in the testator's assets to the testator's **executors**, who will then pass that legal title on to any trustees who have been appointed by the testator, so the issue of 'constitution' of the trust does not arise.

Also, although not discussed further in this chapter, the settlor or testator must have the requisite mental **capacity** to be able to create the trust (with a testator this will be testamentary capacity, as discussed in **2.4.1**).

### 12.2.1 The three certainties

A trust (whether it is an *inter vivos* one or a testamentary one) imposes onerous obligations on the trustee, and so it is very important to be clear about whether or not a trust has been created. The trust will also create new beneficial entitlements for the beneficiary, so again it is important to be clear whether or not a trust has been created. Lastly, once an *inter vivos* trust has been created, the settlor will usually lose their beneficial interest in the property—like a gift, the property will no longer belong to the settlor, and so again it must be clear whether or not a trust has been created.

Accordingly, for an express private trust to be valid, three things need to be clear, or 'certain'. These three things are known as 'the three certainties'. As explained in *Knight v Knight* (1840) 3 Beav 148, there must be:

1 certainty of words (also known as certainty of intention). It must be clear (or certain) that the person intended to create a trust;
2 certainty of subject matter (the subject matter is the trust property that is the subject of the trust); and
3 certainty of objects (the objects are the beneficiaries, ie the persons who are to benefit from the trust).

We will look at each of these three certainties in turn, but it is worth mentioning here that if there is uncertainty regarding one of these three aspects, it can cast doubt on the certainty of the other aspects (as in *Mussoorie Bank v Rayner* (1882) 7 App Cas 321, where uncertainty of subject matter cast doubt on whether there was **certainty** of intention).

### 12.2.1.1 Certainty of intention

It must be clear that the person intended to make a trust. This is because once the trust is created, the trustees will take on obligations to the beneficiaries and the beneficiaries will acquire property rights (as equitable or beneficial owners of the property). With an *inter vivos* trust, the settlor will also cease to be the sole legal and beneficial owner of the property, just as if the settlor had made an outright gift.

It is important, therefore, that the settlor's or testator's intention to create a trust is crystal clear, given the effect it has on the property rights of settlors, of the testator's estate and of beneficiaries, and given the obligations imposed on the trustees.

People sometimes make statements (both oral and written) that might give the impression that they wish to set up a trust, but might in fact not go far enough to clearly show an intention to create a trust.

Oral statements made on a single occasion might be seen as 'loose conversations' and be insufficiently clear to show certainty of intention to create a trust (eg *Jones v Lock* (1865) 1 Ch App 25). In contrast, oral statements made repeatedly on different occasions over a period of time may be sufficient to evidence an intention to create a trust (eg *Paul v Constance* [1977] 1 WLR 527).

Written statements might be worded in a way that is insufficiently clear whether or not a person intended to create a binding trust. Instead, the wording may be seen as merely the expression of a non-binding wish. Such non-binding wording is known as 'precatory' wording (the expression of a prayer, or a wish). If wording is held to be merely precatory then there will be no trust because there is a lack of certainty of intention.

It is not necessary to use the word 'trust' to create a trust (*Re Kayford Ltd* [1975] 1 WLR 279). Equally, the use of the word 'trust' does not automatically mean that there will be a trust (eg *Singha v Heer* [2016] EWCA Civ 424). Instead, the court will look at the meaning of the words used to determine the person's intention (*Re Hamilton* [1895] 2 Ch 370).

It must also be clear that the person intends to create a trust as opposed to, say, wishing to make an outright gift. A trust is different from a gift in that with a trust the legal title to the trust property is held by the trustee and the beneficial or equitable interest belongs to the beneficiary. With an outright gift, though, the person making the gift (the donor) intends to give *both* the legal title *and* the beneficial or equitable interest to the recipient of the gift (the donee). For example, in *Jones v Lock* (1865) 1 Ch App 25, a father indicated an intention to make a gift of a cheque for £900 to his baby son. The gift failed because the father did not complete the gift. It was held that the father had intended an outright gift and so could not have also intended to hold the money on trust for his baby son.

### 12.2.1.2 Certainty of subject matter

The subject matter of a trust must also be certain, or ascertainable. In other words, it must be clear exactly what property is subject to the trust.

There are different rules for *inter vivos* trusts compared with testamentary trusts and different rules seemingly for different types of property.

The first rule, however, is that the subject matter should be described with accuracy. We have seen this already when considering the validity of gifts in wills (see **3.5.1**). The property which is subject to the trust must be described clearly, whether it is a sum of money or an intangible asset (eg a holding of shares), or tangible property (eg an item or items of personal property, or real property—particular land and buildings).

As well as there being an accurate description of the trust property, the subject matter must also be ascertainable. With *inter vivos* trusts there are different rules seemingly for tangible (ie physical) and intangible property.

Tangible property (eg bottles of wine or gold bars and coins) have to be ascertainable, if they form part of a larger number of such items. So, if there is to be a trust over 100 bottles of wine and the settlor has 1,000 bottles of wine, it has to be clear exactly which 100 bottles are subject to the trust. It is not possibly simply to take any 100 bottles for the trust—the exact 100 bottles have to be ascertainable. How might those 100 bottles be ascertainable? The bottles could have been segregated (put into separate crates), labelled or a list might have been drawn up to indicate which 100 bottles were subject to the trust. If those 100 bottles are not ascertainable, the trust will fail due to uncertainty of subject matter (*Re London Wine Co (Shippers) Ltd* [1986] PCC 121). The rule can perhaps be justified on the basis that wine, as a natural product, is likely to vary in terms of quality from one bottle to another, but the same rule has been applied to other types of tangible property, such as gold bars and coins which are effectively identical (*Re Goldcorp (Exchange) Ltd* [1995] 1 AC 7).

The rules on ascertainability are less clear for intangible property, such as money in bank accounts and shares in companies. There are contradictory authorities regarding money in bank accounts over whether the trust's money has to be segregated into a separate bank account from other money. The authority on company shares (*Hunter v Moss* [1994] 1 WLR 452) suggests that it is possible to have a trust over a number of shares which form part of a larger whole (eg a trust over 50 shares out of a larger holding of 950 shares), provided the shares are of the same type (eg all 'ordinary' shares of the same denomination, as opposed to, say, 'preference' shares) in the same company.

However, the rules just mentioned apply to *inter vivos* trusts only. It is possible to have a trust in a will of 100 bottles of wine (out of a cellar containing 1,000 bottles) or a testamentary trust of 50 shares (out of a holding of 950 shares). This is because the selection of the bottles of wine or shares would be in the hands of the executors, in other words, the executors would choose which bottles or shares would be transferred to the trust. Students commonly fail to remember this point, and mistakenly apply the *inter vivos* rules on ascertainability to testamentary provisions.

The beneficial interests of the beneficiaries in the subject matter must also be certain. It is possible to have certainty of subject matter but not know what interests the beneficiaries have in that subject matter; that is, it is not clear who should get what. This was seen in the case of *Boyce v Boyce* (1849) 16 Sim 476, where a father left two houses for his two daughters, Maria and Charlotte. Under the terms of the father's will, Maria could choose which house she wanted and then Charlotte would receive the other house. Unfortunately, Maria died before the testator and so there was no way of knowing which of the two houses should go to Charlotte because this was dependent on a choice that only Maria could make. The subject matter here was certain (the two houses) but Charlotte's beneficial interest in the subject matter was not clear and so the whole trust failed. This is more of a problem with testamentary trusts than with *inter vivos* trusts. If an *inter vivos* trust were to fail, the settlor is usually still alive and so has an opportunity for a second attempt at setting up a trust, but with a testamentary trust the testator has already died and so the trust cannot be re-made.

### 12.2.1.3 Certainty of objects

It must also be clear who is meant to benefit from the trust, namely who are the beneficiaries. There are different tests for certainty of objects for different types of trust and similar provisions.

#### Fixed interest trusts

A fixed interest trust is one where the beneficial interest of each beneficiary is fixed. The beneficiary might be entitled to a fixed sum of money or a particular item of property, but most commonly the beneficiary will have an entitlement to a proportional part of the trust property, say, one-third, one-tenth or one-twelfth, depending on what proportions are specified in the trust instrument.

The rule for certainty of objects of a **fixed trust** is that it must be possible to draw up a complete list of the beneficiaries. This makes complete sense, because if the trust property is to be divided equally between the beneficiaries, it will be necessary to know exactly how many beneficiaries there are and who they are.

**EXAMPLE**

Arthur makes a will in which he leaves his **residuary estate** on trust equally for those of his grandchildren living at his death. This is a fixed trust, as the shares of the beneficiaries will be fixed depending on the number of grandchildren in the class. When Arthur dies, there are five grandchildren living at his death, so each grandchild will be entitled to one-fifth (or 20 per cent) of the trust property.

## Discretionary trusts

In a discretionary trust the beneficiaries do not have a fixed entitlement to an identifiable proportion of the trust property. Instead, the trustees are given the power, within parameters set by the settlor/testator, to decide who should benefit from the trust property.

The trust instrument will specify a class of beneficiaries (eg 'my grandchildren' or 'all the employees, and former employees of X Co Ltd and their relatives and dependants'), but the trustees do not have to divide the trust property equally among all the persons within that class. Instead, the trustees have the discretion to make payments to some beneficiaries but not to others, and to pay different amounts to those beneficiaries who do receive payments.

For certainty of objects of discretionary trusts, it used to be the case that a complete list of beneficiaries was required (*IRC v Broadway Cottages* [1955] Ch 20). However, the test for certainty of objects of discretionary trusts was changed in *McPhail v Doulton* [1971] AC 424, when the House of Lords adopted a test that previously had applied only to 'powers of **appointment**'.

This test was the 'any given postulant test', or 'individual ascertainability test'. It has also been called the 'is in, or is out test'! Under this test, it must be clear whether any given postulant (a postulant is a person who claims they are a beneficiary) falls within the class of beneficiaries or falls outside the class. So, in *McPhail v Doulton*, the class of beneficiaries included the relatives of employees and of ex-employees of a company, and so it had to be clear whether a person was (or was not) a 'relative' of an employee or ex-employee.

Lord Wilberforce identified three aspects to the test.

1 Conceptual (or semantic) certainty—the meaning of the class had to be clear. In the *McPhail v Doulton* litigation, the question was whether the term 'relative' was sufficiently certain. The Court of Appeal judges in the related case of *Re Baden (No 2)* [1973] Ch 9, all agreed that the term 'relative' was conceptually certain, although the three judges disagreed (on a 2 to 1 split) on the meaning of that term. One judge was of the view that 'relative' meant 'next of kin', whereas the other two judges thought that 'relative' meant 'descendants of a common ancestor'. In contrast, there was the suggestion that the term 'friends' was not a conceptually certain term as 'friends' could mean different things to different people.

2 Evidential certainty—if there is no conceptual certainty, then the trust will fail and there is no need to consider evidential certainty. However, if the meaning of the class is conceptually certain, there still has to be evidential certainty. Evidential certainty relates to whether it can be proven that a given postulant is either inside or outside the class of beneficiaries. It has been said that trusts should not fail for evidential uncertainty, namely that it should always be possible to prove whether or not someone is within a class of beneficiaries. Despite this statement, there might be occasions on which proof might be difficult, if not impossible. For example, how could it be proven whether a person voted for a particular political party at a general election, when the ballot is a secret one? However, in most cases it should be possible to prove that any given postulant is inside or outside the class. (Equity and Trusts students spend much time discussing the different approaches of the three Court of Appeal judges in *Re Baden (No 2)*, but in practice proof is not likely to be an issue, so long as the class itself is conceptually certain. In *Re Baden (No 2)*, Stamp LJ was of the view that the trust would fail if it was not possible to determine in all cases whether someone was inside or outside the class, so if there was even only one person in

the world where this was not clear, the trust would fail. This was a very strict approach and, it has to be said, not particularly practical. Sachs LJ was of the more pragmatic view that it was up to the postulant to prove that they were inside the class of beneficiaries, and that if the postulant could not prove this on the balance of probabilities then the postulant was automatically outside the class. Megaw LJ thought a trust would be valid provided there was a 'substantial number' of postulants who were in the class, even though there might be doubt over the status of other postulants; however, the problem with this approach is that it isn't clear what constitutes a 'substantial' number. Arguably, the most practical approach is that of Sachs LJ so that it is up to the postulant to prove that they are inside the class of beneficiaries.)

3 Administrative workability—in fact, Lord Wilberforce referred to trusts being void due to administrative *un*workability, but what was meant was that the class of beneficiaries must be such as to make it workable to administer the trust. The point is that some classes of beneficiaries will be so large as to make a sensible selection by the trustees impossible. Put another way, how can the trustees be expected to exercise their discretion when the class of beneficiaries is, quite simply, enormous? In *McPhail v Doulton*, Lord Wilberforce gave the example of 'the residents of Greater London' as a class of beneficiaries that would be too large, although his comment was *obiter*. However, in the case of *R v District Auditor, ex p West Yorkshire Metropolitan County Council* [1986] RVR 24, a trust for the 'residents of West Yorkshire' was held to be void due to administrative unworkability. The defining factor for administrative unworkability appears to be the sheer size of the class.

Another concept used in connection with powers of appointment is 'capriciousness', whereby provisions are held to be void because there is, essentially, a lack of common sense shown by the settlor in setting the class of beneficiaries in the first place. For example, if a settlor indicated that the class of beneficiaries was 'anyone whose first name is George', this would be seen as capricious because it simply is not a sensible basis for a class of beneficiaries. It is not clear from the authorities whether capriciousness applies to discretionary trusts (or if it applies only to powers of appointment), but settlors would be well advised to avoid trusts which have a nonsensical or bizarre class of beneficiaries.

## Powers of appointment

One of the issues in *McPhail v Doulton* was whether the provision in the trust instrument was a discretionary trust or a **power of appointment**. Superficially, the two can look remarkably similar. The problem was that, prior to *McPhail v Doulton*, the test for certainty of objects of a discretionary trust was the same test as is applied to fixed trusts, namely a complete list of beneficiaries is required. Applying that complete list test, the trust in *McPhail v Doulton* (for the employees, ex-employees, relatives and dependants) would have failed. As said, what the House of Lords did in *McPhail v Doulton* was to change the test for certainty of objects of discretionary trusts to adopt the test which had previously been used for powers of appointment. It then did not matter whether the provision in the trust instrument was a discretionary trust or a power of appointment, as the test for certainty of objects was essentially the same. What is a power of appointment, though, and how does it differ from a discretionary trust?

A power of appointment looks similar to a discretionary trust because a power of appointment gives the person who has the power (called, rather confusingly, the 'donee') the right to make payments from the trust fund in favour of anyone who falls within a particular class of beneficiaries. Powers of appointment are often included in trust instruments and are given to the trustees of a trust. These are both reasons why it is sometimes difficult to distinguish between a 'discretionary trust' and a 'power of appointment'.

However, the key difference between the two is that the trustees of a discretionary trust have an obligation to exercise their discretion. So, although the trustees will have discretion over which beneficiaries should receive payments and how much each beneficiary receives, the trustees are still bound to pay out all of the trust funds. A discretionary trust fund is said to be exhaustive. For example, a settlor creates a discretionary trust for their grandchildren. The trust fund is £1 million. The trustees will have the discretion to make payments to some grandchildren but not others, and can pay different amounts to different grandchildren. However, the trustees have to pay out the whole £1 million: there must be nothing left over.

In contrast, the power of appointment is permissive only. The donee of the power (who remember is often a trustee) has the power to make payments from the trust fund and to select who to make those payments to, but there is no obligation to exhaust the trust fund. Money can be left over. So, if a settlor gave their trustees a power of appointment over £1 million in favour of their grandchildren, the trustees need not pay out the whole £1 million. They could, for example, pay out £250,000 only, leaving £750,000 undistributed.

What then happens to that part of the trust fund that is left? The answer is that the trust instrument will specify what is to happen to any undistributed funds. So, for example, the settlor might indicate that any funds not paid out to the grandchildren under the power of appointment should go to the settlor's daughter. This sort of provision is called a 'gift over', and if there is a gift over in the trust instrument it suggests that the trustees have been given a power of appointment rather than a discretionary trust.

Some of the responsibilities of a donee of a power of appointment are similar to the responsibilities of a trustee of a discretionary trust, though. If the donee is acting in a **fiduciary** capacity (eg they have been appointed as trustee, which is usually the case), then the donee has an obligation to survey the range of objects (ie the class of beneficiaries), and to consider periodically whether to exercise the power of appointment by making payments to beneficiaries. Importantly, however, the donee does not have to make payments to beneficiaries (unlike with a discretionary trust). Also, if the donee does exercise the power and make payments to beneficiaries, the donee must exercise the power correctly, namely they may only make payments to persons who fall within the specified class of beneficiaries.

As said, the House of Lords in *McPhail v Doulton* applied the test for certainty of objects in powers of appointment to discretionary trusts. The test for certainty of objects came from the cases of *Re Gestetner* [1953] Ch 672 and *Re Gulbenkian* [1970] AC 508, and is the 'any given postulant' test, which is described earlier. However, it is not clear whether all of the aspects mentioned by Lord Wilberforce in *McPhail v Doulton* apply to powers of appointment. In particular, there is the suggestion that administrative unworkability is not relevant to powers of appointment because it is possible to have a class of beneficiaries which is anyone in the world. As a result, the size of the class should not matter for a power of appointment. However, it seems that a power may fail due to capriciousness (see earlier), whereas it is not clear whether capriciousness applies to discretionary trusts.

## Gifts subject to a condition precedent

Another form of provision that can cause confusion is a gift subject to a condition precedent. The perspective here is from the viewpoint of the potential beneficiary who may have a gift, but the gift may still be out of property which is being held on trust by trustees.

For example, in *Re Barlow* [1979] 1 WLR 278, a testatrix provided that friends and family members could each purchase a painting from her estate at a discounted price. This was not a discretionary trust or a power of appointment. Instead, each beneficiary could obtain a gift (the discount in the cost of a painting) provided they could satisfy a condition precedent (ie prove that they were indeed a 'friend' or a member of the family). The question arose as to what was a 'friend'. Whilst the term 'friend' might be too imprecise for a class of beneficiaries in a discretionary trust (as indicated in *McPhail v Doulton*), the court in *Re Barlow* took a more relaxed approach to gifts subject to a condition precedent. It was said that if a person could show the trustees that they were, on any measure, a friend, then they could purchase a painting.

The different approaches to certainty of objects of a discretionary trust and of a gift subject to a condition precedent is perhaps unsatisfactory, but one justification for the different approaches is that in a discretionary trust the trustees have to survey the range of objects and make decisions on who should benefit and by how much. With a gift subject to a condition precedent, the trustees' discretion is more limited and all they need do is be reasonably satisfied that a person more or less meets the description chosen by the testator.

## Appointing an expert

One possibility is appointing or nominating an expert in the trust instrument, so that the expert can give an opinion on whether or not a postulant falls within the class of beneficiaries. This happened in *Re Tuck* [1978] Ch 49, when the trust instrument indicated that the question of whether a person was of the Jewish faith could be referred to a chief rabbi.

## 12.2.2 Formalities for the creation of *inter vivos* trusts

We have already considered the formalities requirements for wills in some depth (see **2.4.3**). As seen, a will must comply with the formalities requirements of s9 of the Wills Act 1837. Not all wills contain trusts, but if there is a trust in a will, the validity of that trust depends upon the will being valid. So, if the will does not comply with s9, then the testamentary trust contained in the will is not going to be valid either.

In contrast, there are no formalities requirements for the declaration of most types of *inter vivos* trusts. An *inter vivos* trust can be made orally, as part of a conversation, provided the three certainties mentioned previously are clear. Similarly, a trust can be created in writing, without any particular formalities as to the type of document used (ie no need for a deed or for witnessing, and the writing could be by letter, email or a text on a smartphone).

The only formalities requirement for trusts is in relation to *inter vivos* **trusts of land**. Section 53(1)(b) of the Law of Property Act 1925 provides that any trust over land must be evidenced in writing which (broadly) is signed by the settlor. Note that the trust itself does not have to be in writing—the trust could be created orally, provided that trust is *evidenced* in writing (perhaps a confirmatory letter from the settlor subsequent to the conversation when the trust was created). Also, the effect of non-compliance with s53(1)(b) is that the trust is not enforceable in court; this is subtly different from the trust not being valid. It means that the oral trust of land will be valid and there would be no problem provided no one challenges the trust. If someone does challenge the trust (eg the settlor tries to go back on their word), then the beneficiary of the trust would not, on the wording of s53(1)(b), be able to enforce the trust in court. Having said this, a court might still help the beneficiary of the trust by invoking the equitable maxim that 'statute shall not be used as an engine of fraud', and might impose a constructive trust on the settlor.

Although not a formality for the creation of a trust, it is worth mentioning s53(1)(c) of the Law of Property Act 1925, which provides for formalities requirements when there is a 'disposition of an equitable interest'. (There is a considerable amount of complicated case law on this particular subsection which is often considered in detail on undergraduate trusts modules. We will not consider the detail here, not least because the reported cases are concerned with whether a tax (stamp duty) applied to certain voluntary share transfers, and stamp duty is no longer levied on such transfers.)

Section 53(1)(c) is not relevant to the creation of *new* trusts. The dispositions referred to in the subsection are dispositions of *existing* equitable interests, namely where a beneficiary of an existing trust tries to dispose of their equitable interest to another person. This is likely to be comparatively rare. If a beneficiary wanted to dispose of an existing equitable interest, s53(1)(c) broadly says that the disposition must be in writing and must be signed by the beneficiary disposing of the interest, failing which the disposition will be void (ie of no effect).

Lastly, it should be noted that the formalities in s53(1)(b) and (c) do not apply to the creation of resulting or constructive trusts (due to s53(2) Law of Property Act 1925). Resulting and constructive trusts arise by operation of law and no formalities are required for their creation.

## 12.2.3 Constitution of *inter vivos* trusts

Trusts can be created in a variety of ways. Testamentary trusts are created by a valid will (or codicil). The trustees of a testamentary trust will always be someone other than the creator of the trust, because the creator of the trust (the testator) dies when the trust comes into being.

*Inter vivos* trusts, though, can be created either: (a) by the settlor appointing other persons to be trustees; or (b) by the settlor appointing themselves as trustee. (Sometimes the settlor will appoint a number of trustees, including themselves as one of the trustees.)

The trustee of a trust will take control of the trust property and so needs to receive the legal title to the trust property from the person who has created the trust.

With a testamentary trust, legal title to everything in the testator's estate passes automatically to the testator's personal representatives (PRs) (usually these are the executors appointed in the will) on death, and the PRs will then pass the legal title (of any assets due to the trust) to the trustees.

With an *inter vivos* trust, if the settlor declares themselves as sole trustee, the legal title to the trust property already rests with the settlor, who is also now the trustee. This means there is no need for the settlor to transfer the legal title to the trustee because the trustee is the settlor, and the settlor has the legal title already.

In contrast, if the settlor appoints other persons as trustees, then the settlor will have to transfer the legal title in the trust property to the trustees. Until this transfer is completed, and until the legal title to the trust property is in the hands of the trustees, the trust will not be fully 'constituted'.

Therefore, for some *inter vivos* trusts to be effective, it is necessary for the settlor to transfer the trust property to the trustees. When the legal title passes to the trustees, the trust is said to be fully 'constituted'. However, if the settlor fails to transfer the legal title to the trustees, the trust will fail because it has not been 'constituted'.

As a result, the formalities for the transfer of legal title to different types of property becomes important. It must be stressed, however, that these are not formalities for the declaration of the trust (we considered those rules in the previous section) but are the standard formalities rules that apply to any transfer of property from one person to another. It is just that a trust might fail if those formalities for transfer of the legal title are not completed.

There are different formalities required for the transfer for different types of property. Some key rules are as follows.

- Transfer of land—this is not a property or land law textbook but, in brief, the transferor must complete and sign a transfer deed (which must comply with s52(1) Law of Property Act 1925) and give that deed to the transferee. The transferee then must pay any stamp duty land tax (if in England) or land transaction tax (if in Wales), although neither tax usually applies to a voluntary transfer. Nevertheless, the transferee must register the transfer with HM Land Registry. The legal title to the land will only pass to the transferee when the transferee is registered as the new owner on the computerised land register.
- Transfer of shares in smaller companies—the transfer of shares in large quoted public companies is arranged via the London Stock Exchange's electronic CREST system. For transfer of shares in unquoted companies, though, the transferor should complete and sign a standard stock transfer form and give that (and possibly the share certificate) to the transferee. (The transferor should give the transferee the share certificate if the transfer is of all of the transferor's shares; if the transfer is of some of the transferor's shares, the transferor should lodge the share certificate with the company.) The transferee then gives the stock transfer form (and, if relevant, the share certificate) to the company. The company secretary should then change the company's register of members to show that the transferee is now the owner of the shares. Significantly, the legal title to the shares only passes when the transferee is registered in the company's register of members as the new owner.
- Personal possessions (**chattels**)—legal title to these usually passes on 'delivery', for example the transferor physically handing an item to the transferee. Alternatively, legal title could be passed by symbolic delivery, via a deed or other written document. There have been cases where there has been evidence that a transferor had said they wanted to give chattels to another person but where it was held that there had been no delivery and so legal title had not passed (eg *Re Cole* [1964] Ch 175).

## 12.2.4 Exceptions from the rule that Equity will not assist a volunteer

One of the equitable maxims is 'Equity will not assist a volunteer'. In the context of an incompletely constituted trust (ie one where the settlor has failed to transfer the legal title in the trust property to the trustee), the beneficiary of the trust will not have any rights to have the trust constituted. The beneficiary is merely a volunteer, and Equity will not force the settlor to transfer the legal title in property to the trustees.

A volunteer is someone who has not provided consideration. So, whilst a party to a contract can enforce that contract because they have provided something valuable (the consideration), a volunteer cannot enforce the trust because they have not provided anything valuable.

Having said this, once the trust has been constituted and the trustees have the legal title to the trust property, the volunteer (the beneficiary) does have rights as against the trustee and the trustee owes duties towards the beneficiary. The problem for the beneficiary, therefore, is before the trust is constituted. That is when the beneficiary is regarded as a mere volunteer and when the beneficiary has no recourse to assistance from Equity.

The other type of volunteer is the donee of a gift. When the legal title of the property has passed from the donor to the donee, the gift is said to be 'perfected', and the donee is obviously then the new legal owner of the property. However, before the legal title has passed to the donee, the gift is not perfected and the intended donee is merely a volunteer, and supposedly will not receive any assistance from Equity. If the legal title has not passed to the donee, the gift is said to be 'imperfect'.

However, over time various exceptions to the rule that Equity will not assist a volunteer have been developed. These exceptions mainly occur in relation to imperfect gifts rather than incompletely constituted trusts. In some instances, trusts have been created out of failed gifts when it has been decided that a donor should hold the property on trust for the donee.

The strict position on Equity not assisting a volunteer can be seen in the case of *Milroy v Lord* (1862) 4 De GF & J 264. In that case, it was said that for a gift to be perfected or a trust to be constituted, every formality for transfer of the legal title to the property must have been completed. For example, with shares, the transferee must have been registered as the new member in the company's register of members.

It was also said in *Milroy v Lord* that an imperfect gift will not be saved by treating it instead as a declaration of trust. So, if a transferor intended a gift, the court will not help the donee by treating the gift as a self-declaration of trust by the transferor. We saw this earlier in the case of *Jones v Lock* (1865) 1 Ch App 25. The transferor either intends to make a gift (and transfer the legal title to the transferee) or intends to make a self-declared trust (and retain the legal title, holding the property on trust for the transferee). The transferor cannot intend both things because they are mutually incompatible (either the transferor intends to pass the legal title to the transferee or they do not).

So, following *Milroy v Lord*, if all of the steps necessary to transfer legal title are not completed, a gift will be imperfect and Equity will not assist the volunteer to force the transferor to complete the gift.

However, over time exceptions to this seemingly hard-and-fast rule have been developed by the courts.

- The 'every effort' approach—in the case of *Re Rose* [1952] Ch 499, it was held that once a transferor had done everything in their power to transfer shares, then from that point in time onwards the transferor was holding the shares on trust for the transferee. The rationale behind this rule is that the transferor can only control some of the steps in the process of transferring title in the shares. It is up to the transferor to complete and sign a stock transfer form and hand this (and the share certificate) to the transferee. After that, though, the remaining process is out of the transferor's hands; it is up to the transferee to pass the documents to the company and it is up to the company secretary to register the transferee in the company's register of members. This approach was also applied to a transfer of land in the case of *Mascall v Mascall* (1984) 50 P & CR 119, where a father was not allowed to withdraw from a transfer to his son because the father had taken all of the steps that were required of a transferor.
- Unconscionability—in *T Choithram International SA v Pagarani* [2001] 1 WLR 1, a wealthy philanthropist wished to leave most of his fortune to a trust that he had set up. Although the trust deed was signed and trustees were appointed, he died before transferring his assets to the trust so the trust was not constituted. Significantly, however, he had appointed himself as one of the trustees and so it was held that it would be unconscionable for his PRs not to complete the transfer of the assets to the trust.
- Unconscionability was used in a very different context in *Pennington v Waine* [2002] EWCA Civ 227, where there had been an attempted transfer of shares. The transferor had died without the transferee being registered as a member. Significantly, the transferor had also died before doing everything that she was capable of doing. The transferor had been acting via an **agent** (her accountant), who had assured the transferee that everything was in hand, and the transferee became a director of the company on the strength of that assurance. It was held that it would be unconscionable for the transferor's estate to withdraw from the transfer, given the clear intention of the transferor, the representation by the accountant, and the transferee's reliance on that representation. Another relevant factor might have been the possible detriment that the transferee had suffered in becoming a director. (This decision has been heavily criticised as interfering with a transferor's right to withdraw from a transfer before they have taken every step that they are required to do to in transferring property. There are also conflicting authorities on whether detrimental reliance is required.)

- The rule in *Strong v Bird*—in *Strong v Bird* (1874) LR 18 Eq 315, a testatrix had lent money to her stepson. There was evidence that she wished to release her stepson from the debt and she also appointed the stepson as her executor in her will. When she died, it was held that the release of the debt had been perfected due to the stepson acquiring the legal title to the testatrix's estate, which in turn was as a result of him being her executor. It was also important that the testatrix appeared to have a continuing intention to release her stepson from the debt until she died. The rule in *Strong v Bird* has been extended to imperfect gifts made by a testator and, controversially, to situations where the donee of an imperfect gift is appointed **administrator** after the donor's death.
- ***Donatio mortis causa***—this exception is derived from Roman law. It is a gift which is made in contemplation of death and which is conditional on death. It is sometimes called a 'deathbed' gift, but whilst the gift has to be made relatively close to the date of death, and whilst it must be in expectation of dying from some known illness, the gift can be made some time before death. It is not necessary for the donor to comply with the usual formalities for transferring legal title in order for the property to pass to the intended donee. All that is required is that the donor hand over 'dominion' to the property (an example might be the keys to a motorcar).
- Proprietary estoppel—volunteers may acquire rights to property where they have relied on, and acted to their detriment in response to, a representation or promise that they will inherit that property. Many of the cases on proprietary estoppel involve farm workers who have worked for low (or no) pay on a farm, having been promised by the farm's owner that they will inherit the farm when the owner dies. What then happens is that the owner does not leave the farm to the worker in the owner's will (even if there is one), and so the worker takes action against the owner's estate, claiming an interest in the property based on the estoppel. To bring a successful claim, the claimant must show that there has been a representation, that the claimant relied on the representation to their detriment and that the owner's conduct had been unconscionable (see **12.8**).

## 12.3 Beneficial entitlement

There are many different types of trust and the beneficiaries of trusts may have quite different beneficial entitlements. We will consider only some of these types of trust and beneficial entitlements here.

### 12.3.1 Fixed and discretionary interests

We have already considered some of the differences between fixed trusts and discretionary trusts when considering certainty of objects.

A fixed trust (or fixed interest trust) is one where the beneficiaries have a fixed entitlement to specific property (eg a beneficial interest in a specific house) or a fixed entitlement to the whole or a share of a trust fund (eg a one-third share of a testator's residuary estate).

In contrast, a beneficiary of a discretionary trust has no entitlement to any identifiable part of the trust property. With a discretionary trust, a class of beneficiaries is specified (eg 'my grandchildren') and the trustees are given discretion. Although the trustees have to distribute the trust property by the end of the trust period, the trustees are free to make decisions as to which beneficiaries should receive payments from the trust and how much each beneficiary should receive. So, if a testator created a discretionary trust for their grandchildren and the testator had four grandchildren, the trustees could decide to make payments to only three of those grandchildren (perhaps because the fourth grandchild was addicted to drink, drugs or gambling, or was simply already wealthy enough from other sources). Then, regarding the three grandchildren receiving payments, those payments need not be equal. The trustees could, for example, pay 50 per cent to one of the grandchildren and 25 per cent to each of the other two.

The beneficiaries of a discretionary trust therefore only have a mere hope (or *spes*, to use the Latin term) that the trustees will exercise the discretion in their favour. Put another way, a beneficiary of a discretionary trust cannot demand that the trustees transfer any property to them, because they do not have a fixed interest in any identifiable part of the trust property.

### 12.3.2 Vested and contingent interests

A vested interest is one where the beneficiary has a present entitlement to that property. A beneficiary may have a vested interest in the capital and income of the trust, or perhaps only have a vested interest to the income.

Where the beneficiary has a vested interest to both capital and income, the beneficiary is, effectively, an absolute owner, apart from the fact that the legal title is held by the trustee. The trustee will be holding the trust property merely as a nominee for the beneficiary and the trust is called a 'bare trust'. Bare trusts are comparatively rare, except in situations where the beneficiaries are minors (ie under the age of 18), because when the beneficiaries are minors they will need an adult to look after the trust property for them.

Where the beneficiary has a vested interest to the income only, this is known as an 'interest in possession'. Here, the beneficiary will have no right to the underlying capital assets of the trust but will be entitled to the income generated by those capital assets as and when that income arises.

It is also possible to have interests in possession in other ways. An interest in possession has been defined as the present right to the present enjoyment of property. So, for example, a beneficiary who is given the right to live in a house for life has an interest in possession because they have the present right to the present enjoyment to that house, even though they are not entitled to the capital value of the house.

A contingent interest is different because the beneficiary will not become entitled to the trust property until the beneficiary satisfies some contingency. Usually, this contingency will be to reach a specified age (say, 18, 21 or 25 years of age), but there may be other contingencies, such as marrying someone (perhaps even marrying someone of a particular religious faith). Until the beneficiary satisfies the contingency, they will only have a conditional or presumptive interest to the trust property, or part of it. For example, a testator might leave their residuary estate on trust 'to be divided equally between those of my grandchildren who survive me and attain the age of 25 years'. Four grandchildren survive the testator, but they are all under the age of 25 at the testator's death. They will each have conditional interests in one-quarter of the estate. If one of the grandchildren dies before reaching 25, then the share of the remaining three grandchildren will increase to one-third each.

The main reason for giving beneficiaries conditional interests is a concern that the beneficiaries might squander their inheritance if they were to receive the inheritance at too young an age.

### 12.3.3 The rule in *Saunders v Vautier*

The law is reluctant to allow property to be tied up in a trust unnecessarily. There are rules, for example to prevent private trusts from lasting beyond a certain period of time (the perpetuities rules). In addition, it is clear that beneficiaries have rights to force trustees to transfer the trust property to the beneficiary if the beneficiary requests it.

Under the rule in *Saunders v Vautier* (1841) 4 Beav 115, a beneficiary who is an adult, who has the requisite mental capacity and who has a vested entitlement to the capital and income of the trust property, can demand that the trustee transfer that property to the beneficiary. The trustee must not refuse to do so and the beneficiary could go to court to enforce the rule. This is one reason why bare trusts are comparatively rare, because why would an adult beneficiary wish to leave property on trust when they could have the property themselves in their own name? Obviously, a beneficiary who is a minor (or an adult beneficiary who lacks the requisite mental capacity) cannot force the trustees to make such a transfer.

The rule applies to beneficiaries who are entitled to the whole of the trust property, or a beneficiary who has a fixed share in the trust property.

The rule would also apply in other situations, where the beneficiaries have limited interests, provided all of the beneficiaries are adults, have the requisite mental capacity and collectively require the trustees to distribute the trust property. Theoretically, this is even the case with a discretionary trust—if every person within the class of beneficiaries gets together and requires the trustees to exercise their discretion, then the trustees must do so and transfer the trust property. In reality, this is unlikely to be the case with a discretionary trust as the class of beneficiaries is usually very wide and may include minors (eg the class in *McPhail v Doulton* included the 'relatives' of employees of the company, and so this would have included the minor children of the employees). Even with the testator leaving a discretionary trust for their grandchildren, it is likely that the will trust would be drafted in such a way that the trustees had discretion to add to the class of beneficiaries, so even if the living grandchildren were all adults and had capacity, the fact that the trustees could add more beneficiaries to the class would mean that the *Saunders v Vautier* rule could not be invoked.

## 12.4 The distinction between charitable trusts and non-charitable purpose trusts

Private trusts are meant to be for beneficiaries who are identifiable human individuals (or legal persons, such as limited companies). If there is no identifiable beneficiary, then there is no one who can go to court to take action to enforce the terms of a trust. If a trust is created to further a purpose, such as to care for donkeys at a donkey sanctuary, there is no identifiable human beneficiary who can enforce the trust. This may make the trust invalid because there is an enforceability issue.

However, some purposes can be seen as for the greater good of everyone (including donkeys!) and are regarded as being charitable. Such trusts do not need an identifiable human beneficiary because they qualify as charities—charities are, in effect, purpose trusts, but they are *public* purpose trusts not **private purpose trusts**. A donkey sanctuary, for example, would fall within the specified charitable purpose of 'advancement of animal welfare' in s3(1)(k) of the Charities Act 2011.

We will look first at the problems with private purpose trusts and then consider charitable trusts in brief.

### 12.4.1 Problems with the validity of private purpose trusts

There are three reasons why private purpose trusts may be invalid.

1 Uncertainty—whilst it is comparatively easy to describe a person or persons when creating trusts for individuals, it is harder to specify a purpose with clarity. So, a purpose trust for 'the maintenance of good understanding between nations' and 'the preservation of the independence and integrity of newspapers' was held to be insufficiently certain and so the trust was held to be void (*Re Astor* [1952] Ch 534).

2 Enforceability—this is also known as 'the **beneficiary principle**'. The idea is that there must be a human beneficiary (or a legal person, such as company) capable of enforcing the trust. A purpose cannot enforce a trust—there has to be a person (individual or legal) who can take the trustees to court if the trustees are not carrying out their duties. The trust in *Re Astor* also failed on the basis that there was no human beneficiary capable of enforcing the trust. Some further aspects of enforceability are covered later.

3 Perpetuity—there are rules, called the **perpetuities rules**, which prevent private trusts from lasting more than an allowed period of time. There is a basic economic and social objection to property being tied up in trust 'in perpetuity' (ie forever). Under the Perpetuities and Accumulations Act 2009, many trusts will have a perpetuity period of 125 years. However, s19 provides that the Act does not apply to non-charitable purpose trusts. This means the common law perpetuity period of a 'life in being' plus 21 years usually applies. A 'life in being' is (basically) a person identified in the trust instrument. The problem with many purpose trusts is that there is no such person identified and so the perpetuity period is limited to 21 years. The greater problem, though, is that the trust will fail from the outset if there is only a mere possibility that the trust may last for longer than the perpetuity period. The Perpetuities and Accumulations Act 2009 provides for a process of 'wait and see' whereby trusts are not invalidated at the outset and will effectively be valid for the full perpetuities period, so long as a distribution is made before it ends. However, as said, the Act (and so the wait and see provisions) do not apply to non-charitable purpose trusts. So, if there is a possibility the trust might last beyond the perpetuity period, the trust will not be valid in the first place.

There are some established exceptions to the beneficiary principle, including trusts for the care of particular animals (as opposed to animals in general, which might be charitable) and trusts to erect and care for graves and monuments to the dead.

It is possible also that a trust for a purpose might be regarded as enforceable if there are humans who have a direct or indirect benefit, and so could take action to enforce the trust in court. So, in *Re Denley* [1969] 1 Ch 373, a trust for the maintenance of sports grounds for the use by the employees of a company was held to be valid as the employees had a direct or indirect interest and so could go to court to enforce the trust.

There can be difficulties with gifts to non-charitable unincorporated associations because, unlike a limited company, an unincorporated association does not have its own separate legal personality. Instead, the association is simply a group of persons banding together for a common purpose. The gift cannot be for a purpose as this would go against the beneficiary principle. Yet if the gift was for the individual members of the association, members could leave the association and insist on being paid their share of the association's property. A practical solution was applied in *Re Recher* [1972] Ch 526, whereby the gift was analysed as a gift to the members of the association but subject to the contract that the members had with each other, so that if a member left the association they relinquished any rights they had in the property held by the association.

## 12.4.2 **Charitable trusts**

This section can only cover the very basics of the requirements to be a charity. It is a considerable and detailed subject in its own right.

Although many charities are not run through the medium of trusts (but instead may be run through the medium of, say, a limited company), charities law developed historically as part of the law of Equity and trusts.

Charities enjoy preferential status, both in terms of their favourable tax status (they are often exempt from paying taxes themselves, and there are tax breaks afforded to donors who donate to charity) and in terms of the legal requirements for validity as a trust. The beneficiary principle mentioned earlier does not apply to charities so there is no need for identifiable beneficiaries. A charitable trust is enforced by the Attorney General (a member of the government), so there is no problem with enforceability. Most of the perpetuities rules do not apply to charities. Also, the court will take a more supportive, or 'benignant' approach to the construction of the trust deed when considering the certainty of the wording of the trust deed, so making it more likely that the trust will be valid. It is not all plain sailing for charities, however, as registered charities must comply with the requirements of the Charities Act 2011 and other legislation, and the administration of charities is overseen by the Charity Commission of England and Wales. The sector is highly regulated and becoming more so.

The starting point for determining charitable status is now the Charities Act 2011. Under s1(1), a charity is an institution which is established for charitable purposes only.

This means that it is not possible to be a charity unless the purposes of the institution are 'wholly and exclusively' charitable. For example, a trust that gave the trustees the discretion to make payments to 'charitable or deserving causes' would most likely not be wholly and exclusively charitable because the use of the word 'or' suggests that the trustees could make payments to causes that were 'deserving' but which were not 'charitable'. Also, political purposes (eg the promotion of the interests of a particular political party) are not regarded as being charitable.

Under s2, a charitable purpose is a purpose which:

- is for one of the specified charitable purposes in s3(1) of the Act; and
- is for the public benefit.

The specified charitable purposes in s3(1) include: purposes that had been recognised historically by the common law, such as 'advancement of education' or 'advancement of religion'; other purposes that had either not been clearly stated in case law (eg 'advancement of human rights'); and entirely new purposes ('advancement of amateur sport'). Under s3(1)(m), it is possible to have charitable purposes that are analogous with recognised charitable purposes.

On public benefit, s4 provides that a charity for a specified purpose is not to be regarded automatically as for the public benefit (so, eg, a private school that charges fees for its school places would be for the advancement of education but might not be seen as for the public benefit if the only pupils enrolled were from very rich families that could afford the high fees). Also, s4 effectively provides that 'public benefit' is to be understood in accordance with its meaning in the case law that predated the Act.

There are, in fact, two aspects to 'public benefit'. The first is that there must be an inherent benefit to the activity. So, a school (even a private, fee-charging school) would meet this requirement as the activities of a school (education of children) are seen as inherently beneficial. However, in contrast, a 'school for pickpockets' would not be regarded as inherently beneficial.

The second aspect of 'public benefit' is that the benefit should be available to the public at large, or a sufficient section of the public. The problem with private, fee-charging schools is that only children from wealthy families can attend the school, because less well-off families cannot afford to pay the school fees. Case law suggests that 'the poor' cannot be excluded from benefit otherwise the benefit is not being provided to a sufficient section of the public. As a result, to meet the public benefit requirement, private schools have to offer discounted school places and/or provide benefit to the public in other ways, such as allowing State school pupils to use the private school's facilities—its sports grounds, swimming pool etc (*Independent Schools Council v Charity Commission* [2011] UKUT 421).

Also, for the benefit to be for a sufficient section of the public, there must usually be no connection (or nexus) between the beneficiaries and an individual or company. So, in *Oppenheim v Tobacco Securities* [1951] AC 297, a trust for the education of the children of employees or former employees of British American Tobacco Co Ltd was refused charitable status even though the number of persons who could benefit from the trust was quite substantial (given that there were over 110,000 employees of the company). However, a trust for one particular charitable purpose ('the prevention or relief of poverty') can have a nexus (*Dingle v Turner* [1972] AC 601).

As well as possibly not being wholly and exclusively charitable, there are public benefit objections to awarding charitable status to an organisation with primarily political purposes, as seen in *McGovern v Attorney General* [1982] Ch 321, when Amnesty International (which campaigns for the release of prisoners of conscience and the abolition of torture) was refused charitable status.

Finally, it is worth noting briefly the rules on 'cy-près'. This phrase means 'as near as possible', and there are rules that enable the application of a charity's funds to a similar charitable purpose where the original purposes of a charity can no longer be carried out. This is a considerable simplification of what is a detailed set of rules, which you are not likely to need for the SQE, and specialist texts should be consulted for more detail.

## 12.5 Resulting trusts

A resulting trust is a form of implied trust which arises by operation of law, as opposed to being created deliberately by the settlor or testator.

The defining characteristic of a resulting trust is that the trust property is held on trust for the person who owned the property in the first place. Depending on the circumstances which have given rise to the resulting trust, this will be the transferor, the settlor or the estate of the settlor or testator.

In each case the beneficial interest in the trust property is said to jump back, or result, to the person who had the property in the first place.

Resulting trusts arise in a number of different situations.

- Apparent gifts—this is when a transferor transfers property to a transferee for no consideration. At face value, the transfer appears to be a gift. However, and perhaps surprisingly, in most situations the law presumes that the transferor did not intend a gift. Instead, the law presumes that the transferor intended that the transferee should hold the property on resulting trust for the transferor. This has been called a 'presumed resulting trust'. The presumption can be rebutted by evidence showing that the transferor did indeed intend an outright gift, and the presumption is comparatively weak, so it is usually easy to rebut the presumption.
- In some situations, the law currently applies a different presumption, called the presumption of **advancement**. This presumes that a gift is intended. The presumption of advancement applies where the transferor and transferee have a particular relationship, such as a father transferring property to a child. Again, this presumption can be rebutted by evidence. The presumption of advancement was due to be abolished by s199 of the Equality Act 2010, but this section has still not yet been brought into force.
- It used to be the case that it was not possible to adduce evidence of an illegal purpose (eg pretending that you were a tenant of a property not a co-owner, in order to claim Housing Benefit

fraudulently) if you were still relying on that illegal purpose, but in *Patel v Mirza* [2016] UKSC 42 the Supreme Court indicated that it was possible to adduce evidence of an illegal purpose in some circumstances. The court would consider the public policy reasons behind a prohibition on illegal behaviour and would have to consider whether a refusal to admit evidence of an illegal purpose was necessary to achieve the public policy objectives. It was said that it was not the place of the law of property to enforce rules against illegal behaviour, as there are already existing sanctions in the criminal law and in aspects of the civil law, such as the insolvency legislation, so in most cases evidence of an illegal purpose could be adduced.

- Failed trusts—there are also situations where a trust will fail, or the initial purposes of the trust will have been carried out and there is an excess of trust property left over. For example, a trust may provide funds to educate a child up to and including university level. What happens to any money left over once the child has finished their university education? Alternatively, a trust's initial beneficiaries may die and there is no provision in the trust instrument to say who should then benefit from the remaining trust property. It is said that Equity abhors (ie hates) a vacuum. In other words, there must always be a beneficiary of the trust property. One solution is for the property to be held on resulting trust for the settlor (or the testator's estate). This has been called an 'automatic resulting trust'. Another example of an automatic resulting trust would be where a trust fails due to uncertainty of objects. The trustees of that trust would then hold the subject matter on resulting trust for the settlor (or the testator's estate).
- Contributions to the purchase of property—trusts of the family home (whether the legal title to the property is in the name of one party or both parties) are now dealt with using common intention constructive trust principles, on which see **12.6** and **12.7**. Investment properties and commercial properties are, for the most part, still governed by resulting trust principles. Thus, when there is a dispute over how the sale proceeds of a property should be divided, resulting trust principles will be used and the starting point would be that the parties should have shares proportionate to their financial contribution to the property. This was seen, for example, in *Laskar v Laskar* [2008] EWCA Civ 347, which involved a residential property which a mother and daughter were letting out to tenants. However, in *Marr v Collie* [2017] UKPC 17, common intention constructive trust principles were applied to an investment property held by a couple, even though this was not the family home.
- *Quistclose* trusts—these are trusts where the purpose of the trust has failed and a resulting trust then arises. The name of these trusts comes from the case of *Barclays Bank Ltd v Quistclose Investments Ltd* [1970] AC 567. These trusts involve situations where a lender lends money to a borrower for a specific purpose. If the money is no longer needed for that specific purpose, a resulting trust arises over the amount of the loan which gives the lender greater protection than if there was only a debt owed by the borrower.

## 12.6 Constructive trusts

Resulting trusts are one type of implied trust. The other type of implied trust is the constructive trust. There are, though, different types of constructive trust, and these arise in a variety of situations.

The two main types of constructive trust are 'institutional constructive trusts' and 'common intention constructive trusts'. We will consider institutional constructive trusts in this section and common intention constructive trusts in **12.7**, as the latter are trusts which apply to the family home.

There is a third type of constructive trust, called a 'remedial constructive trust', but at present this type is not recognised in the law of England and Wales, so we will not consider it here.

Institutional constructive trusts arise by operation of law, out of particular circumstances. These circumstances vary, but one common attribute is that the trigger for the trust arising is unconscionability. A constructive trust will thus arise where a person's conscience is, or ought to be, affected by the realisation that they should hold the property on trust for another person rather than treating that property as their own.

Constructive trusts arise in a wide variety of situations, including:

- where the legal title to property has not been transferred to a transferee, but either the transferor has done everything in their power to effect the transfer, as in *Re Rose* [1952] Ch 499 or it is unconscionable for the transferor to go back on the transfer, as in *Pennington v Waine* [2002] EWCA Civ 227;

- where a fiduciary has made a profit (eg a bribe, **secret profit** or an unauthorised profit) due to an opportunity that has come their way by virtue of their fiduciary position (*FHR European Ventures v Cedar Capital Partners* [2014] UKSC 45);
- where the seller of property is holding the property on constructive trust for the buyer between exchange of contracts and completion;
- where a couple have made **mutual wills** (see **3.3.1.3** for more detail on mutual wills), the survivor of them may hold their estate on constructive trust and thus cannot alter their will;
- where someone realises they have received property by mistake (eg when one bank mistakenly makes a payment to another bank).

(This is not a complete list of situations in which a constructive trust arises.)

Constructive trusts are not the same as express trusts because with express trusts the trustees have obligations to manage the property for the benefit of the beneficiaries, and this would include, for example, duties of care and skill and ensuring that trust property is invested wisely. In contrast, the trustee of a constructive trust is really only under a duty to transfer the property to the rightful owner—there are no obligations related to managing the property.

## 12.7 Trusts of the family home: common intention constructive trusts

Disputes over the family home are inextricably linked with relationship breakdown. When a married couple divorce (or registered civil partners seek dissolution of the **civil partnership**), there is a statutory framework, under the Matrimonial Causes Act 1973, that governs the division of property between the parties. However, with couples who are not married (or in a civil partnership), there is no equivalent statutory framework and the question of the parties' respective interests in real property (ie land and buildings) is governed largely by trust principles.

Historically, disputes over the parties' respective interests in a property were usually determined using resulting trust principles, which only recognised the parties' respective financial contributions. However, such disputes are now governed by different principles, those relating to 'common intention constructive trusts'.

These common intention constructive trusts are quite different to the institutional constructive trusts which were considered in **12.6**. Whereas an institutional constructive trust arises out of circumstances where it would be unconscionable for the trustee to treat the property as their own, common intention constructive trusts arise due to the common intention of the couple.

The leading cases on common intention constructive trust are the House of Lords decision in *Stack v Dowden* [2007] UKHL 17 and the Supreme Court decision in *Jones v Kernott* [2011] UKSC 53. Although both cases concerned properties in joint names, a similar approach applies to properties in the sole name of one of the parties.

*Hudson v Hathway* [2022] EWCA Civ 1648 indicates that the party claiming a greater interest than that shown on the legal title must establish detrimental reliance, although this requirement was not stated in either *Stack* or *Jones*.

### 12.7.1 Legal title in the name of one member of the couple

Where one member of the couple is the sole proprietor of the property according to the legal title registered at HM Land Registry, the presumption is that the property is owned wholly by that person. The legal title indicates they are the sole owner, and the equitable presumption is that 'Equity follows the law'.

Thus, if the other member of the couple is to obtain a share of the property, that other member must rebut the presumption that Equity follows the law. If the other member of the couple manages to rebut the presumption, then the court will try to determine what the common intention of the couple was regarding division of the property between them.

### 12.7.2 Legal title in both names

Where both members of the couple are registered proprietors of the property, the presumption is that Equity follows the law and that they own the property in equal shares—namely, a 50:50 split.

Thus, if one member of the couple is to obtain a greater share of the property, they will have to rebut that presumption and show that there was a common intention that the couple were holding the property in unequal shares. This presumption is quite strong, and it is possible that a party seeking to rebut the presumption will not be able to do so. For example, in *Fowler v Barron* [2008] EWCA Civ 377, a man had contributed nearly all of the finance towards purchasing the couple's home, but the legal title was in joint names and he was unable to rebut the presumption that the house was owned by him and his partner in equal shares. However, in both *Stack v Dowden* and *Jones v Kernott*, the presumption of equal share was rebutted: Ms Dowden received around 65 per cent of the value of the property and Ms Jones received 88 per cent.

### 12.7.3 Establishing the parties' common intention

Whether the house is in sole or joint names, if the presumption that the legal title reflects the equitable interests is rebutted, the court then has to determine what shares the parties should have in the property. As has been said, in either situation the court will need to establish the common intention of the parties regarding the beneficial shares in the property.

Whereas historically a resulting trust analysis was used to reflect financial contributions only, in *Stack v Dowden* Baroness Hale identified a wider range of factors that the court should consider in attempting to ascertain the common intention of the couple. These included whether the couple had children and whether the couple had shared finances or kept their finances separate.

The intention of the couple may be express, inferred or imputed. If there was a written document evidencing the couple's intention, then the trust will be an express one, but if their intention was expressed orally, it can be seen as a constructive trust. If there is no evidence of express statements, then the couple's intention may be inferred from surrounding circumstances. However, it might not be possible to infer an intention from the surrounding circumstances, in which case the court might impute an intention, namely decide on the intention that the parties would have had if they had thought about it.

### 12.7.4 Other properties

*Stack v Dowden* and *Jones v Kernott* specifically related to the family home where it was considered inappropriate to apply resulting trust principles based solely on financial contributions. Common intention constructive trust principles have also been applied to situations where persons who are not a couple have purchased a house together to live in.

Other properties, such as an investment property purchased by a mother and daughter for the purpose of letting out to tenants, are seemingly still governed by resulting trust principles (*Laskar v Laskar* [2008] EWCA Civ 347). Similarly, commercial properties should be governed by resulting trust principles rather than common intention constructive trust principles.

However, in *Marr v Collie* [2017] UKPC 17, common intention constructive trust principles were applied to an investment property which was owned by an unmarried couple, even though this was not their family home.

## 12.8 Proprietary estoppel

We have already considered proprietary estoppel when considering the exceptions to the rule that Equity will not assist a volunteer (**12.2.4**).

A successful claim for proprietary estoppel will give a volunteer an equitable interest in a property provided certain elements are present. There are four elements:

1. there must be a representation by the owner of the legal title that the claimant has, or will have, an interest in the property;
2. the claimant must have relied upon that representation;
3. the claimant must have suffered detriment due to the reliance on the representation;
4. the defendant's conduct must have been unconscionable.

Many of the cases on proprietary estoppel concern farms and agricultural land, where farm workers have relied upon representations by the farm owner that the worker will inherit the farm on the farm owner's death, provided the worker works for the owner, often for very low wages (thus suffering a detriment) (eg *Guest v Guest* [2022] UKSC 27). In *Guest*, the Supreme Court said there should be an assumption that the promisor be held to the promise, rather than to precisely compensate the claimant for the detriment.

## KEY POINT SUMMARY

- For a valid express private trust three things have to be certain: (1) certainty of words (or intention); (2) certainty of subject matter (the trust property); and (3) certainty of objects (the beneficiaries). Different rules apply for certainty of subject matter with tangible and intangible property, and different rules for certainty of objects apply to different types of trust, and to similar provisions (eg a power of appointment).
- For a testamentary trust to be valid, the will containing the trust must be valid. This includes complying with the formalities in s9 of the Wills Act 1837. The only formalities requirement for *inter vivos* trusts is that trusts over land must be evidenced in writing and signed.
- A settlor may declare an *inter vivos* trust and appoint themselves as sole trustee. This is a self-declaration of trust and the trust will be fully constituted immediately because the trustee (the settlor) already holds the legal title to the trust property.
- However, if the settlor appoints other persons as trustees, then the settlor must transfer the legal title to the trustees for the trust to be fully constituted. Similarly, if a donor wishes to make a lifetime gift, the legal title must pass to the donee before the gift is perfected.
- If the trust is not constituted, or the gift is not perfected, supposedly Equity will not assist the intended beneficiary of the trust or the intended donee of the gift, because in each case they are a volunteer who has given no consideration. However, a number of exceptions have arisen whereby imperfect gifts may be perfected (as in the rule in *Strong v Bird*), or where a trust will arise out of a failed gift (as in *Re Rose* or as in *Pennington v Waine*).
- Beneficiaries can have different interests in the capital and income of the trust depending on the type of trust created. Beneficiaries who together are entitled to the whole of the trust property may, if they are adults and have mental capacity, require the trustees to bring the trust to an end under the rule in *Saunders v Vautier.*
- There are various reasons why private purpose trusts are not valid. The main reason is the beneficiary principle, in that there have to be identifiable beneficiaries who can enforce the trust. There are, though, some exceptions to the rule and there may be individuals who have a direct or indirect interest who can enforce the trust.
- There is no problem with enforceability of public (ie charitable) purpose trusts, as these are enforced by the Attorney General. Charities enjoy a number of advantages, principally significant tax breaks. To qualify for charitable status, an organisation needs to meet three conditions: (1) the purposes must be for one of the specified charitable purposes listed in the Charities Act 2011; (2) the organisation must be for the public benefit; and (3) the organisation's purposes must be wholly and exclusively charitable. On public benefit, the purpose must be inherently beneficial to the public and it must benefit the public as a whole or a sufficient section of the public.

- There are two types of implied trust—resulting trusts and constructive trusts. Resulting trusts arise by operation of law. Under a resulting trust, the beneficial interest is held for the person who owned the property in the first place. Resulting trusts can arise where there is an apparent gift, where there is a failed trust, when parties contribute to the purchase price of real property and when the purposes of a loan cannot be carried out.
- Most constructive trusts are institutional constructive trusts which arise in well-established and defined circumstances. Mainly, the basis for institutional constructive trusts is unconscionability.
- In disputes between unmarried couples over the family home, resulting trusts have been replaced by common intention constructive trusts. Equity is said to follow the law, so that there is a presumption the property is owned as shown on the legal title. If the property is in the name of one person, the other member of the couple must rebut the presumption to show that the property is owned jointly. Where the title to the property is in the joint names of the couple, the presumption is that the couple own the property in equal shares and evidence would be needed to rebut that presumption. It seems that the party claiming a greater interest than that shown on the legal title will need to show detrimental reliance.
- In either case, if the presumption is rebutted, the court will look at a range of factors (listed in the case of *Stack v Dowden*) to determine the common intention of the couple, and thereby the shares that they should receive from the sale proceeds.

# CHAPTER 13
# Personal Representatives, Trustees and Beneficiaries

## FUNCTIONING LEGAL KNOWLEDGE

This chapter covers the following functioning legal knowledge required to pass the SQE 1 assessments:

**Trustees:**

- who can be a **trustee**, appointment, removal and retirement of trustees
- trustees' duty of care
- trustees' duty to invest (and powers in relation to investment)
- trustees' statutory powers of maintenance and **advancement**

**The fiduciary relationship and its obligations:**

- duty not to profit from fiduciary position
- trustees not to purchase **trust** property
- fiduciary not to put themselves in a position where their interest and duty conflict

**Trustees' liability:**

- breach of trust
- measure of liability
- protection of trustees
- limitation period

**The nature of equitable remedies and the availability of tracing in Equity**

**Liability of strangers to the trust:**

- establishing recipient liability
- establishing accessory liability

## AUTHORITIES UNDERPINNING PRACTICE

Most of the law on Equity and trusts is derived from case law. There are relatively few statutory provisions, compared with other topics; however, the following legislation underpins aspects of this area of practice. Note that for legislation you are linked to legislation.gov.uk.

Although much of the legislation on this government website is available in its amended form, the incorporation of new amendments into the text of legislation can be delayed. You should refer to legal databases to ensure you are referencing the most up-to-date legislation.

- Trustee Act 1925
  **http://www.legislation.gov.uk/ukpga/Geo5/15-16/19/contents**
- Trustee Act 2000
  **http://www.legislation.gov.uk/ukpga/2000/29/contents**
- Trusts of Land and Appointment of Trustees Act 1996
  **http://www.legislation.gov.uk/ukpga/1996/47/contents**

## 13.1 Introduction

In **Chapter 12** we considered most of the core principles of the law of Equity and trusts. Some core principles, though, concerning the powers and duties of **personal representatives** (PRs) and trustees, and the rights and remedies of **beneficiaries**, are considered in this chapter.

## 13.2 Appointment, removal and retirement of trustees

Trustees of **express trusts** will usually have been appointed by the settlor or **testator** in the trust deed or **will**. There are circumstances, however, in which the original trustees will retire or may be removed, and in which replacement or additional trustees may be appointed.

### 13.2.1 Appointment of trustees

There is no limit on the number of trustees who may be appointed by a settlor or testator, but where the trust is a private (ie non-charitable) trust and the subject matter of the trust is land, the maximum number of trustees is four (s34 Trustee Act 1925). Conversely, it is possible to appoint only one trustee of a trust but, if land is to be sold by the trust, the purchaser will want the sale to be made by at least two trustees to overreach the beneficial interests. However, a **trust corporation** can act as the sole trustee and can sell land without the need of a second trustee.

The trust instrument may give one or more persons an express power to appoint new trustees. Often this power is given to the original trustees so that they can appoint replacements.

There is a statutory power to appoint new trustees under s36 of the Trustee Act 1925, although this power may be excluded by the trust instrument. The statutory power can be exercised by persons nominated in the trust instrument or, if none, by the continuing trustees. The appointment can only be made in particular circumstances, such as where one of the original trustees has died.

Under s41 of the Trustee Act 1925, the court may appoint new trustees if it is inexpedient, difficult or impracticable for new trustees to be appointed without the assistance of the court. The court can appoint both replacement and additional trustees. The court may also appoint a judicial trustee as an additional or replacement trustee, under the Judicial Trustees Act 1896. This jurisdiction overlaps with the court's jurisdiction to appoint new PRs under s50 of the Administration of Justice Act 1985.

Under s19 of the Trusts of Land and Appointment of Trustees Act 1996, in certain circumstances the beneficiaries can require the trustees to appoint new trustees (see **13.7.1.5** for more detail).

The situation is different for **implied trusts**. Trustees of **constructive trusts** are not appointed, but rather the trust arises by operation of law out of particular circumstances and the trust is effectively imposed on the trustee by the law. Similarly, **resulting trusts** arise by operation of law, so the trustee of a resulting trust is not appointed as trustee of the resulting trust, but sometimes the resulting trust will arise because there is no identifiable beneficiary of an express trust, and in those circumstances the trustees of the express trust (who will have been appointed by the settlor or testator) will be holding the trust property on resulting trust.

### 13.2.2 Removal and retirement of trustees

Under s39 of the Trustee Act 1925, a trustee may retire provided there will still be two remaining trustees or a trust corporation still acting as trustee. An attempted retirement is not effective if this is not the case. Trustees should seek a formal discharge of liability from the beneficiaries (if the beneficiaries are adults and so able to give it). Trustees will be liable for breaches of trust committed before retiring but not for breaches of trust committed after retirement (unless the trustee has retired in order to commit the breach!).

Under s19 of the Trusts of Land and Appointment of Trustees Act 1996, in certain circumstances the beneficiaries can require the trustees to retire (again, see **13.7.1.5** for more detail).

The trust instrument may give one or more persons the right to remove trustees, either under an express power or a statutory power in s36 of the Trustee Act 1925. Also, trustees may be removed by the court, under the statutory power in s41 of the Trustee Act 1925 or as part of the court's inherent jurisdiction.

Lastly, under s50 of the Administration of Justice Act 1985 the court may remove a PR (and appoint a replacement).

## 13.3 The duties of personal representatives and trustees

In this section we will consider the duties of trustees. Many of these duties also apply to PRs too. Essentially, the duties described in this section apply to trustees of express trusts who have been appointed by the settlor or testator in a trust instrument. As we have seen in **Chapter 12**, a person may be made a trustee of a constructive trust or a resulting trust, but many of the duties described in this section will not apply to those trusts. That is because the trustee of an express trust is expected to manage trust property over a considerable period of time, acting for the benefit of the beneficiaries. However, the duties of a trustee of a constructive or resulting trust are usually limited to ensuring they transfer the legal title in the property to the rightful owner.

### 13.3.1 The duty of care and skill (s1 TA 2000)

Under s1 of the Trustee Act 2000, trustees and PRs have a duty to exercise care and skill when discharging many of their functions. The duty of care and skill applies to the matters set out in Sch 1 to the Act.

Trustees and PRs must exercise such care and skill as is reasonable in the circumstances, having regard to:

- any special knowledge or experience that they have or hold themselves out as having; and
- any special knowledge or experience that it is reasonable to expect of a person acting in the course of a profession, if the trustee/PR is acting as trustee in the course of a business or profession.

The second point above means that a trustee/PR who is a solicitor (and who is acting in their professional capacity) will be expected to exercise such care and skill expected of a solicitor, which is arguably a higher standard of care and skill than would be expected of a lay trustee or PR.

However, the duty of care and skill can be excluded by the trust instrument (Sch 1, para 7).

### 13.3.2 Duties in respect of investment

One of the functions where a PR or trustee must exercise care and skill is in the investment of the estate or the trust fund.

PRs have a primary duty to distribute the estate, but as we have seen there are reasons why the PRs cannot distribute the estate as soon as they have cashed in the deceased's assets. There may be property (land or shares) which needs to be sold, which may be difficult to sell or simply that the sale will take time. There may be potential claims against the estate and the PRs have to wait until they are certain that no claims will in fact be brought. In the meantime, the PRs will be holding substantial sums of money and the PRs will need to consider how best to invest those sums.

Similarly, with a trust, the trust period might last for many years and so the trustees will naturally have to consider how best to invest the trust fund.

Should the PRs or trustees invest in investments which produce a high income, or where the capital value is likely to increase substantially? Should the PRs or trustees invest in potentially lucrative, but high-risk, investments or choose safer, but perhaps less remunerative, investment products? Should they invest in one type of investment or a mix?

As well as the duty of care and skill, the PRs and trustees will have other duties in respect of investment. These duties generally reflect common sense.

- First, PRs and trustees must have regard to the 'standard investment criteria' in s4 of the Trustee Act 2000. PRs and trustees must review the investments from time to time and consider whether those investments should be varied. The PRs and trustees should also consider the suitability of the type of investments and the suitability of the particular investment chosen within that type. For example, would shares in public companies listed on the London Stock Exchange be a suitable type of investment and, if so, which company's shares should the estate/trust invest in? In addition, PRs and trustees must consider the need for diversification of investments, so far as this is appropriate.
- The standard investment criterion of diversification mirrors the 'portfolio' theory developed in case law—the idea is to avoid putting all your eggs in one basket, namely to spread the risk of one investment failing. If all of the trust fund were invested in one investment or one type of investment, the failure of that investment would be catastrophic for the trust, whereas if the trust were invested in a range of investments, the losses could be borne more easily because other investments would not have failed.
- Under s5 of the Trustee Act 2000, PRs and trustees are under a duty to consider proper investment advice from an expert, or from more than one expert, except where the PRs and trustees reasonably conclude that it is not necessary to do so.
- Trustees also have duties of investment from the common law. In particular, trustees must choose investments that are likely to bring the greatest financial return for the beneficiaries, disregarding non-financial considerations such as not investing in tobacco companies or companies with particularly harmful environmental impacts (*Cowan v Scargill* [1985] Ch 270). However, if all of the beneficiaries are adults and have **capacity**, the trustees can take into account the wishes of the beneficiaries in choosing the trust's investments.
- Lastly, as explained in the next section, trustees have to consider the interests of all of the beneficiaries of the trust when deciding on the trust's investments.

It is worth noting that all of the above duties of investment apply whether the trustees are exercising their statutory powers of investment (on which, see **13.6.1.2**) or express powers of investment given to them by the trust instrument.

(Although not strictly trustees' duties, the solicitor who is acting for the PRs or trustees should have regard to the Financial Services and Markets Act 2000 requirements and to any requirements arising under the SRA Accounts Rules 2019.)

### 13.3.3 The duty to consider the interests of all of the beneficiaries

Trustees have a duty to consider the interests of all of the beneficiaries. Sometimes this involves balancing the competing interests of different beneficiaries. For example, a trust might provide for a **life interest** for one beneficiary (who is called the life tenant), with the trust property to pass to other beneficiaries (called the remainder beneficiaries) on the death of the life tenant. The life tenant will be entitled to the income of the trust as and when it arises, and so the life tenant's financial interests will be furthered by investments that produce a high income. However, the remainder beneficiaries will receive the capital of the trust after the death of the life interest, and so their financial interests will be furthered by investments that produce a lot of capital growth. Rarely will investments produce both high income and high capital growth, and so the trustees will have to balance the interests of the life tenant with the interests of the remainder beneficiaries, and invest in a mix of investments that produce a mix of income (for the life tenant) and capital growth (for the remainder beneficiaries).

### 13.3.4 Other duties

Trustees have a range of other duties, for example trustees have a duty to safeguard trust assets and a duty to keep accounts. Trustees are also fiduciaries and so are bound by the **fiduciary duties** considered in the next section.

## 13.4 The fiduciary relationship and its obligations

Trustees are a type of 'fiduciary'. Fiduciaries (sometimes called 'fiduciary agents') owe duties to other persons, called their '**principals**' (sometimes called 'fiduciary principals'). Other types of fiduciary include solicitors (who owe duties to their clients), company directors (who owe duties to their company) and **agents** (who owe duties to their principals).

As can be seen from these categories of fiduciaries, the principal often has to place reliance on the fiduciary (the client relies on the solicitor, for example). Given the principal's reliance on the fiduciary, the fiduciary must be loyal to the principal and must act in the interests of the principal.

The duties of a fiduciary are essentially negative in nature—the duties indicate what a fiduciary should *not* do rather than what a fiduciary should do. In *Bray v Ford* [1896] AC 44, two strict duties were identified:

1 first, fiduciaries have a duty not to let their own interests conflict with the interests of their principals (the 'no-conflict' duty);

2 secondly, fiduciaries must not make a profit from their fiduciary position (the 'no-profit' duty). If a fiduciary makes a profit arising out of their fiduciary position, the fiduciary should account for (ie pay) the profit to their principal rather than keeping the profit for themselves. The fiduciary will hold any such profit on constructive trust for the principal (*FHR European Ventures v Cedar Capital Partners* [2014] UKSC 45).

The two duties are interlinked, and the no-profit duty could be seen as part of the no-conflict duty.

To give some examples of situations when a fiduciary has been held to have breached their fiduciary duties to the principal:

- A trustee cannot buy property from the trust or sell property to the trust. If the trustee does so, this is regarded as '**self-dealing**' and the beneficiaries of the trust can avoid the transaction (ie set it aside). That said, such a transaction cannot be set aside if the beneficiaries had approved the transaction or if the trust instrument permits such a transaction, or if the parties cannot be put back in their original positions or if the beneficiary has delayed too long in taking action.
- In *Keech v Sandford* (1726) Sel Cas 61, a trustee took a lease of the profits of Romford market personally (ie for himself) because the landlord supposedly refused to renew the trust's lease in favour of the trust. The court decided that the trustee should assign the lease to the trust and account for the profits, even though the trustee had acquired the new lease personally. It was said that the trustee was the only person in the world who could not take the benefit of a new lease.
- In *FHR European Ventures v Cedar Capital Partners*, an agent for the purchaser of a hotel in Monte Carlo received a **secret commission** of €10 million from the seller of the hotel. The agent was liable to account for the secret commission to the principal (the purchaser), and the agent held the secret commission on constructive trust for the principal. A similar treatment applies to other secret profits, and to bribes.
- In *Boardman v Phipps* [1967] 2 AC 46, a solicitor to a trust was held liable to account for a profit that he had made from an investment opportunity (purchase of shares in a company) which had come to him by virtue of being a fiduciary for the trust. This was not a secret profit but was seen as merely an 'unauthorised profit'. Controversially, the solicitor had to account to the trust for this profit even though he had offered the investment opportunity to the trust before investing his own money, and even though the solicitor's actions had increased the value of the trust's existing shares in the company. Although not clear from the case itself, a fiduciary will hold an unauthorised profit on constructive trust for the principal.
- A trustee, or other fiduciary, should not receive payment for carrying out their duties. However, the principal can always agree that a fiduciary receive payment, provided they are adults and have capacity. So, a client can agree that the solicitor should be paid, a company can agree to pay director's fees to a director and a principal can by contract agree the agent's remuneration. This is less easy for a trustee, though, as the trust is set up by the settlor or testator not by the beneficiaries. Also, the beneficiaries may be minors and thus not able to

agree that the trustees should be paid. Despite this, trustees may receive payment for their services either through an appropriate clause in the trust instrument or by virtue of ss28 and 29 of the Trustee Act 2000.

## 13.5 The liability and protection of personal representatives and trustees

Trustees are liable to the beneficiaries for loss arising out of a breach of trust. Also, as has been seen, because trustees are fiduciaries, if a trustee makes an unauthorised (or secret) profit, the trustee will be liable to account to the trust for the profit.

Some breaches of trust will involve an element of dishonesty—for example, the trustee misappropriating (ie stealing) the trust property (perhaps emptying its bank accounts and disappearing with the money). Other breaches of trust will be merely negligent—such as failure to exercise a sufficient degree of care and skill in the investment of the trust's money. In each case, however, the trustee will be liable to the trust for any loss caused by the breach of trust. This poses particular problems for those persons who take on the onerous obligations of a trustee, because they may find that they are made personally liable for any loss caused to the trust.

We have already considered in earlier chapters some measures to protect PRs from liability, such as **statutory advertisements** under s27 of the Trustee Act 1925 (**Chapter 9**) and waiting at least six months from the **grant of representation** before distributing (so protecting PRs from liability for successful applications under the Inheritance (Provision for Family and Dependants) Act 1975—see **Chapter 11**).

In addition to this, trustees may be protected from liability to a beneficiary due to the inclusion of a trustee exemption clause in the trust instrument. Alternatively, the court may excuse the trustee from liability under s61 of the Trustee Act 1925.

### 13.5.1 Trustee exemption clauses

Perhaps surprisingly, trustees can be protected from liability for breach of trust by including trustee exemption clauses in the trust instrument. These clauses seek to exempt the trustees for liability to the beneficiaries. Many trust instruments contain such clauses.

The validity and effectiveness of such clauses were considered in *Armitage v Nurse* [1998] Ch 241. The Court of Appeal drew a distinction between the fundamental duties of a trustee and the other duties of a trustee, indicating that liability for a breach of a fundamental duty could never be excluded. Fundamental duties include the duty of honesty and good faith, but the duties of care and skill would not be regarded as fundamental.

The court also distinguished between merely negligent breaches of trust and fraudulent breaches of trust, indicating that an exemption clause could protect a trustee from liability for negligent breaches, but not from liability for fraudulent breaches. For a breach to be fraudulent, the trustee needed to have acted dishonestly. Unlike dishonesty in other contexts, such as accessory liability, dishonesty is to be judged subjectively, so that the trustee has to realise they are acting dishonestly. However, for a trustee who is also a solicitor, the test is more objective as the solicitor–trustee cannot act in a way that is so unreasonable that no reasonable solicitor–trustee would act in that way.

However, in many cases the beneficiary will have no redress against the trustee for negligent breaches of trust, due to the effect of a trustee exemption clause in the trust instrument.

### 13.5.2 Section 61 of the Trustee Act 1925

Even if there is no trustee exemption clause in a trust instrument, the trustee may be excused liability for a breach of trust. Under s61 of the Trustee Act 1925, the court may relieve a trustee from personal liability where it appears to the court that the trustee has acted honestly and reasonably, and ought fairly to be excused for the breach of trust. For example, in *Daniel v Tee* [2016] EWHC 1538 (Ch), the court relieved trustees of liability for breach of trust in circumstances where the trustees had relied upon expert investment advice.

# 13.6 Different types of trustee power: administrative and dispositive powers

Both PRs and trustees have a range of powers to help them in the administration of the estate or trust. Some of these powers derive from the common law, others from statute, and the will or trust instrument may expand the powers available from the general law.

A number of these powers are 'administrative' in nature as they help smooth the administration of the estate or trust. Other powers are described as 'dispositive' as they relate specifically to the transference of estate or trust property to the beneficiaries. We will consider administrative powers first, followed by dispositive ones.

## 13.6.1 Administrative powers

PRs and trustees may benefit from a range of powers given to them by the common law and by statute. These powers assist with the general administration of the estate or trust.

### 13.6.1.1 Charging for professional services

The rule that trustees and PRs must not benefit from their position means that historically trustees and PRs have not been entitled to be paid for the work they undertake in carrying out their role. However, it has always been possible to include a clause in the trust instrument, called a 'charging clause', which gives the trustees and PRs permission (from the settlor or testator) to charge for the work they do. Such charging clauses were particularly important for professional trustees and PRs, such as solicitors, who undertake trust and administration work.

Since 2001, professional trustees and PRs have also been able to charge for the work they do due to provisions in the Trustee Act 2000. Section 29 provides that professional trustees and PRs (including trust corporations) may charge for their services. If the trustee or PR is not a trust corporation, all the other trustees/PRs must agree in writing that remuneration should be paid. Also, under s28 professionals may charge for work that could be carried out by a lay trustee. This covers work during the administration that is not strictly legal or technical, such as reading the deceased's gas meter! Despite the Trustee Act 2000, it is still common to include charging clauses in wills and other trust instruments, if nothing else than to make it clear to the settlor/testator and the beneficiaries that the professional trustees/PRs will be charging for their services.

In the absence of authority from a charging clause or s29 of the Trustee Act 2000, the court has an inherent jurisdiction to permit recovery of fees, but this should only be exercised in exceptional cases (*Shepherd v Brealey* [2022] EWHC 3229 (KB)).

Charging clauses are interpreted strictly against the PR/trustee. In *Da Silva v Heselton* [2022] EWCA Civ 880, a non-professional executor was not permitted to charge for the work she claimed to have undertaken for the estate because the charging clause in the testator's will was interpreted as only permitting professional executors to charge.

### 13.6.1.2 Powers of investment

Under s3 of the Trustee Act 2000, trustees and PRs have a general power of investment. This permits trustees and PRs to make any kind of investment that they could have made if they had been absolutely entitled to the assets of the trust. The investments do not have to be within the UK, but s3 does not permit trustees or PRs to invest in land (other than loans which are secured on land, ie a charge or mortgage).

However, s8 of the Trustee Act 2000 gives trustees and PRs the power to invest in freehold or leasehold land, but only in the UK. Section 8 allows the land to be acquired as an investment or for occupation by a beneficiary, or for any other purpose.

Whilst the general power of investment in s3 is very comprehensive, the restriction of the power to invest in land in s8 to land in the UK means that often trust instruments will contain a wider express power of investment.

Any express power will override the statutory powers even if the express power is more restrictive that a statutory power.

#### 13.6.1.3 Powers of insurance

Under s19 of the Trustee Act 1925, PRs and trustees have the power to insure trust property against risks or damage due to any event, and can pay the premiums on the insurance policy from the estate or trust fund. There used to be restrictions under the previous version of s19, so it used to be common to include an express power to insure in the trust instrument but now the statutory power is a comprehensive one, it is no longer really necessary to have an express power.

#### 13.6.1.4 Other administrative powers

The Trustee Act 2000 gives trustees the power to employ agents (s11) and to appoint persons to hold trust assets—nominees (s16) and custodians (s17). These powers are particularly important in the context of investment.

PRs and trustees may benefit from other powers, such as the inherent power of PRs to run the deceased's business for a limited time with a view to selling the business as a going concern. This power can be expanded by express provisions in the will.

### 13.6.2 **Dispositive powers**

When trustees make payments from the trust to beneficiaries, or transfer specific property from the trust to a beneficiary, the trustees will be exercising their dispositive powers. These powers will come either from the express terms of the trust instrument or perhaps from the general law, particularly from statute.

PRs may be given the power to pay money to which a minor beneficiary is entitled to the parents or guardians of the child by the inclusion of an express infant receipt clause. Failing that, s42 of the Administration of Estates Act 1925 gives PRs the power to appoint trustees for the minor beneficiary and obtain a **valid receipt** from those trustees.

When payments are made to beneficiaries, it is necessary to determine whether the payment is part of the capital of the trust fund or is part of the income earned on the trust fund. Different statutory provisions apply to payments of capital and income.

#### 13.6.2.1 Maintenance out of income

Under s31 of the Trustee Act 1925, trustees may make payments of the trust's income to beneficiaries. This is called an 'application' of income, and the trustees are said to be 'applying' the income for the benefit of the beneficiary.

Under previous versions of s31, trustees had to consider whether the beneficiary's needs were being met by other sources of income before applying the trust's income to the beneficiary, but this is not necessary with the current version of s31. Trustees do not, therefore, have to conduct enquiries to determine if the beneficiary has access to other sources of income before making a payment.

Why might the trustees apply income for the benefit of a beneficiary? This might happen, for example, if the beneficiary needed money for something, such as a school skiing trip or paying for driving lessons.

When might the trustees apply income for a beneficiary under s31? Typically, this power is used where the beneficiaries are either children (ie under the age of 18) or where the beneficiary does not yet have a vested interest in the trust because they have not reached an age specified in the will or trust instrument.

First, considering children, even if a beneficiary has a vested interest in the capital and income of the trust, if the beneficiary is under 18 years of age, they will not be able to demand the money from the trustees. Under s31, the trustees will be able to accumulate any income earned by the trust, if the trustees prefer not to pay that income out to the minor beneficiary. However, the trustees do have the power under s31 to make a payment of income to the minor beneficiary. Of course, the minor beneficiary will probably not be able to deal with the money themselves but the application of income could be for the benefit of the beneficiary, namely the trustees could make a payment for something on behalf of the beneficiary.

Secondly, the other situation in which s31 might be used is where a beneficiary has a contingent interest, for example the beneficiary has to reach the age of 25 years. The trustees might decide to apply the income of the trust (or part of it) for the benefit of a beneficiary who is, say, 20 years of age. That beneficiary is not entitled to the income (because they have not yet reached 25) but the trustees are empowered by s31 to apply some of the income to the beneficiary. As the beneficiary is 20 years old and an adult, the payment of the income can be made direct to the beneficiary.

However, s31 Trustee Act 1925 also provides beneficiaries with an automatic entitlement to income at the age of 18 if the beneficiary has a contingent right to a share of the capital. So, in the example just given, the beneficiary who is aged 20 may already have acquired an entitlement to a share of the trust's income and can demand that income from the trustees as of right. This part of s31 can, though, be overridden by the terms of the will or trust instrument. So, when a testator or settlor wishes to give the beneficiaries interests which are contingent on reaching a later age (eg 21 or 15), it is common to exclude this part of s31 in the will or the trust instrument to prevent the beneficiaries from acquiring a right to the income at the age of 18.

**EXAMPLE**

Anoor makes a will leaving his estate to be divided equally between those of his children who survive him and reach the age of 25. The will specifies that none of the beneficiaries will acquire an automatic right to the income at the age of 18 (ie the relevant part of s31 is excluded).

Anoor is survived by three children—Ravi, Ketan and Priti. All of them are under the age of 25 at Anoor's death. Ravi is the eldest, aged 19.

The trustees decide to exercise their discretion under s31 and pay some of the income of the estate to Ravi so that he can buy a car, which he needs to be able to drive to his work.

### 13.6.2.2 Advancement of capital

Section 31 of the Trustee Act 1925 just considered provides trustees with a power to distribute, or apply, *income* to beneficiaries. In contrast, s32 of the Act gives trustees power to distribute the *capital* of the trust to beneficiaries.

Of course, trustees will distribute capital from the trust to a beneficiary when they distribute the beneficiary's share of capital to the beneficiary. For example, if a beneficiary with a vested interest is under the age of 18, the beneficiary will not be able to give the trustees a valid receipt until the beneficiary reaches 18. When the beneficiary reaches 18, the trustees will pay the beneficiary their share of the capital.

Similarly, if a beneficiary has an interest in capital contingent on reaching a later age (say, 21 or 25), when the beneficiary reaches that age the trustees will pay that beneficiary's share to them.

Neither of the above situations involve an exercise of the trustees' power in s32, though. This is because s32 gives the trustees the power to 'advance' capital to the beneficiary, namely to pay some or all of the capital to the beneficiary *earlier than* the date on which the beneficiary becomes fully entitled.

Therefore with a beneficiary of a vested interest, s32 would give the trustees the power to advance some or all of the beneficiary's capital entitlement to (or more likely, for the benefit of) the beneficiary before the beneficiary reaches 18.

With a contingent interest, s32 gives the trustees powers to advance some or all of the beneficiary's prospective or presumptive interest (ie the interest they would get on reaching the specified age) to the beneficiary before they reach that age. So, in the above example, the trustees of Anoor's trust could advance part or all of Ravi's prospective interest in one-third of the capital. In other words, the trustees could pay one-third of the capital from the trust to Ravi now, even though he is only 19 and has not yet satisfied the contingency of reaching 25. Clearly, although the trustees have the power to do this under s32, they should be very circumspect about exercising the power and should only advance capital if there is a very good reason for doing so.

Under a previous version of s32, trustees could only advance up to one half of the beneficiary's capital entitlement, but this changed in 2014. In practice, you may still see older wills which include clauses designed to override this historical restriction, but such clauses are no longer necessary.

A payment to the beneficiary under s32 is an advancement, or advance payment of capital—the beneficiary is receiving part of the entitlement earlier than they would otherwise receive it. It is not meant to be an additional payment to the beneficiary. The trustees should take the advance payment into account, therefore, when the rest of the beneficiary's entitlement is paid to them. Accordingly, when a minor beneficiary with a **vested gift** reaches 18, or where a beneficiary with a **contingent gift** reaches the specified age (eg 21), the beneficiary will only then be paid whatever is left of their entitlement, having deducted the amount of the advancement. Although this is what s32 provides, it is possible for the trust instrument to override this and provide that no deduction is to be made in respect of an advancement.

**EXAMPLE**

Returning to Anoor's will trust (for those of his children who survive him and reach the age of 25), when Priti (the youngest child) is 22, the trustees decide to exercise the power under s32 and advance £20,000 of Priti's presumptive entitlement to her, to provide her with a deposit for the purchase of a house. Subsequently, when Priti reaches 25 she will receive her one-third of the estate, less the £20,000 which has already been advanced to her.

#### 13.6.2.3 Appointments of capital under an express power

An **appointment** of capital will occur with a **discretionary trust** or with a **power of appointment**.

A trustee of a discretionary trust has to survey the range of objects of the trust (ie the class of beneficiaries) and make a decision about which beneficiaries should receive payments and how much each beneficiary who receives a payment should receive. The process of deciding to make a payment to a particular beneficiary, and of paying that beneficiary, is called an 'appointment'. Put another way, the trustee is said to 'appoint' trust property to the beneficiary. The trustee derives the authority to make this appointment from the express terms of the trust (rather than from statute).

Similarly, a trustee may be given what is called a 'power of appointment'. We have already considered the difference between a discretionary trust and a power of appointment in **Chapter 12**, but the essential difference is that the discretionary trust imposes a binding obligation on the trustees to exercise their discretion, whereas a power of appointment is merely permissive, enabling the donor of the power but not obliging them to exercise the power. However, if the donor exercises a power of appointment, they will also be said to be making an 'appointment' and will 'appoint' property to the beneficiary.

**EXAMPLE**

Dennis makes a will in which he leaves his **residuary estate** on trust to his trustees, giving them discretion to make payments to his children, grandchildren and great-grandchildren. This is a discretionary trust. Following Dennis's death (and following the completion of the administration of his estate), the trustees decide to exercise their discretion and make a payment of £30,000 to one of Dennis's grandchildren, Betty. The trustees will be making an 'appointment' to Betty.

#### 13.6.2.4 Transferring assets to beneficiaries

We saw in **Chapter 9** that PRs have the power to **appropriate** assets to beneficiaries of the estate, in satisfaction or part satisfaction of the beneficiary's entitlement (s41 Administration of Estates Act 1925).

Similarly, trustees have a power to transfer assets to beneficiaries of trusts instead of having to convert all the assets to cash, and then pay money to the beneficiary.

We have seen earlier that under s32 of the Trustee Act 1925, an advancement of capital by the trustees can be by way of transfer of specific items of property.

## 13.7 Beneficiaries' rights and remedies

The beneficiaries of an estate in administration do not have a legal or equitable interest in the property in the estate until such time as the PRs decide that the estate's property is no longer needed for the administration of the estate (eg for paying the debts of the deceased and expenses of the estate). However, the beneficiaries of an estate can expect the PRs to carry out their duties properly.

A beneficiary of a trust has an equitable interest in the trust property (if it is a fixed interest trust), and will have rights as against the trustees of the trust and will have remedies if the beneficiary suffers loss as a result of the trustee's mismanagement of the trust, or as a result of the misappropriation of trust property. Even the beneficiary of a discretionary trust has the right to expect the trustees to carry out their functions properly, and can take action to recover trust property for the benefit of the trust.

We will consider beneficiaries' rights first, followed by beneficiaries' remedies.

## 13.7.1 Beneficiaries' rights

The beneficiaries of estates and of trusts have rights as against the PRs or trustees who are administering the estate or trust. Some of these rights come from case law, others from statute.

### 13.7.1.1 The right to compel due administration of the estate or trust

The beneficiaries of an estate or trust have a right to compel the PRs or trustees to administer the estate or trust properly. For example, a beneficiary of a discretionary trust can take action to compel a trustee to consider the exercise of their discretion. Beneficiaries also have the right to be informed that they are beneficiaries, and the right to see trust documents and to be given certain information about the trust.

If the beneficiaries are concerned by the conduct of the PRs or trustees, they can apply to court. The beneficiaries may take action to ensure the PRs or trustees comply with the terms of the will or trust, to ensure that trust property is preserved or to compel the PRs or trustees to take action against a third party.

### 13.7.1.2 The right to bring a trust to an end (under *Saunders v Vautier*)

As we saw in **12.3**, the beneficiaries of a trust may bring the trust to an end, under the rule in *Saunders v Vautier* (1841) 4 Beav 115, by requiring the trustees to transfer the legal title in the trust property to the beneficiaries.

The beneficiaries have to be adults, with mental capacity, and collectively they must be entitled to the whole of the trust property. As we have seen, although in theory the beneficiaries of a discretionary trust have the same right under *Saunders v Vautier* to bring the trust to an end, in practice it is very unlikely that all the beneficiaries in the class will be able to get together to force the trustees' hand.

### 13.7.1.3 The right to be consulted (s11 TLATA 1996)

The Trusts of Land and Appointment of Trustees Act 1996 (TLATA 1996) gives the beneficiaries of trusts certain rights as against the trustees. Some of these rights only apply to a '**trust of land**', but one of the rights applies to all trusts. A trust of land is a trust where part or all of the trust property is land or an interest in land.

Under s11 of TLATA 1996, the beneficiary of a trust of land has the right to be consulted by the trustee regarding the exercise of any function relating to the land. Also, the trustee should, so far as is consistent with the general interest of the trust, give effect to the wishes of the beneficiaries or the wishes of those with a majority interest in the land. The trustees only have to consult adult beneficiaries with mental capacity who are beneficially entitled to at least an interest in possession in the land.

The right can be excluded by a provision in the trust instrument, and clauses which exclude the right in s11 are sometimes incorporated in wills. Even if the obligation to consult formally is excluded in the will, the trustees would be wise to consult the beneficiaries in practice.

### 13.7.1.4 The right to occupy land (s12 TLATA 1996)

Section 12 of TLATA 1996 also only applies to trusts of land. Under s12, provided certain conditions are met, a beneficiary who has an interest in possession in land has a right to occupy that land. The provisions of TLATA 1996 are complex, but in simple terms it may be possible to restrict the right by specifying in the trust instrument that the purposes of the trust do not include making the land available for the beneficiary.

#### 13.7.1.5 The right to require trustees to retire (s19 TLATA 1996)

Section 19 of TLATA 1996 applies to all trusts, not just trusts of land. Under s19, the beneficiaries of a trust have the right to require the existing trustees to retire and to require the trustees to appoint new trustees of the beneficiaries' choosing. The beneficiaries must be adults, with mental capacity, and must between them own the whole of the trust property.

This right can be excluded by a provision in the trust instrument and it is common in wills to include a clause excluding this right. This is particularly important where professional **executors** and trustees are appointed in a will or trust, because it would not be desirable for the beneficiaries to be able to remove those professional executors and trustees.

### 13.7.2 Beneficiaries' remedies

If a beneficiary suffers loss as a result of a trustee breaching their trust (perhaps by misappropriating, ie stealing, trust property), the beneficiary may have personal and **proprietary remedies**, both against the trustee and against other persons.

#### 13.7.2.1 Personal and proprietary remedies

If a trustee commits a breach of trust (eg the trustee misappropriates trust property), the beneficiary will have a **personal remedy** against the trustee.

The beneficiary's claim will differ depending on the circumstances.

- If the trust (and thus the beneficiary) has suffered loss, then the beneficiary will be able to claim compensation (the equitable equivalent to the common law remedy of damages).
- Alternatively, the trustee might have made a profit as a result of the breach of trust, and in those circumstances the beneficiary should be able to claim that profit from the trustee. The beneficiary will require the trustee to 'account' for that profit to the trust (and thus to the beneficiary).

However, personal claims against the trustee will only be effective if the trustee is able to pay the compensation, or **account of profits**, which has been ordered by the court. If the trustee has disappeared (perhaps overseas), then there may be no point seeking a personal remedy because the trustee cannot be found. Alternatively, if the trustee has become insolvent (eg bankrupt), then any court order would merely make the beneficiary an ordinary **creditor** of the trustee. As the trustee is insolvent, the ordinary creditors of the trustee may recover very little, or nothing, of what they are owed, so the beneficiary is unlikely to recover much, if anything, from the trustee.

Happily, beneficiaries often have the right to a proprietary remedy in addition to their right to a personal remedy. If the trustee has misappropriated trust property and has used that to acquire other property, then the beneficiary can 'trace' the value of the misappropriated trust property into the trustee's newly acquired property. The beneficiary can then exercise a proprietary remedy, which is to 'claim' the trustee's new property. The beneficiary can do this because Equity treats the trustee's new property as if it belongs to the beneficiary.

This is particularly important where the trustee is insolvent, because the beneficiary can claim the specific item of property and that item of property is not then available to the general creditors of the trustee. Also, if the trustee invested the misappropriated trust property wisely and the newly acquired property is worth more than the amount misappropriated from the trust, the beneficiary effectively acquires a windfall as the beneficiary will obtain more valuable property than the trust property which was taken by the trustee in the first place.

However, the proprietary remedy of claiming property is only feasible if it is possible to trace the value of the trust property into other property.

#### 13.7.2.2 Tracing, prior to claiming a proprietary remedy

Tracing is a process that can be contrasted with 'following'. Following is the process of following the *original* trust asset through different hands, which would then enable the beneficiary to claim the *original* property back. This is unlikely to happen often, as usually the original trust property is sold to a bona fide purchaser for value without notice and the trustee may use the sale proceeds to acquire new property. Typically, the trustee will misappropriate the trust's money, which might then be used to purchase land and buildings or investments. In such circumstances, the beneficiary will seek to rely on the process of 'tracing'.

Tracing is the process of identifying how the *value* of the trust's misappropriated property has been used to acquire new property. It is all about showing that new property acquired by the trustee has been acquired, in whole or in part, by using the sale proceeds of the trust's original property. If this can be done, the beneficiary will be able to claim the new property (or a share of it). So, tracing is not a remedy in itself—the remedy is claiming the new property. Instead, tracing is a process which is an essential prerequisite to the proprietary remedy of claiming.

Tracing is possible at common law but it is easier to trace in Equity. For example, it is possible to trace through bank accounts in Equity, whereas this can only be done in simple situations at common law.

There are many specific tracing rules which are too detailed to cover in this chapter. Some main points, though, include:

- It is not possible to trace where the trust money (or proceeds) of it have been 'dissipated' (basically, spent on frivolities).
- It is not possible to trace into property acquired by a bona fide purchaser for value without notice (essentially, a party who has acquired the property for consideration in good faith).
- When tracing into a bank account in which the trust money and the trustee's own money are mixed, everything is presumed against the trustee, so that money used profitably (to buy successful investments) is treated as the trust's money and money that has been dissipated is treated as the trustee's own money.
- If the trust money is mixed with the money of an innocent party and there is insufficient to pay both in full, then the money is usually divided proportionately ('*pari passu*') between the trust and the innocent party.
- Where an asset has been purchased using a combination of the trust's money and the trustee's money, the asset will usually be shared proportionately (*Foskett v McKeown* [2001] 1 AC 102).
- It is not possible to trace into a debt, so if the trust money has been used to pay off a loan, it is not possible to recover the trust money from the lender. However, it might be possible to trace into, and claim, an asset which was purchased with the aid of that loan (eg a house which the trustee acquired with the aid of a mortgage where the trustee has since used trust money to pay off the mortgage). This is known as 'backwards tracing', which is allowed in some circumstances following *Federal Republic of Brazil v Durant International* [2015] UKPC 35. Essentially, there has to be a sufficient connection between the acquisition of the trustee's asset and the use of trust money to pay off the loan.

### 13.7.2.3 Remedies against third parties involved in a breach of trust

Although a beneficiary may have personal and proprietary remedies against the trustee, these may not be effective in practice. As already noted, the trustee may be insolvent and so any personal claim would only rank alongside the trustee's general creditors, so that the beneficiary will only be able to recover a proportion (perhaps only a small proportion) of what the beneficiary had lost. Alternatively, the trustee may have disappeared and so a personal remedy will be useless.

Although proprietary remedies may be more useful where a trustee is insolvent, if it proves impossible to trace the value of the trust's property into other property, then again the beneficiary will be left without an effective remedy.

In certain circumstances, however, the beneficiary will have remedies against a stranger to the trust, also known as a 'third party' (ie someone other than the beneficiary or trustee).

A third party may be made liable to the beneficiary in one of three situations:

1 Trustee *de son tort* (loosely translated, a 'trustee of their own wrong'). This is where the third party has intermeddled (ie involved themselves when they shouldn't have) in the management of the trust, acting as if they were a trustee even though they are not in fact a trustee.
2 Recipient liability (or '**knowing receipt**'). This is where the third party has knowingly received misappropriated trust property (or the proceeds thereof). The third party must have held the trust property (or proceeds) at some point in time in a 'beneficial' capacity. Acting merely as an agent, and having what is called 'ministerial receipt', is not sufficient for

recipient liability. For example, a bank might have receipt of misappropriated trust money when that money passes through its accounts, but the bank would not usually be liable for recipient liability because it only had ministerial receipt, not beneficial receipt, of the money. The recipient must have such knowledge as to make it unconscionable for them to retain the benefit of the property that they had received (*Bank of Credit and Commerce International (Overseas) Ltd v Akindele* [2001] Ch 437). Also, the claimant must have retained an equitable proprietary interest at the time of receipt (*Byers v Saudi National Bank* [2023] UKSC 51).

3 Accessory liability (also called **dishonest assistance**). This is where the third party has assisted the trustee in the misappropriation of the trust property (or its proceeds). For example, a solicitor who assists the trustee to move a trust's money offshore by making the necessary legal arrangements might find themselves liable for accessory liability. However, in order to be liable, the third party must have acted 'dishonestly'. The test for dishonesty comes from the case of *Royal Brunei Airlines v Tan* [1995] 2 AC 378: having taken into consideration certain subjective elements, such as the third party's actual state of knowledge, the court should ask the question—'what would an honest person do in the circumstances?' The third party will be liable for accessory liability if they had not acted as an honest person would have acted. This is an objective test: in *Ivey v Genting Casinos* [2017] UKSC 67, the Supreme Court confirmed that it was not necessary for the third party to realise that they were being dishonest, a question that had been debated in case law and by academics prior to *Ivey*.

For the most part, the beneficiary will only have a personal remedy against a third party (in other words, a proprietary remedy is not usually available). Although a constructive trust (which would entitle the beneficiary to a proprietary remedy) may be imposed on a trustee *de son tort*, the Supreme Court has confirmed that a beneficiary only has personal remedies against a third party in respect of recipient liability and accessory liability (*Williams v Central Bank of Nigeria* [2014] UKSC 10).

Lastly, where payments are made by the PRs of an estate to the wrong beneficiaries, the true beneficiaries of the estate will have a personal claim for reimbursement from the wrong beneficiaries, but only to the extent that the true beneficiaries cannot recover their loss from an action against the PRs (*Ministry of Health v Simpson* [1951] AC 251).

## KEY POINT SUMMARY

- Usually, the settlor or testator will appoint the trustees in the trust instrument. Subsequently, the original trustees may retire or be removed, and may be replaced or joined by newly appointed trustees. There may be express powers to appoint new trustees and there are statutory powers of appointment, retirement and removal.
- Trustees (and personal representatives) have a range of duties which they owe to the beneficiaries of the trust (or estate). There is a duty of care and skill in exercising a number of their functions, including investing the trust fund. Trustees must also consider standard investment criteria and seek expert investment advice when appropriate. Trustees must also consider the interests of all of the beneficiaries of the trust.
- Trustees are a type of fiduciary. Fiduciaries owe duties of loyalty to their principals. Trustees owe duties to beneficiaries, solicitors owe duties to their clients, directors owe duties to the company and agents owe duties to their principals. The duties include the duty not to profit from the fiduciary position and the duty not to allow their own interest to conflict with that of the principal.
- Trustees will be liable to the beneficiaries in respect of losses arising out of the trustees' breaches of trust. Additionally, trustees are liable to account to the beneficiaries for any profit that the trustee has made out of their fiduciary position. However, trustees may be protected from liability by the inclusion of a trustee exemption clause in the trust instrument, or may be excused liability by the court.
- Trustees (and PRs) have a range of powers to deal with the administration of the trust (or estate). There are statutory powers which may be modified or excluded by provisions in

the trust instrument. There are administrative powers (eg the powers of investment and insurance). There are also dispositive powers (eg the power to apply income or to advance capital).

- Beneficiaries have rights as against the trustees. Depending on the circumstances, the beneficiaries may have the right to bring the trust to an end under the rule in *Saunders v Vautier*, the right to be consulted, the right to occupy land and the right to require the trustees to retire and appoint new trustees.
- Beneficiaries may have personal remedies against a trustee. The beneficiary may be able to claim equitable compensation if the trust (and so the beneficiary) has suffered loss. Alternatively, the beneficiary may be able to claim an account of profits if the trustee has made a profit from the breach of trust.
- Beneficiaries may also have proprietary remedies. A personal remedy may not be effective if the trustee cannot be found, or is insolvent, but a proprietary remedy would enable a beneficiary to claim the trustee's property to satisfy a claim. A proprietary remedy will give the beneficiary preference over the general creditors of the trustee, and the beneficiary can claim the trustee's property even if this has increased in value beyond the original amount misappropriated.
- Usually, the original trust property has been converted into other assets by the trustee but the process of tracing makes it possible to trace the value of misappropriated trust property through replacement property in order to enable the beneficiary to claim that replacement property.
- Third parties may be liable to the beneficiaries of a trust if: (a) the third party intermeddles in the management of the trust (and becomes a trustee *de son tort*); (b) the third party knowingly receives the trust property, with such knowledge that would make this receipt unconscionable; or (c) the third party dishonestly assists in the breach of trust or in the misappropriation of trust property subsequently.

# PART F
# Solicitors' Accounts

# CHAPTER 14
# The SRA Accounts Rules

**FUNCTIONING LEGAL KNOWLEDGE**

This chapter covers the following functioning legal knowledge required to pass the SQE 1 assessments:

**Solicitors' Accounts:**

- **client money**:
  - definition
  - requirement to pay client money into a **client account**
  - circumstances in which client money may be withheld from a client account
- client account:
  - meaning and name of account
  - obligation not to use client account to provide banking facilities
  - withdrawals

**Requirement to keep client money separate from money belonging to the authorised body**

**Breach of the SRA Accounts Rules:**

- duty to correct breaches of SRA Accounts Rules promptly on discovery

**Requirement to keep and maintain accurate records in client ledgers, including requirement to carry out reconciliation of client accounts**

**Operation of joint account; operation of a client's own account**

**Third party managed accounts**

**Obtaining and delivery of accountants' reports; storage and retention of accounting records**

**AUTHORITIES UNDERPINNING PRACTICE**

The following rules underpin this area of practice:

- The SRA Accounts Rules 2019
  **https://www.sra.org.uk/solicitors/standards-regulations/accounts-rules/**

## 14.1 Introduction

In **Chapters 14–16** we will consider the obligations placed on solicitors in respect of their accounts. These accounts will not just record normal business transactions but, crucially, a solicitor is usually entrusted with money which belongs to others. This money, which belongs to clients and third parties, is called 'client money', and the SRA Accounts Rules 2019 are largely concerned with keeping that client money safe. One key aspect of this is maintaining a separation between the solicitor's own money (which we will call, for the sake of convenience, '**business money**') and client money. Another key aspect is having appropriate accounting systems and processes to record transactions and keep track of money which belongs to clients and to others.

In this chapter we will look at the SRA Accounts Rules 2019 in detail and consider the requirements of the rules. We will not consider any accounting **entries** in this chapter, though: instead, a consideration of accounting entries is deferred to **Chapters 15** and **16**. In those chapters we will look at the **double entry bookkeeping** system and the forms of **ledger accounts** used by solicitors to record transactions. We will also consider a range of transactions and the accounting entries that will be required in each case.

However, this first chapter is particularly important for the assessment of Solicitors' Accounts in the SQE. This is because the SQE Stage 1 assessments will consist of a series of multiple-choice questions and so you will often be required to apply the Accounts Rules by selecting the appropriate option in the multiple-choice question. This is quite different to the assessment of Solicitors' Accounts on the Legal Practice Course (LPC). On the LPC, students are required to write up whole ledger accounts, making the appropriate accounting entries for a long series of transactions. You will not have to do that in the SQE assessment, but you do need to know what the entries should be in particular situations, which is why they are covered in **Chapters 15** and **16**.

## 14.2 The SRA Accounts Rules 2019

The SRA Accounts Rules 2019 are part of the rules of professional conduct. They form part of the SRA Standards and Regulations, and should be read alongside the SRA Codes of Conduct (the Code of Conduct for Solicitors, RELs and RFLs, and the Code of Conduct for Firms). The SRA Accounts Rules 2019 came into force on 25 November 2019 and replaced the SRA Accounts Rules 2011.

A solicitor can be disciplined by the SRA for a breach of the SRA Accounts Rules 2019, and can be struck off the Roll of Solicitors by the Solicitors' Disciplinary Tribunal for a breach of the Rules.

The case of *Weston v The Law Society* [1998] 6 WLUK 523 is a good example of the importance of ensuring not just that you observe the rules yourself, but also that you ensure (if you are a manager of a law firm) that others within the firm observe the rules too. In *Weston*, one of the partners of the firm was struck off the Roll, even though he had not committed the breaches of the Accounts Rules himself. The breaches had been committed by his fellow partners and he was unaware that the breaches had taken place. However, he had failed to ensure compliance by others in the firm and it was his responsibility, as a partner, to do this. Although he was not directly responsible for the offending transactions himself, he was in breach of the Rules through his failure to pay sufficient attention to the accounts of the firm.

The SRA Accounts Rules 2019 are divided into the following parts:

- Part 1: General
- Part 2: Client money and client accounts
- Part 3: Dealings with other money belonging to clients or third parties
- Part 4: Accountants' reports and storage and retention of accounting records

Parts 2–4 are covered in **14.3–14.5**.

As well as discussing the Accounts Rules themselves, reference will be made to guidance which the SRA has issued on aspects of the Rules.

The Rules, and the guidance, can be found on the SRA's website.

It should be noted that the SRA Accounts Rules 2019 do not specifically mention solicitors. This is because the SRA may regulate other legal services providers. The SRA regulates 'authorised bodies', which includes (but is not restricted to) firms of solicitors. The Accounts Rules apply to all authorised bodies, together with the managers and employers of those bodies. In the context of a solicitors' firm, the managers would include the partners of a traditional partnership, the 'members' of a limited liability partnership (LLP) and the directors of a limited company. The employees of a solicitors' firm would include all the solicitors, trainee solicitors and paralegals, but also anyone else who is an employee of the firm.

The SRA Accounts Rules 2019 helpfully (or unhelpfully, depending on your point of view) refers throughout to 'you', and references to 'you' in the Rules are to be read as references to authorised bodies, their managers and employees (rule 1.1). As your aim is to qualify as a solicitor, we will use 'solicitor' and 'firm' throughout, rather than 'you', but you should bear in mind that the Rules apply to a wider group of persons and organisations, not just to qualified solicitors and solicitors' firms.

The authorised body itself and its managers also are jointly and severally responsible for compliance with the Rules by the authorised body, its managers and employees (rule 1.2).

One type of authorised body is a licensed body. A licensed body is a legal services provider which is an 'alternative business structure' (or ABS). ABSs may be legal services providers which are run otherwise than through a traditional law firm. However, several firms of solicitors have themselves become ABSs. A licensed body may undertake legal services work which is regulated by the SRA but may also undertake other work that is not regulated by the SRA. Rule 1.3 of the SRA Accounts Rules provides that the Accounts Rules only apply in respect of activities of the licensed body that are regulated by the SRA.

## 14.3 Client money and client accounts

Part 2 of the Accounts Rules is entitled 'Client money and client accounts'. It is the largest part of the Rules and the part that we will spend most time considering. It contains the key requirements relating to the management of client money and the separation of client money from the solicitor's own money (which we will call 'business money').

We will consider the meaning of 'client money', how client money should be kept in a special account called a 'client account', how client money should be kept separate from business money and restrictions on the use of client money by the solicitor. A very important aspect of the Rules is that the solicitor should not provide banking facilities through a client account.

### 14.3.1 Client money

Client money is not restricted to money which belongs to the solicitor's clients. It also includes the money of other people ('third parties'). In fact, client money is basically any money other than the money of the solicitor.

The definition is in rule 2.1. Client money is any money held or received by the solicitor:

1 relating to regulated services delivered to a client;

2 on behalf of a third party, in relation to the regulated services of the solicitor;

3 where the solicitor is holding the money as a trustee or as the holder of a specified office or appointment;

4 in respect of the solicitor's **fees** and any unpaid **disbursements** prior to the delivery of a bill.

Note that the money described in point (1) above will not necessarily have been received from the client—it could have been received from a third party (eg receipt of **settlement** monies from a third party in settlement of a claim brought by your client against the third party).

What, then, is the difference between points (1) and (2), as point (2) also relates to money received from third parties? The difference in point (2) is that the client money is held or received 'on behalf of' the third party and so does not necessarily belong to the client. Examples of monies received from third parties under point (2) include money received by a solicitor to be held as **agent** or stakeholder, or held to the sender's order. (This would occur, for example, in conveyancing matters where the solicitor receives money from the third party that is intended to be used for a deposit or in the completion of the purchase of a property.)

Examples of specified offices or appointments under point (3) include the attorney under a power of attorney (this could be any power of attorney—it would not be restricted to a lasting power or attorney), a deputy appointed by the Court of Protection (to manage the affairs of a mentally incapacitated person) or the trustee of an occupational pension scheme (this will rarely be the case, as a pension scheme's money is likely to be retained in the scheme's own bank accounts rather than being paid to the solicitor).

### 14.3.2 Client accounts

Under rule 2.3, a solicitor must pay client money promptly (after receipt) into a 'client account'. Not every account will qualify as a client account under the Rules. 'Client account' has a particular meaning.

Under rule 3.1, a client account must be maintained at a bank or building society in England and Wales. The account may be at a branch or head office of the bank or building society. In most cases, a solicitors' firm will maintain a client account at a branch of one of the large 'High Street' banks, such as NatWest, Barclays, HSBC or Lloyds.

A solicitors' firm may have more than one client account. Firms will usually have a 'general' client account into which the firm will place most of the client money. However, the firm may also maintain other, specified, client accounts, perhaps for individual client matters (see **16.5.1** for more information on separate designated client accounts). Even if some specified client accounts are maintained, though, the bulk of the client money held will be held in the 'general client account'.

There are requirements in the Rules for the naming of client accounts, whichever type is opened by the solicitor. Rule 3.2 provides that the name of any client account must include:

- the name of the authorised body (ie the solicitor's firm); and
- the word 'client'—this is to distinguish the client account from the business accounts of the authorised body.

The second requirement is particularly important, because if the solicitors' firm became, or was about to become, insolvent, the money in the firm's bank accounts would become available to satisfy the claims of the firm's **creditors.** If the client account is properly named, using the word 'client', then the bank will know that the money in that account does not belong to the solicitors' firm but belongs to clients and third parties, and the money in that account would not be available for creditors. If a client account did not have the word 'client' in the name, there is a possibility that the money belonging to clients and third parties would be used to pay creditors.

### 14.3.2.1 Situations in which a solicitor need not maintain a client account

Although most solicitors' firms will maintain a client account and will use this to hold client money, there are situations in which a solicitor will not need to maintain a client account. These are:

- where the solicitor takes advantage of the exception in rule 2.2; and/or
- where the solicitor decides not to operate client accounts to hold client money but instead makes arrangements with providers of third party managed accounts.

Under rule 2.2, a solicitor need not maintain a client account if the only client money held and received is of a particular kind. If the only client money held and received is money in respect of the solicitor's fees and any unpaid disbursements prior to the delivery of a bill, then the solicitor does not have to hold that money in a client account but can instead hold the money in one of the firm's business accounts.

For this exception to apply, though, certain conditions must be met:

- any money held for disbursements must relate to **costs** and expenses incurred by the solicitor on behalf of the client for which the solicitor is liable; and
- the solicitor does not for any other reason maintain a client account.

It is important to realise that the first condition is only met *if the solicitor is liable* for the disbursements, as is the case with **counsel's fees** or expert's fees. The condition is not met if the disbursements are ones for which the client is liable (eg stamp duty land tax or land transaction tax).

Also, for the exception to apply the client must be informed in advance of where and how the money will be held. SRA guidance suggests that the solicitor should explain to the client that their money will not be protected in the event of the firm's insolvency. This is so that the client can make an informed decision about whether they wish to proceed with their money being held outside a client account.

If client money is held outside a client account under this rule, certain other rules in the SRA Accounts Rules 2019 do not apply (see rule 2.2 for the full list).

In practice, it will be difficult for most firms to rely solely on the exception in rule 2.2. A firm undertaking conveyancing work, for example, will need to receive and pay large sums of money from and on behalf of the client, towards payments of deposits and completion monies, and when receiving mortgage advances from lenders and redeeming existing mortgages for the client.

A solicitor undertaking litigation work may need to receive and pay settlement monies to or on behalf of the client. A **probate** practitioner will receive substantial sums of money when administering the deceased's estate. However, the exception might be useful to a criminal practitioner where the only client money received by that practitioner may be from the Legal Aid Agency or from fee-paying criminal clients, in respect of fees and disbursements. It might be possible, therefore, for such a practitioner to manage client money without maintaining a client account.

As said, the other situation in which a solicitor does not need to maintain a client account is where the solicitor decides instead to make arrangements with a provider of third party managed accounts. The money of clients and of third parties will then be held in those third party managed accounts instead of the solicitor holding the money in a client account. See **14.4.3** for more detail. The SRA has also issued guidance on whether a firm needs to operate a client account.

## 14.3.3 Dealings with client money

In this section we will consider a number of the requirements for dealings with client money, including activities which are prohibited.

### 14.3.3.1 Client money should be paid into a client account

Rule 2.3 provides that when a solicitor receives client money, the solicitor must pay that client money into a client account.

Rule 2.3 says that this must be done 'promptly'. There is no definition of 'promptly', and the SRA has declined to provide a definition. Under the 2011 Accounts Rules, client money had to be paid into a client account 'without delay', and this was defined as, in normal circumstances, either the day of receipt or the following working day. Although there is no definition of 'promptly' in this context, the old rule may provide a guide as to what is acceptable.

There are exceptions in rule 2.3 which mean the solicitor does not have to pay client money into a client account in particular situations. These are when:

1 the client money has been received by the solicitor as trustee or the holder of a specified office or appointment, and paying the client money into a client account would conflict with the solicitor's obligations under rules and regulations relating to that office or appointment (see below);

2 the client money is payments received from the Legal Aid Agency for the solicitor's costs (ie fees and disbursements);

3 the solicitor and the client (or third party) agree in writing to an alternative arrangement.

An example of when the solicitor might be permitted not to pay client money relating to an office or appointment into client account (exception (1) above) is when the solicitor has been appointed as a deputy by the Court of Protection. As deputy, the solicitor will be acting on behalf of a mentally incapacitated person (known as 'P'). The stated view of the Office of the Public Guardian (which oversees Court of Protection deputyships) is that P's money should be kept in a separate account. It would not be appropriate, therefore, to pay P's money (which would qualify as 'client money') into a general client account where P's money would be mixed with the money belonging to other people.

### 14.3.3.2 Client money must be available on demand

Rule 2.4 provides that client money must be available on demand unless an alternative arrangement is agreed in writing with the client or third party.

The reason for this is that the solicitor should only be receiving client money if it is needed for a particular purpose (to pay fees and disbursements, to make payments on behalf of the client in respect of the client's legal transactions). It is not usually appropriate, therefore, to put the client money into a deposit account with the bank where an extended period of notice is needed in order to withdraw money. Such deposit accounts with restricted access tend to pay higher rates of interest which is why placing the money on deposit might be considered advantageous. However, as client money should ordinarily be available on demand, the general client account will be an instant access account.

### 14.3.3.3 Client money must be returned at the end of the legal transaction

Under rule 2.5, client money should be returned to its owner (client or third party) as soon as there is no longer any proper reason to hold the funds. So, as soon as the legal services work undertaken by the solicitor has been completed, the remaining client money held by the solicitor should be paid to the client or third party. For example, in conveyancing where the solicitor is acting for the client in the sale of a property (and where there is no related purchase of another property), the solicitor should transfer the net sale proceeds to the client as soon as the sale has been completed.

SRA guidance indicates that solicitors should have checks and controls to make sure client files are closed promptly, and that prompt payments back to clients of any residual **balances** are made.

Despite this, firms may find that occasionally they will have a small 'residual' balance on a client ledger, perhaps because the client cannot be located and so the residual balance cannot be paid to the client. There is nothing in the Rules regarding residual client account balances, but the SRA has issued guidance. This enables solicitors to pay residual balances up to £500 to charity without seeking SRA approval, and a process for seeking SRA approval to withdraw balances exceeding £500.

### 14.3.3.4 Prohibition on providing banking facilities

Linked to rule 2.5 is the prohibition in rule 3.3 on the use of a client account to provide banking facilities to clients or third parties.

The rule makes it clear that payments into, and transfers and withdrawals from, a client account must be in respect of delivery of regulated services (ie the solicitor's legal services in the client's matter, such as conducting litigation for the client or conveyancing work).

Rule 3.3 is an extremely important rule. The SRA are quite rightly very keen that solicitors abide by this rule. There are various reasons for this, as we shall see, but one of the reasons is to reduce the opportunity for criminals to launder dirty money (ie the proceeds of crime) through the solicitor's client bank accounts.

The SRA has issued a 'warning notice' to firms (published in December 2014, updated in March 2023). Aspects of this warning notice are noted later but the full wording is available on the SRA website.

The SRA has also issued guidance, in conjunction with the warning notice, with a number of case studies covering a wide range of practice areas (including trust administration and operating a lasting power of attorney).

The warning notice explains that:

- providing banking facilities through a client account is objectionable in itself because a solicitor is not regulated (as a bank is) to provide such services (also, the solicitor may lose any exemption or exclusion under the Financial Services and Markets Act 2000 if a deposit is taken in circumstances which do not form part of the solicitor's regulated services);
- there must be a proper connection between the delivery of regulated services and the payments the solicitor is asked to make or receive (simply having a retainer with a client is by itself insufficient reason to process funds through a client account–there must be some other reason why the money cannot be paid directly between the client and the other party);
- a client may ask the solicitor to hold or deal with money in a client account to avoid the client's obligations under insolvency legislation (this may result in personal liability to the solicitor if payments from client account are made to the client's creditors); and
- allowing a client account to be used as a banking facility carries with it the additional risk that the solicitor may assist money laundering (rule 3.3 is an important 'first line of defence' against money laundering. However, the obligations under rule 3.3 and the anti-money laundering legislation are separate, and there are good reasons for compliance with rule 3.3 in situations that do not involve money laundering).

The warning notice, which was originally issued in respect of the pre-cursor to rule 3.3 (rule 14.5 of the SRA Accounts Rules 2011), reflects relevant case law, including the decisions in *Fuglers LLP v Solicitors Regulation Authority* [2014] EWHC 179 (Admin) and *Patel v Solicitors Regulation Authority* [2012] EWHC 3373 (Admin).

## 14.3.4 Client money must be kept separate

One of the most important aspects of the SRA Accounts Rules is that the solicitor should keep client money separate from the solicitor's own money.

We have already seen that it is acceptable for the solicitor to mix the money of different clients and third parties in a general client account, although this is provided the solicitor maintains accurate records of how much client money is being held for each client and third party.

However, subject to some limited exceptions, the solicitor is prohibited from mixing client money with the firm's own money in the same bank accounts. The solicitor will operate a business bank account which is separate from the solicitor's client accounts. Inevitably, though, due to circumstances and methods of payment, a limited amount of mixing of business money and client money will occur, but the rules seek to minimise the situations in which this will occur and the length of time over which mixing is permitted. It should be noted that the SRA Accounts Rules 2019 allow the mixing of business money and client money in situations which were not allowed under the 2011 Rules.

We have already seen (in **14.3.2.1**) that there are limited circumstances in which a solicitor does not need to operate a client account, and where certain kinds of client money may be held in another account (eg the firm's business account).

Generally, however, under rule 4.1 a solicitor must keep client money separate from money belonging to the authorised body (ie business money).

A problem arises where the solicitor receives payment from a client which is partly client money and partly business money. This might occur where the client sends the solicitor a sum of money in payment of the solicitor's bill but also in respect of future fees and disbursements. The amount received in payment of the bill is business money; the amount received in respect of future fees and disbursements is client money (rule 2.1(d)).

**EXAMPLE**

Leila is a solicitor and she is acting for Bronwen. Leila has billed Bronwen £400 plus **VAT** (£480 in total).

Bronwen pays £700 to Leila. This is a mixed receipt. £480 of the payment is business money (payment for the bill). The remaining £220 is client money (money on account of future fees and disbursements).

It is likely that the payment by Bronwen has been made electronically and so the payment has been made to a specified bank account. This will either be Leila's business account or, more likely, Leila's client account. Whichever account receives the money, the result will be that business money and client money will be mixed, which would appear to be a breach of rule 4.1.

To address this, rule 4.2 provides that it is acceptable for a solicitor to pay a mixed receipt into either business account or client account, provided that the solicitor allocates funds to the correct account 'promptly'. So, as is likely, if the whole payment is paid into the client account, the business money must be allocated (ie transferred) to the business account promptly. Conversely, although this is less likely, if the whole payment is paid into the business account, the client money must be allocated (ie transferred) to the client account promptly.

This is a sensible rule which reflects modern payment methods, as most payments now are electronic—the solicitor will give the client the details of the bank account to which the solicitor would like the client to transfer the money, and so the money (even if it is a mixed payment) will go into a single bank account.

**EXAMPLE**

Leila instructs Bronwen to transfer the £700 to Leila's general client account and Bronwen does so.

As said, £480 of the £700 payment is business money as it is in payment of the bill, and this £480 does not belong in the client account. Leila must allocate (ie transfer) this £480 to the business account promptly.

As already noted, there is no definition of 'promptly' and the SRA has declined to provide a definition. In this context, under the 2011 Accounts Rules solicitors had up to 14 days after receipt of the money to transfer the solicitor's own money from client account to the solicitor's own account, and this might provide a guide as to what the SRA would regard as prompt action.

Also, under the 2011 Accounts Rules there were (very limited) circumstances in which it was permissible to pay client money into a solicitor's own account. The 2011 Accounts Rules provided that if solicitors wished to pay a mixed receipt into a single account, usually it had to be paid into a client account with a subsequent transfer of the solicitor's own money to the solicitor's own account. The 2019 Accounts Rules have made a significant change, therefore, in permitting the payment of all **mixed receipts** into the business account. However, because solicitors' firms will have accounting practices and systems based on the old Accounts Rules, it is likely that solicitors will continue to pay mixed receipts into the client account rather than the business account. It is also likely to be more prudent to do so, as paying the money into the client account provides better protection for the client money.

Lastly, it is theoretically possible to 'split' a mixed receipt if the payment is made by cheque. The solicitor could instruct their bank to pay part of a cheque into one account and the rest of the cheque into another account. We will look at accounting for mixed receipts and splitting of cheques in **Chapter 15**, although this will rarely now happen in practice. This is because payments by cheque are much less common and also because banks are reluctant to split cheques. With electronic transfers, it would still be open to the solicitor to ask to client to make two payments—one for the amount of the business money to the business account and a second for the amount of the client money to the client account, but this is more cumbersome than receiving one combined payment from the client and then making a subsequent transfer.

## 14.3.5 Payment of the solicitor's costs

Sometimes the solicitor will bill the client for costs and then the client will send the solicitor a payment. However, more often than not the solicitor will be holding client money on account of fees and disbursements, and the solicitor will wish to transfer some or all of this money from client account to business account in order to pay for part or all of the costs.

Under rule 4.3, the solicitor must give the client a bill of costs or other written notification of the costs before the solicitor can transfer client money from the client account to the business account. Any payment must be for the specific sum identified in the bill or other notification of costs, and the solicitor can only transfer the sum required if the solicitor is holding sufficient client money for that client or third party.

Note that rule 4.3 prohibits solicitors from transferring client money to pay for fees and unpaid disbursements before a bill or notification of costs is issued, but does not prohibit solicitors from transferring money from the client account to the business account to reimburse solicitors in respect of paid disbursements. For example, if a solicitor has used their own business money to pay a court fee and then receives money which is paid into the client account, the solicitor should be permitted to transfer money from the client account to the business account to obtain reimbursement for the amount of the court fee without first needing to bill the client for the court fee.

This is because it would not be a transfer of *client* money from the client account to the business account. The definition of 'client money' in rule 2.1(d) only includes money in respect of fees and *unpaid* disbursements, prior to the delivery of a bill. So, if a solicitor receives money from a client, part of which is to cover the cost of a paid disbursement, that part of the money received will be business money not client money. The requirement under rule 4.3 that a bill must be delivered before a transfer can be made does not apply, therefore, because rule 4.3 only regulates transfers of *client* money.

This interpretation of the rules was confirmed by the SRA in guidance issued in September 2020—'Taking money for your costs'. The guidance indicates that rule 5.1(a) allows money for paid disbursements to be transferred from the firm's client account to the business account as the money is being used for the purpose for which it is being held.

However, the SRA also indicates that it would expect the solicitor to explain to the client how and when payments might be made on their behalf from the business account and that the solicitor will then be seeking a reimbursement from the client account in accordance with rule 5.

## 14.3.6 Withdrawals from client account

The SRA Accounts Rules 2019 include restrictions on the withdrawal of client money from a client account.

Rule 5.1 provides that client money can only be withdrawn from a client account:

- for the purpose for which it is being held; or
- following receipt of instructions from the client (or third party); or
- on the SRA's prior written authorisation or in prescribed circumstances.

In most cases, the first point will apply; for example, the solicitor is holding money on account of fees and disbursements in a litigation matter and the solicitor pays a court fee for the client.

Under rule 5.2, all withdrawals from the client account must be appropriately authorised and supervised. Essentially, this means oversight by someone within the firm who has responsibility for compliance with the Rules (eg a manager of the authorised body). SRA guidance indicates that solicitors should establish clear systems and controls for ensuring that persons permitted to authorise the withdrawal of client money from a client account have both an appropriate understanding of the requirements of the Accounts Rules and also sufficient seniority within the firm.

An important rule is rule 5.3, which states that a solicitor may only withdraw client money from a client account if there are sufficient funds being held for the particular client or third party to make the payment. Because the solicitor will pay all or most of the client money received from all clients and third parties into a general client account, there will usually always be sufficient monies in the general client account to make a payment out of it. However, the solicitor has to be careful that the payment for a particular client or third party is made out of money received from that particular client or third party, otherwise the solicitor will find that they have used other people's money to make the payment.

**EXAMPLE**

Imran is a solicitor and he is acting for Peter. Peter paid Imran £500 on account of costs and disbursements.

Imran pays a court fee of £650 for Peter and the payment is made out of the general client account. Imran will have breached rule 5.3 because Imran has made a payment out of the client account of £650 yet he was only holding £500 of Peter's money. This means Imran has used £150 of other clients' money to make this payment on Peter's behalf.

**CONDUCT POINT**

Solicitors should have systems and procedures for checking there is sufficient client money held for a client before making a payment on behalf of a client.

## 14.3.7 Duty to correct breaches on discovery

Many of the Accounts Rules are aimed at preventing solicitors from breaching the Rules. However, what happens if a breach occurs (perhaps inadvertently)? What should the solicitor do when the breach is discovered and how quickly must the solicitor act to remedy the breach?

Rule 6.1 provides that any breach must be corrected promptly on discovery. As already mentioned, there is no definition of 'promptly' and the SRA has refused to provide a strict definition. Therefore, there is no set time period within which the breach must be remedied. In general terms, it is probably fair to say that a breach should be remedied as soon as possible once the breach is discovered.

Often the breach will involve client money being withheld from a client account improperly or client money being withdrawn from a client account improperly. Rule 6.1 provides that the remedy in those cases would be to pay the client money into the client account or replace the client money that has been withdrawn, and in each case this must be done 'immediately'. Where client money needs to be replaced, the solicitor will usually have to use business money to replace the client money that had been withdrawn improperly.

**EXAMPLE**

Continuing the above example, Imran has paid a court fee of £650 for the client, Peter, but had only been holding £500 of Peter's money. Imran has therefore used £150 of other clients' money, in breach of rule 5.3.

Imran should correct the breach promptly on discovery. He should immediately replace the £150 of client money that has been improperly withdrawn from the client account by transferring £150 from the business account to the client account.

### 14.3.8 Payment of interest

Under rule 7.1, a solicitor should account to a client or third party for a fair sum of interest on any client money held on their behalf, although it is possible under rule 7.2 to come to a different arrangement with the client or third party.

The payment of interest is covered in more detail in **16.5**.

### 14.3.9 Client accounting systems and controls

Rule 8.1 provides that the solicitor should maintain certain records which are:

- accurate;
- contemporaneous (ie transactions should be recorded as and when they are made); and
- chronological (ie the records should be in date order).

Under rule 8.1, the solicitor has to maintain the following records:

- a client ledger for each client matter (identified by the client's name and an appropriate description of the matter), showing:
  - all receipts and payments of client money on the client side of the ledger; and
  - all receipts and payments of other money (ie essentially the firm's business money) and bills of costs on the business side of the ledger;
- a list of all the balances on the client ledger accounts showing the liabilities (ie amounts owed) to clients and third parties; and
- a 'cash book' showing the running total of all transactions through client accounts held or operated by the solicitor (NB: rule 8.1 does not require a solicitor to maintain a cash book showing the running total of all transactions through business accounts, but a solicitor will maintain one as well, as this is good practice).

It may be hard to understand what rule 8.1 requires a solicitor to do without seeing the form of ledger accounts themselves. Essentially, rule 8.1 requires the solicitor to have a separate client ledger for each matter and that client ledger must have two sections, or sides—a client side and a business side. By convention, as we will see in **Chapter 15**, the business side of the ledger appears on the left, and the client side appears on the right. You will see the format of these ledger accounts in **15.3.3**.

Rule 8.1 also requires a solicitor to maintain a cash book for any client accounts. Although those client accounts will most likely be bank accounts, and the bank will provide bank statements periodically to the solicitor, the solicitor cannot rely upon those bank statements as a record and must write up their own cash book showing the total of all transactions affecting the firm's client bank accounts. As said previously, although there is no requirement in the Rules for the solicitor to have a cash book showing the transactions in the firm's business bank accounts, the solicitor will still prepare such a cash book. We will see in **15.3.2** that the client and business cash books are combined into one account (called the Cash account in **Chapters 15** and **16**), again with a business section on the left side and a client section on the right side.

In addition to the above, the following checks and records are required:

1 At least every five weeks, the solicitor must obtain statements (from banks, building societies and other financial institutions) for all client accounts and for all business accounts (rule 8.2).

2 For all client accounts, the solicitor must undertake a reconciliation (ie a check), at least every five weeks between, first, the balances shown on those bank or building society statements and, secondly, the balances shown in the solicitor's own accounting records (ie the balance in the cash book *and* the total of the balances on the client ledger accounts). This reconciliation must be signed off by the firm's COFA (Compliance Officer for Finance and Administration) or one of the firm's managers. Any differences in the balances shown by the reconciliation should be investigated promptly (rule 8.3).

3 There should be a readily accessible central record of the solicitor's bills or other notifications of costs (rule 8.4).

The SRA has also issued guidance on keeping accurate client accounting records. Much of this guidance reflects what is said in the Rules and also accepted business practice. For example, the guidance suggests that the firm prepares ledger accounts using double entry bookkeeping principles. (We will look at these principles in **Chapter 15**.)

One matter mentioned in SRA guidance, but which does not appear in the Rules, is that solicitors should keep separate records of inter-ledger transfers (these transfers are discussed in **15.6.2**).

The guidance acknowledges that most firms will have computerised accounting records, and notes that firms will need to consider issues of accessibility to those records with physical controls (eg passwords and PIN numbers) that reduce the risk of a cyber-attack which could result in the loss of client money.

The full wording of the guidance ('Helping you keep accurate client accounting records') is available on the SRA website.

### 14.3.9.1 Acting for a borrower and an institutional lender

When a solicitor is acting for the buyer of residential property, they will frequently also act for the lender of the buyer. Usually, the lender is a reputable and established lender, such as a building society.

The solicitor therefore has two clients and, when the solicitor receives the mortgage advance from the lender just prior to completion of the purchase, the solicitor will be holding client money which belongs to the lender as well as any other client money the solicitor is holding for the buyer.

As the solicitor has two clients, there is a question over whether the solicitor has to open two separate client ledger accounts—one for the buyer and one for the lender.

Under the 2011 SRA Accounts Rules, the position was crystal clear. Rule 29.10 of the 2011 Rules provided that the solicitor need not open two client ledgers but could use just one client ledger, provided the lender was an institutional lender which provided mortgages in the normal course of its business (which would be the case with a bank or building society) and provided the funds belonging to each client were clearly identifiable.

Unfortunately, the 2019 SRA Accounts Rules, perhaps in an effort to make the rules as simple as possible, indicate in rule 8.1 that there is an obligation to record client money in separate client ledgers but fails to specify what happens in the case of a buyer and a lender. There is no equivalent of the old rule 29.10. Does this mean that the solicitor will have to open a separate client ledger account for the lender?

If so, this is not a very practical approach. The old rule 29.10 worked very well, and there are practical problems associated with having to create a new client ledger for the lender. It would make preparing financial statements and checking and moving funds before completion more difficult. There are also issues accounting for the costs of acting for the lender, especially as the buyer usually pays for the work undertaken by the solicitor for the lender.

Advice received from the SRA telephone helpline in November 2019 was that rule 8.1(a) merely confirms the position and is not inconsistent with the old rules, it only simplifies them. Solicitors can still record mortgage advances on the one client ledger in the same way as they previously did under the old rule 29.10. The 2019 Rules now only require that a clear audit trail can be identified. It is therefore up to solicitors' firms to decide if they wish to continue recording the mortgage advance on the client ledger or whether they want to open a separate ledger.

However, it is hoped that the SRA will provide written guidance on this issue to clarify that the absence of a specific rule covering the situation does not prevent solicitors from continuing to use one ledger for the borrower and institutional lender.

## 14.4 Dealings with other money belonging to clients or third parties

As we have seen, not all solicitors have to operate a client account. We have seen that a solicitor can hold client money in a business account in limited circumstances, and if that is the only client money held by the solicitor then the solicitor does not have to operate a client account.

However, there are other ways in which the money of clients might be managed.

The three methods referred to in the Accounts Rules are:

- operating a joint account with a client or third party;
- operating the client's own bank account; and
- using third party managed accounts to hold clients' money.

The first two methods of managing the money of clients are usually specific to particular client matters, with the solicitor holding the money of their other clients in a general client account. In the case of third party managed accounts (see **14.4.3**), though, the method can be an alternative to the solicitor operating a client account at all.

We will look at each method in turn in the following sections.

### 14.4.1 Operation of joint accounts

Occasionally, a solicitor might be one of the holders of a joint account. This might happen, for example, where the solicitor is one of the executors of the deceased and the other executor is a lay person. The money of the estate does not have to be placed in a client account but could be held in an account in the joint names of the solicitor and the other executor.

Many of the rules which apply to client money will not apply to money which is held in such a joint account. Rule 9.1 provides that Part 2 of the Rules does not apply to such an account, but it is still necessary to comply with rule 8.2 and obtain statements at least every five weeks from the bank, building society or other financial institution where the account is held. It is also necessary to comply with rule 8.4 and maintain a central record of bills or other notification of costs.

Guidance produced by the SRA warns that those named on the joint account will have equal access to the account, and so the risks to a client's money could be higher than if the money were kept in the solicitor's client account. The guidance indicates that the solicitor will need to consider in each case the risks to the client's money and any actions the solicitor could take to mitigate those risks. For example, the guidance suggests making sure that the account has a joint signature mandate (ie that both holders of the account have to sign to make withdrawals and payments to avoid one of the joint holders acting unilaterally).

### 14.4.2 Operation of a client's own account

There may also be situations in which the solicitor will be operating a client's own bank or building society account; that is, the solicitor will be a signatory on that account and will be able to make payments and withdrawals from that account. This is most likely to occur in a situation where the client lacks the necessary mental **capacity** to operate their own account, and where the solicitor has been appointed as an attorney under a lasting power of attorney (or enduring power of attorney), or where the solicitor has been appointed as a deputy by the Court of Protection.

In each case, there will be reasons why it will be preferable for the solicitor to operate the client's own account rather than putting the client's money into one of the firm's client accounts.

Some, but not all, of the SRA Accounts Rules apply to the client's own account which is operated by the solicitor as a signatory. Rule 10.1 provides that most of Part 2 of the Rules (which largely deal with requirements for client money and for client accounts) does not apply. It is still necessary to obtain statements from banks, building societies and other financial institutions at least every five weeks (under rule 8.2). It is also necessary to complete reconciliations under rule 8.3 and to keep a central record of bills or other notification of costs under rule 8.4.

However, under guidance issued by the SRA, the SRA recognises that solicitors might not be able to obtain monthly statements in order to comply with rules 8.2 and 8.3. The SRA has indicated that it will not regard the solicitor as being in breach if the solicitor takes reasonable steps to record—and satisfy themselves—that the client's money is not at risk, and to record the position. Guidance indicates that a solicitor should keep a separate record of the transactions carried out in respect of the client's own account.

## 14.4.3 Third party managed accounts

A major change in recent years, reflected in the 2019 Accounts Rules (and rule 11 in particular), is that solicitors can now decide to utilise 'third party managed accounts' (TPMA) to manage receipts and payments of the client's money. TPMAs are bank or building society accounts operated by third party companies that provide a facility for the management of the client's money, and are an alternative to the solicitor managing the client's money through a client account. The TPMA provider should be regulated by the Financial Conduct Authority (FCA). Any money held in a TPMA will not be 'client money' and so will not be subject to the requirements of the SRA Accounts Rules 2019 which relate to 'client money'.

If a solicitors' firm uses TPMAs and the firm does not itself hold any client money, the firm will not have to operate one or more client bank accounts and many of the requirements of the SRA Accounts Rules 2019 will not apply to the firm. This is because most of the provisions of the Rules are intended to protect client money that is in the hands of the firm in a client account.

The rules on payment of interest on client money only apply to client money which the solicitor is holding (or should be holding) in a client account. If the client's money is in a TPMA, the provisions on payment of interest in the Rules do not apply. Obviously, though, the contractual arrangement reached with the TPMA provider must not result in the solicitor breaching the SRA Principles or Codes of Conduct. In particular, Principle 7 is to act in the best interests of the client, and para 4.2 of the SRA Code of Conduct for Solicitors, RELs and RFLs and para 5.2 of the SRA Code of Conduct for Firms provide that the solicitor or firm must safeguard money and assets entrusted to them by clients and others.

Under rule 11.1(b) of the SRA Accounts Rules 2019, the solicitor should take reasonable steps to ensure, before accepting instructions, that the client is informed of and understands the contractual arrangements relating to the use of the TPMA, including how the TPMA provider's fees will be paid and by whom. Clients should also be informed of their right to terminate the agreement and how to dispute payment requests made by the solicitor to the TPMA.

Under rule 11.2, the solicitor must obtain regular statements from the TPMA provider and check those statements to ensure that they accurately reflect all transactions on the account.

Any contractual arrangement reached with a TPMA should take into consideration the question of payment of interest to the client by the TPMA where it is appropriate. As the payment of any such interest would be by the TPMA not by the solicitor, and as the client's money is not being held by the solicitor, the solicitor will not prepare ledger accounts in respect of this money. However, the solicitor should ensure that the money in the TPMA is only used for its designated purpose, as well as maintaining an overview of the transactions on the account and keeping appropriate records to reflect this.

Also, although the solicitor does not need to obtain permission from the SRA to use a TPMA, the solicitor must inform the SRA if a TPMA is to be used, and provide the SRA with details of each TPMA provider.

The SRA has issued guidance on the selection of TPMA providers and the use of TPMAs. Although you do not need to know the detail of this for the SQE, the guidance is available on the SRA website.

## 14.5 Accountants' reports and storage and retention of accounting records

Part 4 of the Rules deals with the question of accountants' reports, and most of the rules in that part relate to the obtaining and delivery of those reports. Part 4 also deals, very briefly, with the storage and retention of accounting records.

### 14.5.1 Obtaining and delivery of accountants' reports

There are rules requiring solicitors' firms to obtain an **accountant's report** and there is also a requirement to deliver certain accountants' reports to the SRA. Most solicitors' firms will need to obtain an accountant's report although it will not always be necessary to deliver the report to the SRA.

An accountant's report provides an important independent check on whether a solicitors' firm is complying with the Accounts Rules. It is a report by a suitably qualified accountant following an examination by the accountant of the accounting records of the solicitors' firm. Under rule 12.8, the solicitors' firm must provide the accountant with details of all bank or building society accounts held or operated by the firm along with all information and documentation that the accountant requires to enable completion of the report.

The accountant will either issue an 'unqualified report', which indicates that no breaches of the Accounts Rules have been discovered, or a 'qualified report', which indicates that some breaches of the Rules have occurred. Some breaches of the Rules will be minor ones and will not mean that there is any risk to client money, but other breaches will be serious ones and these are the breaches that the SRA want to know about.

Only certain accountants are eligible to produce a report. Rule 12.5 provides that the report must be prepared and signed by an accountant who is a member of a specified chartered accountancy body (these bodies are specified in the Glossary to the SRA Standards and Regulations). In addition, the accountant must be, or work for, a registered auditor. Under rule 12.6, the SRA may disqualify an accountant from preparing a report if the accountant has been found guilty of professional misconduct or if the SRA is satisfied that the accountant has failed to exercise due care and skill in the preparation of a report.

#### 14.5.1.1 Obtaining accountants' reports

Under rule 12.1, a solicitors' firm has to obtain an accountant's report if it has, at any time during the accounting period:

- held or received client money; or
- operated a joint account; or
- operated a client's own account as signatory.

(It follows that if the firm does not do any of the above, and the money belonging to clients is managed using third party managed accounts, then an accountant's report is not required.)

However, rule 12.1 is subject to the exceptions in rule 12.2. A firm will not have to obtain a report where:

- all of the client money held or received was money received from the Legal Aid Agency; or
- the balance of the client money held or received on all accounts (including joint accounts and clients' own accounts) did not exceed an average of £10,000 and a maximum of £250,000 (or the equivalent of these figures in foreign currency).

Where an accountant's report is required, it must be obtained within six months of the end of the accounting period.

Under rule 12.9, the accountant must complete the report in a prescribed form, and under rule 12.7 the SRA may, from time to time, specify the matters to be included in the terms upon which the accountant is engaged.

The SRA has issued guidance for reporting accountants, including key risk areas for accountants to check. You do not need to know the detail of this guidance for the SQE, but for reference it is available on the SRA website.

#### 14.5.1.2 Delivery of accountants' reports

Not all accountants' reports have to be delivered to the SRA. Under rule 12.1(b), it is only necessary to deliver an accountant's report to the SRA if the report is 'qualified', such that it shows a failure to comply with the Rules. Not all breaches of the Rules will result in a qualified report. A report should only be qualified if the breach of the Rules is significant, so that money belonging to clients or third parties is, or has been or is likely to be, placed at risk. The SRA recognises that a firm may make minor breaches of the Rules in the course of practice but such minor breaches (unless persistent and numerous) are not likely to require a qualified report.

The SRA guidance is designed to help reporting accountants assess whether their reports should be qualified. The guidance sets out certain factors categorised into the level of seriousness. The presence of a 'serious' factor (eg evidence the client account is being used improperly as a banking facility, in breach of rule 3.3) is likely to lead to a qualification of the report.

Additionally, rule 12.4 provides for other circumstances in which delivery of an accountant's report will be required. The SRA may require delivery of a report upon reasonable notice if:

- the firm ceases to operate as an authorised body and to hold or operate a client account; or
- if the SRA considers that it is otherwise in the public interest to require the delivery of a report.

Guidance issued by the SRA indicates that it will be necessary to deliver an unqualified report if this is a condition of the solicitor's practising certificate or the firm's authorisation.

Where an accountant's report has to be delivered to the SRA, this must be done within six months of the end of the accounting period.

Reporting accountants also have a duty (under s34 Solicitors Act 1974) to immediately report to the SRA any evidence of theft or fraud in relation to client money, or any concerns which the accountant has over whether a solicitor or firm is fit and proper to hold money for clients or third parties.

### 14.5.2 Storage and retention of account records

Rule 13.1 provides that all accounting records must be stored securely and that they should be retained for at least six years.

**KEY POINT SUMMARY**

- The SRA Accounts Rules 2019 are part of the SRA Standards and Regulations and, like the Codes of Conduct, are rules of professional conduct. Solicitors must comply with the Accounts Rules and can be disciplined for breaches of the Rules. The Rules are principally aimed at protecting client money.
- The Rules apply to 'you' which includes all authorised bodies (law firms and alternative business structures) and the managers and employees of those bodies. This includes partners, solicitors, trainee solicitors and paralegals.
- A solicitor will receive, hold and manage money which belongs to others. This is called 'client money' in the Rules and includes money belonging to clients and to third parties. It is basically any money that does not belong to the solicitor or the firm.
- Most firms will maintain at least one client account and will have a general client account into which they will pay the majority of client money received. A solicitor might also have separate designated client accounts for individual client matters. Any client account must be with a bank or building society in England and Wales and must have the word 'client' in the name of the account. This is to protect the client money in the event of the solicitor's insolvency.
- A solicitor need not maintain a client account where the only client money is in respect of the solicitor's fees and certain disbursements (this will only be useful to a limited number of firms). A solicitor may also choose not to operate a client account but to make arrangements with a third party managed account provider.

- When a solicitor receives client money, the solicitor must pay it into a client account 'promptly'. There are some exceptions where client money may be withheld from a client account.
- Client money must be available on demand, so all client money (or an appropriate proportion) needs to be held on an instant access account.
- The solicitor should return any unused client money to the client as soon as there is no longer any proper reason to hold the funds (usually, at the end of the legal transaction).
- A solicitor must not provide banking facilities via a client account. The client money held by a solicitor must be related to an underlying legal transaction and there must be a proper connection between the holding of the money and the regulated services provided by the solicitor. A solicitor is not regulated to hold funds (as is a bank) and there are risks if the client is or becomes insolvent, and there is a risk of assisting the client or third party to launder the proceeds of crime.
- A solicitor must keep client money separate from money which belongs to the solicitor. Client money will be kept in a separate bank account (the client account) although there are limited circumstances in which client money may be paid into the firm's business account. For example, mixed receipts may be paid into either the business account or the client account, with the money being allocated to the correct account subsequently by means of a transfer. Usually, though, mixed receipts will be paid into the client account rather than into the business account.
- A solicitor may not transfer client money from a client account to pay for the solicitor's fees and unpaid disbursements before a bill is issued. However, money in respect of a disbursement that has already been paid is not client money and so money can be transferred from the client to the business account in reimbursement even before a bill is issued.
- There are restrictions on withdrawals from a client account and withdrawals must be properly authorised and supervised. A solicitor should not make a payment of client money for a client unless the solicitor is holding sufficient monies for that client.
- Breaches of the Rules must be corrected promptly on discovery. This includes replacing client money which has been improperly withdrawn from a client account with the firm's own business money.
- A solicitor should account for a fair sum of interest on client money held.
- The Rules provide that the solicitor should maintain accurate, contemporaneous and chronological accounting records. These include separate client ledgers for each client matter, a list of client ledger balances and a cash book for all transactions through client accounts. A solicitor should also obtain bank statements and undertake a reconciliation at least every five weeks, and maintain a central record of bills issued.
- Not all money belonging to clients will be held in client accounts. A solicitor might hold an account jointly with a client or may operate the client's own bank account as a signatory. A solicitor may also decide to make arrangements with a third party managed account (TPMA) provider.
- The SRA requires most firms to obtain an accountant's report within six months after the end of each accounting period. A report will be required if the firm holds client money (or operates certain other accounts), although a report will not usually be required if a firm has held relatively small amounts of client money or the only client money is received from the Legal Aid Agency.
- The solicitor will also have to deliver the accountant's report to the SRA within six months of the end of the accounting period if the report is qualified by the accountant. A report will be qualified if the accountant discovers serious or persistent breaches of the Rules.

# CHAPTER 15
# Accounting Records and Basic Transactions

**FUNCTIONING LEGAL KNOWLEDGE**

This chapter covers the following functioning legal knowledge required to pass the SQE 1 assessments:

**Solicitors' Accounts:**

- **client money**:
  - requirement to pay client money into a **client account**
  - repayment
  - accounting **entries** required
- client account:
  - withdrawals and accounting entries required

**Requirement to keep client money separate from money belonging to the authorised body**

**Requirement to keep and maintain accurate records in client ledgers to include:**

- transfers
- accounting entries required

**AUTHORITIES UNDERPINNING PRACTICE**

The following rules underpin this area of practice:

- The SRA Accounts Rules 2019
  **https://www.sra.org.uk/solicitors/standards-regulations/accounts-rules/**

## 15.1 Introduction

In **Chapter 14** we considered the provisions of the SRA Accounts Rules 2019 without considering accounting entries for recording transactions.

In this chapter and in **Chapter 16** we will look at the system of accounting used by solicitors, and will consider the most common accounting entries made by solicitors in respect of client money and in respect of the firm's own money (which we will call '**business money**').

In this chapter we will look at **double entry bookkeeping** and at the format of the **ledger accounts** used by solicitors. Then, we will consider the accounting entries needed for the receipt and payment of money, and for two very different types of transfer.

In **Chapter 16** we will look at the accounting entries in relation to **costs** and **disbursements**, the payment of interest on client money and some miscellaneous transactions.

## 15.2 Double entry bookkeeping

The modern system of double entry bookkeeping was developed by Italian merchants in the 15th century. It is based upon a simple foundation of recording money that is owed to the merchant and money that the merchant owes to someone else.

A person who owed money to the merchant was called a 'debitor'—the modern word is 'debtor'. A person to whom the merchant owes money was called a '**creditor**'—we still use this word today.

In simple (if not simplistic) terms, the merchant had a big book called a 'ledger'. This book had blank pages and the merchant would use the book, or ledger, to record sums owed to the merchant and sums owed by the merchant. Sums owed to the merchant (by 'debitors') were recorded with **debit entries** in the left-hand column, and sums owed by the merchant (to creditors) were recorded with **credit entries** in the right-hand column.

From this foundation, debits and credits were used to record other things—cash receipts, cash payments, income, expenses—so that every aspect of business accounting could be recorded using a system of debits and credits.

The idea behind double entry bookkeeping is that there are always two aspects to every transaction. For example, if a client pays money to a solicitor and the solicitor puts that money into the firm's general client account, there are two separate things that need to be recorded.

The first thing that needs to be recorded is that the solicitor now has some money in its client account that was not there before. So, there needs to be a record of the receipt of this money. This is, under the double entry bookkeeping system, recorded with a 'debit' entry.

The second thing to be recorded is that the solicitor now owes the client some money, because if the solicitor does not use the money for the client's matter, the solicitor will have to pay that money back to the client. The solicitor thus has acquired a creditor—the client—and this is recorded with a 'credit' entry.

We will see how this works in a set of 'ledger accounts' in **15.3**, but these entries can also be written out as follows:

| | | |
|---|---|---|
| Dr | Cash account (client) | £ |
| Cr | Client ledger (client) | £ |

This format of describing ledger entries (rather than writing up the entries in the ledgers themselves) is a useful shorthand method of stating the accounting entries that are needed for a particular transaction. Entries written out in this way are called 'journal entries'.

You will see journal entries throughout the rest of this chapter and **Chapter 16**. Often, the generic journal entries for a particular type of transaction are shown first, followed by an example in which the specific journal entries for that example are shown. This is then usually followed by the ledger accounts showing how the entries would appear in those accounts.

The SQE assessment consists of multiple-choice questions, rather than exercises where you will be required to write up whole ledgers. You are likely to be asked to select which entries are required in a particular situation and so may be shown a short ledger with a series of options to choose from, or be given a list of journal entries and be asked to select the correct option. You should, therefore, be familiar with both journal entries and how entries appear in ledger accounts.

Some important points to remember about double entry bookkeeping:

- there are two aspects to every transaction, so two entries (at least) are required to record any given transaction;
- one of those entries must be a debit and the other entry must be a credit—you cannot have two debits without a credit or two credits without a debit;
- some transactions (eg transferring money from a client account to the business account) require more than two entries (a transfer from a client to the business account requires four entries), but there will always be an even number of entries (ie it has to be a multiple of two)—there can never be an odd number of entries;
- the amount for each of the two double entries must the same, namely if the amount is £100 in one ledger account, the double entry in the other ledger account must also be £100. They can never be different amounts.

We will now look at the form of the ledger accounts and what the accounting entries look like in those accounts.

## 15.3 Ledger accounts

Most businesses will only have one type of ledger account—a simple ledger account. This is because most businesses do not hold money belonging to other people. However, a solicitor will hold client money and will need to keep that money separate from the solicitor's own money. This means that a solicitor will have combined ledger accounts that show business dealings and dealings with client money, as well as having a number of simple ledger accounts.

### 15.3.1 Simple ledger accounts

These simple ledgers record aspects of the solicitor's own business dealings. They are 'business' ledgers and are not used for recording the movement of client money.

A simple ledger account will have a column for the date of the transaction, a column for a description, two columns to record debit (Dr) and credit (Cr) entries, and then a column for the **balance** on the account (the balance could be either a debit balance (DR) or a credit balance (CR)). By convention, debit entries are shown on the left and credit entries on the right.

**Table 15.1** shows a simple ledger.

**TABLE 15.1**

| Name of ledger account | | | | |
|---|---|---|---|---|
| Date | Description | Dr | Cr | Bal |
| | | | | |

### 15.3.2 Cash accounts

Because solicitors hold and use money which belongs to other people (client money), solicitors will need ledgers to record what is happening with the client's money as well as ledgers recording what is happening with the firm's own money (business money).

Rule 8.1(c) of the SRA Accounts Rules 2019 requires that a solicitor should keep a cash book to record the running total of all transactions through client accounts operated by the solicitor. The solicitor cannot rely solely on the bank statements provided by its bank, and the solicitor must have their own records of the movement of client money.

There is no requirement in the Rules to maintain a cash book for business money but a solicitor will also keep a business cash book as this is accepted good practice.

Therefore, the cash book (or Cash account) maintained by the solicitor will record the movement of monies into and out of the solicitor's client and business bank accounts.

The solicitor will have at least one business account which the solicitor will use for a range of purposes connected with running the business. A solicitor will need somewhere to put the **fees** paid by clients, to store the **VAT** that the solicitor has charged its clients and which the solicitor will have to pass on to HMRC, to hold funds which are used to pay the expenses of the business, including the wages and salaries of staff, and the costs of running the office (rent, light, heat, telephone and broadband, computer equipment, office furniture, stationery, insurance).

The solicitor must keep business money separate from client money and so in addition to the business account, the solicitor will also have at least one client bank account. Client money belonging to the solicitor's various clients will flow into and out of the client bank account.

The Cash account will have more columns than a simple ledger account because there will be entries relating to business money and also entries relating to client money. By convention, the business entries will be on the left and the client entries will be on the right. Within each section, the debit entries will be on the left and the credit entries on the right.

**Table 15.2** shows how a Cash account will look.

**TABLE 15.2**

| Cash account | | | | | | | |
|---|---|---|---|---|---|---|---|
| | | Business | | | Client | | |
| Date | Description | Dr | Cr | Bal | Dr | Cr | Bal |
| | | | | | | | |

Strictly, the Cash account is not regarded as a 'ledger account' but for simplicity's sake and ease of reference we will use the term 'ledger accounts' to describe all of the accounts, including the Cash account. However, when we use the term 'client ledger' we are, of course, referring to the ledger account for that particular client matter.

## 15.3.3 Client ledgers

Rule 8.1 of the SRA Accounts Rules 2019 repeats the long-standing requirement in previous sets of Accounts Rules to have a separate ledger account for each client matter.

The client ledger is, basically, a debtor/creditor account. It shows the money that the client owes to the solicitor (the client is then a debtor of the solicitor), and the money that the solicitor owes to the client (the client is then a creditor of the solicitor).

A client might be a debtor of the solicitor because the solicitor has billed the client for the solicitor's legal services and, until the client pays, the client owes money to the solicitor. As the client is a debtor, bills and other monies owed by the client to the solicitor are recorded as debit entries, and usually will lead to a debit balance (showing the total amount that the client owes to the solicitor).

Why then might a client be a creditor of the solicitor? Well, the answer is that the solicitor will often be holding the client's money. For example, a solicitor might ask a client for a sum of money on account of future costs and disbursements. When the client pays this money to the solicitor, the solicitor will pay the client's money into a client account. Although this client money may be used at some point in the future to pay the solicitor's fees or to pay for a disbursement on behalf of the client, until that happens the firm has a liability to the client in respect of that money. If the client's money is not used to pay for something in connection with the client's matter, then the solicitor will have to return the client's money to the client. A liability is an obligation to pay money to someone either now or at some point in the future. This means that the solicitor has a liability to pay the client money back to the client until such time as the money is used for the client's matter. As the solicitor owes money to the client, the client is a creditor of the solicitor. The liability to the client will be recorded with credit entries and will result in a credit balance in the client ledger.

This may seem confusing, but think of your bank statement. Your bank statement is not a cash account—you do not see your bank's cash account, which is elsewhere in the bank's accounting system and contains entries relating to the money of the bank's other clients as well as entries relating to your money. Your bank statement is not your cash account either, although you might treat it like one. If you were, in fact, to write up a proper cash account for yourself, you would have to reverse the debit and credit entries that you see on your bank statement. Instead, your bank statement is a debtor/creditor account, which is part of your bank's accounting system and which is written from the bank's perspective. If there is a credit balance, this means to the bank that you are a creditor—the bank owes you that money. If there is a debit balance (and you are overdrawn), this means to the bank that you are a debtor—you owe money to the bank.

The client ledger is thus the same way round as a bank statement—a debit balance shows the client owes money to the solicitor and a credit balance shows that the solicitor owes money to the client.

However, an important difference between your bank statement and a client ledger is that the client ledger splits the transactions into two: first, those transactions which involve the solicitor's business money (and other business dealings, such as the issuing of a bill) and, secondly, those transactions which involve the use of client money. This is because the SRA Accounts Rules provide that the solicitor must keep client money separate from the solicitor's own money.

Therefore, like a cash account, a client ledger will have more columns than a simple ledger account. Again, this is because there will be entries relating to business ledgers and also entries relating to client money. By convention, the business entries will be on the left and the client entries will be on the right, and within each section the debit entries will be on the left and the credit entries on the right.

A client ledger will therefore look like the example in **Table 15.3**.

**TABLE 15.3**

| Client ledger: client name and description of matter | | | | | | | |
|---|---|---|---|---|---|---|---|
| | | | Business | | | Client | |
| Date | Description | Dr | Cr | Bal | Dr | Cr | Bal |
| | | | | | | | |

## 15.3.4 Example

The following example shows how transactions are recorded in a solicitor's ledger accounts using the double entry bookkeeping method.

**EXAMPLE**

A solicitor acts for three companies—Alpha Ltd, Beta Ltd and Zeta Ltd—in separate litigation matters.

On 15 January, the following transactions occur in relation to the three matters:

1. Alpha Ltd sends the solicitor £1,000 on account of costs and disbursements. This payment is made to the firm's client account.
2. The solicitor pays a court fee of £350 on behalf of Beta Ltd (Beta Ltd had previously provided the solicitor with £750 on account of costs and disbursements so the payment is made from client account.)
3. The solicitor bills Zeta Ltd for £500 plus VAT (£100).
4. Zeta Ltd had previously provided the solicitor with £800 on account of costs and disbursements, and so on 15 January the solicitor also transfers £600 from the client account to the business account to pay for the costs which have been billed.

The above transactions would be recorded in a set of ledger accounts, as shown in **Table 15.4**. The number of the relevant transactions (1)–(4) above is shown in the example ledgers so that you can track the entries that are made in respect of each individual transaction.

For the moment, do not worry about the detail of the entries shown. We will consider each type of accounting entry in detail later in this chapter and also in **Chapter 16**. The important thing for the moment is that you obtain an impression of how the double entries would appear in the ledger accounts of the firm and that a number of different ledger accounts are used.

Remember also that under double entry bookkeeping principles there must be two entries for every transaction. Some transactions (eg transaction (4)—the transfer of £600 from client account to business account) will require a multiple of two entries (with a client to business transfer, the reason for this is explained in **15.6.1**).

**TABLE 15.4**

| Client ledger: Alpha—litigation | | | | | | | |
|---|---|---|---|---|---|---|---|
| | | Business | | | Client | | |
| Date | Description | Dr | Cr | Bal | Dr | Cr | Bal |
| Jan | | | | | | | |
| 15 | Cash: paid by client (1) | | | | | 1,000 | 1,000CR |

| Client ledger: Beta—litigation | | | | | | | |
|---|---|---|---|---|---|---|---|
| | | Business | | | Client | | |
| Date | Description | Dr | Cr | Bal | Dr | Cr | Bal |
| | (Existing balance) | | | | | | 750CR |
| Jan | | | | | | | |
| 15 | Cash: court fee (2) | | | | 350 | | 400CR |

| Client ledger: Zeta—litigation matter | | | | | | | |
|---|---|---|---|---|---|---|---|
| | | Business | | | Client | | |
| Date | Description | Dr | Cr | Bal | Dr | Cr | Bal |
| | (Existing balance) | | | | | | 800CR |
| Jan | | | | | | | |
| 15 | Costs (3) | 500 | | 500DR | | | |
| | VAT (3) | 100 | | 600DR | | | |
| | Zeta: transfer (4) | | 600 | 0 | 600 | | 200CR |

| Cash account | | | | | | | |
|---|---|---|---|---|---|---|---|
| | | Business | | | Client | | |
| Date | Description | Dr | Cr | Bal | Dr | Cr | Bal |
| | (Existing balances) | | | 200,000DR | | | 800,000DR |
| Jan | | | | | | | |
| 15 | Alpha: paid by client (1) | | | | 1,000 | | 801,000DR |
| | Beta: court fee (2) | | | | | 350 | 800,650DR |
| | Zeta: transfer (4) | 600 | | 200,600DR | | 600 | 800,050DR |

Hopefully, you will have noticed that the entries on each client ledger relate to that client's matter only, whereas entries relating to all three clients appear on the Cash account. This is because the Cash account is a general account, recording the receipt and payment of all monies in the business bank account and general client bank account. (NB: the existing balances shown in the Cash account are to reflect the fact that there will be entries in respect of other clients and other matters, not just these clients' files.)

Most of the double entries (for the entries in the client ledgers) will be seen in the Cash account as the transactions in question involve the movement of cash. However, this is not the case for all transactions, as when the solicitor records the issuing of the bill for Zeta Ltd, the double entries will appear not in the Cash account but in two other ledger accounts—Costs, and VAT as shown in **Table 15.5**.

**TABLE 15.5**

| **Costs account** | | | | |
|---|---|---|---|---|
| **Date** | **Description** | **Dr** | **Cr** | **Bal** |
| | (Existing balance) | | | 395,000CR |
| Jan | | | | |
| 15 | Zeta (3) | | 500 | 395,500CR |

| **VAT account (HMRC)** | | | | |
|---|---|---|---|---|
| **Date** | **Description** | **Dr** | **Cr** | **Bal** |
| | (Existing balance) | | | 15,000CR |
| Jan | | | | |
| 15 | Zeta: costs (3) | | 100 | 15,100CR |

Another point to note before moving on is the information included in the description column for each entry. You should note that the description always begins with the name of the *other* ledger account affected by the double entries. So, in the Alpha Ltd client ledger, the description starts with 'Cash'—that is because the other entry appears in the Cash account. And, in the Cash account, the description starts with 'Alpha' to indicate that the other entry appears in the client ledger for Alpha Ltd. This is important because it ensures that the bookkeeper can follow the accounting entries from one ledger to another. Without such information, the accounts would soon become indecipherable. (In practice, the ledgers will be part of a computer system, and ledger numbers, not names, will be used to identify client ledgers for particular files.)

In the rest of this chapter, and in **Chapter 16**, we will consider the accounting entries for a number of different transactions, starting in this chapter with basic receipts and payments, and with transfers.

## 15.4 **Receipts**

When a solicitor receives a payment from a client (we will call these payments *by* the client 'receipts', as we are looking at it from the point of view of the solicitor), the solicitor will need to determine whether or not the money received is client money or business money, or perhaps a mixture of the two.

Receipts of business money from the client will usually occur when the client pays a solicitor's bill, or where the solicitor has paid for a disbursement on behalf of the client and the client is reimbursing the solicitor.

Receipts of client money will include:

- payments by the client of money on account of costs and disbursements (ie in respect of future costs and disbursements)—until a client is billed or a disbursement is paid by the solicitor, the money received by the solicitor is client money (rule 2.1(d));
- sums paid by the client to the solicitor in respect of the client's matter (eg monies for the deposit on a house purchase or an agreed sum under a contract for the purchase of a business); and
- sums received from third parties which belong to the client (eg the settlement monies paid by the other party at the end of a litigation matter or completion monies on the sale of the client's property).

## 15.4.1 Unmixed receipts

To record the receipt of money, whether it is business money or client money, the basic entries are as follows:

| | | |
|---|---|---|
| Dr | Cash account (business *or* client) | £ |
| Cr | Client ledger (business *or* client) | £ |

Note that if the entry in one ledger account is in the business section, the entry in the other ledger account must also be in the business section. Similarly, if the entry in one ledger account is in the client section, the entry in the other ledger account must be in the client section. It is not possible to have an entry in the business section of one ledger account and the double entry in the client section of the other ledger account.

**EXAMPLE**

A solicitor is acting for Lockdown Ltd in a litigation matter. The solicitor has billed Lockdown £500 plus VAT (£600 in total), but is not holding any money on account from the client. Lockdown sends the solicitor a payment of £600 which is sent to the solicitor's business account. This is perfectly proper, as the payment is not client money within the definition in rule 2.1. The money is received on 3 October.

The entries for the receipt of business money will be as follows:

| | | |
|---|---|---|
| Dr | Cash account (business) | £600 |
| Cr | Client ledger (business) | £600 |

The ledgers for the above example would look as shown in **Table 15.6**.

**TABLE 15.6**

| Client ledger: Lockdown—litigation | | | | | | | |
|---|---|---|---|---|---|---|---|
| | | Business | | | Client | | |
| Date | Description | Dr | Cr | Bal | Dr | Cr | Bal |
| | (Existing balance) | | | 600DR | | | |
| Oct 3 | Cash: paid by client | | 600 | 0 | | | |

| Cash account | | | | | | | |
|---|---|---|---|---|---|---|---|
| | | Business | | | Client | | |
| Date | Description | Dr | Cr | Bal | Dr | Cr | Bal |
| | (Existing balances) | | | 410,000DR | | | 985,755DR |
| Oct 3 | Lockdown: paid by client | 600 | | 410,600DR | | | |

*(Note that the existing balances shown above in the Cash account are to reflect the fact that there will be entries in respect of other clients and other matters, not just this client's file.)*

The receipt of client money is very similar in terms of the accounting entries, with the crucial difference that the solicitor is receiving client money which must be paid into the client account. As we saw in **Chapter 14**, there are only limited circumstances in which client money may be paid into the business account.

## EXAMPLE

A solicitor is acting for Mr Wong in respect of the sale of one house and the purchase of another. In response to the solicitor's request, Mr Wong sends the solicitor £500 on account of costs. This is client money (rule 2.1(d)) and the payment is made to the solicitor's general client account. The money is received on 28 February.

The entries for the receipt of client money will be as follows:

| | | |
|---|---|---|
| Dr | Cash account (client) | £500 |
| Cr | Client ledger (client) | £500 |

**Table 15.7** shows the ledgers for the above example.

**TABLE 15.7**

| Client ledger: Mr Wong—sale and purchase | | | | | | | |
|---|---|---|---|---|---|---|---|
| | | Business | | | Client | | |
| Date | Description | Dr | Cr | Bal | Dr | Cr | Bal |
| Feb 28 | Cash: paid by client | | | | | 500 | 500CR |

| Cash account | | | | | | | |
|---|---|---|---|---|---|---|---|
| | | Business | | | Client | | |
| Date | Description | Dr | Cr | Bal | Dr | Cr | Bal |
| | (Existing balances) | | | 345,695DR | | | 1,315,250DR |
| Feb 28 | Mr Wong: paid by client | | | | 500 | | 1,315,750DR |

*(Note that the existing balances shown above in the Cash account are to reflect the fact that there will be entries in respect of other clients and other matters, not just this client's file.)*

### 15.4.2 Mixed receipts

Often the solicitor will receive a payment from the client (or a third party) which is a mixture of client money and business money. For example, this might happen where the client is paying the solicitor's bill and, at the same time, sending the solicitor more money on account of future costs and disbursements. The part of the receipt which relates to the bill will be business money, and is best paid into the business account. However, the part of the receipt which is on account of future costs and disbursements is (under rule 2.1(d)) client money and should be placed into the client account.

One of the aims of the SRA Accounts Rules is to keep client money separate from the solicitor's own money. This is stipulated in rule 4.1. How, then, should a solicitor deal with a mixed payment in order to keep client money separate from business money?

There are in fact three courses of action that the solicitor could take:

1 instruct the solicitor's bank to split the receipt between the business account and the client account so that the business money is paid into the business account and the client money is paid into the client account; or

2 pay the whole receipt into the client account and transfer the business money subsequently to the business account; or

3 pay the whole receipt into the business account and transfer the client money subsequently to the client account.

With modern methods of payment it is rare that the solicitor will be in a position to instruct the bank to split a receipt. Most receipts are now by electronic transfer rather than by cheque, and the electronic transfer will be paid into one account. So, it will only be possible to split the receipt if the client has paid by cheque. The solicitor would send the cheque to the bank and ask the bank to pay part of the money into the business account and part of it into the client account.

However, in most cases the solicitor will not ask for a cheque to be split because the rules allow the whole receipt to be paid into one account (either the client or the business account). Also, banks are very reluctant to split cheques. It is administratively inconvenient for a bank as it creates extra work in tracking the money when the cheque is split between two accounts.

In short, it is very unlikely that you will split receipts in practice: first, because most payments are not by cheque; secondly, because banks may refuse to split a cheque; and, thirdly, because there are acceptable alternative courses of action under the SRA Accounts Rules.

The accounting entries for the solicitor in splitting a cheque are, though, quite simple. The amount owed to the solicitor (ie the business money) is recorded on the business side of the client ledger and cash account, and the remaining money (ie the client money) is recorded on the client side of the client ledger.

**EXAMPLE**

A solicitor is acting for Mrs Noble in a litigation matter. The solicitor has already billed Mrs Noble £300 plus VAT (£360 in total) but is not holding any money on account from the client. Mrs Noble sends the solicitor a cheque for £500. This is a **mixed receipt**, and the solicitor instructs their bank to split the cheque, which the bank agrees to do. The money is received on 25 March.

The entries will be as follows:

| | | |
|---|---|---|
| Dr | Cash account (business) | £360 |
| Cr | Client ledger (business) | £360 |
| Dr | Cash account (client) | £140 |
| Cr | Client ledger (client) | £140 |

**Table 15.8** shows the ledgers for the above example.

**TABLE 15.8**

| **Client ledger: Mrs Noble—litigation** | | | | | | | |
|---|---|---|---|---|---|---|---|
| | | | **Business** | | | **Client** | |
| **Date** | **Description** | **Dr** | **Cr** | **Bal** | **Dr** | **Cr** | **Bal** |
| | (Existing balance) | | | 360DR | | | |
| Mar 25 | Cash: paid by client | | 360 | 0 | | 140 | 140CR |

| **Cash account** | | | | | | | |
|---|---|---|---|---|---|---|---|
| | | | **Business** | | | **Client** | |
| **Date** | **Description** | **Dr** | **Cr** | **Bal** | **Dr** | **Cr** | **Bal** |
| | (Existing balances) | | | 586,000DR | | | 1,745,000DR |
| Mar 25 | Mrs Noble: paid by client | 360 | | 586,360DR | 140 | | 1,745,140DR |

*(Note that the existing balances shown below in the Cash account are to reflect the fact that there will be entries in respect of other clients and other matters, not just this client's file.)*

As said, though, it is very unlikely that you will be splitting receipts in practice. Instead, you are likely to pay the whole amount into either the business account or, more likely, the client account, and then subsequently transfer out the money that should be in the other account.

This is allowed by rule 4.2, which provides that a solicitor must 'allocate promptly' any funds from mixed payments received to the correct client account or business account. So, for example, the solicitor in the previous example could have paid the whole of Mrs Noble's £500 cheque into the client account, even though £360 of that receipt was business money. However, if the solicitor does this, they must 'allocate promptly' the business money to the business account. In other words, the solicitor must transfer the business money from the client account (where it does not belong) to the business account (where it does belong), and the solicitor must do this 'promptly'. There is no definition of 'promptly' in the SRA Accounts Rules 2019 and, as said in **Chapter 14**, the SRA has declined to provide a definition of 'promptly'. Under the 2011 Accounts Rules, the solicitor had 14 days in which to make a transfer in these circumstances so this might provide a guide, but this is far from certain.

If the whole of a mixed receipt is paid into client account and there is a subsequent transfer of business money to the business account, the entries for the transfer will be as shown later in **15.6.1**.

It is less likely that a solicitor will pay the whole of a mixed receipt into the business account and then transfer client money to client account. This is partly because such a course of action was largely prohibited under the 2011 Accounts Rules, so solicitors' firms are likely to have accounting systems and practices that discourage this or even prevent mixed receipts being paid into the business account. It is also arguably safer to put the receipt into the client account first, rather than into the business account first. Problems could arise if the solicitor's firm became insolvent before a subsequent transfer of client money from the business account to the client account could be effected. The solicitor's bank, as one of the solicitor's creditors, might seek to take any money in the business account, and there will be complications if some of this money is, in fact, client money.

We will not, therefore, look at the entries to transfer client money from the business account to a client account, but the entries are essentially the same as the entries made when remedying a breach when a client's cheque has been dishonoured—see **16.6.1**.

## 15.5 **Payments**

A solicitor may make payments out of the business account or out of a client account.

The money in the business account will be used to make payments in connection with the solicitor's business generally, such as payment of wages and salaries to staff, payment of lighting and heating bills, paying rent on the firm's premises and purchasing computer and other equipment. These are the sort of payments that many businesses will have to make.

However, a solicitor will also make payments on behalf of clients, such as paying the fees of counsel (ie a barrister), paying court fees or the cost of search fees in a conveyancing matter. Where possible, such payments ought to be made out of the client account, using client money which the solicitor has obtained from the client on behalf of costs and disbursements. Nevertheless, it may be that the solicitor will have to use business money to make such payments. We will see in **16.4.2** that some disbursements have to be paid from the business account if the 'principal method' of paying for disbursements applies.

As said, the solicitor will also make payments out of the client account using client money that the client has entrusted to the solicitor for the client's matter. It is best practice to obtain funds from the client in advance, on account of costs and disbursements. This is to ensure that the solicitor will be paid for the work they do for the client.

In contentious (ie litigation) matters, there is a statutory right to obtain a reasonable sum on account of costs and disbursements (s65 Solicitors Act 1974), and the solicitor may terminate the retainer if such a sum is not paid by the client within a reasonable time. There is no such statutory right to money on account in non-contentious matters, but the solicitor's terms of business may be such that money on account is required before the solicitor will commence work for the client.

The sorts of payments that are made from a client account include payments of disbursements (eg court fees in a litigation matter) on behalf of the client, payment of sums of money to third parties (eg deposit or completion monies in a conveyancing matter) and payment of any excess client money to the client at the end of the matter.

The entries for making a payment are straightforward, and are as follows:

| | | |
|---|---|---|
| Dr | Client ledger (business *or* client) | £ |
| Cr | Cash account (business *or* client) | £ |

Hopefully, you will see that the entries are the opposite of the entries used for a receipt of monies into one of the two accounts. As with receipts, though, it is not possible to have an entry in the business section of one ledger account and the double entry in the client section of the other ledger account.

Here are two examples. The first shows the entries and ledgers for a payment from the business account, and the second shows the entries and ledgers for a payment from the client account.

**EXAMPLE**

A solicitor is acting for Xedron Ltd in a litigation matter. The solicitor pays a court fee of £350 on 2 August out of the business account.

The entries for the payment of business money will be as follows:

| | | |
|---|---|---|
| Dr | Client ledger (business) | £350 |
| Cr | Cash account (business) | £350 |

**Table 15.9** shows the ledgers for the above example.

**TABLE 15.9**

| **Client ledger: Xedron—litigation** | | | | | | | |
|---|---|---|---|---|---|---|---|
| | | **Business** | | | **Client** | | |
| **Date** | **Description** | **Dr** | **Cr** | **Bal** | **Dr** | **Cr** | **Bal** |
| Aug | | | | | | | |
| 2 | Cash: court fee | 350 | | 350DR | | | |

| **Cash account** | | | | | | | |
|---|---|---|---|---|---|---|---|
| | | **Business** | | | **Client** | | |
| **Date** | **Description** | **Dr** | **Cr** | **Bal** | **Dr** | **Cr** | **Bal** |
| | (Existing balances) | | | 551,500DR | | | 1,145,890DR |
| Aug | | | | | | | |
| 2 | Xedron: court fee | | 350 | 551,150DR | | | |

*(Note that the existing balances shown below in the Cash account are to reflect the fact that there will be entries in respect of other clients and other matters, not just this client's file.)*

**EXAMPLE**

A solicitor is acting for Mrs Green in the sale of a property. Following completion of the sale and after all the work has been finished on the file, there are net sale proceeds of £76,800. The solicitor pays this sum to Mrs Green on 18 May.

The entries for the payment of client money will be as follows:

| | | |
|---|---|---|
| Dr | Client ledger (client) | £76,800 |
| Cr | Cash account (client) | £76,800 |

The ledgers for the above example are shown in **Table 15.10**.

**TABLE 15.10**

| **Client ledger: Mrs Green—property sale** | | | | | | | |
|---|---|---|---|---|---|---|---|
| | | **Business** | | | **Client** | | |
| **Date** | **Description** | **Dr** | **Cr** | **Bal** | **Dr** | **Cr** | **Bal** |
| | (Existing balance) | | | | | | 76,800CR |
| May | | | | | | | |
| 18 | Cash: paid to client | | | | 76,800 | | 0 |

*(continued)*

**TABLE 15.10** *(continued)*

| Cash account | | | | | | | | |
|---|---|---|---|---|---|---|---|---|
| | | Business | | | Client | | | |
| **Date** | **Description** | **Dr** | **Cr** | **Bal** | **Dr** | **Cr** | **Bal** |
| | (Existing balances) | | | 395,879DR | | | 1,276,800DR |
| May 18 | Mrs Green: paid to client | | | | | 76,800 | 1,200,000DR |

*(Note that the existing balances shown below in the Cash account are to reflect the fact that there will be entries in respect of other clients and other matters, not just this client's file.)*

# 15.6 **Transfers**

There are two types of transfer that we are concerned with in this section:

1 transfers of client money from the client account to the business account; and
2 transfers between client ledgers (also known as inter-client transfers).

## 15.6.1 **Transfers of client money to the business account**

As we saw earlier, often a solicitor will obtain money on account of costs from a client. After the solicitor has billed the client for the solicitor's fees, the solicitor will look to transfer money from the client account to the business account in payment of the bill.

Also, we saw that when a solicitor receives a payment from the client that is partly client money and partly business money, the whole receipt is usually placed into the client account and the solicitor will subsequently make a transfer of the business money out of the client account and into the business account.

When recording transactions using the double entry bookkeeping method, normally we have only two entries but occasionally there may be a need for more than two entries. As said before, because we are using the double entry method, there must always be a multiple of two—we can never have an odd number of entries.

A transfer of client money from a client account to the business account is a good example of a situation where we will need more than two entries. This is because there are, in fact, two transactions occurring, not one. The first transaction is taking money out of the client account, and we need two entries to record that. The second transaction is putting the same money into the business account, and we need a further two entries to record that.

In total, the four entries required are as follows:

**(1) Entries to record money being taken out of client account**

Dr Client ledger (client account)

Cr Cash account (client account)

**(2) Entries to record money being put into the business account**

Dr Cash account (business account)

Cr Client ledger (business account)

**EXAMPLE**

A solicitor is acting for Mr Patel. The solicitor has already billed Mr Patel for £400 plus VAT (£480 in total). The solicitor is holding £600 on the client account for Mr Patel, on account of costs and disbursements. On 1 June, the solicitor transfers £480 from the client account to the business account in payment of the bill.

The entries for the client to business transfer will be as follows:

**(1) Entries to record money being taken out of client account**

| | | |
|---|---|---|
| Dr | Client ledger (client account) | £480 |
| Cr | Cash account (client account) | £480 |

**(2) Entries to record money being put into the business account**

| | | |
|---|---|---|
| Dr | Cash account (business account) | £480 |
| Cr | Client ledger (business account) | £480 |

**Table 15.11** shows the ledgers for the above example.

**TABLE 15.11**

| **Client ledger: Mr Patel** | | | | | | | |
|---|---|---|---|---|---|---|---|
| | | | **Business** | | | **Client** | |
| **Date** | **Description** | **Dr** | **Cr** | **Bal** | **Dr** | **Cr** | **Bal** |
| | (Existing balance) | | | 480DR | | | 600CR |
| Jun 1 | Cash: transfer | | 480 | 0 | 480 | | 120CR |

| **Cash account** | | | | | | | |
|---|---|---|---|---|---|---|---|
| | | | **Business** | | | **Client** | |
| **Date** | **Description** | **Dr** | **Cr** | **Bal** | **Dr** | **Cr** | **Bal** |
| | (Existing balances) | | | 750,000DR | | | 3,250,600DR |
| Jun 1 | Mr Patel: transfer | 480 | | 750,480DR | | 480 | 3,250,120DR |

*(Note that the existing balances shown above in the Cash account are to reflect the fact that there will be entries in respect of other clients and other matters, not just Mr Patel's file.)*

## 15.6.2 Transfers between client ledgers

This is the transfer of the record of the firm's liability to the client. The transfer will be made between the client ledger of one client and the client ledger of another client. The transfer is also called an 'inter-client transfer'.

Usually, the transfer is made between two different ledgers opened for the same client but in respect of different matters. For example, a firm might act on behalf of an insurer defending a large number of personal injury claims, and a separate client ledger will be opened for each claim that is defended. Similarly, a solicitor might act for a property developer and will open a separate client ledger for each sale or purchase. Or, the solicitor might be acting for the client in a range of different matters—the client's divorce, drafting the client's will and the client's house purchase: there would be a separate client ledger for each matter even though there is just the one client. Although a transfer between two ledgers opened for the same client might more properly be described as an 'intra-client transfer', we will use the term inter-client transfer to describe any transfer between two client ledgers.

The entries for an inter-client transfer are:

| | |
|---|---|
| Dr | First client ledger (client account) |
| Cr | Second client ledger (client account) |

Note that there are no entries on the Cash account. This is because the money is staying in the same bank account, namely in the firm's general client account. Before the transfer the money is held in the general client account, and the money remains in the general client account after the transfer.

Put another way, no money is transferred when there is an inter-client transfer. What, then, is transferred? The transfer is really just the movement of a record of a liability—moving the record of the liability from one client ledger to another client ledger. The effect of the transfer is that the firm owes that money either (a) to another client or (b) to the same client but in respect of a different matter.

**EXAMPLE**

The solicitor is acting for Mrs Jones in her divorce from, and financial dispute with, her husband. As part of the settlement, the husband pays £50,000 to Mrs Jones's solicitor. On 1 May, Mrs Jones instructs the solicitor to hold £20,000 of the money so that it can be used as a deposit in the purchase of her new home.

The solicitor transfers £20,000 from Mrs Jones's divorce ledger to a ledger opened for Mrs Jones's house purchase.

The entries for the inter-client transfer will be as follows:

| | | |
|---|---|---|
| Dr | Mrs Jones, divorce ledger (client account) | £20,000 |
| Cr | Mrs Jones, purchase ledger (client account) | £20,000 |

Table 15.12 shows the ledgers for the above example.

**TABLE 15.12**

| Client ledger: Mrs Jones—divorce | | | | | | | |
|---|---|---|---|---|---|---|---|
| | | Business | | | Client | | |
| Date | Description | Dr | Cr | Bal | Dr | Cr | Bal |
| | (Existing balance) | | | | | | 50,000CR |
| May | | | | | | | |
| 1 | Mrs Jones—purchase: transfer | | | | 20,000 | | 30,000CR |

| Client ledger: Mrs Jones—purchase | | | | | | | |
|---|---|---|---|---|---|---|---|
| | | Business | | | Client | | |
| Date | Description | Dr | Cr | Bal | Dr | Cr | Bal |
| May<br>1 | Mrs Jones—divorce: transfer | | | | | 20,000 | 20,000CR |

As can be seen, all that has happened is that the liability of the solicitor to the client for the £20,000 has been moved and is now shown in the different client ledger. There has been no movement of the £20,000 cash—that remains in the solicitor's general client bank account.

## KEY POINT SUMMARY

- Solicitors' firms, like other businesses, will use double entry bookkeeping. This is a universal method of bookkeeping which has been used for hundreds of years. In double entry bookkeeping, there are two entries (or a multiple of two entries) for every transaction. With each double entry, one entry will be a 'debit' entry and the other entry will be a 'credit' entry.
- These debit and credit entries are made in a series of ledger accounts. There are simple ledger accounts, recording aspects of the solicitor's business (eg costs, VAT, **bad debts**, **petty cash**). The solicitor will have Cash account ledgers to show receipts into and payments from the business bank account and client bank accounts. The solicitor will also maintain a client ledger for each client matter, which will show the amounts owed by the client to the solicitor and the amounts owed by the solicitor to the client. With both the Cash account and the client ledgers, there are separate columns for business entries and for client money.
- Receipts of money are recorded with a debit entry in the relevant Cash account and a credit entry in the relevant side of the client ledger.
- Some receipts will be mixed, including money belonging to the solicitor (business money) and client money. Most receipts are electronic and will be paid into the one account. Even if a cheque is received, it is likely this will be paid into the one account. Where a mixed receipt has been paid into one account, the money that does not belong in that account should be transferred to the correct account promptly. It is usual to pay mixed receipts into client account and to transfer out any business money. Alternatively, a solicitor could ask the bank to split a cheque between two accounts, but banks are reluctant to do this.
- Payments of money by the solicitor are recorded with a credit entry in the relevant Cash account and a debit entry in the relevant side of the client ledger. As a matter of good practice, a solicitor should obtain money on account of costs and disbursements from the client, so that client money can be used to pay disbursements where this is possible.
- The solicitor will often have to make entries in respect of transfers from one account to another. However, there are two very different types of transfer. The first is an actual transfer of money from one bank account to another (usually this is transferring money from a client account to the business account). The other type of transfer is a nominal one, where a balance (or part of one) is transferred from one client ledger to another client ledger. This is merely moving the record of the solicitor's liability to the client and does not involve the movement of cash from one bank account to another.

# CHAPTER 16
# Costs and Disbursements, Payment of Interest and Other Transactions

**FUNCTIONING LEGAL KNOWLEDGE**

This chapter covers the following functioning legal knowledge required to pass the SQE 1 assessments:

**Solicitors' Accounts:**

- **client money**:
  - circumstances in which client money may be withheld from a **client account**
  - accounting entries required

**Interest:**

- requirement to pay interest on client money
- accounting entries required

**Breach of the SRA Accounts Rules:**

- duty to correct breaches of SRA Accounts Rules promptly on discovery
- accounting entries required

**Requirement to keep and maintain accurate records in client ledgers, including requirement to keep a record of bills to include:**

- **disbursements** using the **agency** and **principal methods**
- submission, reduction and payment of bills including the VAT element
- accounting entries required

**AUTHORITIES UNDERPINNING PRACTICE**

The following rules underpin this area of practice:

- The SRA Accounts Rules 2019
  **https://www.sra.org.uk/solicitors/standards-regulations/accounts-rules/**

## 16.1 Introduction

In this chapter we will look at the accounting entries that are used to record the issuing of a bill, payment of the bill by the client, reductions in a bill and what happens when it is known that a client will not pay and the bill is written off. We will also look at the accounting treatment of disbursements (payments made by the solicitor on behalf of the client). A key aspect of the accounting treatment of **costs** and disbursements is **value added tax** (VAT), and so we will note some important aspects of the VAT system first, before moving on to the entries relating to costs and disbursements.

We will then look at the solicitor's obligation to pay interest to a client on the client's money held by the solicitor, and the accounting entries required. Lastly, we will consider the accounting entries in a number of other transactions.

As with **Chapter 15**, when accounting entries are discussed, these are stated in 'journal **entry**' form first. An example is then given, with the journal entries that would be used in the situation in that example. The example is then continued by showing what the ledger entries would look like in the relevant **ledger accounts**.

As mentioned in earlier chapters, for the SQE assessment you will not have to write up whole ledgers (as was the case on the Legal Practice Course). For this reason, there are no exercises for you to do. You will simply need to be able to answer multiple-choice questions on the ledger entries in the SQE assessment.

Also, in the office you are very unlikely to be writing up the ledger accounts yourself. You will not have to do **double entry bookkeeping** in practice, therefore. This is usually done by the firm's accounting software. The firm may also have specialist accounts staff who monitor and operate the firm's accounting systems. As a fee earner, you will normally only see the client ledgers on your computer screen, so when you are shown ledgers in this chapter your main focus should be on what is happening in the client ledgers, because it is the client ledgers that you really need to understand: the other ledgers are, though, also shown, to give you a complete picture and so that you have an idea about the double entries made elsewhere in the firm's accounts.

## 16.2 Value added tax

VAT is a tax which is payable on the taxable supply of goods and services by a business that is registered for VAT.

The supply of most goods and services are taxable, although some supplies are exempt from VAT (eg education, healthcare services). Other supplies, whilst taxable, are taxed at 0 per cent (these are called zero-rated supplies and include many types of food and other items, such as children's clothing, which the government wish to keep as affordable as possible).

A business must be registered for VAT, broadly, if its taxable supplies in a year exceed the figure for compulsory registration for VAT. Currently, the registration threshold is £85,000. It is also possible to register voluntarily even if the business's taxable supplies are below this figure. This registration figure is quite low (it is the value of the supplies that is considered, not the profit made by the business) so most businesses, and virtually all solicitors' firms, will be registered for VAT.

The standard rate of VAT, which applies to most supplies, is 20 per cent. (There is a rate of 5 per cent but this applies to a limited range of supplies, including domestic fuel and children's car seats.)

When a business charges VAT to a customer or client, the business must issue a VAT invoice with certain prescribed information.

The VAT that a business charges to its customers is called '**output tax**'. Basically, the business is acting as a collection agency for HMRC, because at the end of each three-month period ('quarter') the business must pay the VAT that it has collected from its customers (ie the output tax) to HMRC.

However, the business may deduct '**input tax**' from its output tax before making this payment to HMRC. The business's input tax will be the VAT that the business has paid to its suppliers on the goods and services that the business has purchased (eg computer and office equipment in the case of a solicitors' firm).

The amount of output tax should exceed the amount of input tax, and it is only the difference (ie the excess output tax) that the business has to pay to HMRC.

For example, a business has output tax of £15,000 for the VAT quarter, but has input tax of £5,000 for the same quarter. The input tax is deducted from the output tax and it is only the difference, namely £10,000, that has to be paid to HMRC.

A business will account for VAT using a VAT ledger account which will look as shown in **Table 16.1**.

**TABLE 16.1**

| VAT account (HMRC) | | | | |
|---|---|---|---|---|
| **Date** | **Description** | **Dr** | **Cr** | **Bal** |
| | | | | |

The business's output tax will be recorded by a series of credit entries on the right-hand side of the ledger and the business's input tax will be recorded by a series of debit entries on the left-hand side. As the output tax is likely to exceed the input tax, there should be a credit **balance** at the end of the VAT quarter, and it is that amount which is payable to HMRC.

In the vast majority of cases, businesses must submit the VAT return online. Businesses can use HMRC's free online service. Alternatively, a business can sign up for the 'Making Tax Digital for VAT' scheme which has certain advantages but the business will need to purchase compatible accounting software to use it.

## 16.3 **Costs**

Virtually all solicitors will be registered for VAT and will charge their clients VAT on the supply of services provided by the solicitor. Information about costs should make it clear to the client that **fees** quoted are exclusive of VAT (eg the cost of making a standard will is quoted at £200 plus VAT). If this is not made clear, a quoted price will be treated as the VAT-inclusive price. Supplies of services by solicitors are standard-rated so the VAT rate is 20 per cent.

Solicitors will issue clients with bills, stating the amount of the solicitors' fees, the VAT charged on the solicitors' fees and any disbursements (and any VAT charged on the disbursements). The solicitor's bill is a VAT invoice, and if the client is themselves a business they can treat the VAT paid to the solicitor as part of the client's input tax.

Strictly, the term 'costs' is defined in the Glossary to the SRA Standards and Regulations as the solicitor's fees *and* disbursements. However, the term 'costs' is often used to indicate the solicitor's fees and it is in this sense that we will use it in this section. Disbursements will be dealt with separately in **16.4**.

### 16.3.1 **Issuing bills**

In order to receive payment from a client for the services that the solicitor has provided, the solicitor should first issue a bill. This will show the charges or fees of the solicitor for professional services (often also called 'costs' or 'profit costs'), the VAT that the solicitor is charging on those fees and any disbursements paid on the client's behalf (and, if relevant, any VAT due on those disbursements).

As we have seen in **Chapter 14**, rule 4.3 provides that the solicitor must first give a bill of costs (or other written notification of the costs) to the client before transferring any client money from the client account to the business account in respect of fees and unpaid disbursements.

We will be considering disbursements in **16.4**, so for the moment we are only concerned with the solicitor's own fees, namely the charges for the work that the solicitor has undertaken on behalf of the client.

What are the accounting entries when a solicitor issues a bill?

There will, in fact, be four entries—one set of double entries to record the fee element of the bill, and another set of double entries to record the VAT element of the bill.

In total, the four entries required are as follows:

**(1) Entries to record the fee element of the bill**

| | | |
|---|---|---|
| Dr | Client ledger (business) | £ |
| Cr | Costs account | £ |

**(2) Entries to record the VAT element of the bill**

| | | |
|---|---|---|
| Dr | Client ledger (business) | £ |
| Cr | VAT account | £ |

## EXAMPLE

On 12 June, a solicitor bills the client (Mr Khan) £200 plus VAT for the preparation of the client's will. The VAT is £40.

The entries will be as follows:

**(1) Entries to record the fee element of the bill**

| | | |
|---|---|---|
| Dr | Client ledger (business) | £200 |
| Cr | Costs account | £200 |

**(2) Entries to record the VAT element of the bill**

| | | |
|---|---|---|
| Dr | Client ledger (business) | £40 |
| Cr | VAT account | £40 |

The fee earner looking at the client ledger on their computer will see two debit entries for a bill on the business side of the client ledger—one **debit entry** for the fee element of the bill and a second debit entry for the VAT.

The credit entries appear in two new ledger accounts that we have not encountered before. In **Chapter 15** we concentrated on entries that affected the client ledger and Cash account, or two client ledgers. Now, we must put entries in other ledgers. These are:

1 The Costs account—this is the ledger which is used to show the amounts which the solicitor has billed to each client. It forms a record of the bills issued, and at the end of the accounting period the balance on the Costs account will be used in the final accounts of the solicitor for that accounting period (in the Profit and Loss account).

2 The VAT account—this is the ledger which records the liability of the solicitor to HMRC in respect of the VAT that the solicitor collects from clients. The VAT charged to clients is the solicitor's 'output tax' and is recorded as a **credit entry** on the right-hand side of the ledger. The VAT which the solicitor pays to suppliers is the solicitor's 'input tax' and is recorded as a debit entry on the left-hand side of the ledger.

As we have seen, the solicitor will deduct the input tax from the output tax and it is only the excess (ie the difference between output tax and input tax) that will be payable to HMRC at the end of the VAT quarter.

The ledgers for the above example are shown in **Table 16.2**.

**TABLE 16.2**

**Client ledger: Mr Khan—preparation of will**

| | | Business | | | Client | | |
|---|---|---|---|---|---|---|---|
| **Date** | **Description** | **Dr** | **Cr** | **Bal** | **Dr** | **Cr** | **Bal** |
| Jun | | | | | | | |
| 12 | Costs | 200 | | 200DR | | | |
| | VAT | 40 | | 240DR | | | |

*(continued)*

**TABLE 16.2** *(continued)*

| Costs account | | | | |
|---|---|---|---|---|
| **Date** | **Description** | **Dr** | **Cr** | **Bal** |
| | (Existing balance) | | | 475,000CR |
| Jun 12 | Mr Khan | | 200 | 475,200CR |

| VAT account (HMRC) | | | | |
|---|---|---|---|---|
| **Date** | **Description** | **Dr** | **Cr** | **Bal** |
| | (Existing balance) | | | 12,500CR |
| Jun 12 | Mr Khan: costs | | 40 | 12,540CR |

*(Note that there are existing balances on both Costs and VAT accounts as these ledgers are used to record transactions in respect of other clients, not just Mr Khan.)*

## 16.3.2 Payment of bills

When a bill is paid there will either be a payment by the client which will go into the business account, or there will be a transfer of client money already held by the solicitor from the client account to the business account. We saw the process of a client-to-business transfer in **15.6.1**, but how would a payment direct from the client be reflected?

Traditionally, clients would pay by cheque but this is now rare and usually payment will be made by electronic transfer.

When the bill is paid, there will be an entry in the cash account (business account) to record receipt of the money, and there will be an entry in the client ledger (business) to show that the client has paid (and that the client no longer owes money to the firm).

Note that there are no entries made in the Costs account or in the VAT account when the bill is paid. Why is this?

- There is no entry in the Costs account, because as said earlier, the Costs account is a record of the amounts which clients have been billed during the accounting period. The solicitor wants to know the total amount of all of the bills that they have issued during that accounting period. If entries were made on the Costs account every time a bill was paid, the Costs account would only end up showing the total of the bills that were still unpaid at the end of the accounting period. For this reason, there is no entry made on the Costs account when a bill is paid.
- As for VAT, the solicitor needs to work out how much VAT needs to be paid to HMRC at the end of the VAT quarter. As we have seen, this will be the total of the VAT charged to clients (the output tax), less the amount of VAT paid to suppliers (the input tax). Regarding the output tax, the amount of VAT payable to HMRC is based on the amount of VAT charged to clients. Subject to what is said in **16.3.4** on **bad debts** and VAT bad debt relief, the VAT charged by solicitors is payable to HMRC *whether or not* the solicitor has been paid the VAT by the client. As the VAT account is recording the indebtedness of the solicitor to HMRC, it does not make sense to make an entry in the VAT account when the client pays the VAT to the solicitor.

The entries on the payment of a bill (assuming there is a direct payment from the client, rather than a client-to-business transfer) are as follows:

| | | |
|---|---|---|
| Dr | Cash account (business) | £ |
| Cr | Client ledger (business) | £ |

**EXAMPLE**

Taking the above example, on 16 June Mr Khan pays the bill by electronic transfer to the solicitor's business bank account.

The entries will be as follows:

| | | |
|---|---|---|
| Dr | Cash account (business) | £240 |
| Cr | Client ledger (business) | £240 |

**Table 16.3** shows the ledgers for the above example.

**TABLE 16.3**

| Client ledger: Mr Khan—preparation of will | | | | | | | |
|---|---|---|---|---|---|---|---|
| | | **Business** | | | **Client** | | |
| **Date** | **Description** | **Dr** | **Cr** | **Bal** | **Dr** | **Cr** | **Bal** |
| Jun | | | | | | | |
| 12 | Costs | 200 | | 200DR | | | |
| | VAT | 40 | | 240DR | | | |
| 16 | Cash: paid by client | | 240 | 0 | | | |

| Cash account | | | | | | | |
|---|---|---|---|---|---|---|---|
| | | **Business** | | | **Client** | | |
| **Date** | **Description** | **Dr** | **Cr** | **Bal** | **Dr** | **Cr** | **Bal** |
| | (Existing balances) | | | 600,000DR | | | 2,125,451DR |
| Jun | | | | | | | |
| 16 | Mr Khan: paid by client | 240 | | 600,240DR | | | |

## 16.3.3 Reduction of bills: abatements

Occasionally, a solicitor will agree to reduce a bill that has already been issued. This might be in response to concerns which the client has raised about the amount of the bill. A solicitor's bill may be assessed (and possibly reduced) by the court, but we are not concerned with assessment of costs by the court here. In this section we are concerned with the situation where the solicitor reduces a bill voluntarily.

Why would the solicitor agree to a reduction in the bill? This does not seem to make good business sense. The reason is to keep clients coming back to the solicitor. It is a 'goodwill' gesture to ensure that the client instructs the solicitor in future. Reducing the bill may mean the client will recommend the solicitor to others rather than complain about the solicitor to other, potential, clients or to the Legal Ombudsman.

Because the bill has already been issued by the solicitor, it will be necessary to adjust the bill and this adjustment is called an '**abatement**'. If there is an abatement, the solicitor will also have to adjust the accounting records by making appropriate entries.

The accounting entries for an abatement are very simple. They are, basically, the exact reverse of the entries made initially when the bill was issued. You should know what entries are needed to record the issuing of the bill, and so it should be easy for you to remember the entries needed to record an abatement.

Four entries will be needed, two for the adjustment of the fee element of the bill and two for the adjustment of the VAT element of the bill.

The four entries are as follows:

**(1) Entries to record the fee element of the abatement**

| | | |
|---|---|---|
| Dr | Costs account | £ |
| Cr | Client ledger (business) | £ |

**(2) Entries to record the VAT element of the abatement**

| | | |
|---|---|---|
| Dr | VAT account | £ |
| Cr | Client ledger (business) | £ |

**EXAMPLE**

On 1 December, the solicitor billed Mrs Smith £2,500 plus VAT (£500) in respect of her divorce. Mrs Smith complains about the amount of the bill and the solicitor agrees to an abatement of £300 plus VAT. The abatement is recorded on 8 December.

The entries to record the abatement will be:

**(1) Entries to record the fee element of the abatement**

| | | |
|---|---|---|
| Dr | Costs account | £300 |
| Cr | Client ledger (business) | £300 |

**(2) Entries to record the VAT element of the abatement**

| | | |
|---|---|---|
| Dr | VAT account | £60 |
| Cr | Client ledger (business) | £60 |

The ledgers for the above example are shown in **Table 16.4**.

**TABLE 16.4**

**Client ledger: Mrs Smith—divorce**

| | | Business | | | Client | | |
|---|---|---|---|---|---|---|---|
| **Date** | **Description** | **Dr** | **Cr** | **Bal** | **Dr** | **Cr** | **Bal** |
| Dec | | | | | | | |
| 1 | Costs | 2,500 | | 2,500DR | | | |
| | VAT | 500 | | 3,000DR | | | |
| 8 | Costs: abatement | | 300 | 2,700DR | | | |
| | VAT: abatement | | 60 | 2,640DR | | | |

| Costs account | | | | |
|---|---|---|---|---|
| **Date** | **Description** | **Dr** | **Cr** | **Bal** |
| | (Existing balance) | | | 350,000CR |
| Dec | | | | |
| 1 | Mrs Smith | | 2,500 | 352,500CR |
| 8 | Mrs Smith: abatement | 300 | | 352,200CR |

*(Note that, obviously, it is likely that other bills would have been issued between 1 December and 8 December, but they are not shown here for the sake of simplicity.)*

| VAT account (HMRC) | | | | |
|---|---|---|---|---|
| **Date** | **Description** | **Dr** | **Cr** | **Bal** |
| | (Existing balance) | | | 9,800CR |
| Dec | | | | |
| 1 | Mrs Smith: costs | | 500 | 10,300CR |
| 8 | Mrs Smith: abatement | 60 | | 10,240CR |

*(Note, similarly, that there would have been other entries in the VAT account between 1 December and 8 December, but they are also not shown for the sake of simplicity.)*

### 16.3.4 **Writing off costs: bad debts**

Unfortunately for the solicitor, not every client will pay the solicitor's bill. Some clients will be unable to do so through becoming insolvent, other clients may simply refuse to pay and it may not be worth the solicitor taking legal proceedings against the client to recover the fees.

This is a good reason to obtain money on account of costs and disbursements from the client at the outset of a matter and as the matter progresses. The solicitor is then holding client money in the client account which can be used to pay any bill which the solicitor issues. The solicitor simply has to transfer money to the business account in order to pay the bill.

If, though, the solicitor does not have money on account and it appears to the solicitor that a client will not be able to, or will almost certainly not be able to, pay a bill, the solicitor should write off the bill as a bad debt. Entries will be needed in the solicitor's accounting records to reflect the fact that the debt has gone bad and has been written off.

Adjustments will be made to the client ledger where the issuing of the bill had been recorded. An entry will also have to be made to a separate ledger account used to record bad debts. Unlike an abatement, no entry is made on the Costs account because the set of final accounts at the end of the accounting period will show the total of the Costs account as part of the solicitor's income for the accounting period, and the total of the Bad Debts account as one of the solicitor's expenses for the accounting period.

The entries relating to VAT will differ depending on whether or not VAT bad debt relief is available. In simple terms, VAT bad debt relief is only available if the bill was issued at least six months before the bill is written off. If the bill is written off sooner than that, VAT bad debt relief will not be available when the bill is written off but can be claimed subsequently.

We will show the entries where the bill is written off within six months of the date of the bill, as this is the most likely scenario.

Assuming the bill is written off within the first six months, the entries will be:

| | | |
|---|---|---|
| Dr | Bad debts account | £ *(the full amount of the bill)* |
| Cr | Client ledger (business) | £ *(the full amount of the bill)* |

Note that the whole of the bill is written off (ie the fee element *and* the VAT element, and these elements are not separated at this stage).

Subsequently, when the six-month period (from the date of the bill) has expired, the solicitor can claim VAT bad debt relief. This is done by reducing the amount of VAT that the solicitor is due to pay to HMRC in a future VAT quarter, and works by posting a debit entry for the amount of the VAT to the VAT account. At the same time, the Bad Debts account is reduced by the amount of the VAT, because at the end of the accounting period the solicitor will only count the VAT *exclusive* amount of the bill (ie the fee element only).

When VAT bad debt relief is claimed, the entries will be:

| | | |
|---|---|---|
| Dr | VAT account | £ (*the VAT element of the bill only*) |
| Cr | Bad debts account | £ (*the VAT element of the bill only*) |

**EXAMPLE**

On 23 January, a solicitor bills Garth Ltd for £500 plus VAT (£100) in respect of litigation, but the solicitor fails to obtain money on account from the company. On 7 March, the solicitor learns that the company has gone into liquidation and the solicitor writes the bill off. The bill is £600 in total (fees of £500 plus VAT of £100).

The entries to record the bad debt will be:

| | | |
|---|---|---|
| Dr | Bad Debts account | £600 |
| Cr | Client ledger (business) | £600 |

Subsequently, following the expiry of the six-month period from the date of the bill, the solicitor claims VAT bad debt relief in respect of the VAT of £100. The solicitor does this on 1 August, and the entries will be as follows:

| | | |
|---|---|---|
| Dr | VAT account | £100 |
| Cr | Bad Debts account | £100 |

**Table 16.5** shows the ledgers for the above example (note that both stages are shown).

**TABLE 16.5**

| Client ledger: Garth Ltd—litigation | | | | | | | |
|---|---|---|---|---|---|---|---|
| | | Business | | | Client | | |
| Date | Description | Dr | Cr | Bal | Dr | Cr | Bal |
| Jan | | | | | | | |
| 23 | Costs | 500 | | 500DR | | | |
| | VAT | 100 | | 600DR | | | |
| Mar | | | | | | | |
| 7 | Bad debts | | 600 | 0 | | | |

| Bad Debts account | | | | |
|---|---|---|---|---|
| **Date** | **Description** | **Dr** | **Cr** | **Bal** |
| | (Existing balance) | | | 8,000DR |
| Mar | | | | |
| 7 | Garth Ltd | 600 | | 8,600DR |
| Aug | | | | |
| 1 | VAT: bad debt relief | | 100 | 8,500DR |

*(Note that, obviously, it is likely that other bills would have been written off between 7 March and 1 August, but they are not shown here for the sake of simplicity.)*

| VAT account (HMRC) | | | | |
|---|---|---|---|---|
| **Date** | **Description** | **Dr** | **Cr** | **Bal** |
| | (Existing balance) | | | 15,750CR |
| Aug | | | | |
| 1 | Bad debts: bad debt relief | 100 | | 15,650CR |

## 16.4 Disbursements

Disbursements are sums which the solicitor pays on behalf of the client in the course of dealing with the client's matter.

Disbursements are defined in the Glossary to the SRA Standards and Regulations as 'any costs or expenses paid or to be paid to a third party on behalf of the client or trust (including any VAT element) save for office expenses such as postage and courier fees'.

Disbursements range from court fees in litigation proceedings, to search fees in conveyancing transactions, to **probate** fees or the cost of **statutory advertisements** in the administration of an estate. There are many other types of disbursement. The solicitor can charge the client for such items in addition to charging for the solicitor's own professional services.

As can be seen from that definition, some items which the solicitor has to pay for, such as the cost of postage, printing or travel to see the client or to attend court, are not regarded as disbursements which the solicitor can charge for separately. Instead, the solicitor is meant to include the costs of such items when setting the fee for professional services. So, the cost of these items is not itemised on the solicitor's bill to the client. Instead, the solicitor will charge a fee that takes into account the cost to the solicitor of such items.

Some disbursements are not subject to VAT, for example court fees and probate fees. However, other disbursements are subject to VAT. Types of disbursement which attract VAT include the services of a barrister ('counsel') or of an expert. The barrister or the expert will charge a fee and, as with the solicitor's own fees, the barrister or expert will charge VAT on top. For example, a barrister delivers a written opinion to the solicitor and charges the solicitor £600 plus VAT (so £720 in total).

### 16.4.1 Disbursements for VAT purposes

Unfortunately, the VAT rules relating to disbursements are very complicated and recent case law has cast doubt on traditional practices for dealing with disbursements and introduced considerable uncertainty for solicitors.

Due to the VAT rules, the solicitor will have to consider carefully how to deal with and account for disbursements. This is because the meaning of a disbursement for VAT purposes is, seemingly, narrower than the accepted, traditional view of what is a disbursement.

If an item of expenditure is treated as a disbursement under VAT rules, the solicitor can obtain reimbursement from the client without the solicitor having to charge the client VAT on the amount of the disbursement.

If, though, the item of expenditure is not treated as a disbursement under VAT rules, the solicitor will have to treat the cost of the expenditure as part of the expense to the solicitor of providing professional services to the client. If the solicitor wishes to cover the cost of this expenditure from the client, the solicitor will have to bill the client for the expenditure as part of the solicitor's professional fees, and the solicitor will have to charge the client VAT on the expenditure.

This is contrary to the established business practices of solicitors, particularly in the area of conveyancing where solicitors' firms traditionally have charged the client for a range of search fees without charging VAT on top of those search fees.

Whilst it has been accepted practice not to treat some expenses, such as postage or travel costs, as disbursements, there are many payments made on behalf of a client, like search fees, that have been treated as disbursements.

As a result of recent case law, however, it would seem that in many cases the solicitor should be treating search fees as part of the cost of the solicitor's professional services, and should be charging VAT on top of the cost of the search fees. The solicitor can do this in one of two ways:

1 increasing the fees charged for the solicitor's professional services to ensure that the solicitor recovers sufficient money from the client to cover the solicitor's expenditure; or
2 itemising the expenditure in the solicitor's bill so that the client is charged for the amount of the expenditure.

Whichever option is chosen, the net result is that the client will end up paying for the amount of the disbursement and a further 20 per cent VAT on the amount of the disbursement. This interpretation is thus likely to make legal services more expensive for clients. It has to be wondered whether this is just an attempt by HMRC to increase the amount of VAT paid into the government's coffers!

In the case of *Brabners LLP v HMRC* [2017] UKFTT 666 (TC), HMRC successfully persuaded the First-tier Tribunal that solicitors should be charging their clients VAT on the cost of electronic searches obtained in conveyancing matters for the clients. This was on the basis that the search costs were part of the solicitor's professional services and could not therefore be regarded as a disbursement for VAT purposes. The First-tier Tribunal reached this decision despite the existence of a concession from HMRC that solicitors could treat postal searches (ie searches made by post rather than electronically) as disbursements.

The First-tier Tribunal accepted HMRC's argument that the electronic searches were undertaken in order to allow the solicitors to provide their professional services to the client. Put another way, the solicitor did not merely pass the results of the searches on to the client, but instead the solicitor evaluated the results of the searches and provided advice to the client based on those results.

This line of reasoning was supported by the Court of Appeal in an *obiter* statement in *British Airways v Prosser* [2019] EWCA Civ 547, when it was said that an item of expenditure could not be regarded as a disbursement for VAT purposes if the solicitor acted as 'more than a postbox' for the client.

The Law Society has disputed this interpretation of the rules. However, in the absence of a decision from a higher court (remember the Court of Appeal statement in the *Prosser* case was *obiter*), and given the uncertainty caused by the *Brabners* decision, the Law Society in its guidance has cautioned solicitors to consider whether expenditure should be accounted for in accordance with the narrow interpretation of the rules. (This is to avoid HMRC seeking substantial sums in respect of 'unpaid' VAT from firms which have not charged their clients VAT on disbursements.)

Although the *Brabners* decision concerned VAT on electronic searches, in June 2020 HMRC announced that they were withdrawing the concession on postal searches, with effect from 1 December 2020. The result of this is that solicitors have to charge their clients VAT on the cost of all searches, whether obtained electronically or by post.

Having said this, some payments made by solicitors on behalf of clients are accepted as disbursements for VAT purposes by HMRC. These include court fees, probate fees, company incorporation fees, stamp duty land tax (or land transaction tax in Wales) and Land Registry registration fees.

The solicitor is able to make these payments on behalf of the client and seek reimbursement from the client without having to charge VAT on top.

## 16.4.2 **Methods of accounting for disbursements subject to VAT**

In this section we will look at the situation where the solicitor pays a disbursement where the supplier of the service has charged VAT on the supply. This would be relevant to the services of a professional, such as counsel or an expert. It could also be relevant to a search fee or other payment on which the supplier had charged VAT (VAT is charged on some search fees, such as enquiries of a local authority (CON29 and CON29O) but not on others, such as a local land charge search (LLC1)).

Where a disbursement contains a VAT element (ie where the supplier has charged VAT), there are two methods of accounting for the payment of the disbursement by the solicitor. These two methods are known as the 'agency method' and the 'principal method'.

### 16.4.2.1 Agency method

The basis of the agency method is that the solicitor is simply making a payment on behalf of the client, namely the solicitor is acting as the **agent** of the client. The agency method will apply when the invoice of the supplier is addressed to the client rather than to the solicitor. Although the supplier is charging VAT on the service, the supply of services is to the client not to the solicitor. The client is the person who is liable to pay the invoice, not the solicitor, so the solicitor is just acting on the client's instructions to make the payment to the supplier on the client's behalf.

Usually, this payment will be using the client's money as the client will have provided the solicitor with monies on account of costs and disbursements. However, the agency method can still be used if the payment is made using the solicitor's own money.

When the agency method applies, the accounting records will show one set of double entries. The VAT-inclusive amount is shown (ie the total cost which includes the VAT). There is no need to separate the fee element of the disbursement and the VAT element of the disbursement. Using the agency method, the payment can be made from the client account or from the business account. Obviously, it is better for the solicitor to have obtained sufficient money on account of costs and disbursements from the client in order to make the payment using the client's money rather than the solicitor's own money.

The entries for payment of a disbursement using the agency method are:

| | | |
|---|---|---|
| Dr | Client ledger (client *or* business) | £ |
| Cr | Cash account (client *or* business) | £ |

**EXAMPLE**

The solicitor is acting for Mr George in a claim over a defective conservatory. The solicitor has already obtained £1,000 from Mr George on account of costs and disbursements. The solicitor instructs an expert to give a structural report on the conservatory, and the expert submits the report together with an invoice for £600 plus VAT. The expert's invoice is addressed to the client, Mr George. The solicitor pays the expert on 21 September, using the agency method, and making the payment from the client account. (The total cost of the expert's report is £600 plus VAT of £120 = £720).

The entries will be as follows:

| | | |
|---|---|---|
| Dr | Client ledger (client) | £720 |
| Cr | Cash account (client) | £720 |

The ledgers for the above example would look as shown in **Table 16.6**.

**TABLE 16.6**

| Client ledger: Mr George | | | | | | | |
|---|---|---|---|---|---|---|---|
| | | Business | | | Client | | |
| Date | Description | Dr | Cr | Bal | Dr | Cr | Bal |
| | (Existing balance) | | | | | | 1,000CR |
| Sep 21 | Cash: expert's fees | | | | 720 | | 280CR |

| Cash account | | | | | | | |
|---|---|---|---|---|---|---|---|
| | | Business | | | Client | | |
| Date | Description | Dr | Cr | Bal | Dr | Cr | Bal |
| | (Existing balances) | | | 215,620DR | | | 1,245,900DR |
| Sep 21 | Mr George: expert's fee | | | | | 720 | 1,245,180DR |

## 16.4.2.2 Principal method

Conversely, if the supplier's invoice is addressed to the solicitor, then usually the principal method has to be used. This is because under the VAT system the supply of services is being made to the solicitor. The solicitor must therefore make the payment out of the solicitor's business account and cannot use client money. Also, the solicitor must treat the VAT element of the supply of services as part of the solicitor's input tax, and record this in the firm's VAT ledger.

Of course, the solicitor is only making the payment because the solicitor is undertaking work for the client, and ultimately the client will have to pay the cost of the disbursement. But, for this to happen, the solicitor will have to *re-supply* the services to the client and the solicitor does this by billing the client for those services. In other words, the solicitor has to issue a bill to the client, charging the client for the same services. This may be on a bill which also includes charges for the solicitor's own fees or may be done separately.

It is important to realise that the principal method is a product of the VAT system and it is the VAT rules which determine whether the solicitor can use the agency method or has to use the principal method. The accounting treatment of these disbursements is determined by the VAT rules not by the SRA Accounts Rules, and there is nothing in the SRA Accounts Rules about the agency and principal methods.

The accounting entries for the principal method are more complicated than the entries for the agency method. This is because the disbursement is treated as a supply of services to the solicitor, who must then bill the client in order to re-supply the client. It is a bit like the owner of an electrical goods shop who buys a television from the manufacturer and pays VAT to the manufacturer. The owner of the shop then sells the television to a customer and charges VAT to the customer on the same television.

Similarly, if the solicitor engages the services of a barrister ('counsel'), the solicitor will pay VAT to the barrister. The work the barrister has undertaken, though, is for the benefit of the client and so the solicitor will re-supply the barrister's services to the client by billing the client, and will then charge the client VAT on the barrister's services.

There are two sets of accounting entries therefore:

- when the solicitor pays the disbursement; and
- when the solicitor bills the client for the disbursement.

## Principal method: paying the disbursement

The payment has to be made from the solicitor's business account because the invoice is addressed to the solicitor and the solicitor is the person liable for the disbursement not the client. There will be entries, therefore, recording a payment from the firm's business account and there will be an entry in the VAT account to note the 'input tax' that the solicitor has paid.

There are four entries needed at this point and these will be as follows (it is better here to show the two credit entries first and then the two debit entries):

| | | |
|---|---|---|
| Cr | Cash account (business) | £ (for the fee element of the disbursement) |
| Cr | Cash account (business) | £ (for the VAT element of the disbursement) |
| Dr | Client ledger (business) | £ (the fee element of the disbursement) |
| Dr | VAT account | £ (the VAT element of the disbursement) |

This is difficult to understand without an example:

### EXAMPLE

A solicitor is acting for Drainflex Ltd in a contractual dispute. The solicitor has obtained £2,000 from the company on account of costs and disbursements. The solicitor instructs a barrister ('counsel') to give an opinion on the prospects of a successful claim, and counsel submits the opinion together with counsel's fee note of £700 plus VAT. The solicitor pays counsel using the principal method. This is done on 30 November.

The entries will be as follows:

| | | |
|---|---|---|
| Cr | Cash account (business) | £700 |
| Cr | Cash account (business) | £140 |
| Dr | Client ledger (business) | £700 |
| Dr | VAT account | £140 |

**Table 16.7** shows the ledgers for the above example (it is best here to show the Cash account first).

**TABLE 16.7**

| Cash account | | | | | | | |
|---|---|---|---|---|---|---|---|
| | | Business | | | Client | | |
| Date | Description | Dr | Cr | Bal | Dr | Cr | Bal |
| | (Existing balances) | | | 188,900DR | | | 987,455DR |
| Nov | | | | | | | |
| 30 | Drainflex: counsel's fee | | 700 | 188,200DR | | | |
| | VAT: counsel's fee for Drainflex | | 140 | 188,060DR | | | |

*(There have to be two separate entries in the Cash account because the double entry for part of the payment to counsel is in the client ledger and the other double entry is in a different account, the VAT account. Note the additional description in the second entry, to identify the particular client.)*

*(continued)*

**TABLE 16.7** *(continued)*

| **Client ledger: Drainflex Ltd** | | | | | | | |
|---|---|---|---|---|---|---|---|
| | | **Business** | | | **Client** | | |
| **Date** | **Description** | **Dr** | **Cr** | **Bal** | **Dr** | **Cr** | **Bal** |
| | (Existing balances) | | | 0 | | | 2,000CR |
| Nov | | | | | | | |
| 30 | Cash: counsel's fees (VAT of £140) | 700 | | 700DR | | | |

*(Note (1) although the solicitor is holding client money, this cannot be used to make a payment via the principal method; (2) there is a reference to the amount of the VAT in the description even though there is no entry for this amount in the client ledger at this point in time.)*

| **VAT account (HMRC)** | | | | |
|---|---|---|---|---|
| **Date** | **Description** | **Dr** | **Cr** | **Bal** |
| | (Existing balance) | | | 22,300CR |
| Nov | | | | |
| 30 | Cash: counsel's fee for Drainflex | 140 | | 22,160CR |

*(Note the additional description in the entry, to identify the particular client.)*

## Principal method: billing the client

When the solicitor subsequently bills the client for the disbursement, there is one set of double entries:

| | | |
|---|---|---|
| Dr | Client ledger (business) | £ (for the amount of the VAT) |
| Cr | VAT account | £ (for the same amount) |

**EXAMPLE**

The solicitor bills Drainflex Ltd on 9 December. The bill is for the solicitor's own fees of £1,000 plus VAT (£200) and for counsel's fee, which is mentioned above.

There will be the usual entries for the bill in relation to the solicitor's own fees of £1,000, and the VAT on those fees of £200. These entries are not listed below.

The additional entries needed for the VAT on **counsel's fees** will be as follows:

| | | |
|---|---|---|
| Dr | Client ledger (business) | £140 |
| Cr | VAT account | £140 |

The ledgers for the above example would look as shown in **Table 16.8**. (NB: only the client ledger and the VAT account are shown here, although there would also be a credit entry for £1,000 in the Costs account.)

**TABLE 16.8**

| **Client ledger: Drainflex Ltd** | | | | | | | | |
|---|---|---|---|---|---|---|---|---|
| | | **Business** | | | **Client** | | | |
| **Date** | **Description** | **Dr** | **Cr** | **Bal** | **Dr** | **Cr** | **Bal** | |
| | (Existing balances) | | | 0 | | | 2,000CR | |
| Nov | | | | | | | | |
| 30 | Cash: counsel's fees (VAT of £140) | 700 | | 700DR | | | | |
| Dec | | | | | | | | |
| 9 | Costs | 1,000 | | 1,700DR | | | | |
| | VAT: on costs | 200 | | 1,900DR | | | | |
| | VAT: on counsel's fees | 140 | | 2,040DR | | | | |

| **VAT account (HMRC)** | | | | |
|---|---|---|---|---|
| **Date** | **Description** | **Dr** | **Cr** | **Bal** |
| | (Existing balance) | | | 22,300CR |
| Nov | | | | |
| 30 | Cash: counsel's fee for Drainflex | 140 | | 22,160CR |
| Dec | | | | |
| 9 | Drainflex: VAT on costs | | 200 | 22,360CR |
| | Drainflex: VAT on counsel's fee | | 140 | 22,500CR |

*(Note that there would have been other entries in the VAT account between 30 November and 9 December, but they are not shown for the sake of simplicity.)*

### Concessionary treatment for counsel's fees

According to VAT principles, the principal method should be used when paying counsel's fees. However, HMRC have agreed a concession with the Law Society and the Bar so that solicitors can pay counsel's fees using the agency method instead. To take advantage of this concession, the solicitor should amend counsel's fee note by hand, so that the fee note is then addressed to the client. The solicitor should give the amended fee note to the client (so that the client can treat any VAT as the client's input tax). HMRC indicated in August 2021 that this concession was under review, but it still applies as of the time of writing (March 2024).

## 16.5 The requirement to pay interest on client money

Under rule 7.1 of the SRA Accounts Rules 2019, solicitors must account to clients (or to third parties) for a 'fair sum of interest on any client money held ... on their behalf'.

It is possible under rule 7.2 to come to a different arrangement with the client or third party, but there must be a written agreement and the solicitor must provide sufficient information to enable the client or third party to give informed consent.

These are the only provisions of the Accounts Rules which deal with payment of interest on client money. In contrast, the 2011 SRA Accounts Rules, which preceded the 2019 Rules, included a number of very specific rules and were supplemented by detailed guidance. Although the SRA has issued guidance on various aspects of the 2019 Rules, currently there is no issued guidance on the payment of interest on client money.

In determining whether interest should be paid, and also what is a fair sum of interest in a given situation, it may be worth considering some of the rules and guidance which applied before November 2019. Under the 2011 Rules, the solicitor would have to take into account the amount of client money held, and the length of time over which that money was held. It would still make sense to consider these points now even though they are not made explicit in the 2019 Rules.

Similarly, under guidance that accompanied the 2011 Rules, the solicitor had to consider the rates of interest paid by the solicitor's own bank, and usually could not apply the very lowest rate available although it was not necessary to apply the highest rate available.

One rule that has found its way into the 2019 Rules is the stipulation that client money should be readily available. Rule 2.4 of the 2019 Rules provides that a solicitor should ensure that client money is available on demand unless an alternative agreement in writing is reached with the client or third party. This means that client money cannot usually be placed in a deposit account where a long period of notice (say, three months) is required in order to withdraw money. Such deposit accounts typically pay a higher rate of interest than deposit accounts where the account holder can withdraw money on demand: usually, rates of interest on 'on demand' accounts have always been low.

The guidance to the 2011 Rules also indicated that solicitors could adopt a *de minimis* policy. This meant that if the amount of interest was less than a certain amount, then the interest would not have to be paid to the client (or third party). Under a previous set of Accounts Rules, there was a standard *de minimis* provision of £20 which applied to all solicitors' firms. This was changed some years ago when the Rules were changed so that each firm had to have its own written policy on payment of interest and could decide on its own *de minimis* figure, although many continued to use £20 as the *de minimis*. It is likely that a firm will, even now, apply a *de minimis* provision, although this may well be more than £20.

It is also worth noting, as we saw in **Chapter 14**, that solicitors should not be providing banking facilities to clients, as indicated by rule 3.3 of the 2019 Rules. Payments into, and transfers or withdrawals from, a client account must be in respect of delivery by the solicitor of regulated (ie legal) services. Solicitors should not be holding large sums of money for clients over long periods of time, simply in order to provide a place where the client can keep their money or in order to provide the client with interest on that money. A solicitor should only request money from the client in order to undertake the legal work for which the solicitor has been instructed, for example some money on account of costs and disbursements. Alternatively, a solicitor might legitimately ask a client for money for a specific purpose related to the client's instructions, such as payment of stamp duty land tax in England (or land transaction tax in Wales). Even then, the money should only be requested when the anticipated payment is in the near future. As we saw in **Chapter 14**, severe penalties may be applied by the SRA against solicitors who breach this prohibition and who are regarded as having provided banking facilities to clients and others.

As result of this prohibition, generally solicitors will not or should not be holding very large sums of client money for long periods of time and so the situations in which interest should be paid are reduced in number.

At the time the SRA Accounts Rules 2019 came into force, interest rates were at historic lows, and remained so until rates began to rise significantly in 2022. The Bank of England base rate is currently 5.25 per cent. Despite this, unless the amount held by a solicitor is very large and/or is held for a significant period of time, the amount of interest is going to be relatively small. The prohibition against providing banking facilities (which should reduce the number and frequency of times when a solicitor is holding large sums of money for a long time), and the likelihood that all firms will have a *de minimis* provision, means that payments of interest by a solicitor to a client should still occur infrequently, therefore.

We will now consider the two methods for accounting for interest. These are not mentioned in the 2019 Rules but reflect the two ways of paying interest in practice. The two methods are:

1 putting the client's money into a separate designated client account; and

2 holding the client's money in a general client account and calculating a sum in lieu of interest at the end of the matter.

We will now consider each method in turn.

### 16.5.1 Interest on separate designated client accounts

Normally, if the solicitor holds client money and operates a general client account, the solicitor will keep most client money in the one, general client account, and will not put the money of individual clients into separate accounts for each client.

It is possible, though, to have more than one client account. In addition to the firm's general client account, the firm might open a series of other accounts for individual client matters. Under the 2011 Rules, these accounts were called 'separate designated client accounts'. There is no mention of such accounts in the 2019 Rules, but equally there is no prohibition on a solicitor opening more than one client account so it is still possible for a solicitor to operate a general client account and a number of separate designated client accounts for particular client matters.

Opening separate client accounts for particular client matters is perhaps less common than it once was. One reason for opening a separate client account is that a greater sum of interest could sometimes be earned on a separate account, if the account had, say, restrictions on withdrawing money on demand. Although there was an equivalent rule under previous sets of Accounts Rules that client money should be available on demand, this has never been an absolute rule and can be departed from, depending on circumstances. Also, in the 2019 Rules, it is possible to hold client money otherwise than on demand if a written agreement is reached with the client or third party for whom the money is held.

Separate designated client accounts have been more prevalent in situations where the solicitor has no option other than to hold client money for long periods of time. This is the case with the administration of an estate, where the monies should not be distributed to the **beneficiaries** until the **personal representatives** (PRs) are satisfied that all debts, expenses and tax liabilities have been paid. It may not be possible to distribute all monies from the estate because the administration is being held up by, say, the sale of the deceased's house, which may take months or years to achieve. A solicitor acting for the PRs may be holding client money for a considerable period of time and it may be more appropriate to put most of that money into a separate deposit account which attracts a higher rate of interest, leaving sufficient money from the estate in the general client account so there is some client money on demand to meet the day-to-day costs of the administration.

Similarly, if the solicitors are acting for the trustees of a trust, it may be years before the beneficiaries of that trust come of age or reach a specified contingency age. The solicitors might be holding money for several years and, again, it might be appropriate to have separate client accounts for the bulk of the trust's money.

(As against that, the PRs and trustees will have duties of investment and may need to consider investing the money of the estate or trust in a range of investments some of which have potentially higher income than a deposit account at a bank or building society, and/or which have the potential for making capital gains. The bulk of an estate's money or a trust's money might not therefore be held by the solicitor in a client account.)

If the solicitor puts the client's money into a separate designated client account, the process of calculating interest will be very simple. The interest earned on the money in that account will be added to the account by the bank, and the solicitor need do nothing other than to pay the closing balance (which includes the interest earned) to the client when the account is closed. The solicitor does not, therefore, have to calculate the amount of interest because this job is done by the bank where the account is held.

**EXAMPLE**

A solicitor decides to hold a client's money in a separate designated client account rather than in the general client account. The amount invested is £100,000. After six months, the account is closed by which time the bank has paid £1,500 interest on the account. The closing balance is £101,500. The solicitor pays £101,500 to the client.

(Although the above example shows the mechanics of how the separate client account works, you must remember that a solicitor is prohibited from providing banking facilities to a client, under rule 3.3 of the 2019 Rules. In the above example, you would have to wonder at the reason why the £100,000 was being held when the whole amount (plus interest) was simply returned to the client rather than being used in connection with legal services provided to the client.)

The accounting entries related to separate designated client accounts are complex, and vary depending on whether the solicitor puts money directly into the separate account when the money is first received or transfers money that had already been paid into the general client account.

The form of ledger accounts will also vary. As a result of rule 8.1, records of client money (however held) must be maintained. Records need to be made of client money in separate designated client accounts as well as the client money held in the general client account.

These records will require a client ledger in respect of each separate designated client account. This could be a separate client ledger for each account or the main client ledger for the particular client matter could be expanded by adding extra columns to the right-hand side to record client money that is held on deposit. An expanded client ledger would have the columns shown in **Table 16.9**.

**TABLE 16.9**

| Client ledger: Mrs Hussain | | | | | | | | | | |
|---|---|---|---|---|---|---|---|---|---|---|
| | | Business | | | Client | | | Client Deposit | | |
| Date | Description | Dr | Cr | Bal | Dr | Cr | Bal | Dr | Cr | Bal |

However, the examples below show the other approach, which is to have a separate client ledger for the monies on deposit in the separate client account.

It will also be necessary to have a separate Deposit Cash account for each separate designated client account or, alternatively, a separate Deposit Cash account for all client monies held on deposit in the firm's various separate designated client accounts. Again, there could be an entirely separate Deposit Cash account or additional deposit columns could be added to the main Cash account as shown in **Table 16.10**.

**TABLE 16.10**

| Cash account | | | | | | | | | | |
|---|---|---|---|---|---|---|---|---|---|---|
| | | Business | | | Client | | | Client Deposit | | |
| Date | Description | Dr | Cr | Bal | Dr | Cr | Bal | Dr | Cr | Bal |

However, in the following example we will take the approach of having a separate ledger for the Deposit Cash account.

## EXAMPLE

Using the figures mentioned in the previous example, a solicitor receives £100,000 in client money (from Mrs Hussain) on 1 February. Although this is paid into the general client account first, the solicitor decides to keep the client's money in a separate designated client account and transfers the money across on 2 February. The account is closed on 5 August and the bank pays £1,500 interest on the account. The closing balance is £101,500. This sum is transferred back to the general client account on 5 August and the solicitor pays £101,500 to the client on 6 August.

We have already seen the entries required for the receipt and payment of client money in **Chapter 15**, so these are not repeated here. The other entries will be:

**(1) Entries to record the transfer from general client account to the separate deposit account**

| | | |
|---|---|---|
| Dr | Client ledger (client) | £100,000 |
| Cr | Cash account (client) | £100,000 |
| Dr | Deposit cash account (client) | £100,000 |
| Cr | Deposit client ledger (client) | £100,000 |

**(2) Entries to record the payment of the interest by the bank**

| | | |
|---|---|---|
| Dr | Deposit cash account (client) | £1,500 |
| Cr | Deposit client ledger (client) | £1,500 |

**(3) Entries to record the transfer from separate deposit account to the general client account**

| | | |
|---|---|---|
| Dr | Deposit client ledger (client) | £101,500 |
| Cr | Deposit cash account (client) | £101,500 |
| Dr | Cash account (client) | £101,500 |
| Cr | Client ledger (client) | £101,500 |

This is a lot of entries and is quite confusing. It is easier to understand the flow of transactions by looking at the ledger accounts. Hopefully, this is made clearer by showing the two client ledger accounts first, and then the two cash accounts. As said, as a fee earner you will only usually see the client ledgers on your computer screen (you won't see the cash accounts) and you might only see the main client ledger (not the deposit client ledger).

**Table 16.11** shows how the ledgers would look.

**TABLE 16.11**

| Client ledger: Mrs Hussain | | | | | | | |
|---|---|---|---|---|---|---|---|
| | | Business | | | Client | | |
| Date | Description | Dr | Cr | Bal | Dr | Cr | Bal |
| Feb | | | | | | | |
| 1 | Cash: receipt from client | | | | | 100,000 | 100,000CR |
| 2 | Cash: transfer to deposit account | | | | 100,000 | | 0 |
| Aug | | | | | | | |
| 5 | Cash: transfer from deposit account | | | | | 101,500 | 101,500CR |
| 6 | Cash: paid to client | | | | 101,500 | | 0 |

*(continued)*

**TABLE 16.11** *(continued)*

| Deposit client ledger: Mrs Hussain | | | | | | | |
|---|---|---|---|---|---|---|---|
| | | Business | | | Client | | |
| Date | Description | Dr | Cr | Bal | Dr | Cr | Bal |
| Feb | | | | | | | |
| 2 | Deposit cash: transfer from general client account | | | | | 100,000 | 100,000CR |
| Aug | | | | | | | |
| 5 | Deposit cash: interest paid by bank on deposit | | | | | 1,500 | 101,500CR |
| | Deposit cash: transfer to general client account | | | | 101,500 | | 0 |

*(Note that in the Cash accounts below all other transactions, for other clients, are ignored for the sake of simplicity. There are therefore no existing balances shown.)*

*Remember that this first Cash account shows the position in the general client account in the 'Client' columns.*

| Cash account | | | | | | | |
|---|---|---|---|---|---|---|---|
| | | Business | | | Client | | |
| Date | Description | Dr | Cr | Bal | Dr | Cr | Bal |
| Feb | | | | | | | |
| 1 | Mrs Hussain: receipt from client | | | | 100,000 | | 100,000DR |
| 2 | Mrs Hussain: transfer to deposit account | | | | | 100,000 | 0 |
| Aug | | | | | | | |
| 5 | Mrs Hussain: transfer from deposit account | | | | 101,500 | | 101,500DR |
| 6 | Mrs Hussain: paid to client | | | | | 101,500 | 0 |

*This second 'Deposit' Cash account shows the position in respect of sums held on separate designated client accounts in the 'Client' columns.*

| Deposit cash account | | | | | | | |
|---|---|---|---|---|---|---|---|
| | | Business | | | Client | | |
| Date | Description | Dr | Cr | Bal | Dr | Cr | Bal |
| Feb | | | | | | | |
| 2 | Mrs Hussain deposit: transfer from general client account | | | | 100,000 | | 100,000DR |
| Aug | | | | | | | |
| 5 | Mrs Hussain deposit: interest paid by bank on deposit | | | | 1,500 | | 101,500DR |
| | Mrs Hussain deposit: transfer to general client account | | | | | 101,500 | 0 |

Do not worry if you cannot remember all of this, as it is unlikely that questions in the SQE will be on the detail of the transactions shown in the above example.

Also, although the above example has been provided to show how interest on a separate designated client account is recorded, in practice solicitors should avoid situations where they may be seen to be providing banking facilities to clients. As already indicated, it would not usually be appropriate to accept a deposit of £100,000 from a client for a six-month period when there is no obvious underlying legal transaction.

## 16.5.2 **Interest on money held in general client account**

More usually, the solicitor will put a client's money into the general client account. As we have seen, this is a bank account which is holding the money of most (if not all) of the client money entrusted to the solicitor. Also, as we have seen, although the money of many clients is mixed in one account, the accounting records kept by the solicitor (in particular the client ledgers) keep track of how much money belongs to each client.

However, this presents a problem if a solicitor has to account for interest to a client. If the money is held on general client account, it will only be a small part of a much larger balance in that account, and any interest paid by the bank to the solicitor will be on the whole balance in the account. The solicitor will therefore need to work out the amount of interest that the client's money would have earned if it had been put into a separate account. When the solicitor has calculated this amount, the solicitor pays this amount (called a sum *in lieu of* interest) to the client.

The sum paid in lieu of interest must be recorded on the client ledger. The payment of the sum is treated as an expense of the firm so will also be recorded in an expense account. In addition, the solicitor will have to pay the sum to the client which will usually be done by transferring the sum from the business Cash account to the client Cash account.

**EXAMPLE**

A solicitor is instructed by a client in the sale of the client's current house and the purchase of a new one. The sale and purchase are not contemporaneous and it is anticipated that there will be a one-month gap between the completion of the sale and the completion of the purchase. The net sale proceeds (after payment of the costs of sale) are £120,000, and the solicitor holds this sum of money for one month in the general client account before the money is used in the completion of the purchase.

The solicitor calculates how much interest would have been earned on the £120,000 if it had been in a separate account. Assuming an interest rate of 2 per cent per annum (which might perhaps be on the low side given current interest rates), the interest on £120,000 over one month is roughly £200.

The solicitor probably has a *de minimis* policy but this sum is likely to exceed most *de minimis* limits. If the solicitor does pay a sum in lieu of interest, the solicitor will add £200 to the other money owed to the client. In this situation, it is likely the solicitor will ask the client for £200 less when the solicitor requests additional funds to complete the purchase of the new home.

The entries for recording the payment of the sum of £200 in lieu of interest would be as follows:

| | | |
|---|---|---|
| Dr | Interest payable account | £200 |
| Cr | Client ledger (business) | £200 |

Then, the entries to record the transfer of the £200 interest from the business account to the client account would be as follows (these are the reverse of the client to business transfer considered in **Chapter 15**):

| | | |
|---|---|---|
| Dr | Client ledger (business) | £200 |
| Cr | Cash account (business) | £200 |
| Dr | Cash account (client) | £200 |
| Cr | Client ledger (client) | £200 |

It is not easy to understand this without looking at how it would appear in the ledgers shown in **Table 16.12**.

**TABLE 16.12**

| **Interest payable account** | | | | |
|---|---|---|---|---|
| **Date** | **Description** | **Dr** | **Cr** | **Bal** |
| | (Existing balance) | | | 4,500DR |
| Oct 31 | Mrs Ali | 200 | | 4,700DR |

| **Client ledger: Mrs Ali** | | | | | | | |
|---|---|---|---|---|---|---|---|
| | | **Business** | | | **Client** | | |
| **Date** | **Description** | **Dr** | **Cr** | **Bal** | **Dr** | **Cr** | **Bal** |
| | (Existing balances) | | | 0 | | | 120,000CR |
| Oct 31 | Interest payable | | 200 | 200CR | | | |
| | Cash: transfer of interest | 200 | | 0 | | 200 | 120,200CR |

| Cash account | | | | | | | | |
|---|---|---|---|---|---|---|---|---|
| | | Business | | | Client | | | |
| Date | Description | Dr | Cr | Bal | Dr | Cr | Bal |
| | (Existing balances) | | | 695,250DR | | | 1,400,000DR |
| Oct | | | | | | | |
| 31 | Mrs Ali: transfer of interest | | 200 | 695,050DR | 200 | | 1,400,200DR |

Remember also that the solicitor should not provide banking facilities to a client and, combined with the firm's likely *de minimis* provision, there should be relatively few situations in which the payment of a sum in lieu of interest will be necessary.

As can be seen, the payment of a sum in lieu of interest is treated as an expense of the solicitor's business. Obviously, any expense will reduce the profits made by the business, but solicitors can cover this expense by earning interest on the general client account monies. A properly run solicitors' firm will have an arrangement with the bank whereby interest is paid to the solicitor on the client money deposited in the client account, or rather a proportion of the monies held. Although client money must be available on demand, a solicitors' firm will rarely need all of the client money on demand, and so a proportion of the overall client money can be placed in an interest-earning account.

Because the balance on the general client account (or the proportion of the money that is on deposit) is usually quite large, the bank will pay a higher rate of interest than would be paid on a smaller deposit. This means that the interest earned on the client money held by the firm will exceed the sums in lieu of interest that have to be paid to the client, because the sum in lieu of interest is calculated on the basis of the interest that the individual client's money would earn if it were deposited in a separate account.

**EXAMPLE**

A solicitor holds £500,000 for a client for two weeks between the sale of one property and the purchase of another.

The firm is holding a large amount of client money at any one time, and £20 million of this is on deposit.

The solicitor calculates a sum in lieu of interest on the client's money. The interest rate that the bank would pay on a deposit of £500,000 is 3 per cent per annum. A year's interest will be £15,000 and two weeks' interest at this rate would be around £575.

However, the interest rate on the £20 million client money on deposit is 4 per cent per annum. So, the interest that the solicitor will have received in respect of the client's £500,000 is around £770.

Therefore, the interest paid by the bank to the solicitor should more than cover any sum in lieu of interest that the solicitor has to pay to the client.

(Note that the interest rates stated above are for illustration purposes and are not necessarily realistic ones.)

## 16.6 Other transactions

In this section we will consider some of the issues and accounting entries needed in respect of particular selected transactions. You should note this is not a comprehensive list and there are other transactions that you might encounter in practice.

### 16.6.1 Cheques

For many years, many (if not most) of the payments to and by solicitors were made by cheque.

A cheque is a promissory note whereby the payer promises to pay the payee a certain amount of money. The cheque is linked to (it is said to be 'drawn on') a particular bank account and the cheque will have the bank account's details pre-printed on it. The payee of the cheque can present the cheque to their own bank and then the respective banks of the payee and payer will arrange for a transfer of the amount of money from the payer's bank account into the payee's bank account.

Until relatively recently, electronic methods of payment were relatively inconvenient, and sometimes expensive. Bank transfers had to be arranged in advance and there was usually a charge levied by the bank, so these were confined to large transactions such as transferring sale proceeds or purchase monies in conveyancing transactions. There was no PayPal, no Apple Pay and no internet banking.

This meant that cheques were the preferred method of payment when clients paid money to the solicitor and when the solicitor made payments on behalf of the client (eg when paying court fees). The alternative to using cheques (apart from expensive bank transfers) was to pay in cash and this is simply not practical in the majority of cases, not to mention the potential money laundering that could be facilitated by accepting large sums of cash from a client or a third party.

Today, cheques are comparatively rare and many more payments are made using credit and debit cards and by direct transfer from one bank account to another using internet and telephone banking. In some cases, though, payment by cheque is still required (eg probate applications which are not made online have to include a cheque in payment of the probate fees). However, it is still possible that a solicitor might receive a cheque from a client or a third party and, if so, the solicitor needs to know what to do with it.

The first point to note is that the solicitor can only pay the cheque into one of the firm's bank accounts if the firm is the payee written on the cheque. If the firm is not the payee of the cheque, the solicitor cannot pay the cheque into one of the firm's bank accounts.

If, say, the solicitor receives a cheque made payable to the client personally, then the solicitor should pass the cheque to the client who will then be able to pay it into their own bank account. Similarly, if the client gave the solicitor a cheque made payable to a third party (say, the other side in litigation proceedings), then the solicitor could not pay that cheque into one of the firm's bank accounts but would have to pass the cheque on to the third party.

However, the firm should keep a record on the file of the receipt and forwarding of the cheque, and ideally should have a central record of cheques received and forwarded.

If, though, the cheque is payable to the solicitor's firm, then the cheque should be paid into one of the firm's accounts (the business bank account or a client bank account). Sometimes, as we saw in **Chapter 15**, the solicitor will ask the bank to split the cheque between the business and client accounts, but this is rare as banks are reluctant to do this.

A particular problem with receiving payment by cheque is that it takes time for a cheque to 'clear'. This is the process mentioned earlier—the payee's bank contacting the payer's bank and arranging a transfer of funds between them to the payee's bank account. Apart from possible frustration due to the delay, there is an issue if the solicitor makes a payment on behalf of the client, using client money, and then subsequently the client's cheque is dishonoured (ie the client's bank refuses to make the payment to the solicitor's bank, usually because the client's bank account is overdrawn).

There is nothing in the SRA Accounts Rules that prevents a solicitor from making a payment on a client's behalf prior to a cheque clearing. However, if the solicitor makes such a payment and the cheque does not clear, the solicitor would then have breached the Accounts Rules because, in effect, other clients' money will have been used to make the payment on the client's behalf.

**EXAMPLE**

A solicitor is acting for Kidnetic Ltd in a litigation matter. Proceedings are due to be issued and the solicitor asks Kidnetic for £1,000 on account of costs and disbursements. Kidnetic sends the solicitor a cheque for this amount, and the receipt of the cheque is recorded on 6 July. On 10 July, the solicitor issues proceedings and pays the court fee of £650 out of the general client account. On 11 July, the solicitor's bank informs the solicitor that the client's cheque has been dishonoured.

In effect, whilst the solicitor thought they had been put in funds by Kidnetic, the solicitor is actually holding no money from Kidnetic. Although it has been possible to make the payment of the court fee from the general client account, it is only because there was other clients' money in that account. So, the solicitor has used other clients' money to pay the court fee for Kidnetic.

This is a breach of rule 5.3 which says that the solicitor must only withdraw client money from a client account if sufficient funds are held on behalf of that specific client or third party to make the payment.

Under rule 6.1, there is a duty to correct any breaches upon discovery. In the above example, the solicitor must do this on 11 July when they realise that the client's cheque has been dishonoured. The breach is remedied in the manner mentioned in rule 6.1, which is to replace the money which has been improperly withdrawn from client account and **business money** will be used to do this. This will involve a transfer of money from the business account to the client account.

There will need to be six entries to record this transaction—two entries to reverse the entries which had been made when the client's cheque was received, and four entries to record the transfer of business money to client account.

The entries for the above example will be:

**(1) Entries to reverse the entries made when the cheque was received**

| | | |
|---|---|---|
| Dr | Client ledger (client) | £1,000 |
| Cr | Cash account (client) | £1,000 |

**(2) Entries to record money being taken out of business account**

| | | |
|---|---|---|
| Dr | Client ledger (business) | £650 |
| Cr | Cash account (business) | £650 |

**(3) Entries to record money being put into the client account**

| | | |
|---|---|---|
| Dr | Cash account (client) | £650 |
| Cr | Client ledger (client) | £650 |

Table 16.13 shows the respective ledgers.

**TABLE 16.13**

| **Client ledger: Kidnetic Ltd** | | | | | | | | |
|---|---|---|---|---|---|---|---|---|
| | | **Business** | | | **Client** | | | |
| **Date** | **Description** | **Dr** | **Cr** | **Bal** | **Dr** | **Cr** | **Bal** | |
| Jul | | | | | | | | |
| 6 | Cash: receipt from client | | | | | 1,000 | 1,000CR | |
| 10 | Cash: court fee | | | | 650 | | 350CR | |
| 11 | Cash: dishonoured cheque | | | | 1,000 | | 650DR | |
| | Cash: transfer from business to client account | 650 | | 650DR | | 650 | 0 | |

*(Note that in the Cash account below all other transactions for other clients are ignored for the sake of simplicity. There are therefore no existing balances shown.)*

*(continued)*

**TABLE 16.13** *(continued)*

| Cash account | | | | | | | |
|---|---|---|---|---|---|---|---|
| | | Business | | | Client | | |
| Date | Description | Dr | Cr | Bal | Dr | Cr | Bal |
| Jul | | | | | | | |
| 6 | Kidnetic: receipt from client | | | | 1,000 | | 1,000DR |
| 10 | Kidnetic: court fee | | | | | 650 | 350DR |
| 11 | Kidnetic: dishonoured cheque | | | | | 1,000 | 650CR |
| | Kidnetic: transfer from business to client account | | 650 | 650CR | 650 | | 0 |

Obviously, this should not be the end of the story, as the solicitor should contact the client to find out why the cheque was dishonoured and to obtain reimbursement from the client for the business money that the solicitor has had to use to remedy the breach.

In practice, it is obviously best if solicitors do not make payments on behalf of clients who have paid by cheque until the solicitor can be sure that the client's cheque has cleared.

## 16.6.2 **Petty cash**

Traditionally, each firm has kept a small amount of physical cash (notes and coins) just in case it has to pay for something small by cash. Increasingly, these small payments will be electronic as even small payments can now be made using debit and credit cards, often in contactless transactions.

Sometimes, though, cash will be useful and so firms may keep a small amount of notes and coins in a box, tin or safe in the office. This cash is known as '**petty cash**'. The amount of petty cash will be topped up every now and again to replace cash which has been used for payments.

The cash is likely to have been withdrawn from the firm's business bank account in the first place. Perhaps confusingly, in the ledger accounts the bank accounts are referred to as 'cash' accounts. However, when you see the ledger for the firm's Cash account, you are in fact looking at a record of the movement of money in and out of the firm's business bank account and general client bank account.

There will be a separate ledger account for petty cash. When notes and coins are withdrawn from the firm's business account and are put into the petty cash box, the entries will be:

| | | |
|---|---|---|
| Cr | Cash account (business) | £ |
| Dr | Petty cash | £ |

Even if petty cash is used to make a payment for something, the fee earner will rarely see an entry on the client ledger for the fee earner's client. This is because cash might be used to pay for something like postage stamps or photographs which, as we have seen, are not regarded as disbursements. These small cash payments are treated as being part of the expenses of the firm in providing its services to its clients, and such small items should not be itemised on the bill to the client but should instead be factored into the fees charged by the firm.

The fee earner would only see an entry relating to petty cash on the client ledger if the cash payment was treated as a disbursement for which the solicitor would charge the client separately. There are now very few such costs. One of the main examples where the fee earner would see entries for petty cash was in probate and administration matters, where it was necessary to use petty cash to pay another solicitor or a commissioner for **oaths** to administer the oath sworn or affirmed by the personal representative(s). However, as we saw in **Chapter 8**, oaths were replaced by **statements of truth** (which have since been replaced by standard probate application forms), and there is now no need to pay petty cash to another solicitor or a commissioner for oaths when applying for a grant of representation.

The entries that would be made when using petty cash to pay an expense are as follows:

| | | |
|---|---|---|
| Dr | Relevant expense account (eg postage costs) | £ |
| Cr | Petty cash | £ |

If, although unlikely, the petty cash payment was in relation to something that would show on the client ledger of a client, the entries would instead be as follows:

| | | |
|---|---|---|
| Dr | Client ledger (business) | £ |
| Cr | Petty cash | £ |

Due to the limited circumstances in which the fee earner would see petty cash entries appearing in the client ledger, no example is given and so no ledger entries are shown here.

### 16.6.3 **Remedying breaches**

As already noted, under rule 6.1 the solicitor is under a duty to correct a breach of the Accounts Rules promptly on discovery. There is no definition of 'promptly' and the SRA has declined to provide a definition. We cannot say, therefore, whether 'promptly' means within two working days, within 14 days or within any other standard period of time. Clearly, although there is some flexibility in the concept of 'promptly', if a solicitor discovers a breach the solicitor would be well advised to correct the breach immediately or as soon as possible.

Often the breach will involve a solicitor withholding client money from a client account (perhaps by placing the money, mistakenly, in the business account). Alternatively, the breach might involve a solicitor withdrawing money improperly from client accounts, such as we saw in **16.6.1**, when a client's cheque has been dishonoured and the money of other clients has been used. In either case, the remedy (which is referred to in rule 6.1) is to replace the client money which has been improperly withheld or withdrawn from the client account, and usually the solicitor must use the firm's own business money to do this.

The entries are the same entries as we saw for a transfer of cash from the business account to a client account in **16.6.1**:

**(1) Entries to record money being taken out of business account**

| | | |
|---|---|---|
| Dr | Client ledger (business) | £ |
| Cr | Cash account (business) | £ |

**(2) Entries to record money being put into the client account**

| | | |
|---|---|---|
| Dr | Cash account (client) | £ |
| Cr | Client ledger (client) | £ |

As there is an example of this in **16.6.1**, no ledgers are shown here to illustrate the point.

**KEY POINT SUMMARY**

- VAT is charged on the supply of goods and services. This includes the services that solicitors provide to their clients. The standard rate of VAT is 20 per cent. Solicitors will collect the VAT and pay this to HMRC. Payments of VAT to HMRC are made quarterly.
- The VAT that solicitors charge is a solicitor's 'output tax'. At the same time, the solicitor will have paid VAT on goods and services received by the solicitor (eg computer and office equipment and the fees of counsel). The VAT paid by a solicitor on the supplies received is called 'input tax'. The solicitor can deduct input tax from output tax, and this will reduce the

amount of VAT payable to HMRC at the end of the VAT quarter. The solicitor will account for both output tax and input tax in a VAT ledger account.

- When a solicitor issues a bill, there will be accounting entries in the client ledger, the Costs account and the VAT account. There is no movement of cash when the bill is issued so there is no entry in the Cash account.
- The bill may be paid by means of a transfer of client money from the client account to the business account. Alternatively, if the solicitor is not holding client money for the client, the client will send a payment to the solicitor.
- Occasionally, the solicitor will agree to a reduction in a bill in the interests of good relations with the client. The reduction in the bill is called an abatement, and the accounting entries are the reverse of the entries needed for issuing a bill.
- Sometimes it becomes obvious that a client will not be able to pay a bill and the solicitor will have to write off the bill and record a bad debt. The entries will differ depending on whether VAT bad debt relief is available at the point in time when the bill is written off.
- VAT is charged on some disbursements (eg counsel's fees), although there is no VAT on other disbursements (eg court fees).
- A disbursement will only be regarded as a disbursement for VAT purposes if the supply (eg a search result) is passed on to the client without comment by the solicitor. If the solicitor advises on the result of the search, recent case law suggests that the expenditure is part of the solicitor's professional services and either the solicitor should increase their fees to cover the cost or the search or the solicitor should charge for the disbursement separately in the solicitor's bill, charging VAT on the amount of the disbursement.
- If a disbursement is subject to VAT (eg counsel's fees) there are two methods of accounting for it. In most cases, the invoice will be addressed to the client and the solicitor can use the agency method. There is no need to account for the VAT separately with this method.
- However, if the invoice or fee note is addressed to the solicitor, the principal method must be used. The supply of services will be to the solicitor not the client, and the solicitor has to record the VAT on the disbursement as part of their input tax. The solicitor will then have to bill the client for the disbursement, charging the client VAT. There is a concessionary treatment for counsel's fees whereby the agency method can be used if counsel's fee note is amended.
- If the solicitor is holding client money, the solicitor must consider whether interest should be paid on the money held. There are two methods of accounting for interest. If the solicitor places the client money in a separate designated client account, then the interest earned on that account will be added to the amount due to the client. Alternatively, the solicitor may hold the client money in the general client account and account to the client for a sum in lieu of interest.
- However, the solicitor should not be providing banking facilities to clients. Client money should only be held in connection with the legal services being provided by the solicitor. Also, usually client money should be available on demand which rules out deposit accounts which pay a better rate of interest. The firm may also have a *de minimis* provision within its policy on the payment of interest so in many cases interest will not be paid.
- Most payments are now by electronic transfer but the solicitor may receive some payments by cheque. Caution needs to be taken before drawing on client funds before a cheque has cleared, because the solicitor may find they have used other clients' money to make a payment on behalf of the client if the client's cheque is dishonoured. Any breach must be corrected promptly on discovery.
- Occasionally, the solicitor will need to make a payment in cash. The firm will keep a small amount of notes and coins in a petty cash box for this purpose. The payment will usually be for something that is an expense of the business (eg buying postage stamps) and there will not usually be entries relating to petty cash in the client ledger.
- As said, any breach of the rules must be remedied promptly on discovery. The breach will often involve wrongly withholding or withdrawing client money from a client account, and the remedy will often involve paying the firm's own money (business money) into the client account.

# APPENDIX
# Forms, Guides and Useful Websites

Here is a list of web links to the court forms, guides and useful websites mentioned in this manual.

## Guides and useful websites

- SRA Accounts Rules 2019
  https://www.sra.org.uk/solicitors/standards-regulations/accounts-rules/
- SRA Code of Conduct for Solicitors, RELs and RFLs 2019
  https://www.sra.org.uk/solicitors/standards-regulations/code-conduct-solicitors/
- SRA Code of Conduct for Firms 2019
  https://www.sra.org.uk/solicitors/standards-regulations/code-conduct-firms/
- SRA's Enforcement Strategy
  https://www.sra.org.uk/sra/corporate-strategy/sub-strategies/sra-enforcement-strategy/
- SRA Standards and Regulations
  https://www.sra.org.uk/solicitors/standards-regulations/
- The Public Trustee
  https://www.gov.uk/government/organisations/official-solicitor-and-public-trustee
- Claiming against an estate which is bona vacantia—Government Legal Department
  https://www.gov.uk/government/organisations/bona-vacantia
- General Register Office of England and Wales
  https://www.gov.uk/general-register-office
- Tell Us Once service
  https://www.gov.uk/after-a-death/organisations-you-need-to-contact-and-tell-us-once
- SRA Transparency Rules
  https://www.sra.org.uk/solicitors/standards-regulations/transparency-rules/
- Inheritance tax accounts and other forms
  https://www.gov.uk/government/collections/inheritance-tax-forms
- British government stock IHT direct payment scheme
  https://www.gov.uk/paying-inheritance-tax/british-government-stock
- HMCTS Guidance notes on online applications to assist professional applicants apply for probate
  https://www.gov.uk/government/publications/myhmcts-how-to-apply-for-probate-online/apply-for-probate-with-myhmcts
- London Gazette
  https://www.thegazette.co.uk/
- SRA warning notice on improper use of a client account as a banking facility (December 2014)
  https://www.sra.org.uk/solicitors/guidance/warning-notices/improper-use-of-client-account-as-a-banking-facility--warning-notice/
- SRA guidance, 'Helping you keep accurate client accounting records'
  https://www.sra.org.uk/solicitors/guidance/ethics-guidance/helping-you-keep-accurate-client-accounting-records/

- SRA guidance on the selection of Third Party Managed Account (TPMA) providers and the use of TPMAs
  https://www.sra.org.uk/solicitors/guidance/ethics-guidance/third-party-managed-accounts/
- SRA guidance for reporting accountants
  https://www.sra.org.uk/solicitors/guidance/ethics-guidance/planning-for-and-completing-an-accountant-s-report/

# Forms

- IHT400
  https://assets.publishing.service.gov.uk/media/65a907fa94c997000daeb9e5/IHT400_English.pdf
- IHT205
  https://assets.publishing.service.gov.uk/government/uploads/system/uploads/attachment_data/file/459092/IHT205_2011_.pdf
- IHT217
  https://assets.publishing.service.gov.uk/government/uploads/system/uploads/attachment_data/file/886025/IHT217.pdf
- IHT405
  https://assets.publishing.service.gov.uk/government/uploads/system/uploads/attachment_data/file/715280/IHT405_online-v3.pdf
- IHT406
  https://assets.publishing.service.gov.uk/government/uploads/system/uploads/attachment_data/file/497808/IHT406.pdf
- IHT407
  https://assets.publishing.service.gov.uk/government/uploads/system/uploads/attachment_data/file/729929/IHT407.pdf
- IHT410
  https://assets.publishing.service.gov.uk/government/uploads/system/uploads/attachment_data/file/497875/IHT410.pdf
- IHT411
  https://assets.publishing.service.gov.uk/government/uploads/system/uploads/attachment_data/file/497883/IHT411.pdf
- IHT412
  https://assets.publishing.service.gov.uk/government/uploads/system/uploads/attachment_data/file/774315/IHT412.pdf
- IHT417
  https://assets.publishing.service.gov.uk/government/uploads/system/uploads/attachment_data/file/373600/IHT417.pdf
- IHT419
  https://assets.publishing.service.gov.uk/government/uploads/system/uploads/attachment_data/file/705315/IHT419_012018_online-v2.pdf
- IHT404
  https://assets.publishing.service.gov.uk/government/uploads/system/uploads/attachment_data/file/517451/IHT404.pdf
- IHT409
  https://assets.publishing.service.gov.uk/government/uploads/system/uploads/attachment_data/file/497813/IHT409.pdf

- IHT418
  https://assets.publishing.service.gov.uk/government/uploads/system/uploads/attachment_data/file/373603/IHT418.pdf
- IHT403
  https://assets.publishing.service.gov.uk/government/uploads/system/uploads/attachment_data/file/917890/IHT403-05-20.pdf
- IHT435
  https://assets.publishing.service.gov.uk/media/64f9a1fdfdc5d10014fce7b7/IHT435-2023.pdf
- IHT413
  https://assets.publishing.service.gov.uk/government/uploads/system/uploads/attachment_data/file/705300/IHT413_0118_online-v2.pdf
- IHT414
  https://assets.publishing.service.gov.uk/government/uploads/system/uploads/attachment_data/file/373595/IHT414.pdf
- IHT38
  https://assets.publishing.service.gov.uk/government/uploads/system/uploads/attachment_data/file/885993/IHT38_filliable_0520.pdf
- IHT30
  https://assets.publishing.service.gov.uk/government/uploads/system/uploads/attachment data/file/902810/IHT30-07-20.pdf
- PA15
  https://assets.publishing.service.gov.uk/media/60b74244e90e0732b2acacb6/PA15_0421_save.pdf
- PA8A
  https://assets.publishing.service.gov.uk/media/6356861 1d3bf7f0bd9d94377/PA8A_0922_save.pdf
- PA1S
  https://assets.publishing.service.gov.uk/media/60ed615ad3bf7f568ffe8704/PA1S_0721.pdf
- PA1P
  (NB: professional applicants can only now use this form in specified circumstances, and will otherwise have to apply online)
  https://www.gov.uk/government/publications/form-pa1p-apply-for-probate-the-deceased-had-a-will
- PA1A
  (NB: professional applicants can only now use this form in specified circumstances, and otherwise have to apply online)
  https://www.gov.uk/government/publications/apply-for-probate-by-post-if-there-is-not-a-will
- AS1
  https://assets.publishing.service.gov.uk/government/uploads/system/uploads/attachment_data/file/808672/AS1__2019-06-17_.pdf
- FR1
  https://assets.publishing.service.gov.uk/government/uploads/system/uploads/attachment_data/file/882099/FR1-2020-04-28.pdf
- C4
  https://assets.publishing.service.gov.uk/government/uploads/system/uploads/attachment_data/file/371960/c4_2.pdf
- 64-8
  https://assets.publishing.service.gov.uk/government/uploads/system/uploads/attachment_data/file/815650/authorise_agent_64-8.pdf

- SA900
  https://assets.publishing.service.gov.uk/government/uploads/system/uploads/attachment_data/file/870489/sa900_2020.pdf
- SA100
  https://www.gov.uk/self-assessment-tax-return-forms
- R185 (estate income)
  https://assets.publishing.service.gov.uk/government/uploads/system/uploads/attachment_data/file/871580/R185_Estate_.pdf

# Glossary

**Abatement (of legacies)** Where the estate is solvent but there is insufficient money to pay all of the legacies in full, each legacy will be reduced proportionately.

**Abatements (Solicitors' Accounts)** A reduction to a solicitor's bill of costs, agreed by the solicitor voluntarily (as opposed to costs which are reduced following assessment by a court).

**Account (of profits)** Where a fiduciary breaches their fiduciary duties and makes a profit out of their position, the principal can claim that profit from the fiduciary. The fiduciary is then said to account for their profit to the principal.

**Accountant's report** Under the SRA Accounts Rules 2019, firms which hold client money must obtain an accountant's report. If a report is qualified by the accountant (due to significant breaches of the Accounts Rules), the firm must submit the report to the SRA.

**Ademption** A gift in a will of specific property will fail if the testator no longer owns the property at the time of death. The gift is said to 'adeem'. The gifted property may have been lost or sold or given away by the testator during their lifetime.

**Administration period** The period of time starting with the death of the deceased and ending with the final distribution of the deceased's estate.

**Administrator** A personal representative who is appointed by the court (following a grant application to the Probate Service). The female equivalent is 'administratrix'.

**Advancement (presumption of)** In connection with resulting trusts, there is a presumption of advancement where there is a lifetime transfer, depending on the relationship between the transferor and transferee.

**Advancement (trustees' powers)** Trustees have a statutory power of advancement to pay part of all of a beneficiary's capital entitlement to them earlier than they would otherwise receive it.

**Affidavit** A formal statement, where the person making the statement swears to the truth of the statement on a holy book or affirms the statement as a secular alternative.

**Agency method (VAT)** A method of accounting for disbursements which are subject to VAT. The disbursement is treated as being made directly to the client and so the solicitor does not have to account for the VAT separately through the firm's accounts.

**Agent** Someone who acts on behalf of another person (who is called the principal). Agents owe fiduciary duties to their principals.

**Appearance** If the person wishing to take out a grant of representation issues a warning against a caveator, the caveator can enter an appearance. This will be a permanent block on a grant of representation, until such time as the caveator withdraws the caveat or the matter is determined by court action.

**Appointment** This term is used to describe the situation where the trustee of a discretionary trust decides to pay part or all of the trust property to a beneficiary. The trustee is said to 'appoint' the trust property to the beneficiary.

**Appropriation** Personal representatives have the power to transfer items of property to beneficiaries of the estate, in part or full satisfaction of the beneficiaries' entitlement to the estate.

**Assent** An indication by the personal representatives that they no longer need certain property for the administration of the estate. The personal representatives transfer the property in question to the beneficiary. The formal document for transferring land is also called an assent.

**Attestation** A properly drafted will should include an attestation clause, which (if it is properly worded) will provide prima facie evidence that the will has been executed in accordance with the formalities requirements of s9 of the Wills Act 1837.

**Bad debt** A debt where the debtor (eg a solicitor's client) is not likely to pay, perhaps because the debtor has become insolvent. Businesses need to 'write off' such bad debts in their accounts.

**Balance (Solicitors' Accounts)** The difference between the debits and credits in a ledger account. The SRA Accounts Rules 2019 provide that running balances need to be kept, following each transaction.

**Beneficiary** The person who is entitled to the equitable or beneficial interest in the trust property. The beneficiary may have an absolute or a limited interest in the trust property. The trustees have to act in the interests of the beneficiaries.

**Beneficiary principle** This principle says that a private trust must have human beneficiaries. In other words, it is not possible to have a private trust for a purpose. The rationale for the rule is that there must be beneficiaries who can enforce the trust.

**Bequest** A gift of chattels (ie personal possessions) in a will.

**Bona vacantia** Where an intestate is not survived by any of the relatives specified in s46 of the Administration of Estates 1925, the estate will pass to the Crown as bona vacantia (literally, 'vacant goods').

**Burden (IHT)** The question of burden of IHT concerns which persons should ultimately bear the cost of the IHT which has been paid.

**Business money (Solicitors' Accounts)** Not a defined term. Under the old (2011) SRA Accounts Rules, a solicitor's own money was called 'office money'. There is no equivalent definition in the SRA Accounts Rules 2019, but the term 'business money' is used in this book to signify the solicitor's own money.

**Capacity** To undertake a valid legal act, a person must have the requisite mental capacity. Generally, only adults (those aged 18 or over) have capacity, and an adult's capacity may be impaired by illness, disease or conditions they were born with. Capacity is assessed on a decision-by-decision basis.

**Capital Gains Tax (CGT)** A tax on gains made when a chargeable person disposes of chargeable assets.

**Caveat** An old fashioned term for a process of stopping a grant from being issued in an estate. The person lodging the caveat is called a caveator.

**Certainty** The provisions of a trust or of a will must be clear, or certain. For a valid express private trust, there must be certainty of intention, certainty of subject matter (the trust property) and certainty of objects (the beneficiaries).

**Cessate grant** A grant obtained by a person who was initially unable to obtain a grant in their own right, usually because they were under 18 years of age when the deceased died. When a minor (who is entitled to a grant) reaches 18 they can obtain a cessate grant, and will replace the original personal representative.

**Chain of representation** When a proving executor dies before completing the administration of the deceased's estate, but the proving executor themselves appoints an executor who proves their will, the executor of the executor can complete the administration of the deceased's estate without having to obtain a second grant to the deceased's estate.

**Charitable trust** A trust which has charitable status. The trust must be for a recognised charitable purpose (or be analogous to one), it must be for the public benefit and it must be wholly and exclusively charitable.

**Chattels** Items of personal property, namely personal possessions.

**Citation** A process used to try and force a personal representative to take out a grant. Used to compel a reluctant or dilatory personal representative.

**Civil partnership** An alternative to marriage. Civil partners acquire similar legal rights and responsibilities towards each other, and obtain similar tax advantages, as married couples. Originally introduced for same-sex couples at a time when same-sex couples could not marry, civil partnerships are now available to opposite-sex couples.

**Clearance (IHT)** The personal representatives should seek to obtain clearance from HMRC once they think that all of the IHT has been paid.

**Client account (Solicitors' Accounts)** An account at a bank or building society in England and Wales, which is used by a solicitor to hold client money. The name of the account must include the word 'client' in order to protect the client money from the solicitor's insolvency.

**Client money (Solicitors' Accounts)** Money which belongs to the solicitor's client or indeed any money which does not belong to the solicitor's own business. See **Chapter 14** for a more accurate definition.

**Codicil** A document that is supplementary to a will. A testator can make more than one codicil to a will. If there are any codicils to a will, these will be proved alongside the will when the grant application is made.

**Commorientes** A Latin term used for the rules that determine the order of death between two or more persons when the order of death is not known. Usually, the elder of two persons is deemed to have died before the younger, but this is a simplification of the rules.

**Constitution (of trusts)** If the settlor creates a trust where the settlor appoints other persons as trustees, the settlor must transfer the legal title in the trust property to the trustees for the trust to be constituted (and valid).

**Constructive trust** A form of implied trust. The main type is an 'institutional' constructive trust. The other type of constructive trust recognised by the law of England and Wales is the common intention constructive trust.

**Contingent gift** A gift which is contingent on the happening of a certain event, usually the beneficiary reaching a specified age. Used in practice to postpone the age at which beneficiaries will inherit, so that beneficiaries have to wait until, say, 21 or 25 before inheriting.

**Coroner** A judicial appointment—coroners are appointed to investigate certain deaths (violent or unnatural deaths; where the cause of death is unknown; deaths in custody). A coroner will consider whether there should be a post-mortem and whether to hold an inquest.

**Corrective account (IHT)** Following submission of the main IHT account, it is sometimes necessary to submit a corrective account, for example where fresh assets are discovered subsequently.

**Costs (Solicitors' Accounts)** The fees charged by the solicitor for the solicitor's legal services and any disbursements paid for by the solicitor on behalf of the client.

**Counsel's fees** The fees of a barrister ('counsel').

**Credit entry (Solicitors' Accounts)** Part of the double entry bookkeeping system. A credit entry is shown on the right-hand side of a ledger account, and is used to record increases in liabilities, income and decreases in assets.

**Creditor** A person to whom you owe money. The personal representatives of a deceased person must ensure that they pay all of the deceased's debts, namely that they pay the deceased's creditors.

**De bonis non administratis (grant of)** A second grant of administration obtained in order to complete the administration of an estate. This will be required where the original personal representative has died (except where the chain of representation applies).

**Death certificate** Formal evidence of a person's death. Asset holders will usually require sight of an official copy of the death certificate, which can be obtained from the register office when the death is registered.

**Debit entry (Solicitors' Accounts)** Part of the double entry bookkeeping system. A debit entry is shown on the left-hand side of a ledger account, and is used to record increases in assets (such as cash or debtors), expenses and decreases in liabilities.

**Demonstrative gifts** A gift which is to be paid for out of a designated fund. Quite rare. Most pecuniary legacies will be general gifts and most gifts of personal or real property will be of specific items of property.

**Devise** A gift of real property (ie land and/or buildings) in a will.

**Disbursements** Payments made by a solicitor on behalf of a client, for example court fees, conveyancing search fees, counsel's (ie a barrister's) fees. There are rules on the VAT treatment of such payments, and the meaning of 'disbursements' for VAT purposes is more specific.

**Disclaimer** The process by which a beneficiary (under a will or on intestacy) decides not to accept their entitlement from the estate. It is not possible to disclaim part of an entitlement, but it is possible to disclaim one of a number of distinct gifts.

**Discretionary trust** A trust where the trustees are given the discretion to divide the trust fund as they see fit among a specified class of beneficiaries. Each beneficiary in the class does not have an entitlement to a specified portion of the trust fund, but only has a mere *spes* (or hope) that the trustees will exercise the discretion in their favour.

**Dishonest assistance** A form of third party liability in the law of trusts. A person may be liable towards a beneficiary who has suffered loss as a result of a breach of trust by the trustee, if the person has assisted the trustee in the breach of trust. The person must have acted dishonestly to be liable.

**Disposal (CGT)** The event which triggers a possible charge to capital gains tax (CGT). If there is no disposal, there is no CGT. For example, there is no CGT on death because there is no disposal on death.

**Donatio(nes) mortis causa** A doctrine from Roman law whereby a person may transfer assets to another on their death by making a gift in contemplation of death. The person must anticipate their death in the near future and must pass 'dominion' over the property to the donee (eg the keys to a motorcar).

**Double entry bookkeeping** The established system for recording business transactions, used worldwide for centuries. Called double entry because there will always be two entries to make for every transaction—one debit entry and one credit entry.

**Double probate (grant of)** A grant obtained by an executor to whom power was reserved initially. The executor who obtains the grant of double probate will join the executor(s) who obtained the original grant of probate, or replace them if the other executor(s) have died or are otherwise incapable of continuing.

**En ventre sa mère** A French phrase (roughly translated as 'being carried by their mother'). It is used to signify a child who has been conceived but not yet born. A gift to 'my children who survive me' would include a child who was *en ventre sa mère* at the date of the testator's death.

**Entry (Solicitors' Accounts)** A recording made in a ledger account, relating to a new accounting transaction.

**Equity** A body of rules developed over time by the courts, based upon a concept of fairness and initially used to mitigate the harshness of the common law in specific cases. There is now a substantial body of case law and precedent.

**Estate accounts** At the end of the administration period, the personal representatives will produce a set of accounts showing the assets and debts of the estate, the income and expenses and how the estate has been distributed.

**Excepted estate** An estate which is excepted from the requirement to submit an inheritance tax account.

**Execution (of wills)** A slightly unfortunate term, given the context of wills and administration of estates! This has nothing to do with capital punishment, but is a word sometimes used to describe the process of signing and witnessing a document. So, a will is said to be 'executed' or the testator and the witnesses are said to 'execute' the will.

**Executor** A personal representative that is appointed by a testator in the testator's will. Executors derive their authority from the will and the grant of probate confirms that authority. The female equivalent is 'executrix'.

**Express trust** A trust created by a settlor or testator in a document (such as a will) or orally.

**Family provision claim** A phrase used often in practice to describe an application for reasonable financial provision under the Inheritance (Provision for Family and Dependants) Act 1975.

**Fees (Solicitors' Accounts)** The charges of the solicitor for the work undertaken by the solicitor.

**Fiduciary** A person who owes a duty of loyalty to another (who is called the principal). A fiduciary must not allow their interests to conflict with the interests of the principal. Trustees are fiduciaries of beneficiaries, solicitors are fiduciaries of clients, and company directors are fiduciaries of their companies.

**Fiduciary duty** A fiduciary owes a duty of loyalty to their principal. The fiduciary duties are essentially negative in nature—the duty not to allow their interests to conflict with those of the principal and the duty not to profit from their fiduciary position.

**Fixed net sum** More commonly called the 'statutory legacy' in practice. On an intestacy, where a spouse (or civil partner) and issue survive the deceased, the spouse (or civil partner) will be entitled to a fixed net sum of up to a certain amount, plus interest from the date of death to the date of payment.

**Fixed trust** A trust where the interests of each beneficiary are fixed. The trustees have no discretion over the amounts each beneficiary will receive.

**Forfeiture** A rule of public policy preventing a person from inheriting from the estate of a person that they have unlawfully killed. It is possible to obtain relief from forfeiture on application to the court. If this relief is granted, the person is allowed to inherit despite the unlawful killing.

**Formalities** In general, rules which require certain prescribed steps to be taken in order to make a document or transaction legally binding. For example, for a will to be valid, the will must comply with the formalities requirements set out in s9 of the Wills Act 1837.

**Gain (CGT)** Capital gains tax (CGT) is charged on gains made on disposals of chargeable assets. The gain is, in simple terms, the difference between the value of the asset when acquired and the value of the asset on disposal. However, the gain can be reduced by other costs.

**General gifts** Gifts which can be paid for out of the estate generally. Pecuniary legacies are usually general gifts.

**Gift** The voluntary transfer of both the legal title and the equitable interest in property from a donor to a donee. The donee will provide no consideration for the transfer.

**Gift subject to a reservation (IHT)** Where the transferor has made a lifetime transfer but has retained a benefit in the gifted property. The value of the gifted property at the date of death is aggregated with the value of the deceased's IHT estate, and so will be subject to IHT on the deceased's death. There are legitimate ways to avoid the reservation rules applying.

**Grant (of representation)** A grant of representation, which is issued by the Probate Service. The grant provides proof of an executor's authority and confers authority on an administrator. The grant is used by personal representatives as proof that they are entitled to act in the administration of an estate.

**Grant of letters of administration** A grant of representation where the deceased died intestate. Sometimes described as 'simple' administration, due to the lack of a will.

**Grant of letters of administration with the will annexed** A grant of representation where the deceased left a will, but there are no executors able and willing to take a grant of probate.

**Grossing up (IHT)** Where a transferor pays for the IHT on a chargeable lifetime transfer, the amount of the transfer (and the IHT on it) will have to be grossed up, and the IHT paid will be greater than if the transferee pays the IHT.

**Guardians (testamentary)** Under the Children Act 1989, a person with parental responsibility for a child can appoint a guardian for the child. The guardian is appointed to care for the child after the person's death. A guardian may be appointed in a number of ways, but if the guardian is appointed by the person's will, the guardian is often referred to as a testamentary guardian.

**Half blood (intestacy)** Used in the intestacy rules to describe a situation where two people share only one parent.

**Implied trust** A trust which arises due to a particular set of circumstances. Implied trusts include resulting trusts and the different forms of constructive trusts.

**Income tax** A tax on various sources of income, including employment income, income of a trade or profession, rental income, savings income and dividends. Individuals pay income tax during their lifetime and personal representatives will have to account to HMRC for income tax on the estate's income during the administration period.

**Incorporation by reference** A doctrine whereby the terms of a document may be incorporated into a will, provided the document is in existence before the date the will is made, and provided the will specifies the document is a pre-existing document.

**Individual Savings Account (ISA)** A form of investment which enjoys income tax advantages. There are cash ISAs which are bank or building society accounts, and there are stocks and shares ISAs.

The income on ISAs is free of income tax, although there are limits on the amounts a person can invest in an ISA each tax year.

**Inheritance tax (IHT)** A tax mainly on the estates of deceased persons, but also on the value of certain transfers made during a person's lifetime. However, due to the IHT rules many lifetime transfers (if made more than seven years before death) will not be taxed. It is necessary to submit an inheritance tax account when a person dies.

**Inheritance tax account** A form in which the personal representatives report details of the deceased's assets and liabilities, and any relevant lifetime transfers. The personal representatives can also use the account to claim exemptions and reliefs.

**Input tax (VAT)** VAT which a business pays on the supplies of goods and services it receives (eg the VAT paid on counsel's fees). A business can set its input tax against any output tax, before accounting to HMRC for VAT at the end of each VAT quarter.

**Inquest** Court proceedings, presided over by a coroner, to determine who died and how, when and where a death happened.

**Insolvent estate** An estate where the debts and expenses exceed the value of the assets.

**Instalment option (IHT)** IHT on certain types of property (including land) may be paid by instalments over a ten-year period, although the sale of the property in question will result in the outstanding balance being due immediately.

**Intention** A person must have the requisite intention to make a will, a trust or a gift. It must be clear from the written or oral words used that there is such an intention. For a will to be valid, a testator must know and approve the terms of the will.

**Inter vivos** A Latin phrase to describe something which happens during someone's lifetime. For example, a lifetime transfer is often described as an *inter vivos* transfer.

**Intestacy** Where the deceased does not leave a will dealing with their estate, the rules of intestacy from the Administration of Estates Act 1925 will govern who will inherit.

**Issue** Children and other lineal descendants (such as grandchildren and great-grandchildren).

**Joint property** Property which is owned by more than one person. Such property may be owned as tenants in common or as joint tenants in equity.

**Joint tenancy in equity** A form of joint ownership of property, where each person does not have an identifiable share or proportion of the property, and where the surviving joint tenant(s) inherits automatically by survivorship the interest of a deceased joint tenant. A joint tenant in equity cannot leave their interest in the property by will, but the joint tenancy can be severed. If so, the property is then held as tenants in common and the person can then leave their share by will.

**Judicial separation** Where a married couple (or civil partners) separate but do not wish to divorce (or dissolve the partnership), they may obtain a judicial separation instead. The marriage (or civil partnership) continues but there are changes to their legal rights as against one another.

**Knowing receipt** A form of third party liability in the law of trusts. A person may be liable towards a beneficiary who has suffered loss as a result of breach of trust by the trustee, if the person received trust property (or the sale proceeds of it). The person need no longer have the property (or proceeds) but the person will be liable if they knew they had received the property as a result of a breach of trust.

**Lapse** A gift in a will fails if the beneficiary dies before the testator. The gift is said to lapse.

**Ledger accounts (Solicitors' Accounts)** Grid-style accounts which are used to record business transactions, using the double entry bookkeeping system.

**Legacy** A gift of money or chattels in a will. Most commonly used to describe a gift of a specified sum of money (which is also called a 'pecuniary' or 'monetary' legacy).

**Liability (IHT)** Persons may be liable for paying IHT to HMRC even if they are not in receipt of all of the property on which IHT is payable. For example, the personal representatives of the deceased are liable to HMRC for the IHT due in respect of the interest of a joint tenant in equity, which passes by survivorship and so does not pass to the personal representatives.

**Life interest** A limited interest where the beneficiary (who is called the life tenant) is entitled to the income from the trust property for life, but has no entitlement to the capital of the trust. When the life tenant dies, the capital passes to the remainder (or reversionary) beneficiaries.

**Lifetime chargeable transfer (LCT)** Lifetime chargeable transfers are lifetime transfers which are chargeable to IHT when they are made. In other words, there may be IHT to pay at the time. Lifetime transfers to companies and to most forms of trust are LCTs.

**Mirror wills** Not a technical phrase, but one used to describe the very common situation where two members of (usually) a married couple make wills that largely mirror each other. Mirror wills do not restrict the freedom of the survivor of the couple to make a fresh will (unlike mutual wills).

**Mixed receipts (Solicitors' Accounts)** A receipt of money which is partly client money and partly the firm's own money (business money).

**Mutual wills** Mutual wills involve a contract between two persons that the survivor of them should not change their will following the first death. If the survivor changes their will this would be a breach of contract, which is enforced through the imposition of a constructive trust.

**Nil rate band (IHT)** An inheritance tax rate of 0 per cent applying to the first portion of the cumulative total on a chargeable transfer.

**Nominated property** Includes limited categories of property, such as deposits in certain accounts, which could be left to another person on death by nomination without the need for a will. Comparatively rare. Not to be confused with nominations of pension scheme benefits.

**Non-residuary gifts** Gifts of specific amounts of money or specific items of property which are given to specified beneficiaries, before the rest (or residue) of the testator's estate is distributed.

**Oath** A formal statement, where the person submitting the statement swears to the truth of the statement on a holy book or affirms the statement as a secular alternative. All grant applications were made by oath prior to November 2018. They were replaced by statements of truth.

**Output tax (VAT)** VAT which a business charges its customers. For example, the VAT that a solicitors' firm charges its clients will be the firm's output tax. A business will pay the excess of output tax (over input tax) to HMRC at the end of each VAT quarter.

**Partial intestacy** Where a testator's will fails to indicate how the whole estate is to be distributed. Part of the estate will be distributed according to the terms of the will and the other part will be distributed according to the rules of intestacy.

**Pecuniary legacies** Legacies of amounts of money. Also called monetary legacies.

**Per capita** A Latin phrase used to describe a pattern of entitlement based on each person (*per capita* = per head).

**Per stirpes** A Latin phrase used to describe a pattern of entitlement based on branches of a family.

**Perfection (of gifts)** The donor of a gift must pass the legal title to the gifted property to the donee in order to perfect the gift. If the donor fails to do this, the gift will not be perfected and the donee may have no rights or redress as a mere volunteer.

**Perpetuity rules** Rules to prevent property being tied up in trust indefinitely. The Perpetuities and Accumulations Act 2009 provides for a perpetuity period of 125 years for most new trusts.

**Personal remedy** If there is a breach of trust, the beneficiary will have a personal remedy against the trustee. This could be for equitable compensation for loss or for an account of profits from the trustee. The beneficiary may also have a personal remedy against third parties. A beneficiary may also have a proprietary remedy.

**Personal representative (PR)** The person or trust corporation appointed to administer the estate of a deceased person. The assets of the deceased (which pass by will or intestacy) devolve upon the personal representatives, who will then distribute the estate to the beneficiaries. There are two types of personal representative—executors and administrators. You will see the abbreviation—PRs—throughout this book.

**Petty cash (Solicitors' Accounts)** A small amount of notes and coins kept by the solicitors' firm, to pay for items where cash is required. With the advent of contactless and electronic payment methods, the need for petty cash has reduced greatly.

**Post-mortem** A physical examination of the corpse to determine cause of death. A post-mortem will be ordered in suspicious circumstances, or in a situation where the cause of death is not clear.

**Potentially exempt transfer (PET)** A type of lifetime transfer for IHT purposes. Most gifts to individuals are PETs. The PET is 'potentially exempt' because if the transferor survives by seven years, the transfer then becomes exempt from IHT. However, if the transferor dies within seven years of the PET, the transfer becomes chargeable to IHT.

**Power of appointment** A power given to someone, usually in a will or other trust instrument, enabling that person to make payments to others who are in a specified class of objects. The person with the power is called the 'donee'. Often the power will be given to the trustees of the trust. However, unlike a discretionary trust, the donee of the power does not have to exercise the power.

**Power reserved** The process by which an executor does not take out a grant of probate initially, but stands in reserve, allowing other executors to take out the grant. An executor to whom power is reserved remains as executor and may subsequently take out a grant of double probate to join or take over from the executors who took out the initial grant.

**Precatory trust** A precatory trust is not a trust at all. It is merely an expression of wishes, and is not binding on an executor or trustee. The term 'precatory' comes from the Latin verb for 'to beg'.

**Principal** The person who appoints the agent. The agent owes fiduciary duties to the principal.

**Principal method (VAT)** Where the disbursement is treated as being made to the firm, not to the client, the firm will have to account for VAT on the disbursements separately through the firm's accounts. The solicitor will have to bill the client for the disbursement to recover any VAT paid by the firm.

**Private purpose trust** A purpose trust created to carry out a private (ie non-public or non-charitable) purpose. In general, private purpose trusts are not valid, but there are exceptions.

**Probate** The word comes from Latin and the verb 'to prove'. An executor will apply for a grant of probate, and is said to be 'proving' the will.

**Proprietary estoppel** A doctrine whereby a person may acquire an interest in real property through acting to their detriment on the strength of a representation by the owner of the property that the person will inherit the property.

**Proprietary remedy** A beneficiary may have a proprietary remedy in addition to any personal remedy in respect of a breach of trust. The proprietary remedy will be to claim particular items of property, but to do this it will usually be necessary to trace the value of the trust property into the property which the beneficiary is claiming.

**Public Trustee** The Public Trustee is a public official who can be appointed as executor of an estate and who provides other trust services to the public. Very much an option of last resort as most estates are administered by individuals and trust corporations.

**Purpose trust** A trust which is created to benefit a purpose, rather than particular persons.

**Reasonable financial provision** Applications to the court under the Inheritance (Provision for Family and Dependants) Act 1975 are for reasonable financial provision. The court will consider whether such provision has been made by the deceased for the applicant and, if not, what provision would be reasonable for the applicant to receive.

**Rectification** Under s20 of the Administration of Justice Act 1982, the court may rectify a will if there has been a clerical error or a failure on the part of the person drafting the will to understand the testator's instructions.

**Remainder interest** A beneficial interest in property following the ending of a prior interest in that property. Typically, a remainder interest is preceded by a life interest. For example, a spouse might be given a life interest and, on their subsequent death, the children have a remainder interest.

**Renunciation** The process by which an executor declines to act, and then ceases to be an executor. An executor may only renounce probate if they have not already intermeddled in the estate (ie not taken active steps in administering the estate).

**Residence nil rate band (IHT)** An inheritance tax rate of 0 per cent applying to the first portion of a person's residence, provided the residence is left on death to specified relatives. A downsizing alternative is available.

**Residuary estate** One of the terms used to describe the rest of a person's estate after payment of any specific legacies and other non-residuary gifts.

**Residuary gifts** Gifts of the whole or part of a person's residuary estate. Often there will be a series of substitutional gifts specified, to cover the eventuality of the original beneficiaries dying before the testator.

**Residue** One of the terms used to describe the rest of a person's estate after payment of any specific legacies and other non-residuary gifts.

**Resulting trust** A form of implied trust where the property is held for the original owner of the trust property. The trust property is said to 'result' (or jump back to) the original owner. A resulting trust may arise in the case of an apparent gift or a failed express trust.

**Reversionary interest** Another name for a remainder interest.

**Revocation** The process of cancelling a will. Most wills are revoked by making a new will but a will may be revoked in other ways, such as destroying the will (with the intention of revoking it) or automatic revocation due to a subsequent marriage or civil partnership.

**Secret profit/commission** A profit or commission obtained secretly by a fiduciary, without the knowledge of the principal.

**Self Assessment** The name given to the system for submitting income tax returns and payment of income tax. The Self Assessment system is also used for reporting and paying CGT on most capital gains.

**Self-dealing** Where a trustee buys trust property from the trust or sells their personal property to the trust. In each case, the trustee is both buyer and seller which is why it is called 'self-dealing'.

**Settled land** Land which is subject to a 'strict settlement' under the Settled Land Act 1925. Comparatively rare, especially as it has not been possible to create new strict settlements since 1996.

**Settlement** Another name for a trust. Sometimes used to signify a larger trust. The term settlement is also used at times in tax statutes.

**Severance** The process of converting a joint tenancy in equity into a tenancy in common. Usually achieved by completing a notice of severance and serving this on the other joint tenant.

**Specific gifts** Gifts of particular items of personal property (personal possessions, choses in action) or real property (land and buildings).

**Standing search** A process to check whether a grant has been issued in an estate, and to provide notice if a grant is issued in the same estate within a period of time (six months) after the search has been made. A standing search can be renewed.

**Statement of truth** A replacement for sworn or affirmed statements (eg oaths and affidavits). The maker of the statement signs a statement of truth at the end of the statement. There is no need for the statement to be witnessed.

**Statutory advertisement** In the context of an estate in administration, an advertisement in *The Gazette* and/or other media, inviting claims from any unknown creditors and beneficiaries of the deceased. The advertisement provides a period of time within which the personal representatives should be notified of claims.

**Statutory legacy** A name used commonly in practice for the 'fixed net sum' on intestacy. Where a spouse (or civil partner) and issue survive the deceased, the spouse (or civil partner) will be entitled to a statutory legacy up to a fixed amount, plus interest at a fixed rate from the date of death to the date of payment.

**Statutory trusts** In the context of an estate, the trusts imposed by the Administration of Estates Act 1925 on property which is subject to intestacy. The statutory trusts provide for substitutional entitlement to the children (and other issue) of certain relatives who have predeceased but who would otherwise have been entitled.

**Statutory will** A will made on behalf of a person who lacks testamentary capacity. An order of the Court of Protection is required.

**Strict settlement** A settlement under the Settled Land Act 1925. It has not been possible to create new strict settlements since 1996.

**Taper relief (IHT)** The rate of IHT due on a lifetime transfer reduces if the transfer survives the transfer by at least three years. The rate tapers downwards the longer the transferor survives.

**Tell Us Once** A service that enables a person to notify various government departments (such as HMRC and the Department for Work and Pensions), without having to contact each department separately.

**Tenants in common** A form of joint ownership of property, where each person has an identifiable share or proportion of the property. Each tenant in common can leave their share in the property by will.

**Testamentary capacity** To make a valid will, a person must have testamentary capacity. The testator must know three things: (1) the nature of the act (making a will) and its effects; (2) the size and nature of their estate; and (3) the persons who they would ordinarily be expected to benefit in the will. The testator must also not be suffering from any delusions which affect the wishes expressed in the will.

**Testator** The person who makes a will. The female equivalent is 'testatrix'.

**Third Party Managed Account** Under the SRA Accounts Rules 2019, a solicitor may use the services of a third party account provider to hold the money of clients (and other persons), as an alternative to operating a 'client account'. The solicitor who uses a Third Party Managed Account would not then hold client money and would not have to comply with certain of the SRA Accounts Rules 2019.

**Tracing** The process of linking misappropriated trust property with new property that is in the hands of the trustee or third party. If it is possible to trace then the beneficiary can claim the new property (or a proportion of it) from the trustee or third party.

**Transfer of value (IHT)** IHT is payable on a transfer of value. A lifetime transfer of value is equal to the value by which the transferor's estate is reduced. The transfer of value on death is everything the deceased was entitled to immediately before death.

**Trust** A legal mechanism whereby one person (the trustee) holds the legal title to property on behalf of another person (the beneficiary) who owns the underlying equitable or beneficial interest. The trustee must act in the interests of the beneficiary.

**Trust of land** A trust of land under the Trusts of Land and Appointment of Trustees Act 1996. Trusts of land replaced trusts for sale in respect of all trusts which included land from 1 January 1997.

**Trust corporation** A company set up to provide estate and trust services. Originally, trust corporations were confined to subsidiaries of the high street banks, but in recent years solicitors' firms have set up their own trust corporations to undertake estate and trusts work.

**Trustee** The person or company who holds the legal title to the trust property and who must act in the interests of the beneficiaries of the trust. Trustees have duties towards the beneficiaries, including fiduciary duties. Trustees may be trustees of express trusts, or of implied trusts (eg resulting and constructive trusts).

**Undue influence** Where one person exerts such pressure or influence on another, typically in order to prefer the first person in some way financially, by making a will that favours them, or a lifetime gift. The pressure must be such as to effectively remove the person's free will in the decisions that they make.

**Valid receipt** Personal representatives need to obtain a valid receipt from beneficiaries when distributing money or property. This will also act as a discharge of the personal representatives' responsibilities to the beneficiary. Only an adult with capacity may provide a valid receipt, unless the will provides otherwise.

**Value added tax (VAT)** A tax levied on the supply of goods and services. For example, a solicitors' firm will charge its clients VAT on the supply of legal services made by the firm. The standard rate of VAT is 20 per cent.

**Variation (post-death)** The process by which the distribution of the deceased's estate is varied by the beneficiaries of the estate. The beneficiaries have to be adults with capacity. The variation is usually achieved using a formal deed of variation.

**Vested gift** An absolute or outright gift. The gift may be of capital and/or income.

**Volunteer** A term used in Equity and trusts to describe a person who has not provided consideration for an attempted transfer. It is said that Equity will not assist a volunteer, but there are exceptions to this rule.

**Warning** If a caveat has been entered, the person who wishes to take out a grant of representation may 'warn off' the caveator. If the caveator does not enter an 'appearance' within a given period of time the person can proceed with the grant application.

**Whole blood (intestacy)** Used in the intestacy rules to describe a situation where two people share the same two parents.

**Will** A document containing a series of declaration indicating what a person wishes to happen following their death. The main purpose of the will is to indicate how a person's estate should be distributed, but the testator can also appoint executors, trustees and testamentary guardians, and express wishes about the funeral and the disposal of the body.

**Witness** To be valid, certain documents have to be signed and the signature has to be witnessed by another person. At least two witnesses are needed as part of the formalities for a valid will.

# Index

Printed and bound by CPI Group (UK) Ltd, Croydon, CR0 4YY